Domesday Book contains a great many things, including the most comprehensive, varied, and monumental legal material to survive from England before the rise of the Common Law. This book argues that it can – and should – be read as a legal text.

When the statistical information present in the great survey is stripped away, there is still a remarkable amount of material left, almost all of which stems directly from inquest testimony given by jurors impaneled in 1086, or from the sworn statements of lords and their men. This information, read in context, can provide a picture of what the law looked like, the ways in which it was changing, and the means whereby the inquest was a central event in the formation of English law.

The volume provides translations (with Latin legal terminology included parenthetically) for all of Domesday Book's legal references, each numbered and organized by county, fee, and folio.

ROBIN FLEMING is Associate Professor of History, Boston College. Her publications include *Kings and Lords in Conquest England* (1991).

Domesday Book and the law

Society and legal custom in early medieval England

ROBIN FLEMING

CAMBRIDGE
UNIVERSITY PRESS

PUBLISHED BY THE PRESS SYNDICATE OF THE UNIVERSITY OF CAMBRIDGE
The Pitt Building, Trumpington Street, Cambridge CB2 1RP, United Kingdom

CAMBRIDGE UNIVERSITY PRESS
The Edinburgh Building, Cambridge, CB2 2RU, United Kingdom   http://www.cup.cam.ac.uk
40 West 20th Street, New York, NY 10011–4211, USA   http://www.cup.org
10 Stamford Road, Oakleigh, Melbourne 3166, Australia

First published 1998

Printed in the United Kingdom at the University Press, Cambridge

Typeset in Bembo 11/13 pt   [CE]

A catalogue record for this book is available from the British Library

ISBN 0 521 63038 X hardback

In memory of C. Warren Hollister

Darwin only said that change must be
incremental, copious, and undirected.
It was someone else who said the flight
of birds is a fortunate consequence.

"Origins"
Sandra Steingraber

Contents

Figures

Tables

Acknowledgments

I should like to thank the following friends and scholars for their help. The two readers for Cambridge University Press provided comments and suggestions at a critical, early stage of this project that helped me understand what exactly it was that I was trying to do, and made me see the ways to do it. Various others have soldiered through the texts, indexes, and/or the introductory chapters. David Bates, Paul Dalton, J. C. Holt, John Hudson, Chris Lewis, Bruce O'Brien, and Mary Frances Smith each offered suggestions that made me rethink and rewrite. Bruce O'Brien and Mary Frances Smith also 'test-drove' the texts, and their responses to the experience helped me bind texts and indexes more tightly together. I would also like to thank William Davies, Jean Field, and Jayne Matthews at Cambridge University Press. A number of friends and colleagues at Boston College also deserve my gratitude, although most are unrepentant Modernists and have indeed escaped reading the manuscript. They need to be thanked, nonetheless, because they have made the Department of History at Boston College a place in which serious and sustained research can be thought about, written, and completed. First among these is Jim Cronin, under whose regime as Chair this book was written, and with whose advocacy I received both time off from teaching and money for research. But there are others to be thanked as well: Paul Breines, Burke Griggs, Patricia Halpin, Lynn Johnson, Deborah Levenson, Andrew Lowerre, Lynn Lyerly, David Northrup, Tom O'Connor, Kevin O'Neill, Alan Rogers, John Rosser, Christine Senecal, Paul Spagnolli, Karine Ugé, and Peter Weiler. A fellowship from the Mary Ingham Bunting Institute at Radcliffe College and a year-long sabbatical from Boston College made the writing of this book a pleasure.

Abbreviations

ANS	*Proceedings of the Battle Conference on Anglo-Norman Studies*, ed. R. Allen Brown, 1–4 (1979–82), continued from 1983 as *Anglo-Norman Studies*
ASC	*Anglo-Saxon Chronicle* [references are to J. Earle and C. Plummer, *Two of the Saxon Chronicles Parallel* (2 vols., 1892, 1899), or to the translation in D. Whitelock, D. C. Douglas, and S. I. Tucker (eds.), *The Anglo-Saxon Chronicle: A Revised Translation* (London, 1961)]
ASE	*Anglo-Saxon England*
BIHR	*Bulletin of the Institute of Historical Research*
Campbell, *Essays*	James Campbell, *Essays in Anglo-Saxon History* (London, 1986)
Cart. Rams.	*Cartularium Monasterii de Rameseia*, ed. W. H. Hart and P. A. Lyons, 3 vols., Rolls Series (London, 1884–93)
Chron. Ab.	*Chronicon Monasterii de Abingdon*, ed. Joseph Stevenson, 2 vols., Rolls Series (London, 1858)
Chron. Ev.	*Chronicon Abbatiae de Evesham*, ed. William Dunn Macray, Rolls Series (London, 1863)
Chron. Rams.	*Chronicon Abbatiae Rameseiensis*, ed. W. D. Macray, Rolls Series (London, 1886)
Dalton, *Conquest*	Paul Dalton, *Conquest, Anarchy and Lordship: Yorkshire 1066–1154* (Cambridge, 1994)
DB	Domesday Book [references are to *Domesday Book seu liber Censualis Wilhelmi Primi Regis Angliae*, ed. A. Farley, 2 vols. (1783); vols. II, IV, ed. H. Ellis (1816), or to *Domesday Book, Facsimile Edition*, ed. Robert Erskine and Ann Williams]
Domesday Studies	*Domesday Studies*, ed. J. C. Holt (Woodbridge, Suffolk, 1987)
EHR	*English Historical Review*
F	Fleming. Domesday texts cited by F and text number

Fleming, *Kings and Lords*	Robin Fleming, *Kings and Lords in Conquest England* (Cambridge, 1991)
Harmer, *Writs*	Florence Harmer, *Anglo-Saxon Writs*, 2nd edn. (Stamford, 1989)
Hemming	*Hemingi Chartularium Ecclesiae Wigorniensis*, ed. T. Hearne, 2 vols. (Oxford, 1727)
HSJ	*Haskins Society Journal*
Hudson, *Land*	John Hudson, *Land, Law and Lordship in Anglo-Norman England* (Oxford, 1994)
Hugh Candidus	*The Chronicle of Hugh Candidus*, ed. W. T. Mellows (Oxford, 1949)
ICC	*Inquisitio Comitatus Cantabrigiensis*, printed in *Inquisitio Comitatus Cantabrigiensis, Subjicitur Inquisitio Eliensis*, ed. N. E. S. A. Hamilton (London, 1876)
IE	*Inquisitio Eliensi*, printed in *Inquisitio Comitatus Cantabrigiensis, Subjicitur Inquisitio Eliensis*, ed. N. E. S. A. Hamilton (London, 1876)
Lawsuits	*English Lawsuits from William I to Richard II*, 2 vols., ed. R. C. van Caenegem, Selden Society, 106–7 (London, 1990)
LE	*Liber Eliensis*, ed. E. O. Blake, Camden Third Series, 92 (London, 1962)
Leg. Ed. Conf.	Bruce O'Brien, *God's Peace and King's Peace: The Confessor's Laws in Twelfth-Century England* (Philadelphia, forthcoming)
LHP	*Leges Henrici Primi*, ed. and trans. L. J. Downer (Oxford, 1972)
Mon. Ang.	W. Dugdale, *Monasticon Anglicanum*, revised edn., J. Caley, H. Ellis, and B. Bandinel, 6 vols. in 8 parts (London, 1817–30)
OV	Orderic Vitalis, *The Ecclesiastical History*, ed. and trans. Marjorie Chibnall, 6 vols. (Oxford, 1969–80)
Placita	*Placita Anglo-Normannica: Law Cases from William I to Richard I*, ed. Melville Madison Bigelow (New York, 1879)
Reassessment	*Domesday Book: A Reassessment*, ed. P. H. Sawyer (London, 1985)
Regesta	*Regesta Regum Anglo-Normannorum*, 4 vols., ed. H. W. C. Davis and others (Oxford, 1913–69)
Robertson, *Charters*	*Anglo-Saxon Charters*, ed. and trans. A. J. Robertson (Cambridge, 1939)
Royal Writs	*Royal Writs in England from the Conquest to Glanvill*, ed. R. C. van Caenegem, Selden Society, 77 (London, 1959)

RS	Rolls Series
S	*Anglo-Saxon Charters: An Annotated List and Bibliography*, ed. Peter Sawyer, Royal Historical Society (London, 1968) (charters cited by S and text number)
Stenton, *English Justice*	Doris Mary Stenton, *English Justice between the Norman Conquest and the Great Charter 1066–1215* (Philadelphia, 1964)
Tabuteau, *Transfers*	Emily Zack Tabuteau, *Transfers of Property in Eleventh-Century Norman Law* (Chapel Hill, 1988)
Textus	*Textus Roffensis*, ed. P. Sawyer, 2 vols., Early English Manuscripts in Facsimile, VII, IX (Copenhagen, 1957–62)
TRC	*Tempore regis Cnuti*
TRE	*Tempore regis Eadwardi*
TRHS	*Transactions of the Royal Historical Society*
TRW	*Tempore regis Willelmi*
VCH	*Victoria County History (1900–)*
Williams, *The English*	Ann Williams, *The English and the Norman Conquest* (Woodbridge, Suffolk, 1995)

Two brief notes on the texts and indexes

Nearly all the short legal narratives found in part II are taken from the Exchequer Domesday Book or Little Domesday Book. Ten entries, however (F 377, 383, 453, 460, 486, 493, 501, 1394, 1409, and 1414), have been emended with information found in the *Liber Exoniensis*, or Exon. Domesday, an earlier draft of the Domesday survey dealing with the south-west of England. Legal information for these entries was edited out in the final version of the Exchequer Domesday. Exon's *Terra Occupatae* have not been given separate entries in this volume.

An attempt has been made in the subject index to index separately different Latin terms for similar actions. Thus Domesday's rich vocabulary for giving is reflected in the index with separate entries for *deliberavit*, *liberavit*, *dedit*, *donavit*, *concessit*, and the like. The index does not, however, take into account variant spellings, of which there are many. Thus *escangio* and *escagio* appear under *excambio*; *accomodavit* under *accommodavit*, and *foresfecit* is indexed under *forisfecit*.

Table of F numbers by county

County	Number
Exchequer Domesday Book	
Bedfordshire	1–72
Berkshire	73–134
Buckinghamshire	135–61
Cambridgeshire	162–251
Cheshire	252–98
Cornwall	299–320
Derbyshire	321–38
Devonshire	339–457
Dorset	458–501
Gloucestershire	502–81
Hampshire	582–675
Herefordshire	676–758
Hertfordshire	759–816
Huntingdonshire	817–72
Kent	873–941
Leicestershire	942–64
Lincolnshire	965–1195
Middlesex	1196–1209
Northamptonshire	1210–39
Nottinghamshire	1240–54
Oxfordshire	1255–86
Ribble and Mersey	1287–1304
Rutland	1305–6
Shropshire	1307–35
Somerset	1336–1464
Staffordshire	1465–75
Surrey	1476–1536
Sussex	1537–63
Warwickshire	1564–84
Wiltshire	1585–1638
Worcestershire	1639–87
Yorkshire	1688–1794
Little Domesday Book	
Essex	1795–2159
Norfolk	2160–751
Suffolk	2752–3217

Frequency of legal information across counties and circuits

Circuit	F nos.	Total	Sq. miles per no.
Circuit I			
Kent	873–941	69	22
Sussex	1537–63	27	53
Surrey	1476–1536	61	13
Hampshire	582–675	94	17
Berkshire	73–134	62	12
		(= 313)	
Circuit II			
Wiltshire	1585–1638	54	26
Dorset	458–501	44	22
Somerset	1336–1464	129	13
Devonshire	339–457	119	22
Cornwall	299–320	22	61
		(= 368)	
Circuit III			
Middlesex	1196–1209	14	20
Hertfordshire	759–816	58	11
Buckinghamshire	135–61	27	27
Cambridgeshire	162–251	90	10
Bedfordshire	1–72	72	6
		(= 261)	
Circuit IV			
Oxfordshire	1255–86	32	23
Northamptonshire	1210–39	30	36
Leicestershire	942–64	23	36
Warwickshire	1564–84	21	42
		(= 106)	
Circuit V			
Gloucestershire	502–81	80	16
Worcestershire	1639–87	49	15
Herefordshire	676–758	83	10
Staffordshire	1465–75	11	109
Ribble and Mersey	1287–1304	18	—
Shropshire	1307–35	29	47
Cheshire	252–98	47	28
		(= 317)	
Circuit VI			
Huntingdonshire	817–72	56	6
Derbyshire	321–38	18	58

Nottinghamshire	1240–54	15	56
Rutland	1305–6	2	—
Yorkshire	1688–1794	107	66
Lincolnshire	965–1195	231	11
		(= 429)	
Circuit VII			
Essex	1795–2159	365	4
Norfolk	2160–751	592	3
Suffolk	2752–3217	466	3
		(= 1,423)	

Introduction

Disputes and the inquest

One of the striking things about the legal information preserved in Domesday Book is just how much was in dispute at the end of the Conqueror's reign. Evidence concerning several thousand complaints can be found in the text, accusing those who had possession of land, or rights, or men of holding them outside the law. Sometimes these complaints in Domesday Book are both specific and double-sided and include the arguments of litigators and the responses of local witnesses and juries. The survey's Hampshire folios, for example, include a detailed description of a suit between William de Chernet and Picot the Sheriff:

Picot holds two and a half virgates from the King. TRE Vitalis held them as a manor in alod from King Edward . . . William de Chernet claims this land, saying that it belongs to the manor of Charford in the fee of Hugh de Port, through the inheritance of his antecessor. He brought his testimony for this from the better and old men from all the county and hundred. Picot contradicted this with his testimony from the villeins, common people, and reeves, who wished to defend this through an oath or the judgment of God, that he who held the land was a free man and could go where he wished with the land. But William's witnesses would not accept any law but the law of King Edward, until it is determined by the King.[1]

Such detailed descriptions are rare, but they do suggest that behind the more typically laconic accounts of disputes in Domesday lay angry argument and loud, heartfelt opinion.

More often Domesday Book recounts only one side of a story. In Northamptonshire, for example, Guy de Raimbeaucourt's fee included land in Isham. Although this holding was recorded under Guy's rubric, Domesday ends its description of that place by noting that the Bishop of Coutances claimed "three little gardens" there.[2] We are not told what Guy thought of this statement or how he defended himself against it, but it is clear from this notice that the matter was discussed during the inquest. At other times seemingly extraneous discussions of livery are included in the text that could only have originated from the *ex parte* pleading of lords at the inquest who

---

[1] F 622.
[2] F 1230.

were making claims or fending them off. In Derbyshire, for example, Domesday Book details the way Walter d'Aincourt came into the thegn Wada's land in Brampton and Wadshelf, explaining that "Walter vouches the King to warranty, and Henry de Ferrers as having given him livery."[3] Because the whole of Walter's fee in the county, with the exception of this land, had once belonged to the thegn Swein Cild, it looks as if Walter felt it necessary or was required to explain how exactly it was that he had come into the holdings of another Englishman.[4] Similarly, oddly detailed entries in Domesday which give potted histories of estates suggest that some argument or threat to title had been raised at the inquest, hence the information's presentation in the text. Although, for example, no clear complaint was registered in Domesday's description of Kenchester, Herefordshire, it seems likely, nonetheless, that Hugh the Ass had made one during the inquest: "Hugh the Ass holds four hides in Kenchester . . . Hugh loaned a hide of this land to [the long-dead] Earl William, and the earl, in turn, gave it to King Maredudd. His son Gruffydd now has two bordars there."[5] Although litigious words like *reclamavit* or *invasit* are not used here, Hugh apparently worried over his hide of land.

Such anxieties and complaints form the bulk of information in Domesday Book not concerned with the text's manorial or tenurial accountings. It has long been recognized that much of Domesday's most familiar information – its data on hidation, values, peasant population, livestock, and fields – was probably taken from administrative records such as geld rolls, lists of dues from royal estates, and manorial surveys,[6] or from returns drawn up by tenants-in-chief specifically for the inquest.[7] This information may have been approved of or improved by Domesday's jurors, but it is unlikely that it was generated by them or discussed at any great length during the inquest.[8] Of

---

[3] F 331.

[4] DB, i, 276v.

[5] F 752.

[6] For the kinds of administrative documents that stand behind Domesday Book, see S. P. J. Harvey, "Domesday Book and its predecessors," *EHR*, 86 (1971), 753–73 and "Domesday Book and Anglo-Norman governance," *TRHS*, 5th series, 25 (1975), 175–93. For the texts of surviving vernacular administrative records, see Robertson, *Charters*, nos. 39, 52, 54, 84, 104, 109, 110, appendix 1, nos. 4, 5, appendix 2, nos. 3, 9.

[7] This is the impression left by the fullest entries of "Evesham A" and "Bath A," which represent material drawn up by tenants-in-chief before the Domesday inquest, and which include information on hundreds, vills, TRE and TRW tenants, values, peasants, livestock, and plowteams. For the texts of these two surveys, see P. H. Sawyer, "Evesham A, a Domesday text," *Worcester Historical Society, Miscellany*, 1 (1960), 3–36 and *Two Cartularies of Bath Priory*, ed. W. Hunt, *Somerset Record Society*, 6 (1893), 67–8. That lay tenants-in-chief were also capable of providing detailed written surveys for the inquest is suggested by Guy de Raimbeaucourt's returns, which are probably preserved in a text published in G. H. Fowler, "An Early Cambridgeshire feodary," *EHR*, 46 (1931), 442–3. For other important discussions of these returns in the making of *DB*, see P. H. Sawyer, "The 'original returns' and Domesday Book," *EHR*, 70 (1955), 177–97; and H. B. Clarke, "The Domesday satellites," in *Reassessment*, 50–70. For marginalia in Little Domesday Book indicating that tenants provided such returns, see below, subject index, XI.2, under "returns." See also H. C. Darby, *Domesday England* (Cambridge, 1977), 105–10, 118, and appendixes 5, 6, and 7.

[8] As H. B. Clarke so cogently put it, "the nature of these satellites gives strength to the argument that the prime concern of the hundredal juries was with landholders and landholding and that the wealth of

the 1,000 explicit references to inquest testimony in Domesday Book, less than a dozen concern the survey's brute statistics. But much of the text is taken up with the kinds of detail that would not have been included in the written documents used to generate the statistics of the survey. Discussions of grants, livery, mortgages, sales, antecession, and the like are much more likely to have resulted from the conversations of jurors or the complaints of lords: indeed these topics are often linked specifically in the text with oral testimony.[9] The facts and figures of the survey were important to the Conqueror and his administrators: when William commissioned the survey in late 1085, and when orders were sent out to begin its compilation, such material was demanded by the King.[10] Too often, however, these figures are seen as the sole reason behind the inquest and the sole reason for using it. But the courts called together in 1086 and the commissioners sent out by the King to preside over them were very much concerned with the survey's more anecdotal information. Imbedded in Domesday's otherwise brutalist prose are several thousand short narratives which describe legal customs or legal or illegal activity that have little to do with the accounting of swine pastures or the numbers of slaves. These narratives have fossilized much of the real work of the 1086 courts – that is, sorting through complaints over title. Such disputes are not, as is often thought, confined to the *clamores* and *annexationes* that form the appendices of a few northern and eastern shires, but are, rather, found scattered across the whole of Great and Little Domesday.[11]

The abundance of legal narratives in the survey suggests that we should take more seriously the twelfth-century view of Richard fitz Nigel, that one of the central reasons for the holding of the Domesday inquest was "in order that every man be content with his own rights and not encroach unpunished on those of others."[12] Many of the survey's fragmentary legal narratives speak unambiguously of unjust actions and employ the vocabulary of evasion or annexation (see table 1). Other of Domesday's legal anecdotes are not linked explicitly in the text to an assault on title or to questions over seisin, but it is difficult to imagine any other reason for their discussion at the inquest or their inclusion in the survey (see table 2). And when these narrative passages are read in context, this connection is made manifest. One hundred and thirty-four post-Conquest grants by named laymen, for example, are preserved in Domesday Book. It is easy to think of these rather gnomic descriptions of grants as accidental asides. But when read together, their

---

manorial detail was added behind the scenes by stewards, bailiffs, or village reeves" (Clarke, "Domesday satellites," p. 45).

[9] See below, chapter 2.

[10] *ICC*, 97; *ASC* (E), 1085; J. C. Holt, "1086," in *Domesday Studies*, 47, 49.

[11] See figures 1 and 2.

[12] Richard fitz Nigel, *Dialogus de Scaccario*, ed. Charles Johnson (London, 1950) and revised F. E. L. Carter and Diana E. Greenway (Oxford, 1983), 63. This view is said in the *Dialogus* to be that of Henry of Blois, Bishop of Winchester and grandson of William the Conqueror (ibid, 63).

Table 1. *Frequency of select illegal actions*

Words for	Number of times used in Domesday Book
Annex	135
Claim	512
Disseise	24
Keep back	32
Seize	48
Take away	168
Total	919

Table 2. *Frequency of select legal actions*

Words for	Number of times used in Domesday Book
Deliver	71
Grant	344
Gift	100
Lease	46
Livery	70
Mortgage	46
Purchase	79
Seise	71
Total	827

purpose is evident. Of the 134 grants, 18 concern property given by men living and thriving in 1086; and of these, 13 represent gifts to monasteries. The remaining 116 grants, however, are notices of the gifts of deceased or disgraced donors or former sheriffs, mostly to laymen; in other words grants that were difficult to warrant in 1086.[13] Notices of these grants, therefore, do not represent some arbitrary or idiosyncratic set of asides, but are, rather, a relic of 1086 testimony generated by insecure title. Similarly, mortgages

---

[13] The grants of dead donors are F 11, 15, 51–2, 68, 110, 112, 124, 156–7, 377, 420, 468, 472, 497–9, 505, 507, 512–13, 521, 523–4, 526, 530–1, 539, 544, 548, 561–2, 568, 573, 576, 583, 591, 621, 673, 693–4, 699–700, 703, 705, 707–8, 713, 723, 725, 730–1, 733–5, 737, 739–40, 745, 751–2, 755, 757–8, 768, 801, 803, 828, 845, 879, 891–2, 901, 925, 927, 929, 933, 935, 1000, 1058, 1079, 1262–3, 1297, 1300, 1302, 1304, 1326, 1386, 1430, 1499, 1502, 1510, 1520, 1591, 1615, 1662, 1677, 1802, 1829, 2029, 2042, 2049, 2174, 2186–7, 2192, 2232, 2268, 2275, 2284, 2286, 2429, 2472, 2474, 3097, 3216. The gifts of the living are F 104, 111, 549, 616, 729, 753, 842, 1233, 1238, 1318, 1390, 1514, 1534, 1547, 1678, 1851, 1891, 2781. Of these, two deal with gifts of Countess Judith, whose husband Waltheof had been disinherited (F 842, 1238), and thirteen are grants to monasteries (F 104, 111, 549, 616, 842, 1233, 1238, 1318, 1390, 1514, 1648, 1851, 2781).

appear in Domesday Book not in an arbitrary fashion, but pointedly in association with testimony, as an explanation for title or as part of a claim.[14] Between Domesday's descriptions of testimony given and legal or illegal actions taken, the survey preserves the fragments of several thousand legal transactions and disputes. This class of evidence, then, although less systematic than Domesday's endless accountings of mills and pasture, is no less astonishing or precious, since it gives us thousands of glimpses of the workings of the eleventh-century court and the actions of lived law.

Yet in spite of its riches, the legal information in Domesday Book, with the exception of that found in the survey's borough customals, is little used. On occasion scholars have picked through the survey for a perfect example or a legal anecdote, but few have examined the information systematically in the context of the rest of the survey. This is due in part to the hyper-specialized knowledge needed to interpret the text. Most historians of the period have been trained on charters and narrative sources, and only reluctantly turn to Domesday for very specific and localized information. Indeed, the bulk of the period's specialists tend, in the words of Sally Harvey, to approach Domesday Book "with the air of one requested to defuse an explosive device."[15] A few historians in recent years have looked more closely at Domesday's legal information. J. C. Holt and Paul Hyams have studied those descriptions which illuminate the reasons behind William's inquest. R. C. van Caenegem has published 111 passages referring to Domesday lawsuits (taken for the most part from J. M. Bigelow's *Placita*, published long ago) and Patrick Wormald has published a paper on royal pleas held in 1086 which includes an appendix giving citations for 339 such cases.[16] Yet in spite of these efforts, the legal information in Domesday Book remains as intractable as ever.

The argument that stands behind this book is that Domesday Book can and should be read as a legal text. It is, of course, many things; but Domesday's mind-numbing detail and its figures, its intricate accountings and its pains-taking attention to castrated sheep, dairy maids, and eel-renders have blinded us to the fact that Domesday is the most comprehensive, varied, and monumental legal text to survive from England before the rise of the Common Law. When the statistical information present in the great survey is stripped away, one is still left with a remarkable amount of material, almost all of which stems directly from inquest testimony given by jurors impaneled in

---

[14] For mortgages that operated in this way in DB, see F 48, 60, 141, 199, 461, 482, 484–5, 581, 651, 775, 807, 844, 903, 973, 1028, 1065, 1107–8, 1142, 1157, 1173, 1179, 1196, 1353, 1502, 1574, 2011–12, 2023, 2230, 2680, 2750, 2860, 2936, 3063, 3155, 3191. The exceptions are F 374, 412, 774, 951, 1285, 1581, and 1636.

[15] Sally P. Harvey, "Recent Domesday studies," *EHR*, 94 (1979), 130.

[16] Holt, "1086," in *Domesday Studies*, 41–64; P. R. Hyams, " 'No register of title': the Domesday inquest and land adjudication," *ANS*, 9 (1986), 127–41; *Lawsuits*, nos. 21–131; *Placita*, 37–61; Patrick Wormald, "Domesday lawsuits: a provisional list and preliminary comment," in *England in the Eleventh Century: Proceedings of the 1990 Harlaxton Symposium*, ed. Carola Hicks, Harlaxton Medieval Studies (Stamford, Lincs., 1992).

1086, or from the sworn statements of lords and their men. One of the clearest things that emerge when Domesday is treated thus is just how much was being contested in 1086. Through the inquest testimony itself we can see the ways in which the English past and the Norman present complicated tenure and created ambiguous title. This, in turn, gives us new insights into the nature of the Norman settlement, the troubles of the Conqueror's reign, and the absolute necessity of the inquest. Domesday Book read as a legal text also tells us much about the mechanics of justice; about the ways men of the Conqueror's generation protected what they had been given and what they had taken on their own. We can see, as well, both how much they depended on old, familiar legal customs to defend property and how they developed new ways of protecting land at law. Domesday's legal information hammers home the oral and public nature of law in the period and the importance of communal memory in legal custom, and it shows us how much life was lived in the glare of other men's view. Domesday's testimony not only provides us with the contours of legal practice across the eleventh century, but shows us that the law of land, because of the particular circumstances of the Conquest, was developing rapidly during William's reign. Finally, such a reading makes manifest the fact that the Domesday inquest itself was the crucible in which a new, hybrid Anglo-Norman law was forged. Thus the legal information in Domesday Book, if read in context, can provide us with a picture of what the law looked like, the ways in which it was changing, and the means whereby the inquest was a central event in the formation of English law.

What follows is an attempt to make Domesday's legal information more accessible to students and scholars. The 3,217 short texts printed in this volume include all of the legal information in the Exchequer Domesday and in Little Domesday Book – "legal" having been defined broadly. All legal

---

1355 i, 87v (2-9) Bishop of Winchester; Taunton: To the manor of Taunton have been added land in Lydeard St. Lawrence and Leigh (in Lydeard St. Lawrence), which a thegn held in parage TRE. This thegn could go to whatever lord he wished. TRW these lands are held by Wulfweard and Alweard, who hold them from the Bishop of Winchester through a grant (*concessionem*) of King William. King William granted (*concessit*) these lands to St. Peter and Bishop Walkelin, as he himself acknowledged at Salisbury in the hearing of the Bishop of Durham, whom he ordered to write down this grant of his in the returns (*recognovit apud Sarisberiam audiente episcipo Dunelmensi, cui praecepit, ut hanc ipsam concessionem suam in brevibus scriberet*).

complaints in the text are here, as are notices of inquest testimony, legal customs, and annexations. So, too, are references to legal transactions such as grants, sales, mortgages, and warranty, as are all specific references to antecession and forfeiture. This volume provides translations (with Latin legal terminology included parenthetically) for all of Domesday Book's legal references, each numbered and organized by county, fee, and folio. Each entry has been assigned a unique number (in bold), a folio number to the manuscripts of Exchequer or Little Domesday, the identification number assigned by the Phillimore edition of Domesday Book (the edition most used by undergraduates), the name of the tenant-in-chief under whose rubric the passage can be found, and the placename to which the description has been appended. The small roman numeral signifies the DB manuscript vol. i = Exchequer Domesday and ii = Little Domesday. Readers can thus locate the text in the manuscripts, the facsimile, the nineteenth-century edition, or the Phillimore edition, and can identify the fee and the vill in which the action described pertains. This identifying information is then followed by a short paraphrase of the entry, giving details on the TRE and TRW holders of the land and the property's hidation. The legal information then follows as it appears in Domesday Book itself.

Part I
Domesday Book and the law

1 The inquest and the mechanics of justice

For over thirty years scholarly attention has been fixed on those shadowy written records lurking behind Domesday Book. V. H. Galbraith, Peter Sawyer, Sally Harvey, H. B. Clarke, and David Roffe have brought to light the mass of written evidence used in the making of Domesday; and their investigations have sharpened our understanding of the workings of eleventh-century government and clarified our thinking about the ways in which the survey's mass of detail was collected and compiled in a single year. Less attention, however, has been paid to oral testimony, the great survey's other source of information. The verbal pronouncements of individuals and groups, so commonplace in Domesday, represent intelligence gathered during the inquest itself, and are the places we can hear most clearly the voices of eleventh-century men speaking about the laws and customs of their world. Because the identity of witness-bearing assemblies and individuals can often be discerned, it is also possible to stitch together the political, social, and legal context for the 1086 inquest, for the assemblies that were convened, and for the jurors who gave sworn testimony. By studying both those who bore witness and the pronouncements they made, the continuities of law and legal customs in England are illuminated, as are the many ways in which 1086 stands at one of the great fault lines of English legal history.

Jurors and the inquest

During the great inquest of 1086 large numbers of men gathered, swore oaths, and gave testimony, and some made judgments as well. According to the prologue of the *Inquisitio Eliensis* (*IE*), one of Domesday's satellite texts, the oral answers to verbal inquiries – one of the central components of the Domesday inquest – were made under oath by various individuals and groups; by the sheriff of each shire,[1] barons and their Norman retainers, hundreds, and by delegations of priests, reeves, and peasants from every village.[2] Indeed, testimony from all of these groups – even the evidence given by clutches of villeins – is preserved in both Exchequer and Little Domesday

---

[1] *ICC*, 97. The *ICC*, following the list of jurors for Staploe Hundred, specifically adds that Picot the Sheriff gave sworn testimony (*ICC*, 1).

[2] The *IE* specifically notes that six villeins from each Cambridgeshire vill were to take an oath and give testimony (*IE*, 97). Village priests and reeves along with heads of tithings, many of whom must have been

Book.[3] Simultaneously, two groups of men that the *IE* left out, those representing the whole of each county and the borough, were impaneled.[4] In some shires still other bodies, representing local districts such as lathes or ridings,[5] were brought together, and there are scattered references, as well, to the corporate testimony of the great episcopal and abbatial *familiae*.[6]

The *IE* names eight jurors for each Cambridgeshire hundred, and this may or may not have been the typical number of men who made up all the local assemblies participating in the inquest. Evidence found in the laws and in the narrative descriptions of disputes, dating both before the Conquest and after, suggests that the more typical number for sworn groups acting as compurgators, jurors, or judges, was twelve. As early as Æthelstan's reign, the heads of tithings, which were apparently organized around London by hundred, were admonished to meet as twelve men – probably as ten tithing men, a reeve, and a priest. At these meetings tithing men, like other guild brothers, were to share a common meal and give alms, but they were also instructed to swear an oath and verify that Æthelstan's laws were being upheld.[7] Æthelred's code, issued at Wantage, describes in detail wapentake moots in which twelve elder thegns and a reeve were to accuse the guilty after swearing oaths on relics.[8] The same twelve thegns were to give a single judgment.[9] Earl Godwine, when he was accused of treason in 1051, was ordered to appear before the King with twelve thegns,[10] and groups of twelve permanent *judices* or *lagemanni* can be found operating in eleventh-century Chester, Lincoln, Stamford, and York.[11] Twelve jurors were also present in the 1080s in a dispute concerning the privileges of the Archbishop of York,[12] and two sets of twelve men deliberated around the same time over Rochester's rights to land in Suffolk.[13] It is likely that at least some of Domesday's impaneled

the moral equivalent of the *IE*'s six villeins, had long been required to act as sworn witnesses to make sure that everyone within the community had given alms and fasted (VII Æthelred 2§5) (all laws are cited from *Die Gesetze der Angelsachsen*, ed. F. Liebermann, 3 vols. [Halle, 1903–16], by king and code).

3   F 622, 1561, 2762, 3011.

4   For testimony of burgesses, see F 75, 520, 906, 939, 966, 971, 1315, 1500, 1689–90, 1694. For testimony of the county, see below, subject index, IX.3, under "county."

5   For the testimony of the men of the lathe see F 939. For testimony of the riding see below, subject index, IX.3, under "riding". For the testimony of the men of Holland see F 1191–2, 1194.

6   F 109, 632, 748, 928, 1510, 1538, 1697, 1826; *Placita*, 288.

7   VI Æthelstan 3, 7§1. This same group had to testify, again after swearing that almsgiving and fasting had been carried out within the hundred (VII Æthelred 2§5).

8   III Æthelstan 3§1.

9   III Æthelred 13§2. If they did not, the opinion of eight would override the others, who were hit with a stiff monetary penalty.

10 *ASC* (E) s. a. 1048 (*recte* 1051).

11 F 269, 965, 984. We are told of four judges in York (F 1688), but twelve men, probably *lagemanni*, witnessed a document of *c.* 1080 detailing the privileges of the Archbishop in the city of York (F. Liebermann and M. H. Peacock, "An English document of about 1080," *Yorkshire Archaeological Journal*, 18 (1905), 412–16). We are not told their number, but we know lawmen were present in tenth-century Cambridgeshire (they meet and give testimony at Ditton, in a court summoned by Ealdorman Byrhtnoth (*LE*, ii, 33). The lawmen of Cambridge are also mentioned (again without number) in F 164. They can also probably be found in the *Abingdon Chronicle*, *c.* 1071, among the unnumbered English *causidici* (*Chron. Ab.*, II, 2).

12 Liebermann and Peacock, "An English document," 412–16.

13 *Textus*, ii, fos. 175v-176v.

groups, in particular in the borough courts where lawmen were present, would have been made up of twelve jurors rather than the *IE's* eight. But whatever their number, across the kingdom and in different assemblies, it is clear that large numbers of sworn men gathered as a result of King William's "deep speech" at the Christmas court of 1085.[14]

From the Domesday text itself, it is clear that the groups of jurors representing different hundreds, like the ones so carefully enumerated in the *IE* and the *Inquisitio Comitatus Cantabrigiensis (ICC)*, were assembled and impaneled at the same time and in the same place in each county, doubtless in the chief borough of every shire;[15] and that these juries of sworn hundredmen were convened with county and borough panels and with individuals and their men. That all these assemblies met at once in each county is made evident by the fact that the testimony of different groups of sworn men and individuals appears side by side in Domesday Book, countering, lending support to, or supplementing the memories of other juries. In Hampshire, for example, both the hundred and the shire produced testimony supporting the Abbess of Nunminster's claim to an estate at Itchen Abbas;[16] and in Hertfordshire the men of the shire testified about the illegal imposition of cartage on King's Walden, while the hundred spoke of a royal official's arrogation of this land.[17] On some occasions a confusion of voices was raised. In Kent the hundred of Dover and the burgesses there, the men of St. Augustine's Abbey and the Lathe of Eastry all provided testimony on the Edwardian history of a single estate.[18] The echoings of conversations between a number of impaneled groups are present in these and in dozens of other cases in Domesday.[19]

These combined courts manifest themselves in their most extravagant and baroque form in the Domesday inquest, but they are one of the most distinctive features of the late Anglo-Saxon and early Anglo-Norman legal system. By the time of the inquest there was a long history of joint judicial meetings, predating 1086 by a century or more, and in the tenth, eleventh, and early twelfth centuries these joint-assemblies were central in maintaining the peace, providing warranty, and settling disputes. This is particularly true for paired meetings of hundreds. The Abbots of Peterborough, for example, can be seen from the second half of the tenth century onward purchasing land

---

[14] *ASC*, s. a. 1086 (E).

[15] With the exception of the Derbyshire and Nottinghamshire inquest, which was held in tandem (DB, i, 280v). For a discussion of particular joint-assemblies before the Conquest, see Harmer, *Writs*, 503–4; and Helen Maud Cam, "Early groups of hundreds," in *Liberties and Communities in Medieval England: Collected Studies in Local Administration and Topography* (Cambridge, 1944), 91–105. For single meetings of multiple courts during the Domesday inquest, see F. W. Maitland, *Domesday Book and Beyond* (Cambridge, 1897), 11, n. 1; V. H. Galbraith, *The Making of Domesday Book* (Oxford, 1961), 70, 73; R. Welldon Finn, *The Domesday Inquest*, 99; G. H. Martin, "Domesday Book and the boroughs," in *Reassessment*, 159.

[16] F 642; and the estate, according to a marginal note in Domesday Book, was restored.

[17] F 765.

[18] F 939.

[19] See below, subject index, IX.3, under "more than one group testifies."

in full view of combined assemblies of two or more hundreds.[20] Not only were purchases of land made, but disputes were aired or reconciled by and in the presence of groups of hundreds. In the late tenth century, to take but one example, men from eight Northamptonshire and East Anglian hundreds gathered at Wansford to adjudicate a dispute over an estate at Downham between the land-grabbing Bishop Æthelwold and the widow Siflæd.[21] Joint-assemblies also monitored and punished criminal behavior. The triple hundred was used in cases involving untrustworthy men. The *ungetreowe* man could not exculpate himself within a single hundred by a simple oath, but was required to produce compurgators from three neighboring hundreds; and presumably he had to clear himself in front of the men of their coacting assemblies.[22] Groups of shires or districts headed by different boroughs also met together long before the Domesday inquest. In the tenth-century Danelaw, breach of peace was determined, pronounced, and publicized at great meetings of the Five Boroughs.[23] Shire courts, too, sat together: in the Confessor's reign, or in the years just preceding his accession, Westminster Abbey's rights to Datchworth and Watton in Hertfordshire were assessed at a meeting of nine shires.[24]

Different types of assemblies – not just shire and shire or hundred and hundred – were convened jointly as well to hear local pleas. After the so-called anti-monastic reaction, for example, the monks of Ely made a claim on lost property at a collective meeting of the borough of Cambridge and the double hundred of Ely;[25] and a dispute over a Kentish estate was reconciled in front of the men of both east and west Kent, who often met separately, and a panel of Canterbury burgesses.[26] Criminal activity could be assessed at similar hybrid meetings. At the time of the Domesday inquest, for example, the fine for breach of the king's peace in many parts of the Danelaw was levied at a borough meeting which included suitors from wapentake or shire assemblies.[27]

After the Conquest these joint-pleas continued. In the Conqueror's reign

---

[20] Robertson, *Charters*, no. 40. The *Leges Henrici Primi*'s casual treatment of these combined moots suggests that they were commonplace: the author advised the consolidation of two or more hundreds as a regular matter of course (*LHP*, 7§5).

[21] *LE*, ii, 11.

[22] II Cnut 22§1, and by extension II Cnut 30, 30§2. At the Domesday inquest double hundreds had twice the number of jurors as single hundreds, suggesting that assemblies of two or three hundreds would empanel double or triple the number of sworn men that meetings of single hundreds would have. (See *IE*, 100 for the names of the thirty-two jurors from the double hundreds of Ely and Broadwater.)

[23] III Æthelred 1§1.

[24] S 1123.

[25] *LE*, ii, 24. The plea concerned Stonea, which now lies in North Witchford Hundred, but which lay, in the early Middle Ages, in the double hundred of Ely (P. H. Reaney, *The Place-Names of Cambridgeshire and the Isle of Ely*, English Place-Name Society, 19 [Cambridge, 1943], 265–6). For Ely's use of joint-assemblies in the later tenth century, see Alan Kennedy, "Law and litigation in the *Libellus Æthelwoldi episcopi*," *ASE*, 24 (1995), 131–83, at 140–2.

[26] S 1456; Nicholas Brooks, "The creation and early structure of the kingdom of Kent," in *The Origins of Anglo-Saxon Kingdoms*, ed. Steven Bassett (Leicester, 1989), 67–74.

[27] F 980, 1243.

Æthelwig abbot of Evesham and Wulfstan bishop of Worcester made claims and counter-claims at a meeting of four shires over which the Bishop of Bayeux presided.[28] St. Wulfstan also made claims at another meeting of four shires, this one held in front of Queen Mathilda.[29] And in 1080 another amalgamated assembly – a meeting of the counties of Essex, Hertfordshire, Huntingdonshire, and Bedfordshire – was held at Kentford to discuss Ely's rights and property.[30] Thus, in 1086 administrators and litigators who had survived twenty years of Norman rule were long practiced at airing their grievances at great meetings of multiple courts, not only because they had done so in the uneasy decades of the 1070s and 1080s, but because such practice had been commonplace since at least the days of Edgar and Æthelred.

Clearly, the practice of convening more than one assembly at a time stretches back into the tenth century; nonetheless, evidence suggests that the assemblies held during the Domesday inquest to substantiate and adjudicate were much larger and more administratively complex than any assembly that had met before. Besides the King's commissioners, the sheriffs, reeves, and priests who were required to attend,[31] at least eight men from every hundred were present. We know, thanks to the *ICC*, that there were 128 jurors for Cambridgeshire alone, and other counties may have had either larger numbers of jurors representing each hundred or included all the hundred's freemen in their meetings.[32] From Domesday and from contemporary descriptions of the inquest we know that royal officials came to these assemblies with helpers; that the sheriff, for example, sometimes appeared at these proceedings with underlings,[33] and that Remigius bishop of Lincoln, acting as a royal commissioner, came to the Worcestershire pleas with a clerk, a priest, and at least two monks.[34] There would have been claimants at these meetings as well, along with their followers and witnesses. Abbots and bishops, for example, who were the most practiced litigators in the kingdom, appeared at some of these inquests, in the same way as they had appeared at judicial assemblies long before the Conquest, with their households in tow.[35] The Abbot of

---

[28] This meeting was held at *Ildeberga* (F 1674). The *Evesham Chronicle*, however, claims that this meeting was composed of five shires (*Chron. Ev.*, 96–7). On the business of this meeting, see R. R. Darlington, "Æthelwig, abbot of Evesham," *EHR*, 48 (1933), 18–21.

[29] F 1567.

[30] *LE*, ii, 116. For the dating of this meeting, see J. H. Le Patourel, "Geoffrey of Montbray, bishop of Coutances, 1049–93," *EHR*, 59 (1944), 129–61. These joint-assemblies continued long after the death of the Conqueror. Under William Rufus a judgment in favor of Thorney was given "in the presence of the first men of Northamptonshire and Leicestershire' (*Lawsuits*, no. 158). The same king ordered a meeting of three and a half hundreds held to hear the claims of the Abbot of Ramsey (*Regesta*, I, no. 449). In the second half of Henry I's reign, nine hundreds gathered to remember, swear, and give currency to a bargain struck by the Abbot of Ramsey and Roger Bigod in William the Conqueror's reign (*Cart. Rams.*, I, 148). For the whole twelfth and thirteenth-century history of the merging of groups of hundreds, see Cam, "Early groups of hundreds," 91–105.

[31] *IE*, 97.

[32] C. P. Lewis, "The Domesday jurors," *HSJ*, 5 (1993), 18.

[33] F 663. For earlier evidence of sheriffs' underlings, see William Alfred Morris, *The Medieval English Sheriff to 1300* (Manchester, 1927), 9.

[34] *Placita*, 288.

[35] For pre-Conquest examples of this, see S 1456 and 1458.

Abingdon's monks were present at the Berkshire inquest,[36] the monks of St. Augustine's accompanied their abbot to the pleas held in Canterbury,[37] the monks of Chertsey were present at the Surrey hearings,[38] and "all the convent of the church of Worcester" was assembled at the Worcestershire pleas.[39] Laymen, too, brought gangs of men to support their claims or to stymie their enemies. The most excessive example of this in Domesday was William de Chernet's rallying of the better and older men from both the county of Hampshire and the hundred of Fordingbridge to his support (these, no doubt, were the county and hundred jurors), while Picot the Sheriff, not to be outdone by the clamoring of William's supporters, disputed his testimony with a pack of "villeins, common people and reeves," all of whom were willing to swear an oath or undertake the judicial ordeal to prove the truth of their testimony.[40] This crowd of peasants, thegns, reeves, and Frenchmen was brought together to dispute the seisin of a mere two and a half virgates of land. Similar mobs of sureties and supporters must have appeared when more valuable holdings were contested, or when title to large amounts of thegnland was being deraigned. Pre-Conquest descriptions of disputes occasionally claim over a thousand unnamed witnesses or oath-takers.[41] This number is no doubt a spectacular exaggeration, but it intimates, nonetheless, that people traditionally turned out in droves to rally round their kith and kin when property was at risk. Thus, it appears that the great assemblies held in county towns during the Domesday inquest, although they did not, as one near-contemporary claimed, include "almost all the inhabitants of the land,"[42] would have numbered in the hundreds. Across all of England in all the county assemblies, perhaps as many as seven or eight thousand people attended the inquests. As a result, these meetings were considerably larger and more cumbersome than even the grandest of the land pleas of the 980s or the 1070s.

The prodigious size of these proceedings goes a long way in explaining why the Domesday inquest so profoundly marked the imagination of the period's chroniclers; but it must have made a similar impression on all those who participated in or witnessed the inquest. The men who were accessories in this enterprise were an uncommonly diverse lot: not only were the greatest of the King's tenants-in-chief involved and his officials, but so, too, were middling undertenants. Villeins and reeves were there, as were newly enriched Frenchmen and their more distressed thegnly neighbors. The inquests, held before large crowds, were adorned with all the gaudy trappings of the eleventh-century law court – with the relics of the saints,[43] vats of

---

[36] F 109.

[37] F 928.

[38] F 1510.

[39] For pre-Conquest examples of this, see S 1456 and 1458. For examples from the Domesday inquest, see F 109, 928, 1510; *Placita*, 288.

[40] F 622.

[41] S 1458; *LE*, ii, 25.

[42] *Feudal Documents from the Abbey of Bury St Edmunds*, ed. D. C. Douglas (London, 1932), 3.

[43] For oaths, which would have been taken on relics, see below, subject index, V.3, under "oath."

boiling water and bars of heated iron,[44] bishops and abbots in the company of their households, the best men of the hundred and members of the urban patriciate. These inquests, in the end, were grand celebrations of the new order and were ritual reenactments of the Conquest itself, set in the theater of the Anglo-Saxon joint-assembly. The recounting of the new tenurial order in public, under the gaze of such a polyglot and socially variegated company and in the language of the law must have done much to legitimate and enroot twenty years of settlement and predation. These gatherings transformed the Norman Conquest into a licit and enduring enterprise by detailing ten thousand petty appropriations in front of convocations of all the great and little men who made law and upheld it. Thus, it appears that the Domesday inquest played an axial role in ensuring the durability of title.[45]

Jurors in social and political context

Sworn men sat at the heart of all hundred, borough, and shire meetings in the tenth and eleventh centuries, and they formed the core of the great joint-assemblies held during the Domesday inquest. These men, like the assemblies themselves, need to be put into the context of late Anglo-Saxon and early Anglo-Norman legal practice, so that we might understand both the ways in which the inquest produced testimony and the nature of the information it collected and preserved. The Domesday jurors appear in Domesday Book itself as corporate, faceless, and disinterested; and they are universally portrayed in the historiography as neutral and competent. They are Sir Frank Stenton's men "learned in the law," Patrick Wormald's "local opinion," and J. H. Round's downright Tolkienian "freemen of the shiremoot." Domesday proper, of course, gives few details about the individuals who offered testimony during the inquest, but some of their names are preserved in the *ICC* and the *IE*. Together, these two texts record the names of all the jurors for fifteen Cambridgeshire and three Hertfordshire hundreds. C. P. Lewis has studied the eighty Englishmen and seventy-eight Frenchmen listed in the two texts, and has located them socially, economically, and geographically among minor tenants who had middling and intensely local interests.[46] The validity of these jurors' opinions on local matters was guaranteed, apparently, by their participation in the most local of societies. Although historians have some-times expressed concern over the validity of information offered up to the

---

[44] For the use of the ordeal at the inquest, see below, subject index, V.3, under "ordeal."

[45] For other arguments, based on different evidence, which support Domesday's role in this, see Fleming, *Kings and Lords*, 210–14; Holt, "1086," in *Domesday Studies*, 41–64; Paul Hyams, "'No register of title': the Domesday inquest and land adjudication," *ANS*, 9 (1987), 127–41. For arguments against this position, see Maitland, *Domesday Book and Beyond*, 25; Patrick Wormald, "Domesday lawsuits: a provisional list and preliminary comment," in *England in the Eleventh Century: Proceedings of the 1990 Harlaxton Symposium*, ed. Carola Hicks (Stamford, 1992), 61–102.

[46] Lewis, "Domesday jurors," 19–25.

royal commissioners by tenants-in-chief, no such suspicion has ever been cast on the opinions of the sworn men impaneled during the 1086 inquest. Our faith in Domesday testimony is due, in part, to the fact that jurors in the eleventh century had serious strictures on their behavior and opinions. A ruined local reputation could complicate a public liar's life, since law-worthy status was essential for the commonplace activities of daily life – for the buying of cattle, the selling of surplus, and the compurgation of dependents and allies.[47] The state, too, such as it was, occasionally prosecuted perjurous jurors by lopping off their hands or levying fines against them of breathtaking severity.[48] In Cambridgeshire, for example, a decade or so after the Conquest, twenty-four jurors accused of perjury were amerced the prodigious fine of 72,000 silver pennies.[49] Opinions given under oath were also clothed in awesome ritual, and God-fearing jurors would, no doubt, anxiously adhere as closely as they could to the truth, not wishing to find themselves in the company of the witches and whores with whom the swearers of false oaths were placed by the crafters of laws and homilies.[50] But truth is elusive, contentious, and not at all straightforward. And to take the opinions offered by men impaneled during the Domesday inquest as uncontested versions of simple fact is unwise.

The opinions produced by juries during the great joint-assemblies, more-over, should not be dissociated from the personal relationships upon which the minor landholders who were jurors depended to prosper in the world and to keep their enemies at bay. The effects of the social and political hierarchy on local judicial opinion are not always clear in Domesday Book, but the tug and pull of great men's desires on little men's decisions are sometimes elaborated in the labyrinthine descriptions of other pleas held during the Conqueror's reign. Sometime between 1077 and 1082, for example, conten-tion rose between Gundulf bishop of Rochester and Picot the Sheriff over land in Isleham, Cambridgeshire, which formed an outlying appurtenance of Freckenham in Suffolk. The case was a complicated one, much less straightforward than the narrative of the plea found in the partisan *Textus Roffensis*. It looks as if the whole complex of land and rights belonging to Freckenham and Isleham had been in the King's hands before the Conquest. He held some of the land there in demesne, but a number of his sokemen held there as well, as did one of his huntsmen and his sheriff.[51] The bishopric of Rochester, however, appears to have had some claims to land in the two vills, and it may have been in Harold Godwineson's short reign that a portion of Rochester's land – all of Freckenham and part of Isleham – was granted

---

[47] E.g. II Cnut 36§1.
[48] II Cnut 6, 36,
[49] See below, 19. Indeed their punishment is reminiscent of Henry I's retribution against moneyers. Perhaps the outsize fine was to discourage further incidents of perjury without constant enforcement.
[50] E.g. VI Æthelred 7; Wulfstan, *Sermo Lupi ad Anglos*, ed. D. Whitelock, 2nd edn. (Exeter, 1976), 39–40.
[51] *Domesday Book*, i, 189v, 190v, 195v, 199r; ii, 381a.

out by Harold to two of his men, possibly his housecarls.[52] By the time of the plea, Rochester was not only claiming a hide in Isleham and ten carucates in Freckenham, but was apparently pressing without right for another hide and a half of land and twenty acres in Isleham. And Picot himself, who was managing and probably farming the King's land in Isleham, seems to have lost yet another hide and a half and twenty acres there to Hugh de Port. So interests on both Picot's and Rochester's sides were eroding away. When the community of Rochester, urged on by Lanfranc, challenged the King's (and therefore the omnivorous Picot's) rights to Isleham and Freckenham, the King called a meeting of the shire of Cambridgeshire to adjudicate the dispute.[53] At this assembly the men of the shire, meeting under the watchful eye of Picot, sheriff of that county, affirmed that Isleham was the King's. Odo of Bayeux, who heard the plea, had his doubts about this decision, and he insisted that twelve men be chosen especially from the assembled crowd to swear an oath affirming the veracity of the court's opinion. The *Textus* gives the names of six of these jurors, five of whom are identified with toponymic bynames. All five were from Staploe Hundred, where Isleham lay, suggesting that the shire meeting described in the *Textus* was actually one of those hybrid judicial meetings of combined shire and hundred courts. The affirma- tion handed down by the sworn men of Staploe Hundred was given, according to the *Textus*, because Picot terrorized the jurors during their deliberations. Thus, the land remained under the power of the sheriff. But later, in that same year, the old monk-reeve of Freckenham contested this decision, claiming that the men of Staploe Hundred had given false judgment and, furthermore, that one of the jurors certainly knew better, since he had been under the monk when he was reeve. The unfortunate juror was brought before Odo, and he confessed to perjury. Odo then summoned the "man who swore first," and he confessed as well. Odo then ordered the sheriff (who was, of course, Picot) to send the whole miserable lot to London, along with twelve of the other "better men of the county," who had also attended the Cambridgeshire assembly. At London all twelve of the original jurors were found guilty of perjury. The second set of jurors – the men of the original shire court who had not actually sworn an oath – were required to prove that they had not been in agreement with the perjurous dozen, but all twelve failed the ordeal of hot iron. The twenty-four together were then penalized with a huge fine, and Rochester was triumphant.

This is a salutary tale, not only for jurors as a warning against the hazards of false testimony, but for historians interested in the Domesday inquest. It allows us a glimpse at the real-world politics that must have operated at every court in the tenth and eleventh centuries, including the ones that produced Domesday Book. The story of Picot, Isleham, and the jurors illustrates the

---

difficulties that arose in determining legal seisin throughout the Conqueror's reign. Oftentimes more than one party had real and legitimate claims to the same property; and all sides were willing to pressure the courts ruthlessly to elicit favorable judgment.[54] The case also makes clear that if anyone paid the price for an overturned decision, it was jurors and not the great men who suborned their testimony. Picot, one of the greatest scoundrels in Domesday Book, must have found this bit of intelligence encouraging! The Isleham case also demonstrates the many ways in which sheriffs could influence testimony, and articulates how lords like Picot with great (if sometimes surrogate) interests in a hundred, could sway jurors' opinions. Finally, and interestingly, the case illustrates how those found guilty of perjury did not always meet a tragic end. At least one of the twelve original Staploe jurors, Ordmær of Badlingham, although tried, fined, and presumably chastened in London, remained active in the legal life of his community: in 1086 he was there at the great Cambridgeshire joint-assembly, acting as one of the Domesday jurors.[55]

It is with the saga of Ordmær of Badlingham in mind that the relationship between Domesday jurors, Domesday lords, and Domesday testimony should be examined. As the Rochester case reveals, one of the most powerful filters through which facts passed as they were determined by jurors was lordship. Although the relations between Domesday jurors and their lords can rarely be recovered from Domesday Book alone, it is possible to unearth such links for Cambridgeshire and for three hundreds in Hertfordshire because of the list of jurors preserved in the *ICC* and the *IE*. These names, enrolled by hundred in the satellite surveys, often include a toponymic byname (e.g. Roger of Childerley) or a quasi-surname that designates a juror's lord (e.g. Tibbald man of Hardwin).[56] Well over half of the jurors in the *ICC* and the *IE* can be traced back to Domesday Book itself, and the lords of those with toponymic bynames can often be discovered simply by finding where and under whom these jurors held their lands TRW. An examination of jurors and their lords in this small corner of England produces results which are suggestive. First, it is clear in Cambridgeshire, where we know the names of all the hundred jurors, that some tenants-in-chief commanded the loyalty of a disproportionate number of jurors (see table 3.) Of the forty-plus tenants-in-chief in Cambridgeshire, only sixteen can be identified as the lords of jurors. Obviously, if we were fully informed on these matters, more tenants-in-chief would be represented. Nonetheless, with over half of the lords known, it is probably safe to assert that not all tenants-in-chief in Cambridgeshire would have had men sitting on hundred juries. The jurors whose lords can be

---

[54] Picot's activities are clear from the *Textus*. Rochester, however, may have been up to no good as well. They may have forged a charter for the occasion. Both Isleham and Freckenham appear in a forged Rochester charter, which is purportedly a charter of Alfred the Great (S 349). This charter does not appear in the *Textus*, but it can be found in Rochester's fourteenth-century *Liber Temporalium*, fo. 10r, printed in *Registrum Roffense*, ed. J. Thorpe (London, 1769), 357–8.

[55] *ICC*, 1.

[56] Lewis, "Domesday jurors," 20–1.

Table 3. *The lords of Domesday jurors*

	Number of jurors	
Overlord	Cambridgeshire	Hertfordshire
Abbot of Chatteris	—	1
Abbot of Ely	20	1
Abbot of Ramsey	2	1
Abbot of Westminster	—	1
Alan of Richmond	12	—
Aubrey de Vere	4	—
Azelina Taillebois	1	—
Bishop of London	—	2
Countess Judith	1	—
Edgar the Ætheling	—	1
Eudo Dapifer	2	—
Eustace of Boulogne	1	1
Eustace of Huntingdon	1	—
Geoffrey de Bec	—	1
Geoffrey de Mandeville	4	2
Gilbert of Ghent	3	—
Gosbert de Beauvais	—	1
Hardwin de Scales	6	1
Odo bishop of Bayeux	—	2
Peter de Valognes	—	3
Picot the Sheriff	7	—
Ralph Baynard	—	1
Remigius bishop of Lincoln	2	—
Robert count of Mortain	—	1
Robert Fafiton	1	—
Robert Gernon	—	2
Sigar de Chocques	—	1
Walter Giffard	2	—
William d'Eu	—	1
William de Warenne	4	—
Total	73	24

discovered, moreover, were distributed very unevenly among the county's tenants-in-chief. Four men, the Abbot of Ely, Alan of Richmond, Hardwin de Scales, and Picot the Sheriff, were the lords of forty-five men – fully two-thirds of all the jurors whose lords are known. And the top seven barons were the lords of 80 percent of these jurors.[57]

---

[57] The percentage remains the same if the Abbot of Ely and the jurors of the double hundred of Ely are removed.

Why were some tenants-in-chief in Cambridgeshire the lords of more men than others? A group of explanations presents itself. The size of a tenant-in-chief's fee certainly played a role. Many of the most successful collectors of jurors had large demesne holdings within the county. Count Alan, for example, held about £170 there in demesne (and another £140 enfeoffed) – between a third and a quarter of his entire demesne holding.[58] Clearly, Alan was a local force with which to be reckoned, and twelve Cambridgeshire jurors can be shown to have been associated with him. Eustace of Boulogne, on the other hand, a man with landed interests equal to those of Count Alan (over £900 in all) held only £41 of land in the county (and only £29 of it in demesne) – a mere 4 percent of his total demesne holdings.[59] Clearly, Cambridgeshire was not a region in which Eustace was particularly involved, and, not surprisingly, only one Cambridgeshire juror can be shown to have been his man. Aubrey de Vere, on the other hand, in comparison to Eustace a man of little consequence, held roughly the same amount of land in Cambridgeshire as Eustace – £39. Unlike Eustace, however, he kept almost all of this land in demesne (£38 10s.), and Aubrey's interests there represented about a quarter of his demesne holdings across the kingdom.[60] All of this suggests that Cambridgeshire was an important place for Aubrey, and one of the centers of his activity. Such local involvement provides the explanation for why so many of Aubrey's men acted as jurors in 1086, and why he is recorded as the lord of more jurors than Eustace, despite his more humble endowment across the kingdom and equal landed interests in Cambridge-shire.

It also looks as if the location of estates, like the configuration of tenants-in-chief's holdings, was a critical factor in determining whose men served as jurors. Lords who controlled land in vills where hundred courts traditionally met – for example, the Abbot of Ramsey and Alan of Richmond in Longstow,[61] or Hardwin de Scales in Thriplow and Papworth[62] – appear to have had a better chance of placing their men on juries than other lords. Sheriffs, too, may have been more savvy than others about "jury rigging" and the good judgments such activity could bring. The sheriffs Aubrey de Vere, Eustace of Huntingdon, Geoffrey de Mandeville, Picot the Sheriff, and the wife of the sheriff Ralph Taillebois all had men in Cambridgeshire who were jurors.[63] Indeed, all the sheriffs holding in Cambridgeshire, even Eustace of Huntington, who held a paltry £3 5s. in the shire, can be attributed with jurors.[64] Similarly, those tenants-in-chief who were involved in pre-

---

[58] DB, i, 193v-95v; Fleming, *Kings and Lords*, 219.

[59] DB, i, 196r; Fleming, *Kings and Lords*, 219.

[60] DB, i, 199v.

[61] DB, i, 192v, 195r.

[62] DB, i, 191r, 199r.

[63] Judith Green, "The sheriffs of William the Conqueror," *ANS*, 5 (1983), 140–1. Peter de Valognes, who held in Hertfordshire, was the lord of a juror in that county (DB, i, 141r).

[64] DB, i, 199v.

Domesday inquests within the shire – men like Eudo Dapifer, Ralph Taillebois, Picot the Sheriff, and Hardwin de Scales, all of whom were commissioners in the inquiry held in 1075 to inventory Ely's chattels – were lords of Cambridgeshire jurors. Indeed, they were the lords of a third of all known jurors in the county.[65] Men, therefore, with experience in royal and legal administration can be shown to have been the lords of a disproportionately large number of Cambridgeshire jurors. If these figures are remotely representative of the relationship between jurors and important tenants-in-chief throughout the kingdom, they are worth some rumination. They do suggest that the faceless and dispassionate "men of the hundred" may not have been altogether disinterested in the disputes presented to them when they involved a handful of the shire's most powerful men – men who just happened to be their lords.

It is not unreasonable, given what we know about lordship and about local assemblies, to think that the lords of jurors had some sort of impact on the verdicts presented by the courts and on the tenor of the descriptions of adjudication that were eventually incorporated into the great survey. Contemporaries certainly understood the dangers lordship presented to jury testimony, and sometimes they sought to keep plaintiffs' men from judging pleas.[66] Tantalizing hints of lordship's impact on judgment are produced by matching jurors' lords with hundreds and hundreds with disputes (see table 4). One of Count Alan's men, for example, was a juror in Flendish Hundred. There, according to Domesday Book, the "men of the hundred" supported Count Alan's claim of a hide in Fulbourn against John fitz Waleran.[67] Or again, in Thriplow Hundred, where a man of Geoffrey de Mandeville sat as juror, the men of the hundred testified in no uncertain terms that Robert Gernon had stolen a half a mill from Geoffrey.[68] Similarly, in Wetherley Hundred at least two of the hundred's jurors were Picot the Sheriff's men; and it was at the hundred court that the illegal seizure of three of Picot's men by Roger de Montgomery was discussed.[69] These and other examples suggest that the complaints of jurors' lords were more likely to be aired and to receive a sympathetic hearing by hundred assemblies packed with wronged lords' dependants than in hundreds where the men of their enemies and expropriators were confirming or disputing testimony.

Still, descriptions of wrongdoing can be found in Domesday in hundreds where a lord's men sat as jurors. In Armingford Hundred, for example, where a man of Hardwin de Scales was a juror, Hardwin was repeatedly reproached by the testimony of the men of the hundred. Indeed, three different claims in

---

[65] *LE*, ii, 114. And if the double hundreds of Ely are removed, this figure goes up to 45 percent.

[66] In an early twelfth-century dispute over Sandwich, a decision was made under oath by twelve men of Sandwich and twelve men of Dover "qui non sunt homines archiepiscopi nec homines abbatis," the two claimants (Stenton, *English Justice*, appendix 1, 118–19).

[67] F 242.

[68] F 198.

[69] F 184.

Table 4. *Cambridgeshire jurors' lords by hundred*

Hundred/lord	Number of jurors
Armingford	
Alan of Richmond	1
Azelina Tallebois	1
Eudo Dapifer	1
Geoffrey de Mandeville	1
Hardwin de Scales	1
Chesterton	
Remigius bishop of Lincoln	2
Robert Fafiton	1
Cheveley	
Alan of Richmond	2
Aubrey de Vere	2
Countess Judith	1
Chilford	
Alan of Richmond	3
Aubrey de Vere	2
Picot the Sheriff	1
Ely	
Abbot of Ely	16
Flendish	
Abbot of Ely	1
Alan of Richmond	1
Longstow	
Abbot of Ely	1
Abbot of Ramsey	1
Alan of Richmond	1
Eudo Dapifer	1
Picot the Sheriff	1
Northstow	
Picot the Sheriff	2
Papworth	
Abbot of Ely	1
Abbot of Ramsey	1
Eustace the Sheriff	1
Gilbert of Ghent	2
Hardwin de Scales	2

Hundred/lord	Number of jurors
Radfield	
Abbot of Ely	1
Alan of Richmond	1
William de Warenne	2
Staine	
Alan of Richmond	1
Hardwin de Scales	1
Walter Giffard	2
Staploe	
Alan of Richmond	2
Geoffrey de Mandeville	1
William de Warenne	1
Thriplow	
Geoffrey de Mandeville	1
Hardwin de Scales	1
Picot the Sheriff	1
William de Warenne	1
Wetherley	
Eustace of Boulogne	1
Picot the Sheriff	3
Whittlesford	
Alan of Richmond	1
Hardwin de Scales	1
Total	72

Armingford Hundred represent Hardwin as the wrongdoer.[70] This suggests that jurors could sometimes suppress the skullduggery of their lords, but not in the most flagrant of cases. And since testimony was gathered at great joint-assemblies, there were some practical impediments to prevarication, because neighbors from nearby hundreds, who were men of competing lords, could contest or at least witness perjurous testimony. The production of written evidence, moreover, by organized and archive-keeping religious communities had a powerful impact on the ways in which jurors remembered past arrangements or gave judgment. In Northstow Hundred, where one of Picot's men served as juror, it was reported that Picot had come into six hides and three virgates formerly held by an Englishman on lease from the Abbot of

[70] Against Ely in Meldreth (F 205–6); against Roger de Montgomery in Steeple Morden (F 183); and as a tenant of Richard fitz Gilbert against the King in Whaddon (F 194).

Ely.[71] The jurors decided that the sheriff's tenancy was illegal. Jurors' memories were only so flexible.

Similarly, having one's rivals' men on the same hundred juries as one's own must have mitigated some of the bullying and influence peddling so clear in the Isleham case. On such occasions, having one's men sitting on a hundred jury could guarantee neither a favorable decision nor the suppression of evil deeds. Evidence for this is provided by Domesday's descriptions of Great Abington in Chilford Hundred. This vill was the locus of a number of disputes aired by Chilford Hundred's jury, which included a man each of Alan of Richmond, Aubrey de Vere, and Picot the Sheriff. Firmatus, one of Chilford's jurors, held the whole of Great Abington from Aubrey de Vere. Aubrey's (and therefore Firmatus's) rights to one of the six hides there were contested by Count Alan, whose man Brian de Scalers was also on Chilford's jury, and who "claims this hide from Aubrey's men, so the hundred testifies."[72] Presumably, Firmatus was one of the "men of Aubrey" against whom Alan claimed the land. Aubrey had also annexed a half a hide of land in Great Abington against the King. Picot the Sheriff, some time before the Domesday inquest, had ruled that the holding was illegal, and had taken it back "for" the King. (In fact Picot himself was holding this half hide in 1086 *sub manu regis*.[73]) Walter de Clais, both Picot's man and a Chilford Hundred juror, must have testified to this. But the interests of the sticky-fingered Aubrey, too, were represented. Twice in the Cambridgeshire folios we are told that the men of Chilford Hundred testified that Picot, when he repossessed the King's half virgate, had illegally distrained 380 of Aubrey's sheep and one of his plows.[74] Between all these descriptions of sheep rustling and land stealing something was said at court in defense of all three of the tenants-in-chief with both interests in Great Abington and men serving as Chilford Hundred jurors. The one set of interests in the vill, however, that is not discussed at all in Domesday Book is that of Ramsey Abbey, and this in spite of the fact that Ramsey had suffered the greatest loss of anyone holding in the vill. Apparently Ramsey had claim to the five hides in Abington which Aubrey had inherited from his antecessor Wulfwine. Wulfwine, according to Ramsey's chronicle, held the land on lease from the abbey.[75] This transaction does not appear in Ramsey's cartulary, nor is there a royal charter, so Ramsey may have lost its bid for reseisin due to the lack of a diploma: certainly this happened elsewhere. The fact, however, that no mention at all is made of Ramsey's claim to the five hides in Domesday Book may be because none of the jurors in Chilford Hundred were the Abbot of Ramsey's men. Ramsey

[71] F 236.
[72] F 213.
[73] F 171.
[74] F 171, 215. The misappropriation of chattels is only very rarely mentioned in Domesday Book. This may be a case of distraint of chattels, used as a first step in moving against a wrongdoer, for details of which, see Hudson, *Land*, 30–3.
[75] *Chron. Rams.*, 152–3.

held no land in the hundred in the time of King William; and because of this the abbey's interests against other jurors' lords there may not have been effectively represented.

Finally, the physical presence of powerful lords and royal officials must also have influenced jurors' memories about the past. We know, for example, that when the jurors of Whittlesford, Armingford, Longstow, and Wetherley Hundreds offered testimony, Picot himself was present, because Domesday Book tells us that he testified in person.[76] Domesday Book records no complaints against Picot in these hundreds, which is quite extraordinary, considering the sheriff's penchant for other people's property.[77]

Great men's ability to receive favorable judgments at local courts was hardly a Norman innovation: it had a long history in England, reaching far back into the Anglo-Saxon past. Two disputes that arose after Edgar the Peaceable's death illustrate this neatly. Both Ely and Rochester had won possession of disputed lands during Edgar's reign, but both were stripped of their titles in local courts soon after the King's death. In Ely's case, "powerful men" – an East Anglian ealdorman and his brother – impugned an earlier assembly's decision made in Ely's favor, and when the two renewed their suit at a newly constituted local assembly, the brothers prevailed; "and they annexed the land and claimed it for themselves."[78] In the case of Rochester, an earlier settlement in St. Andrew's favor concerning two estates was overturned when laymen, with some claim to the land, took it back through "illegal seizure" (*on reatlace*). This annexation, so it turns out, was not instituted through force, but rather via an unfavorable judgment at a local court, held under the auspices of Ealdorman Edwin and decided by "the people who were God's enemies" – no doubt the men of the hundred or shire court.[79] On both occasions, local courts were called and manipulated by local noblemen, and both pleas were settled in their favor. These two examples suggest that the "anti-monastic reaction" was perpetrated not so much by thegns on the rampage as by local *boni homines* working through local courts. Indeed much of the violence done to monastic communities in the decade after Edgar's death was committed in legally constituted assemblies. The imprint of lordship, therefore, on the decisions of hundred and shire courts is visible across the tenth and eleventh centuries. As Eric John noted, although local courts "were in a sense public courts administering public law . . . they were also assemblies of landed warriors quarreling and bargaining amongst themselves."[80] The dependence of local courts on local lords, then, was not limited to private sokes or honorial courts. Every court meeting apart from the *curia regis* in the tenth and eleventh centuries could be

---

[76] F 184, 220, 222, 225–6.

[77] Odo's imprisonment, on the other hand, may explain why so many complaints could be registered against him in Surrey (F 1478–9, 1483, 1487–8, 1491–3, 1495–6, 1499, 1501, 1513).

[78] *LE*, ii, 7.

[79] S 1457.

[80] Eric John, *Orbis Britanniae* (Leicester, 1966), 149.

manipulated by great thegns, or counts, or abbots, and used to bolster aristocratic interests in the countryside, not because local magnates had any formal rights to do so, but because their private relationships with the local men enabled them to do so.[81]

Local courts and royal writs

The miracle, of course, is that some time between the tenth and the late twelfth centuries, the king made impressive inroads into many of these regional assemblies, and increased his ability to direct their actions and suitors in ways that would have been inconceivable in Edgar's reign. I would argue that an important step in this process, tentative though it was, was taken both because of William I's Conquest and because of his inquests. The King's control in 1086, as we can surmise from the vulnerability of jurors, was far from complete. But his presence was more directly felt in local courts in 1086 and after than it had been at any time before the Norman Conquest. This transformation is best seen in the rapid evolution of the Anglo-Norman writ, that instrument of written administration yoking such courts to royal will. The metamorphosis of regional courts, as seen through writs, and the role of William I's reign and inquests in this, can be discerned by comparing royal use of local assemblies before and after 1066 and by locating the arenas in which kings of England promulgated written orders on either side of the Norman Conquest. The meetings of the regular shire, borough, and hundred courts were convened, according to the prescriptive legislation of pre-Conquest kings, twice, three times, and twelve times each year.[82] In some ways, these meetings can be read as moments when royal power manifested itself in the localities, since the neighborhood judgments made there were produced under the aegis of king's men – his ealdormen, bishops, sheriffs, and hundred reeves.[83] In Cnut's reign, for example, a meeting of the county of Herefordshire, called to settle a thorny dispute between a mother and her son, was overseen by a bishop, an earl, a sheriff, and Tovi the Proud, "who came there on the King's business."[84]

These courts were also places where Old English kings' needs could more directly be revealed through their writs or messengers.[85] Royal desires made known through legates or writs coalesced, before the Conquest, in interesting

---

[81] Patrick Wormald has exposed a similar nexus of personal relationships and testimony for the pleas surrounding Oswaldslow in the Conqueror's reign (Patrick Wormald, "Lordship and justice in the early English kingdom: Oswaldslow revisited," in *Property and Power in the Early Middle Ages*, ed. Wendy Davies and Paul Fouracre [Cambridge, 1995], 114–36).

[82] Hundred Ordinance (a. k. a. I Edgar) 1; III Edgar 5§1.

[83] H. R. Loyn, "The hundred in England in the tenth and early eleventh centuries," in *British Government and Administration*, ed. H. R. Loyn and H. Hearder (Cardiff, 1974), 4.

[84] S 1462.

[85] Domesday Book examples of royal writs directed at shires, hundreds, and boroughs are plentiful. For examples of writs directed to hundreds, see F 61, 662–3, 1134, 1753, 2967. For a writ of the Queen

ways around a limited number of concerns. First of all, the king used local courts in conjunction with writs or legates to announce grants of land which had come to him through forfeiture,[86] to pardon geld,[87] or to herald the appointment of a new official.[88] Writs were also apparently expected at local assemblies when land in the king's farm was leased,[89] when the sheriff acquired rights to *terra regis*[90] or when land was granted out in return for service to the king.[91] All of these things can be seen as central to the king's household administration – actions involving the management of his own resources and the policing of his own officials.[92] Regular meetings of local assemblies, therefore, were often harnessed by the king through his writ, and employed to promote royal rights or to oversee royal property, dues, and administrators; and if we look beyond the writs preserved in monastic cartularies, and which served, for the most part, to notify shire courts of grants or confirmations of land or privileges, and give equal weight to the large number of writs described in Domesday Book, we have ample evidence that pre-Conquest writs functioned as "written instruments . . . of current government,"[93] as long, that is, as we are willing to view government as the safeguarding of royal income. From the surviving evidence, we can only conclude that before the Norman Conquest this was one of the king's

---

directed to a hundred, see S 1241. For writs directed to a borough, see F 844, 980. See also S 1153. For writs directed to a shire, see F 122, 663, 766, 1567 and the vast majority of pre-Conquest writs. For the use of special messengers from the king, see F 199, 252, 658, 1056, 1525, 1527, 1812, 1865, 2708.

[86] S 991. It may be this practice that accounts for the detailed descriptions of forfeitures to the King found in Æthelred's charters (Simon Keynes, "Crime and punishment in the reign of King Æthelred," *People and Places in Northern Europe 500–1000*, ed. I. Wood and N. Lund [Woodbridge, Suffolk, 1991], 67–81, at 76–8). Earlier, during Alfred's reign, during one phase of the dispute involving Fonthill, an agreement was reached at the King's court, and a charter drawn up and read at the meeting (Simon Keynes, "The Fonthill letter," *Words, Texts and Manuscripts*, ed. M. Korhammer [Cambridge, 1992], 53–97, at 70–1).

[87] S 1113. Apparently the county or hundred court expected notification through the king's writ of new grants of beneficial hidation. The clearest example of this can be found under the Domesday Book entry for Pyrford, an estate of twenty-seven hides. When Earl Harold acquired it, its assessment fell to sixteen hides *ad libitum Heraldi*. The men of the hundred, however, protested that they had never seen a writ *ex parte regis*, which lowered this land's assessment (F 1503). For another TRE example, see F 662. For TRW examples, see F 574, 636.

[88] For use of the writ to publicize the appointment of a new bishop, see, for example, S 1111, 1151. Writs were probably also used to notify local courts of the appointment of secular officials.

[89] F 122, 663, 863. For a TRW example, see F 1499.

[90] F 95, 122, 199, 663; and for post-Conquest examples, see F 766, 1523.

[91] F 95 and perhaps 1688. See also Queen Edith's writ, directed to a hundred, which orders that the hundred give a lawful judgment concerning the actions of a certain Wudumann, probably a local reeve, who had withheld rent from Edith for six years (S 1241).

[92] James Campbell has argued that royal revenues in the late Anglo-Saxon period were largely paid in cash, and that they were collected or farmed in some way by the sheriff of each shire. The complexity of this system is revealed in Domesday Book, and it would, as Campbell notes, have required a good system of account (James Campbell, "The Anglo-Norman state in administrative history," in Campbell, *Essays*). The writ may well have played a central role in the accounting of royal dues and farms in this period, as it clearly did by the mid-twelfth century (fitz Nigel, *Dialogus de Scaccario*, 33, 89–91). For other indications of the use of the written word in royal administration before the Conquest, see also James Campbell, "The significance of the Anglo-Norman state in the administrative history of Western Europe," in Campbell, *Essays*, 171–89, at 173–5, and "Some agents and agencies of the late Anglo-Saxon State," in *Domesday Studies*, 201–18, at 214–15; Simon Keynes, "Royal government and the written word," in *The Use of Literacy in Early Medieval Europe*, ed. Rosamond McKitterick (Cambridge, 1990), 226–57.

[93] *Royal Writs*, 110.

primary uses of the writ and, therefore by extension, the regional assembly. And it suggests that much of the effort of pre-Conquest state-building was spent developing the means through which kings could intervene locally in fiscal matters – in the raising of taxes, in the management of dues, and in the exploitation of the *terra regis*. The king and the state before 1066 were closest to local communities in these matters.

Before the Conquest the king also utilized local meetings in conjunction with writs to publicize agreements that had been brokered not at a meeting of the shire, borough, or hundred, but rather in his own presence and at his court,[94] or to confirm and give force to ancient bequests which may in some way have been threatened.[95] The king also periodically directed local courts to take action. Writs, for example, could be sent to shire or borough courts to grant individuals the king's peace.[96] Only very occasionally in the pre-Conquest period, however, did royal writs instruct local assemblies to remedy particular legal claims. Æthelred the Unready admonished the thegns of east and west Kent, through his writ and seal, to settle a dispute over Snodland;[97] and he ordered a shire meeting in Berkshire, by the same means, to adjudicate a lawsuit between Wynflæd and Leofwine.[98] Edward the Confessor, through a writ directed to the shire of Norfolk, demanded that the assembly make a judgment against a certain Samær.[99] These three examples, spanning the years *c*. 990 to 1052, are the sum total evidence for pre-Conquest kings' use of writs as precepts compelling local courts to adjudicate specific pieces of litigation: together they make up only a tiny fraction of known writs.[100] Clearly, the king interfered in the legal life of local courts from time to time. But our evidence suggests that it was not actually until after the Conquest that writs were *regularly* issued by the king mandating that assemblies remedy particular disputes;[101] and it was not until the Conqueror's reign and after that writs which are wholly judicial come to be preserved in monastic

---

[94] S 1116, 1123.

[95] S 1153. The majority of the writs in Domesday Book, which have not been preserved in ecclesiastical archives, deal not with confirmations of title but rather with a much broader range of administrative uses (F 14, 17, 19, 22, 61–2, 95, 109, 122, 128, 199, 252, 474, 531, 574, 594, 636, 658, 662–3, 766, 809, 844, 863–4, 868, 872, 980, 997, 1050, 1056, 1134, 1243, 1265, 1353, 1496–7, 1499, 1503, 1510, 1517, 1523, 1525, 1527, 1530 1567, 1576, 1688, 1690, 1701, 1753, 1792–3, 1812, 1825, 1830, 1832, 2342, 2373, 2410, 2637, 2708, 2834, 2881, 2934, 2962, 2967, 3063, 3071). See Campbell, "The Anglo-Norman state," 175–6.

[96] F 252, 980, 1243, 1265, 1701. Powerful laymen could also grant individuals peace (S 1243), as could earls (F 252, 1702), earls' officials (F 252), sheriffs (F 1307, 1640) and King's legates (F 252).

[97] S 1456.

[98] S 1454.

[99] S 1077.

[100] Two other writs survive through which two royal wives, Edith and Ælfthryth, attempted to meddle in local judicial decisions, suggesting that intervention into the legal life of shires, hundreds, and boroughs did not constitute an exclusively royal prerogative, but was rather a commonplace practice among the powerful (S 1240, 1242).

[101] See, for example, *Regesta*, I, nos. 155, 184, 242, 383, 449; *Mon. Ang.*, I, 602; A. W. Levison, "A report on the Penenden trial," *EHR*, 27 (1912), 719; *ICC*, xviii, no. 3; Stenton, *English Justice*, appendix 1, 116–23; *Historians of the Church of York*, II, 353; *Memorials of Bury St. Edmunds*, 60–7. See also John, *Orbis Britanniae*, 151. For a list of post-Conquest judicial writs see *Royal Writs*, 181–2, 189–94.

archives.[102] This proliferation of judicial writs marks the Conqueror's and his sons' increasing intrusion into the judicial business of local communities in the decades following the Conquest.

Not surprisingly, this same period also witnessed the rise of royal writs as a means of proving seisin in local courts.[103] The century before the Conquest, of course, witnessed royal intervention in local courts to bolster the rights of important local thegns and ecclesiastical communities. But this practice was apparently popularized in William I's reign to such an extent that by his death even small men were sometimes expected to produce royal writs to confirm their rights to virgates and acres.[104] Although it has been argued that this was a pre-Conquest practice,[105] this seems unlikely in light of the evidence in Domesday Book. There are some two dozen TRW writs described in the survey pointing to this use, but only six from Edward's reign, and these six deal either with the confirmatory writs of large ecclesiastical houses or with *terra regis* and sheriff's land – and the latter, I would argue, are administrative writs and not writs dealing with seisin.[106] Here, again, is evidence for expanded royal participation in local courts.

Other changes in the proximity of king and local assembly can be located to this same period. Pre-Conquest writs, for example, when not dealing directly with royal officials or dues, were generally reactive rather than pro-active, and few bear much resemblance to Sir Frank Stenton's "brief notifications . . . of the king's will addressed to men who must carry it out."[107] The writs themselves give ample evidence that local courts before the Conquest were habitually convened independent of royal desire, and that the king's writ typically followed rather than precipitated such assemblies. Monasteries and donors, for example, often forged agreements under the gaze of a local assembly, then traveled to the king's court to obtain a writ of confirmation, and finally published the writ back home at yet another local meeting. *Circa* 1044, for example, Cnut's housecarl Ork and his wife Tole granted property to Abbotsbury in full view of the local "good men" (*godre manna*) – clearly the suitors of a hundred or shire court. More than a decade later, after Ork's death, the Abbot of Abbotsbury felt it necessary to travel to the royal court, to procure a confirmatory writ in which the King promised to be a "protector and guardian" of Abbotsbury and its property, and to publish this writ at a Dorset assembly.[108] The king, therefore, did not

---

[102] Evidence of two of the above writs is preserved in descriptions of lawsuits (S 1454, 1456), and the actual surviving writ which contains judicial instructions (S 1077) is mainly concerned with other matters.

[103] For the few pre-Conquest examples, see F 1056, 1467, 1688, 2934, 2967. For post-Conquest examples, see F 14, 17, 19, 61–2, 128, 531, 594, 658, 664, 766, 809, 1050, 1134, 1496, 1510, 1517, 1525, 1527, 1530, 1690, 1753, 1792–3, 2637, 2962, 3071.

[104] F 61–2, 594, 658, 809, 1530; Campbell, "Agents and agencies," *Domesday Studies*, 201–18, at 214. For the growing popularity of the writ of right under the Anglo-Norman kings, see Judith Green, *The Government of England under Henry I* (Cambridge, 1986), 103–4.

[105] Campbell, "Agents and agencies," 15.

[106] F 95, 122, 199, 474, 663, 1792.

[107] F. M. Stenton, *The Latin Charters of the Anglo-Saxon Period* (Oxford, 1955), 89.

[108] S 1064.

participate in the legal dealings of Ork, Abbotsbury, or the Dorset shire court until years after the initial gift, and then only after his involvement had been solicited especially by the Abbot. Or again, when the abbots of Ramsey and Thorney were disputing rights over a valuable stretch of fenland, they called a meeting themselves and hammered out a concord. It was only after this that the two abbots went to the King's court – and as the Confessor's writ says, "and they have notified me that this agreement was made between them." Only at this point did the King confirm their agreement with a writ.[109] These examples illustrate how before the Conquest local assemblies, under the guidance of great country lords, dealt independently with provincial issues, and how the king was inserted into regional affairs only after local assemblies had cobbled together agreements, and then only at the request of the parties involved.[110]

The metamorphosis of the writ across the eleventh century, then, reveals something important about the changing ecology of regional assemblies in the years following the Battle of Hastings. The king (or his orders in the form of a writ) took an active role before the Conquest in local assemblies when he wished to administer his own holdings and officials or to uphold the actions of local lords who had come to his court in search of a royal confirmation. But these assemblies, when dealing with warranty, disputes, or criminal behavior, almost always operated in the shadow of important local magnates and their followings. In no way can we view the bulk of judicial assemblies that met apart from the royal court before 1066 as regular and profound manifestations of royal power in the localities, in the way that the tenth-century Hundred Ordinance intimates that they were.[111] In reality, up-country thegns met and made decisions according to local power, needs, and interests. Beginning in William the Conqueror's reign, however, there is ample evidence for a deepening royal involvement in regional assemblies.[112] By William Rufus's reign the King, through his writ, routinely mandated the holding of county courts, the investigation into specific claims and the final resolution of complaints.[113] This does not, of course, mean that Anglo-Norman kings had absolute control over local courts: but they had gained an important foothold there. Anglo-Norman kings, on the whole, were less effective in their fiscal management of local communities than late Anglo-

---

[109] S 1110; *Chron. Rams.*, 166; *Cart. Rams.*, I, 188. For a discussion of this suit, see Stenton, *English Justice*, 13–14.

[110] *Facsimiles of English Royal Writs to A.D. 1100*, ed. T. A. M. Bishop and P. Chaplais (Oxford, 1957), xii-xiii. See Simon Keynes, "Regenbald the Chancelor (*sic*)," *ANS*, 10 (1988), 187 and n. 9, and 213 for the role of an early royal secretariat in the production of royal writs and its role in empowering local interested ecclesiastics to draw them up.

[111] Hundred Ordinance 1, 2, 3§1. The dogged legislation of tenth-century kings concerning these assemblies creates the powerful but spurious illusion that already functioning local assemblies operated under the authority of West Saxon kings.

[112] *Regesta*, I, nos. 98, 242, 244, 258; F 1134; *ICC*, xviii, no. 3. By Henry I's reign, royal writs ordered that specific tenants provide service to their lords, suggesting that lords still requested royal backing, which resulted in writs, which helped them act more effectively against recalcitrant tenants (Hudson, *Land*, 38).

[113] See, for example, *Regesta*, I, no. 383.

Saxon kings, particularly when it came to levying geld and managing coinage. But they appear to have intensified their judicial control over the localities. Thus, Anglo-Norman royal power on a local level, which was dependent on many of the same institutions and mechanisms as royal power before 1066, appears to have shifted and transformed in interesting ways.

The amplification of royal power within regional assemblies can be attributed, in part, to the tenurial crisis unleashed by the Norman settlement. New Norman lords and old ecclesiastical corporations, for their part, had a pressing need to establish warranty after the Conquest. And King William, for his part, was compelled to keep disputes over the tricky business of seisin, spawned by the Norman settlement, from erupting into unmanageable violence, and from escaping out from under royal control.[114] These twinned needs of king and lords worked in concert to broaden royal power in local courts. The king's deepening involvement with local assemblies also, no doubt, was brought about by the Domesday inquest itself, because this grand event required the hasty assembling of every regularly constituted court in England, and charged these assemblies to give evidence on the tenurial status of every holding in England. In doing so, the inquest swiftly routinized the employment of the writ as a proof of seisin and as a way of bringing disputes to law. It also encouraged lords and men to take disputes concerning both disciplinary and proprietary cases out of seigniorial courts and into the royal assemblies called especially for the Domesday inquest, a habit that helped to erode Anglo-Norman seigniorial jurisdiction just as it was being established.[115] Clearly the inquest also generated a mass of pleas, which in turn required other writs and other court meetings.[116] It looks very much as if the accelerated evolution of the writ and royal justice during this period parallels the swift transformation of the two in the first decade of Henry II's rule, a development which John Hudson has argued occurred in direct response to the crush of litigation carried over from Stephen's troubled reign.[117] King William, therefore, not only dramatically extended royal power (at least in theory) by granting every man his land, but by guaranteeing possession practically and concretely by providing a more mechanized means of guaranteeing seisin in court. But Domesday Book, itself, also played an important role in the widening of royal involvement in regional courts. As J. C. Holt has reminded us, Domesday Book, above all else, looks like a practical, administrative document, the purpose of which was to bind together sheriff, treasury, and the localities.[118] The production and layout of Domesday Book opened up the possibility for an intensified intimacy

[114] See below, chapter 4.
[115] Dalton, *Conquest*, 262–3.
[116] For a Ramsey plea, held in William Rufus's reign in response to the Domesday inquest, and for the two writs this plea generated, see David Bates, "Two Ramsey Abbey writs and the Domesday survey," *BIHR*, 63 (1990), 337–9.
[117] Hudson, *Land*, 71.
[118] Holt, "1086," 55.

between king and shires, because it provided royal administrators with the details they needed in each county to keep track of tenure, succession, royal rights, escheats, and wardships: and it gave them the ability to pen quick and dirty writs to sheriffs, so that the sheriff, in turn, could direct local courts in the manner in which king and *curia* desired. This capacity was prerequisite for the eventual elaboration of the centralizing procedures of royal justice and for the genesis of the system of eyres, which eventually bound local courts to the machinery of central government.

Conclusion

A study of the courts and testimony of 1086 has both obvious lessons and more subtle implications. On the most concrete level, an examination of the assemblies gathered to produce sworn evidence in 1086 provides us with the legal and political background against which Domesday Book should be read, and it contextualizes the disputes and claims enumerated in the survey. Jurors and their testimony also highlight the inquest's dependence on the institution of the Anglo-Saxon joint-assembly, and they emphasize that the types of disputes and conflicts recorded in Domesday Book were often shaped by the structures of lordship. A look at Domesday's assemblies and juries also offers evidence of the rapid and immediate expansion of royal power in regional assemblies after the Norman Conquest, and it shows the very real gains in royal power over local interests in the first generation of Norman rule. At the same time, of course, we can see how very far the king and his administrators had to go before they could fully co-opt local assemblies.

On a more abstract level, the oral aspect of Domesday's proceedings reveals something about the hierarchy of textuality and orality both in William the Conqueror's century and in our own. Our stock-in-trade as historians is the written word, and we are dazzled by texts. Indeed oftentimes we are so intently focused on the written word that we forget about the clamoring noise of oral culture, a thing that cohabited with textual culture in the eleventh century, and indeed overshadowed it. Our fixation on the iconic text of Domesday Book is clear evidence of this: so interested have we become in the great survey and in the written sources hidden beneath it, that we have forgotten about the Domesday inquest. And when we think at all about that great, noisy assembly, we tend to conflate it with Domesday Book. The inquest and the Book obviously share an intimate relationship, but they are not the same thing. The meaning of the *descriptio* to its sponsor and authors must have been entirely different than the meaning of the performance of the inquest for those who witnessed it. Oral testimony was central to the purpose of the inquest, and it provided the means through which neighbors of all social classes witnessed and recognized the permanence of the Norman settlement: and the inquest rather than the book became the means through which the whole of the tenurial revolution (much of which had been accomplished without written order or public sanction) came clearly and finally into every man's view, and it was the way in which the Conquest was at last fitted snugly and publicly within the law. For this purpose, it did not matter that some disputes dredged up by the proceedings remained unresolved in 1086. Oral legal culture, by its very nature, is noisy, heterodox, and confusing; and it contains many points of view. But it is also public spectacle, and as such it ritualized the whole process of the Norman settlement, and it informed all of those who upheld law, whether in villages, boroughs, or shires, about the permanence of England's tenurial transformation. The inquest also provided a highly regulated forum in which complaints could be made and compromises could be begun, with perhaps the threat of violence, but without actual breach of peace.

When the stories of the inquest, however, were transformed into text and retold in Domesday Book, they were given a single, monolithic voice. The writing of Domesday Book transformed the enterprise of the inquest from a communal event that took place across the whole of England into a private record. The voice of Domesday Book, unlike the voices of the inquest, is that of royal administration: it is organized, authoritative, and rational. In this translation from event to text, the many points of view aired in the courts were domesticated by editing and by indexes, rubrics, and gatherings. Such a transformation determined the book, and made it a separate enterprise from the inquest itself. The text of Domesday – and not the inquest – informed the King and his officials about his and other men's rights, and made possible a more mechanized running of the state. The information in Domesday Book, at least in theory, freed royal officials and administrators from a reliance on their own memories of the proceedings and the memories of the thousands of sworn men who participated in it, and it allowed them instead to concentrate their efforts on organizing and calculating about the information that Domesday's author chose to preserve in writing. The application of this knowledge would have been inconceivable without the transformation of inquest into text. This is probably what the Conqueror had in mind all along. It is, however, an altogether different accomplishment than that of the inquest.

2   Living in the shadow of the law

The business of local assemblies

Sworn men, as we have seen, sat at the heart of the Domesday inquest, and their words and their memories were the source of almost all the information in Domesday Book related to legal customs, legal activity, and disputes. The range of these men's knowledge is astonishing. Men living in boroughs could describe in detail regulations about weights and measures,[1] about the proscriptions of certain types of behavior on holy days,[2] about the fines for adultery, and about the punishments for theft, rape, arson, and homicide.[3] Their familiarity with the penalties of sin and breach of peace was doubtless grounded in practical experience: they themselves lived in the shadow of legal custom, and many would have participated in accusing and judging individuals within their communities of social and legal transgressions. Their special expertise in the weaknesses of their neighbors and in the regulation of bad behavior shows how much of life was lived in full view of the community and indicates how often the private lives of burgesses were policed by deep-rooted social institutions manned by groups of curious neighbors.

The jurors in rural hundred courts and shire assemblies also knew a great deal about the lives of the families and individuals with whom they lived. During the 1086 inquest they were able to rehearse for the King's commissioners a whole universe of infractions — moral, familial, legal, and political. Members of hundred and shire assemblies, for example, knew who in their communities were thieves and who had carried out illegal feuds,[4] and they could name those who held land without proper warranty.[5] They remembered when their neighbors had lost land because of the shame of an adulterous affair or an uncanonical marriage.[6] They could testify about the mendacious,[7] and about those who had attempted to use forged writs.[8] They also knew how the families in their acquaintance hung together or fell apart.

[1] F 268.
[2] See below, subject index, VIII.2.
[3] See below, subject index, VIII.4, under "adultery," "theft," "rape," "arson," and "homicide."
[4] F 1797, 1969, 2220, 3038; 1501.
[5] F 66, 176, 2125–6.
[6] F 1555; 2424.
[7] F 3192.
[8] F 1830.

They could provide detailed information on the kinds of arrangements kinsmen made who held land in parage,[9] and they could air their suspicions about bequests gone wrong.[10] Local men could also describe to the King's legates the ways in which brothers came, in troubled times, to one another's aid,[11] and how husbands, fathers, sons, and brothers made donations to local religious communities for the souls of their loved ones.[12] They knew when a son had given his father's heriot to the sheriff,[13] and they had mastered the particular property arrangements made between individual husbands and their wives.[14] Their knowledge was not only legal, but political. They could identify those within their community who had been impoverished or "ruined" by the Conquest;[15] and they knew whose status had once been freeman and now was villein.[16] They could name those who exacted unjust customs and rents and denounce those who were in prison.[17] And many had incriminating stories about sheriffs and reeves that they were eager to rehearse in front of the King's commissioners.[18] Jurors could speak with authority about the ways in which those who had lost their lords sought the protection of other men.[19] They could describe, in detail, the circumstances behind many outlawings,[20] and they knew whose fortunes had been made on the backs of the dispossessed.[21]

The *Libellus Æthelwoldi*, a tract on Ely Abbey's late tenth-century litigation, gives us some indication of the world in which the Domesday's jurors moved and explains quite clearly why they knew so much.[22] The county society portrayed in the *Libellus* was an intensely public and populated one, one in which absolutely everyone transacted business at court and pursued their

---

[9] F 1014, 1073.
[10] F 1058.
[11] F 1534.
[12] F 548, 615, 707, 809.
[13] F 3186.
[14] F 38, 578, 609, 996, 1735.
[15] See below, subject index, V.5, under "ruined."
[16] F 1795.
[17] See below, subject index, V.10, under "unfair payments"; F 3047, 3207, and below, index of names, under "Odo bishop of Bayeux."
[18] For the misdeeds of sheriffs, see F 8, 26, 37, 55, 91–2, 94, 98, 116, 122, 150, 154, 162–4, 170, 177, 199, 218–19, 221, 224–5, 227–41, 246, 387, 389, 468–9, 470–1, 475, 490, 492, 494, 496, 502, 525, 539, 561, 614, 627, 633, 709–10, 767–8, 802, 806, 808–9, 813, 817–20, 836–9, 844–5, 863, 868, 903, 972, 977, 983, 1236, 1284, 1460, 1477, 1523, 1526–8, 1617, 1619, 1623–5, 1667, 1669, 1674, 1676, 1682–4, 1796–7, 1823, 1838, 1947–8, 1950, 1954, 1960, 1962, 1994, 2043, 2073–80, 2083–4, 2131, 2141, 2148, 2201, 2637, 3063, 3193. For the misdeeds of reeves, see F 283, 590, 608, 693, 760, 808, 900, 1486, 1478–9, 1694, 2050, 2122, 2124, 2126, 2163, 2172, 2380, 2422, 2473, 2499, 2722, 2749, 2934, 2942, 3206.
[19] See below, pp. 73–4.
[20] E.g. F 1001, 1172, 1951, 1832, 1835; and below, 44–5.
[21] See, for example, below, subject index, X.4, X.5, X.6.
[22] A new edition of this important text, along with a translation and discussion are being prepared by Simon Keynes and Alan Kennedy, and will be published as *Anglo-Saxon Ely: Records of Ely Abbey and its Benefactors in the Tenth and Eleventh Centuries*. A version of the *Libellus* was incorporated into the *LE*, and can be found in Blake's edition, along with a discussion of the text (*LE*, ix–xviii). See also Kennedy, "Law and litigation," 131–3.

enemies and interests there – ex-slaves on-the-make,[23] gouty thegns,[24] priestly wide-boys,[25] even ruthless women.[26] Although they are harder to identify, a similar cast of characters turned out for the Domesday inquest – the formidable widow of Hugh fitz Grip,[27] the perjurer Ordmær of Badlingham,[28] the thieving clerk of Eustace of Boulogne.[29] The assemblies described in the *Libellus* were also full of named witnesses, warrantors, and sureties, as well as wrongdoers paying pledges for good behavior.[30] The Domesday inquest, too, had all of these.[31] But what the *Libellus* does that Domesday does not, is place those active in the law into a nexus of personal relationships, and it pays meticulous attention to the friendships and alliances that enabled thegns, abbots, and ealdormen to buttress their rights through law. Kinsmen, especially, are omnipresent in the *Libellus*. There are in the text, widows, children, and assorted cousins pursuing claims across decades and generations, and priests pressing the landed interests of their families as enthusiastically as any laymen. There is also much talk in the *Libellus* about the protection and advocacy of important local figures and accounts of the money paid and the land given out to cement such alliances and assure success at law.[32] The lists of jurors preserved in the *IE* and the *ICC* suggest that the same sorts of men (although half now were French) were gathered at the Domesday inquest, men whose names linked them to a village, a kindred, or some greater man's affinity – jurors like Ælmær son of Blæc, Huscarl of Swaffham, and Leofsige the Abbess of Chatteris's man.[33] Supporters of litigants and members of local assemblies had, however, shifted in some ways in the century separating the *Libellus* from Domesday Book. When individual witnesses or jurors are identified in Domesday or one of its satellite surveys, they are almost always great lords speaking on behalf of their followers, men testifying on behalf of their lords,[34] or officials giving evidence on behalf of their masters.[35] Lordship, which was important in the *Libellus*, but not perhaps as important as kinship, is much more visible in the legal actions of Domesday Book, and here the kindred seems to be receding in the face of lordship.

Whether the jurors of tenth and eleventh-century hundred assemblies had different competencies than other jurors – say the men of the shire court – is

---

23 *LE*, ii, 10.
24 *LE*, ii, 11.
25 *LE*, ii, 32.
26 E.g., *LE*, ii, 7, 11.
27 See below, index of names, under "Hugh fitz Grip."
28 See above, chapter 1, 20.
29 F 1812.
30 For references in the *LE* and a discussion of them, see Kennedy, "Law and litigation," 158–61.
31 See below, subject index, IX.3, under "individuals who testified"; V.3, under "pledge, and "surety"; V.9, under "warranty."
32 *LE*, ii, 10; 18, 27, 31; 30, 31; 33.
33 Lewis, "Domesday jurors," appendix 1, 35–44 has a complete list of jurors found in the *IE* and the *ICC*.
34 F 3, 6, 7, 27, 32, 35, 41, 49, 132, 144, 199, 385, 492, 578, 775, 806, 861, 939, 961, 1209, 1517, 1836, 1913, 1961, 1964, 1986, 1998, 2031, 2038, 2070, 2124, 2166, 2255, 2326, 2342–3, 2360, 2399, 2403, 2447, 2458, 2568, 2583, 2708, 2724, 2729, 2758, 2767, 2934, 2942, 2973, 3053, 3060, 3097, 3185.
35 F 508, 594, 663, 711, 385, 903, 1499, 1639, 1642, 2165, 2187, 2255, 2326, 2343, 2448, 3012, 3192.

not at all clear. Historians earlier in this century struggled with this issue, attempting to assign to the hundred, the shire, and the king's court specific duties. J. E. A. Jolliffe claimed that disputes over bookland were heard exclusively by the king;[36] Florence Harmer argued that pleas revolving around the ownership of land were settled at the shire court;[37] it was F. Zinkeisen's contention that the shire court dealt mainly with civil pleas;[38] and J. W. Corbett believed that the hundred served as the venue for criminal cases in the pre-Conquest period.[39] Such absolute distinctions between the responsibilities of one court during this period and the work of another have now been abandoned. Recently scholars have quite sensibly argued that although there was, in this period, a very strong notion that local assemblies should strive to create lasting settlements between litigating parties before complaints were taken to the king,[40] there was no area of law that was strictly limited to one kind of assembly or another and no absolute hierarchy of courts. Complaints over bookland, for example, could be adjudicated at the king's court or at a meeting of the shire court;[41] and thievery was worried over by hundred, shire, and borough courts as well as great royal assemblies.[42] Oftentimes, one imagines, the choice of venue was simply left to the litigating or needy parties.[43]

One of the proofs of the varied use of local assemblies can be found in the tenth-century records of Peterborough and Ely. Between 963 and 992 the abbots of Peterborough purchased land for their house in front of a variety of assemblies – in front of eight hundreds at Wandsford, at a meeting of the whole army at Northampton, in a single wapentake assembly, three hundreds at *Wyðreðe* cross, two hundreds meeting at "the dyke", a joint meeting of two other hundreds, three hundreds attached to Oundle, and twice with the witness of eight hundreds at Oundle.[44] And Ely Abbey purchased land and defended its property in the presence of an extraordinary array of assemblies – in front of the borough court of Cambridge,[45] the King's court at London,[46] the shire courts of Cambridgeshire, Hertfordshire, Northamptonshire, and Huntingdonshire,[47] as well as assemblies of individual hundreds and vills.[48]

---

[36] J. E. A. Jolliffe, "English book-right," *EHR*, 50 (1935), 1–21.

[37] Harmer, *Writs*, p. 46.

[38] F. Zinkeisen, "The Anglo-Saxon courts of law," *Political Science Quarterly*, 10 (1895), p. 136.

[39] W. J. Corbett, "England from A.D. 954 to the death of Edward the Confessor," *The Cambridge Medieval History*, III, ed. H. M. Gwatkin, J. R. Whitney, J. R. Tanner, and C. W. Previté-Orton (Cambridge, 1936), 371–408, at 376–7.

[40] Alan Harding, *A Social History of English Law* (Harmondsworth, 1966), 21; A. G. Kennedy, "Disputes about 'bocland': the forum for their adjudication," *ASE*, 14 (1985), 175–95; III Edgar 2, 2§1; II Cnut 17; *The Will of Æthelgifu*, ed. D. Whitelock (Oxford, 1968).

[41] Kennedy, "Disputes about 'bocland' ", *ASE*, 175–95.

[42] Keynes, "Crime and punishment," 76–8, and Simon Keynes, "The Fonthill letter," 70–1.

[43] See above, chapter 1.

[44] Robertson, *Charters*, no. 40.

[45] *LE*, ii, 19, 20, 24, 26.

[46] *LE*, ii, 11.

[47] *LE*, ii, 11, 18; 10; 10, 11; 25.

[48] *LE*, ii, 11a.

But the abbot also did business at combined assemblies of two, three, and eight hundreds,[49] in the presence of the most important thegns settled beyond Upware,[50] in the borough court of Thetford (which sometimes met in conjunction with the double hundred of Ely),[51] and at the borough court of Cambridge meeting in association with a variety of unnamed hundreds.[52] Taken together, this evidence suggests that in the late Anglo-Saxon period the purchasing and granting of land, along with the disputes stemming from these transactions, occurred more often at hundred or joint-assemblies than in shire or borough courts, but there were, nonetheless, frequent exceptions.[53]

In many ways Domesday's evidence about the competencies and labors of particular courts mirrors this earlier picture, and it, like the charters and narratives of the tenth century, suggests that there remained in the eleventh century enormous flexibility in the choice of venue for particular classes of legal transactions. Nonetheless, the general pattern of judicial interests and competencies at the Domesday inquest, illustrated by the testimony of lords and their men, hundred jurors, and men of the shire, is suggestive of some broad patterns of business with which these various groups commonly dealt by the 1080s. Of the 1,000 instances of testimony imbedded in the survey, just over 120 cannot be attributed to any specific group or individual: the text simply states that "they testify" or that "the men say."[54] Several dozen other cases represent the voices of assemblies not much mentioned in relation to testimony – those of lathes, villages, or the like.[55] The remaining 800 or so specific descriptions of testimony represent sworn statements given by hundred and shire jurors or individuals and their men.[56] Since so much testimony is unidentified, and since much of the information in the survey, although unattributed, was clearly the result of some man's assertion, it is impossible to speak with great precision about real numbers in relation to oral testimony. Nonetheless, patterns emerge.

In Exchequer Domesday it looks as if hundred jurors gave testimony something like three times as often during the inquest as those of the shire courts, and that individuals or their men offered testimony about half as often again as did the men of the shire. Apparently, then, it was hundred and wapentake assemblies in 1086 whose knowledge was most frequently called upon and whose memories were most often invoked when problems concerning land were aired. Nonetheless, the voices of tenants-in-chief and their men were often heard; thus testimony of individuals was central to the inquest. The particular knowledge these different groups had that the King's

49 *LE*, ii, 18; 11a, 48; 34.
50 *LE*, ii, 11
51 *LE*, ii, 12, 16, 18.
52 E.g. *LE*, ii, 31.
53 E.g. Robertson, *Charters*, 40; *LE*, ii, 10, 11, 11a, 12, 16, 17, 18, 48.
54 See below, subject index, IX.3, under "men/they."
55 Ibid., under "lathe" and "villeins."
56 Ibid., under "county," "hundred," "individuals who testify," "men of," "shire," and "wapentake."

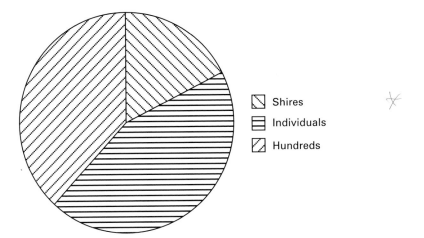

Figure 1 Distribution of testimony concerning grants and seisin

commissioners were anxious to tap can be broken down into a number of broad categories – matters concerning the *terra regis*, royal rights, and geld; the activities of sheriffs and reeves; grants and seisin; manorial appurtenances; tenurial arrangements; antecession; and information related to the rights and possessions of the Church (see figure 2). Hundreds were ten times more likely to testify about antecessors than were county assemblies or individuals and their men; seven times more likely to speak about manorial appurte-nances; five times more likely to offer testimony about the misdeeds of reeves; and they were about twice as likely to offer information concerning an estate's tenurial arrangements. Hundred testimony was less dominant, however, in other areas. Although hundreds did give testimony concerning grants and seisin, this information more often came from lords or their men (see figure 1). The opinions of shire courts were more often heard than hundreds in matters concerning geld or the skullduggery of sheriffs, although hundreds had things to say about these matters as well; and hundreds and counties spoke about equally regarding the rights of local Churches and the King (see figure 2).

These loose patterns of testimony are suggestive of the kinds of activities that normally took place in particular venues. Clearly, men who habitually participated in the regular meeting of the hundred, and who were impaneled once again for the Domesday inquest, witnessed, as the usual business of their frequent and local assemblies, a number of activities of interest to the Domesday commissioners. It was the men of the hundred who were most likely to witness the misdeeds of reeves. It was usually the hundred rather than the shire that viewed the negotiations and rituals associated with the selling, mortgaging, or granting of land and could, therefore, more often speak to the veracity of a lord's claims and the specifics of his tenure. It was the hundredmen in Domesday Book who most often judged that mills, urban

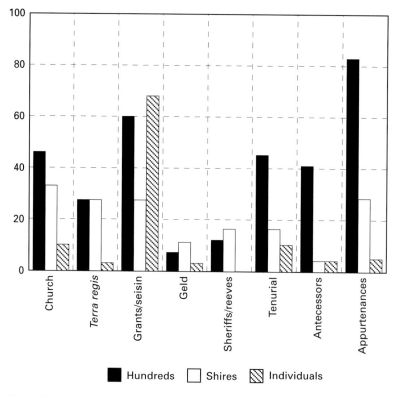

Figure 2 Patterns of testimony in the Exchequer Domesday Book

tenements, woodland, and the like – the bits and pieces of estates – belonged or did not belong to a manor, suggesting that some of the jurors in earlier years had walked bounds during the disputes of the 1060s, 1070s, and 1080s, or had overseen the details of property transference, and many had participated in those informal meetings at the boundaries of estates alluded to in the *Leges Henrici Primi*[57] (see figure 3). That hundreds more often testified about antecessors than any other group not only suggests that hundred jurors remembered dispossessions or dispossessing, but that hundred courts were intimately involved in the legal machinations that enabled Norman barons to step into the shoes of English thegns (see figure 4).

The shire courts in Domesday Book can often be seen confirming the testimony of others, doubtless when those decisions were controversial in

---

[57] *LHP.* According to the *Leg. Ed. Conf.*, hundred courts dealt with cases between "vills and neighbors, and if there are fines, compensatory payments and agreements about pastures, meadows, harvests and disputes between neighbors and many things of this sort, which commonly arise" (28§1). Or again, when the Bishop of Worcester brought a claim against the son of a patron who had illegally taken back his father's estate, those at the shire meeting at Worcester set a day and ordered that "the same people who had traced the boundaries for him," no doubt local men of the hundred, should go back to the estate and "then the bishop and the man who sold him the estate and those who had been witnesses came and went to the estate and they all road around the boundaries" (Robertson, *Charters,* no. 83).

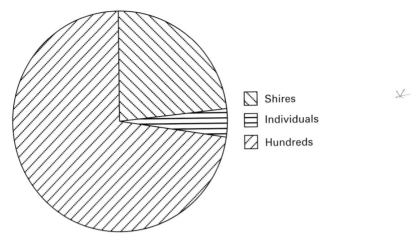

Figure 3 Distribution of testimony concerning appurtenances

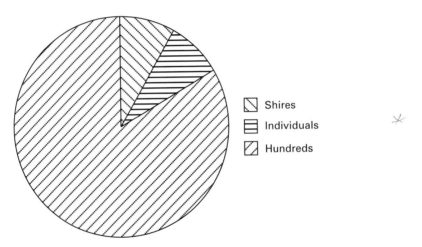

Figure 4 Distribution of testimony concerning antecession

some way, and the shire seems to have offered authority to the more problematic decisions of local assemblies. Both hundred and county jurors dealt with the deeds and misdeeds of sheriffs, but not unsurprisingly county jurors presented more testimony about the king's chief representative in the shire than did the hundred. Both groups testified about geld infractions, but the county dealt with these more commonly, which must mean that in spite of the role hundreds played in the collection of tax, the power of the state in enforcing gelds was organized at the level of the county.

In spite of the tendency of one court to provide particular types of information to the King's commissioners in 1086, no single group held a monopoly on any class of legal action. Different courts seem to have had overlapping expertise, doubtless because there were occasions on which a variety of local judicial institutions would have either met together at a joint-meeting or had to work together to effect a judgment. This is illustrated neatly by the Domesday jurors' discussions of outlawry. Much of what we know about the mechanisms of outlawry comes from Domesday's borough customals, suggesting that shire courts, which were convened by the eleventh century as a matter of course in county towns, were the sites in which the rituals and acclamations surrounding outlawry took place. The King, the earl, and the sheriff could all, apparently "expel an outlaw from the realm,"[58] and this expulsion was then publicly supported or acclaimed by the "men of the shrievalty," doubtless the worthies who participated in the shire court.[59] In most cases, however, and in most places, only the King could restore peace to an outlaw, again, probably at the shire court.[60] Although the meeting of the shire court was the occasion at which a man's outlawry became known, it was apparently the men of the hundred courts who had to enforce the dispossession that followed such infamy. At the inquest it was the hundred and wapentake jurors who provided the most detailed information about forfeiture and antecession, suggesting that these courts were often used to effect dispossessions.[61] Hundreds could also recall tenurial details that impinged upon dispossession. In Lincolnshire, for example, hundred jurors agreed that a thegn named Hereweard had been exiled and had lost his land, but they also testified that the land which his Norman successor was holding was not rightfully his, because Hereweard had, in fact, leased the land from the Abbot of St. Guthlac's, and further, that the abbot had repossessed it before the Conquest because Hereweard had not met the terms of their agreement.[62] This kind of detailed, local knowledge about the dealings of outlaws would have been essential to affect a lawful confiscation of land. It also appears that the followers of the disgraced, who would have been required by law to find another lord, made public their new arrangements at the hundred court.[63] Finally, hundred jurors, more than any other group, provided the King's commissioners with detailed information about the particulars of outlawings. In 1086 they were able to reminisce, for example, about how one of Earl Harold's housecarls had gone to York, where he died an outlaw, and they knew that the Abbot of Ramsey had fled to Denmark.[64]

[58] F 981, 1703, 2721. See also *Leg. Ed. Conf.* 6§1.
[59] F 981.
[60] Or in the case of Yorkshire and Lincolnshire, at the riding court. F 253, 981. But see also F 1703 for the circumstances under which the earl and sheriff could recall an outlaw and give him peace. See also *Leg. Ed. Conf.* 18, 18§1.
[61] At the Domesday inquest hundred courts were impressively well informed about the parade of disgraced thegns and barons who had held some estates in rapid succession. In Lincolnshire, for example, a local wapentake court knew that the thegn Elaf, soon after the Conquest, had lost his land to another Anglo-Scandinavian, Rainer the Deacon, but that Rainer was given Elaf's land only to lose it himself as an outlaw (F 1083). Or again, in Norfolk and Suffolk, hundreds testified both that Walter de Dol had inherited the land of disinherited freemen, and that he in turn had forfeited it to others (F 3053, 2962).
[62] F 1172.
[63] F 2834, 2839; and II Æthelstan 2.
[64] F 1951, 851.

There is, by Domesday standards, an unusual immediacy in the language hundred jurors used to describe the disgraced: they told of the day when Asfrith and Hereweard "fled," when Tonni "was captured," and when Skalpi "died in outlawry."[65] The color of the language used suggests that English jurors were remembering the ruination of old friends, lords, or neighbors, and Norman jurors were thinking about posses that they had organized and the skirmishes they had fought, or about the beginnings of their lords' and their own fortunes. In outlawry we can see borough, shire, and hundredmen working in tandem to do the business of the state.

The various regional judicial assemblies participating in the inquest, then, did not specialize absolutely in the business they oversaw, but they had a tendency to participate in certain kinds of legal transactions. Simultaneously, a variety of local courts often worked together to effect decisions made at law. Thus no hierarchy of courts existed, but intersecting, overlapping, and conjoining groups of law-worthy men kept the peace, did justice, and looked out for the rights of the king.

The legal lives of lords and their men

Many men gave testimony during the inquest not as members of hundred or shire courts, but as individuals representing their own interests or those of their lords.[66] About a third of those whose names are recorded in Domesday Book as having given testimony are English. Some are either explicitly called or look very much like minor royal functionaries – beadles, reeves, and the like – and they can be seen providing the court with information about small parcels of land that belonged by right to the King.[67] Englishmen, however, also testified on their own behalf, claiming rights to hides and virgates attached to royal estates either by King William's gift or through the actions of one of his sheriffs.[68] Two brave souls, Arnketil of Withern and Ulfkil of Asterby, testified about the taking of illegal tolls in Lincolnshire, possibly because they were looking after the King's interests.[69] The appearance of English reeves again and again as the givers of testimony at the inquest reminds us of their long history as the overseers of the most local and particular interests of kings and lords at neighborhood assemblies.[70] Their ubiquitous presence at the inquest underscores, as well, their survival as a class after 1066; and lowly

---

[65] F 1128, 1172, 1050, 1951.

[66] The testimony of only one woman, Edith the Nun, is recorded in Domesday Book, and this may well have been testimony presented in writing (F 1658).

[67] F 95, 119. 953, 997, 3089. Unnamed royal reeves testified in F 508. French reeves also testified, making claims on several occasions about the values of farms – either about how the Englishmen were making them too low, or that they were having to pay too high a farm to the King (F 903, 2767).

[68] F 73, 457, 483, 651, 653, 953, 967, 1016. F 161 and 2050 are claimed by these men as forfeitures to the King. For claims of land held through sheriffs, see F 63, 205.

[69] F 1074.

[70] Campbell, "Some agents," 205–9.

though they were, by the time of the inquest they were the highest-level category of secular survivor in the kingdom. Certainly by 1070 x 1075 English earls, English sheriffs, English bishops, and the greatest English thegns – the men who had once called, presided over, and controlled the local courts harnessed by the inquest – had been replaced almost to a man by more reliable friends of King William. As the most important figures of local society and administration were purged, it was the cooperation of petty English agents that allowed Normans to use native legal institutions to collect taxes, consolidate their power, and dispossess their enemies. Thus, English reeves participated in crucial ways in the preservation of traditional social structures that had long been used to keep the peace, provide warranty, and adjudicate disputes; and their cooperation with the new elite during the period of intense disinheritance and settlement allowed the Normans to acquire land in shires and hundreds through the law rather than by the sword. These petty agents, by 1086, were also used to doing business at local assemblies now dominated by the conquerors, and as a result they were perhaps more sanguine than other Englishmen about the ways in which such courts could be utilized for their own interests under the new regime. Perhaps, as well, because of their access to royal land and customs, and thus to temptation, and because they were one of the most prosperous groups of English survivors, they were called upon more often than other men to explain their actions.[71]

Most of the remaining Englishmen who testified as individuals during the inquest were involved in legal altercations stemming from lordship. These men were usually fighting for what remained of their landed fortunes, which were in dispute in 1086 because they had maintained an interest in their land by becoming tenants of Normans settled nearby. Some were being sued in 1086 by abbots and abbesses from whose houses they had long ago leased their land. A few were willing to chance the collective memory of the hundred to maintain that their land was, by right, part of a Norman's fee. In these cases we see thegns and freemen in effect upholding their new lords' claims to land, which they themselves now held as tenants, explaining at the inquest how various Roberts or Rogers had come to be their lords, or how the hides and virgates they now held from a Norman had been unencumbered before the Conquest by lease or mortgage.[72]

The Normans who gave testimony did so under quite different circumstances. England's sheriff-magnates and princes of the Church are the men most often seen in the survey giving testimony. There are a number of reasons for this. Both groups were habitués of local judicial assemblies, and sheriffs and churchmen alike had official duties there. Sheriffs and bishops acted as presidents of various local courts, and abbots and bishops were often

---

[71] See above, pp. 73–4.
[72] F 928, 1844, 2458, 2868.

the holders of extraordinary judicial rights and privileges. Because of their familiarity with court procedure, these men were doubtless among the most accomplished and successful litigators in the kingdom. Moreover, although most had come from the Continent only a generation before, they had mastered the intricacies of court procedure through their regular attendance, and they had modified these courts' personnel and judgments by asserting themselves as the lords of local jurors.[73] And because all had been involved in the wide-ranging and protracted pleas held to deraign rights to thegnland, they were more familiar than most men with the hybrid legal practices evolving after the Conquest.[74]

The testimony of abbots and bishops along with monks and canons is preserved for fourteen different counties, suggesting that nearly all the important male communities personally gave witness concerning their rightful possessions and their tribulations in 1086.[75] On a number of occasions local hundred courts could not substantiate churchmen's testimony concerning gifts of oblation,[76] donations from pious benefactors,[77] loan-land or gifts from King William.[78] In such cases bishops and abbots often testified that they had royal writs to support their claims, although there were times when hundred jurors swore that these writs were unknown to them.[79] The tenor of this testimony indicates that while much pious giving was done or confirmed, before the Conquest, in the sight of local courts, some had nonetheless taken place within ecclesiastical precincts and churches, where monks, nuns, or canons and members of the donor's family would gather to witness and solemnize grants or leases. The disagreements arising between churchmen and panels of jurors point to the fact that notification of such *conventiones* were not always confirmed in the public courts.

Lay followers of ecclesiastics also attended the same inquests as their ecclesiastical lords to lend weight to their just causes.[80] In shires where abbots and bishops held the bulk of their patrimonies, it appears that they came to the inquest with large groups of witnesses drawn from their estates. Thus, the Abbot of St. Augustine's was supported in the Kent county court, an inquest he himself attended, by a crowd of men; and Bury's men were testifying

---

[73] See above, chapter 1.

[74] See below, chapter 4.

[75] Bishops, abbots, and their households testify in Berkshire, Dorset, Essex, Hampshire, Herefordshire, Huntingdonshire, Kent, Norfolk, Somerset, Suffolk, Surrey, Sussex, Warwickshire, and Yorkshire. The following heads of English ecclesiastical houses or their *familiae* testify: Abbotsbury (F 492), Abingdon (F 109), Bury (F 2934), Chertsey (F 1510), Christchurch (F 1538), Ely (F 3106), Exeter (F 103), Lincoln (F 872), London (F 775), Ramsey (F 617, 2284, 2286), St. Augustine's (F 928), Old Minster, Winchester (F 632, 1349), Worcester (F 1567), York (F 1697).

[76] F 109.

[77] F 1510, 2284, 2286.

[78] F 103, 632, 928; 872, 1826.

[79] F 872, 1510. See below, chapter 3.

[80] Lay followers of the Abbot of Bury (F 2934), the Abbot of St. Augustine's (F 939), the Bishop of Durham (F 1836), and the Bishop of London (F 775) are named specifically in the text as giving testimony at the inquest.

alongside the abbot in Norfolk.[81] The interests of great ecclesiastical lords were also at times represented by secular retainers, who can be found testifying on their lords' behalf, when the great men themselves could not attend.[82] These men were representing churchmen whose widespread diocese and far-flung estates made it impossible for them to attend inquests in every shire in which they held land. Thus, the Bishop of Durham's men, who had been settled by him on his Essex estates, testified at the inquest about their lord's important manor of Waltham Holy Cross, located hundreds of miles south of the bishop's main holdings.[83]

Sheriffs, like bishops and abbots, are seen testifying everywhere in Domesday Book. Almost half the 1086 sheriffs, and the bulk of these the richest and most powerful of that species – Geoffrey de Mandeville, Haimo Dapifer, Hugh de Beauchamp, Hugh de Port, Peter de Valognes, Picot, Ralph Baynard, Robert Malet, Roger Bigot, Urso d'Abetot, and Waleran – appear specifically in the text giving testimony.[84] The sheriffs' active participation is not surprising. In part, their presence must have been required and their testimony a formal part of the inquest. And as royal farmers, sheriffs had been obliged to manage various business associated with the royal estates over which they had charge – leasing, mortgaging, setting farms – in front of hundred or shire assemblies, and local courts expected to see or hear writs affirming changes in the status of the *terra regis* made by the sheriff.[85] Sheriffs, therefore, were expected to be sheriffs in full view of local communities. They, along with a number of high-level royal farmers,[86] played an extremely vocal part at the 1086 proceedings, fighting to reestablish regalian rights or regain berewicks, men, and minor tenancies that had been part of the *terra regis* before the Confessor's death, but no longer were.[87] But they were also there on their own behalf. They were experienced litigators and adjudicators, who had had to spend a good deal of every year at the shire court before 1086,[88] and therefore, knew how to use the courts. And, like reeves, sheriffs often had sticky fingers and local enemies, so they were called to account again and again during the inquest over the mismanagement of royal resources or because of their appropriation of other men's land. As entrepreneurs *par excellence*, they had much to answer for by 1086, and were accused of malfeasance more often than any other group of men in England.[89]

---

[81] F 939, 2934.

[82] In Essex, Hertfordshire, Kent, and Suffolk.

[83] F 1836.

[84] Judith Green, "The sheriffs of William the Conqueror," *ANS*, v (1983), 129–45, at 140–1; F 1838, 1949, 1952, 2038; 1945; 58; 641, 648; 809, 2012; 184, 220, 222, 225–6; 1983; 2222, 2258; 2258, 2368, 2722, 2724, 2767, 2873, 3187; 1639, 1642, 1667, 1669; 488.

[85] See above, chapter 1.

[86] Included among these are Godric Dapifer (F 2164, 2223, 2268, 2535); Robert Gernon (F 1838, 1967, 1970, 1975, 1979, 2036); Roger de Raismes (F 1811, 2021, 2886, 2890, 3100).

[87] See, for example F 184.

[88] W. A. Morris, *The Medieval English Sheriff* (Manchester, 1927), 20–1; Judith A. Green, *English Sheriffs to 1154* (London, 1990), 9–13.

[89] The exception is the incredibly straight-laced William de Cahaignes, who, unlike every other sheriff in

Sheriffs' men testified during the inquest as well. Geoffrey de Mandeville, Roger Bigot, and Ralph Baynard, as well as the recently deceased Hugh fitz Grip and Ralph Taillebois, were supported during the inquest by the testimony of their men.[90] Their words suggest that they had quite detailed knowledge of their lord's official responsibilities and activities. One sheriff's *ministri*, for example, swore that land belonged to the King's farm.[91] Peter de Valognes's men knew the circumstances behind his acquisition of parcels of land: they swore that one of his holdings came to him as a forfeiture, because its geld had not been paid.[92] Ralph Taillebois's management of the *terra regis* was also remembered by his men: that he had placed land in Sewell, with the King's consent, in the manor of Houghton Regis in order to increase his profits there.[93] The testimony of sheriff's men indicates that sheriffs long before the inquest had been accompanied at local shire court meetings by a following of retainers and petty administrators, and that these men gave their lord-sheriff counsel concerning many of his dealings, and that they helped him transact both the King's business and his own.

The most conspicuous absence among the inquest's named witnesses are the very greatest magnates in England – the King's half-brothers, Roger de Montgomery, Richard fitz Gilbert, William de Warenne, Hugh d'Avranches, Eustace of Boulogne, Geoffrey of Coutances, Alan of Richmond – Corbett's famous "Class A" barons.[94] Some of these men may indeed have given testimony at the inquest, testimony that was not attributed explicitly to them in the text. But judging from the long list of those we know to have given testimony, it does look as if it was the barons of middle and lower rank who came and watched after their own interests in 1086, and that the very greatest of William's magnates may have been there, but that they came not on their own behalf, but rather as representatives of the King. Geoffrey bishop of Coutances is one of the few named commissioners at the inquest, but other of these men doubtless were as well. Some, moreover, may have been with the King, as they had been when he gave his "deep speech," ready to judge the most intractable, troublesome, or important cases, cases that we know were periodically sent on by the commissioners to the King for judgment.[95]

Domesday Book, has not a single complaint registered against him. For the extra-legal activity of sheriffs, see Richard Abels, "Sheriffs, lord-seeking and the Norman settlement of the south-west midlands," *ANS*, 19 (1997), 19–50.

[90] F 199, 1209, 1961, 1964; 2724; 1986, 2568; 492; 3, 32, 35. The sheriff of Hampshire, Hugh de Port, was also supported by the testimony of his *ministri* (F 663).

[91] This is in spite of the fact that the hundred and shire denied this (F 663).

[92] The shire denied this, as did the hundred (F 806).

[93] F 3.

[94] This list of Corbett's "Class A" barons includes some men left out by Corbett, but who have the requite £750 of land (W. J. Corbett, "The development of the duchy of Normandy and the Norman Conquest of England," *The Cambridge Medieval History*, V, ed. J. R. Tanner, C. W. Previté-Orton, and Z. N. Brooke (Cambridge, 1926), 481–520, at 505–13; C. W. Hollister, "The greater Domesday tenants-in-chief," in *Domesday Studies*, 219–48, at 220, 242). The only "Class A" baron to testify is Geoffrey de Mandeville, who like the other sheriffs, played a highly visible and vocal role at the inquest.

[95] F 103, 1174.

The final group whose testimony is found everywhere in Domesday is the men of tenants-in-chief. Through the testimony offered up by these lords' men, we can discern what kinds of activities most often took place not in the long-standing public courts, where English jurors expected actions concerning landholding to occur, but rather in the "privacy" of the King's court or in a local lord's own court. Men, for example, often gave testimony concerning their lords' royal gifts,[96] suggesting that a significant number of grants made by the King were given at the royal court, without benefit of a follow-up writ of notification to local hundred or shire courts where the gift lay. Judging from the evidence of Domesday Book, there was a clear expectation, at least on the part of local jurors, that they should have received formal notification of such gifts. Again and again, however, at the inquest local courts were questioning title to land that a lord or his men were willing to swear was a special, royal gift. A lord's own men, no doubt, were able to swear to the veracity of such gifts, because they had either witnessed King William's act of generosity themselves, or because they had long heard their lord's tales about the glorious moment when the King had shown his particular favor. They were often able to provide details about the livery of their lord's holdings as well.[97] Finally, men and their lords commonly testified during the inquest about exchanges, of which local courts seemed to know nothing,[98] and the *conventiones* behind such private estate-swappings certainly seem to have taken place in front of lords' men, but not before hundred or shire courts. Thus, the "private" lives of lords were lived out at times not in the glare of the old, public assemblies, but rather in the more intimate setting of their own halls.

Men were also, if their testimony at the inquest is anything to go by, intimately involved in the running of their lords' estates. They were often competent to give detailed information about the value of their lords' manors, sometime disagreeing with hundred jurors on the issue, as did the Bishop of Durham's men, when they were assessing the value of the land their lord had been given at Waltham; or as Count Alan's men did when they discussed how much an Englishman rendered to their lord each year.[99] They also knew when their lords should have customs from men who lived on their lands, and were competent to provide information about the kinds of rights their lords' antecessors had held over land TRE.[100] Geoffrey de Mandeville's men, for example, claimed that Ordgar, the Edwardian sheriff of Cambridgeshire, had mortgaged some land for seven marks and two ounces of gold, presumably to Esger the Staller, Geoffrey's antecessor (although the hundred denied having any knowledge of this transaction).[101] Men testified

---

[96]   F 49, 578, 1961, 1964, 2166, 2342, 3097.
[97]   F 2070, 3060.
[98]   F 6, 7, 32, 35, 144, 961, 1517, 1913, 1964.
[99]   F 1836; 2360.
[100] F 2447, 2458.
[101] F 199.

when meadow land should be held by their lord, and not some other man;[102] and they made claims on their lord's behalf for rights to freemen and their acres.[103] They claimed land from others as part of their lord's fee.[104] They also testified about the number of carucates that had been delivered to their lords, and about whether they had been delivered as one manor or two.[105] They knew if land had been beneficially hidated by King William,[106] and they knew when estates had not been sufficiently productive.[107] They were also quite capable of giving detailed histories of their lord's estates as well as information about its former English and Norman holders.[108] They knew, for example, what other Normans' fees their lord's land had been in before a disgrace.[109] They also knew when their lord held land not through antecession, but for some other reason.[110] Clearly, men knew these things because they helped administer their lord's estates, accompanied him to the king's court, and helped attend to his legal needs both in the hundred and shire courts and at his own honorial court. Men also organized their legal memories around the activities of their lords. Geoffrey de Mandeville's men, for example, remembered that he had gained possession of some land in Spelthorne Hundred before "he went across the sea in the service of the King,"[111] and they recalled when an Englishman had become Geoffrey's man of his own accord.[112] Peter de Valognes's men knew that Queen Edith had given a freeman named Spearhavoc to Peter de Valognes, and that after her death the King had granted the same man to him.[113] They also knew whom their lords had subinfeudated on his estates.[114] And men were loyal to their lords, not only helping to shape the memories of local juries, and not only willing to give sworn evidence, but they were often willing to undergo the ordeal, in order to prove that their lords' claims were just.[115] Oaths and God's wrath, however, did temper men's testimony, and from time to time they were unwilling to give an account or justify their lords' actions.[116] Men's eagerness, for the most part, to testify, argue, or undergo the ordeal concerning their lord's actions is hardly surprising, since they seem so often to have witnessed what he did. Roger Bigot, for example, wished to prove

---

[102] F 41.
[103] F 2729.
[104] F 3185,
[105] F 3060, 1998.
[106] F 578.
[107] F 2708.
[108] F 2342, 3053.
[109] F 2301, 2399, 2942.
[110] F 27.
[111] F 1209.
[112] F 1964.
[113] F 3097.
[114] F 3053.
[115] F 2255, 2301, 2360, 2447, 2458, 2742, 2767. They were also willing, at times, to go against the testimony of a local abbot, and swear that their lord held from a monastery, in spite of the fact that the abbot denied it (F 492).
[116] F 132; 2343, 2583, 2124, 2343.

how much a royal manor he farmed paid, "wishing to prove this through those men who were at his agreement."[117] Thus, through the haze of Domesday testimony, we can see the dim outlines of honorial courts and the bands of retainers who helped administer great men's honors.

[117]   F 2767.

3 Disputes and the Edwardian past

Remembering the past in 1086

By 1086 there were countless reasons for title to be questioned or claims against holders to be raised. First among these were the long-standing arrangements attached to new acquisitions, some of which were painfully complicated. Take, for example, Domesday's description of Leighs in Essex:

In the time of King Edward, Esger [the Staller] held two and a half hides and fifteen acres of land in Leighs. Now W. holds it from Geoffrey de Mandeville [Esger's successor]. Esger gave this manor to [Earl] Harold, and Harold then gave it to Skalpi, his housecarl. Skalpi then gave it to his wife in dower, in the sight of two men – Roger the Marshal and an Englishman. The hundred testifies that they heard these men acknowledge Skalpi. Skalpi himself held it after King William came into this land, until he went to York, where he died in outlawry.[1]

After the Conquest, the men who had gained rights to Earl Harold's and Skalpi's possessions could challenge Geoffrey de Mandeville's title to Leighs, and so, too, perhaps could Skalpi's widow or surviving heirs. At other times it was impossible, twenty years on, to trace unambiguous title back through the confusing entitlements of English leaseholders, lords, and litigants. This was certainly the case with the Bishop of Worcester's estate of Alveston:

In the time of King Edward, Beorhtwine held seven and a half hides there. Archbishop Ealdræd had the sake and soke, and toll and team, and churchscot, and all other forfeitures from this land except those four which the King has throughout his whole kingdom. Beorhtwine's sons, Leofwine and Eadmær, and four others testify to this, but they do not know from whom Beorhtwine held this land – perhaps the Church or Earl Leofric, whom he served. They say, however, that they themselves held it from Earl Leofric and could turn where they wished with the land. Beorhtnoth and Alwig held the remaining seven and a half hides in the vill, but the county does not know from whom they held. Bishop Wulfstan, however, says that he established his claim to this land before Queen Mathilda in the presence of four sheriffdoms, and he has King William's writs for it and also the testimony of the county of Warwick.[2]

---

[1] F 1951.
[2] F 1567. For a detailed account of Worcester's claim to Alveston, see *The Cartulary of Worcester Cathedral Priory*, ed. R. R. Darlington, Pipe Roll Society, new ser., 38 (London, 1968), no. 8, and Ann Williams, "A vice-comital family in pre-Conquest Warwickshire," *ANS*, 11 (1989), 282–3.

Here rights to land in 1086 were complicated by failed memory and the puzzling expectations of long-dead lords and their tenants. More explicitly political events, some dating back as much as thirty years, could also precipitate disputes in William's reign. This can be seen in a long narrative passage in Little Domesday, which preserves the discussion of Domesday jurors regarding an Edwardian rebellion and its impact on land once held by a certain Eadric and his men:

> Before King Edward died this Eadric was commended to Eadric of Laxfield, Robert Malet's antecessor. Eadric of Laxfield was outlawed, and King Edward seised all of his land. Later, he was reconciled to King Edward, and the King granted him his land. The King gave him a writ and seal, so that whichever of his commended freemen might wish to return to him could return with the King's consent. King Edward was seised, in his own hand, of this particular Eadric. Afterwards the hundred did not see Eadric return to his lord Eadric of Laxfield, but this Eadric himself says that he did, and offers the ordeal that he returned, as did the freemen whom he has under his commendation. He vouches Robert Malet as warrantor.[3]

In all three of these cases, the contested versions of the dead regime's rebellions, local alliances, and land market are recorded in Domesday Book because they had led to questions or disputes over title. The ambiguities generated by these intricate and untidy arrangements fueled complaint. These examples, along with dozens of others lodged in the survey, illustrate how the tenurial complexities governing so many Anglo-Saxon estates and the ways in which they were forgotten or remembered often meant that more than one party had an argument in 1086 on which to pin a legitimate claim.

Even the more straightforward tenures created in the 1030s, 1040s, and 1050s haunted landholders in the 1070s and 1080s. Many religious houses, for example, were defending their rights in 1086 to *post-obitum* gifts made by prosperous thegns during the Confessor's reign, but which were held or claimed by these same thegns' Norman successors. Such donations were all too often lost.[4] Still, bishops and abbots or their surrogates did their best to secure or reclaim them. Some, for example, recollected during the Domesday inquest that such benefactions, while they had admittedly been compromised because of their association with donors whose lands had since been confiscated, had been given nonetheless by thegns who had propitiously died or made their gifts in those ten months between King Edward's death and Harold's defeat; in other words, before the donors had fought against King William. This was one of Westminster Abbey's favorite gambits. Its claim to four hides in Upper Tooting was argued thus:

---

[3] F 2834.

[4] For examples of the loss of thegnly gifts in Domesday Book, see F 145, 545, 617, 870, 2438, 2456, 2498, 2944, 3182. Other lost gifts can be found by comparing the estates bequeathed to the Church in thegnly wills dating from Edward's reign with information in Domesday Book on TRW holders. See, for example, S 1516, 1519, 1528.

TRE Swein held four hides in Upper Tooting from the King . . . TRW it is held by Westminster Abbey . . . Earl Waltheof took this land from Swein after the death of King Edward and mortgaged it to Æthelnoth of London for two marks of gold. Æthelnoth then granted it to St. Peter's for his soul.[5]

Here Westminster was asserting that its rights to Tooting were greater than those of either Swein's or Æthelnoth Cild's successors, because the estate had been granted to St. Peter's before Æthelnoth's and Earl Waltheof's disgrace. In much the same way the Abbey based its rights to Paglesham on the fact that a thegn had presented it to the community "when he went with Harold to the battle in York."[6] In a similar fashion Eadsige the Sheriff, so the monks of New Minster recalled, had given half a hide of land in Tatchbury to the community "after King Edward's death, but before King William came" – in other words, in that legally ambiguous period between TRE and TRW.[7]

In a slightly more complicated case, Evesham was trying to rescue a gift of oblation, made during Edward's reign and then leased, from the clutches of Urso d'Abetot:

Wulfgeat donated this land to Evesham Abbey, and put his gift on the altar when his son Ælfgeat was made a monk there. This was done in the fifth year of King Edward's reign. Afterward Abbot Æthelwig leased this land to his uncle for as long as the uncle should live. This man later died in Harold's battle against the Norse, and the abbey again took his land before King William came into England.[8]

Evesham's claim was based on the fact (whether true or invented for the occasion) that this land, although held TRE by a thegn who was later disseised, had been illegally confiscated, since the uncle had never fought against William at Hastings. In each of these cases it appears that what stood out most clearly about the past for Norman sheriffs or successors at the inquest was the act of disinheritance, and what was most important in the memory of the communities defending their property was the moment of the gift. These competing views of what was significant about an estate's past led to competing conclusions about its just fate after Hastings.

Westminster's, New Minster's, and Evesham's legal skirmishes all involved recent transactions. But the permanent bestowal of pious bequests was often postponed before the Conquest for generations by wheedling kinsmen through litigation, gifts of money, annual renders, or assurances of future reversion.[9] But with the Conquest the mechanisms whereby both the

---

[5] F 1502.

[6] F 1835. It is interesting to note that these two similarly argued claims were made in the courts of two different counties, the first in Surrey and the second in Essex.

[7] F 614. This argument for the gifts of disgraced thegns' land may have been echoed at other times by arguments made by religious communities concerning the loss of church treasures, some given to religious houses by disgraced thegns, and some stored in monasteries for safe-keeping and never redeemed (*ASC*, s. a. 1070 (C, D); *Chron. Ab.*, I, 480, 486; *LE*, ii, 113–14).

[8] F 1683.

[9] For an outline of the general contours of this practice, see Barbara H. Rosenwein, *To Be a Neighbor of St. Peter: The Social Meaning of Cluny's Property 909–1049* (Ithaca, 1989), 49–77; Stephen D. White, *Customs,*

promise of gifts and the names of patrons were kept alive were undermined; and the two interlocking systems of memory – that of thegnly families and that of religious *familiae* – were ruptured. Hundreds of hides of land granted to the Church, but not yet given outright, were at risk after Hastings because of this; and many of these perpetually promised estates, along with the dues and social bonds they generated, were lost to the Church when thegnly families were displaced by a new and essentially disengaged aristocracy. Thus, in spite of the occasional inspired argument, large numbers of *post-obitum* bequests to the Church, some dating back generations, were lost during the cataclysm of the Conquest.

Written evidence and collective memory in legal action

Many of these pre-Conquest reversionary grants are disguised, both in charters and in Domesday Book, as leases. Whether leased land was land granted to a Church by a thegn and then leased back to his family, or land held outright by the Church and then loaned temporarily to an ally, it was acutely vulnerable after the Conquest.[10] The most celebrated example of appropriated loan-land involves the holdings deraigned at Penenden Heath in the famous pleas held between Odo of Bayeux and Archbishop Lanfranc. There Odo was determined to uphold his rights to all of the lands of his Kentish antecessors, and Lanfranc, for his part, was resolved to regain the land these antecessors had leased from Christ Church in Cnut's or Edward's reigns.[11] Canterbury's complaints, its long years of litigation, and its limited success mirror the experience of other religious establishments during the period of Norman settlement. As a result, the sad fate of Church lands leased to dead or disgraced Englishmen is a favorite topic of the narrative sources produced by monastic houses two or three generations after William's reign; and the loss of loan-land represents the period's best-documented category of legal complaint.[12] Domesday Book not only corroborates the evidence of cartulary-chronicles for this, but it extends our knowledge of the scope of the

---

Kinship, and Gifts to Saints: The Laudatio Parentum *in Western France,* 1050–1150 (Chapel Hill, 1988). In England the cycle of the giving of *post-obitum* gifts followed by renegotiation is seen most clearly in the stories of the *Libellus Æthelwoldi.* For another example of a century's worth of prevarication, renegotiation, etc., see the case discussed in Patrick Wormald, "Charters, law and the settlement of disputes in Anglo-Saxon England," in *The Settlement of Disputes in Early Medieval Europe,* ed. Wendy Davies and Paul Fouracre (Cambridge, 1986), 149–68, at 157–9.

[10] Susan Kelly, "Anglo-Saxon lay society and the written word," in *The Uses of Literacy in Early Mediaeval Europe,* ed. Rosamond McKitterick (Cambridge, 1990), 36–62, at 48, n. 42. For a similar practice in Normandy of combining *post-obitum* gifts, sales, mortgages, and leases into hybrid transactions, see Tabuteau, *Transfers,* 229.

[11] *Lawsuits,* 5a–k; David Bates, "The land pleas of William I's reign: Penenden Heath revisited," *BIHR,* 51 (1978), 1–19.

[12] For Abingdon, see *Chron. Ab.,* I, 484, II, 3; for Ely, see *LE,* appendix D, 426–32; for Peterborough, see Hugh Candidus, 69; for Ramsey, see *Chron. Rams.,* 145–6, 152–3; for Worcester, see Hemming, I, 254–69. For a general discussion of these pleas, see David Bates, "The land pleas of William I's reign," 1–19 and Edward Miller, "The Ely land pleas in the reign of William I," *EHR,* 62 (1947), 438–56.

problem, and it deepens, considerably, our understanding of the mechanisms used in the pursuit of title both before and after the Conquest.

In many cases, Domesday Book provides more information about a house's losses than its own sources do, as if two or three generations after the Conquest communities were either uninterested in marshaling the necessary texts to document their losses to Norman laymen, or that they had some difficulty remembering the particulars of the feast on Church land. Christ Church's late eleventh-century cartulary, for example, preserves no information whatsoever on the lands the community leased during Cnut's and Edward's reigns and then subsequently lost during the Norman settlement.[13] Similarly, Old Minster Winchester's magnificent twelfth-century cartulary, although it incorporates large numbers of Anglo-Saxon charters and includes title deeds to long-lost property, contains only four eleventh-century leases: without the evidence of Domesday Book, we should never know how serious the community's loss of loan-land was.[14] Even houses that wrote narratives about the period of Norman settlement recorded only the sketchiest of anecdotes concerning the erosion of their endowments. Ramsey Abbey's chronicle and its cartulary, for example, contain a few tales of lost loan-land, but neither accounts for more than a fraction of the land represented as such in Domesday Book.[15] There is no trace, for example, in Ramsey's cartulary of the house's loss of three estates in Huntingdonshire and Essex, and only a garbled story of two of these lands appears in its chronicle.[16] According to the testimony of Domesday jurors, however, the community had loaned this land to the thegn Ælfric of Yelling. Ælfric, according to Domesday, was killed at the Battle of Hastings – an act of treason against the Norman king – and as a consequence all of his lands, leased as well as demesne, were confiscated and given over to Aubrey de Vere. Twenty long years after Hastings, Ramsey was still trying to get its loan-land back.[17] In this case, and in many others like it, the survey increases our knowledge of the losses sustained even by those houses that cultivated their archives and wrote their own histories. And for those that did not, it is our only source.

Domesday's abundant material on the loss of loan-land and later monastic chronicles' less concrete complaints may tell us something about the ways in which religious communities in the eleventh century went about remembering what they had and what they had lost. This, in turn, sheds important light on contemporary notions concerning the relationship between written evidence and law, and about the ways in which the inquest itself worked. A

---

[13] Fleming, "Christ Church Canterbury's Anglo-Norman cartulary," in *Anglo-Norman Political Culture*, ed. C. Warren Hollister (Woodbridge, Suffolk, 1997), 83–155, at 103. The only extant eleventh-century lease surviving from Christ Church is S 1471.

[14] S 1391, 1402–3, 1476; F 131, 603, 605, 607, 617, 629–30, 632, 1355; Alexander R. Rumble, "The purposes of the *Codex Wintoniensis*," *ANS*, 4 (1982), 153–66, at 159–60. See also F 598–9, 602, 604.

[15] For Ramsey's Domesday claims, see F 23, 188, 201, 218, 791, 817, 820, 825, 830, 833, 843, 847, 850–1, 870, 1002, 1167, 1189, 1236, 2174, 2262, 2291, 2293, 2438, 2550, 3091.

[16] *Chron. Rams.*, 152–3.

[17] F 843, 850.

case can be made that one community – the bishopric of Worcester – developed the habit in the tenth and eleventh centuries of using written texts during legal action. The bishops of Worcester probably defended land promised to them or leased from them through the production and collection of formal, written leases: copies of nearly one hundred of them survive in either Worcester's early eleventh-century cartulary or in Hemming's cartulary compiled a century later.[18] These leases were probably also used by Bishop Wulfstan at the Domesday inquest, not only to shape the survey's discussion of Oswaldslow, Worcester Abbey's liberty, but also as evidence for Worcester's rights to thegnland and as an explanation for the community's varied and complex tenurial arrangements.[19] Certainly no other fee in the whole of Domesday Book provides such painstaking descriptions of the arrangements governing tenants' obligations towards their lords.[20] The community's apparent use of these leases at law may well explain the texts' careful preservation. Worcester's interest in its written leases, their use and their preservation was, however, exceptional. There is no evidence that any other house in England during this period collected and organized its leases thus, nor any indication that other abbeys or bishoprics systematically used such documents as legal proof at hundred and shire courts or at the Domesday inquest.

Although other monasteries besides Worcester were enthusiastic partici-pants in written culture – drawing up and preserving charters, and commem-orating the names of gifts and donations in *libri vitae* and obituaries – their use of written leases, mortgages, and the like was much less systematic. Some communities, like Christ Church Canterbury, had, by the year 1086, been writing and collecting charters for nearly half a millennium and had accumulated impressive archives of legal material.[21] Nonetheless, in the eleventh century it appears that Christ Church's dealings with patrons and clients were neither consistently recorded nor preserved.[22] The lands we now know to have been leased during Archbishops Eadsige's and Stigand's

---

[18] S 1297–1375, 1381, 1384–5, 1388, 1392–7, 1399, 1405–7, 1409. Of these, S 1326, 1347, 1385, 1393, 1394, 1399 and 1405 are originals. For Worcester's cartularies, see N. R. Ker, "Hemming's cartulary: a description of the two Worcester cartularies in Cotton Tiberius A. xiii," in *Studies in Medieval History Presented to Frederick M. Powicke*, ed. R. W. Hunt, W. A. Pantin, and R. W. Southern (Oxford, 1948), 49–75. If the Worcester material is excluded, only a few such eleventh-century transactions survive. One mortgage survives (S 1387), nine leases (S 1390–1, 1402–3, 1459, 1468, 1470–1, 1476) and two descriptions of purchases (S 1469, 1473). Of these, only a handful are contemporary copies (S 1390, 1469, 1471, 1473). For a discussion of pre-Conquest leases, see Kelly, "Anglo-Saxon lay society," 48–50.

[19] For the ways in which Worcester, with the aid of its dossier of legal material, helped to shape Domesday Book's description of Oswaldslow, see Wormald, "Lordship and justice," 114–36, and "Oswaldslow: and 'immunity'?," in *St. Oswald of Worcester*, ed. Nicholas Brooks and Catherine Cubitt (London, 1996), 117–28. The original book of leases may have proven awkward for use at court during the Domesday inquest, hence Hemming's reorganization of his information by shire.

[20] For examples of Worcester's detailed descriptions of tenure in Domesday Book, possibly made with the aid of Worcester's early cartulary, see F 1644–6, 1651, 1658, 1660.

[21] Nicholas Brooks, *Early History of the Church of Canterbury* (Leicester, 1984).

[22] Later monastic histories sometimes allude to texts like these, which were still extant, but not incorporated in their houses' cartulary: several ninth and tenth-century private charters, for example, were cited by

pontificates are not represented in Christ Church's extant archives: so, if these transactions were ever commemorated in writing, they were not preserved.[23] It also looks as if the bulk of the thegnly benefactions (many of which would have been *post-obitum* gifts) received by the community during the eleventh century were never written up as charters. A decade or two after the Conquest, when Christ Church produced its first cartulary, the author had to invent charters for Christ Church's eleventh-century gifts based on notations made in obituary lists used in the community's commemorative liturgy.[24] Similarly, it looks as if Hugh Candidus's account of Peterborough's eleventh-century leases and thegnly benefactions was founded not on charters, which the author bitterly laments were lacking, but on the community's *liber vitae*.[25]

By the eleventh century Shaftesbury Abbey may also have kept track of its gifts in non-diplomatic ways. The nunnery's pre-Conquest archive is now represented by thirty documents – twenty-nine of which are royal diplomas.[26] Domesday Book, along with a variety of Anglo-Norman and Angevin records make it clear that many of the nunnery's estates had been leased before the Conquest, and that there was a long tradition at the nunnery of collecting gifts of oblation from the parents of new girls. Indeed, a periodically updated post-Conquest list of these gifts survives.[27] A similar extra-diplomatic method of accounting for thegnly gifts may well have been employed by Shaftesbury before the Conquest; if so, this method of gift commemoration may have been used in lieu of more formal private charters. In any event, during the inquest Shaftesbury established title to some of its land by exhibiting a writ of King Edward.[28] But there is no evidence that the nunnery's lost loan-land and confiscated thegnly gifts were defended there by a similar display of pre-Conquest leases or thegnly charters.

At Christ Church, Peterborough and Shaftesbury it looks as if formal records of transactions between the communities and their thegnly benefac-

historians of St. Augustine's Abbey in the thirteenth and fourteenth centuries, but they are nowhere to be found in the community's twelfth-century cartulary (*Charters of St. Augustine's Abbey Canterbury and Minster in Thanet*, ed. Susan E. Kelly [Oxford, 1995], 183–4).

23 Fleming, "Christ Church Canterbury's Anglo-Norman cartulary," 103–7.
24 Ibid.. A similar habit of recording gifts in non-diplomatic ways on the Continent during this period has been found for Ottonian Germany (Timothy Reuter, "Property transactions and social relations between rulers, bishops and nobles in early eleventh-century Saxony: the evidence of the *Vita Meinwerci*," in *Property and Power*, 165–99) and in France (Arnoud-Jan A. Bijsterveld, "Patrons and gifts in chronicles: the evidence from the diocese of Liège, 11th-12th centuries," presented at the Third International Congress on Medieval Studies, Leeds, England, July, 1996).
25 Hugh Candidus's account of these grants and agreements is similar to the description found in Peterborough's *Liber Niger*, an account that cites the *liber vitae* as its source for information for the community's late Anglo-Saxon gifts (Hugh Candidus, 67; London Society of Antiquaries, MS. 60, fo. 64r).
26 *Charters of Shaftesbury Abbey*, ed. Susan E. Kelly (Oxford, 1996), xvi.
27 Ann Williams "The knights of Shaftesbury," *ANS*, 8 (1986), 214–37. One post-Conquest (1089 x 1121) list of dowries given by the families of nuns survives from Shaftesbury. It is found in BL MS. Harley 61 fo. 54r, printed in *Mon. Ang.*, II, 482–3. For a discussion of this list, see Kathleen Cooke, "Donors and daughters: Shaftesbury Abbey's benefactors, endowments and nuns c. 1086–1130," *ANS*, 12 (1990), 29–45. For a general background on similar Continental practices, see Léopold Deslisle, *Etudes sur la condition de la classe agricole et l'état de l'agriculture en Normandie au Moyen Age* (Evreux, 1851), 55.
28 F 474.

tors were hardly ever drawn up in the eleventh century into the kind of record documents that we recognize as charters. This can only be because the three communities had found other ways of keeping track of and securing gifts and leases, and that the strategies they developed for remembering and securing their endowment did not put them at any greater risk than the graphomaniacal community at Worcester. This in turn suggests that when relations between professional religious and their neighbors soured, and they were forced to resort to law, written proofs of disputed arrangements were not expected and probably not often used, at least in the courts around Huntingdon, Dorchester, and Canterbury. One of the results of the poverty of archival sources relating to thegnly gifts and loans at Christ Church, Peterborough and Shaftesbury was that their houses' later attempts at historical writing and cartulary production were distinctly weaker than Worcester's. But what may lie at the root of these communities' dearth of eleventh-century records is that their legal strategies during the period were simply different from Worcester's.

Evidence for the collection and cultivation of leases and thegnly grants at other communities in the eleventh century is more mixed, suggesting that in some monasteries more effort was made to write and preserve charters having to do with thegnly gifts and leases, but that these efforts were not very systematic. The fenland monasteries in particular seem to have written and stored a quantity of vernacular documents.[29] Still, these texts were not *bona fide* legal documents: they rarely functioned as actual conveyances of land, and they were almost always *ex parte* and written *ex post facto*.[30] Bury St. Edmund's is a case in point. Its cartulary contains a few leases, two from the eleventh century. Originally the two documents were drawn up as chirographs, with copies going both to Bury and to the lessees. The first of these leases commemorates an agreement made *c.* 1043 in front of a large, public assembly, probably the Norfolk shire court.[31] The transaction represents the forging of an important political alliance, since it was made with Æthelmær, brother of Stigand, the up-and-coming bishop of East Anglia. Besides local thegns, the whole of the communities of Bury, Ely, and St. Benet of Holme were witness to the transaction. In spite of the temporary nature of Bury's arrangements with Æthelmær, and in spite of a later written bequest drawn up by him, Bury lost the land to Æthelmær's Norman successor, William bishop of Thetford. No mention of Bury's rights to this land is found in Domesday Book, and no reference is made there to either the chirograph or the bequest.[32] Bury's second lease, also dating from the mid-1040s, describes

---

[29] For their variety and number see Kelly, "Anglo-Saxon lay society," 36–62; Alan Kennedy, "Law and litigation," 167.

[30] Kennedy, "Disputes about 'bocland,'" 178. Patrick Wormald believes a will was presented at court as evidence in one case, but the word for the documents viewed is *libri*, which suggests diplomas (Wormald, "Charters, law and the settlement of disputes," 157).

[31] S 1468, 1499.

[32] *DB*, ii, 192r.

a much more modest affair, an agreement drawn up between the community and a local thegn and his wife. By 1086 Bury had lost this land as well.[33] This lease was not invoked during the inquest, but the terms of another, obviously later, lease were discussed there, one not found in the cartulary. It may be that this second agreement was never made in writing.[34] There is, therefore, no evidence that the two extant written leases were used by Bury during the 1086 inquest to bolster its claims to lost loan-land. There is also no indication that in the dozen or so other disputes related to Bury's loan-land aired during the inquest, written leases were brought to the proceedings to prove Bury's claim to these lands, and no interest, a century later, in enshrining such texts (if they ever existed) in Bury's cartulary.[35] In short, it seems as if there was no relationship between Bury's written leases and the proceedings of the Domesday inquest. Domesday does, however, specifically note that some of Bury's claims were supported by the showing of writs. We are told, for example, that the abbot offered the writ and seal of King Edward as a means of establishing that Bury held Onehouse in Suffolk as the King's gift.[36] Evidence from both Shaftesbury and Bury, then, suggests that writs were shown at the inquest, but that documents drawn up concerning temporary alienations or the gifts of thegns were not used at the proceedings as a form of legal proof. Domesday's discussion of Bury's claims also makes it clear that the abbot was much more dependent on the testimony of local jurors to prove the rights of his case than any evidence drawn from his archives.[37] As far as most abbots, abbesses, and courts were concerned in 1086, it was either royal writs or communal memory, rather than old chirographs, that protected the property given, loaned, or mortgaged by thegnly benefactors.[38]

Although writs and public testimony were both used as proof of title during the inquest, the two forms of evidence were not carefully coordinated: writs and testimony were invoked at various times by ecclesiastics, but the use of memory and writ were not apparently viewed as two necessary and closely associated components of a single legal maneuver. Abingdon Abbey, for example, according to Domesday Book, was holding the large ten-hide estate of Fawler in Berkshire in 1086. The men at the inquest knew that a certain Eadric had held this manor during the Confessor's reign, and that he had granted its farm to Abingdon when his son became a monk there. Furthermore, jurors remembered that there had been an understanding between Eadric and the monks that after his death the son should have the manor. The

---

[33] S 1470; F 3182.

[34] F 3182. Occasionally charters were updated (e. g. S 106, 287, 332, 1211), but examples of this are very rare, and there are no examples of updated leases among extant originals.

[35] F 2235, 2576, 2603, 2686, 2763, 2770, 2918, 2919, 2930, 2941–2, 3090, 3111, 3142, 3182.

[36] F 2934.

[37] F 2603, 2686, 2941–2, 3142.

[38] For a similar emphasis, in the later tenth century, on the necessity of the public witness in land transactions, and the corollary lack of use of written documentation as evidence, see Kennedy, "Law and litigation," 156–8. For Norman monastic archives' similar dearth of eleventh-century records dealing with conditional or temporary transactions, see Tabuteau, *Transfers*, 9.

men of the shire, however, did not know if this agreement had been finalized, and, so Domesday reports, "they have seen neither the King's writ nor his seal." Nonetheless the Abbot and his monks testified that Eadric's son had indeed given the manor to the abbey, and that the community in fact had King Edward's writ and seal for it.[39] Here it appears that the original dealings between Eadric and Abingdon had been witnessed by men of the shire court. At some later date the abbot obtained a writ from King Edward confirming that the son had given Fawler to the monastery. Apparently, however, the abbot had never bothered to have the son's grant or the royal writ published at the local court. Thus, the initial gift was first and foremost safeguarded by the public witness of law-worthy men. The existence of the royal, written confirmation had been sought separately as an extra safeguard, but only after the transfer of land had been made. The writ, moreover, had not come to light until the extraordinary circumstances of the Domesday inquest. The existence of the writ helped Abingdon establish title to Fawler at the 1086 inquest, but it did so because the Conqueror, over the course of his reign and as the outcome of a number of local complaints and inquests, had come to support the notion that land granted by thegns to the Church or loaned by the Church to thegns was to be returned if a royal writ were produced. This clear-cut remedy was a neat, but extremely limited solution to a major problem. Religious communities before the Conquest had only sporadically sought and/or preserved writs to prop up their agreements with local thegns.[40] On the fortuitous occasions after the Conquest when such writs were available, the Church found quick relief to illegal alienation. In most cases, however, there were no writs. Thus the Church was forced, during the pleas of the Conqueror's reign, to rely heavily on the memories of local men.

The habit, in England, of relying on human memory and public witness was a long-standing one, and can be seen operating as clearly in the late tenth century as it can in the late eleventh. At one end of the period stands that curious text, the *Libellus Æthelwoldi*, a narrative history of Ely Abbey's legal life in the later tenth century.[41] Domesday Book, of course, stands at the other. Although the reasons for the genesis of the two texts and the circumstances of their production were dramatically different, and although they are separated by a century, the legal worlds they portray are, in many ways, strikingly similar. Although the two texts are different in their attention to detail, they can often be used together, the one adding flesh to the account of the other. Both, for example, give detailed accounts of the reliance of lords on local courts. Both demonstrate landholders' dependence on personal relationships, on public warranty and on the testimony of good men in matters of law, in particular in the making or breaking of sales, leases,

[39] F 109.
[40] See above, chapter 1.
[41] Kennedy, "Law and litigation," 167.

exchanges, and purchases.[42] And both the *Libellus* and Domesday Book provide overwhelming evidence for the importance of living memory in law and for law's pronounced sociability.

The two accounts also betray a similar attitude towards the written word. The *Libellus* contains a dramatic description of the drawing up and "cutting" of a chirograph – a document made to shore up the bequest of a dying thegn. The text also casually mentions charters three times in contexts that leave little doubt that landbooks were collected and preserved by local thegns.[43] Clearly, texts played a crucial role in particular circumstances in the later tenth century. Nonetheless, the descriptions of particular classes of actions in the *Libellus* – the selling and leasing of property, the disputing of title and the making of concords – suggest that these activities depended more on the eyes and ears of respected witnesses than on the production of written evidence.[44] The *Libellus*, for example, is bristling with descriptions of discussions and arguments, and it gives detailed accounts of the public examination of proof, the swearing of oaths, and the reconciliation of litigators. All of these are lived actions, and their validity was insured, according to the text, by the memory of the crowds that witnessed them. At the same time, the kind of private documents we know that thegns, ealdormen, and monks often drew up – descriptions of litigation, leases, or sales – are never invoked by the hundred juries, oath-helpers, or witnesses whose voices can be heard in the text. The absence of these documents from law courts at the end of the tenth century and again at the end of the eleventh, suggests that they had little to do with formal legal remedies against encroachment.[45] It is unclear to what use these documents, which look so pragmatic, were actually put: they were doubtless used for administrative purposes and as aids to memory in preparation for disputes, but perhaps they were also drawn up to mark the making of a *conventio* or the end of a dispute. They may even have been written up because this was something that people of substance did. Indeed, their production and collection may have served as an important social marker, an activity in which gentlemen and women participated and their creation may, therefore, have been not simply pragmatic, but symbolic. Similar, seemingly pragmatic practices, for example the thegnly uses of seals, judging from the surviving seal matrices themselves, were as much about dignity and social status as they were about utility. It looks, for example, as if Anglo-Saxon seal matrices were worn by their aristocratic bearers, either as pendants or as brooches, displayed as an advertisement of social prominence, closeness to the king and participation in written culture. Like seals, perhaps private charters

---

[42] See above, chapter 2.

[43] LE, ii, 27, 32, 37. See also Eric John, *Land Tenure in Early England* (Leicester, 1960), 51–3; Simon Keynes, *Diplomas*, 31–3; Wormald, *Bede and the Conversion of England*, 19–23; Kelly, "Anglo-Saxon lay society," 45–6.

[44] Kennedy, "Law and litigation," 167–9, 173.

[45] At times in the tenth century charters were produced for courts, as in S 1456. But probably, for the most part, these were royal diplomas.

were rather like Rolex watches, which do tell the time, but are procured and worn for less practical reasons as well.[46] Whatever their use, according to the account of the *Libellus*, documents like these were not for the most part being read, shown, or discussed at court in tenth-century Cambridgeshire.

The lived quality of the law portrayed by the *Libellus* bears a striking resemblance to the actions described in Domesday Book. At the inquest jurors often based their testimony on what they "had heard" or what they "had seen";[47] and in many cases inquest jurors testified that they "did not know" about some action or other, the implication being because they had not seen it with their own eyes.[48] And like the *Libellus*, Domesday Book only rarely mentions *cartae*. Only seven charters are invoked in the whole of Great and Little Domesday Book:[49] at the same time there are 1,000 explicit references to oral testimony. While there are hints that a few other diplomas might have been incorporated into Domesday,[50] it is certain, nonetheless, that the survey's fulsome details of sales, leases, and seisin were founded not on texts, but on men's memories of actions carried out in full view of public courts.

There are two significant differences between the legal actions recorded in Domesday Book and the *Libellus*, which point towards the important legal transformations taking place in the eleventh century. The first and most striking variation between the texts concerns royal writs and seals,[51] and the second the presence of sheriffs and royal reeves: writs and royal officials are very much in evidence in 1086, but are nowhere to be seen in the *Libellus*.[52] Clearly, here we can see changes both in the use of the written word and royal administrators, two developments linked to the rapid evolution, over the course of the eleventh century, of the writ, first as a centralizing administrative tool, and then as an instrument of law.[53]

The habit, so clear in the *Libellus* and Domesday Book, of relying on communal memory persisted throughout the Conqueror's and his sons' reigns. Just months before the Domesday inquest, King William, when attempting yet again to solve the vexing problems surrounding Ely's

[46] For seals and social status, see T. A. Heslop, "English seals from the mid-ninth century to 1100," *Journal of the British Archaeological Association*, 133 (1980), 1–16; P. Chaplais, "The Anglo-Saxon chancery: from the diploma to the writ," *Journal of the Society of Archivists*, 3 (1966), 160–76, at 160.

[47] For examples of testimony based on what had been heard, see below, subject index, IX.1, under "heard"; IX.2, under "did not hear." For testimony based on what had been seen, see subject index, IX.1, under "saw" and IX.2, under "had not seen."

[48] See below, subject index, IX.2, under "did not know."

[49] F 360, 1050, 1673, 1680, 1683–4, 3000.

[50] For two possible examples, one from Lichfield and the other from Evesham, see F 1680 and 1683.

[51] For the invocation of seals and writs and for their lack, see below, subject index, VII.4, under "seal" and "writ."

[52] For actions taken by sheriffs in leases, see F 63, 153, 903, 1490, 1631, 1696, 3012; in the delivery of land see F 1690, 2610, 2627; in mortgages, see F 199, 903, 3063; in sales, see F 1677. For actions taken by royal reeves in leases, see F 339, 483, 1486; in sales, see F 676, 2163, 2172. Although there is some evidence for the use of writs in the ninth and tenth centuries, it appears that they were not fully exploited until the eleventh (Campbell, "Some agents," 214–15). Kennedy, however, believes that the King's reeves may have been active in Cambridgeshire during Edgar's reign, but not after his death (Kennedy, "Law and litigation," 146).

[53] See above, chapter 1.

patrimony, did not order his commissioners to go through Ely's archives to find out the truth about the history of its estates, but rather commanded that the Bishop of Coutances and the Bishop of Winchester gather proper oral testimony regarding this and then write it down. They were to:

> inquire who had the lands of St. Ætheldreda recorded and sworn to, in what way the oaths were taken, and who took them, and who heard them, and what the lands are, and of what kind, and how many, and how they are named, and who holds them, and have these things noted and written down.[54]

Later, in Henry I's reign, jurors who were called to give an oath about the profits of Sandwich were each made to swear that what they had testified was based on what "I have learned from my ancestors and seen and heard from my youth up to now, so help me God and these holy gospels."[55] Communal memory bolstered by religious sanction was used across the whole of the late Anglo-Saxon and early Anglo-Norman periods as the primary form of proof in disputes centering on title. This traditional Anglo-Scandinavian reliance on memory fit comfortably into the legal practices of the Normans: in pre-Conquest Normandy it was public witness rather than charters that constituted legal proof.[56] Its survival at the time of the inquest and beyond is not, therefore, surprising.

The contrast between the legal strategies of most religious houses and Worcester is, therefore, striking, and suggests that individual communities' use of the written word in legal transactions varied dramatically. It doubtless also points to wide regional variations in the use of the written word in law, since the ways in which local textual communities protected themselves in local courts must have done much to shape the ways in which law operated in neighborhood and shire assemblies. Although an argument can be made that Worcester carefully marshaled and then put to use a variety of documents in courts of law, it looks as if most other religious communities in England used texts in a much more circumscribed fashion. The bulk of a house's transactions with thegnly neighbors – the leasing of estates, the collection of *post-obitum* grants, the gifts of oblation, the creation of mortgages – could be commemorated in writing, but these writings were not used formally as proof of title or conveyance during disputes. The memory of these transactions, which often came due only after the death of a donor and the donor's spouse and heirs, was primarily kept alive, not with a charter, but with yearly,

---

[54] *LE*, ii, 125. Written evidence was not excluded during the Ely land pleas, but it does seem as if it was limited to diplomas and writs. One of William's writs concerning Ely states that, "I want you allow the abbey to have the customs now that it had in the time of King Edward, such as the abbot will be able to plead by his charters and his witnesses (*per cartas suas et per testes suos eas deplacitare poterit*)" (*LE*, ii, 124). These customs were likely to be those protected by the confirming writs typical of Edward's reign.

[55] Stenton, *English Justice*, appendix 1, 116–23.

[56] Tabuteau, *Transactions*, 212–22.

witnessed rituals such as masses for the dead donor or the payment of small annual gifts or food-rents.[57]

In general, therefore, it seems that the use of writing in legal matters was broad rather than deep; that most abbots and bishops in the generation before the Conquest were enthusiastic collectors of royal writs which provided generic confirmations of privileges, and they acquired and treasured diplomas given to them by the king when he made donations. Texts associated with the king had long held an important place in the actions of local courts, where they were examined as evidence in legal disputes as early as the ninth century.[58] Given the long history of the legal utility of royal diplomas and William's own emphasis on the place of writs in law, it is hardly surprising that in the twelfth century, when cartularists began collecting and organizing their houses' land documents, they were primarily concerned with diplomas and writs, and that in houses like St. Augustine's, Canterbury, where ancient leases and thegnly grants could still be found, such documents were not for the most part included in cartularies.[59] Finally, the utility of particular classes of documents explains why post-Conquest forgers were uninterested in concocting pre-Conquest private charters, but penned writs and royal diplomas on a grand scale.

Conclusion

In the legal world of tenth and eleventh-century England, where archives were uneven and certain classes of written records were not given much weight at court, there was nothing incongruous about landholders defending their patrimonies by marshaling an untidy, and to our eyes schizophrenic, array of evidence. Thus, after the Norman Conquest, as survivors and settlers began arguing over enormously complex and contentious claims based on conflicting memories of the Anglo-Saxon past, there was nothing curious about one ecclesiastical litigant bringing writs or diplomas to court, another bringing relics, another the *vitae* of his community's saints, and another the testimony of the better and older men of the shire.[60] All constituted valid and recognized forms of proof and legal argumentation, both for Englishmen and for Normans, and all helped protect rights to property. Throughout the

---

[57] See, for example S 1482, 1530; Robin Fleming, "History and liturgy at pre-Conquest Christ Church," *HSJ*, 6 (1994), 67–83 at 71–2.

[58] For ninth-century examples of diplomas brought to court, see S 137, 1187, 1433, 1434. For tenth-century examples, see S 1445, 1456 (the word used is *swutelunga*; but the context suggests royal diplomas) and *LE*, ii, 25, 27. For eleventh-century examples, see F 360, 1050, 1673, 3000. For a discussion of the use of diplomas in court, see Kennedy, "Disputes about 'bocland'," 181–4; and Kennedy "Law and litigation," 161–3.

[59] See above, n. 22.

[60] *Vita Wulfstani*, 24–6; *Lawsuits*, 9a, 15; Fleming, "History and liturgy," 76–82; Richard Sharpe, "Eadmer's letter to the monks of Glastonbury concerning St. Dunstan's disputed remains," in *The Archaeology and History of Glastonbury Abbey*, ed. Leslie Abrams and James P. Carley (Woodbridge, Suffolk, 1991), 205–15.

Conqueror's reign landholders used the courts and the law in ways we moderns recognize as legal to regain or keep hold of land, rights, or men. Bury St. Edmund's, Ely, Evesham, Canterbury, and Worcester litigated hard in local courts, using men skilled in the law.[61] And Archbishop Lanfranc, along with the Abbot of Bury, the Bishop of Wells, and the Bishop of Worcester, sought to protect their patrimonies by strengthening their archives.[62] But the powers of the unseen world were also marshaled by Christ Church, Evesham, Glastonbury, and Worcester in their bid to win pleas, and it seems as if such eschatological remedies were part and parcel of law and justice. Thus could the oaths of compurgators and trial by battle coexist in 1086 alongside the inspection of diplomas.[63] Meanwhile, the Abbot of Abingdon combated annexation by beating a royal reeve with a stick,[64] and the Archbishop of York did so by chastising the King in his own court.[65] These are a very broad range of responses to legal problems – to our minds legal, quasi-legal and extra-legal. All were used by landholders to bring relief to the problems that rose out of the past history of estates and their entanglements with long-dead laymen. These strategies suggest that there was no rigid definition in the late eleventh century of law as a small, neat, circumscribed world requiring a close adherence to set legal procedures and written forms. The law was this, but it was more, encompassing a wide universe of strategies and rememberings that eleventh-century people thought of in some way as legal action, but that we no longer do.

[61] For Bury, see Antonia Gransden, "Baldwin, abbot of Bury St. Edmund's, 1065–1097," *ANS*, 4 (1982), 65–76; for Ely, see Miller, "The Ely land pleas," 438–56; for Evesham, see R. R. Darlington, "Æthelwig, abbot of Evesham," *EHR*, 48 (1933), 1–22, 177–98; for Canterbury, see Bates, "The land pleas of William I's reign," 1–19; for Worcester, see Ann Williams "The spoliation of Worcester," *ANS*, 19 (1997), 383–408.

[62] Margaret Gibson, *Lanfranc of Bec* (Oxford, 1978), 153; S. D. Keynes, "Giso, bishop of Wells (1061–88)," *ANS*, 19 (1997), 203–72; Gransden, "Baldwin, abbot of Bury," 68–74; Emma Mason, *St. Wulfstan of Worcester c. 1008–1095* (Oxford, 1990), 209–18.

[63] For the use of oaths, see F 622, 688, 1295, 1301, 1354. For the use of trial by battle, see F 1190, 1534, 2255, 2356, 2399, 2458, 2724. For the showing of charters, see F 360.

[64] *Lawsuits*, 12. The Abbot of Abingdon's forceful response is echoed in an early twelfth-century Thorney Abbey suit. The Abbot, after an unsuccessful attempt at getting back land given out by his predecessor, went to the manor in question and "broke" the tenant's houses and "stubbed his holt," before hurrying off to get a writ from the King (Stenton, *English Justice*, Appendix 4, 140–7).

[65] *Historians of the Church of York*, ed. James Raine, RS (1879–94), II, 350–3; Emma Mason, "Changes and continuity in eleventh-century Mercia: the experience of St. Wulfstan of Worcester," *ANS*, 8 (1986), 154–76 at 167; Henry Mayr-Harting, "Function of a twelfth-century recluse," *History*, 60 (1975), 337–52.

4 Disputes and the Norman present

Disputes and the Norman settlement

Not all disputes aired in 1086 were the product of prelapsarian circumstance. Many of the inquest's conflicts were newly minted, and came into being in the first two decades of Norman settlement. Sometimes the claims brought forth in 1086 were between rightful TRW holders and successful predators: in these cases we can identify both saints and sinners. In the *invasiones* of Suffolk, for example, we are told that Richard fitz Gilbert, "the bad neighbor," had taken a carucate of land in Bradley. Presumably Richard's local sobriquet, *malus vicinus*, was awarded because of his relentless encroachments.[1] In Bedfordshire, William de Warenne not only dispossessed William Speke of some land in Dean, but he stole a couple of horses there from William Speke's men.[2] And while Bertran de Verdun was in France on the King's business other lords settled near him took advantage of his absence: Geoffrey de Mandeville disseised him of half a hide, and Ralph Taillebois built a mill on Bertran's land.[3] These and other of Domesday's most blatant annexations share two important characteristics. First, Domesday Book assigns unambiguously condemning words to these actions: "seized," "annexed," "encroached," "stole," or the like.[4] Second, the actions found in association with these verbs are often concerned not with whole estates, but rather with pieces of them. Hundreds of small encroachments, involving the theft of a mill or the seizure of woodland and meadow, were the subject of litigation in 1086.[5] Clearly, liminal and valuable possessions like these were common objects of desire, but without the evidence of Domesday we should never know it. Only a few examples of such activity survive in the charters and narratives of the Conqueror's reign, small stories compared to the dramas of Penenden Heath or *Ildeburga*. In one, a monk of St. Alban's lamented his house's loss, sometime in the 1070s, of a beautiful stretch of woodland to the scheming Abbot of Westminster, who, it appears, undertook a series of lawsuits to solidify his encroachment. The abbot's "litigations and sophistry,"

---

[1] F 3198.
[2] F 19.
[3] F 154.
[4] See below, subject index, I.10.
[5] For the illegal seizure of mills, woodland, meadow, and the like, see below, subject index, I.2, under "manorial appurtenance claimed, disputed, etc."

so we are told, broke Abbot Frederick's heart and sent him to an early grave.[6] Similarly, Fécamp was fighting with William de Braose over woodland in Sussex, and Robert de Courcy tried to encroach upon one of Bury's pastures.[7] These three narratives alone give no indication of the typicality or uniqueness of such events. It is only when they are situated within the legal context provided by Domesday Book that it becomes clear that the boundaries of estates and their more distant appurtenances were a prime source of legal discord in William's reign.

An important minority of disputes in 1086 did, however, concern the annexation of substantial estates. Gilbert fitz Thurold, for example, had given land in Sheriff's Lench, Worcestershire, to Evesham Abbey,

> for the soul of Earl William with the consent of the King. Consequently, one monk was put in the Church. Abbot Æthelwig gave a gold mark to King William for the other two hides. The King granted this land to the Church for his soul, by testimony of Gilbert fitz Thurold, who took the gold for the King's use. Evesham Abbey was seised of these four hides for many years, until the Bishop of Bayeux took them away from the Church and gave them to Urso [d'Abetot].[8]

Although men at the inquest could remember the complicated negotiations and rituals of conveyance that stood behind Evesham's possession of Sheriff's Lench, Odo of Bayeux had managed to seize it nonetheless, and grant it to another.[9] In Sheriff's Lench and elsewhere jurors were able to make the distinction between legal seisin and possession outside the law, and they were willing to assert that great and especially disgraced magnates like Odo held their manors "unjustly" or "through force."[10]

Many of the complaints aired during the inquest, however, were the product of a more complicated set of legal factors, and in these cases it is difficult to separate victim from predator. Any kind of opacity of title caused neighbors and competitors to encroach and to litigate, and ambiguities to title are more likely to have increased over the course of William's reign rather than diminished. Throughout the central Middle Ages land and its possession were especially vulnerable at particular moments: in the later Anglo-Norman period the most common circumstances for complaint were the ending of limited-term grants, the succession of new lords (especially those without clear-cut antecessors), and remarriage.[11] In 1086 these factors lay at the heart

---

6   *Gesta Abbatum Monasterii Sancti Anblani*, ed. H. T. Riley, RS (London, 1867–9), I, 43–4.
7   *Regesta*, I, appendix 1, 32; Hermann, *Liber de Miraculis Sancti Eadmundi*, in *Memorials of St. Edmund's Abbey*, ed. Thomas Arnold, 3 vols., RS (1890–6), I, 79.
8   F 1677.
9   Evesham's chronicle tells the story of Odo's encroachments against Evesham, including Sheriff's Lench, and suggests that Odo had trumped up a legal pretext for his confiscation of the abbey's land (*Chron. Ev.*, 96–7). For the various rituals that surrounded the conveyance of gifts after the Conquest, see Hudson, *Land*, 157–66.
10   For actions described as "unjust" or done through force, see below, subject index, VII.3, and VII.5, under "justice."
11   John Hudson, "Maitland and Anglo-Norman law," *The History of English Law: Centenary Essays on "Pollock and Maitland,"* *Proceedings of the British Academy*, 89 (1996), 21–46, at 35–6.

of nearly every secular tenancy in England, so it is hardly surprising to find challenges to title raised twenty years on by hopeful sons, new husbands, or old tenants.[12] Even in the more placid days of good King Edward, land over time became burdened with a host of other people's expectations and disappointments simply because landlords lived, died and managed their estates, but in the period of the Conquest the usual complications of title were intensified by the rapid and massive redistribution of land and by the ambiguous circumstances of so many acquisitions.

Some of these conflicts rose out of honest mistakes, stemming from that incendiary combination of land rush and attenuated bureaucracy. Something like half of all the estates in England were given out after the Conquest to new lords, and in some regions and at some times this upheaval occurred at breakneck pace. Indeed, in some years, the King and his most trusted *familiares* were granting out hundreds of thousands of acres of stocked, cultivated, and populated land, and they were doing so without much written instruction and with few clear-cut accountings of what exactly it was they were doing. That the King and his officials did not always know what they were doing when they handed out land, or what they had done after granting land away, is evident from a series of Ely writs, in which King William, as a result of a local inquest, attempted to undo the damage he had done by granting out land that was not his to give. In these writs he ordered that "if anyone says that he has [Ely land] by my gift, let me know the size of the land and how he claims it; and according to what I hear, I shall give him land in exchange or do something else."[13] Soon Norman tenants-in-chief were settling their own followers on estates, or making accommodations with the thegnly survivors still squatting on their old manors. At this level, written accountings are even less likely to have been used.

That conflicting claims were created in this environment is hardly surprising. Domesday Book preserves a number of disputes stemming from the fact that the same land, rights, or men had been given away twice or even three times to different beneficiaries by muddled officials or open-handed, but disorganized lords. In the reign of King Edward, for example, a freeman commended to the thegn Wigulf had held five acres of land in Hemingstone, Suffolk. Twenty years on, this land was held in Roger Bigot's fee. Roger de Raismes, however, claimed all the land of Wigulf, along with the lands of his freemen. De Raismes based his claim on the simple fact that the men and the land of Wigulf had been delivered to him *before* they had been delivered to

---

[12] For the relationship between marriage and the transfer of property during the Norman settlement, see Eleanor Searle, "Women and the legitimization of succession at the Norman Conquest," *ANS*, 3 (1981), 159–71; Williams, *The English*, 198–202. Norman successors, for example, were occasionally challenged by English heirs, some of whom were fortunate enough to have writs, and some of whom won back the fields and farms of dead relatives (F 609, 648, 657, 971, 1353, 2834). And the rights of English heiresses married to Normans may have come into conflict with the rights of others. The long-winded description of William Goizenboden's rights found in F 560 may suggest that others felt they had better rights than he.

[13] *Lawsuits*, 18d, 18e, 18f.

Roger Bigot. This created a legal conundrum, since both men had been given the same land. It is hardly surprising that those hearing the dispute of the two Rogers complained that they did not "know how to tell the truth in this."[14]

The disputes resulting from serial seisin could last for years. In Falkenham, Suffolk, for example, Domesday records the fate of twenty-six acres of land held, in the time of King Edward, by a man called Beorhtmær:

This Beorhtmær had several manors, and part was delivered on the King's behalf to Engelric, and the other parts to Ranulf brother of Ilger and to Ralph Pinel. This particular manor was delivered to Ralph Pinel, so Ralph himself says. He also produces the testimony of the hundred that he was seised *first*. But they are ignorant as to whether or not he was seised on the King's behalf. They say that Ranulf brother of Ilger claimed this land against Ralph, and that Roger the Sheriff named a specific time to them that they should come together. Ranulf came, but Ralph did not. Therefore the men of the hundred judged that Ranulf be seised. He now holds it, but Ralph Pinel denies that he was summoned regarding this plea.[15]

Here is a case where more than one tenant was seised of the same land, and, despite earlier complaints and pleading, the problem had yet to be resolved.

Greater tenants-in-chief seem to have come across this problem quite a lot, often enough in any case that they were willing to maintain amity among themselves until a resolution could be negotiated. In Ashfield, Suffolk, for example, there were a series of claims and counter-claims between Roger Bigot and Hugh of Chester arising out of serial seisin. But the two great men were content to maintain a temporary and amiable accord concerning Ashfield, until the King or his ministers could settle things between them:

TRE Swærting the Priest, a freeman in the soke and commendation of the Abbot, held thirty acres of land in Ashfield. Walter de Dol had been seised of this priest when Walter forfeited his land. Afterwards, Earl Hugh was seised, so the hundred testifies. Northmann says that the King sent him a writ that he should seise Ralph de Savenay [an undertenant of Roger Bigot, who was a tenant of the Bishop of Bayeux] of all the freemen over whom Hubert de Port had seised the Bishop. Northmann thus seised Ralph de Savenay of the priest. Northmann, however, does not know if Hubert had first seised the Bishop of the priest. When they came into the county [for the Domesday inquest], the King's barons found the priest in peace between Roger Bigot and Earl Hugh, and so he shall be in peace until this be adjudged.[16]

The case of Ashfield suggests that so common were the problems of serial seisin that great tenants-in-chief and royal officials alike had become habituated to them.

Title was also complicated by less innocent mistakes. It was fairly common during the inquest for two tenants, both of whom had warranty for a holding,

---

[14]   F 2890.
[15]   F 3105. This is an early example of an essoin. The other examples of this in Domesday Book are F 3047, 3207 and 3211.
[16]   F 2962.

to have legitimate claims to the same piece of land: it was their lords whose title was questionable. In Hertfordshire, for example, a King's reeve was disseised of half a hide of land by the Bishop of Bayeux, who then gave it to Eudo Dapifer. Eudo must have assumed that his possession was secure, since the land had been given to him by the King's half-brother and occasional surrogate. Eudo then granted the hide to his man Humphrey. When Humphrey (legally) acquired this land from his lord – land that had been taken illegally, so it turns out, from the reeve – "he got with it 68 oxen, 250 sheep, 150 pigs, 50 goats, [and] a mare . . . [and] cloth and vessels [together worth] 20s."[17] Here is a rare example in Domesday Book of a list of chattels disputed along with title to an estate. In 1086 it was not only land that was in dispute, but substantial herds of animals, woodlands full of swine, and the kinds of household goods that fill Carolingian inventories. Here the competing interests of the King and his reeve on the one hand and Eudo Dapifer and his man on the other could be delineated by jurors but they could never be resolved to everyone's satisfaction, since more than one man sincerely maintained that he had legal title.

Other problems rose out of the very mechanisms through which land redistribution had occurred. The most convenient and stable method of settlement, of course, was antecession, that practice begun by William soon after Hastings, of rewarding loyal followers with all of the lands of a single, disgraced thegn. In 1086, twenty years after William's victory, the names of antecessors were invoked to prove legal title more often than any other rationale, including the possession of a writ, the claim of a royal grant or the warranty of a lord. But the simple logic of antecession was confounded both by pre-Conquest habits of lordship and landholding, and by the other means whereby Normans received English lands.

 In particular, the intricacies of pre-Conquest lordship, with its perplexing separation of tenurial, personal, and jurisdictional rights, and the freedom it offered so many men to "go where they would with their land," interfered with antecession and led to a confusing press of claims. In Suffolk, for example, Domesday Book records that:

TRE Balki, commended to Æthelstan, held forty acres of land in Helmingham. In the same place Blachmann, a freeman half commended to a man commended to Eadric, Robert Malet's antecessor, and half commended to Saxi, held twenty-four acres of land; and Godric, a freeman half commended to a man commended to Eadric, Robert Malet's antecessor, and half commended to Saxi, held twenty acres of land. Also in Helmingham there were eleven freemen with seventy-one acres of land. Saxi, Ranulf Peverel's antecessor, had the commendation of two and a half of these men, and another half was commended to a man commended to Eadric, Robert Malet's antecessor. Now Odo of Bayeux holds all of this.[18]

---

[17] F 801. James Campbell suggests that this is another example of distraint of chattels (Campbell, "Some agents," 215).
[18] F 2958.

Although Balki, Blachmann, and Godric did not, themselves, have specially designated successors after the Conquest, the men to whom they were commended did: Æthelstan was the antecessor of Peter de Valognes, Eadric of Robert Malet, and Saxi of Ranulf Peverel. In other places each of these Normans had in their power or made claims to the commended men of their antecessors.[19] But here in Helmingham Odo of Bayeux gained hold of all of these antecessors' men and acres. The detailed tallying of Odo's holdings in the vill and the text's careful articulation of its old, Edwardian affinities does suggest that some at the inquest questioned at least a portion of Odo's rights in Helmingham. Across the folios of Little Domesday and in the Exchequer Domesday accountings of Bedfordshire, Buckinghamshire, and Cambridge-shire, where the rich detail of pre-Conquest lordship and dependency is preserved, Normans can be seen fighting one another in court, arguing, depending on the situation of the moment, either that old ties of commenda-tion conferred title to designated successors, or that they did not. Thus those who succeeded in acquiring the commended men of their antecessors were being challenged in 1086 by those who felt their own rights had been compromised; and those who did not gain their antecessors' men were complaining as well. Since every man was required by the legal customs current in Anglo-Saxon England to have a lord,[20] and since many a thegn was both the antecessor of a particular Norman and the man of another Norman's antecessor, the potential for conflict was enormous.[21]

Lordship complicated title in other ways. Surviving English landholders scrambled for lords in the months following the Battle of Hastings, as their own lords died, fled, or became powerless. William de Warenne, for example, held a hide and a virgate of land in Easton, which had been held TRE by a man called Authgi, who could grant or sell his land to whomever he pleased:

Afterwards, King William [re]granted this land to Authgi and commended him to Ralph Taillebois through his writ, so that [Ralph] might have custody of Authgi as long as he lived. On the day Authgi died, [however,] he said that he was William de Warenne's man, and William, therefore, has been seised of this land.[22]

Like the Berkshire thegn Thorir, Authgi probably commended himself to his new Norman neighbor "for his own protection," and doubtless, like an unnamed Wiltshire thegn, he had put himself "voluntarily" under the power of his new lord.[23] Apparently Authgi, after some careful thought, had decided that William's lordship was more efficacious than Ralph's, and it looks very much as if he and his land walked out of Ralph's fee and into William's. The consequence of this action was that in 1086 Ralph Taillebois was waving his

[19]　See for example F 3096.
[20]　E.g. II Æthelstan 2.
[21]　Fleming, *Kings and Lords*, 113–23; Abels, "Sheriffs and lord-seeking," 25–33.
[22]　F 22.
[23]　F 102, 1621.

writ around the Bedfordshire inquest, while William, in possession of the land, was insisting that he was Authgi's ultimate and therefore legitimate lord. Both Ralph and William had golden claims, the one based on a royal grant bolstered by a writ and the other on the pervasive and powerful rights of lordship.

In the case of Authgi, and in countless more, the lands of Englishmen in 1086 were being accounted for in the fees of the Normans with whom they had made private arrangements. The rights of a thegn's new Norman lord, however, could and did come into conflict with the Englishman's other and older obligations. In Berkshire, for example, the sons of Algeard had held seven hides in Lyford before the Conquest from the Abbot of Abingdon: "They could not go to another lord without the abbot's permission. Nonetheless, they commended themselves to Walter Giffard TRW, without the abbot's order."[24] In 1086 Walter was holding this land himself, not as part of his fee, but from the abbot, an obvious compromise whereby the abbot asserted his rights to loan-land and Walter Giffard maintained land that had come to him through a kind of entrepreneurial lordship.

Sometimes the rights conferred by the private arrangements made between English survivors and Norman settlers conflicted with that quintessential Conquest right – that of antecession. According to a claim in Lindsey's South Riding, Robert Dispensator claimed land in Scremby through his antecessor Vighlak. But the riding testified that Vighlak, although he may have been the antecessor of Robert, had made himself a man of Gilbert of Ghent after the Conquest; and when Vighlak had forfeited, he forfeited this land "to the loss of his lord Gilbert." The riding, therefore, decided that Gilbert, the lord, rather than Robert, the successor, had title to Scremby.[25] Similarly, in Norfolk we find that Hugh de Montfort's antecessor had held a freeman with six acres of land. After the Conquest, however, the freeman "became a man" of Bishop Herfast, and in 1086 it was the Bishop's successor, rather than Hugh de Montfort, who held the freeman and his land.[26]

Some of the legal troubles generated by commendation and lord-seeking doubtless came about because of the wide gulf separating Continental and English practices of lordship and were the result of honest confusion. But there must also have been a willful blurring of distinctions between Continental and English customs, with Normans cannily claiming whatever rights they could through the contradictory principles of rights to their antecessors' commended men and rights to Englishmen who sought protection from them. Thus, the vagaries of Old English lordship and the scramble by thegns and sokemen for lords after the Conquest caused the settlement to be less regular and clear-cut than antecession on its own would have been. This combination of willful reinterpretation and genuine misunderstanding

[24]   F 107.
[25]   F 1071.
[26]   F 2419.

spawned enormous numbers of disputes during William's reign. Their adjudication and resolution at the inquest may have been a first step towards the genesis of a new, streamlined lordship in England which more tightly bound together personal, jurisdictional, and territorial lordship, collapsing them into the compact honorial rights that were to become ubiquitous in the twelfth century.[27]

Lordship was not the only challenge to antecession. In some parts of the kingdom land was granted out not only by antecessor, but also on the basis of hundred.[28] After the earliest wave of disinheritance and antecessorial acquisition, the remaining estates in some hundreds and wapentakes, particularly those in the northern Danelaw, were sometimes handed over to one of William's favorites. Like grants based on antecession, territorial grants had a certain straightforward logic – either land lay in a hundred or it did not. But these hundredal grants were complicated in the same ways as antecessorial grants: during the inquest those holding by antecession and those holding by hundred often came into conflict. Geoffrey Alselin, for example, was the successor of Toki son of Auti throughout the kingdom, and Roger de Bully had received a territorial grant based on the Yorkshire wapentake of Strafforth. During the inquest, both Roger and Geoffrey laid claim to ten carucates of Toki's land within the wapentake; the former on the basis of territory and the latter on the basis of antecession.[29] Similarly Osbern d'Arques claimed the land of his antecessor Wulfberht in Skyrack Wapentake, a wapentake which apparently had the same boundaries as Ilbert de Lacy's castelry:

The men of Barkston Wapentake and Skyrack Wapentake produce testimony for Osbern d'Arques that his antecessor Wulfberht had all of Thorner – that is, four manors of eight carucates of land. They do not know by whose gift. But all of Thorner sits within the boundary of Ilbert's castle, according to the first measurement. But it sits outside it according to the newest measurement.[30]

Here it seems that Ilbert had been arguing that anything within the bounds of Skyrack Wapentake was a legitimate part of his fee, but Osbern d'Arques was claiming land there on the basis of antecession. The case was made all the more difficult by the fact that the men of this wapentake and its neighbor of Barkston could not agree on the boundary between the two, and therefore the territorial delineation of Ilbert's rights.[31]

To further confuse matters, it was not absolutely clear how an estate's outlying appurtenances and rights – its extensive sokes and berewicks – should be affected by antecession and by territorial redistribution. Whose rights over berewicks and sokes within a wapentake were greatest: the

---

[27] Maitland, *Domesday Book and Beyond*, 67, 294, 311.
[28] For hundredal grants, see Fleming, *Kings and Lords*, 145–82; Dalton, *Conquest*, 19–78.
[29] F 1769, 1772; Fleming, *Kings and Lords*, 161.
[30] F 1754. See also F 1755.
[31] Fleming, *Kings and Lords*, 149–65; Dalton, *Conquest*, 76.

successor of a well-defined antecessor who had gained hold of the *caput* of a manor, or the man in whose territory outlying rights and fields lay? The Yorkshire and Lincolnshire *clamores* are very much concerned with this question. For the most part, pre-Conquest soke-rights and berewick-rights were carefully upheld by Domesday's jurors. Nonetheless great men, when it suited their needs, pressed claims to sokes and berewicks on the basis of their hundredal grants.[32]

Clearly, lords strove to maximize their holdings by founding their complaints on whatever legal pretext was advantageous to them. Sometimes they insisted that title came to them through antecession; at other times they based a claim on the Edwardian commendation of their English tenants; and sometimes they argued for land or rights on the basis of a hundredal grant. Henry de Ferrers, by no means the most litigious of the Conqueror's followers, was involved in several dozen disputes in 1086, and the grounds upon which he, his followers, or his reeves based their claims shifted wildly depending on the particular circumstances of each dispute. In Berkshire, for example, where Henry acted as sheriff, he took possession of as much of the land of his Edwardian predecessor, Godric the Sheriff, as he could. Thus his holdings in the county included both bits of land that had been attached to the *terra regis*, and long used to support the Sheriff of Berkshire,[33] and that land which Godric, at least in theory, held not as sheriff, but through inheritance, dowry, lease, or purchase.[34] Godric's two sets of land were hopelessly entangled, a state of affairs encouraged by Henry. Jurors at the Domesday inquest testified that much of Henry's land in the county, land he claimed through antecession, was actually part of the King's farm, and that Henry was abusing his office by claiming land for his own fee that he held, in actual fact, from the King as sheriff. Henry was also pushing claims to land that Godric had seized illegally after the Battle of Hastings,[35] and land that he had leased from Abingdon Abbey.[36] Thus, in Berkshire, Henry made claims on the basis of his office and on antecession, boldly asserting that he was entitled to every piece of land associated with Godric, no matter how weak or temporary that association might have been. In Derbyshire, however, Henry was a much less enthusiastic supporter of the rights of successors. Here Henry had been granted a territorial fee based on Appletree Wapentake and was, therefore, defending his rights to land given out as part of a hundredal grant. Some of his Derbyshire possessions ran roughshod over the rights of antecession: he took possession, for example, of all the lands in the wapentake that Geoffrey Alselin's antecessor, Toki son of Auti, had held, and was fighting Geoffrey's claims at the Derbyshire inquest.[37] Henry's legal sensibil-

---

[32] Fleming, *Kings and Lords*, 133–4.
[33] F 90–5, 97, 115, 118–19, 122.
[34] F 94–5, 117, 120.
[35] F 116.
[36] F 117.
[37] F 327.

ities shifted yet again at the Lincolnshire pleas, where he or his men were battling Geoffrey de la Guerche, whose fee was centered on Epworth Wapentake, and who had possession of Henry's antecessor Siward Barn's land there.[38] Here Henry argued that antecessorial grants took precedence over territorial ones.

As Henry's litigation shows, lords in 1086 pressed claims not on the basis of some sort of well-understood hierarchy of legal rights and principles, but rather on whatever point of law suited a very particular and local set of needs. The land law of King Edward's day, the legal habits of the Norman aristocracy and the confusion and opportunism spawned by the mechanics of land redistribution created a ragged and haphazard pattern of settlement, and because of this, the particulars of landholding were often contentious, and were the source of countless legal claims and hard feelings across William's reign and kingdom. It seems likely, however, that the common sources and causes of dispute, displayed again and again during the Domesday inquest, helped to clarify the thinking of royal administrators and local jurors, and helped to standardize and routinize their settlement. It is at the inquest itself that we should look for the rapid evolution of a clearer set of legal norms and principles concerning succession and possession.

Disputes and the politics of William's reign

This environment of contested rights was complicated exponentially by the political and personal misadventures of some of the Conqueror's most important magnates. In order to fully appreciate the complexities of title *c.* 1086, it is important to see how the problems of settlement, discussed above, were compounded by the politics of William's reign. Many of the events that rocked the Conqueror's court and preoccupied twelfth-century chroniclers also precipitated abrupt and wide-ranging tenurial transformations, transformations that reconfigured many of the great fees in the kingdom and spawned large numbers of disputes in their wake. These events, described by John Gillingham as "the ordinary accidents of medieval politics," happened at an extraordinary rate during the Norman settlement.[39] The most dramatic of these events were the early deaths or rebellions of some of William's closest and richest *familiares*. These crises, most of which occurred in the first decade of William's rule, had a profound and unsettling effect on landholding. Because of them, many lords came into possession of land, men, and rights through exceptional circumstances rather than antecession, territory, or lordship; and there were hundreds of complaints aired before Domesday's

---

[38] F 1121; Fleming, *Kings and Lords*, 161.

[39] John Gillingham, "Some observations on social mobility in England between the Norman Conquest and the early thirteenth century," in *England and Germany in the High Middle Ages*, ed. Alfred Haverkamp and Hanna Vollrath (Oxford, 1996), 333–56.

commissioners in 1086, the roots of which could be traced back, not to antecession or to lordship, but rather to the most shocking political moments of the reign. Indeed the complaints in Domesday Book serve to remind us that problems that came about because of the death or disgrace of a great man were rarely resolved within the year it happened, an impression left by Orderic Vitalis, John of Worcester, and the rest, but that they continued to dog the King, sometimes for a generation or more. Domesday Book, therefore, provides us with a window into the local and social ramifications of high politics, and shows us the ways in which great landholders and middling undertenants alike were plagued by the doings of the rich and the famous.

The most sensational reason for acquisition was the redistribution of land following a forfeiture. The periodic regranting of disgraced magnates' possessions over the course of the Conqueror's reign complicated title, and by the time of the inquest there were many in the kingdom who felt that they had unjustly lost out as a result of some great man's forfeiture. Most pronounced among such cases are those stemming from the disgrace of Ralph Wader, son of Edward the Confessor's staller, Robert fitz Wimarc, and Earl of Norfolk when he rebelled in 1075.[40] On the day, as Domesday puts it, that "he wronged the King," Earl Ralph was in possession of a large and valuable honor centered on Norfolk and Suffolk. Ralph, before his fall, also had charge of a number of royal estates in East Anglia, estates for which a whole series of Norman sheriffs, bailiffs, and stewards assumed responsibility after his rebellion.[41] Ralph, like royal farmers everywhere, had worked assiduously in the days in which he was much favored by the King both to preserve royal rights and to profit from them.[42] In 1086 Ralph was repeatedly accused of having annexed freemen or acres that belonged by right to the King. Some of these *invasiones* were done through brute force, but other of his encroachments stood, in many ways, within the law. One of Earl Ralph's men, for example, traded a bridle to a King's reeve for the rights to five freemen, and when the Earl forfeited, these men and their land were considered by some as part of Ralph's fee and by others as something that the King needed to recover.[43] Ralph had also rented freemen from royal manors before his fall and purchased rights, land, and men for cash.[44] It was not at all clear in 1075 whether these purchases should revert to the crown or be passed on to lords succeeding Ralph. Did the purchase of land by a great man from a grubby little reeve constitute legal seisin? What happened to such a purchase after that man forfeited? Did the rights held by a disgraced magnate to those

---

[40] *ASC*, s. a. 1075 (D, E); David C. Douglas, *William the Conqueror* (Berkeley, 1964), 230–4. The rebellion of his fellow-traveler Roger de Breteuil also necessitated various complicating adjustments in Hereford's tenurial geography (C. P. Lewis, "The Norman settlement of Herefordshire under William I," *ANS*, 7 [1985], 195–213, at 201).

[41] F 2163–4, 2172, 2194, 2202, 2207, 2213, 2216, 2219–20, 2227, 2232, 2686, 2708.

[42] The farming of royal estates by great men can be seen in many places in England. For Earl William's and Roger's activities, for example, see Lewis, "The Norman settlement of Herefordshire," 198.

[43] F 2163.

[44] F 2207; 2172.

complex and diffuse estates of the King, over which he had charge, have to be given out to other retainers, or should they be returned to the King? Local circumstances, administrative mix-ups and the longings of great men created different answers in different places to these same questions. The resulting lack of uniformity in the redistribution of Earl Ralph's fee led to hundreds of vexing claims. In 1086, a full decade after Ralph's dispossession, East Anglian lords, royal officials, and hundred juries were still wrestling with them.

A host of men came into the earl's land after his fall, confusing title further, especially since the disposition of much of the earl's property seems not to have been governed by an ordered, carefully planned redistribution, but accomplished rather by *ad hoc* decisions and opportunism. Count Alan,[45] Earl Hugh,[46] Ivo Taillebois,[47] the Bishop of Norwich,[48] Odo of Bayeux,[49] Richard fitz Gilbert,[50] Robert de Verly,[51] Walter Giffard,[52] William d'Ecouis,[53] and William de Warenne[54] were all holding bits and pieces of the earl's fee in 1086. There are easy explanations for some of the Conqueror's largess. Odo of Bayeux, William de Warenne, and Richard fitz Gilbert, all of whom were instrumental in putting down Ralph's rebellion, were rewarded by the King with pieces of the Earl's fee.[55] Godric Dapifer, Robert Blunt, William de Noyers, and Roger Bigot, all hardworking royal officials, profited from Ralph's disgrace because the Conqueror shared between them the rights once vested in Ralph to oversee the East Anglian royal demesne. Others, like the Abbot of Ely and the Abbot of St. Benet of Holme, managed to gain hold of portions of Ralph's fee, holdings that had probably belonged to their houses before the Conquest.[56] The consequences of all of this were that no single man, but rather dozens of men, believed in 1086 that they had legitimate claims to pieces of the earl's honor.

Besides having to determine what belonged to Earl Ralph in-chief and what belonged to the royal estates over which he had been given custody, Domesday jurors also had to deal with the competing and powerful interests of those who had come into the earl's land, and the rights of these men *vis-à-vis* the King. Roger Bigot, for example, asked the King for a number of Ralph's estates, and the King granted them to him.[57] Roger also oversaw a number of royal estates after the rebellion that Earl Ralph at one time had either had custody of or had pillaged; and Roger, like his predecessor,

---

[45] F 2360, 2403, 2775.
[46] F 2741, 2810.
[47] F 2207, 2538.
[48] F 2425.
[49] F 2946.
[50] F 3022.
[51] F 2595.
[52] F 2531.
[53] F 2482.
[54] F 2280, 2708.
[55] OV, IV, 316–17; Douglas, *William the Conqueror*, 232; F 2946, 2280, 2708, 3022.
[56] F 2465, 2475.
[57] F 2379, 2873, 2880.

sometimes blurred the distinction between the King's holdings and his own. He acknowledged, for example, during the proceedings of 1086, that he had been given custody of royal land in Stoke Holy Cross, in Norfolk, but he argued that he held it, nonetheless, as part of his own fee, claiming it to be among King William's gifts to him.[58] Similarly, Robert Blunt, another royal farmer who had profited from Earl Ralph's fall, had managed to acquire custody of 140 of the King's acres in Witton after the earl's disgrace, but he had transferred them to his fee, and was treating them as his own. Some time before the inquest, however, legal action was taken on the King's behalf, and a writ was sent out ordering that the land be restored to him. This story is found in Little Domesday to explain why a King's thegn named Ulfkil had rights to land in 1086 that had once been held by Earl Ralph.[59] Had there been no conflict of interest, no complaint, neither the earl's interest in Witton nor Robert Blunt's would be known to us.

Ralph's surviving tenants were also pressing claims in 1086. In a slightly later period, tenants were often more secure than their great lords; and sometimes this was the case with Ralph's men.[60] Although an impoverished nun, who held a small parcel of land from Earl Ralph, lost her four acres after his disgrace to a follower of the King,[61] many of Ralph's tenants, who refused to participate in his rebellion, kept hold of their mesne tenancies, but not without controversy. In Bradenham, for example, William de Warenne held half a carucate of land which had probably come to him through Earl Ralph as a mesne tenancy, since both William's supporters and the hundred court insisted that both men had held the land before Ralph's forfeiture. After Ralph's disgrace, according to the hundred, Robert Blunt was allowed by the King to farm the land, and after him Godric Dapifer was given the same privilege. Later still, the land was held directly by the King. In 1086, in spite of the fact that no one at the inquest could remember ever seeing a writ or a legate giving William seisin, he was holding the land.[62] William, Roger, Godric, and the King all had compelling claims to this land, and it is difficult to imagine how they could be resolved. Similarly, another of Earl Ralph's former tenants, Warengar, had come into possession of some of the demesne of Earl Stonham, in Suffolk, before 1075. In 1086 he was holding the same land from Roger Bigot, having simply transferred his allegiance and his land from one powerful man to another. Warengar was still holding the land from Roger in 1086, although men at the inquest felt that this land, by right, belonged to Count Alan, since he had been granted the rest of the manor.[63]

---

[58] F 2379.

[59] F 2637.

[60] J. C. Holt, "Politics and property in early medieval England," *Past and Present*, 57 (1972), 3–52, at 30–6, and "Feudal society and the family in early medieval England: I. The revolution of 1066," *TRHS*, 5th ser., 32 (1982), 193–212, at 207–10.

[61] F 2612.

[62] F 2708.

[63] F 2794.

Or again, Earl Ralph had given one of his English followers, Godwine Healfdene, some freemen and land in Thorpe St. Andrew, and Godwine had managed to keep hold of the land after his lord's disgrace. But at the inquest the hundred was questioning the efficacy of this gift, and felt that the land should be returned to the royal estate from which it had been detached.[64] Although many of Ralph's tenants persevered in East Anglia, their tenancies were sometimes judged dubious.

Freemen and sokemen who held acres that made up Earl Ralph's estates also drifted into other lordships after his rebellion, taking their lands with them. In Framingham Pigot, for example, in the reign of King Edward, a freeman had been commended to the thegn Edwin. After the Conquest, Edwin's land, like the land of so many others, had fallen to Earl Ralph, who made Godric Dapifer Edwin's successor. But when Earl Ralph fell, the freeman ended up in the power of Bishop Æthelmær, the defrocked and unseated former Bishop of Elmham, who was apparently living quietly in the Norfolk countryside. Æthelmær had been a great lord of men before the Conquest, and perhaps, out of habit, the freeman had sought his protection after Ralph's disgrace. When Æthelmær died, the freeman drifted once again, this time into Roger Bigot's lordship, and both he and his land, in 1086, were accounted for in Roger's fee.[65] In this way a dozen East Anglian lords were enriched or impoverished. It was difficult for jurors to evaluate the legality of such actions.

The untimely deaths of some of the most trusted of the Conqueror's followers also created an opportunity for lords to expand their interests. William Malet, one of the men who fought with the Conqueror at Hastings and one of those the King sent north to quash the rebellion there, was given wide responsibilities, including those of sheriff, and vast amounts of land before his death in 1071. William Malet had been the beneficiary of some early celebrity forfeitures – the most important of which was his succession in East Anglia to the lands of Eadric of Laxfield, one of the richest men and greatest lords in the Confessor's England. In Yorkshire, on the other hand, where William seems to have held something like 200 carucates of land, his holdings were made up of the lands of dozens of men who fell at Fulford or Stamford Bridge, or individuals who had, for one reason or another, gone into exile in the first months of the Conqueror's reign. After his death, the bulk of William's fee in Yorkshire was lost by his son and heir Robert. In 1086 men testifying at the Yorkshire inquest believed that the devolution of William's fee in Yorkshire was illegal, and in cases of disputed tenure they always settled in favor of Robert Malet. Restitution, however, was impossible. Most of the Malet fee in the North had been divided between the King

---

[64] F 2232.
[65] F 2354. See also F 2393.

and nine of his tenants-in-chief, and by 1086 had been held by them for more than a decade.[66] Thus title had been granted, in a sense, three times; first to William Malet, while the wars of Conquest raged in the North, then to Robert Malet, as his father's heir, and finally to other men, either through rights of antecession or through territorial grants based on hundreds or wapentakes. This led to dozens of disputes between Robert Malet and other lords in Yorkshire. The Malet fee in East Anglia was equally controversial. By 1086 the problem of the Malet fee was, in a very real sense, irresolvable.

Like the piecemeal regranting of Earl Ralph's fee, the collapse of William Malet's fee suggests that the very great honors forming and consolidating during the first decade of the Conqueror's reign were probably not sufficiently organized and administered to have solidified into sturdy honorial blocks, and that there was a tendency for some of them to atomize after their original holders died or were disinherited.[67] Indeed the great honors in this period appear to have been so fluid and temporary that no one thought to redistribute them in one or two shares. The fact that Ralph's and William's fees were given away piecemeal in the 1070s led to extraordinary problems in the second half of the Conqueror's reign. Indeed the contested title that came about because of the dismantling of these fees took up more time at the inquest than any other problem, and it marked the imaginations of jurors, who often organized their legal memories around the time when William Malet died or the day Earl Ralph rebelled.[68] All of this suggests that early on in the Conqueror's reign, honors were inchoate and porous, and that this fragility of new tenurial configurations was the source of tension and dispute. In 1086, however, the exposure of this problem, coupled with the demand that tenants-in-chief survey their own estates as the first step of the inquest, and with the careful organization of landholdings by tenancy-in-chief in Domesday Book, honors became hardier tenurial units, and developed into the building blocks of aristocratic power and royal patronage that they were to become in Henry I's reign. Indeed after the making of Domesday Book, the honors of disgraced or heirless men were no longer arbitrarily shattered, but given out more rationally on the basis of the barony.

Conclusion

It is an inescapable fact of the Conquest that between 1066 and 1086 the Old English elite was replaced completely and irreversibly by William's favored followers. It is also certain that much of the resulting transfer of land was governed by some combination of the exigencies of Conquest, the opportu-

---

[66] Fleming, *Kings and Lords*, 159–60.
[67] For the best discussion of Norman settlers' attempts to organize their fees, see Dalton, *Conquest*, 19–79.
[68] For Earl Ralph's career and rebellion as a point of reference, see below, subject index, X. 5. For William Malet's career and death as a point of reference, see subject index, X.10.

nities of private enterprise, and the traditions of Continental lordship and tenure. These processes of settlement had a profound impact on the conventions that structured landholding in England until the later twelfth century. At the same time, however, the disruption of the Norman settlement was mitigated in crucial ways by older, native ideas about law and landholding. The landed interests of King William (founded as they were on the Anglo-Saxon *terra regis*), and the needs of powerfully entrenched ecclesiastical communities (most of whom by the early 1070s were headed by ecclesiastical followers of the new king), were best protected by the ancient laws and customs of England.[69] These interests must have bolstered continuity in English land law. There were also the long-standing legal and administrative practices of local English courts and royal agents, working without interruption across the great divide of 1066: these were essential components of William's kingship and also strong forces for the conservation of English legal culture. Finally, there was the central ideology of William's reign – that William ruled as Edward's legal heir, and was, therefore, by necessity, the upholder of the old king's laws. As a result of these peculiar circumstances, England in the 1070s and 1080s was a kingdom in which there was no single set of legal norms or customs to govern the transfer and the holding of land, but a place in which overlapping and sometimes conflicting sets of customs vied with one another in the courts and in the minds of the landholding classes. It was, in short, a kingdom of dangerously ambiguous legal practices, where the expectations of Norman profiteers, English survivors, reeves, and law-worthy men came into conflict at almost every turn. In the most placid of times, this would have been a crippling problem; but in a period in which perhaps 40,000 hides of land changed hands, it was perilous. By 1085 some types of tenure and acquisition were doubtless already considered more secure than others. Property which the Church held by royal diploma or writ, for example, was supported again and again both by royal fiat and by the decisions of local courts.[70] But the murkier forms of acquisition, alongside the complicating politics of the period, led to endless conflict. As things stood in 1085, in spite of periodic inquests like those held at Kentford, "Ildeburga," and Penenden Heath, England's legal practices remained blatantly *ad hoc*. Had large numbers of local landholders decided to rely on self-help as the remedy for their tenurial disappointments rather than the King and his courts, there could have been a rapid devolution of royal power.

These are the legal circumstances of the Domesday inquest. Although local inquests had been held throughout the Conqueror's reign it was only in 1086 that every piece of property in England came under the scrutiny of local courts, the sheriff, and the King's commissioners. It was in the process of

---

[69] See, for example, the invocation of such ancient laws and customs by Christ Church Canterbury (*Lawsuits*, 5b; Eadmer, *Eadmeri Historia Novorum in Anglia*, 17); Abingdon (*Lawsuits* 4, 146); Worcester (*Lawsuits*, 15); Ely (*LE*, ii, 120, 124).
[70] E.g. *Lawsuits*, 4, 9, 18b, 146; *LE*, ii, 125.

hearing many thousands of complaints over the course of a few short months
that those responsible for the making and enforcing of law began forming a
consensus about the legal norms determining what gave men rights to land.
The inquest, for example, seems to have formalized the notion that
inheritance (whether from a fictive Anglo-Saxon antecessor or a real Norman
father) was one of the best forms of title. This was a familiar notion for well-
to-do Normans, but this precept was confirmed literally thousands of times
during the course of the inquest, and must, as a result, have become one of
the commonplaces of English land law. There seems, as well, to have been a
grudging consensus forming at the Domesday proceedings, that formal
notification at a hundred or shire court, either by the King's writ or his
legate, was a powerful guarantee of title, as was the warranty of one's lord.
Here we can see agreement forming across England, in the minds of hundred
jurors and tenants-in-chief, about the importance of inheritance and a
particular set of legal procedures. In these cases, and in others, we are seeing,
through the hyper-active adjudications of 1086, the formation of a common
set of very loose, very broad legal assumptions across regional courts, among
landholders with far-flung estates and in royal administrative circles, concerning a new and hybrid set of legal norms and practices used to govern
tenure and title. Some of this was rooted in English custom and Anglo-
Scandinavian administrative practices, and some developed out of the nexus
of relationships and obligations found in Continental lordship. In their
crudest and most basic form, the courts and commissioners of 1086 upheld
the notion that land inherited from a Norman father or an English antecessor,
if it had been taken away, should be restored; that acquisitions (in the sense of
land not "inherited') were more open to claim, and that if such acquisitions
were unlawful, they should be taken away. They also formalized the notion
that the day "King Edward was alive and dead" marked the limits of legal
memory in the law of property.[71] This broad set of norms governing rights to
land sounds very much like those J. C. Holt believes lay at the heart of the
1153 "Treaty of Winchester," an agreement that ended the anarchy of
Stephen's reign. In this later settlement, setting legal memory to the day
Henry I was alive and dead, "inheritances," as Holt persuasively argues,
"were to be restored; acquisitions were at risk; unlawful acquisitions would
be revoked."[72] This very general set of solutions to disputes over land that
arose during the civil wars of Stephen's reign bears a striking resemblance to
the pragmatic judgments of the Domesday inquest. And like the hierarchy of
rights to property worked out at the Domesday inquest, the provisions of the
1153 settlement were workable because they provided only the broadest of
guidelines, and could be enforced in radically different ways, depending on
the parties involved, the desires of the king, and the circumstances of the

---

[71] Obviously, this was one of the legal standards forming earlier in William's reign.
[72] J. C. Holt, "1153: the Treaty of Winchester," in *The Anarchy of King Stephen's Reign*, ed. Edmund King
(Oxford, 1994), 291–316, at 297, 302–4.

dispute.[73] This was not Common Law statute and procedure. But it was a hardy and flexible mix of Norman and English legal custom, and it provided just enough structure to legal expectations, and just enough support for predictable resolution, that the King and his laws, rather than private war, was looked upon as the primary means of resolving land disputes. It does appear as if the settlement at the end of Stephen's reign in some way simply restored the most basic norms governing rights to land worked out at the Domesday inquest, and that what we are looking at, both in 1086 and in 1153, are the founding conventions of Anglo-Norman land law, which took their first formal shape at the Domesday inquest, and which remained the guiding legal principles for landholding, acquisition, and inheritance for the century separating the Domesday inquest from the Angevin "leap forward."

[73] Holt, "1153," 298–304.

Part II
The texts

Exchequer Domesday Book

Bedfordshire

1.   i, 209r (B) <u>Bedford</u>: The land of Bedford was never hidated, nor is it now, except for one hide which lay TRE in alms in St. Paul's, London. TRW it lies by right (*recte*) there, but Remigius bishop of Lincoln unjustly (*iniuste*) put (*posuit*) it outside the alms of St. Paul's, so the men say, and now he holds it and all that belongs to it.

2.   i, 209r (1-1b) <u>Terra Regis; Leighton Buzzard</u>: TRE Wynsige the Chamberlain held ten hides from King Edward in Leighton Buzzard and Starcher, a thegn of King Edward, held seven hides there. Ralph Taillebois put (*apposuit*) these seventeen hides in the King's manor of Leighton Buzzard where they did not belong TRE.

3.   i, 209v (1-4) <u>Terra Regis; Sewell</u>: TRE Wælhræfn, a man of Queen Edith, held Sewell, and could grant it to whom he wished. It lay in 'Odecroft' Hundred. Ralph Taillebois put (*apposuit*) it in the King's manor of Houghton Regis with King William's consent (*concedente*), through the increase (*per crementum*) it gave him. This is what Ralph's men state, according to what they heard him say.

4.   i, 210r (3-6) <u>Bishop of Coutances; Easton [Hunts.]</u>: TRW four sokemen hold three virgates of land from the Bishop of Coutances in Easton. TRE the same sokemen held this land. They were Burgræd's men and could grant to whom they wished. In these three virgates, the Bishop of Coutances claims (*reclamat*) twenty acres of woodland against Sigar de Chocques. They lay in Easton TRE. This the men of the hundred testify.

5.   i, 210r (3-8) <u>Bishop of Coutances; Bolnhurst</u>: TRE Guthmund, a man of King Edward, held three virgates in Bolnhurst, and could sell to whom he wished. Now the Bishop of Coutances holds them in exchange (*pro excambio*) for Bleadon [Som.].

6.   i, 210r (3-10) <u>Bishop of Coutances; land in Willey Hundred</u>: TRW the Bishop of Coutances holds four hides in Willey Hundred in exchange (*pro excambio*) for Bleadon [Som.], so his men say. TRE Thorbert, a man of King Edward, held this manor and could sell.

7.   i, 210r (3-11) <u>Bishop of Coutances; Turvey</u>: TRW the Bishop of Coutances holds four hides in Turvey. TRE three sokemen, men of King Edward, held this manor and could grant and sell. The Bishop of Coutances has this land in exchange for (*pro excambio*) Bleadon [Som.], so his men say.

8.   i, 210r (4-2) <u>Bishop of Lincoln; Easton [Hunts.]</u>: TRW William de Cairon holds half a hide and half a virgate in Easton from Remigius bishop of Lincoln. William de Cairon claims (*reclamat*) sixty acres in this manor – arable and woodland – against Hugh de Beauchamp. Ralph Taillebois

disseised (*desaisiuit*) William's father of them, despite the fact that William's father, according to the testimony of the men of the hundred, held this land TRE.

9   i, 210v (5-1) <u>Bishop of Durham; Millow</u>: TRW the Bishop of Durham holds four and a half hides in Millow. King Edward gave (*dedit*) Millow to Waltham Abbey, so the men of the hundred testify.

10   i, 210v (6-1) <u>Bury St. Edmund's; Biddenham</u>: TRE Wulfmær, a priest of King Edward, held half a hide in Biddenham and could grant to whom he wished; but Ordwig the Reeve took it away (*abstulit*) from him when he was reeve of Bedford as a forfeiture (*pro quidam forisfactura*). Now Ordwig holds it from the Abbot of Bury St. Edmund's, but the men of the hundred say that he has seized (*occupavit*) it unjustly (*iniuste*).

11   i, 210v (6-2) <u>Bury St. Edmund's; Kinwick</u>: TRE two sokemen held three hides and three virgates in Kinwick, and they could grant them to whom they wished. In the time of King William, Earl Waltheof and his wife Countess Judith gave (*dederunt*) Kinwick to Bury St. Edmund's in alms. Now the abbot holds it.

12   i, 210v (8-2) <u>Ramsey Abbey; Barton-le-Clay</u>: TRE and TRW Ramsey Abbey holds eleven hides in Barton-le-Clay. Along with this manor, the abbot claims (*reclamat*) twelve acres of meadow against Nigel d'Aubigny and Walter the Fleming. They lay in Barton-le-Clay TRE. John de Roches has disseised (*desaisiuit*) the abbot unjustly (*iniuste*). This the hundred testifies.

13   i, 211r (10-1) <u>Thorney Abbey; Bolnhurst</u>: TRW Thorney Abbey holds two hides and a virgate in Bolnhurst. TRE Alflæd held this manor from King Edward and could grant to whom she wished. Nonetheless, the men of the hundred testify that it lay in the monastery of Thorney on the day King Edward was alive and dead.

14   i, 211r (12-1) <u>Bishopric of London; Caddington</u>: TRE Leofwine Cild held five hides in Caddington; now the canons of St. Paul's hold it. The canons have a writ (*brevem*) from King William, which has it that the King gave (*dedit*) this manor to St. Paul's.

15   i, 211r (13-1) <u>Church of St. Paul, Bedford; Biddenham</u>: TRE Leofgeat the Priest held three virgates in Biddenham in alms, first from King Edward and later from King William. When he was dying, Leofgeat granted (*concessit*) one virgate of this land to the Church of St. Paul, Bedford, and Ralph Taillebois added another two virgates to this church in alms. Now all three are held by St. Paul's, and Osmund, a canon of St. Paul's holds them.

16   i, 211r (13-2) <u>Church of St. Paul, Bedford; Biddenham</u>: TRE Mærwynn held a virgate in Biddenham and could sell to whom she wished. Now it is held by Ansfrid the Canon. Ralph Taillebois put (*apposuit*) this land in the alms of St. Paul's.

17   i, 211r (14-1) <u>Earnwine the Priest; Harrowden</u>: TRW Earnwine the Priest holds one hide in Harrowden. TRE his father held it and was a man of King Edward. Earnwine, however, has neither livery nor writ (*liberatorem nec*

brevem) for this land, but has seized (*occupavit*) it against the King, so the hundred testifies.

18 i, 211v (16-3) <u>Walter Giffard; Marston Moretaine</u>: TRE two thegns held two hides less half a virgate in Marston Moretaine and could grant to whom they wished. TRW Hugh de Bolbec holds them from Walter Giffard. Herfast, Nigel d'Aubigny's man, claims (*reclamat*) half an enclosure (*sepem*) here, which lay in the manor of Herfast's antecessor, so the men of the hundred testify.

19 i, 211v (17-1) <u>William de Warenne; Dean (Upper or Lower)</u>: TRW William de Warenne holds two hides in Dean and three sokemen hold from him. William Speke was seised (*fuit saisitus*) of half a hide and half a virgate of this land through the King and through livery (*liberatorem*); but William de Warenne disseised him without the King's writ (*sine breve regis eum desaisiuit*) and also took away (*abstulit*) two horses from William Speke's men. He has not yet returned (*reddidit*) them. This the men of the hundred attest.

20 i, 211v (17-2) <u>William de Warenne; Tilbrook [Hunts.]</u>: TRW William de Warenne holds five hides in Tilbrook, and a number of sokemen hold from him. TRE these same sokemen held the manor. They were so far from the King's sake and soke that they could grant and sell their land to whomever they wished, and they could withdraw to another lord without permission of the lord they were under. Hugh de Beauchamp claims (*reclamat*) Tilbrook against William de Warenne. The men of the hundred bear (*portant*) testimony to the fact that Ralph Taillebois, Hugh's antecessor, was seised of Tilbrook through the King (*per regem saisitus fuit*), and that he held it.

21 i, 211v (17-4) <u>William de Warenne; Easton [Hunts.]</u>: TRW William de Warenne holds a virgate in Easton. TRE Authgi, a man of Eskil of Ware, Hugh de Beauchamp's antecessor, held it. He could sell to whom he wished, but Eskil kept the soke in his manor in Colmworth. Hugh de Beauchamp claims (*reclamat*) this land against William de Warenne, and all the sworn men of the sheriffdom (*omnis qui iuraverunt de vicecomitatu*) bear testimony that this land does not belong to William.

22 i, 211v (17-5) <u>William de Warenne; Easton [Hunts.]</u>: TRW William de Warenne holds a hide and a virgate of land in Easton. TRE Authgi held it, and he could grant it to whom he wished. Afterwards, King William granted this land to Authgi and commended him to Ralph Taillebois through his writ, so that he might have custody of Authgi as long as he lived (*concessit et per suum brevem . . . commendavit, ut eum servaret quamdiu viveret*). On the day Authgi died, he said that he was William de Warenne's man, and William, therefore, has been seised (*saisitus est*) of this land.

23 i, 212r (19-1) <u>Miles Crispin; Clapham</u>: TRW Miles Crispin holds five hides in Clapham. TRE Beorhtric, a thegn of King Edward, held it from Ramsey Abbey. The abbot and the monks of Ramsey claim (*reclamant*) this manor, since it was for their victualing TRE. The whole hundred bears testimony for this.

24 i, 212r (19-2) <u>Miles Crispin; Milton Ernest</u>: TRW there are two sokemen in Milton Ernest with sixteen acres of land. They gave (*dederunt*) their *warram* in Milton Ernest, but they could grant or sell their land to whom they wished. Robert d'Oilly unjustly put (*apposuit iniuste*) these sokemen in Clapham, because they never belonged there TRE, so the men of the hundred say.

25 i, 212r (21-1) <u>Eudo Dapifer; Eaton Socon</u>: TRE Wulfmær of Eaton, a thegn of King Edward, held Eaton Socon. There were two sokemen there as well, who could grant and sell their land. TRW Eudo Dapifer holds Eaton Socon, and it is assessed at twenty hides. Theobald, Countess Judith's man, claims (*reclamat*) one of these hides, of which Eudo disseised (*desaisiuit*) him after he came to Eaton Socon.

26 i, 212r (21-6) <u>Eudo Dapifer; Sandy</u>: TRE Wulfmær of Eaton, a thegn of King Edward, held sixteen hides and a virgate in Sandy. TRW Eudo Dapifer holds it. In the same vill Eudo claims (*reclamat*) three acres of woodland against Hugh de Beauchamp, which Wulfmær of Eaton had held, but of which Ralph Taillebois disseised (*desaisiuit*) him when he was sheriff. Because of this, Eudo has refused to give tax (*noluit dare warras*) from this woodland. This the men of the hundred attest.

27 i, 212v (21-12, 13) <u>Eudo Dapifer; Beeston</u>: TRW Northmann holds four hides in Beeston from Eudo Dapifer, and Roland holds three hides. TRE this same Northmann held all seven hides. Now Eudo has them from the King, so his men say, but it is not from Lisois's fee.

28 i, 212v (22-1) <u>William Peverel; Tilsworth</u>: TRE Leofric son of Osmund, a thegn of the King, held ten hides in Tilsworth. Now William Peverel holds it from the King, and Ambrose holds from him. TRE it had a woodland at 100 pigs, so the hundred says, but Oswig took it away (*abstulit*).

29 i, 212v (23-2) <u>Hugh de Beauchamp; Riseley</u>: TRW Hugh de Beauchamp holds a hide in Riseley, which is a berewick of Keysoe. TRE his antecessor Eskil of Ware held it.

30 i, 212v (23-7) <u>Hugh de Beauchamp; Goldington</u>: TRW Hugh de Beauchamp holds three hides and a virgate in Goldington, which lie in Putnoe. TRE nine sokemen held them and could grant or sell to whom they wished. Ralph Taillebois has two hides and three virgates of this land in exchange (*pro excambio*) for Ware [Herts.].

31 i, 213r (23-12) <u>Hugh de Beauchamp; Stotfold</u>: TRW Hugh de Beauchamp holds Stotfold, which is assessed at fifteen hides. TRE Eskil of Ware, a thegn of King Edward, held nine and a half of these hides. Seven sokemen held the remaining land and could sell to whom they wished. One of these hides, however, belongs to St. Albans Abbey, and the men of the hundred say that it lay there TRE.

32 i, 213r (23-16) <u>Hugh de Beauchamp; Salph End</u>: TRW Hugh de Beauchamp holds five hides in Salph End, and eleven sokemen, who held it TRE, hold it from him. Ralph Taillebois had this land in exchange (*pro excambio*) for Ware [Herts.], so his men say.

33 i, 213r (23-24) Hugh de Beauchamp; Easton [Hunts.]: TRW Hugh de Beauchamp holds half a hide in Easton, and Wimund holds from him. TRE Wulfgeat, Eskil of Ware's man, held this land, and could grant and sell it. The soke, however, always lay in Colmworth, Eskil's manor.

34 i, 213v (23-41, 42, 43) Hugh de Beauchamp; Goldington: TRW Hugh de Beauchamp holds six hides in Goldington. Earlier, however, Ralph Taillebois held them in exchange for (*pro excambio de, est escambium de*) Ware [Herts.].

35 i, 213v–214r (23-49, 50, 51, 52, 52, 53, 54, 55) Hugh de Beauchamp; Cople: TRW Hugh de Beauchamp holds ten hides and three virgates of land in Cople. TRE it was held by Eskil of Ware and a number of sokemen. Ralph Taillebois had this land in exchange for (*pro excambio de*) Ware [Herts.], so his men say.

36 i, 214r (24-12) Nigel d'Aubigny; Maulden: TRW John de Roches unjustly seized (*occupavit iniuste*) twenty-five acres in Maulden against the men who hold the vill. Now Nigel d'Aubigny has them.

37 i, 214r (24-14) Nigel d'Aubigny; Clophill: TRE two thegns, men of Earl Tosti, held five hides in Clophill. Now Nigel d'Aubigny holds them. Of these five hides, Nigel claims (*clamat*) one virgate which his antecessor held TRE, but of which Ralph Taillebois has disseised (*desaisiuit*) him. Nigel, however, was seised (*saisitus fuit*) of it after he came into the honor (*ad honorem venit*).

38 i, 214v (24-18) Nigel d'Aubigny; Streatley: TRE Leofwine Cild and three other thegns of King Edward held four and a third hides in Streatley, and they could sell their land to whom they wished. TRW Pirot holds the land. He holds one and a third of these hides from Nigel in fee, and the three remaining hides from his wife's marriage portion (*de maritagio suae feminae*).

39 i, 214v (25-1) William Speke; Hulcote: TRE Alweard Belrap, a man of Alric, held four hides in Hulcote. He could sell to whom he wished. TRW William Speke holds this land in exchange for (*de excambio de*) Toddington, which he gave in exchange (*excambiavit*), and Ralph Passwater holds from him.

40 i, 214v (25-4) William Speke; Biddenham: TRE eleven sokemen held four hides less a virgate and a half in Biddenham, and they could grant and sell their land to whom they wished. TRW Ralph and Serlo de Rots hold them from William Speke. William says that he has this land in exchange for (*pro excambio de*) Toddington.

41 i, 215r (25-7) William Speke; Chawston: TRW William fitz Rainward holds seven hides and a virgate in Chawston from William Speke. TRE twelve sokemen held this land and could sell to whom they wished. Of this land, William Speke's men claim (*reclamant*) an acre and a half of meadow against Eudo Dapifer's men, and the hundred testifies that his antecessor held it TRE. William also claims (*reclamat*) another seven acres of land against a man of Hugh de Beauchamp, of which he was disseised (*desaisitus*), but of which his antecessor was seised (*fuit saisitus*). Eudo Dapifer claims (*reclamat*) one acre of this land against Riwallon, Hugh de Beauchamp's man.

42 i, 215r (28-1) <u>Robert d'Oilly; Thurleigh</u>: TRW Robert d'Oilly holds half a hide of land in Thurleigh, and Richard Basset holds from him. TRE Wulfgeat, a thegn of King Edward, held it and could sell to whom he wished. Eudo Dapifer's men claim (*clamant*) this land through the antecessor of their lord, all of whose lands King William donated (*donavit*) to him.

43 i, 215r (29-1) <u>Ranulf brother of Ilger; Pavenham</u>: TRW Ranulf brother of Ilger holds five hides in Pavenham, and Robert fitz Nigel holds from him. TRE Godwine, a thegn of King Edward, held them. Of this land Ranulf claims (*reclamat*) twelve acres against Gilbert fitz Solomon and four acres of meadow against Hugh de Grandmesnil, of which Ranulf has been unjustly disseised (*desaisitus est iniuste*). The men of the half-hundred say that this land, which is now held by Hugh and Gilbert, lay TRE in the lands which Ranulf brother of Ilger holds.

44 i, 215v (31-1) <u>Alvred of Lincoln; Wymington</u>: TRW Alvred of Lincoln holds three hides in Wymington, and Gleu holds from him. TRE Godwine Frambolt held this manor and could sell. With these three hides Alvred claims (*reclamat*) half a hide against Walter the Fleming, of which Walter unjustly disseised (*iniuste desaisiuit*) him. The men of the hundred bear testimony for this, because his antecessor was seised (*saisitus fuit*) of it TRE; and the same Alvred afterwards was seised (*fuit saisitus*). Beside this land, Alvred claims (*reclamat*) a woodland for 100 pigs against Geoffrey bishop of Coutances, which his antecessor held TRE, but of which the bishop has disseised (*desaisiuit*) him unjustly (*iniuste*), so the men of the hundred testify.

45 i, 215v (32-1) <u>Walter the Fleming; Totternhoe</u>: TRW Walter the Fleming holds Totternhoe and Osbert holds from him. TRE it was assessed for fifteen hides, but after King William came to England, it answered for only ten hides. The men who held and hold these hides kept and keep back (*retinuerunt et retinent*) all the King's customs and rent (*gablum*).

46 i, 215v (32-7) <u>Walter the Fleming; Wymington</u>: TRW Walter the Fleming holds half a hide in Wymington. TRE Godwine Frambolt held it and could grant it to whom he wished. Alvred of Lincoln claims (*reclamat*) it against Walter the Fleming.

47 i, 215v (32-14) <u>Walter the Fleming; Southill</u>: Walter the Fleming holds half a hide of woodland in Southill, which his antecessor held TRE.

48 i, 215v (32-15) <u>Walter the Fleming; Southill</u>: TRW Alric holds a virgate from Walter the Fleming in Southill. TRE Leofwine, a thegn of the King, held this land in mortgage (*in vadimonio*), but after King William came to England the same man who had mortgaged this land redeemed it (*ille ipse qui invadiavit hanc terram redemit*), and Sihere seized (*occupavit*) it against the King, so the hundred testifies.

49 i, 216r (33-2) <u>Walter brother of Sihere; Silsoe</u>: TRW Walter brother of Sihere holds four hides in Silsoe, and Hugh holds from him. TRE Leofnoth, a thegn of King Edward, held this manor. Three sokemen held half a hide there and could grant or sell to whom they wished. Hugh holds this half hide from the King, so his men say.

50   i, 216r (38-1, 2) Richard fitz Gilbert; Sudbury, Wyboston: TRW Richard fitz Gilbert holds a virgate in Sudbury and two hides and a half virgate in Wyboston. The monks of St. Neot's hold Wyboston from him. TRE this land lay in the Church of St. Neot in alms.

51   i, 216r (40-3) William the Chamberlain; Totternhoe: TRW William the Chamberlain holds seven hides less a virgate from the King in Totternhoe. TRE Leofwine, a man of Earl Waltheof, held this manor. Along with this land William claims (*reclamat*) two hides, which were held TRE by his antecessor, so the hundred testifies. But Odo bishop of Bayeux took them away through force (*per vim ei abstulit*) and gave (*dedit*) them to Æthelwulf his chamberlain.

52   i, 216v (46-1) Osbern the Fisherman; Sharnbrook: TRW Osbern the Fisherman holds half a hide in Sharnbrook from the King. TRE Tovi, a housecarl of King Edward, held this land and could sell. Along with this land Osbern also claims (*reclamat*) one and a fourth virgates, which were held by his antecessor TRE. But after King William came to England, he refused to give the rent due from this land (*ille gablum de hac terra dare noluit*). Ralph Taillebois took (*sumpsit*) the land as a forfeiture (*pro forisfacto*) and then granted (*tribuit*) it to one of his knights.

53   i, 217r (53-3) Countess Judith; Wilstead: TRE eight sokemen held Wilstead and could grant and sell, but the soke always lay in Kempston. TRW Countess Judith holds it, and the nuns of St. Mary's, Elstow hold from her. The Countess gave (*dedit*) it to St. Mary's in alms.

54   i, 217v (53-20) Countess Judith; Potton: [The information on TRE holders for this entry hints at Earl Tosti's 1065 dispossession. The entry notes that "King Edward held [Potton]. It was Earl Tosti's."]

55   i, 217v (54-2) Adelaide wife of Hugh de Grandmesnil; Houghton Conquest: TRW Adelaide holds four and a half hides in Houghton Conquest. TRE three sokemen held them, and they could grant and sell their land to whom they wished. In the same place Adelaide claims (*reclamat*) a virgate and thirty acres of woodland and field against Hugh de Beauchamp. The men of the hundred bear testimony that TRE this land lay with the other land which Adelaide holds, and that he who held this land could grant or sell it to whom he wished. Ralph Taillebois seized this land unjustly (*iniuste occupavit*) when he was sheriff.

56   i, 217v (54-3) Adelaide wife of Hugh de Grandmesnil; Chalton: [The information on TRE holders for this entry hints at Earl Tosti's 1065 dispossession. The entry notes that "King Edward held this manor. It was Earl Tosti's."]

57   i, 218r (55-5, 6, 7, 8, 9, 11, 12) Azelina wife of Ralph Taillebois; Eyeworth, Cockayne Hatley, Stanford, Warden, Henlow, Chicksands: These lands are part of Azelina's marriage portion (*de maritagio*) or dowry (*de dote sua*).

58   i, 218r (55-9) <u>Azelina wife of Ralph Taillebois; Henlow</u>: TRW Azelina holds a hide and three virgates of land in Henlow, and Widrus holds from her. TRE Eskil of Ware held it. It was a berewick of Stotfold. Hugh de Beauchamp claims (*clamat*) this land against Azelina, saying that she has it unjustly (*iniuste*), and that it was never part of her dowry (*nec eius dotem unquam fuisse*).

59   i, 218r (56-2) <u>Burgesses of Bedford; Biddenham</u>: TRW Godwine the Burgess holds one hide and the fourth part of a virgate in Biddenham from the King. TRE this same Godwine held half a hide of this land and could grant it to whom he wished. However, he bought (*emit*) another half hide and the fourth part of the virgate after King William came to England, but he did not do service for them, either to the King or to anyone else, nor did he have livery (*liberatorem*) for them. Against him, William Speke claims (*reclamat*) a virgate and the fourth part of a virgate, for which he was given livery (*liberata fuit*), but which he has subsequently lost (*perdidit*).

60   i, 218r (56-3) <u>Burgesses of Bedford; Biddenham</u>: TRW Ordwig the Burgess holds one hide and the third part of half a hide from the King in Biddenham. TRE the same Ordwig held half a hide and the fourth part of a virgate of this land, and he could grant it to whom he wished. But he held one virgate in mortgage (*in vadimonio*) TRE, and holds it still, so the men of the hundred testify. The same man bought (*emit*) a virgate and the fourth part of a virgate after King William came to England, and he pays no service for it to the King or to anyone else.

61   i, 218r (56-5) <u>Burgesses of Bedford; Hinwick</u>: TRW Edward holds half a hide in Hinwick from King William. TRE his father held it and could sell. King William granted (*concessit*) this land to Edward in alms. Edward has the King's writ (*brevem regis*) for it and the testimony of the hundred.

62   i, 218r (56-6) <u>Burgesses of Bedford; Sharnbrook</u>: TRW Almær holds half a virgate of land in Sharnbrook from King William. TRE his father held it. King William returned this land to him through his writ (*per brevem suum reddidit*).

63   i, 218v (57-1) <u>King's reeves, beadles, and almsmen; Eversholt, Woburn, Potsgrove</u>: TRW Herbert the King's reeve holds land in Eversholt, Woburn, and Potsgrove in the King's service (*in ministerio regis*). They did not lie there TRE, but Herbert says that after Ralph Taillebois was sheriff, he had these through a grant (*per concessionem*) of the King.

64   i, 218v (57-2, 3i-vi) <u>King's reeves, beadles, and almsmen; Potsgrove, Priestley, Maulden, Tempsford, Edworth, Holme, Sutton</u>: TRW, when Ralph Taillebois was sheriff, he put all this land to the King's service (*apposuit . . . in ministerio regis*). They were not there TRE. Those who hold them now, so they say, hold them by a grant (*concessione*) of the King.

65   i, 218v (57-4) <u>King's reeves, beadles, and almsmen; Streatley</u>: TRW the reeve of the hundred holds two-thirds of a virgate in Streatley for the use of the King. They now lie in the King's manor of Luton, but did not TRE.

Bondi the Staller put (*apposuit*) them in this manor, and Ralph Taillebois found them there.

66 i, 218v (57-6) <u>King's reeves, beadles, and almsmen; Carlton</u>: TRW Ketilbert, a man of Queen Edith, holds three and a half virgates in Carlton. He held a virgate of this land TRE and could grant it to whom he wished. However, he seized (*occupavit*) the other two and a half virgates, for which he has found neither livery nor a warrantor (*nec liberatorem nec advocatum*). TRE this land was held by Alli, a thegn of King Edward.

67 i, 218v (57-7) <u>King's reeves, beadles, and almsmen; Wymington</u>: TRW five brothers and their mother hold three virgates in Wymington from her dowry (*de dotem*). TRE their father Lant held this land. He could grant and sell.

68 i, 218v (57-8) <u>King's reeves, beadles, and almsmen; Goldington</u>: TRW Alric Wintermelc holds half a hide from King William in Goldington. He held it TRE. He was a man of King Edward and could grant this land to whom he wished. Afterwards, Alric gave (*dedit*) this land to the canons of St. Paul's under King William, and has granted that they should have it all after his death (*ut post mortem suam haberent omnio concessit*).

69 i, 218v (57-11) <u>King's reeves, beadles, and almsmen; Beeston</u>: TRW Alwine holds a virgate and a half in Beeston. This land was put in the King's service (*apposita est in ministerio regis*), where it was not TRE, when Dot held it and could grant and sell.

70 i, 218v (57-13) <u>King's reeves, beadles, and almsmen; Dean (Upper or Lower)</u>: Eleven of King William's sokemen hold seven and a quarter virgates in Dean. TRE the same sokemen held this land and could grant it to whom they wished. Ralph Taillebois put (*apposuit*) this land in the King's service (*in ministerio regis*), where it did not lie TRE.

71 i, 218v (57-19) <u>King's reeves, beadles, and almsmen; Turvey</u>: TRW Alwine the Priest holds the third part of half a hide in Turvey from the King. He himself held it TRE and could do with it what he wished. Later King William granted (*concessit*) this land to Alwine in alms, for which he performs mass each week on Monday for the souls of the King and Queen.

72 i, 218v (57-20) <u>King's reeves, beadles, and almsmen; half a hide in Willey Hundred</u>: TRW Osgeat the King's reeve holds half a hide. TRE a sokeman held it. King William loaned (*commendavit*) the sokeman with his land to Osgeat the Reeve, so that as long as the sokeman lived, Osgeat should supply (*praeberet*) food and clothing to him.

Berkshire

73 i, 56r (B-1) <u>Borough of Wallingford</u>: TRW the son of Alsige of Faringdon holds one of the urban tenements in Wallingford that were destroyed (*sunt . . . destructae*) for the castle. Alsige says that the King gave (*dedit*) it to him.

74 i, 56r (B-1) <u>Borough of Wallingford</u>: Similarly, Humphrey Visdeloup has one of these urban tenements. He claims the King's warranty (*reclamat ad warant*) for it.

75   i, 56r (B-1) <u>Borough of Wallingford</u>: Nigel also has one of these urban tenements, through the inheritance (*per hæreditatem*) of Swærting, but the burgesses testify that he never had it.

76   i, 56r (B-1) <u>Borough of Wallingford</u>: King Edward had fifteen acres of land in Wallingford on which his housecarls lived. TRW Miles Crispin holds it, but they do not know how. One of these acres lies in Walter Giffard's manor of Long Wittenham.

77   i, 56r (B-4) <u>Borough of Wallingford</u>: TRW Henry de Ferrers holds six urban tenements, which gave (*dederunt*) 62d. through custom both in the times of King Edward and King William. Now they give nothing (*nichil dant*).

78   i, 56v (B-6) <u>Borough of Wallingford</u>: TRW St. Albans Abbey holds a single urban tenement, and it is in dispute (*est in calumnia*).

79   i, 56v (B-7) <u>Borough of Wallingford</u>: TRW two priests named Almær, along with Brunmann, Eadwig, Edmund, William fitz Osmund, Leofflæd, Lambert the Priest, Alweald, and Godric have the rent (*gablum*) from their houses and the fines from bloodshed (*sanguinem*), if blood is shed there, if the accused man shall be taken (*receptus fuerit*) there before he is charged by the King's reeve (*calumnietur a praeposito regis*), except on Saturday, when the King has the forfeiture (*forisfacturam*) because the market is held then. The aforementioned men have the forfeitures for adultery and theft in their own houses (*forisfacturam et de adulterio et latrocinio habent ipsi emendam in suis domibus*), but the other forfeitures (*forisfacturae*) are the King's.

80   i, 56v (B-10) <u>Borough of Wallingford</u>: TRE if anyone was summoned for an expedition, but did not go, he forfeited (*forisfaciebat*) all his land to the King. If, however, some one stayed behind, promising to send another in his place, but that man stayed behind, his lord was acquitted (*quietus erat*) for a payment of 50s.

81   i, 56v (B-10) <u>Borough of Wallingford</u>: Upon the death of a thegn or a soldier of the King's demesne (*miles regis dominicus*), he sent all his arms and a horse with a saddle and another without to the King as a relief (*pro relevamento*). But if he had dogs or hawks, they were presented to the King, who could take them if he wished.

82   i, 56v (B-11) <u>Borough of Wallingford</u>: If anyone killed a man who had the King's peace (*occidet hominem pacem regis*), he forfeited his body and all his property (*corpus suum et omniem substantiam forisfaciebat*) to the King.

83   i, 56v (B-11) <u>Borough of Wallingford</u>: Whoever broke into (*effringebat*) Wallingford at night paid a fine (*emendabat*) of 100s. – not to the sheriff but to the King.

84   i, 56v (B-11) <u>Borough of Wallingford</u>: A man who was summoned for game-beating for the hunt, but did not go, paid a fine (*emendabat*) of 50s. to the King.

85   i, 57r (1-9) <u>Terra Regis; Wantage</u>: King Edward held Wantage. TRW it is

King William's. In this manor Bishop Peter held two-thirds of the church with four hides. They are now in the King's hand, because they were not the bishopric's.

86   i, 57r (1-11) <u>Terra Regis; Charlton (near Wantage)</u>: TRW King William holds Charlton. Almær, a free man, held it TRE for eight hides. A mill belongs there, which Walter Giffard holds unjustly (*iniuste*), so the hundred says.

87   i, 57r (1-12) <u>Terra Regis; Betterton</u>: TRE Wulfric, a free man, held Betterton for ten hides; now it is the King's. The King has half a virgate there as well, which Wulfflæd held TRE. She could go where she wished. Robert holds this in the farm of Wantage, but it never belonged there TRE.

88   i, 57r (1-13) <u>Terra Regis; Sutton Courtenay</u>: TRW the King holds half a virgate in Sutton Courtenay, which Leofflæd held TRE. She could go where she wished. Robert holds it in the farm of Sutton Courtenay, but it did not belong there.

89   i, 57r (1-14) <u>Terra Regis; Warfield</u>: TRE Queen Edith held Warfield, which was assessed at ten hides. Now King William holds it. A priest of Geoffrey de Mandeville has one of these hides, which was always part of this manor. But, he put (*misit*) it in his lord's manor.

90   i, 57v (1-25) <u>Terra Regis; Compton (near Aldworth)</u>: King Edward held two and three quarter hides of land in Compton. Now it is held by King William. Henry de Ferrers holds the woodland.

91   i, 57v (1-26) <u>Terra Regis; Kintbury</u>: King Edward held two hides in Kintbury. Now King William holds them. Henry de Ferrers holds forty-three acres of this manor's land, which were in the King's farm TRE, so the shire says. They say, moreover, that Godric the Sheriff made a pasture there for his horses, but they do not know how.

92   i, 57v (1-27) <u>Terra Regis; Shalbourne [Wi]</u>: King Edward held six and a half hides in Shalbourne. Now they are held by King William. Two and a half hides of this manor were put (*sunt . . . missae*) in Henry de Ferrers's manor. One of these hides was reeveland, one was villeins' land and the remaining half hide belonged to the King's farm. In the time of Godric the Sheriff, however, this land was put outside (*foris missa*) Shalbourne. This the whole shire attests.

93   i, 57v (1-32) <u>Terra Regis; Kingston Lisle</u>: King Edward held ten hides in Kingston Lisle. TRW King William holds them. Henry de Ferrers, however, holds a virgate of this land, along with twelve acres of meadow and a dairy, at six weys of cheese. All this remained in the King's farm when Godric lost (*perdidit*) the sheriffdom, according to the testimony of the shire.

94   i, 57v (1-37) <u>Terra Regis; Sutton Courtenay</u>: King Edward held Sutton Courtenay, which was assessed at twenty-three hides and a virgate. TRW King William holds it. Henry de Ferrers holds 120 acres of land and 3 acres of meadow from the King's demesne. This is because Godric the Sheriff, his antecessor, ploughed this land with his own ploughs when he was sheriff.

The hundred, however, says that in justice (*iuste*) it belongs to the King's court. Indeed Godric has seized it unjustly (*occupavit iniuste*).

95 i, 57v (1-38) <u>Terra Regis; Hendred (East or West)</u>: King Edward held Hendred, and it was assessed for four and a half hides. Now King William holds it. Henry de Ferrers holds a hide there, which was in the King's farm. TRE Godric held it. Ælfric of Thatcham says that he has seen the King's writ (*brevem*) by which it was given (*dederit*) to Godric's wife as a gift (*in dono*), because she cared for the King's dogs. But there is no one in the hundred who has seen the writ besides Ælfric.

96 i, 57v (1-39) <u>Terra Regis; Steventon</u>: TRE Earl Harold held Steventon, and it was assessed for twenty hides. Now King William holds it. Thirteen urban tenements in Oxford belonged to this manor, as well as a meadow. Now the men of the hundred say that they suspect (*suspicantur*) that Robert d'Oilly holds them. They know nothing else, because it is in another shire.

97 i, 58r (1-42) <u>Terra Regis; Borough of Reading</u>: TRW Henry de Ferrers has an urban tenement and half a virgate of land in Reading, along with three acres of meadow. Godric the Sheriff held it TRE *ad hospitium* (for lodging?; at lodging?), therefore Henry holds it. Regenbald, the son of Bishop Peter, held an urban tenement in Reading, which he drew into (*trahebat*) his manor of Earley. Now it is in the King's hand.

98 i, 58r (1-43) <u>Terra Regis; Pangbourne</u>: TRE Pangbourne lay in the King's farm. Later Alweald the Chamberlain held it, but the hundred does not know how. Afterwards Froger the Sheriff put (*misit*) it in the King's farm without plea or law (*absque placito et lege*).

99 i, 58r (1-45) <u>Terra Regis; Wokefield</u>: TRW King William holds Wokefield. It lies in his manor in Aldermaston, which belonged to Earl Harold TRE. Beorhtweard held Wokefield by Harold's gift (*de dono*).

100 i, 58r (2-3) <u>Bishop of Winchester; Brightwell-cum-Sotwell</u>: TRE Bishop Stigand held twenty hides in Brightwell. Now Bishop Walkelin holds them. Twenty-five shillings come from the pleas of the land (*de placitis terrae*) that belongs to this manor in Wallingford.

101 i, 58r (3-1) <u>Bishop of Salisbury; Sonning</u>: TRW Osmund bishop of Salisbury holds sixty hides in Sonning in demesne from his bishopric. Aubrey de Coucy held twenty hides from the berewicks of this manor in East Ilsley, which in justice (*iuste*) belong to the Bishop's manor. Robert the Priest, too, holds a church in Wallingford, which in justice (*iuste*) belongs to this manor.

102 i, 58r (3-2) <u>Bishop of Salisbury; land in Wantage Hundred</u>: TRW Bishop Osmund holds one and a half hides from the King in Wantage Hundred, and Thorir holds from him. TRE Thorir's father held this land and could go where he wished, but for his protection, he commended himself (*pro sua defensione se commisit*) to Bishop Herman. Thorir similarly commended himself to Bishop Osmund.

103 i, 58v (5-1) <u>Bishop of Exeter; Buckland</u>: TRE Wulfric Kemp lived in

Buckland. TRW Bishop Osbern holds Buckland in demesne from his bishopric, so he says. Concerning this matter, they did not state a judgment (*iudicium non dixerunt*), but sent it before the King, so that he might judge it (*sed ante regem ut iudicet dimiserunt*). It was then assessed at fifteen and a half hides; now for eight.

104 i, 58v (7-7) Abingdon Abbey; Shippon: TRW Abingdon holds Abingdon. TRE it was assessed at sixty hides, now for forty. Of these hides, Reginald holds the manor of Shippon, for five hides from the abbot in mortgage (*in vadimonio*). TRE Eadnoth the Staller held it, but it was not in the abbey. Earl Hugh gave (*dedit*) it to the abbey.

105 i, 58v (7-15) Abingdon Abbey; Beedon: TRE Northmann held Beedon from the Abbot of Abingdon. He could not go where he wished. It was assessed at fifteen hides, but they say that King Edward pardoned (*condonavit*) it for eleven hides.

106 i, 58v (7-16) Abingdon Abbey; Benham: TRW Walter de Rivers holds two hides in Benham from the Abbot of Abingdon. Edith held them TRE and could go where she wished. This land was not of the abbey TRE, but it has been quit to the King (*sed est quieta regi*).

107 i, 59r (7-24) Abingdon Abbey; Lyford: TRE Algeard's sons held seven hides in Lyford from the abbot. They could not go to another lord without the abbot's permission. Nonetheless, they commended (*commendaverunt*) themselves to Walter Giffard TRW, without the abbot's order (*praecepto*). Now Walter holds this land from the abbot.

108 i, 59r (7-31) Abingdon Abbey; Winkfield: TRE and TRW Abingdon holds Winkfield, which was assessed at ten hides, now for three and a half hides. A man holds half a hide there against the wishes (*voluntate*) of the abbot, and does so unjustly (*iniuste*). Four other hides are in the King's forest.

109 i, 59r (7-38) Abingdon Abbey; Fawler: TRW Ansketil holds ten hides in Fawler from the Abbot of Abingdon. TRE Eadric held it in alod from the King, and could go where he wished. Concerning this manor, the shire attests that Eadric delivered (*deliberavit*) this manor to his son, who was a monk in Abingdon, to hold at farm, so that he might be provided with the necessities of life for as long as he lived (*ut ad firmam illud teneret, et sibi donec viveret necessaria vitae inde donaret*). After Eadric's death, the son should have the manor. Therefore, the men of the shire do not know what belongs to the abbey, because they have seen neither the King's writ nor his seal (*brevem regis vel sigillum*). Concerning this, the abbot testifies that TRE Eadric's son put (*misit*) the manor in the abbey, to which he belonged. The abbot has the writ and seal (*brevem et sigillum*) of King Edward for it, and all his monks attest (*attestantibus*) to this.

110 i, 59v (10-1) New Minster, Winchester; Chaddleworth: TRW New Minster, Winchester holds Chaddleworth. TRE two freemen held it from Countess Gytha and her son Earl Gyrth as two manors. Then it was assessed at sixteen hides, now at ten. Oda of Winchester gave (*dedit*) this manor to

Robert, Hugh de Port's steward, but the men of the shire do not know how the abbey has it.

111 i, 59v (12-1) <u>St. Albans Abbey; West Hendred</u>: TRE three thegns held West Hendred, and they could go where they wished. TRW St. Albans holds it. Then it was assessed at ten hides, now at four. Nigel d'Aubigny gave (*dedit*) it to the abbey.

112 i, 59v (14-1) <u>Nunminster, Winchester; Coleshill</u>: TRE Edmund held eight hides in Coleshill from King Edward in alod. Walter de Lacy gave (*dedit*) it to Nunminster with his daughter, but the shire does not know how. TRW Nunminster holds this land for two and a half hides.

113 i, 59v (15-1) <u>Battle Abbey; Brightwalton</u>: TRE Earl Harold held Brightwalton, and it was assessed at ten hides. The thegn who held it before Harold, however, paid geld for fifteen hides. The Abbot of Battle now holds this land from the King.

114 i, 60r (20-2) <u>Walter Giffard; West Hanney</u>: TRE Earl Tosti held West Hanney. TRW Walter Giffard holds it. Then it was assessed at fourteen hides, now for seven. Two mills are included in this manor. One, according to the hundred, belongs to the manor of Charlton.

115 i, 60v (21-6) <u>Henry de Ferrers; Bagshot</u>: TRW Henry de Ferrers holds Bagshot. TRE Godric the Sheriff held it from King Edward as a manor. Two hides did not pay geld there, because they were of the King's farm. They have been claimed (*calumniatae sunt*) for the King's use.

116 i, 60v (21-13) <u>Henry de Ferrers; land in Wantage Hundred</u>: TRW Henry de Ferrers holds three hides and a virgate of land in Wantage Hundred. TRE four freemen held it. Henry says that this land belonged to his antecessor Godric the Sheriff, but the hundred testifies that Godric seized (*occupavit*) it against the King after the Battle of Hastings, and that he never held it TRE.

117 i, 60v (21-15) <u>Henry de Ferrers; Fyfield</u>: TRW Henry de Ferrers holds ten hides in Fyfield and Henry holds from him. TRE Godric the Sheriff held it from the Abbot of Abingdon. He could not go where he wished with this land.

118 i, 60v (21-16) <u>Henry de Ferrers; Fyfield</u>: TRW Henry de Ferrers holds Fyfield. TRE Godric the Sheriff held it from King Edward. It was assessed at ten hides, now for five, because King Edward pardoned (*condonavit*) it, so the hundred testifies.

119 i, 60v (21-17) <u>Henry de Ferrers; Hendred (East or West)</u>: TRW Henry holds a hide in Hendred from Henry de Ferrers. TRE Godric the Sheriff held it from King Edward. This is the hide that lay in the King's farm, concerning which Ælfric offered (*detulit*) testimony.

120 i, 60v (21-18) <u>Henry de Ferrers; Stanford in the Vale</u>: TRW Henry de Ferrers holds Stanford in the Vale. TRE Siward Barn held it from King Edward, and it was assessed at forty hides. They say, however, that King Edward pardoned (*condonavit*) it for thirty hides.

121 i, 60v (21-20) <u>Henry de Ferrers; Burghfield</u>: TRW Henry de Ferrers holds one and a half hides of land in Burghfield. TRE two alodiaries held it. One served Queen Edith and the other served Bondi the Staller. These two men still hold it from Henry, but the hundred does not know for what reason.

122 i, 60v (21-22) Henry de Ferrers; Woolhampton: TRW Henry de Ferrers holds three hides in Woolhampton. TRE Godric the Sheriff held them from King Edward, who gave (*dedit*) this land to Godric from his farm. The men of the county have seen his seal (*sigillum*) for it. Godric also received another virgate from the King's farm, for which the county has not seen the King's seal.

123 i, 61r (23-2) William d'Eu; Denford: TRW William d'Eu holds Denford. TRE Alweard held it in alod from King Edward, and it was assessed for ten hides; now it is assessed for five. Along with this manor William holds half a hide, which two freemen held TRE. It never belonged to this manor, so the shire says.

124 i, 61r (30-1) Walter fitz Poyntz; Eaton Hastings: TRW Walter fitz Poyntz holds Eaton Hastings from the King. Gyrth held it in alod from King Edward. Then it was assessed for twenty hides; now for six. The villeins there did not give geld. Walter's father, Poyntz, gave (*dedit*) three hides of this manor to New Minster, Winchester for his soul (*pro anima sua*).

125 i, 61v (31-3) Walter fitz Othere; Bucklebury: TRW Walter fitz Othere holds a hide in Bucklebury, and one of his men holds from him. TRE Ælfhild Dese held it from King Edward. It lies in the forest and never paid geld, so the shire says.

126 i, 61v (31-4) Walter fitz Othere; Kintbury: TRW Walter fitz Othere holds half a hide in Kintbury, which King Edward gave (*dedit*) to Walter's antecessor from his farm, exempt (*solutam*) from all customs because of his custody of the forest, except for the King's forfeitures, that is, theft, homicide, housebreaking, and breach of peace (*excepta forisfactura regis sic est latrocinium, homicidium, heinfara et fracta pax*).

127 i, 62r (41-5) Robert d'Oilly; Ardington: TRW Robert d'Oilly holds Ardington. TRE Sæwine, a freeman, held it. Then it was assessed at nine hides; now at four hides and three virgates. There are two mills there. Cola the Englishman claims (*calumniatur*) one of them, but Alwine, Godwine, and Ælfric testify that it always lay in Ardington.

128 i, 62r (41-6) Robert d'Oilly; land in Wantage Hundred: TRW Robert d'Oilly holds a hide in Wantage Hundred, which Azur, King Edward's steward (*dispensator*), held TRE. He could go with it to whom he wished. TRW this same Azur holds from Robert, but the men of the hundred testify that he ought to hold from the King, since King William returned (*reddidit*) this land to him at Windsor, and gave him a writ for it (*brevem suum inde ei dedit*). Robert, therefore, holds it unjustly (*iniuste*), because no one has seen the King's writ nor, on Robert's behalf, the man who seised him of it (*brevem regis vel ex parte eius hominem qui eum inde saisisset*).

129 i, 62r–v (43-1) Richard Poynant; Lollingdon: TRE Almær, a free man, held

Lollingdon. TRW Richard Poynant holds it. Then it was assessed at three hides; now at nothing. When Richard took (*accepit*) this manor, he found it in the farm of Cholsey. Now it is outside it.

130   i, 62v (44-1) <u>Roger d'Ivry; Eling</u>: TRE Sæwine held a virgate in Eling from King Edward in the King's manor of Hendred. TRW Roger d'Ivry holds it. He put (*misit*) it in his manor of Harwell, where it never lay, so the shire says, nor has it ever paid geld.

131   i, 62v (46-4) <u>Ralph de Mortimer; Burghfield</u>: TRW Ralph de Mortimer holds one and a half hides in Burghfield, and a knight holds from him. TRE and after Æthelsige abbot of St. Augustine's, Canterbury held it from Old Minster, by testimony of the shire, until he was made an outlaw (*utlage fuit*).

132   i, 63r (58-2) <u>Hugolin the Steersman; Irish Hill</u>: TRE Herling held a hide in Irish Hill. Hugolin the Steersman held it until now. The shire testifies that this manor did not belong to Hugolin's antecessor, through whom he claims it (*per quem reclamat*). His men, however, refused to give an account of it (*noluerunt inde reddere rationem*). He has also transferred (*transportavit*) the hall, the other houses, and the livestock to another manor.

133   i, 63v (65-7) <u>Oda and other thegns; "Lierecote"</u>: TRW Alsige of Faringdon holds 'Lierecote' by the King's gift (*de dono regis*). Harold held it TRE. It was then assessed at five hides; now at two.

134   i, 63v (65-18) <u>Oda and other thegns; Inglewood</u>: TRW Ralph de Fougères holds two and a half hides in Inglewood, which lay in Inkpen, so the shire says.

Buckinghamshire

135   i, 143r (B-11) <u>Buckingham</u>: TRW William de Castellion has two burgesses from the fee of the Bishop of Bayeux. TRE they were the men of Earl Leofwine. They pay 16d., but nothing to the King. In the time of King Edward, however, they paid 3d.

136   i, 143v (1-2) <u>Terra Regis; Wendover</u>: King William holds the manor of Wendover for twenty-four hides. There are two sokemen there who hold one and a half hides of land. It did not lie there TRE.

137   i, 143v (3a-1) <u>Bishop of Lincoln; Stoke Mandeville</u>: TRW Remigius bishop of Lincoln holds eight hides in Stoke Mandeville. TRE Bishop Wulfwig of Dorchester held it. From the eight hundreds which lie around Aylesbury, each sokeman who has a hide or more pays a *summa* of corn to the Church. Moreover TRE each sokeman paid (*solvebant*) an acre of corn or 4d. to the Church. But after the coming of King William, this payment (*redditum*) was not made.

138   i, 144r (4-5) <u>Bishop of Bayeux; Weston Turville</u>: TRW Roger holds twenty hides in Weston Turville from the Bishop of Bayeux. TRE Earl Leofwine held nine and a half hides of this land. Godric the Sheriff had three and a half

hides as a manor. Two of Godric's men had three and a half hides, a man of Earl Tosti two hides, and two of Earl Leofwine's men had a hide and a half. All these men could sell. The men whom Roger now holds in Weston Turville did not belong to Earl Leofwine TRE.

139   i, 144v (4-17) <u>Bishop of Bayeux; West Wycombe</u>: TRW Roger holds half a hide from the Bishop of Bayeux in West Wycombe. TRE a man of Archbishop Stigand held this land. He could not sell or grant it outside of Stigand's manor of Wycombe, so the hundred testifies.

140   i, 144v (4-20) <u>Bishop of Bayeux; Radnage</u>: Theodwald held three hides of land from the Bishop of Bayeux, which is now in the King's farm. TRE Frithebert, a man of Earl Leofwine, held two and a half of these hides. Alric Gangemer and his sister held the other half hide, which was unjustly taken away (*iniuste ablata est*) from them TRE.

141   i, 145r (5-6) <u>Bishop of Coutances; Simpson</u>: TRE Queen Edith held eight hides and three virgates in Simpson. Now the Bishop of Coutances holds them as a manor in mortgage (*in vadimonio*) from William Bonvallet.

142   i, 145r (5-10) <u>Bishop of Coutances; Tyringham</u>: TRW Ansketil holds two and a half hides and three-quarters of a virgate from the Bishop of Coutances in Tyringham. TRE two thegns held them. One was Earl Waltheof's man. This land is in exchange (*de excambio*) for Bleadon [Som.].

143   i, 145v (5-15) <u>Bishop of Coutances; Lavendon</u>. TRW William holds four hides and two-thirds of a virgate from the Bishop of Coutances in Lavendon as a manor. TRE eight thegns held this land. One of them, Alli, was senior to the others (*senior aliorum*).

144   i, 145v (5-18) <u>Bishop of Coutances; Clifton Reynes</u>: TRW Morcar holds a hide and a half from the Bishop of Coutances in Clifton Reynes. TRE Alli, a thegn of King Edward, held this land and could sell. This land is in exchange (*de excambio*) for Bleadon [Som.], so the bishop's men say.

145   i, 145v (7-1) <u>Westminster Abbey; Denham</u>: TRW the Abbot of Westminster holds ten hides in Denham. Wulfstan, a thegn, gave (*dedit*) this manor to Westminster, and it lay there in demesne on the day on which King Edward was alive and dead.

146   i, 146r (12-5) <u>Count of Mortain; West Wycombe</u>: TRW William holds half a hide from the count in West Wycombe. TRE a sokemen, who was a man of Archbishop Stigand, held this land. He could not grant or sell it outside the manor of Wycombe TRE, so the hundred testifies.

147   i, 146v (12-16, 17, 18, 19) <u>Count of Mortain; Pitstone</u>: TRW the Count of Mortain holds Pitstone. Ralph holds three hides and a virgate of this land from the count as a manor. TRE Ælfgeat of Aylesbury held it and could sell. In the same vill, Bernard holds three hides and a virgate from the count as a manor. TRE two men of the Abbot of St. Albans held this land and could sell. In the same vill Fulcold holds a hide and a virgate of land from the count. TRE Glædwine, a man of the Abbot of St. Albans, held this land and could sell. Thorgisl, a man of the count, took (*sumpsit*) six hides from the manor of Pitstone, which the count himself holds unjustly (*iniuste*) in his demesne.

148   i, 148v (17-2) <u>William fitz Ansculf; Ellesborough</u>: TRW Ralph holds thirteen and a half hides from William fitz Ansculf in Ellesborough. TRE Earl Harold held them. Ansculf de Picquigny exchanged (*excambiavit*) this manor with Ralph Taillebois for half of Risborough, by order (*iussu*) of King William.

149   i, 148v (17-16) <u>William fitz Ansculf; Marsh Gibbon</u>: TRW Æthelric holds four hides from William fitz Ansculf in Marsh Gibbon as a manor. He also held it TRE, but now he holds it at farm from William in oppression and misery (*graviter et miserabiliter*).

150   i, 148v (17-20) <u>William fitz Ansculf; Bradwell</u>: TRW William fitz Ansculf holds three virgates in Bradwell. TRE Alweard, a man of Goding, held them and could sell. When he was sheriff, Ansculf unjustly (*iniuste*) disseised (*desaisiuit*) William of Cholsey of this land, so the men of the hundred say, and without the King's or anyone else's livery (*sine liberatore regis vel alicuius*).

151   i, 149r (18-3) <u>Robert de Tosny; Clifton Reynes</u>: TRW William de Bosc-le-Hard and his brother Roger hold four hides in Clifton Reynes as a manor from Robert de Tosny. TRE Oswulf, a thegn of King Edward, held this manor and could sell. Sigefrith and Thorbert hold three virgates of this vill, which William and Roger have seized and concealed (*habent occupatas et celatas*) against the King, so the men of the hundred say.

152   i, 149r (19-1) <u>Robert d'Oilly; Iver</u>: TRW Robert d'Oilly holds seventeen hides in Iver. TRE Toki, a thegn of King Edward, held this manor, and there were three sokemen there. One, Toki's man, held three virgates and could not sell his land without Toki's permission. The second, Queen Edith's man, held two and a half hides. The third, Sæwulf's man, had two and a half hides. These last two men could grant or sell to whom they wished, and they did not belong to the manor. Robert exchanged (*excambiavit*) this manor with Clarenbold du Marais for Padbury. It is from his wife's fee.

153   i, 149r (19-3) <u>Robert d'Oilly; Oakley</u>: TRW Robert fitz Walter holds five hides and three virgates in Oakley from Robert d'Oilly. TRE Ælfgyth, a girl, held two of these hides, and she could grant them to whom she wished. She held another half hide from King Edward's demesne farm, which Godric the Sheriff granted (*concessit*) to her for as long as he was sheriff, so that she might teach his daughter how to embroider in gold. Robert fitz Walter now holds this land, so the hundred testifies.

154   i, 151v (38-1) <u>Bertran de Verdun; Farnham</u>: TRE Countess Gode held ten hides in Farnham. Now Bertran de Verdun holds them. Geoffrey de Mandeville holds half a hide of this manor in Amersham, of which he disseised (*desaisiuit*) Bertran while he was across the sea in the King's service: this the hundred testifies. Ralph Taillebois built a mill on Bertran's land, which was not there TRE, so the hundred testifies.

155   i, 151v (40-1) <u>Nigel de Berville; Drayton Parslow</u>: TRW Nigel de Berville holds two hides and a virgate in Drayton Parslow. TRE Leofwine of

Nuneham held this manor from the King. Later, in King William's time, Ralph Passwater held this land from the same Leofwine. He found two breastplated men for the guard of Windsor (*loricatos in custodia Windesores*). The Bishop of Coutances disseised (*desaisiuit*) Ralph of this and delivered (*liberavit*) it to Nigel.

156   i, 153r (56-1) Ælfsige; Chesham: TRW Ælfsige holds four hides in Chesham from the King. TRE Queen Edith held it. She gave (*dedit*) it to Ælfsige after the coming of King William.

157   i, 153r (56-2) Ælfsige; "Sortelai" (lost in Quainton): TRW Ælfsige holds four hides in "Sortelai." TRE Wulfweard, Queen Edith's man, held this land. The Queen gave (*dedit*) it to Ælfsige with Wulfweard's daughter.

158   i, 153r (56-3) Ælfsige; Shipton Lee: TRW Ælfsige holds two hides from the King in Shipton Lee. He took this land with his wife (*sumpsit cum uxore sua*).

159   i, 153r (57-10) Leofwine of Nuneham; Wendover Dean: TRW Leofwine of Nuneham holds half a hide in Wendover Dean. He held it in the time of King Edward as well and could sell. Ralph put (*apposuit*) this land in Wendover, but it was not there TRE.

160   i, 153r (57-11) Leofwine of Nuneham; Wendover: TRW three men hold a hide from the King in Wendover. They held it in King Edward's time as well and could sell. Now they are in the King's farm in Wendover, where they were not TRE.

161   i, 153r (57-18) Leofwine of Nuneham; Soulbury: TRW Godwine the Beadle holds half a hide from the King in Soulbury. TRE Alric Bolest held it. Godwine says that this land was forfeited (*fuit forisfacta*) after the coming of King William.

Cambridgeshire

162   i, 189r (B-11) Cambridge: TRE the burgesses of Cambridge lent (*accommodabant*) their ploughs to the sheriff three times each year. Now they are demanded (*exiguntur*) nine times. Furthermore, in the time of King Edward, they found neither cartage nor carts, but TRW they do, through the imposition of a custom (*per consuetudinem impositam*). The burgesses also claim (*reclamant*) the common (*communem*) pasture against Picot the Sheriff, which was taken away from them through and by him (*per eum et ab eo ablatam*).

163   i, 189r (B-12) Cambridge: TRW Picot the Sheriff has made three mills in Cambridge, which have taken away (*auferebantur*) the pasture and destroyed (*destruuntur*) many houses.

164   i, 189r (B-13, 14) Cambridge: Picot the Sheriff had £8, a palfrey, and the arms of a soldier as heriot (*harieta*) from the lawmen (*lagemannorum*). When Ælfric Godricson was sheriff, he had a heriot (*herietam*) of 20s. from one of them.

165   i, 189v (1-2) Terra Regis; Fordham: King Edward held the manor of Fordham. Now King William has it at five and a half hides. In this vill a sokeman named Brunmann holds a hide of the King's soke. TRE he could grant his land to whom he wished, but he always provided either cartage or 8d. in service of the King, and paid his forfeitures (*forisfacturam emendabat*) to the sheriff.

166   i, 189v (1-3) <u>Terra Regis; Isleham</u>: King William has six hides and forty acres in Isleham. King Edward held them. Four of King Edward's sokemen were in this manor. They held a hide and forty acres and could grant or sell to whom they wished. They paid their forfeitures to the sheriff (*forisfacturam suam vicecomiti emendabant*).

167   i, 189v (1-11) <u>Terra Regis; Woodditton</u>: TRW William de Noyers holds Woodditton from King William. TRE it lay in Ely Abbey, but Archbishop Stigand took (*sumpsit*) it, although the men of the hundred do not know how. Then it was assessed at ten hides; now for one.

168   i, 189v (1-12) <u>Terra Regis; Exning [Suffolk]</u>: TRW King William holds thirteen and a half hides in Exning. TRE Eadgifu the Fair held them. Seven of Eadgifu's sokemen were there. They could withdraw without her permission, but she had their soke. Each of them also provided cartage or 8d. in the King's service, or a pledge (*mancipium*).

169   i, 189v (1-13) <u>Terra Regis; Soham</u>: TRW King William has six hides and forty acres in Soham in his return (*in breve suo*).

170   i, 190r (1-14) <u>Terra Regis; Fulbourn</u>: TRW Picot the Sheriff holds twenty-six sokemen who have four hides in Fulbourn. He holds them under the King's hand. They pay £8 a year weighed and assayed, along with twelve horses and twelve watchmen if the King comes into the sheriffdom (*vicecomitatus*): if he does not come, they pay 12s. 8d. TRE these sokemen paid nothing to the sheriff except cartage and watch and ward or 12s. 8d. Picot has annexed (*invasit*) the rest against the King.

171   i, 190r (1-16) <u>Terra Regis; Great Abington</u>: TRE Almær held half a virgate in Great Abington and could grant and sell. TRW Picot the Sheriff holds it under the King's hand, and Sigar the Sokeman holds from him. Aubrey de Vere annexed (*invasit*) this land against the King, and Picot established title (*deratiocinavit*) against him. Concerning the stock (*pecunia*) which he took (*sumpsit*) from it, Aubrey still keeps back (*retinet*) 380 sheep and a plow, so the men of the hundred testify.

172   i, 190v (3-5) <u>Bishop of Lincoln; Histon</u>: TRW Bishop Remigius holds a hide and two-thirds of a virgate in Histon, and Picot the Sheriff holds from him. TRE Wulfwine, the Abbot of Ely's man, held it and paid a sester of honey each year. Bishop Remigius annexed (*invasit*) this land against the abbot, so the hundred testifies.

173   i, 190v (5-2) <u>Abbot of Ely; Stetchworth</u>: TRE and TRW Ely Abbey holds eight and a half hides and half a virgate in Stetchworth. Seric d'Auberville took (*sumpsit*) a virgate and a half of this land from the demesne farm of the Abbot of Ely, and put (*posuit*) it in St. Wandrille's manor, so the hundred testifies.

174 i, 190v (5-3) <u>Abbot of Ely; Westley Waterless</u>: TRW Ely Abbey holds three hides in Westley Waterless. This land lies and always lay in the demesne of Ely Abbey, by testimony of the hundred.

175 i, 191r (5-21) <u>Abbot of Ely; Thriplow</u>: TRE Ely Abbey held a hide in Thriplow. TRW Hardwin de Scales holds it under the abbot from the abbot's demesne, which is for the victualing of the monks, through a certain postponement (*quoddam respectum*) of the abbot, until he speaks with the King about it (*donec cum rege inde loquatur*).

176 i, 191r (5-22) <u>Abbot of Ely; Thriplow</u>: TRW Hardwin de Scales was holding two acres of the abbot's land in Thriplow, for which he had neither warrantor nor livery (*non habet advocatum nec liberatorem*). Hardwin seized (*occupavit*) this against the abbot, so the men of the hundred testify.

177 i, 191r (5-24) <u>Abbot of Ely; Harston</u>: TRW Picot the Sheriff holds a hide and a half in Harston from the Abbot of Ely, by order (*iussu*) of the King. TRE a sokeman held it under the Abbot of Ely. He could withdraw without the abbot's permission, but the soke remained with the abbot.

178 i, 191r (5-26) <u>Abbot of Ely; Shelford</u>: TRW Hardwin de Scales holds two and a half hides, nine acres, and a minster-church from the demesne farm of the monks of Ely in Shelford. They were in the demesne farm of the abbey TRE, so the hundred testifies. Now the abbot does not have them.

179 i, 191r (5-29) <u>Abbot of Ely; Whaddon</u>: TRW Hardwin de Scales holds two and a half hides in Whaddon. This land is assessed with Hardwin's land. Nonetheless, TRE one of these hides was held by Thorbiorn White from the Abbot of Ely. He could not separate this land from the Church outside the farm of the monks. The other hide and a half was held by twelve sokemen. They could sell, but the soke remained with the abbot.

180 i, 191r–v (5-32) <u>Abbot of Ely; Meldreth</u>: TRW Hardwin de Scales holds half a hide and a minster-church in Meldreth, which was of the demesne farm of the monks of Ely. The monks held them during the life and at the death of King Edward, so the men of the hundred testify.

181 i, 191v (5-33) <u>Abbot of Ely; Meldreth</u>: TRW Guy de Raimbeaucourt holds ten sokemen in Meldreth. One of them could not sell TRE, but the others could. This the hundred testifies.

182 i, 191v (5-44) <u>Abbot of Ely; rubric</u>: [The rubric reads: "The two hundreds of Ely which meet (*conveniunt*) at Witchford."]

183 i, 193r (13-2) <u>Roger of Montgomery; Guilden Morden</u>: TRW Earl Roger holds half a hide and half a virgate in Guilden Morden. TRE Goda held it under Earl Ælfgar. It belongs to Shingay. Hardwin de Scales seized (*occupavit*) four acres of this land against the earl, so the hundred testifies.

184 i, 193v (13-8) <u>Roger of Montgomery; Orwell</u>: TRW Earl Roger holds a hide, a virgate, and a third of a virgate in Orwell. TRE six sokemen held this land and could grant and sell it. One of them was King Edward's man, and he found ward and watch for the sheriff. Picot the Sheriff lent (*accommodavit*) three of these men to Earl Roger to hold his pleas (*placita sua tenenda*), but afterwards the earl's men seized (*occupaverunt*) them and kept (*retinuerunt*) them with their lands, without livery (*sine liberatore*). The King has neither had nor has any service from them, so the sheriff himself says.

185   i, 194v (14-30) Count Alan; Whaddon: TRW two men hold a virgate in Whaddon from Count Alan. TRE two sokemen held this land. One was Kolsveinn's man. The other was of the soke of Ely Abbey. He could sell, but the soke remained with the abbey.

186   i, 195r (14-57) Count Alan; Willingham: TRW a sokeman holds a virgate of land from Count Alan in Willingham. TRE Oswulf, a man of Eadgifu the Fair, held this land. He could sell, but the soke remained with Ely Abbey.

187   i, 195r (14-59) Count Alan; Landbeach: TRW Walter holds four and a half hides less twelve acres of land in Landbeach from Count Alan. TRE Eadgifu the Fair held it. A sokeman held two hides and a virgate under her. He could grant to whom he wished, but Ely Abbey had the sake and soke of the virgate.

188   i, 196r (17-1) Walter Giffard; Bottisham: TRW Walter Giffard holds ten hides in Bottisham. TRE Earl Harold held eight of these hides, and Alric the Monk had the other two, which he could neither grant nor sell without the permission of the Abbot of Ramsey, whose man he was.

189   i, 196r (17-2) Walter Giffard; Swaffham Bulbeck: TRW Hugh holds seven and a half hides and ten acres in Swaffham Bulbeck from Walter Giffard. Alwig the Harper held three hides and the mill from the demesne farm of the monks of Ely. The monks held them themselves during the life and at the death of King Edward, and Alwig could not withdraw without the abbot's permission. Three sokemen, who were the Abbot of Ely's men, held two and a half hides and ten acres of this land, and they could not withdraw without the abbot's permission. Nineteen sokemen, who were King Edward's men, held two hides and could not withdraw without their lord's permission.

190   i, 196r (17-3) Walter Giffard; Swaffham Bulbeck: TRW Hugh holds three virgates from Walter Giffard in Swaffham Bulbeck. TRE Wulfwine, the Abbot of Ely's man, held them, and he could not withdraw from Ely without the abbot's permission.

191   i, 196r–v (18-3) William de Warenne; Weston Colville: TRW William de Warren holds seven hides in Weston Colville. TRE Toki held this land from the Abbot of Ely. He could not separate it from the abbey, because it was in Ely's demesne farm, so the men of the hundred testify.

192   i, 196v (18-7) William de Warenne; Trumpington: TRE Toki held four and a half hides in Trumpington from Ely Abbey. He could not grant, sell, or separate this land from the abbey. Afterwards, Frederick, William de Warenne's brother[-in-law] had this land. Now William de Warenne holds it.

193   i, 196v (19-1) Richard fitz Gilbert; Papworth: TRW Richard fitz Gilbert has a virgate of land in Papworth, and William holds it from him. TRE Ælfric the Priest held it from the Abbot of Ely and could not withdraw from him. The soke always lay in Ely. Richard seized (*occupavit*) this land against the King, and took 20s.-worth of stock (*pecuniae*) from it.

194 i, 196v (19-4) <u>Richard fitz Gilbert; Whaddon</u>: TRW Hardwin de Scales holds a virgate from Richard fitz Gilbert in Whaddon. TRE Sægifu held this land under Eadgifu the Fair, and she could grant it to whom she wished. This land did not belong to Richard's antecessor, nor was he ever seised (*saisitus fuit*) of it. Ralph Wader held it on the day he wronged (*deliquit*) the King.

195 i, 196v (21-4) <u>Robert Gernon; Harston</u>: TRW Ranulf holds a hide and a virgate in Harston from Robert Gernon. TRE a sokeman held this land under King Edward and found a watchman. He could sell his land, but the soke remained with the King.

196 i, 196v–197r (21-5) <u>Robert Gernon; Barrington</u>: TRW Robert Gernon holds seven hides and two and a half virgates in Barrington. TRE Eadric "Pur" held three virgates of this land under King Edward and could sell. This same Eadric also held another half virgate of this land, which lay in Chatteris Abbey. Robert Gernon annexed (*invasit*) it against the abbess, so the men of the hundred testify.

197 i, 197r (21-7, 8, 9) <u>Robert Gernon; Conington, Boxworth, Swavesey</u>: TRW Robert Gernon holds a hide and a virgate in Conington, and Picot holds from him. TRE a man of Earl Waltheof held this land, and its soke lay in Long Stanton. Picot holds another three and a half hides in Boxworth, which Leofsige, a man of Earl Waltheof held and could sell. Robert also holds a hide in Swavesey, and Picot the Sheriff holds from him. TRE Leofsige, a man of Earl Waltheof, held this land, and he could grant and sell. Picot the Sheriff holds these lands from Robert Gernon as part of his wife's marriage portion (*in maritagio*).

198 i, 197r (22-5) <u>Geoffrey de Mandeville; Foxton</u>: TRW Robert Gernon seized (*occupavit*) half a mill in Foxton against Geoffrey de Mandeville, so the men of the hundred testify.

199 i, 197r (22-6) <u>Geoffrey de Mandeville; Chippenham</u>: TRW Geoffrey de Mandeville holds five hides in Chippenham. TRE Ordgar, King Edward's sheriff, and later a man of Esger the Staller, held it. It answered for ten hides TRE, but the sheriff put (*misit*) them at five hides through a grant (*concessionem*) of the King because the farm oppressed (*gravabat*) him. Five hides of this land were in King Edward's farm. Two sokemen had three of these hides from the King and could grant their land to whom they wished, but each found 8d. and a horse for the King's service, and for their forfeitures (*forisfactura*) they made restitution (*faciebant rectitudinem*) in Fordham. Ordgar the Sheriff had three hides of this land himself and could grant to whom he wished. Ordgar put this land in mortgage (*posuit . . . in vadimonio*) for seven marks and two ounces of gold, so Geoffrey's men say, but the men of the hundred have seen neither a writ (*brevem*) nor a legate (*legatem*) of King Edward, nor do they produce (*perhibent*) testimony.

200 i, 197v (25-9) <u>Eudo Dapifer; Gamlingay</u>: TRW Eudo Dapifer holds eighteen hides in Gamlingay. TRE Wulfmær of Eaton held them. Nine sokemen were also there, who held four hides which they could grant and sell. In addition to these hides, the sokemen held a virgate which belongs to Little Gransden, the Abbot of Ely's manor. Lisois de Moutiers seized (*occupavit*) it against the abbot, so the hundred testifies.

201   i, 197v (26-2) <u>Hardwin de Scales; land in Staploe Hundred</u>: TRW Hardwin de Scales holds half a hide from the King in Staploe Hundred. Turch, the Abbot of Ramsey's man, held it TRE. He could not withdraw without the abbot's permission.

202   i, 198r (26-9) <u>Hardwin de Scales; Horseheath</u>: TRW five villeins hold half a hide from Hardwin de Scales in Horseheath. TRE Leodmær held half a virgate of this land under the antecessor of Aubrey de Vere, and he could not withdraw without his permission.

203   i, 198r (26-17) <u>Hardwin de Scales; Hauxton</u>: TRW Hardwin de Scales holds a hide and a half in Hauxton. TRE Bondi held three virgates of this land from the Abbot of Ely. He could sell it, but the soke remained with the abbot.

204   i, 198r (26-18) <u>Hardwin de Scales; Shelford</u>: TRW Hardwin de Scales holds six hides, a virgate, and seven acres in Shelford. During the reign of King Edward and on the day he died, two and a half hides and nine acres of this land and a minster-church were in the demesne of Ely Abbey. They are now in the demesne farm, so the hundred testifies. Seven sokemen held a hide and half and six acres of this land from the Abbot of Ely's soke. They could not withdraw with the land, and the soke remained with Ely Abbey.

205   i, 198v (26-29) <u>Hardwin de Scales; Meldreth</u>: TRW Hardwin de Scales holds a virgate in Meldreth. TRE Almær held it under the Abbot of Ely and could sell. The soke, however, remained with Ely.

206   i, 198v (26-30) <u>Hardwin de Scales; Meldreth</u>: TRW Hugh holds a hide and a half from Hardwin de Scales in Meldreth. During King Edward's life and at his death, this land belonged to Ely Abbey in the monk's demesne, so the men of the hundred testify.

207   i, 198v (26-33) <u>Hardwin de Scales; Shepreth</u>: TRW Hugh holds half a virgate from Hardwin de Scales in Shepreth. It lay in the demesne of Ely Abbey during King Edward's life and on the day he died, so the men of the hundred testify.

208   i, 199r (26-48) <u>Hardwin de Scales; Over</u>: TRW Ralph holds two hides and a virgate from Hardwin de Scales in Over. TRE a sokeman held half a hide of this land under the Abbot of Ely. He could not grant or sell outside the Church, without the abbot's permission. Two other sokemen had three virgates of this land. They could sell them, but the soke remained with the Abbot of Ely. The other seven sokemen who held land in Over TRE, had one hide. They were the Abbot of Ramsey's men, and they could sell the land, but without the soke.

209   i, 199r (26-49) <u>Hardwin de Scales; Dry Drayton</u>: TRW Payne holds five hides and three virgates from Hardwin de Scales in Dry Drayton. TRE nineteen sokemen held this land. Five of them were the Abbot of Ely's men:

four of these held one hide and could sell without the soke, but the fifth had half a virgate under the abbot and could not sell. Four others were the men of Croyland Abbey. They held a hide and a virgate from the abbey's demesne farm.

210   i, 199r (28-2) Hugh de Port; Snailwell: TRW Hugh de Port holds five hides of land in Snailwell from the fee of the Bishop of Bayeux. TRE it lay in the demesne farm of Ely Abbey, but the abbot leased (*praestitit*) it to Archbishop Stigand, so the hundred testifies. Now Simeon abbot of Ely claims (*reclamat*) it through his antecessors. Six sokemen, who were Archbishop Stigand's men, were also there, and they could withdraw without his permission and grant and sell their land. The soke, however, remained with the Archbishop.

211   i, 199v (29-4) Aubrey de Vere; Swaffham Prior: TRW Aubrey de Vere holds half a hide and twenty acres in Swaffham Prior. TRE a sokeman of King Edward held this land. He could not withdraw without permission, and he provided cartage for the King's sheriff. Aubrey's antecessor did not have this land, so the men of the hundred testify. Instead, Aubrey himself seized (*occupavit*) it against the King.

212   i, 199v (29-6) Aubrey de Vere; Wilbraham: TRW Reginald holds half a hide and thirty acres of land from Aubrey de Vere in Wilbraham. TRE Godric, a man of King Edward, held it. He did not hold it from Aubrey's antecessor, so the men of the hundred testify. Nonetheless, Aubrey seized (*occupavit*) it against the King.

213   i, 199v (29-10) Aubrey de Vere; Great Abington: TRW Aubrey de Vere holds six hides in Great Abington, and Firmatus holds from him. TRE Wulfwine, King Edward's thegn, held this manor. A priest, however, held a hide of this land from Eadgifu the Fair, and could not withdraw without her permission. Now Count Alan claims (*reclamat*) this hide from Aubrey's men, so the hundred testifies.

214   i, 199v (29-11) Aubrey de Vere; Babraham: TRW Firmatus holds half a virgate in Babraham from Aubrey de Vere. TRE Godwine held it under Wulfwine, Aubrey's antecessor. He could not withdraw.

215   i, 199v (29-12) Aubrey de Vere; Great Abington: TRW a sokeman has half a hide in Great Abington from the King, which is in the custody of Picot the Sheriff. TRE Almær, a sokeman of King Edward, held it, and he could grant or sell to whom he wished. Aubrey de Vere annexed (*invasit*) this land from the King's soke, but Picot the Sheriff established title (*deratiocinavit*) against him. He still keeps back (*retinet*) a plow and 380 sheep, which Aubrey has from this land, so the men of the hundred testify.

216   i, 199v–200r (31-1) Guy de Raimbeaucourt; Meldreth: TRW Guy de Raimbeaucourt holds three hides and a virgate in Meldreth. TRE sixteen sokemen held this land. Ten of them had two hides and half a virgate from the soke of Ely Abbey. One of these sokemen could neither grant nor sell his land. The other nine could grant and sell to whom they wished, but the soke of all remained in Ely.

217 i, 200r (31-2) <u>Guy de Raimbeaucourt; Meldreth</u>: TRW Guy de Raimbeaucourt holds five hides and one and a quarter virgates in Meldreth. Eight sokemen, men of the Abbot of Ely, held two hides and half a virgate of this land. They could sell their lands, but their soke remained with the Abbot of Ely.

218 i, 200r (32-1) <u>Picot the Sheriff; Stow cum Quy</u>: TRW Picot the Sheriff holds four and a half hides and ten acres in Stow cum Quy. TRE two men of the Abbot of Ramsey – Alric the Monk and Godric – held three and a half hides of this land. They could not withdraw without the Abbot of Ramsey's permission. Four sokemen, who were King Edward's men, held a hide and ten acres there. They could neither grant nor sell without the King's permission.

219 i, 200r (32-2) <u>Picot the Sheriff; Stow cum Quy</u>: TRW Picot the Sheriff holds three hides and three virgates in Stow cum Quy. TRE two sokemen of the Abbot of Ely held this land. They could not sell without his permission.

220 i, 200r (32-4) <u>Picot the Sheriff; Hinxton</u>: TRW Picot the Sheriff holds fifteen and a half hides in Hinxton. He took (*recepit*) this land as two manors, so he says. Twenty sokemen held it TRE.

221 i, 200r (32-5) <u>Picot the Sheriff; Harston</u>: Picot serves (*servit*) the abbot from a hide and a half of land in Harston. He holds it by order (*iussu*) of the King. TRE Frithebert held it from the Abbot of Ely and could withdraw with his land. The soke, however, remained with the abbey.

222 i, 200v (32-10) <u>Picot the Sheriff; East Hatley</u>: TRW Picot the Sheriff holds two hides in East Hatley. TRE eight sokemen held this land. Picot says that he has a hide of this land in exchange (*pro excambio*) for Eynesbury [Hunts.], and he had the other in exchange (*pro excambio*) for Rushden [Herts.], because Ilbert of Hertford delivered (*liberavit*) it to him.

223 i, 200v (32-21) <u>Picot the Sheriff; Kingston</u>: TRW Ralph holds five and a half hides and sixteen acres from Picot the Sheriff in Kingston. TRE fourteen sokemen held this land. One of them, the abbot of Ely's man, held a virgate of the abbot's soke. He could withdraw.

224 i, 200v (32-22) <u>Picot the Sheriff; Toft</u>: TRW two knights hold one and a half hides and ten acres from Picot the Sheriff in Toft. TRE a man of the Abbot of Ely held half a hide and six acres of this land and could withdraw with it, but the soke remained with the abbot.

225 i, 200v–201r (32-23) <u>Picot the Sheriff; Bourn</u>: TRW Picot the Sheriff holds thirteen hides in Bourn. In total twenty-two men held this land TRE. One, a thegn, held three hides under King Edward. Two priests, this thegn's men, held a hide, but they could not separate outside the Church. Picot says that he had taken (*recepisse*) this land as two manors.

226 i, 201r (32-25) <u>Picot the Sheriff; Hatley St. George</u>: TRW Picot the Sheriff holds a hide in Hatley St. George. TRE three of King Edward's sokemen held this land. Picot says that he has it in exchange (*pro excambio*) for Rushden, which Sigar holds.

227 i, 201r (32-27) <u>Picot the Sheriff; Fen Drayton</u>: TRW Picot the Sheriff holds a hide in Fen Drayton and Roger holds from him. TRE two sokemen held this land. One of them, the Abbot of Ely's man, could sell his land without the soke.

228 i, 201r (32-28) <u>Picot the Sheriff; Over</u>: TRW Sæwine holds half a hide in Over from Picot the Sheriff. TRE a man of the Abbot of Ramsey held this land and could sell without the soke.

229 i, 201r (32-29) <u>Picot the Sheriff; Willingham</u>: TRW Roger holds a virgate from Picot the Sheriff in Willingham. TRE Golda held this land under the Abbot of Ely. He could neither grant nor sell.

230 i, 201r (32-30) <u>Picot the Sheriff; Long Stanton</u>: TRW Guy holds three hides from Picot the Sheriff in Long Stanton. TRE fifteen sokemen held them. Three of these men held a hide under the Abbot of Ely and could sell, but the soke remained with the abbot.

231 i, 201r (32-31) <u>Picot the Sheriff; Rampton</u>: TRW Roger holds four and a half hides in Rampton from Picot the Sheriff. TRE six sokemen held them, and they were assessed at six hides. Five of these men were the Abbot of Ely's men. Of these, four could sell their land, but the soke remained with the abbot. The fifth had a virgate and half and could not withdraw.

232 i, 201r (32-32) <u>Picot the Sheriff; Lolworth</u>: TRW Robert holds nine hides from Picot in Lolworth. A sokeman, who was a man of the Abbot of Ely, held a hide and a half of this land. His soke remained with the abbey.

233 i, 201r (32-33) <u>Picot the Sheriff; Madingley</u>: TRW Picot the Sheriff holds eleven hides and two and a half virgates in Madingley. TRE twelve sokemen held this manor. Five were the Abbot of Ely's men and had three hides and one and a half virgates. Of these men, four could withdraw; but the fifth, who held half a hide, could not.

234 i, 201r (32-35) <u>Picot the Sheriff; Oakington</u>: TRW two knights hold three hides, a virgate, and ten acres in Oakington from Picot the Sheriff. A third knight holds half a hide, nine acres, and three gardens from Picot. TRE a man of the Abbot of Ely had one and a half hides and ten acres of this land. He could sell, but the soke remained with the abbot.

235 i, 201r (32-36) <u>Picot the Sheriff; Impington</u>: TRW Walter holds three and a half hides from Picot the Sheriff in Impington. TRE three sokemen of the Abbot of Ely held them. Two of them held a hide and a virgate, and they could sell but the soke remained with the abbot. The third held two hides and a virgate, and he could not sell.

236 i, 201v (32-37) <u>Picot the Sheriff; Milton</u>: TRW Ralph holds twelve hides from Picot the Sheriff in Milton. TRE Æthelbeorht, the Abbot of Ely's steward, held six hides and three virgates of this manor, on the condition that he could neither sell nor separate from the Church, and that after his death, the land should be restored (*restitueret*) to Ely Abbey. Four sokemen held another four hides and two and a half virgates under the Abbot of Ely, and they could sell without the soke.

237 i, 201v (32-39) <u>Picot the Sheriff; Waterbeach</u>: TRW Mucel holds six hides from Picot the Sheriff in Waterbeach. TRE Æthelbeorht, the Abbot of Ely's man, held a hide of this land, which he could neither sell nor separate from the Church. Another man of the abbot had a virgate and could sell. The soke, however, remained with the abbot.

238 i, 201v (32-40) <u>Picot the Sheriff; Cottenham</u>: TRW Roger holds five hides from Picot the Sheriff in Cottenham. TRE a sokeman, who was a man of Ely Abbey, held three and a half hides less fourteen acres, and he could not grant them because they were in the demesne of the Church. Another man of the abbot had one and a half hides and could grant without the soke.

239 i, 201v (32-41) <u>Picot the Sheriff; Cottenham</u>: TRW Picot the Sheriff holds forty acres and a garden in Cottenham from the demesne of Ely Abbey.

240 i, 201v (32-42) <u>Picot the Sheriff; Cottenham</u>: TRW Picot the Sheriff holds forty acres of land and five acres of meadow in Cottenham from the demesne of Croyland Abbey.

241 i, 201v (32-43) <u>Picot the Sheriff; Westwick</u>: TRW Odo holds three hides in Westwick from Picot the Sheriff. TRE a sokeman of the Abbot of Ely had forty acres of this land. He could withdraw, but the soke remained with the abbot.

242 i, 201v (35-1) <u>John fitz Waleran; Fulbourn</u>: TRW John fitz Waleran holds six hides in Fulbourn. TRE three men of Eadgifu the Fair held a hide of this land, and they could not withdraw from her. Count Alan claims (*reclamat*) this hide. The men of the hundred testify for him.

243 i, 201v (35-2) <u>John fitz Waleran; Teversham</u>: TRW John fitz Waleran holds three and a half hides in Teversham. The antecessor of Simeon abbot of Ely bought (*emit*) a hide of this vill from Earl Ælfgar. Up to this time it had found cartage, but after the abbot bought it, it lay in the Church and did not find cartage. A church in Teversham lies with this hide, so the men of the hundred testify.

244 i, 201v (37-1, 2) <u>William de Cahaignes; Comberton, Barton</u>: TRW William de Cahaignes holds a virgate and a half in Comberton. TRE a man of Earl Waltheof held this land, and he could grant and sell. The Bishop of Bayeux delivered (*liberavit*) this land to William, but the men of the hundred do not know for what reason. William holds another two and a half hides in Barton in the same manner. TRE Barton was held by four of Earl Waltheof's sokemen. Two could grant and sell their land, but the other two, who held a hide and two and a half virgates, could not withdraw without Waltheof's permission.

245 i, 202r (38-2) <u>Robert Fafiton; Trumpington</u>: TRW Robert Fafiton holds two hides in Trumpington. TRE a man of King Edward held a virgate of this land and provided cartage for the sheriff. He could, however, withdraw with the land. Robert seized (*occupavit*) this land against the King, so the hundred testifies.

246 i, 202r (39-2) <u>David d'Argenton; Croxton</u>: TRE three of Earl Ælfgar's men and a man of Earl Waltheof held six hides in Croxton and could sell. TRW David d'Argenton holds them. Eustace of Huntingdon seized (*occupavit*) this land against David, so the whole hundred testifies.

247   i, 202r (39-3) <u>David d'Argenton; Westwick</u>: TRW Robert holds a hide from David d'Argenton in Westwick. TRE Guthmund, a man of Earl Waltheof, held it. The soke, however, remained with the Abbot of Ely.

248   i, 202r (40-1) <u>King's Carpenters; Waterbeach</u>: TRW two carpenters hold five hides in Waterbeach from the King. TRE Oswig, a man of the Abbot of Ely, held three and a half hides of this land. He could not sell or separate from the Church, so the men of the hundred testify.

249   i, 202v (41-14) <u>Countess Judith; Over</u>: TRW Roger holds half a hide in Over from Countess Judith. TRE Godwine, a man of Earl Waltheof, held this land and could grant it. The soke, however, remained with the Abbot of Ramsey.

250   i, 202v (43-1) <u>Wife of Boselin de Dives; Oakington</u>: TRE Siward, Earl Waltheof's man, held a hide and a half in Oakington, and he could sell. The soke, however, remained with the Abbot of Ely. TRW the wife of Boselin de Dives holds this land, which the Bishop of Bayeux delivered (*liberavit*) to her; but the men of the hundred do not know for what reason.

251   i, 202v (44-2) <u>Erchenger; Toft</u>: TRW Erchenger the Baker holds a hide in Toft from the King. TRE five sokemen of the Abbot of Ely held this land. In the time of King Edward and at his death, they could not grant or sell outside Ely Abbey.

Cheshire

252   i, 262v (C-3) <u>Borough of Chester</u>: If peace, given by the King's hand, his writ, or his legate was broken (*pax data manu regis vel suo brevi vel per suum legatum fuisset infracta*) by anyone, the King had 100s. If, however, the same peace, given by the earl on the King's order (*iussu*) was broken, the earl had the third penny of the 100s. given for the breach. If the same peace, given by the King's reeve or the earl's official (*ministro*) was broken, a fine was paid (*emendabatur*) of 40s.; the third penny was the earl's.

253   i, 262v (C-4) <u>Borough of Chester</u>: If a freeman broke (*infringens*) the peace given by the King, or if he killed a man in a house (*in domo hominem occidisset*), all his land and his goods (*pecunia*) were the King's, and he became an outlaw (*utlagh*). The earl was entitled to the same penalty, but only over his own man who made this forfeiture (*forisfacturam faciente*). No one, however, could restore peace to an outlaw (*utlagh nullus poterat reddere pacem*) except through the King.

254   i, 262v (C-5) <u>Borough of Chester</u>: He who shed blood (*sanguinem faciebat*) between Monday morning and Saturday at nones paid a fine (*emendabat*) of 10s. But from nones on Saturday to Monday morning he was fined

(*emendabatur*) 20s. Similarly, he who shed blood during the twelve days of the Nativity, on the Purification of St. Mary, on the first day of Easter, on the first day of Pentecost, on Ascension Day, the Assumption, and Nativity of Saint Mary, or on the feast of All Saints paid (*solvebat*) 20s.

255   i, 262v (C-6) <u>Borough of Chester</u>: He who killed (*interficiebat*) a man on one of these holy days was fined (*emendabatur*) £4. On other days the fine was 40s. Similarly, he who committed housebreaking (*heinfaram*) or robbery (*forestel*) during these feast days or on Sunday discharged himself (*exsolvebat*) with £4; on all other days, 40s.

256   i, 262v (C-7) <u>Borough of Chester</u>: He who failed to seize a thief (*hangeuuitham*) in Chester gave 10s. If, however, the King's reeve or the earl committed this offense (*forisfacturam faciens*), he paid a fine (*emendabat*) of 20s.

257   i, 262v (C-8) <u>Borough of Chester</u>: He who committed robbery (*revelach faciebat*), theft (*latrocinium*), or did violence to a woman in a house (*violentiam feminae in domo inferabat*) was fined (*emendabatur*) 40s.

258   i, 262v (C-9) <u>Borough of Chester</u>: If a widow had unlawful intercourse (*non legitime commiscebat*) with anyone, she paid a fine (*emendabat*) of 20s. A maid paid 10s. for the same thing.

259   i, 262v (C-10) <u>Borough of Chester</u>: He who seised (*saisibat*) another man's land in the city and could not establish his title to it (*non poterat diratiocinare suam*) paid a fine (*emendabat*) of 40s. Similarly, he who made a claim (*clamorem*) to this land but could not establish that it ought to be his (*esse debere non posset diratiocinare*), paid the same fine.

260   i, 262v (C-11) <u>Borough of Chester</u>: He who wished to pay relief in Chester (*relevare volebat*) on his own or his kinsman's (*propinqui*) land gave 10s. But, if he could not or would not, the reeve took the land into the King's hand.

261   i, 262v (C-12) <u>Borough of Chester</u>: He who did not pay rent (*gablum*) as he ought at the end of term (*ad terminum*) paid a fine (*emendabat*) of 10s.

262   i, 262v (C-13) <u>Borough of Chester</u>: If a fire burnt the city, the man from whose house the fire came paid a fine (*emendabat*) of three *ora* of pence, and he gave 2s. to his near-neighbor (*propinquori vicino*).

263   i, 262v (C-14) <u>Borough of Chester</u>: Of all these forfeitures (*forisfacturarum*), two-thirds went to the King, and a third to the earl.

264   i, 262v (C-15) <u>Borough of Chester</u>: If ships came to or left port without the King's permission, the King and the earl had 40s. from each man who was on the boat.

265   i, 262v (C-16) <u>Borough of Chester</u>: If a ship came against the King's peace (*contra pacem regis*) and against his prohibition (*prohibitionem*), the King and the earl had the ship and its men, along with everything else on it.

266   i, 262v (C-17) <u>Borough of Chester</u>: If, however, the ship came with the King's peace and his permission, those who were in it sold (*vendebant*) what they had peacefully (*quiete*). But when the ship left, the King and the earl had 4d. from each load (*lesth*).

267   i, 262v (C-17) <u>Borough of Chester</u>: If the King's reeve ordered (*iuberet*) those

who had marten-skins not to sell (*venderent*) to anyone until they were first shown to him, so that he could make his purchase, but the man with the pelts did not observe (*observabat*) this, he paid a fine (*emendabat*) of 40s.

268   i, 262v (C-18) <u>Borough of Chester</u>: A man or a woman who gave false measure (*falsam mesuram*) in the city paid a forfeiture (*dephensus . . . emendabat*) of 4s. Similarly, anyone making bad beer was either put on a privy-stool (*cathedra ponebatur stercoris*), or gave the reeves 4s. The official (*minister*) of the King or the earl took this forfeiture (*forisfacturam*) in the city no matter on whose land the crime occurred, whether it was the bishop's or another man's. Similarly with toll; anyone who kept it back (*detinebat*) for more than three nights paid a fine (*emendabat*) of 40s.

269   i, 262v (C-20) <u>Borough of Chester</u>: There were twelve judges (*iudices*) in the city. They were men of the King, the bishop, and the earl. If any of them stayed away (*remanebant*) from the hundred on the day it sat (*sedebat*), without a clear excuse (*sine excusatione manifesta*), he paid a fine (*emendabat*) of 10s., which was divided between the King and the earl.

270   i, 262v (C-21) <u>Borough of Chester</u>: For the rebuilding of the city wall and bridge, the reeve commanded (*edicebat*) that one man come from each hide in the county. The lord of any man who did not come paid a fine (*emendabat*) of 40s. to the King and the earl. This forfeiture (*forisfactura*) was in addition to the farm.

271   i, 262v (C-22) <u>Borough of Chester</u>: Chester paid £45 of farm and three timbers of marten pelts. The third part was the earl's, two-thirds the King's.

272   i, 262v (C-24) <u>Borough of Chester</u>: Mundret held Chester from the earl for £70 and one mark of gold. Mundret also had £50 from the farm and a gold mark from all the earl's pleas in the county and the hundreds (*omnia placita comitis in comitatu et hundretis*) except Englefield.

273   i, 262v (C-25) <u>Borough of Chester</u>: The land on which the Church of St. Peter stands, which Robert of Rhuddlan claimed (*clamabat*) for thegnland, never belonged to a manor outside the city, so the county established (*diratiocinavit*). It belonged instead to the borough and always paid customs to the King and the earl, just like the land of the other burgesses.

274   i, 263r (B-1) <u>Bishop of Chester; Chester</u>: The Bishop of Chester has these customs in the city: if a freeman works on a holy day, the bishop has 8s. If, however, a male or female slave breaks (*infringente*) a holy day, the bishop has 4s.

275   i, 263r (B-2) <u>Bishop of Chester; Chester</u>: If a merchant coming to Chester with a bale of goods (*trussellum*) should break it open without permission of the bishop's official (*ministri*) between nones on Saturday and Monday, or on any other feast day, the bishop has 4s. as a forfeiture (*forisfactura*). If a man of the bishop finds any man loading within the territory (*levvam*) of the city, the bishop has a forfeiture (*foresfactura*) of 4s. or two oxen.

276   i, 263r (B-6,7) <u>Bishop of Chester; Eyton</u>: TRE St. Chad's (i.e. the bishopric of Lichfield) held Eyton. King Edward gave (*dedit*) King Gruffydd all the

lands which lay beyond the River Dee. But after Gruffydd forfeited (*forisfecit*) to the King, he took this land away (*abstulit*) from Gruffydd and returned (*reddidit*) it to the Bishop of Chester (i.e. the Bishop of Lichfield) and all his men, who had held it before. [There is an "r", for "*reclamatio*" written in the margin.]

277   i, 263r (B-13) <u>Bishop of Chester; Bettisfield</u>: TRW the Bishop of Chester claims (*calumniatur*) two hides in Bettisfield, in the manor of Robert fitz Hugh. They belonged to the bishopric in the time of King Cnut, and the county testifies that St. Chad's (i.e. the bishopric of Lichfield) lost them unjustly (*iniuste perdit*).

278   i, 263v (1-8) <u>Earl of Chester; Frodsham</u>: TRW Earl Hugh holds three hides of land in Frodsham. TRE Earl Edwin held it, and the third penny from the pleas (*de placitis*) of this hundred belonged to Frodsham.

279   i, 264r (1-35) <u>Earl of Chester; Stanney</u>: TRE Ragenvald held a hide in Stanney as a free man. TRW Restald holds it from the Earl of Chester. Of this land, the county testifies that the fifth acre was and ought to be in the Church of St. Werburgh, Chester. The canons claim (*calumniantur*) it, because they lost it unjustly (*iniuste perdunt*).

280   i, 264r (2-1) <u>Earl of Chester; Bettisfield</u>: TRE Earl Edwin held Bettisfield, which was assessed at seven hides. TRW Robert fitz Hugh holds it from Earl Hugh. The Bishop of Chester claims (*calumniatur*) two hides of this manor, which St. Chad's (i.e. the bishopric of Lichfield) held in the time of King Cnut, but the bishop pleads (*plangit*) that they have been lost (*amisisse*) from then until now.

281   i, 264r (2-2) <u>Earl of Chester; Iscoyd</u>: TRE Earl Edwin held Iscoyd, which was assessed at five hides. TRW Robert fitz Hugh holds it from Earl Hugh. The Bishop of Chester claims (*calumniatur*) a hide and a half of this manor and a salthouse.

282   i, 264r (2-5) <u>Earl of Chester; Tilston</u>: TRE Earl Edwin held Tilston, which paid geld for four hides. TRW Robert fitz Hugh holds it from Earl Hugh. The Bishop of Chester claims (*calumniatur*) half a hide of this manor's land, but the county does not testify that this land is from his bishopric.

283   i, 264v (2-21) <u>Earl of Chester; Burwardsley</u>: TRE Ælfric, Colibert, and Ramkel held three hides in Burwardsley as three manors and were free men. TRW Humphrey holds from Robert fitz Hugh, who holds from Earl Hugh. A hide of this land was taken away (*fuit ablata*) from the Church of St. Werburgh, Chester. The reeves of Earl Edwin and Morcar sold (*vendiderunt*) it to Ramkel.

284   i, 265r (8-16) <u>Earl of Chester; Acton (near Nantwich)</u>: TRE Earl Morcar held Acton, which paid geld for eight hides. TRW William Malbank holds this land from Earl Hugh. This manor has its pleas in the hall of its lord (*suum placitum in aula domini sui*).

285   i, 268r (27-3) <u>Earl of Chester; Gresford</u>: TRW Hugh, Osbern, and Rainwald hold Gresford from Earl Hugh. TRE Thorth held it as a free man, and paid

geld for thirteen hides. One of these hides lay in the Church of St. Chad (i.e. the bishopric of Lichfield), half a hide in "Chespuic" and a half in Radnor. The county testifies to this, but does not know how the Church lost it (*perdiderit*).

286 i, 268r (S3-1) Northwich: Northwich was at farm for £8. The same laws and customs (*leges et consuetudines*) were in Northwich as in Nantwich and Middlewich, and the King and the earl similarly divided the payments (*redditiones*).

287 i, 268r (S3-2) Northwich: Anyone from another shire who brought a cart with two or more oxen gave (*dabat*) a 4d. toll. Any man from the same shire gave (*dabat*) 2d. a cart within the third night of the time he returned from whence he came. If the third night passed, he paid a fine (*emendabat*) of 40s. A man from another shire with a pack-horse gave (*dabat*) 1d., a man from the same shire gave a mite (*minutam*) within three nights, as has been said.

288 i, 268r (S3-3) Northwich: If a man who lives in this hundred brought a cart of salt through the county for the purpose of selling it, he gave 1d. for each cart every time he loaded it. If he carried the salt by horse, for the purpose of selling, he paid a penny on the feast of St. Martin. He who did not pay within this time, paid a fine (*emendabat*) of 40s.

289 i, 268r (S1-5) Nantwich: All the salthouses, both of the commune and the demesne (*communes et dominicae*), were enclosed on one side by a river and on the other by the fosse. He who incurred a forfeiture (*forisfecisset*) within these bounds (*metam*) could pay a fine (*poterat emendare*) of 2s. or thirty boilings of salt, except for homicide (*homicidio*) or a theft for which the thief was sentenced to death (*furto de quo ad mortem iudicabatur latro*). If these crimes were committed there, amends were made (*emendabant*) as in the whole shire.

290 i, 268r (S1-6) Nantwich: If anyone was proven (*probatus*) to have taken away (*detulisset*) the toll on salt outside the bounds of the salthouses to anywhere else in the county, he came back (*referebat*) and paid a fine (*emendabat*) of 40s. if he was a freeman, or 4s. if he was not. But if he carried it off (*adportabat*) into another shire, he paid the fine where the claim was made (*ubi calumniabatur ibidem emendabat*).

291 i, 268r (S1-7) Nantwich: TRE Nantwich paid £21 in farm, including all the pleas (*placitis*) of the hundred.

292 i, 268r (S2-1) Middlewich: Although there were no demesne salthouses in Middlewich, it had the same laws (*leges*) and customs (*consuetudines*) as in Nantwich.

293 i, 268r (S2-2) Middlewich: Anyone who so overloaded a cart that the axle broke within a league of either Middlewich or Nantwich paid 2s. to an official (*ministro*) of the King or the earl, if he could be overtaken (*posset consequi*) within the league. Similarly, anyone who so overloaded a horse that he broke its back, paid 2s., if overtaken (*consecutus*) within the league. Beyond the league, he paid nothing.

294 i, 268r (S2-3) Middlewich: Anyone who made two packloads of salt out of

one paid a fine (*emendabat*) of 40s., if an official (*minister*) could catch (*posset consequi*) him. If he could not be found, he paid no fine (*emendabat*) through anyone else.

295   i, 269r (FT2-19) <u>Earl of Chester; Rhuddlan</u>: There is a new borough with eighteen burgesses in Rhuddlan, divided between Hugh earl of Chester and Robert of Rhuddlan. Hugh and Robert allowed (*annuerunt*) these burgesses the laws and customs (*leges et consuetudines*) found in Hereford and Breteuil; that is, throughout the whole year they only give 12d. for any forfeiture (*forisfactura*) except homicide (*homicidium*), theft (*furtum*), and premeditated housebreaking (*heinfar praecogitata*).

296   i, 269r (FT2-19) <u>Earl of Chester; Rhuddlan</u>: In the year of this inquest (*descriptionis*) the toll of this borough was given out at a farm of 3s.

297   i, 269r (G-1) <u>Earl of Chester; North Wales</u>: Robert of Ruddlan holds North Wales from the King at farm, except for the land which King William had given (*dederat*) him in fee and except for the land of the bishopric.

298   i, 269r (G-2) <u>Earl of Chester; Arwystli</u>: Robert of Rhuddlan claims (*calumniatur*) a hundred called Arwystli, which Roger of Montgomery holds. The Welsh testify that this hundred is one of the hundreds of North Wales.

Cornwall

299   i, 120r (1-4) <u>Terra Regis; Lanow</u>: TRE Earl Harold held five hides in Lanow. Now King William holds them. Two manors, Poundstock and St. Gennys, which are assessed at a hide and a half, have been taken away (*ablata sunt*) from this manor. Iovin holds them from the Count of Mortain.

300   1, 120r (1-6) <u>Terra Regis; Blisland</u>: TRE Earl Harold held four hides in Blisland. Now King William holds them. A hide in Pendavey has been taken away (*ablata est*) from this manor. Boia the Priest holds it from the Count of Mortain.

301   i, 120r (1-7) <u>Terra Regis; Pendrim</u>: TRE Earl Harold held a hide in Pendrim. Now King William holds it. Two and a half hides in Bonyalva, Bucklawren, and Bodigga have been taken away (*sunt ablatae*) from this manor. The canons of St. Stephen's, Launceston hold them from the Count of Mortain.

302   i, 120v (1-15) <u>Terra Regis; Coswarth</u>: King William holds a hide and three virgates in Coswarth. TRE Beorhtric Algarson held this land, and St. Petroc's had 30d. or an ox from this land by custom. Afterwards, Queen Mathilda held this land.

303   i, 120v (2-2) <u>Bishop of Exeter; Methleigh</u>: TRE and TRW the Bishop of Exeter holds a hide in Methleigh. The Count of Mortain has this manor's market, but the bishop held it TRE.

304   i, 120v (2-6) <u>Bishop of Exeter; St. Germans</u>: TRE and TRW the Church of Exeter holds a manor called St. Germans at twenty-four hides. There is a

Sunday market in this manor, but it has been reduced to nothing (*adnichilum redigitur*) by the Count of Mortain's market which is nearby.

305   i, 120v (2-12, 13, 14, 15) <u>Bishop of Exeter; Church of St. Germans</u>: A hide, which paid a cask of ale and 30d. by custom to the Church of St. Germans, has been taken away (*est ablata*) from the Church, as has an acre and a virgate of land. TRE St. Germans held this land in demesne, and Leofric bishop of Exeter held it. Now Reginald and Hamelin hold from the Count of Mortain.

306   i, 120v (4-1) <u>Church of St. Michaels; Truthwall</u>: TRE Beorhtmær held two hides in Truthwall. TRW the Church of St. Michael holds it. The Count of Mortain took away (*abstulit*) one of these hides.

307   i, 120v (4-2) <u>Church of St. Michael; St. Stephen's (by Launceston)</u>: TRW the canons of St. Stephen's hold St. Stephen's. The Count of Mortain has taken away (*abstulit*) the market, which lay there TRE.

308   i, 121r (4-21) <u>Church of St. Petroc; one hide</u>: Earl Harold unjustly (*iniuste*) took away (*abstulit*) a hide of land from St. Petroc's, concerning which King William ordered a judgment to be held (*praecepit iudicamentum teneri*), and the saint to be reseised through justice (*per iusticiam resaisiri*).

309   i, 121r (4-22) <u>Church of St. Petroc; Coswarth</u>: TRW the King holds Coswarth. TRE the Church of St. Petroc held it, and it paid an ox and seven sheep through custom to the Church.

310   i, 121r (4-22) <u>Church of St. Petroc; rubric</u>: TRE a virgate in Tregona, a half hide in Trevornick, a virgate in Trenhale, half a hide in Tolcarne (in Newquay), half a hide in Tremore, a virgate in Lancarffe and a virgate in Treninnick were held by St. Petroc's. These lands have been taken away (*sunt ablatae*) from St. Petroc's. Now the Count of Mortain holds them, and his men hold from him.

311   i, 121r (4-26) <u>Canons of St. Piran; Perranzabuloe</u>: TRE and TRW the canons of St. Piran's hold three hides in Perranzabuloe. Two lands have been taken away (*ablatae sunt*) from this manor. They paid four weeks' farm to the canons and 20s. to the dean through custom. Berner holds one of them from the Count of Mortain. The other is held by Odo, who holds it from St. Piran's; the count, however, has taken away (*abstulit*) all the livestock (*pecuniam*).

312   i, 121r (4-28) <u>Clerks of St. Neot's; St. Neot</u>: TRE and TRW the clerks of St. Neot's hold two hides in St. Neot. Count Robert has taken away (*abstulit*) all this land except for an acre, which the priests still hold. Odo holds from the count.

313   i, 121r (4-29) <u>Church of St. Constantine; half a hide</u>: TRW St. Constantine's holds half a hide of land, which was quit from all service TRE. But after Count Robert took (*accepit*) the land, it paid geld unjustly (*iniuste*) as villeins' land.

314   i, 121r (3-2) <u>Tavistock Abbey; Antony</u>: TRW Ermenald holds half a hide in Antony from Tavistock Abbey. The Abbot of Horton claims (*calumniatur*) it.

315   i, 121v (3-7) <u>Tavistock Abbey; Boyton, Illand, Trebeigh, Trewanta</u>: TRE the Count of Mortain unjustly (*iniustae*) holds four manors – Boyton, Illand,

Trebeigh, and Trewanta. The Abbot of Tavistock claims (*calumniatur*) them, because they have been taken away (*ablata sunt*) from the Church.

316 i, 123v (5, 6-6) Count of Mortain; Lancarffe: TRW Nigel holds a virgate in Lancarffe from Robert count of Mortain. TRE Alweald held it. It is from the honor of St. Petroc's.

317 i, 123v (5, 7-6) Count of Mortain; Poundstock: TRE Countess Gytha held a hide in Poundstock. Now Iovin holds it from the Count of Mortain. This land is of Lanow.

318 i, 123v (5, 8-10) Count of Mortain; "Tregrebri": TRE Eadwig held a hide in "Tregrebri." TRW Berner holds it from the Count of Mortain. This is from the possessions (*de possessione*) of St. Piran's.

319 i, 125r (5, 24-14) Count of Mortain; Treroosel: TRE Eadmær held two acres in Treroosel. Now Wimarc holds it from the Count of Mortain. This land belongs to the honor of St. Kew.

320 i, 125r (5, 25-5) Count of Mortain; Truthwall: TRE Beorhtmær held a hide in Truthwall. Now Blohin holds it from the count of Mortain. The Count took this land away (*abstulit*) from the Church of St. Michaels.

Derbyshire

321 i, 272v (1-27) Terra Regis; Bakewell: King Edward held a manor of eighteen carucates in Bakewell along with Bakewell's eight berewicks. Now King William holds this. Henry de Ferrers claims (*calumniatur*) a carucate in Haddon, one of Bakewell's berewicks.

322 i, 273r (1-35) Terra Regis; Mapperley: TRE Stapolwine held four bovates in Mapperley. Now William Peverel has charge of them through the King. There is also a half carucate of land there, which is of the soke of Spondon, a manor of Henry de Ferrers.

323 i, 273r (3-2) Burton Abbey; Appleby Magna: TRE and TRW the Abbot of Burton has a manor in Appleby Magna, which is assessed at five carucates. Of this land, Abbot Leofric leased (*prestitit*) a carucate to Countess Gode. The King now has it.

324 i, 273r (3-3) Burton Abbey; Winshill [Staffs.]: TRE and TRW the Abbot of Burton has a manor in Winshill, which is assessed at two carucates. King William put (*apposuit*) six sokemen there, who belong to Repton.

325 i, 273r (3-6) Burton Abbey; Caldwell: TRE Ælfric held two carucates in Caldwell. Now Burton Abbey holds them. King William gave (*dedit*) this manor to the monks for his spiritual benefit (*pro beneficio suo*).

326 i, 273v (4-1, 2) Earl of Chester; Markeaton: TRE Earl Siward held a manor in Markeaton assessed at nine and a half carucates. TRW Earl Hugh holds it. Kniveton, Mackworth, and Allestree are the berewicks of this manor, and they have four carucates between them. One of these carucates lies in Ednaston, Henry de Ferrers's manor.

327 i, 274v (6-27, 28, 48) Henry de Ferrers; Scropton, Sudbury, Hatton: TRE Toki held a manor in Scropton with three berewicks. They were assessed at six carucates. Now Henry de Ferrers holds it, and Geoffrey Alselin claims (*calumniatur*) it. [A "k," for *klamor*, is written in the margin, to mark this claim. Other of Henry's possessions – half a bovate and a sixth of a bovate of soke in Sudbury, six and a half bovates of soke in Hatton, and a bovate and a half of thegnland in Hatton, which all belong to Scropton – are marked with marginal crosses, probably to relate them to Geoffrey's claim.]

328 i, 275r (6-58, 59) Henry de Ferrers; Osmaston (near Ashbourne), Wyaston, Edlaston: TRE Waltheof and Æthelgeat held two carucates in Osmaston as two manors. TRW Henry holds them, and Elfin holds from him. TRE Earl Edwin held two carucates in Wyaston and Edlaston. Now Orm holds them from Henry. These last two vills are from the King's farm in Rocester [Staffs.], except for a bovate, which lies in Osmaston.

329 i, 275r (6-62) Henry de Ferrers; Rodsley: TRE Brun held twelve bovates in Rodsley as a manor. Now John holds them from Henry de Ferrers. The Abbot of Burton claims (*clamat*) the soke of this vill.

330 i, 276r (6-99) Henry de Ferrers; Radbourne: TRE Wulfsige held three carucates in Radbourne as a manor. Now Henry de Ferrers holds them. Ralph fitz Hubert claims (*calumniatur*) a third of Radbourne, and the wapentake testifies for him.

331 i, 276v (8-2) Walter d'Aincourt; Brampton, Wadshelf: TRE Wada held three and a half bovates and four acres in Brampton and Wadshelf. TRW Walter d'Aincourt holds them. Walter vouches the King to warranty (*advocat Walterus regem ad protectorem*), and Henry de Ferrers as having given him livery (*ad liberatorem*).

332 i, 277v (13-2) Gilbert of Ghent; Shipley: TRE Brun and Othenkarl held two carucates of land in Shipley as two manors. Now Gilbert of Ghent holds this land, and Mauger holds from him. The sworn men (*homines qui iuraverant*) say that this land did not belong to Ulf Fenisc TRE, but instead to two thegns who could grant or sell to whom they wished.

333 i, 278r (16-1) Roger de Bully; Breaston: TRE Ligulf and Leofwine Cild held three carucates in Breaston as a manor. Fulk, a man of Roger de Bully, now holds them. Ligulf also had a half carucate of soke, which Fulk de Lisors stole from (*interceptam super*) Gilbert of Ghent.

334 i, 278r (16-2) Roger de Bully; Risley: TRE Wulfsige and Godric each held five and a third bovates in Risley. Now Fulk holds this land from Roger de Bully. Earnwine claims (*calumniatur*) it. [There is a "k," for *klamor*, written in the margin opposite this entry.]

335 i, 278v (17-9) King's thegns; Calow: TRE Esbiorn and Hakun held a carucate in Calow as two manors. TRW two King's thegns, Stenulf and Dunning, hold it, but Dolgfinnr claims (*calumniatur*) it. [There is a "k," for *klamor*, written in the margin opposite this entry.]

336 i, 280r (B-1) Borough of Derby: From rent (*census*), tolls, forfeitures (*forisfactura*) and all customs of Derby, the King had two-thirds and the earl a third.

337 i, 280r (B-15) <u>Borough of Derby</u>: The two pennies of the King and the third penny of the earl, which come from Appletree Wapentake in Derbyshire, are in the hand or rent (*in manu vel censu*) of the sheriff, according to the testimony of the two shires of Derbyshire and Nottinghamshire.

338 i, 280r (B-16) <u>Borough of Derby</u>: Concerning Stori, Walter d'Aincourt's antecessor, they say that he was able to make himself a church on his land and in his soke without anyone's permission, and put (*mittere*) the tithe where he wished.

Devonshire

339 i, 100r (1-4) <u>Terra Regis; Exminster</u>: King Edward held a hide in Exminster; now King William holds it. Eccha the Reeve lent (*accommodavit*) a furlong of this land to a priest TRE. Now the monks of Battle hold it. William d'Eu holds another half virgate which belonged TRE to Exminster.

340 i, 100r (1-5) <u>Terra Regis; Braunton</u>: King Edward held Braunton; now King William holds it. It was assessed at one hide. One virgate has been taken away (*est ablata*) from this manor, which paid 20s. to the King's farm. Robert de Pont-Chardon holds it. Another virgate has been added to this manor, which belonged TRE to Baldwin the Sheriff's manor of Filleigh.

341 i, 100r (1-6) <u>Terra Regis; South Molton</u>: King Edward held a virgate and a half in South Molton; now King William holds it. A half virgate of land called 'Ringedone' has been added to this manor.

342 i, 100r–v (1-11) <u>Terra Regis; Axminster</u>: King Edward held Axminster; now King William holds it. Charlton, a manor of the Bishop of Coutances, owes 15d. to Axminster; 30d. are owed from Honiton (near Axminster), a manor of the Count of Mortain; 30d. are owed from Smallridge, a manor of Ralph de la Pommeraye; 30d. from Membury, a manor of William Chevre; and 30d. from Rawridge, a manor of St. Mary's Abbey, Rouen. The King has not had these pence now for many years. Furthermore, two virgates in Deneworth, which Æthelric held TRE, have been added to this manor. A virgate in Undercleave has also been attached to this manor. Eadric the Cripple held it from the King in alms. Now Edward son of Eadric holds it.

343 i, 100v (1-15) <u>Terra Regis; Diptford</u>: King Edward held three virgates in Diptford; now King William holds them. A virgate in Farleigh, which a thegn held freely TRE, was added to this manor in the time of William de Vauville.

344 i, 100v (1-18) <u>Terra Regis; Yealmpton</u>: King William holds two and a half hides in Yealmpton. King Edward held it. The clerks of Yealmpton hold a hide of this land. The King grants (*concedit*) it to them in alms.

345 i, 100v (1-22) <u>Terra Regis; Walkhampton</u>: King Edward held Walkhampton.

Now King William holds it. A virgate in Maker [Corn.] has been taken away (*est ablata*) from Walkhampton. TRE it paid £6 less 30d. to the King's farm.

346 i, 100v (1-23) <u>Terra Regis; Ermington</u>: TRE Esger held three hides in Ermington. Now King William holds them. The following customs belong to this manor: 30d. from Fardel and the customs of the hundred; similarly from the two Dinnatons, Broadaford, and Ludbrook. The Count of Mortain's men hold these lands and keep back (*retinent*) the King's customs – that is, 30d. from each vill and the customs of the hundred. This manor is in exchange (*de excambio*) for Bampton.

347 i, 100v (1-24) <u>Terra Regis; Blackawton</u>: TRE Esger held six hides in Blackawton. Now King William holds them. This manor is in exchange (*de excambio*) for Bampton.

348 i, 100v (1-25) <u>Terra Regis; Lifton</u>: TRE Queen Edith held three and a half virgates in Lifton. Now King William holds them. Two lands, Landinner [Corn.] and Trebeigh [Corn.], belonged to this manor TRE. Now the Count of Mortain holds them.

349 i, 100v (1-29) <u>Terra Regis; South Tawton</u>: TRE Countess Gytha held three hides and a virgate in South Tawton. Now King William holds them. A virgate and a half in Ash (in South Tawton), which Wulfric held as a manor TRE, has been attached to South Tawton. This land was seized (*est occupata*) into South Tawton in King William's time.

350 i, 100v (1-32) <u>Terra Regis; Witheridge</u>: TRE Countess Gytha held a virgate in Witheridge. Now King William holds it. Three furlongs, the land of two thegns,have been added to this manor. They held them freely TRE.

351 i, 101r (1-40) <u>Terra Regis; Tawstock</u>: TRE Earl Harold held five hides in Tawstock. Now King William holds them. A virgate and a half in Langley, which was attached to this manor in the time of King Edward, has been taken away (*est ablata*). This land lies unjustly (*iniuste*) in High Bickington.

352 i, 101r (1-41) <u>Terra Regis; Molland (in West Anstey)</u>: TRE Earl Harold held four hides and a furlong in Molland. Now King William holds them. A half hide in Blackpool, which Æthelweard held as a manor TRE, has been joined to Molland. "Nimete" has been unjustly (*iniuste*) attached to this manor. The third penny of North Molton, Bampton, and Braunton Hundreds along with the third animal on the moorland pasture belong to Molland.

353 i, 101r (1-46) <u>Terra Regis; Colaton Raleigh</u>: TRE Earl Harold held three hides in Colaton Raleigh. Now King William holds them. A half virgate, which a thegn held freely TRE, has been added to this manor.

354 i, 101r (1-45) <u>Terra Regis; Moretonhampstead</u>: King William holds Moretonhampstead. The third penny of Teignbridge Hundred belongs to this manor.

355 i, 101r (1-49) <u>Terra Regis; King's Nympton</u>: TRE Earl Harold held three hides in King's Nympton. Now King William holds them. A half virgate has been added to this manor, which a thegn held freely TRE.

356 i, 101r (1-50) <u>Terra Regis; Werrington [Corn.]</u>: TRE Countess Gytha held six and a half hides in Werrington. Now King William holds them. The Count of Mortain holds half a hide of this land, which belonged there TRE.

357   i, 101r (1-55) <u>Terra Regis; Langford (in Ugborough)</u>: TRE Earl Leofwine held three hides in Langford. Now King William holds them. The borough of Totnes paid 20s. to the King's farm here. The King granted (*concessit*) these shillings to Iudhael.

358   i, 101r (1-60) <u>Terra Regis; Bideford</u>: TRE Beorhtric Algarson held three hides in Bideford, and later Queen Mathilda held them. Now King William holds this land. A fishery was attached to this manor TRE.

359   i, 101v (1-67) <u>Terra Regis; High Bickington</u>: TRE Beorhtric Algarson held a hide and two and a half virgates in High Bickington. Later Queen Mathilda held them. Now King William holds this land. Langley has been added to this manor and pays £4 in High Bickington. It belonged to Tawstock TRE.

360   i, 101v (2-1) <u>Bishop of Exeter; Crediton</u>: TRW the Bishop of Exeter holds fifteen hides in Crediton. He also holds three hides in Newton St. Cyres with this manor. Bishop Osbern showed (*ostendit*) his charters (*cartas*) for this manor, which testify that the Church of St. Peter had been seised (*fuisse saisitam*) of it before King Edward reigned. In the time of King William, moreover, the bishop established (*diratiocinavit*) that this land was his before the King's barons (*coram baronibus regis*). Dunna holds it.

361   i, 101v (2-9, 10) <u>Bishop of Exeter; Haxton, Benton</u>: The bishop holds two virgates in Haxton, which Ordwulf held TRE, and a virgate in Benton, which Eadnoth held freely. Both have common (*communis*) pasture with Bratton Fleming. Benton has been added to Haxton. The Count of Mortain gave (*dedit*) these two manors to the bishop in exchange (*pro excambio*) for a castle in Cornwall.

362   i, 102r (3-2) <u>Bishop of Coutances; Exeter</u>: Drogo holds six houses in Exeter from the Bishop of Coutances. Four of them were quit TRE. The other two paid 16d. in customs. Drogo keeps back (*retinet*) these pence.

363   i, 102r (3-8) <u>Bishop of Coutances; Bovey Tracey</u>: TRE Eadric held Bovey Tracy; now the bishop holds it. The land of fifteen thegns has been added to this manor in Little Bovey, Warmhill, Scobitor, "Brungarstone," Elsford, Woolleigh (in Bovey Tracey), Hawkmoor, Hatherleigh (in Bovey Tracey), and Pullabrook. Of this land, the fifteen thegns have two hides and half a virgate. They pay £4 30d. in rent (*de censu*) to Bovey Tracey.

364   i, 102r (3-11) <u>Bishop of Coutances; Horton</u>: TRE Oswulf held a virgate in Horton. It has been joined with the Bishop of Coutances's manor of Horwood, but it did not belong there TRE. Now Drogo holds it from the bishop.

365   i, 102r (3-19) <u>Bishop of Coutances; Roborough</u>: TRE Wulfgifu held a hide and a half in Roborough. Now Drogo holds it from the Bishop of Coutances. A virgate in Barlington, which Alfred held freely TRE, has been added to Roborough.

366   i, 102v (3-26) <u>Bishop of Coutances; West Down</u>: TRE Algar held half a hide

in West Down; now Drogo holds it from the Bishop of Coutances. The lands of three thegns, which were held freely TRE and which paid geld for half a hide, have been added to this manor.

367 i, 102v (3-30) <u>Bishop of Coutances; High Bray</u>: TRE Alwine held a virgate and a half in High Bray; now the Bishop of Coutances holds it and Drogo holds from him. A virgate in Whitefield (in High Bray) has been added to this manor. Sæwine held it as a manor TRE.

368 i, 102v (3-32) <u>Bishop of Coutances, virgate of land</u>: TRE Beorhtric held a virgate of land, which before this time was in the King's manor of Braunton. In the time of King William, William de Vauville put it back (*remisit*) in Braunton. The Bishop of Coutances claims (*calumniatur*) this land, but the thegns do not know how Beorhtric had it.

369 i, 103r (3-76) <u>Bishop of Coutances; "Celvertesberie"</u>: A virgate in Coombe (in Templeton), which Weland held TRE, has been added to the manor of "Celvertesberie." Now the Bishop of Coutances holds this land, and Drogo holds from him.

370 i, 103r (3-80) <u>Bishop of Coutances; Thelbridge</u>: TRE half a hide and half a virgate in Thelbridge was held by Wulfgifu. Now the Bishop of Coutances holds it, and Drogo holds from him. A half virgate in Middlewick has been added to this manor. Beorhtmær held this half virgate as a manor TRE.

371 i, 103r (3-92) <u>Bishop of Coutances; Tapeley</u>: TRE Wulfgifu held a hide in Tapeley. Now Osbern holds it from the bishop. A virgate has been taken away (*ablata est*) from this manor, which was there TRE. Roger holds it from the bishop.

372 i, 103v (5-2) <u>Tavistock Abbey; Milton Abbot</u>: TRE and TRW Tavistock Abbey holds half a hide in Milton Abbot. The Abbot holds two lands with this manor – Leigh (in Milton Abbot) and Liddaton – which were held TRE by two thegns as two manors. These lands paid geld for half a hide.

373 i, 103v (5-8) <u>Tavistock Abbey; Burrington (near Chulmleigh)</u>: TRE and TRW Tavistock Abbey holds three hides in Burrington. Two lands – which two thegns held as two manors and which were gelded for half a hide – have been added to this manor. William Chevre and Geoffrey now hold them from the abbot.

374 i, 103v (5-15) <u>Tavistock Abbey; Exeter</u>: TRW the Abbot of Tavistock has a house in Exeter in mortgage (*in vadimonium*) from a burgess. It used to pay 8d. in customs to the King.

375 i, 104r (7-4) <u>Horton Abbey; Beer</u>: TRE and TRW the Abbey of Horton holds half a hide in Beer. A furlong of land and four salthouses have been taken away (*ablatae*) from this manor. Drogo holds them from the Count of Mortain.

376 i, 104r (10-2) <u>St. Mary's Abbey, Rouen; Rawridge</u>: TRE Wulfgifu held three hides in Rawridge. King William gave (*dedit*) them to the Church of St. Mary, Rouen.

377 Exon (for 13a-2) <u>King's Clerks; Swimbridge</u>: TRW Sæwine the Priest holds

three virgates in Swimbridge from the King. Beorhtfrith [his uncle] held it TRE. [Exon fo. 194b: Queen Mathilda gave (*dedit*) him this land in alms.]

378 i, 104v (15-12) <u>Count of Mortain; Buckland Brewer</u>: TRW Ansgar the Breton holds three hides less half a virgate in Buckland Brewer from the Count of Mortain. TRE Eadmær Atre held them. A half virgate in Galsworthy has been added to this manor. Eadwig held it as a manor TRE.

379 i, 104v (15-30) <u>Count of Mortain; Densham</u>: [Following the entry for Densham, the manuscript notes that: "The Count of Mortain holds these aforementioned seventeen lands with the land of Eadmær Atre, which have been delivered (*deliberata est*) to him. But the aforementioned thegns held them freely TRE."]

380 i, 105r (15-37) <u>Count of Mortain; Bolberry</u>: TRE Eadmær held a hide in Bolberry. Now Hugh holds it from the Count of Mortain. A virgate in Buckland (in Thurlestone), which Eadgifu held freely TRE, has been added to this manor.

381 i, 105r (15-40) <u>Count of Mortain; Bratton Fleming</u>: TRW Erchenbald holds a hide in Bratton Fleming from the Count of Mortain. Ordwulf held it TRE. Three lands, which were held freely TRE by three thegns as three manors, have been joined to this manor. Two of these thegns were Ordwulf's men; the third was not. They paid geld for three virgates.

382 i, 105r (15-46, 53) <u>Count of Mortain; Bere Ferrers, "Wederige"</u>: [The following rubric appears after the entry for Bere Ferrers: "The count holds the seven below-written lands with the land of Ordwulf." After the entry for "Wederige," another rubric appears, which states: "Up to this point, these are added lands."]

383 Exon (for 15-53) <u>Count of Mortain; "Wederige"</u>: TRW Reginald holds "Wederige" from the Count of Mortain. Ottar held it TRE. [Exon fo. 222b: The above Ottar held this land in parage. Now it has been added to Ordwulf's land.]

384 i, 105r (15-57) <u>Count of Mortain; Donningstone</u>: TRW Mauger de Carteret holds half a hide in Donningstone from the Count of Mortain. TRE Dunning held it. Three virgates in "Alwinestone," which Alwine held TRE, have been added to this manor.

385 i, 105v (15-67) <u>Count of Mortain; Fardel</u>: TRW Reginald holds a hide in Fardel from the Count of Mortain. TRE Dunna held it. Thirty pence in customs are owed from this manor to the King's manor of Ermington, as well as the customs for the pleas (*consuetudine placitorum*), so the King's men say.

386 i, 105v (15-79) <u>Count of Mortain; Lipson</u>: TRW Reginald holds half a hide in Lipson from the Count of Mortain. TRE Godwine held it freely and in parage. This has been added to Algar's lands.

387 i, 105v (16-7) <u>Baldwin the Sheriff; Bridestowe</u>: TRW Ralph de la Pommeraye holds half a hide and half a furlong in Bridestowe from Baldwin the Sheriff. Eadmær held it TRE. With this manor Baldwin holds the land of six thegns, who did not belong there in the time of King Edward – Sæwine,

Dodda, Dodda, Godwine, Godwine, and Abbot Sihtric. This land was assessed at half a hide and a furlong and a half.

388 i, 106r (16-33) <u>Baldwin the Sheriff; Parkham</u>: TRW Richard holds two hides in Parkham from Baldwin the Sheriff. TRE Algar held them. A virgate in Sedborough, which Beorhtmær held, was attached to this manor TRE.

389 i, 107r (16-74) <u>Baldwin the Sheriff; Blakewell</u>: TRW Robert de Pont-Chardon holds a virgate in Blakewell from Baldwin the Sheriff. This land, so the men of the hundred say, is from the King's manor of Braunton.

390 i, 107r (16-80) <u>Baldwin the Sheriff; Filleigh</u>: TRW Baldwin the Sheriff holds a hide in Filleigh. Osfrith held it TRE. A virgate of land called Lobb has been taken from this manor and added to the King's manor of Braunton.

391 i, 107r (16-83) <u>Baldwin the Sheriff; Lincombe</u>: TRW Robert holds two hides in Lincombe from Baldwin the Sheriff. TRE Beorhtmær held them. A virgate of land called Yarde (in Ilfracombe) was added to this manor. Godric held it TRE.

392 i, 107r (16-92) <u>Baldwin the Sheriff; West Clyst</u>: TRW the canons of St. Mary's hold two and a half virgates in West Clyst from Baldwin the Sheriff. Wulfgifu held them TRE. A furlong has been taken away (*est ablata*) from this manor, which belonged there TRE. It has been added to Odo's manor of Poltimore.

393 i, 107r (16-94) <u>Baldwin the Sheriff; Whimple</u>: TRW Baldwin the Sheriff's wife holds two hides and a virgate in Whimple. TRE Almær held them. A half hide called Larkbeare belonged to this manor TRE, which Almær held. Now Alvred Brito holds it.

394 i, 108r (16-144) <u>Baldwin the Sheriff; Creacombe (near Witheridge)</u>: TRW Ansgar holds three furlongs less the fourth part of a furlong in Creacombe from Baldwin the Sheriff. TRE Siward held them. A furlong and a quarter in Creacombe, which Leofgar held freely and in parage TRE, has been added to this manor.

395 i, 108v (17-13) <u>Iudhael of Totnes; Marytavy</u>: TRW Nigel holds a virgate in Marytavy from Iudhael of Totnes. TRE Beorhtwig held it. A virgate of land, the land of three thegns – Ælfric, Alwine, and Ealdwulf – has been added to this manor. These men held this land as three manors TRE and could go where they wished.

396 i, 108v (17-16) <u>Iudhael of Totnes; Tetcott</u>: TRW Iudhael of Totnes holds half a hide in Tetcott. TRE Ealdræd held it. A furlong of land, which Alwine held freely and in parage TRE, has been added to this manor.

397 i, 110r (17-92) <u>Iudhael of Totnes; Baccamoor</u>: TRW Ralph holds half a hide in Baccamoor from Iudhael of Totnes. TRE Elous held it. Another Baccamoor has been added to this manor. Sigeric held it TRE. These two lands together pay geld for half a hide.

398 i, 110r (17-105) <u>Iudhael of Totnes; Woodford</u>: TRW Ralph holds half a hide in Woodford from Iudhael of Totnes. TRE Almær held it. A half hide in another Woodford has been added to this land. Ælfric held it TRE.

399 i, 110r (19-6) <u>William Chevre; Eastleigh</u>: TRW Ansketil holds half a hide in Eastleigh from William Chevre. Alweard held it TRE. A half virgate of land has been added to this manor. It has been concealed (*celata est*), and because of this, the King has not had geld from it.

400 i, 110v (19-17, 18) <u>William Chevre; Lyn, Badgworthy</u>: TRW William Chevre holds three virgates in Lyn. Algar held them TRE. A virgate in Badgworthy has been added to Lyn, which Fulcold holds from William.

401 i, 110v (19-35) <u>William Chevre; Cruwys Morchard</u>: TRW William Chevre holds a hide in Cruwys Morchard. Almær held it TRE. He took it away (*abstulit*) from Æthelweard Tokison after King William came to England. William holds this land with Æthelweard's land.

402 i, 110v (19-37) <u>William Chevre; Oakford</u>: TRW William Chevre holds a hide in Oakford. Beorhtmær held it TRE. A virgate in Mildon, which Edith held TRE, has been added to this manor.

403 i, 110v (19-40) <u>William Chevre; Bradford (in Witheridge)</u>: TRW Beatrice, William Chevre's sister, holds a virgate in Bradford from William. TRE Almær held it. A half virgate in Thorne, which Ælfric held freely and in parage TRE, has been added to this manor.

404 i, 111r (20-10) <u>William de Falaise; Cockington</u>: TRW William de Falaise holds three hides in Cockington. Alric held them TRE. Of this land, Alric held a virgate in "Deptone" (lost in Widecombe in the Moor). This land has been added to Cockington, and William holds it as a manor.

405 i, 111r (21-9, 10, 11) <u>William de Poilley; Blagrove, Pedley, "Assecote"</u>: TRW William de Poilley holds a virgate in Blagrove, and Ralph holds from him. Hache held it TRE. Hache also held two and a half furlongs in Pedley. TRE Almær held half a furlong in "Assecote." Now Hildwine holds it from William. These two lands – Pedley and "Assecote" – have been joined to Blagrove.

406 i, 111v (22-1) <u>William d'Eu; Powderham</u>: TRW William d'Eu holds half a hide in Powderham from the King, and Ranulf holds from him. TRE Thurs held it. In this manor there is half a virgate of land which lay in Exminster TRE.

407 i, 111v (23-5) <u>Walter de Douai; Bampton</u>: TRW Walter de Douai holds Bampton. King Edward held it. This land never paid geld. To this manor is attached a hide of land which five thegns held in parage as five manors TRE. Now Rædmær, Rædmær, and Gerard hold it from Walter. William de Mohun unjustly (*iniuste*) took (*accepit*) half a furlong of this hide against Walter.

408 i, 111v (23-6) <u>Walter de Douai; Dipford</u>: TRW Wulfric holds half a hide in Dipford from Walter de Douai. TRE two thegns held it in parage as two manors. Walter holds this manor from the Queen. Concerning this, he vouches the King (*inde regem advocat*).

409 i, 112r (23-20) <u>Walter de Douai; Greenway</u>: TRW Ludo holds a hide in Greenway from Walter de Douai. TRE Æthelsige held it. A hide in

Shapcombe, which lay in Beorhtric's land Broadhembury TRE, has been added to this manor.

410 i, 112r (23-23) Walter de Douai; Coleridge (in Stokenham): TRW Alric holds a virgate in Coleridge from Walter de Douai. TRE Bicca held it and could go where he wished with the land. This manor has been added to Esger's lands.

411 i, 112r (23-24) Walter de Douai; Widdicombe: TRW Alric holds half a hide in Widdicombe from Walter de Douai. TRE Eadric held it and could go where he wished. This land has been added to Esger's land.

412 i, 112r (23-27) Walter de Douai; Exeter: TRW Walter de Douai has a house in mortgage (*in vadimonium*) from a burgess. Its customs have been kept back (*est retenta*).

413 i, 112r (24-5) Walter de Claville; Washford Pyne: TRW Walter holds a hide less a furlong in Washford Pyne from Walter de Claville. Two thegns held it TRE. A furlong has been added to this manor.

414 i, 112r (24-8) Walter de Claville; Craze Lowman: TRW Walter de Claville holds three virgates in Craze Lowman. TRE Ælfrun held it. A virgate in Kidwell, which Ælfrun held freely TRE, has been added to this manor.

415 i, 112r (24-18) Walter de Claville; Buckland-tout-Saints: TRW Walter de Claville holds half a virgate in Buckland-tout-Saints. TRE Wudumann held it. This land has been added to Beorhtric Algarson's lands. It was free in the time of King Edward.

416 i, 112v (24-22) Walter de Claville; unidentified land: TRW Walter de Claville holds a virgate of land, which belongs to the King's manor of Iddesleigh. Ælfgifu the Thief held it TRE, and she could not separate it from the King's manor.

417 i, 112v (25-3) Goscelm; Newton Tracey: TRW Walter holds half a hide in Newton Tracey from Goscelm. Ælweard held it TRE. Kolsveinn, a man of the Bishop of Coutances, has taken away (*aufert*) the common (*communem*) pasture, which was attached to this manor in the time of King Edward, and for five years afterwards in the time of King William.

418 i, 112v (25-20) Goscelm; Ash Thomas: TRW Godfrey holds half a hide in Ash Thomas from Goscelm. TRE Ælfgifu, a free woman, held it. This land has been added to Beorhtric's lands.

419 i, 113r (25-25) Goscelm; Buckland-tout-Saints: TRW Baldwin holds half a hide in Buckland-tout-Saints from Goscelm. TRE Ælfric held it, and he was a free man. This land has been added to Beorhtric's lands.

420 i, 113r (27-1) Roger de Bully; Sampford Peverell: TRW Roger de Bully holds three and a half hides in Sampford Peverell from the King. Beorhtric held it TRE. The Queen gave (*dedit*) this land to Roger with his wife.

421 i, 113r (28-16) Robert d'Aumale; Widey: TRW Oswulf holds half a hide in Widey from Robert d'Aumale. TRE Wadilo held it. A half hide in Whitleigh, which Wadilo held freely and in parage TRE, has been added to this manor.

422 i, 113v (30-4) <u>Richard fitz Thurold; Exeter</u>: TRW Richard has a house in Exeter from which he keeps back (*retinet*) the customs of the King, that is 8d.

423 i, 114r (34-2) <u>Ralph de la Pommeraye; Dunsdon</u>: TRW Ralph de la Pommeraye holds three virgates in Dunsdon. Tovi held them TRE. A virgate has been taken away (*ablata est*). The Count of Mortain holds it.

424 i, 114r (34-5) <u>Ralph de la Pommeraye; Ash (in Bradworthy)</u>: TRW Ralph de la Pommeraye holds a virgate in Ash. Leodmær held it TRE and was a free man. Ralph annexed (*invasit*) it, so the French and English testify.

425 i, 114r (34-10) <u>Ralph de la Pommeraye; Ashcombe</u>: TRW Ralph de la Pommeraye holds Ashcombe. TRE Ælfric held it. Three lands have been added to Ashcombe, which three thegns held freely and in parage TRE as three manors. These four lands paid geld for two hides.

426 i, 114r (34-14) <u>Ralph de la Pommeraye; Brendon</u>: TRW Ralph de la Pommeraye holds a hide in Brendon. TRE Æthelweard held it. A furlong in Lank Combe has been added to this manor. Edwin held it TRE.

427 i, 114v (34-34) <u>Ralph de la Pommeraye; "Heppastebe"</u>: TRW Ralph holds a virgate in "Heppastebe." Wulfweard held it TRE. Ralph was seised (*saisiuit*) of this land with another manor, Aunk.

428 i, 114v (34-43) <u>Ralph de la Pommeraye; Chevithorne</u>: TRW Beatrice holds a virgate in Chevithorne from Ralph de la Pommeraye. TRE Almær held it. A virgate and a furlong in Uplowman have been added to this manor. Alwine held them TRE. Now the same Alwine holds this land from Ralph.

429 i, 114v (34-45) <u>Ralph de la Pommeraye; Ivedon</u>: TRW Ralph de la Pommeraye holds a virgate in Ivedon. Sæmær held it TRE. Ralph has added this land to Awliscombe.

430 i, 114v (34-46) <u>Ralph de la Pommeraye; Dunstone (in Widecombe in the Moor)</u>: TRW Ralph holds half a virgate in Dunstone from Ralph de la Pommeraye. TRE Edwin held it. A virgate in Blackslade, which Edwin held TRE, has been added to this manor.

431 i, 114v (34-49) <u>Ralph de la Pommeraye; Afton</u>: TRW Ralph de la Pommeraye holds three virgates in Afton. TRE Æthelsige held it. A virgate of land, which a woman held freely and in parage TRE, has been added to this manor.

432 i, 114v (34-52, 53, 54) <u>Ralph de la Pommeraye; Weycroft, Bruckland, Radish</u>: Viking held a hide in Weycroft TRE; now Roger holds it from Ralph de la Pommeraye. TRE Æthelheard held a hide in Bruckland. TRW Geoffrey holds it from Ralph. TRE two thegns held half a hide in Radish. TRW Geoffrey holds it from Ralph de la Pommeraye. These three manors have been given (*data fuerunt*) to Ralph in exchange (*in excambio*) for a manor of one virgate.

433 i, 114v (34-55) <u>Ralph de la Pommeraye; Keynedon</u>: TRE Eadwig held half a hide in Keynedon. Now Roger holds it from Ralph de la Pommeraye. Pool has been added to this manor, which Eadwig held freely and in parage TRE.

434 i, 114v (34-57) <u>Ralph de la Pommeraye; half a virgate</u>: TRE Ælfric held half a virgate of land in parage. TRW Roger holds it from Ralph de la Pommeraye. It has been added to Weycroft.

435 i, 114v (34-58) <u>Ralph de la Pommeraye; Exeter</u>: TRW Ralph holds six houses in Exeter, from which he has kept back (*retinuit*) the King's customs, that is 3s. 4d.

436 i, 114v (35-4) <u>Ruald Adobed; Panson</u>: TRE Leofgar held a virgate in Panson. TRW Alvred holds it from Ruald Adobed. Ruald holds this land in exchange (*pro excambio*) for Bruckland and Radish (in Southleigh).

437 i, 115r (35-10) <u>Ruald Adobed; Weare Giffard</u>: TRE Ordwulf held a hide in Weare Giffard. TRW Ruald Adobed holds it. The Count of Mortain holds half a virgate of this manor.

438 i, 115v (36-25) <u>Theobald fitz Berner; Rifton</u>: TRE Æthelmær held half a hide in Rifton. TRW Aubrey holds it from Theobald fitz Berner. A virgate has been added to this manor, which a thegn held freely TRE.

439 i, 115v (36-25) <u>Theobald fitz Berner; Rifton</u>: TRE Æthelmær held half a hide in Rifton. Now Aubrey holds it from Theobald fitz Berner. A virgate, which a thegn held freely TRE, has been added to this manor.

440 i, 115v (36-26) <u>Theobald fitz Berner; Widworthy</u>: TRE Æthelmær held a hide in Widworthy. Now Oliver holds it from Theobald fitz Berner. A half hide in Wilmington has been added to this manor. Alweard held it TRE.

441 i, 115v (38-1) <u>Alvred d'Epaignes; Arlington</u>: TRE Alwig held a hide in Arlington. Now Alvred d'Epaignes holds it. A virgate in Twitchen (in Arlington) has been added to this manor, which Beorhtweald held freely TRE.

442 i, 116r (39-10) <u>Alvred Brito; Larkbeare</u>: TRE Ulf held half a hide in Larkbeare. Now Alvred Brito holds it. A half hide, which belongs to Whimple, Baldwin's manor, has been added to this manor.

443 i, 116r (39-14) <u>Alvred Brito; Battisborough</u>: TRE Almær held a hide in Battisborough. Now Alvred Brito holds it. A half hide in Creacombe (in Newton Ferrers), which Almær held in parage as a manor TRE, has been added to this manor.

444 i, 116r (39-16) <u>Alvred Brito; Moreleigh</u>: TRE Ælfric held half a hide in Moreleigh. TRW William holds it from Alvred Brito. This land has been added to the manor of Grimpstonleigh.

445 i, 116r (40-4) <u>Ansgar; Cheldon</u>: TRE Mahthild held a virgate and a half in Cheldon. Now Ansgar of Montacute holds it. A half virgate and half a furlong have been added to this manor, which Beorhtmær held TRE as a manor.

446 i, 116r (40-6) <u>Ansgar; Sutton (in Halberton)</u>: TRE Godric held half a hide in Sutton. TRW Ansgar of Montacute holds it. This land has been unjustly (*iniuste*) added to the land of Beorhtric.

447 i, 116r (40-7) <u>Ansgar; Dolton</u>: TRE Eadric held two virgates in Dolton and could go where he wished. TRW Ansgar of Montacute holds them. This land has been unjustly (*iniuste*) added to Beorhtric's land.

448 i, 116v (42-16) <u>Odo fitz Gamelin; Broadhembury</u>: TRW Odo fitz Gamelin holds four hides in Broadhembury. TRE Beorhtric held them. A hide in Shapcombe was attached to this manor TRE. Ludo holds it unjustly (*iniuste*) with Walter's land.

449 i, 116v (42-21) <u>Odo fitz Gamelin; West Worlington</u>: TRE Ælfric held a furlong in West Worlington. Now Alwig holds it from Odo fitz Gamelin. The land of nine thegns has been added to this manor, which they held freely and in parage TRE. It paid geld for three virgates. Another two virgates have also been joined to this manor. Two thegns held them as two manors in parage TRE.

450 i, 116v–7r (43-3) <u>Osbern de Sacey; Shilstone</u>: TRW Osbern de Sacey holds a virgate in Shilstone. TRE Eadric held it. A virgate of land was attached to this manor TRE. No one holds it.

451 i, 117r (43-6) <u>Osbern de Sacey; Exeter</u>: TRW Osbern de Sacey has a house in Exeter, from which he keeps back (*detinet*) the King's customs, that is, 8d.

452 i, 117r (44-1, 2) <u>Hervey d'Helléan; Ashton, Hackworthy</u>: TRW the wife of Hervey d'Helléan holds a hide and two furlongs in Ashton from the King. TRE Almær held it. Two virgates and half a furlong have been added to this manor. TRE two thegns held them as two manors in parage. Hervey's wife has these three lands as one manor. She also holds a virgate in Hackworthy, which Eadric held TRE. She holds these lands in exchange for (*pro excambio*) Chilton.

453 Exon (for 48-12) <u>Nicholas the Balistarius; Northleigh</u>: TRE Sumarlithr held a virgate in Northleigh. Now Nicholas the Balistarius holds it. [Exon fo. 473a adds: This manor is from Nicholas's exchanges (*de escangiis Nicholai*).]

454 i, 117v (51-2, 3) <u>King's officials; Taw Green, Crooke Burnell</u>: TRE Godric held a virgate of land in Taw Green and Æthelweard held three virgates in Crooke Burnell. Now William the Usher holds this land. These two manors are from William's exchange (*excambio*) of land.

455 i, 117v (51-4, 5, 6, 7, 8, 9, 10) <u>King's officials; a virgate of land, Cadeleigh, Raddon (in Thorverton), Blackborough, Bolham (in Tiverton), Ilsham, Sutton (in Widworthy)</u>: TRE two thegns held a hide in Cadeleigh freely and in parage. Edward held two and a half virgates in Raddon; Leofwine held a hide and a virgate in Blackborough; Beorhtric held three virgates in Bolham; Bera held a hide in Ilsham; and Wulfwine held a hide in Sutton. Now William the Usher holds all of this land. It is from William's exchanges (*de excambiis Willelmi*).

456 i, 118r (52-33) <u>King's thegns; Sedborough</u>: TRE Beorhtmær held a virgate in Sedborough. Now Ansgot holds it. TRE this Sedborough belonged to Parkham, Baldwin the Sheriff's manor.

457 i, 118r (52-34) <u>King's thegns; Newton St. Cyres</u>: TRW Dunna holds three hides in Newton St. Cyres. TRE the same Dunna held this land from King Edward, and he now says that he holds it from King William.

Dorset

458 i, 75r (1-8) <u>Terra Regis; Puddletown</u>: TRE Earl Harold held Puddletown. Now it is the King's. The third penny of the whole shire of Dorset is attached to this manor.

459 i, 75v (1-13) <u>Terra Regis; Loders</u>: TRE Earl Harold held Loders, and it paid geld for eighteen hides. Now King William holds it. There are two hides of thegnland in this manor which do not belong there. Two thegns held them TRE.

460 Exon (for 1-20) <u>Terra Regis; Witchampton</u>: TRE two thegns held four and two-thirds hides in Witchampton. Now the King holds them. Azelin used to hold it from the Queen. He never paid geld on the two-thirds hide [fo. 30a].

461 i, 75v (1-24) <u>Terra Regis; Tarrant</u>: TRE Ælfric held three and a half hides in Tarrant. Afterwards, Hugh fitz Grip held them from Queen Mathilda. Now King William holds. A virgate of land belongs to this manor, which Ælfric had in mortgage (*in vadimonio*) for half a mark of gold. It has not yet been redeemed (*necdum est redempta*).

462 i, 75v (1-30) <u>Terra Regis; Melcombe Horsey</u>: TRE Earl Harold unjustly took away (*iniuste abstulit*) ten hides in Melcombe Horsey from Shaftesbury Abbey. Now King William holds this land. Furthermore, TRE twelve acres of meadow, which belong to this manor, were leased (*praestitae fuerunt*) to Wulfgar White. Now William Bellett holds them. Countess Gode added three and a half virgates to this manor, which were held by three free thegns TRE. These virgates are in Buckland Hundred.

463 i, 77r (2-6) <u>Bishop of Salisbury; Sherborne</u>: TRE Queen Edith held forty-three hides in Sherborne, and before her Bishop Ælfweald held them. Now the Bishop of Salisbury holds this land.

464 i, 77r (3-1) <u>Sherborne Abbey; Sherborne</u>: TRW the monks of the Bishop of Salisbury hold nine and a half carucates of land in Sherborne. In addition to this land, Sinod holds a hide from the bishop in the same vill. Alweard held it from King Edward TRE, but it had previously belonged to the bishopric of Ramsbury.

465 i, 77r (3-6) <u>Sherborne Abbey; Stalbridge</u>: The Bishop of Salisbury held and holds twenty hides in Stalbridge. TRW Manasseh holds three virgates of this land, which William Rufus, the King's son, took away (*tulit*) from Sherborne without the consent (*sine consensu*) of the Bishop and monks.

466 i, 77r (3-14, 15, 16, 17, 18) <u>Sherborne Abbey; "Cerne," Bardolfeston, Athelhampton, Bowood, Buckham, Wellwood</u>: TRW the following land is held by the Bishop of Salisbury in exchange (*pro excambio*) for Shipley: one and a half hides and ten acres in "Cerne"; four hides in Bardolfeston; four hides in Athelhampton; six hides in Bowood; three hides in Buckham; and one hide in Wellwood.

467 i, 77v (9-1) <u>New Minster, Winchester; Piddletrenthide</u>: TRE Almær and Æthelfrith held thirty hides in Piddletrenthide as two manors from King

Edward. They could not go to whichever lord they wished with this land. Later Roger Arundel held this land from King William. Now New Minster holds it.

468 i, 77v (10-1) <u>Cranborne Abbey; Gillingham</u>: In the time of King William Hugh fitz Grip took (*accepit*) Gillingham from the King's farm and gave (*dedit*) it to Cranborne Abbey.

469 Exon (for Do 11-5) <u>Cerne Abbey; Affpuddle</u>: Cerne Abbey held and holds nine hides in Affpuddle as a manor, and five and a half hides in Bloxworth. When the abbot acquired (*recepit*) them they were valued at 100s. more than they now pay, because the land has been devastated on account of Hugh fitz Grip (*pro Hugone filio Grip fuerunt depredati*).

470 i, 78v (13-1) <u>Abbotsbury Abbey; Abbotsbury</u>: Abbotsbury Abbey held and holds twenty-one hides in Abbotsbury. TRW Hugh fitz Grip unjustly took and kept back (*accepit iniuste et retinuit*) one of these hides, which was for the victualing of the monks TRE. His wife still keeps it back by force (*vi detinet*).

471 i, 78v (13-4) <u>Abbotsbury Abbey; Portisham</u>: Abbotsbury Abbey held and holds twelve hides in Portisham. TRW Hugh fitz Grip unjustly took (*iniuste accepit*) a virgate of this land, and his wife still holds it by force (*vi*). TRE it was for the victualing of the monks.

472 i, 78v (17-1) <u>St. Stephen's, Caen; Frampton</u>: TRW Countess Gytha held twenty-five and a half hides in Frampton. TRW St. Stephen's Abbey, Caen holds them. Two hides belong to this manor, which were given (*dederunt*) to St. Stephen's by Queen Mathilda.

473 i, 78v (19-10) <u>Shaftesbury Abbey; Kingston (in Corfe Castle)</u>: Shaftesbury Abbey held and holds sixteen hides in Kingston. King William holds one of these hides, upon which he built Wareham Castle. For this hide he gave (*dedit*) Shaftesbury the church of Gillingham with its dependencies. William de Braose also has a virgate of this manor. Shaftesbury held it TRE.

474 i, 78v (19-14) <u>Shaftesbury Abbey; Cheselbourne</u>: TRE Earl Harold had taken away (*abstulerat*) both Cheselbourne and Stour from Shaftesbury Abbey. King William, however reseised (*fecit resaisiri*) them, because a writ with the seal of King Edward has been found (*inventus est brevis cum sigillo Regis Edwardi*) in the Church itself, which ordered that these lands be restored to the Church (*praecipiens ut aecclesiae restituerentur*) along with Melcombe Horsey, which the King still holds. Earl Harold also took Piddle away (*abstulit*) from Shaftesbury Abbey. Robert count of Mortain holds it.

475 i, 79r (23-1) <u>St. Mary's, Montivilliers; Waddon</u>: Hugh fitz Grip gave (*dedit*) six hides in Waddon to St. Mary's, Montivilliers. Three thegns held them TRE. TRE Abbotsbury Abbey had six acres of crops from this land and three churchscots by custom, but Hugh never gave (*dedit*) them.

476 i, 79v (26-40) <u>Count of Mortain; Witchampton</u>: TRE a thegn held two hides in Witchampton. Now Hubert holds them from the Count of Mortain. He has never given (*dedit*) geld on one and a third virgates there.

477 i, 80r (27-2) <u>Earl of Chester; Ilsington</u>: TRW William holds two hides in

Ilsington from Earl Hugh. Eadnoth the Staller held them TRE, through (*per*) Earl Harold, who took them away (*abstulit*) from a clerk.

478 i, 80r (27-9) <u>Earl of Chester; South Perrott</u>: TRW Hugh earl of Chester holds five hides of land in South Perrott, and William holds from him. TRE Eadnoth the Staller bought (*emit*) it from Ælfweald bishop of Sherborne for his lifetime (*in vita sua*), with the following agreement: that after his death the land should be restored (*tali conventione ut post eius mortem restitueretur*) to Sherborne.

479 i, 80r (27-10) <u>Earl of Chester; Catsley</u>: TRW Hugh earl of Chester holds a hide in Catsley, and William holds from him. TRE Eadnoth the Staller bought (*emit*) it from Ælfweald bishop of Sherborne for his lifetime, with the agreement that after his death the land should return to Sherborne (*ea conventione ut post eius mortem ad aecclesiam rediret*). There is also a virgate of land in this manor on which the geld has been concealed (*celatus est geldum*) in the time of King William.

480 i, 80r (27-11) <u>Earl of Chester; Burstock</u>: TRW the Earl of Chester holds three hides of land in Burstock, and William holds from him. A thegn held it TRE. Eadnoth the Staller took it away (*tulit*) from him in the time of King William.

481 i, 80v (30-4) <u>Robert fitz Gerald; Povington</u>: TRW Robert fitz Gerald holds eight and a half hides in Povington. TRE Almær held them. This manor's mill has been claimed (*calumniatus est*) for the King's use.

482 i, 80v (34-6) <u>William d'Eu; Blandford St. Mary</u>: TRE Tholf held three and a half hides in Blandford St. Mary. TRW William holds them from William d'Eu. In this vill William also holds half a hide which Tholf held through a mortgage (*per vadimonio*). It was redeemed (*fuit adquietata*), but Ralph de Limesy took (*cepit*) it with the other land. Later, the King did not have geld from it.

483 i, 80v (34-8) <u>William d'Eu; Swyre</u>: TRE Tholf held nine hides in Swyre. Now William holds them from William d'Eu. Besides these nine hides, William holds some land there, which was never gelded TRE, but was instead in the King's demesne and farm. A King's reeve leased (*prestiterat*) it to Toxus the Priest, but then took it back (*resumpsit*) into the King's hand. Toxus was seised (*fuit saisitus*) of it again through King Edward, so he says, and thus he held it on the day King Edward lived and died. Similarly, he held it in the time of Harold. Previously it was pasture, now it is for seed (*seminabilis*).

484 i, 82r (34-14) <u>William d'Eu; Stock Gaylard</u>: TRW Hugh holds a hide in Stock Gaylard from William d'Eu. TRE Tholf held it in mortgage (*in vadimonio*) from the lands of Sherborne Abbey.

485 i, 82r (35-1) <u>William de Falaise; Silton</u>: TRE Wulfweard White held eight hides in Silton. TRW William de Falaise holds it. William holds a hide and half a virgate in the same vill, which Wulfweard White held in mortgage (*in vadimonio*) TRE from one of his reeves. William also holds another hide, which Wulfweard held in Silton. He bought (*emit*) it from the Bishop of Exeter. This hide did not belong to Wulfweard's eight-hide manor in Silton.

486   Exon (for 36-6) <u>William de Mohun; Chilfrome</u>: TRE three thegns held ten hides in parage on the day King Edward was alive and dead. William de Mohun now claims these three manors as two [fo. 48b].

487   i, 81v (36-8) <u>William de Mohun; Chelborough (East or West)</u>: TRE Godric held three hides in Chelborough. TRW Ranulf holds it from William de Mohun. The son of Odo the Chamberlain claims (*calumniatur*) this land.

488   i, 82r (40-7) <u>Waleran; Church Knowle</u>: TRE a thegn held a hide in Church Knowle, and he was free with his land. TRW Beulf holds them from Waleran. Waleran held it from Earl William. Now he says he holds it from the King.

489   i, 83r (49-16) <u>Æthelwulf the Chamberlain; Long Crichel</u>: TRE Ælfric held four hides in Long Crichel. TRW Æthelwulf holds it from the King as long as he is sheriff.

490   i, 83r (49-17) <u>Æthelwulf the Chamberlain; Farnham</u>: TRE a thegn held half a hide in Farnham from Shaftesbury Abbey, and he could not be separated from it. TRW Æthelwulf holds it.

491   i, 83r (54-8) <u>Hugh d'Ivry and other Frenchmen; Tyneham</u>: TRE Beorhtric held three hides in Tyneham. Now Ansketil fitz Amelina holds it. Ansketil says that he held this land from the Queen, but after her death he did not ask the King for it (*regem non requisiuit*).

492   i, 83v (55-3) <u>Wife of Hugh fitz Grip; Little Cheselbourne</u>: TRE Algar and Alstan held two hides in Little Cheselbourne. TRW Hugh fitz Grip held it from the Abbot of Abbotsbury, so his men say, but the abbot denies (*negat*) it.

493   Exon (for 55-16) <u>Wife of Hugh fitz Grip; Turners Puddle</u>: TRE Gerling held six hides in Turners Puddle. TRW Walter holds them from the wife of Hugh fitz Grip. A half hide, four acres, and a garden never paid geld, but have been concealed (*celatus est*) [fo. 56b].

494   i, 83v (55-17) <u>Wife of Hugh fitz Grip; Winterborne Houghton</u>: TRE Wulfgar held two hides and a virgate in Winterborne Houghton. TRW Hugh holds them from the wife of Hugh fitz Grip. Along with this land, Hugh fitz Grip held another virgate there unjustly (*iniuste*), which belongs to William de Mohun.

495   i, 83v (55-21) <u>Wife of Hugh fitz Grip; Farnham</u>: TRE Alwine held half a hide in Farnham from Shaftesbury Abbey, and he could not be separated from it. TRW Ilbert holds it from the wife of Hugh fitz Grip.

496   i, 83v (55-23) <u>Wife of Hugh fitz Grip; Tatton</u>: TRE two thegns held two hides in Tatton by lease (*prestito*) from the Abbot of Cerne. These hides were from the abbey's demesne. Hugh fitz Grip took (*accepit*) the land against the abbot, and his wife now holds it.

497   i, 84r (55-47) <u>Wife of Hugh fitz Grip; Orchard (in Church Knowle)</u>: TRW the wife of Hugh fitz Grip holds Orchard. Four thegns held it TRE, and it paid geld for one and a half hides. Hugh fitz Grip gave (*dedit*) one of these hides to Cranborne Abbey for the sake of his soul (*pro anima sua*).

498   i, 84r (56-19) <u>King's thegns; Hampreston</u>: TRW Thorkil holds three and a

third virgates in Hampreston. The Queen gave (*dedit*) this land to Schelin; now the King has it in demesne.

499 i, 84r (56-20) <u>King's thegns; half a hide</u>: TRW Dodda holds half a hide. The Queen gave (*dedit*) this land to him in alms.

500 i, 84v (56-36) <u>King's thegns; Waddon</u>: TRW Beorhtwine holds two hides in Waddon. Alweard held them TRE. Hugh fitz Grip exchanged (*cambiuit*) this land with Beorhtwine for land which Robert count of Mortain now holds. The exchange itself is worth twice as much (*ipsum scambium valet duplum*).

501 Exon (for 58-3) <u>Countess of Boulogne; Swanage</u>: TRE Wulfgifu held a hide and a third of a virgate in Swanage. TRW the Countess of Boulogne holds it. King William has never had geld from this manor [fo. 33a].

Gloucestershire

502 i, 162r (G-4) <u>Gloucester</u>: Geoffrey de Mandeville holds six messuages. TRE they paid 6s. 8d. with other customs. William fitz Baderon holds two messuages at 30d.; William the Scribe holds a messuage at 51d.; Roger de Lacy holds a messuage at 26d.; Bishop Osbern one messuage at 41d.; Berner one messuage at 14d.; William the Bald one messuage at 12d.; Durand the Sheriff two messuages at 14d.; Durand also holds a messuage at 26d. and another messuage which pays no customs. Hadewine holds a messuage in Gloucester which gives rent (*gablum*), but keeps back (*retinet*) other customs. Gosbert has one messuage; Dunning one messuage; and Widard one messuage. Arnulf the Priest has one messuage, which pays rent (*gablum*). He keeps back (*retinet*) other customs. All these messuages paid royal customs TRE. Now King William has nothing from them, nor has Robert his official (*minister*). These messuages were in the farm of King Edward on the day he was alive and dead. Now they have been taken away (*sunt ablatae*) from the farm and customs of the King.

503 i, 162r (G-4) <u>Gloucester</u>: TRE the King's demesne in the city was for hospitality or clothing. When Earl William acquired (*recepit*) it at farm, it was similarly for clothing.

504 i, 162r (W-4) <u>Wales</u>: There are thirteen vills under Waswic the Reeve, fourteen vills under Elmui, thirteen vills under Bleio, and fourteen vills under Iudhael. Walter the Balistarius has a piece of wasteland, Berdic the King's jester has three vills, Morin one vill, Cynesige one, Waswic's son one, Sessisbert one, and Abraham the Priest has two vills. Earl William put (*misit*) these men in the customs of King Gruffydd, with permission of King William.

505 i, 162r (W-8) <u>Wales</u>: All of the villages enumerated in no. 504, along with four vills wasted by King Caradoc – a vill which belongs to the Church, and which pays two pigs and one hundred loaves with ale at Martinmas for the King's soul; a carucate which belongs to St. Michael's and another which belongs to St. Dewy's; and a half carucate held by Belward of Caerwent –

together pay £40 12s. 8d. Durand the Sheriff gave (*dedit*) them to William d'Eu for £55 at farm.

506 i, 162r (W-16) <u>Wales</u>: TRW William d'Eu has £9 from the customs of Chepstow, so he says. But Gerard and the other men say that he has nothing more in justice (*iuste*) from the £10 of Chepstow's customs, even if it were assessed at £100.

507 i, 162r (W-16) <u>Wales</u>: Earl William gave (*dedit*) Ralph de Limesy fifty carucates of land, as is done in Normandy (*sicut fit in Normannia*). This is testified by Hugh and the others who gave livery (*alii liberatores*): that William granted (*concessit*) it to Ralph in this way. Now William d'Eu says that he himself has only thirty-two carucates of this land.

508 i, 162r (W-18) <u>Wales</u>: Thurstan fitz Rolf has seventeen plows between the Rivers Usk and Wye. The King's reeves claim (*calumniantur*) five and a half carucates of this land, saying that Thurstan took them without gift (*sine dono assumpsit*).

509 i, 162v (B-1) <u>Winchcombe</u>: TRE the borough of Winchcombe paid £6 in farm. Of this Earl Harold had the third penny, that is, 40s.

510 i, 162v (1-2) <u>Terra Regis; Barton (near Gloucester)</u>: King Edward had nine hides in Barton. Now King William holds them. TRE Ealdræd Archbishop of York leased (*prestitit*) Brawn, a berewick of this manor. It was assessed at three virgates. Now Miles Crispin holds it. TRE Alwig the Sheriff also leased (*prestitit*) another berewick, assessed at one hide, called Upton St. Leonards. TRW Humphrey holds it. TRE Alwig also leased (*prestitit*) another berewick called Maisemore. There are three virgates there. Nigel the Physician now holds it.

511 i, 162v (1-3, 4, 5) <u>Terra Regis; Haresfield, Down Hatherley, Sandhurst, Harescombe, Brookthorpe</u>: TRE a thegn, Eadmær, had three manors assessed at two hides in Haresfield, Down Hatherley, and Sandhurst, and he could grant and sell his land to whom he wished. Wigflæd held three virgates of land in Harescombe in the same manner as Eadmær held his; and Ælfric held three virgates in Brookthorpe. After King Edward's death, Earl Harold took away (*abstulit*) these five lands. Roger d'Ivry put (*posuit*) them at farm for £46 13s. 4d.

512 i, 162v (1-6) <u>Terra Regis; unnamed land in the hundred near Gloucester</u>: TRE Wulfweard held half a hide from King Edward which adjoined Gloucester. In the time of King William, Earl William gave (*dedit*) it to one of his cooks, because Wulfweard was made an outlaw (*utlag factus est*).

513 i, 162v (1-8) <u>Terra Regis; Cirencester</u>: TRE a freeman held two hides of land in Cirencester, and paid 20s. in farm and served the sheriff throughout the whole of England. Earl William put (*misit*) this land outside the farm and gave (*dedit*) it to one of his men.

514 i, 162v–163r (1-10) <u>Terra Regis; Lower Slaughter</u>: TRW King William holds seven hides in Lower Slaughter. King Edward held them, and the sheriff paid what he wished for this manor. They do not, therefore, know its value.

515 i, 163r (1-11) <u>Terra Regis, Westbury-on-Severn</u>: King Edward held thirty hides in Westbury-on-Severn; now King William holds them. Four years after the death of King Edward, six hides in Kyre [Worcs.], ten hides in Clifton upon Teme [Worcs.], eight hides in Newent and Kingstone (in Weston under Penyard) [Hereford] and one hide in Edvin Loach [Hereford] were taken away (*ablatae sunt*) from this manor. The Abbot of Cormeilles, Osbern and William fitz Richard now hold them. The sheriff, however, finds the whole farm from the remainder. The men of the county also say that the firwood lay in King Edward's farm in Westbury-on-Severn.

516 i, 163r (1-12) <u>Terra Regis; Upper Clopton [War.]</u>: King Edward held eight hides in Upper Clopton and eight in its berewick of Meon. Now King William holds them. TRE the sheriff paid what came from this manor to the farm. Now the manor pays £15 with the two hundreds that the sheriff put (*apposuit*) there.

517 i, 163r (1-13) <u>Terra Regis; Awre</u>: King Edward held five hides in Awre; now King William holds them. There are three berewicks outside this manor which were always and ought to be within it, so the men of the county testify. They are Purton, Etloe, and Bledisloe. Purton is in Earl William's fee. Roger of Berkeley holds Etloe, and William fitz Baderon holds Bledisloe. Alwig the Sheriff put (*misit*) them outside the farm.

518 i, 163r (1-16) <u>Terra Regis; Cromhall</u>: TRE two brothers held five hides in Cromhall in the King's manor of Berkeley, and they could turn where they wished with the land. Earl William loaned (*comendavit*) them to the reeve of Berkeley, so that he might have their service. So says Roger.

519 i, 163r (1-19) <u>Terra Regis; Sharpness</u>: Five hides in Sharpness belong to Berkeley. Earl William put (*misit*) them outside Berkeley in order to build a small castle. Roger claims (*calumniatur*) them.

520 i, 163r (1-21) <u>Terra Regis; Barton (in Bristol), Bristol</u>: The manor of Barton (in Bristol) and Bristol pay 110 marks of silver to the King. The burgesses say that Bishop Geoffrey has thirty-three marks of silver and one mark of gold beyond the King's farm.

521 i, 163v (1-37) <u>Terra Regis; Clifford Chambers [War.]</u>: TRE seven hides in Clifford Chambers belonged to Beorhtric Algarson's manor of Tewkesbury. TRW Queen Mathilda gave (*dedit*) this land to Roger de Bully.

522 i, 163v (1-39) <u>Terra Regis; Rubric</u>: [A rubric notes that "Beorhtric Algarson held Tewkesbury TRE. He had the lands of other thegns, written below, completely in his power (*in sua potestate habuit*)."]

523 i, 163v (1-42) <u>Terra Regis; Wincot [War.]</u>: TRE a thegn held three hides in Wincot. In the time of King William, Queen Mathilda gave (*dedit*) this land to Regenbald the Chaplain.

524 i, 163v (1-44) <u>Terra Regis; Twyning</u>: TRE four villeins held two hides and another thegn held half a hide in Twyning. In the time of King William, Queen Mathilda gave (*dedit*) this land to John the Chamberlain.

525 i, 163v (1-48) <u>Terra Regis; Old Sodbury</u>: TRE Beorhtric Algarson held ten hides in Old Sodbury; now they are held by King William. A virgate in Droitwich [Worcs.] belongs to this manor. It paid twenty-five sesters of salt, but Urso the Sheriff so oppressed (*vastavit*) the men, that they cannot now pay the salt.

526 i, 163v–164r (1-50, 51) <u>Terra Regis; Fairford</u>: TRE Beorhtric Algarson held twenty-one hides in Fairford. Afterwards Queen Mathilda held this manor. The Queen gave (*dedit*) four hides of this manor to John the Chamberlain and three hides and three virgates to Baldwin.

527 i, 164r (1-53) <u>Terra Regis; Dymock</u>: King Edward held twenty hides in Dymock, and the sheriff paid what he wished for the manor. Afterwards King William held it in his demesne for four years. Later Earl William and his son Roger had it, but the men of the county do not know how.

528 i, 164r (1-54) <u>Terra Regis; Naas</u>: TRE Earl Harold held five hides in Naas. It was not at farm, but Earl William joined it to two other manors – Poulton (in Awre) and Purton. Purton is in dispute (*est in calumnia*) for the King's farm.

529 i, 164r (1-55) <u>Terra Regis; Lydney</u>: In the time of King William, Earl William made a manor from four lands, which he took (*accepit*) from their demesne. He [took] three hides from the Bishop of Hereford's demesne, and he [took] six hides from the demesne for the victualing of the monks of Pershore.

530 i, 164r (1-56) <u>Terra Regis; Tidenham</u>: TRE the Abbot of Bath held thirty hides in Tidenham. This manor did not pay rent (*censum*) TRE, except for the victualing of the monks. Archbishop Stigand was holding it when Earl William took (*accepit*) it. Earl William gave (*dedit*) a virgate of this land to his brother, Bishop Osbern. He gave (*dedit*) Walter de Lacy two fisheries on the Severn and half a fishery on the Wye. He gave (*dedit*) Ralph de Limesy two fisheries on the Wye. He gave (*dedit*) the Abbot of Lyre half a hide and the manor's church with its tithes.

531 i, 164r (1-59, 60) <u>Terra Regis; Beckford [Worcs.], Ashton under Hill [Worcs.]</u>: TRE Rotlesc, King Edward's housecarl, held eleven hides in Beckford. TRW Earl William gave (*dedit*) three of these hides to Ansfrid de Cormeilles. TRE Thorbert, a thegn of Earl Harold, held eight hides in Ashton under Hill. Earl William gave (*dedit*) the Abbey of Cormeilles the tithes and churches of these two vills with three virgates of land. The men of the county, having been questioned, said that they never saw the King's writ which said that this land had been given (*homines de comitatu inquisiti dixerunt se nunquam vidisse brevem regis qui hanc terram diceret datam esse*) to Earl William.

532 i, 164r (1-62) <u>Terra Regis; Hempsted</u>: TRE Eadric Lang, a thegn of Earl Harold, held five hides in Hempsted. Earl William took (*cepit*) this manor in demesne. It was not at farm, but the sheriff has put (*posuit*) it at farm for 60s. by tale.

533 i, 164r (1-63) <u>Terra Regis; Woodchester</u>: TRE Gytha, Earl Harold's mother, held Woodchester. Earl Godwine bought (*emit*) it from Azur and gave (*dedit*) it to his wife, so that she could live from it when she stayed at Berkeley. She did not want to eat anything from the manor, because of the destruction (*destructione*) of the abbey. Edward holds this land unjustly (*iniuste*) in the farm of Wiltshire, so the county says, because it does not belong to any farm. No one has rendered an account (*rationem*) of this manor to the King's legates (*legatis*), nor have any of them come to this survey (*descriptionem*).

534 i, 164r (1-64) <u>Terra Regis; Modesgate</u>: TRE Beorhtric held three hides in Modesgate. The King has two fisheries in demesne, and Roger de Lacy has a fishery and half a hide. The Abbot of Malmesbury has a fishery with half a hide by the King's gift (*dono regis*), so they say. William d'Eu has two hides and claims (*calumniatur*) these four fisheries on the Wye.

535 i, 164r (1-65) <u>Terra Regis; Down Ampney</u>: TRE Eadnoth held fifteen hides in Down Ampney. King Edward pardoned (*perdonavit*) five of these hides for Eadnoth, so the county says, and afterwards this manor paid geld for ten hides.

536 i, 164v (2-4) <u>Archbishop of York; Oddington (Lower or Upper)</u>: TRE Archbishop Ealdræd held Oddington with its berewick of Condicote. This land never paid geld. Now Archbishop Thomas holds it. St. Peter's, Gloucester had it in demesne until King William came to England.

537 i, 164v (2-8) <u>Archbishop of York; Northleach</u>: TRW Walter fitz Poyntz holds a manor of twelve hides, which belongs to the manor of Northleach. St. Peter's, Gloucester held it TRE, and Archbishop Ealdræd held it with the abbey. Archbishop Thomas claims (*calumniatur*) it.

538 i, 164v (2-9) <u>Archbishop of York; Compton Abdale</u>: TRE Archbishop Stigand held nine hides in Compton Abdale; now Archbishop Thomas holds them. A man of Roger d'Ivry holds three hides which belong to this manor. The archbishop himself claims (*calumniatur*) them.

539 i, 164v (2-10) <u>Archbishop of York; Standish</u>: TRE Archbishop Ealdræd held fifteen hides in Standish. It was in the demesne of St. Peter's, Gloucester. Now Archbishop Thomas holds this land. The Abbot of Gloucester by law (*iure*) holds and ought to hold a hide of this land. Earl Hugh unjustly (*iniuste*) holds another hide. Durand the Sheriff holds three more hides, which Earl William gave (*dedit*) to his brother Roger. Archbishop Thomas claims (*calumniatur*) these hides.

540 i, 164v (3-1) <u>Worcester Abbey; Westbury on Trym</u>: Worcester Abbey held and holds fifty hides in Westbury on Trym. Osbern Giffard holds five of these hides, and he does no service (*nullum servitum facit*).

541 i, 165r (3-7) <u>Worcester Abbey; Bishop's Cleeve</u>: Worcester Abbey held and holds thirty hides in Bishop's Cleeve. Bernard and Reginald hold seven hides of this land in Stoke Orchard. They refuse to do service to St. Mary's (*servitium S Marie nolunt facere*).

542 i, 165r (7-1) <u>Bath Abbey; Olveston</u>: Bath Abbey held and holds five hides in Olveston. Three of these hides are gelded and two are not, by consent (*concessu*) of Kings Edward and William.

543 i, 165r (7-2) <u>Bath Abbey; Cold Ashton</u>: TRW Bath Abbey holds five hides in Cold Ashton. Two of these hides are quit from geld by consent (*concessu*) of Kings Edward and William.

544 i, 165v (10-13) <u>Gloucester Abbey; Duntisbourne Abbots</u>: TRW Walter de Lacy's wife gave (*dedit*) Gloucester Abbey a manor of five hides in Duntisbourne Abbots for the soul of her husband (*pro anima viri sui*), by consent (*concessu*) of King William.

545 i, 165v (11-14) <u>Winchcombe Abbey; Windrush</u>: TRE Bolla held three and a half hides from Winchcombe Abbey in Windrush, and could go where he wished with his land. He gave (*dedit*) it to the abbey. TRW Ælfsige of Faringdon holds it from the abbot. It unjustly (*iniuste*) lay in Salmonsbury Hundred after Bolla was dead. Now it lies in Barrington Hundred, by the judgment (*iudicio*) of the men of that hundred.

546 i, 165v (12-1) <u>Evesham Abbey; Maugersbury (near Stow on the Wold)</u>: TRE and TRW Evesham Abbey holds Maugersbury. In King Edward's time there were eight hides. A ninth lies near St. Edward's Church. King Æthelred gave (*dedit*) it quit.

547 i, 166r (12-8, 9) <u>Evesham Abbey; Lark Stoke [War.], Hidcote Bartrim</u>: TRW there are two hides in Lark Stoke and three in Hidcote Bartrim. The abbot has loaned (*commendatas*) these two vills to two of his knights.

548 i, 166r (16-1) <u>Cormeilles Abbey; Newent</u>: King Edward held six hides in Newent. Now Cormeilles Abbey holds them. Earl Roger gave (*dedit*) this land to the Church for the soul of his father, with the consent (*pro anima patris sui, concessu*) of King William. There are two haies there for which the King has seisin (*habet saisitas*). William fitz Baderon holds a virgate of this manor through force (*per vim*).

549 i, 166r (17-1) <u>Lyre Abbey; Duntisbourne Leer</u>: TRE Eadmær held a hide and a virgate in Duntisbourne Leer. Now Lyre Abbey holds a hide and a virgate there. Roger de Lacy gave (*dedit*) this land to the Church.

550 i, 166r (19-1, 2) <u>Westminster Abbey; Deerhurst</u>: TRW Westminster Abbey holds fifty-nine hides in Deerhurst. Besides these hides, Gerard the Chamberlain holds eight hides in Kemerton [Worcs.] and three hides in Boddington, which have always paid geld and done all service in Deerhurst Hundred. But after Gerard had this land, he paid neither geld nor service.

551 i, 166v (24-1) <u>Troarn Abbey; Horsley</u>: TRE Gode, King Edward's sister, held ten hides in Horsley. Now Troarn Abbey holds them by gift of King William (*dono regis Willelmi*).

552 i, 166v (28-3) <u>Earl of Chester; Edgeworth</u>: TRW Earl Hugh holds half a hide in Edgeworth, which, by testimony of the county, Roger de Lacy claims (*calumniatur*).

553 i, 166v (28-7) <u>Earl of Chester; land in Longtree Hundred</u>: TRE Alnoth and Leofwine held two manors of four hides. Now Earl Hugh holds them. There was no one who answered (*responderet*) for these lands, but they are assessed through the men of the county at £8.

554 i, 166v (31-2) <u>William d'Eu; Allaston</u>: TRE Bondi the Staller held three hides in Allaston; now William d'Eu holds them. Henry de Ferrers claims (*calumniatur*) this land because Bondi held it. But Ralph de Limesy, William d'Eu's antecessor, held it.

555 i, 166v (31-4) William d'Eu; Wyegate: TRE Ælfstan of Boscombe held six hides in Wyegate. Afterwards William d'Eu held them, but Ralph de Limesy held them before him. Now, by the King's order (*iussu*), it is in his forest.

556 i, 166v (31-7) William d'Eu; Daglingworth: TRE Ælfstan of Boscombe held five and a half hides in Daglingworth. Now Ralph holds this manor from William, and it pays geld. But he keeps back (*retinet*) the geld on three hides.

557 i, 167r (31-10) William d'Eu; Culkerton: TRE Scirweald held three virgates and five acres in Culkerton. Now Herbert holds them from William d'Eu. Ralph de Limesy held this land, but it was not Ælfstan's.

558 i, 167r (32-9) William fitz Baderon; land in Westbury Hundred: TRW William fitz Baderon holds two and a half virgates in Westbury Hundred. His antecessor Wihanoc held them, but the county affirms (*affirmat*) that this land is from the King's demesne farm in Westbury-on-Severn.

559 i, 167r (32-12) William fitz Baderon; Hewelsfield: TRE Wulfheah held three hides in Hewelsfield. Afterwards William fitz Baderon held them. This land, by the King's order (*iussu*), is in the forest.

560 i, 167r (34-8) William Goizenboded; Guiting Power: King Edward held ten hides in Guiting Power and loaned (*accomodavit*) them to Alwine his sheriff so that he might have them for his life (*ut in vita sua haberet*). The King did not, however, give this as a gift (*non tamen dono dedit*), so the county testifies. When Alwine died, King William gave his wife and land to Richard, a youth (*dedit Ricardo cuidam iuveni uxorem eius et terram*). Now William Goizenboded, Richard's successor, holds this land.

561 i, 167r (34-12) William Goizenboded; half a hide in Westbury Hundred: TRW Alwine the Sheriff held half a hide and half a fishery in Westbury Hundred. He gave (*dedit*) them to his wife. They were, however, from the King's farm in Westbury-on-Severn.

562 i, 167r (35-1, 2) William fitz Guy; Dyrham: In the time of King William, William fitz Guy holds seven hides in Dyrham, which Ælfric had held TRE. William also held three other hides in this manor. Durand the Sheriff had seised (*saisierat*) Pershore Abbey of these hides by the King's order (*iussu*). Earl William had given (*dederat*) them to Thurstan fitz Rolf with this manor.

563 i, 167v (37-3) William fitz Norman; Mitcheldean: TRW William fitz Norman holds two hides and two and a half virgates in Mitcheldean. TRE three thegns – Godric, Alric, and Earnwig – held them. King Edward granted (*concessit*) these lands quit from geld in return for taking custody of the forest.

564 i, 167v (38-2) William Leofric; Hailes: TRE Asgot held eleven hides; now William Leofric holds them. There were twelve slaves there whom William made free (*liberos fecit*).

565 i, 167v (39-8) Roger de Lacy; Painswick: TRE Earnsige held a hide in Painswick and could go where he wished. Now Roger de Lacy holds it. St.

Mary's, Cirencester holds a villein and part of the woodland. King William granted (*concessit*) these to St. Mary's.

566   i, 168r (39-18) Roger de Lacy; Siddington: TRE Godric and Leofwine held six hides in Siddington as two manors. TRW Roger de Lacy holds them, and his mother holds them as her dowry (*de sua dote*).

567   i, 168r (41-1) Roger d'Ivry; Hampnett: TRW Roger d'Ivry holds ten hides in Hampnett. TRE Archbishop Ealdræd held them. King Edward gave (*dedit*) him two of these ten hides quit, so they say.

568   i, 168r (41-5) Roger d'Ivry; Hazelton (in Rodmarton): TRE Alnoth held three hides and three virgates in Hazelton. In the time of King William, Roger held this manor from the Bishop of Bayeux for £16. Later the Bishop gave (*dedit*) it to Roger d'Ivry along with the farm.

569   i, 168r (44-2) Ralph Pagnell; a virgate and a half in Longstree Hundred: TRW Roger d'Ivry held a virgate and a half of land from Ralph Pagnell, which they have both relinquished (*dereliquerunt*).

570   i, 168v (50-2) Osbern Giffard; Oldbury: TRE Æthelric held a hide in Oldbury, and he could go where he wished. Now Osbern Giffard holds it, but it did not belong to the man Duns, whose lands, so the shire says, Osbern holds.

571   i, 168v (53-6) Durand of Gloucester; Whaddon: TRW Durand of Gloucester holds five hides in Whaddon. TRE five brothers held them as five manors, and they could go where they wished. They were equals (*pares erant*).

572   i, 168v (54-1) Drogo fitz Poyntz; Frampton on Severn: TRE Earnsige held ten hides in Frampton on Severn. TRW Drogo fitz Poyntz holds them from the King. Roger de Lacy unjustly (*iniuste*) holds one hide of this manor.

573   i, 169r (56-2) Walter fitz Roger; South Cerney: TRW Walter fitz Roger holds fourteen hides and a virgate in South Cerney. Archbishop Stigand held them TRE. This manor is claimed (*calumniatum est*) by Abingdon Abbey, but all the county testified that Archbishop Stigand held it for ten years while King Edward lived. Earl William gave (*dedit*) this manor to Roger the Sheriff, Walter's father.

574   i, 169r (59-1) Henry de Ferrers; Lechlade: TRW Henry de Ferrers holds Lechlade. TRE Siward Barn held it. Fifteen hides were gelded there TRE, but the King granted (*concessit*) six hides quit from geld. This all the county testifies, as does Henry, who offered the King's seal (*detulit sigillum regis*).

575   i, 169v–70r (68-1, 8, 13) Ansfrid de Cormeilles; Winstone, Duntisbourne Abbots: TRE Wulfweard held five hides in Winstone, and Almær held one hide in Duntisbourne Abbots. TRW Ansfrid de Cormeilles had these hides from Walter de Lacy, when Ansfrid took Walter's niece (*cum eius neptem accepit*).

576   i, 170r (69-6, 7) Humphrey the Chamberlain; Iron Acton, Wickwar: TRE Harold, a man of Alwig Hiles, held two and a half hides in Iron Acton; and three men of Beorhtric Algarson held four hides in Wickwar as three manors. All of these men could go where they wished. Queen Mathilda gave (*dedit*) these two vills to Humphrey.

577 i, 170r (72-2) <u>Sigar de Chocques; Hazleton (near Andoveresford)</u>: TRE Gode held ten hides in Hazleton. TRW Sigar de Chocques holds them. King William granted (*concessit*) three of these hides quit from geld, so the county testifies.

578 i, 170r (72-3) <u>Sigar de Chocques; Yanworth</u>: TRE Gode held Yanworth. TRW Sigar de Chocques holds it. There are five hides there. Three of them are quit from geld through (*per*) King William, so Sigar's man says.

579 i, 170r (75-2) <u>Roger fitz Ralph; land in Swinehead Hundred</u>: TRW Roger fitz Ralph has a hide of land in Swinehead Hundred. There was no one who answered for this land (*non fuit qui de hac terra responderet*).

580 i, 170v (78-9) <u>King's thegns; Leckhampton</u>: TRW Beorhtric holds four hides in Leckhampton from the King. The same Beorhtric had two of these hides in King Edward's time. Ordric held the other two hides. King William, when he went into Normandy, granted (*concessit*) these six hides to Beorhtric.

581 i, 170v (78-15) <u>King's thegns; Wheatenhurst</u>: TRW Hearding holds five hides in Wheatenhurst in mortgage (*in vadimonio*) from Beorhtric. Beorhtric himself held them TRE.

Hampshire

582 i, 38r (1-2) <u>Terra Regis; Neatham</u>: King Edward held Neatham; now King William holds it. They did not say how many hides there are. A virgate of land, which was held by Leofwine the Forester, has been taken away (*ablata est*) from this manor, so the hundred testifies.

583 i, 38r (1-8) <u>Terra Regis; Mapledurham</u>: TRE Wulfgifu held twenty hides in Mapledurham. Afterwards Queen Mathilda held them. Now King William holds Mapledurham in demesne, and it is assessed at thirteen hides. Theobald holds three and a half hides of this manor. Richard of Tonbridge gave (*dedit*) them to him, when he held the land from the Queen. Now they do not know through whom he holds this land.

584 i, 38r (1-12) <u>Terra Regis; Hayling Island</u>: King William holds two and a half hides in Hayling Island. TRE Leofmann held them from the King in parage. When Harold annexed the kingdom (*regnam invasit*) he took them away (*abstulit*) from Leofmann and put (*misit*) them in his farm, where this land still is.

585 i, 38r (1-13) <u>Terra Regis; Soberton</u>: King William holds Soberton, which is assessed at nothing. TRE Leofmann held it from Earl Godwine for four hides and could not withdraw where he wished. They say that this land was in Chalton in parage. Harold took Soberton away (*abstulit*) when he reigned (*regnabat*), and put (*misit*) it in the King's farm, where it still is.

586 i, 38r (1-14) <u>Terra Regis; Soberton</u>: King William holds Soberton. TRE Godwine held it from King Edward in parage, and he could not withdraw elsewhere. Then it answered for three hides; now for nothing. Harold took it away (*abstulit*) from him and put (*misit*) it in his farm.

587   i, 38r (1-16) Terra Regis; East Meon: King William holds East Meon. TRE Archbishop Stigand held it for the use of the monks, and afterwards he had it as long as he lived (*post quamdiu vixit habuit*). There were seventy-two hides.

588   i, 38v (1-17) Terra Regis; Barton Stacey: King Edward held Barton Stacey. Now King William holds it. They did not say the number of hides.

589   i, 38v (1-19) Terra Regis; Over Wallop: King William holds Over Wallop. TRE Countess Gytha held it from Earl Godwine. It was then gelded for twenty-two hides; now for nothing. In the time of King Edward the third penny of six hundreds belonged to this manor.

590   i, 38v (1-21) Terra Regis; Broughton: King William holds Broughton. King Edward held it in demesne. They have not given an account (*rationem*) of the hides. A woodland, which is in the hand of Bishop Walkelin of Winchester, belongs to this manor, but thus far it has not been adjudged (*non est diratiocinata*). TRE some land was given (*fuit data*) for one of this manor's mills; but in the time of King William the reeve took (*accepit*) the mill and has both the land and the mill.

591   i, 38v (1-25) Terra Regis; Upper Clatford: King William holds Upper Clatford. It is from Earl Roger's fee. Saxi held it from King Edward TRE. It was then gelded for eleven hides; now for four and a half. Adelina the Jester holds a virgate of this land. Earl Roger gave (*dedit*) it to her.

592   i, 38v (1-27) Terra Regis; Eling: King William holds Eling in demesne. They do not know the number of hides. Two berewicks belong to this manor on the Isle of Wight and three outside of it. When Hugh de Port acquired (*recepit*) this manor, they were missing (*defuerunt*), and Earl William held them. Sixteen villeins' and three bordars' messuages were seized (*sunt occupatae*) into the forest. There was also a woodland at 280 pigs from pannage and three sesters of honey – all of which are now missing (*sunt minus*). These things are assessed together at £26.

593   i, 39r (1-41) Terra Regis; Andover: King William holds Andover. King Edward held it. They did not say the number of hides.

594   i, 39r (1-42) Terra Regis; Basingstoke: King William holds Basingstoke. It was always a royal manor, and it never gave geld. In Winchester four *suburbani* paid 13s. less 1d. Geoffrey the Chamberlain holds the land of one of these men, but neither the sheriff nor the hundred has ever seen the King's seal (*regis sigillum*) for this.

595   i, 39r (1-43) Terra Regis; Kingsclere: King William holds Kingsclere in demesne. It was of the farm of King Edward and belongs to the day's farm of Basingstoke. They did not know the number of hides.

596   i, 39r (1-44) Terra Regis; Hurstbourne Tarrant: King William holds Hurstbourne Tarrant in demesne. It was from King Edward's farm. They do not have the number of hides.

597   i, 39v (1-47) Terra Regis; King's Somborne: King William holds King's Somborne. It was a royal manor and was not assessed in hides. The soke of two hundreds belongs to this manor. The reeve claims (*calumniatur*) a virgate

of land and a pasture, which they call Down, for the use of this manor. The Count of Mortain holds it, but the hundred testifies that it ought to lie in the King's demesne farm. It was there TRE, along with the meadow.

598 i, 40r (2-1) <u>Bishop of Winchester; Alresford</u>: TRE and TRW the Bishop of Winchester held and holds Alresford. TRE it answered for fifty-one hides; now for forty-two. Of this land, Robert holds three and a half hides, Walter two hides, and Durand four hides in Soberton and six in Beauworth. Wulfric Cepe, Robert's antecessor, could not go where he wished, nor could Osbern, Walter's antecessor, nor Edward and Alric, Durand's antecessors.

599 i, 40r (2-10) <u>Bishop of Winchester; Overton</u>: TRE and TRW the Bishop of Winchester holds forty-one hides in Overton. Of this manor's land, Robert the Clerk holds two hides, his brother Gilbert two hides, and Geoffrey holds five hides in Bradley. TRE their antecessors – Alnoth, Wulfstan, and Alric – could not go where they wished.

600 i, 40v (2-15) <u>Bishop of Winchester; Fareham</u>: TRE and TRW the Bishop of Winchester holds Fareham. TRE and now it answers for twenty hides. There are, however, thirty hides there in number; but King Edward granted it thus, because of the Vikings, and because Fareham is beside the sea (*ita donavit causa Wichingarum quia super mare est*).

601 i, 40v (2-17) <u>Bishop of Winchester; Meon (in Titchfield)</u>: TRW the Bishop of Winchester holds a hide in Meon. Tovi had half of this hide through Earl William. He had the other half from the King through his own money, and it was through this that Tovi held this land (*medietatem huius hidae habuit Tovi per Willelmum comitem, et aliam partem per pecuniam suam habuit a rege et per hoc quod Tovi tenuit hanc terram*). The bishop now has it through the King's gift (*per donum regis*).

602 i, 40v (2-20) <u>Bishop of Winchester; Houghton</u>: TRE and TRW the Bishop of Winchester holds twenty-four hides in Houghton. William Peverel holds a hide of this manor, but he does not wish to give geld (*non vult dare geldum*).

603 i, 41r (3-1) <u>Monks of Old Minster, Winchester; Chilcomb</u>: TRW the Bishop of Winchester holds a hide in Chilcomb. Six hides were attached to this manor TRE, which Ralph de Mortimer now holds, but he does no service (*nullum servitium facit*) to the Church.

604 i, 41r (3-3) <u>Monks of Old Minster, Winchester; Chilbolton</u>: TRE and TRW Old Minster, Winchester holds Chilbolton. Then it answered for ten hides, now for five. The Bishop has only five hides and three virgates of this manor's land. Richard Sturmid holds the other hides. A reeve held them and could not go where he wished. He held two of these hides as if he were a villein (*habuit quasi villanus*).

605 i, 41v (3-9) <u>Monks of Old Minster, Winchester; Droxford</u>: TRE and TRW Old Minster, Winchester holds Droxford. Then it answered for sixteen hides, now for fourteen. Ralph de Mortimer holds half a virgate from the caput of this manor through force (*per vim*). The monks, however, acquit (*adquietant*) it of geld. This land was in the caput TRE.

606 i, 41v (3-12) <u>Monks of Old Minster, Winchester; Alverstoke</u>: TRE and TRW Old Minster, Winchester holds Alverstoke. TRE it answered for sixteen hides, but King Edward pardoned (*condonavit*) it to be ten hides, and so it is now.

607 i, 41v (3-15) <u>Monks of Old Minster, Winchester; Bransbury</u>: Richere the Clerk claims (*reclamat*) that he holds four hides from the bishop in Bransbury. TRE Abbot Æthelsige held it from Archbishop Stigand and the monks. It was for their victualing.

608 i, 42r (4-1) <u>Archbishop of York; Mottisfont</u>: TRW Archbishop Thomas holds a church and six chapels along with five hides less a virgate in the manor of Mottisfont, with all customs of the living and the dead (*cum omni consuetudine vivorum et mortuorum*). His antecessor similarly held them from King Edward. Of this land, the King's reeves, so the hundred says, took away (*abstulerunt*) one hide, twelve and half acres of meadow, a grove, and a pasture. Cava the Reeve did this without the knowledge (*nesciente*) of Hugh de Port.

609 i, 42v (6-16) <u>New Minster, Winchester; Micheldever</u>: TRW New Minster, Winchester holds Micheldever in demesne. TRE it answered for 106 hides; now for eighty-three hides and half a virgate. Hugh de Port holds twenty-two and a half hides and a virgate of this manor's land from the Abbot. TRE four freemen held them from the abbey as the four manors of Cranbourne, Drayton, West Stratton, and Popham. They could not withdraw with their land, so the men of the hundred testify. Ealdræd brother of Oda of Winchester holds another hide and a half of this land. His wife held it in dowry (*in dote*) TRE.

610 i, 42v (6-17) <u>New Minster, Winchester; Abbots Worthy</u>: TRE and TRW New Minster, Winchester holds seven hides in Abbots Worthy, which never paid geld. The Abbey has seventy-two acres of meadow there, which King Edward gave (*dedit*) the Church, along with pasture, which they call Hyde Moors (in Winchester), and eighty acres of meadow.

611 i, 43r (6-1) <u>New Minster, Winchester; Alton</u>: TRE Queen Edith held five hides in Alton. Now the Abbot of New Minster, Winchester holds them in demesne, but they are not gelded. The county testifies that the abbot took this manor unjustly in exchange (*iniuste accepit pro excambio*) for a house of the King, because the house was already the King's.

612 i, 43r (6-5) <u>New Minster, Winchester; Lomer</u>: TRW Ruald holds three hides in Lomer. TRE Alweard held it from the abbot. He bought it in the time of King Edward so that he might hold it for his life only (*emit ut tantummodo in vita sua teneret*), and he paid ten sesters of wine to the abbot each year.

613 i, 43r (6-9) <u>New Minster, Winchester; Kingsclere</u>: TRE Queen Edith held a church, four hides and a virgate of land in Kingsclere. Now New Minster, Winchester holds them. King William gave (*dedit*) all of this to the Church in exchange (*pro excambio*) for the land in Winchester on which the King's house is situated. TRE it answered for four hides and a virgate; now for nothing. They call the King regarding its geld (*revocant regem pro geldo*).

614   i, 43r (6-10) <u>New Minster, Winchester; Tatchbury</u>: TRE Eadsige the Sheriff held half a hide in Tatchbury in parage from King Edward. After King Edward's death, but before King William came, Eadsige gave (*dedit*) it to the Church for his soul (*pro sua anima*). Now New Minster, Winchester holds it.

615   i, 43r (6-12) <u>New Minster, Winchester; Laverstoke</u>: In the time of King Edward Wulfgifu Beteslau held ten hides in Laverstoke from New Minster, Winchester until her death. After she died, King William returned (*reddidit*) this manor to the Church for his soul and the soul of his wife (*pro sua anima et uxoris suae*).

616   i, 43r (7-1) <u>Gloucester Abbey; Linkenholt</u>: TRE Eadric held Linkenholt from King Edward. Now Gloucester Abbey holds it. Arnulf d'Hesdin gave (*dedit*) it to the Church by grant (*concessione*) of King William. Then it answered for five hides; now for one. The others are in demesne.

617   i, 43v (10-1) <u>Jumièges Abbey; Hayling Island</u>: TRE Wulfweard White held Hayling Island in alod from Queen Edith. Now the Abbey of Jumièges holds it. It paid geld for twelve hides in the time of King Edward; now for seven. The monks of Old Minster claim (*calumniantur*) this manor, because Queen Emma had given (*dederit*) it to the Church of St. Peter and St. Swithun, and then she seised (*saisiuit*) the monks of half. She handed over the other half to Wulfweard White for his life only (*in vita sua tantum ita dimisit*), on condition that after his death, he should be buried there and the manor should be returned to the monastery (*quatinus post obitum suum ipse sepeliendus et manerium rediret ad monasterium*). And so Wulfweard held half of the manor from the monks until he died, in the time of King William. This is so attested by Æthelsige abbot of Ramsey and by the whole hundred.

618   i, 44r (18-2) <u>Count Alan; Funtley</u>: TRW Count Alan holds a hide in Funtley. TRE Wulfweard held it from Earl Godwine. Ealdræd and the men of the hundred testify that this manor does not belong to Crofton.

619   i, 44v (20-1) <u>Count Eustace; Bishop's Sutton</u>: TRE Earl Harold held Bishop's Sutton. TRW Count Eustace holds it from the King. There are twenty-five hides there. Now it answers for ten, and it did so TRE, so the hundred says.

620   i, 44v (21-1) <u>Roger of Montgomery; Boarhunt</u>: TRE three freemen held Boarhunt in alod from King Edward. TRW Earl Roger holds it from the King. It answered for eleven and a half hides TRE; now for four hides and a virgate and a half. Oda of Winchester claims (*calumniatur*) half a hide of this manor, which he says does not belong to Boarhunt.

621   i, 44v (21-7) <u>Roger of Montgomery; Sunwood</u>: TRW Walter holds three hides in Sunwood from Earl Roger. TRE Tunbi held it from Earl Godwine. The men of the hundred say that Sunwood did not lie in the Earl's manor of Chalton, because Earl William, who gave (*dedit*) Chalton to him, did not grant (*concessit*) him Sunwood.

622   i, 44v (23-3) <u>Hugh de Port; two and a half virgates in Fordingbridge Hundred</u>: TRW Picot holds two and a half virgates from the King. TRE Vitalis held them as a manor in alod from King Edward. William de Chernet

claims (*calumniatur*) this land, saying that it belongs to the manor of Charford in the fee of Hugh de Port, through the inheritance of his antecessor (*per hereditatem sui antecessoris*). He brought his testimony for this from the better and old men from all the county and hundred (*adduxit de melioribus et antiquis hominibus totius comitatus et hundredus*). Picot disputed this with his testimony from the villeins, the common people, and the reeves, who wished to defend this through an oath or the judgment of God (*Picot contraduxit suum testimonium de villanis et vili plebs et de praepositis qui volunt defendere per sacramentum aut per diem iudicum*), that he who held the land was a free man and could go where he wished with the land. But William's witnesses refused to accept any law but the law of King Edward, until it is determined by the King (*sed testes Willelmi nolunt accipere legem nisi regis Edwardi usque dum diffiniatur per regem*).

623 i, 45r (23-16) <u>Hugh de Port; Houghton, Awbridge</u>: TRW Heldræd holds two and a half hides in Houghton and one and a half hides in Awbridge from Hugh de Port. Godwine held them TRE. Hugh acquired (*recepit*) these two manors as one. He claims (*calumniatur*) three messuages, a corner of a meadow, and a virgate and five acres of land for this manor's use against Thurstan the Chamberlain. The whole hundred bears (*fert*) testimony of this: that his antecessors were seised (*saisiti erant*) of them, and were holding on the day King Edward was alive and dead.

624 i, 45v (23-25) <u>Hugh de Port; Chawton</u>: TRW Hugh de Port holds Chawton. TRE Oda held it from King Edward in alod. There were ten hides there, but King Edward put this land at service and geld (*misit ad servitium et geldum*) for four hides and a virgate.

625 i, 45v (23-44) <u>Hugh de Port; Amport</u>: TRW Hugh de Port holds Amport. TRE Eadric held it from King Edward as a manor in alod. Then it was gelded for ten hides; now for six. Ralph de Mortimer holds five hides which belong to this manor. Eadric's brother held them under the following agreement (*conventione*): that as long as he was good to Eadric, he would hold the land from him. If he wished to sell it, he was not allowed to grant or sell to anyone except Eadric (*quod quamdiu bene se haberet erga eum tam diu terram de eo teneret, et si vendere vellet, non alicui nisi ei de quo tenebat vendere vel dare liceret*). This the hundred testifies.

626 i, 46v (25-1) <u>William de Percy; Hambledon</u>: TRE Alwine held a hide in Hambledon from King Edward. Now William de Percy holds it. He took it with his wife (*cum femina sua accepit*).

627 i, 46v (27-1) <u>Edward of Salisbury; Bramshott</u>: TRE two freemen held six hides in Bramshott from King Edward in alod. Now Edward of Salisbury holds it from the King. William Mauduit claims (*clamat*) a hide of this land, which lies in Hartley Mauditt. This the hundred and shire testify.

628 i, 46v (28-1) <u>Robert fitz Gerald; Church Oakley</u>: TRE Tovi held a hide and a half from King Edward in Church Oakley. Now Robert fitz Gerald holds it from the King. Robert put (*apposuit*) half a virgate of Malshanger, which

Bolla held in alod from King Edward, in Church Oakley. The hundred says, however, that it never belonged there.

629 i, 46v (29-1) <u>Ralph de Mortimer; Otterbourne</u>: TRW Ralph de Mortimer holds four hides in Otterbourne. TRE Cypping held it from the bishopric of Winchester, and could not withdraw from the Church.

630 i, 46v (29-3) <u>Ralph de Mortimer; Headbourne Worthy</u>: TRW Ralph de Mortimer holds a hide in Headbourne Worthy. TRE Cypping held it from King Edward. This manor was bought out of the Church in the time of King Edward, through a pact and agreement that after the third heir (*extra aecclesiam emptum fuit eo pacto et conventione ut post tercium haeredem*) the bishopric of Winchester should take (*reciperet*) the manor back with all its stock (*cum omni pecunia*). Now Ralph is the third heir (*est tercius haeres*).

631 i, 46v–47r (29-6) <u>Ralph de Mortimer; Botley</u>: TRE Cypping held two hides in Botley from King Edward. Now Ralph de Mortimer holds them. The woodland is missing (*deest*).

632 i, 47r (29-9) <u>Ralph de Mortimer; Swampton</u>: TRW Ralph de Mortimer holds a hide in Swampton. TRE Cypping held it from the Bishop and monks of Winchester. It was always of the monastery, and was granted to Cypping to hold during his life only. After his death, it ought to have returned to the Church (*concessa est eidem in vita sua tantum tenere, et post mortem eius ad aecclesiam debebat redire*). This is what the monks say, but the hundred knows nothing of this agreement (*nil scit de conventione*). The hundred, however, knows that this land was of the monastery, and that it did not nor does not now give geld. They do not know why it has remained Ralph's (*nesciunt quare remansit*).

633 i, 47r (30-1) <u>Eudo Dapifer; Ashe</u>: TRE Ailwacre held Ashe from Earl Harold. Now Eudo Dapifer holds it from the King. It then answered for eight hides; now for three. TRE the value was £7; afterwards and now it is valued at £6 10s., and this for half a hide which is missing through (*minus est per*) Hugh the Sheriff.

634 i, 47r (32-3) <u>William d'Eu; Malshanger</u>: TRE Edward held half a virgate and four acres in Malshanger from King Edward in alod. TRW William d'Eu holds it. Now it has been put (*est appositum*) with Deane, a manor held by William d'Eu. It belongs there, so the hundred says.

635 i, 47r (33-1) <u>William de Braose; half a hide in Neatham Hundred</u>: TRW Ricoard holds half a hide in Neatham Hundred from William de Braose, who holds it from the King. TRE Wynsige held it from King Edward. He held it at custom, as did his antecessor, who was a goatherd.

636 i, 47v (35-2) <u>William Mauduit; Hartley Mauditt</u>: TRW William holds Hartley Mauditt. TRE Gyrth held it from King Edward in alod. Then answered for six hides; later for three, but the county has seen neither a writ nor the King's seal for this (*non vidit inde brevem vel sigillum regis*).

637 i, 47v (39-4) <u>Bernard Pancevolt; Chilworth</u>: TRE Godwine held two hides in Chilworth. TRW Bernard Pancevolt holds them. TRE the value was £10 and afterwards £8. Now it is valued at £4 because Bernard does not have power in his woodland (*non habet potestatem in silva sua*).

638   i, 48r (41-1) Richard Sturmid; Chilbolton: TRW Richard Sturmid holds Chilbolton. TRE Ordweald held it from the Bishop of Winchester. It was the monastery's, and Ordweald could not go with it where he wished. Then it answered for three hides and three virgates; now for one hide.

639   i, 48r (43-4) Gilbert de Breteuil; Bramshill: TRW Gilbert de Breteuil holds two hides less a virgate in Bramshill with the King's manor of Swallowfield, which is in Berkshire. TRE Alwig and Alsige held this land from the King in alod as two manors. This manor never belonged to the King's manor, so the hundred says.

640   i, 48r (43-5) Gilbert de Breteuil; Stratfield Saye: TRW Gilbert de Breteuil holds Stratfield Saye with the King's manor of Swallowfield. But the hundred says that it never belonged there. TRE Edward held it from the King in alod. Then it was gelded for a hide. Now it is not gelded. Hugh holds it from Gilbert.

641   i, 48r (43-6) Gilbert de Breteuil; one hide in Somborne Hundred: TRW Gilbert de Breteuil holds a hide in Somborne Hundred from the King. TRE Alnoth held it from King Edward. Hugh de Port claims (*calumniatur*) this hide, saying that it belongs to his manors of Charford and "Eschetune" and that his antecessors held it there. The whole hundred testifies to this.

642   i, 48r (44-1) Hugh fitz Baldric; Itchen Abbas: TRW Hugh fitz Baldric holds Itchen Abbas from the King. Nunminster held it TRE. Then it answered for twelve hides; now for three and a half. The Abbess of Nunminster claims (*calumniatur*) this manor, and the whole hundred as well as the whole shrievalty produce testimony (*testimonium perhibet*) that it was Nunminster's in the time of King Edward, and ought, in justice (*iuste*) to be in the time of King William. [Written in the margin of this entry is the following statement: "The King returned (*reddidit*) this to the Church."]

643   i, 48r (44-3) Hugh fitz Baldric; Stratfield Saye: TRE Bondi held Stratfield Saye from the King in alod. Now Hugh fitz Baldric holds it. Then it was gelded for fifteen hides; now for seven and a half. [Written in the margin of this entry is the statement "four hides were seized (*sunt occupatae*) against the King."]

644   i, 48r (44-4) Hugh fitz Baldric; South Warnborough: TRE Bondi held South Warnborough from the King. Now Hugh fitz Baldric holds it, and Guy holds it from him with Hugh's daughter. It then answered for eleven hides; now for six.

645   i, 48r (45-1) Waleran the Huntsman; Winkton: TRE Earl Tosti held Winkton from King Edward in alod. Now Waleran the Huntsman holds it from the King, and Robert holds from him. Then it was gelded for seven hides; now for three hides and a virgate. King William gave (*dedit*) a virgate of this land to a priest.

646   i, 48r (45-2) Waleran the Huntsman; Outwick: TRW Waleran the

Huntsman holds a virgate and a half in Outwick, and Jocelyn holds from him. TRE Aghmund held it from the King in alod. It belonged to West Wellow, so the hundred and shire say.

647 i, 48v (48-1) <u>William son of Manni; Newton Stacey</u>: TRE Ælfric held a hide in Newton Stacey. TRW William son of Manni holds it. He took (*recepit*) it with his wife.

648 i, 48v (53-2) <u>William the Balistarius; Compton</u>: TRW William the Balistarius holds Compton. TRE five thegns held it from King Edward and could go where they wished. Then it answered for four and a half hides; now for three. Ealdræd brother of Oda claims (*calumniatur*) a virgate of this manor, and says that he held it on the day King Edward was alive and dead, and was disseised (*disaisitus fuit*) after King William crossed the sea. He established his title to it in front of the Queen (*dirationavit coram regina*). Hugh de Port is a witness of his (*est testis eius*), as are the men of the whole hundred.

649 i, 48v (54-2) <u>Herbert fitz Remigius; Farley Chamberlain</u>: TRE Northmann held half a hide from the King in Farley Chamberlain. Now Herbert fitz Remigius holds this land. William d'Eu claims (*calumniatur*) this hide, saying that it belongs to his manor. But the men of the hundred do not testify that he ought to have it, but that it was encroached upon (*praeoccupatam esse*) against the King.

650 i, 49r (56-3) <u>Henry the Treasurer; Nutley</u>: TRE four freemen held Nutley in alod from the King. Now Henry the Treasurer holds it. Then it answered for five hides; now for two and a half. Geoffrey the Marshal holds half a hide of this manor, which belongs there, so the hundred says.

651 i, 49r (67-1) <u>Geoffrey the Chamberlain; Hatch Warren</u>: TRW Geoffrey, chamberlain of the King's daughter, holds Hatch Warren from the King. TRE Alsige held it. Then it answered for a hide; now for three virgates. Oda of Winchester claims (*calumniatur*) this hide, saying that he had it from Alsige in mortgage (*in vadimonio*) for £10, by grant (*concessione*) of King William. He therefore lost it unjustly (*iniuste eam perdit*). Geoffrey, however, holds it from the King for the service he did for William's daughter Mathilda.

652 i, 49v (68-4) <u>King's officials; Northam</u>: TRW Eskil son of Osmund holds a virgate from the King in Northam. TRE Eadsige held it from King Edward, and it was from the King's farm. In his time it was put outside (*fuit missa foris*) the farm, but the hundred does not know how.

653 i, 49v (69-4) <u>King's thegns; Oakhanger</u>: TRW Edwin holds a hide and a virgate in Oakhanger because, so he says, he bought (*emit*) it from King William. The shire, however, does not know this (*nescit hoc*). Richard now holds it from Edwin. TRE Alwig held it from King Edward. The King's reeve claims (*calumniatur*) half a hide of this manor for pasture for the King's oxen. The shire, however, testifies that he can have neither the pasture nor pannage from the King's woodland as he claims, except through the sheriff (*sic calumniatur nisi per vicecomitem*).

654 i, 49v (69-6) <u>King's thegns; Preston Candover</u>: TRE Esbiorn held Preston

Candover from Queen Edith. Now Cypping holds it from the King. Then it was gelded for two and a half hides; now for two. A half hide was taken away (*ablata est*) from this manor and put (*est missa*) in Odiham, so the hundred says.

655   i, 49v (69-11) <u>King's thegns; Stratfield Saye</u>: TRE Godric and Siward held two hides in Stratfield Saye from King Edward as two manors in alod. Ælfric has held them until now without any warrantor (*sine ullo warant*).

656   i, 50r (69-12) <u>King's thegns; Hartley Wespall</u>: TRE Alric held a hide in Hartley Wespall from King Edward in alod. Now Ælfric holds it. He says that he bought (*emit*) this land from Earl William for two marks of gold, but never had it before.

657   i, 50r (69-13) <u>King's thegns; "Sudberie"</u>: TRE Eadnoth and Eadwig held two and a half hides in "Sudberie" from King Edward in alod. After his death they also died. A kinsman (*proximus*) of theirs, Cola of Basing, redeemed (*redemit*) the land from Earl William. Now Walter holds it in pledge (*in vadium*) from the son of Cola.

658   i, 50r (69-16) <u>King's thegns; Tytherley (East or West)</u>: TRE three freemen held Tytherley as three manors from King Edward in alod. Two of them were killed in the Battle of Hastings. TRW Alwig son of Thorbert holds them from the King. Then they were gelded for four hides and a virgate; now for three hides and a virgate. The men of the hundred say that they have never seen the seal nor the legate of the King, which seised (*sigillum vel legatum regis, qui saississet*) Alwine Ret, the antecessor of the man who now holds this manor. And unless the King were to testify, Alwig has nothing there (*nisi rex testificetur, nichil habet ibi*).

659   i, 50r (69-20) <u>King's thegns; "Mulceltone"</u>: TRW Edmund holds half a hide in "Mulceltone" from the King. TRE Edmund's father held a virgate of this land from King Edward. The other virgate was given to Edmund for an exchange with (*data est ei pro excambio de*) Walter Giffard. Sceua held this virgate from King Edward in alod.

660   i, 50r (69-22) <u>King's thegns; East Wellow</u>: TRW Aghmund holds five hides of land in East Wellow from the King. The same man held it from King Edward in alod. Waleran took away (*abstulit*) a virgate and a half of this manor and put it outside (*misit foras . . . et misit*) the county, in Wiltshire.

661   i, 50r (69-28) <u>King's thegns; Enham</u>: TRE Wulfgifu held one and a half hides in Enham from King Edward in alod. Now Alsige Berchenistre holds it from the King. The monks of Old Minster have a £12 pledge (*de vadio*) on this manor, which a man who died handed over (*dimisit*) to them.

662   i, 50r (69-30) <u>King's thegns; Rockbourne</u>: TRE Wulfgeat held a hide in Rockbourne from King Edward in alod. TRW Alwig holds it. The hundred says that a virgate of this hide which Wulfgeat claimed (*calumniabatur*), was quit and exempt (*quieta et soluta fuit*) in the time of King Edward, and that Alwig has King Edward's seal (*sigillum*) for it.

663   i, 50r (69-33) <u>King's thegns; Rockbourne</u>: TRW Sæwine holds half a hide in

Rockbourne from the King. He held it himself TRE from King Edward in alod. The officials (*ministri*) of the sheriff say that this half hide belongs to the King's farm, but the hundred and the shire say that King Edward gave (*dedit*) this land to Sæwine, and that Sæwine has his seal (*sigillum*) for it.

664 i, 50v (69-38) <u>King's thegns; half a hide in Redbridge Hundred</u>: TRW Alric holds half a hide in Redbridge Hundred. His father held it from King Edward, but he did not ask (*requisiuit*) the King for it after his uncle Godric, who had charge of it (*qui eam custodiebat*), died.

665 i, 50v (69-40) <u>King's thegns; two hides in Kingsclere Hundred</u>: TRW Alwine the White holds two hides in Kingsclere Hundred. He also held it in the time of King Edward, under Wigot for protection (*pro tuitione*). Now he holds it under Miles Crispin. It was delivered (*fuit deliberatus*) through Humphrey Visdeloup to Wigot in exchange (*in excambio*) for Broadwater [Sussex], so he himself says. But the hundred knows nothing of this.

666 i, 50v (69-41) <u>King's thegns; two hides in Kingsclere Hundred</u>: TRW Edwin the Huntsman holds two hides from the King's farm in Kingsclere Hundred. King Edward gave (*dedit*) them to him.

667 i, 50v (69-53) <u>King's thegns; two hides in Redbridge Hundred</u>: TRW Ælfric the Small holds a virgate in the forest. Colibert held it in the King's farm. Now Ælfric claims (*reclamat*) it from the Bishop of Saintes.

668 i, 50v (NF10-2) <u>Langley</u>: TRE four alodiaries held a hide in Langley in parage. Now Hugh de St. Quentin holds it through the Bishop of Bayeux, so he says, in exchange (*pro excambio*) for a mill which he had from a man.

669 i, 51v (NF9-40) <u>Hugh, Oda and others; Milford</u>: Ælfric holds Milford from the King in exchange (*de excambio*) for forest. Sæwulf held it from King Edward. Then it answered for a hide; now for half a hide because the church's part is in the forest.

670 i, 51v (NF9-42) <u>Hugh, Oda and others; "Utefel"</u>: TRE Lyfing and Ketil held a virgate and a half in "Utefel." Ælfric now holds it. He bought (*emit*) it from them in the time of King William.

671 i, 52r (S2) <u>Borough of Southampton</u>: In the time of King Edward, these men had land in Southampton quit by the King (*ab ipso rege*): Oda of Winchester, Eskil the Priest, Ketil, Fugel, and Tosti. The sons of Alric had sixteen acres of land and Gerin had eighteen acres. Cypping had three houses quit (*quietas*); now Ralph de Mortimer holds them. Godwine had three houses; Bernard Pancevolt holds them.

672 i, 52r (S3) <u>Borough of Southampton</u>: The brief description of Southampton ends with a list of men who have the customs of their houses by consent (*concessu*) of King William: Bishop Geoffrey has the customs of one house; the Abbot of Cormeilles one; the Abbot of Lyre one; the Count of Evreux two; Ralph de Mortimer two; Gilbert de Breteuil two; William fitz Stur two; Ralph de Tosny one; Durand of Gloucester two; Hugh de Port one; Hugh de Grandmesnil two; the Count of Mortain five; Æthelwulf the Chamberlain five; Humphrey, Æthelwulf the Chamberlain's brother one; Osbern Giffard one; Nigel the Physician four; Richere des Andelys four; Richard Poynant one; Stephen the Stirman two; Thurstan the Chamberlain two; Thurstan Machinator two; Ansketil fitz Osmund three; and Reginald fitz Croc one.

673   i, 52r (IOW1-6) <u>Terra Regis; Wilmingham</u>: TRE Wulfgeat the Huntsman held a hide in Wilmingham in parage. Now the King holds it in demesne. Reginald fitz Croc holds a virgate of this manor, and he says that Earl Roger gave (*dedit*) it to his father.

674   i, 52r (IOW1-7) <u>Terra Regis; Bowcombe</u>: TRE Bowcombe was in the farm of King Edward. Now King William holds it. Then it answered for four hides; now for nothing. The monks of Lyre hold a church with a virgate of this manor. Of this virgate, Humphrey holds as much land as where eight men pay 5s., and William fitz Azur holds two and half acres where he has four houses. Humphrey and William hold this against the wishes (*absque voluntate*) of the priest.

675   i, 54r (IOW9-15) <u>King's thegns; Knighton</u>: TRE Bondi held half a virgate in alod in Knighton from King Edward. Now Tovi holds it by gift of the King (*de dono regis*).

Herefordshire

676   i, 179r (C-2) <u>City of Hereford</u>: If anyone wished to depart from the city of Hereford, he could, with the consent (*concessu*) of the reeve, sell (*vendere*) his house to another man who was willing to owe service for it (*servitium debitum inde facere*). The reeve had the third penny of this sale (*venditionis*). If, however, anyone could not make up the service because of his poverty, he relinquished (*relinquebat*) his house to the reeve without payment, and the reeve saw to it (*providebat*) that the house did not remain empty and that the King was not without service.

677   i, 179r (C-3) <u>City of Hereford</u>: Within the city walls, he who had a horse proceeded three times each year with the sheriff to the pleas and hundred (*ad placita et ad hundrez*) at Wormelow.

678   i, 179r (C-5) <u>City of Hereford</u>: When a burgess serving with a horse died, the King had his horse and his arms. If the burgess who died did not have a horse, the King had either 10s. or he had the man's land with its houses. If anyone did not bequeath (*non divisisset*) what was his because of unanticipated death (*morte praeventus*), the King had all his goods (*pecuniam*).

679   i, 179r (C-9) <u>City of Hereford</u>: When a moneyer of the King died, the King had 20s. of relief (*de relevamento*). If, however, he died without dividing his wealth (*non diviso censu suo*), the King had all his income (*censum*).

680   i, 179r (C-10) <u>City of Hereford</u>: If the sheriff went into Wales with an army, the men of Hereford went with him. But if anyone ordered (*iussus*) to go did not, he paid a fine (*emendabat*) of 40s. to the King.

681   i, 179r (C-13) <u>City of Hereford</u>: The King had three forfeitures (*forisfacturas*) in his demesne; that is, breach of peace (*pacem suam infractam*), housebreaking (*heinfaram*), and robbery (*forestellum*). Any man who did one of these, paid a fine (*emendabat*) of 100s. to the King, no matter whose man he was.

682   i, 179r (C-14) <u>City of Hereford</u>: King William has the city of Hereford in his demesne, and the English burgesses living there have their former customs (*suas priores consuetudines*). The French burgesses, however, have all their forfeitures (*forisfacturas*) quit for 12d. except for breach of peace, house-breaking, and robbery.

683   i, 179r (C-15) <u>City of Hereford</u>: The city of Hereford pays £60 to the King by tale of blanched pence. Between the city and the eighteen manors which pay their farm in Hereford, £335 18s. are reckoned for, besides the pleas of the hundred and county (*placitis de hundredo de comitatu*).

684   i, 179r (A-1) <u>Archenfield</u>: The King has three churches in Archenfield. When one of the priests of these churches dies, the King has 20s. from him through custom.

685   179r (A-2) <u>Archenfield</u>: If a Welshman steals (*furatur*) a man, woman, horse, ox, or cow, when he is convicted (*convictus*), he first returns (*reddidit*) what was stolen (*furtum*), and then gives 20s. as a forfeiture (*pro forisfactura*). But for stealing (*furata*) a sheep or a bundle of sheaves, he pays a fine (*emendat*) of 2s.

686   i, 179r (A-3) <u>Archenfield</u>: If anyone has killed (*occiderit*) a man of the King and committed housebreaking (*facit heinfaram*), he gives the King 20s. as a payment (*de solutione*) for the man, and 100s. as a forfeiture (*de forisfactura*). If anyone has killed (*occiderit*) a thegn's man, he gives 10s. to the dead man's lord.

687   i, 179r (A-4) <u>Archenfield</u>: If a Welshman has killed (*occiderit*) a Welshman, the kinsmen of the slain man gather (*congregantur parentes occisi*), and rob (*praedantur*) the killer and his kinsmen (*propinquos*) and burn (*comburunt*) their houses until the body of the dead man is buried on the morrow around mid-day. Of this plunder (*praeda*), the King has a third, and the kinsmen have the other two-thirds quit.

688   i, 179r (A-5) <u>Archenfield</u>: A man who sets a house on fire (*domum incenderit*) and is accused of it (*accusatus fuerit*), defends himself through forty men (*per xl homines se defendit*). If he cannot, he shall pay a fine (*emendabit*) of 20s. to the King.

689   i, 179r (A-6) <u>Archenfield</u>: If anyone conceals (*celaverit*) a sester of honey [owed] by custom, on proof of this (*probatus inde*) he pays five sesters for one, if he holds as much land as ought to give it.

690   i, 179r (A-7) <u>Archenfield</u>: If the sheriff calls them to the shiremoot (*evocat eos ad siremot*), six or seven of the better men (*meliores*) go with him. He who does not go when called gives 2s. or an ox to the King. He who stays away from the hundred (*hundret remanet*) pays (*persoluit*) as much.

691   i, 179r (A-8) <u>Archenfield</u>: He who is ordered (*iussus*) by the sheriff to go with him into Wales but who does not go, is fined (*emendat*) similarly.

692   i, 179v (1-3) <u>Terra Regis; Kingstone (near Hereford)</u>: King Edward held four

hides in Kingstone; now King William holds them. There is a woodland named Treville there, which pays no customs except hunting. The villeins who lived there in the time of King Edward carried the hunt to Hereford, but did no other service, so the shire says.

693   i, 179v (1-4) <u>Terra Regis; Marden</u>: King Edward held Marden. There were many hides there, but only two were gelded. Now King William holds them. Earl William put (*posuit*) a virgate of this land outside the manor and gave (*dedit*) it to a burgess of Hereford. Ansketil holds forty acres of this land between fields and meadow, which King Edward's reeve leased to his kinsman (*prestavit suo parenti*).

694   i, 179v (1-5) <u>Terra Regis; Kingsland</u>: King Edward held fifteen hides in Kingsland; now King William holds them. Roger de Lacy holds two hides at Hopleys Green, which are attached to this manor. He holds another hide at Street and another at Lawton. He also holds half a hide which a swineherd held TRE. Earl William gave (*dedit*) all this land to Walter de Lacy.

695   i, 179v–180r (1-8) <u>Terra Regis; Cleeve</u>: TRE Earl Harold held fourteen and a half hides in Cleeve; now King William holds them. Roger de Lacy holds half a fishery, which belonged to this manor in the time of King Edward. Twenty-five measures of salt from Droitwich [Worcs.] were also there. At that time there were also two hides less a virgate, which are in Ashe Ingen. Alvred of Marlborough holds them now. Earl Harold held all of this when he died. The shire says that they are from this manor.

696   i, 180r (1-10a-b) <u>Terra Regis; Leominster</u>: TRE Queen Edith held Leominster with its sixteen berewicks. Now King William holds it. This manor is at farm for £60, besides the victualing of the nuns. The county says that if they were released (*deliberant esset*), this manor would be assessed at £120.

697   i, 180r (1-12) <u>Terra Regis; Wapley</u>: TRW Osbern fitz Richard, so he says, holds two hides in Wapley by the King's gift (*de dono regis*). He held it himself TRE.

698   i, 180v (1-38) <u>Terra Regis; Leominster</u>: The land that Ralph de Mortimer holds in Wigmore paid geld and customs to Leominster. Now it does not pay.

699   i, 180v (1-39) <u>Terra Regis; Martley [Worcs.]</u>: TRE Queen Edith held ten hides and a virgate in Martley. Now King William holds them. Earl William gave (*dedit*) St. Mary's, Cormeilles the church and the tithe of this manor with the land that belonged there. The earl also gave (*dedit*) Ralph de Bernay two radmen and put (*misit*) them outside this manor with the land that they held. The same earl gave (*dedit*) Droard a virgate of land, which he still holds.

700   i, 180v (1-40) <u>Terra Regis; Feckenham [Worcs.]</u>: TRE five thegns held ten hides in Feckenham from Earl Edwin and could go where they wished. Now King William holds this land. The woodland has been put outside (*foris est missa*) this manor and into the King's woodland, as has one hide of land, which Earl William gave (*dedit*) to Jocelyn the Huntsman. Earl William also gave (*dedit*) St. Mary's, Cormeilles the tithe, the church, and the priest of this manor, along with two virgates of land.

701 i, 180v (1-41) <u>Terra Regis; Hollow [Worcs.]</u>: TRE Siward, a thegn and kinsman (*cognatus*) of King Edward, held three hides in Hollow. Now King William holds them. There is a park for wild beasts, but it has been put outside (*missum est extra*) this manor with all the woodland. There are two houses that belong to Feckenham [Worcs.], which have been put outside (*extra missae sunt*) this manor. They pay nothing.

702 i, 180v (1-44) <u>Terra Regis; Bushley</u>: TRW King William holds Bushley. TRE Beorhtric held it. He bought (*emit*) it from Lyfing bishop of Worcester for three marks of gold. He bought, as well, a house in Worcester which pays a mark of silver each year and a woodland a league in length and another in breadth. He bought (*emit*) all of this and held it quit, so that he did not serve any man from it (*ut inde non serviret cuiquam homini*). There is one hide in this manor.

703 i, 180v (1-45) <u>Terra Regis; Queenhill [Worcs.]</u>: TRE Æthelric brother of Bishop Beorhtric held a hide in Queenhill. Now King William holds it. Earl William gave (*dedit*) the tithe of this manor, along with a villein who holds half a virgate of land, to St. Mary's, Lyre.

704 i, 180v (1-46) <u>Terra Regis; Eldersfield [Worcs.]</u>: TRE Regenbald the Chancellor held five hides in Eldersfield. Earl William exchanged (*excambiavit*) Eldersfield with him. Now King William holds it.

705 i, 180v (1-47) <u>Terra Regis; Suckley [Worcs.]</u>: TRE Earl Edwin held five hides in Suckley. Now King William holds them. Earl Roger gave (*dedit*) Richard half a virgate of land here in complete freedom (*in solida libertate*).

706 i, 181r (1-49) <u>Terra Regis; Archenfield</u>: If a freeman dies in Archenfield, the King has his horse with his arms. When a villein dies there, the King has an ox. King Gruffydd and Bleddyn wasted this land TRE. It is not, therefore, known what it was like in Edward's time.

707 i, 181r (1-61) <u>Terra Regis; Westwood</u>: King Edward held six hides in Westwood. Now St. Peter's, Gloucester holds it. Durand gave (*dedit*) it to St. Peter's for the soul of his brother Roger (*pro anima fratris sui Rogerii*). Roger de Lacy holds part of this manor, and Odo holds from him. Earl William gave (*dedit*) it to Roger.

708 i, 181r (1-65) <u>Terra Regis; Old Radnor</u>: TRE Earl Harold held fifteen hides in Old Radnor. Now the King holds them. They were and are waste. Hugh the Ass says that Earl William gave (*dedit*) him this land, when he gave (*dedit*) him the land of his antecessor Thorkil.

709 i, 181r (1-70) <u>Terra Regis; Woonton (in Almeley)</u>: TRE Algar and Alwine held a hide and a half in Woonton as two manors and could go where they wished. When Ralph de Bernay was sheriff he unjustly put (*misit . . . iniuste*) these two lands in the farm of Leominster. They now pay 62d. to the King's farm.

710 i, 181r (1-72) <u>Terra Regis; Newarne</u>: There were two and a half hides which met and did work (*conveniebant et operabantur*) in Herefordshire. In the time of Earl William, however, Roger de Pîtres transferred (*divertit*) them to Gloucestershire.

711   i, 181r (1-75) Terra Regis; Yatton: TRE Hwætmann held a hide in Yatton and could go where he wished. This land was thegnland, but after the time of King Edward it was converted (*conversa est*) to reeveland. The legates of the King (*legati regis*) say that this land and the rent (*census*) which comes from it are being secretly taken away (*furtim auferuntur*) from the King.

712   i, 181v (2-2) Bishopric of Hereford; Didley, "Stane": Walter bishop of Hereford held the two manors of Didley and "Stane." There are ten hides between the two, and by right (*recte*), they belong to the bishopric. Now part of this land is in Alvred of Marlborough's castlery of Ewyas Harold, and part is in the King's enclosure.

713   i, 181v (2-8) Canons of Hereford; Eaton Bishop: TRE Earl Harold held five hides in Eaton Bishop. Earl William gave (*dedit*) them to Bishop Walter for land on which the market now is, and for three hides in Lydney [Glos.].

714   i, 181v (2-12) Canons of Hereford; Holme Lacy: TRW Roger de Lacy holds six hides in Holme Lacy under the Bishop of Hereford. Earl Harold held this manor unjustly (*iniuste*), because it was for the victualing of the canons. King William returned (*reddidit*) it to Bishop Walter.

715   i, 182r (2-22) Canons of Hereford; Whittington (in Staunton): TRW there are three hides in Whittington which, by right (*recte*), belong to the bishopric. They were and are waste.

716   i, 182r (2-26) Canons of Hereford; Ledbury: TRW the canons of Hereford hold five hides in Ledbury. TRE Earl Harold unjustly (*iniuste*) held a hide of this manor in Hazle, and Godric held from him. King William returned (*reddidit*) it to Bishop Walter.

717   i, 182r (2-31) Canons of Hereford; Colwall: TRW the canons of Hereford hold three hides in Colwall, which lie in Cradley [another of their properties]. Earl Harold held this manor unjustly (*iniuste*), and Thurmoth held from him. King William returned (*reddidit*) it to Bishop Walter.

718   i, 182r (2-32) Canons of Hereford; Coddington: TRW the canons of Hereford hold three hides in Coddington. TRE Earl Harold held this manor unjustly (*iniuste*). King William returned (*reddidit*) it to Bishop Walter.

719   i, 182r (2-33) Canons of Hereford; Hampton Bishop: TRW the canons of Hereford hold four hides in Hampton Bishop. TRE Earl Harold held it unjustly (*iniuste*). King William returned (*reddidit*) it to Bishop Walter.

720   i, 182r (2-37) Canons of Hereford; Sugwas (in Stretton Sugwas): TRW the canons of Hereford hold two hides in Sugwas. TRE Earl Harold held it unjustly (*iniuste*). King William returned (*reddidit*) it to Bishop Walter.

721   i, 182v (2-48, 50) Canons of Hereford; Bridge Sollers, Collington: TRW the canons of Hereford hold five hides in Bridge Sollers and three hides in Collington. Earl Harold held them unjustly (*iniuste*) in the time of King Edward. King William returned (*reddidit*) them to Bishop Walter.

722 i, 182v (2-57) <u>Canons of Hereford</u>: In total, there are three hundred hides in the bishopric of Hereford, although the bishop's men have given no account (*rationem non dederint*) of thirty-three of them.

723 i, 182v (2-58) <u>Bishopric of Hereford; Priors Frome</u>: TRE Eadwig Cild held a hide and a virgate of land in Priors Frome. TRW St. Peter's, Hereford holds it. Walter de Lacy gave (*dedit*) it to the Church, with the consent (*concessu*) of King William.

724 i, 182v (3-1) <u>Abbey of Cormeilles; Kingstone</u>: TRW the Abbey of Cormeilles holds two hides in Kingstone. These hides are gelded in Gloucestershire and do service (*operant*) there, but the men who live in Kingstone assemble for pleas (*ad placita conveniunt*) in this hundred of Bromash, so that they might give and receive justice (*ut rectum faciant et accipiant*).

725 i, 182v (5-2) <u>Gloucester Abbey; Lea</u>: TRE Ansgot held a hide in Lea and could go where he wished. TRW St. Peter's, Gloucester holds it by gift (*dono*) of Walter de Lacy.

726 i, 183r (7-1) <u>Nigel the Physician; Bartestree</u>: TRW Nigel the Physician holds two hides in Bartestree from the land of St. Guthlac's. TRE Leofflæd held it. One of these hides is gelded, by testimony of the county. A berewick is attached to this manor. Leofflæd held it. There are two hides there: one of them is gelded, by testimony of the county.

727 i, 183r (8-1) <u>Ralph de Tosny; Clifford</u>: TRW Ralph de Tosny holds the castle of Clifford. It is in the kingdom of England, but it is not subject to any hundred or customs (*est de regno Angliae, non subjacet alicui hundret neque in consuetudine*).

728 i, 183r (8-7) <u>Ralph de Tosny; Dinedor</u>: TRE Godric and Wulfheah held six hides in Dinedor as two manors. Now Ralph de Tosny holds it and William and his brother Ilbert hold from him. No one fishes in the river without permission.

729 i, 183r (8-8) <u>Ralph de Tosny; Westhide</u>: TRE Edith held two hides and a virgate of land in Westhide and could go where she wished. TRW Ralph de Tosny holds it. He gave (*dedit*) half a hide of this land to one of his knights: the manor, therefore, pays less.

730 i, 183v (9-2) <u>Ralph de Mortimer; Downton on the Rock</u>: TRE Almær and Ulfkil held four hides in Downton on the Rock as two manors and could go where they wished. Earl William gave (*dedit*) this land to Thurstan of Flanders. Now Ralph de Mortimer holds it and Odilard holds from him.

731 i, 184r (10-1) <u>Roger de Lacy; Ewyas Harold</u>: Earl William gave (*dedit*) Walter de Lacy four carucates of waste land in the castlery of Ewyas Harold. Roger de Lacy, his son, holds them, and William and Osbern hold from him.

732 i, 184r (10-2) <u>Roger de Lacy; Longtown</u>: Roger de Lacy has a land called Longtown in the territory (*in fine*) of Ewias. This land does not belong to the castlery, nor to the hundred. Roger has fifteen sesters of honey and fifteen pigs when the men are there and he decides pleas over them (*placita super eos*).

733 i, 184r (10-5) <u>Roger de Lacy; Ocle Pychard</u>: TRE six freemen held seven hides in Ocle Pychard as six manors, and they could go where they wished. Now Roger de Lacy holds them. Walter de Lacy gave (*dedit*) two carucates of this land to St. Peter's, Hereford with the consent (*concessu*) of King William.

734 i, 184v (10-37) <u>Roger de Lacy; Leadon</u>: TRE Thorkil held half a hide in Leadon and could go where he wished. TRW St. Peter's holds it from Roger de Lacy by his father's gift and with the consent of King William (*de dono patris eius et concessu Willelmi regis*). [A cross is written in the margin of this entry.]

735 i, 184v (10-41) <u>Roger de Lacy; Street</u>: King Edward held a hide in Street. Earl William gave (*dedit*) it to Ewen the Breton. Now William holds it from Roger de Lacy.

736 i, 184v (10-46) <u>Roger de Lacy; Eardisley</u>: TRE Eadwig held Eardisley. Now Roger de Lacy holds it, and Robert holds from him. This land is not gelded, nor does it give (*dat*) customs, nor does it lie in any hundred. It is in the middle of a woodland, and there is a fortified house.

737 i, 184v (10-48) <u>Roger de Lacy; Weobley</u>: TRE Eadwig Cild held three and a half hides in Weobley. TRW Roger de Lacy holds them. There are ten villeins there. St. Peter's holds one by gift (*dono*) of Walter de Lacy.

738 i, 184v (10-50) <u>Roger de Lacy; King's Pyon</u>: King Edward held five hides in King's Pyon. Ewen the Breton held this land from Earl William. King William, however, gave (*dedit*) it to Walter de Lacy. Now Roger de Lacy holds it.

739 i, 185r (10-66) <u>Roger de Lacy; Wolferlow</u>: TRE Alwine the Sheriff held six hides in Wolferlow and could go where he wished. Earl William gave (*dedit*) four and a half of these hides to Walter de Lacy, and King William gave (*dedit*) one and a half hides to Roger de Lacy. Now Hugh and Walter hold this land from Roger.

740 i, 185r (10-75) <u>Roger de Lacy; Hanley</u>: TRE Alnoth held half a hide in Hanley and could go where he wished. Now Roger de Lacy holds it, and St. Peter's holds it in alms by gift (*dono*) of Walter de Lacy.

741 i, 185v (14-1) <u>William d'Ecouis; Caerleon</u>: TRW William d'Ecouis holds eight carucates in the castlery of Caerleon, and Thurstan holds from him. There are three Welshmen there who live under Welsh law (*lege Walensi viventes*).

742 i, 185v (14-2) <u>William d'Ecouis; Maund Bryan</u>: TRE Edwin held a hide in Maund Bryan. Now William d'Ecouis holds it. The clerks of St. Guthlac's claim (*calumniantur*) this manor.

743 i, 185v (15-1) <u>William fitz Baderon; Hope Mansell</u>: TRE Leofric and Eadwulf held four hides in Hope Mansell as two manors. Now William fitz Baderon holds them, and Soloman holds from him. By testimony of the county, a third of this manor lay in the Church of St. Peter's, Gloucester TRE.

744 i, 185v (16-3, 4) <u>William fitz Norman; Venn's Green, Vern</u>: TRE Stenulf held a hide and a half in Venn's Green and two radmen held half a hide in Vern. Now William fitz Norman holds them. These two manors were attached to the farm of the King's manor of Marden.

745 i, 186r (19-1) <u>Alvred of Marlborough; Ewyas Harold</u>: TRW Alvred of Marlborough holds the castle of Ewyas Harold from King William. The King granted (*concessit*) him the lands which Earl William, who had refortified (*refirmaverat*) the castle, had given (*dederat*) to him – that is, five carucates of land there, and five at Monnington. The King also granted (*concessit*) Alvred the land of Ralph de Bernay, which belonged to the castle.

746 i, 186r (19-2, 3) <u>Alvred of Marlborough; Burghill, Brinsop</u>: TRE Earl Harold held eight hides in Burghill. Now Alvred of Marlborough holds them. TRE the third penny of the two hundreds of Stretford and Cutsthorn belonged to this manor. Earl Harold also held five hides in Brinsop, which Richard now holds from Alvred of Marlborough. Osbern, Alvred's uncle, held these two manors TRE, when Godwine and Harold were outlawed (*erant exulati*).

747 i, 186r (19-4) <u>Alvred of Marlborough; Monnington</u>: TRE Earl Harold held five hides in Monnington. Now Alvred of Marlborough holds this land. Ralph de Bernay unjustly (*iniuste*) took (*abstulit*) a hide away from there.

748 i, 186r (19-8) <u>Alvred of Marlborough; Pembridge</u>: TRW Alvred of Marlborough holds eleven hides less a virgate in Pembridge. TRE Earl Harold held them. The canons of St. Guthlac's claim (*calumniantur*) this manor, and they say that Earl Godwine and his son Harold unjustly took it away (*abstulerunt iniuste*) from St. Guthlac's.

749 i, 186r (19-10) <u>Alvred of Marlborough; Much Cowarne</u>: TRE Earl Harold held Much Cowarne. There were fifteen hides gelded, but King William pardoned (*condonavit*) six hides quit from geld. TRW Agnes, the daughter of Alvred and the wife of Thurstan of Wigmore, holds this manor. TRE the third penny of three hundreds belonged to this manor. It has now been taken away (*ablata est*).

750 i, 186v (22-8) <u>Durand of Gloucester; Litley</u>: TRE Reuer and Alwine held a hide in Litley as two manors. TRW Widard holds it from Durand of Gloucester. King William gave (*dedit*) this land to Roger de Pîtres.

751 i, 187r (25-9) <u>Gilbert fitz Thurold; Ailey</u>: TRE Earl Harold held two hides in Ailey. Earl William gave (*dedit*) them to Gilbert fitz Thurold for four hides.

752 i, 187r (29-1) <u>Hugh the Ass; Kenchester</u>: TRW Hugh the Ass holds four hides in Kenchester. TRE Wulfwig Cild held them and could go where he wished. Godric bought (*emit*) half a hide of this land from Wulfwig and held it as a manor. Hugh loaned (*accommodavit*) a hide of this land to Earl William, and the earl, in turn, gave (*dedit*) it to King Maredudd. His son Gruffydd now has two bordars there.

753 i, 187r (29-2) <u>Hugh the Ass; Fownhope</u>: TRE Thorkil the White held fifteen hides in Fownhope. Now Hugh the Ass holds them. Hugh gave (*dedit*) a berewick of this manor to one of his knights.

754 i, 187r (29-16) <u>Hugh the Ass; "Bernoldune"</u>: TRE Thorkil the White held two hides in "Bernoldune." Now Hugh the Ass holds them. There is a large woodland there, but how much has not been stated (*quantitas non fuit dicta*).

755 i, 187r (29-18) <u>Hugh the Ass; Chickward</u>: TRE Earl Harold held a hide and a virgate in Chickward. Now Hugh the Ass holds them. Earl William gave (*dedit*) them to Hugh.

756 i, 187v (30-1) <u>Urso d'Abetot; Wicton</u>: TRE Alwine held a hide and a virgate in Wicton and could go where he wished. Now Urso d'Abetot holds it. Roger de Lacy holds this manor through an exchange with (*per cambitionem de*) Urso.

757 i, 187v (31-1) <u>Gruffydd son of Maredudd; "Mateurdin"</u>: TRE Earl Harold held two-thirds of a hide in "Mateurdin." Earl William gave (*dedit*) this land to King Maredudd. Now Gruffydd son of Maredudd holds it.

758 i, 187v (31-7) <u>Gruffydd son of Maredudd; Lye</u>: TRE Owen and Almær held three hides of waste in Lye as two manors. Earl William gave (*dedit*) them to King Maredudd. Now Gruffydd holds them. King William pardoned (*condonavit*) the geld for King Maredudd, and later for his son. Ralph de Mortimer holds this manor's woodland along with fifty-seven acres of land.

Hertfordshire

759 i, 132r (B-3) <u>Borough of Hertford</u>: TRW Eudo Dapifer has a house in Hertford which was Wulfmær of Eaton's. It does not pay customs.

760 i, 132r (B-5) <u>Borough of Hertford</u>: Humphrey d'Anneville holds two houses and a garden in Hertford under Eudo Dapifer. One of these houses was loaned (*accommodata fuit*) to the King's reeve; the other, with its garden, belonged to a burgess. The burgesses now claim (*reclamant*) they were unjustly taken away (*iniuste ablatas*) from them.

761 i, 132r (B-7) <u>Borough of Hertford</u>: TRW Peter de Valognes has two churches with a house in Hertford, which he bought (*emit*) from Wulfwig of Hatfield. Wulfwig could grant and sell them TRE.

762 i, 132r (B-10) <u>Borough of Hertford</u>: TRE Aki held fourteen houses in Hertford. TRW Hardwin de Scales holds them, and he calls the King to warranty (*advocat . . . regem ad protectorem*) for them. Hardwin has another house there by the King's gift. It belonged to a burgess TRE.

763 i, 132r (1-1) <u>Terra Regis; Wymondley</u>: TRW King William holds eight hides in Wymondley. This manor was in the demesne of Chatteris Abbey, but three years before the death of King Edward, Earl Harold took it away (*abstulit*), so the whole shire testifies. He put (*apposuit*) it in his manor of Hitchin.

764 i, 132v (1-5) <u>Terra Regis; Westoning [Bd]</u>: TRW King William holds five hides in Westoning. Earl Harold held this manor TRE. Since King Edward's death it has not acquitted (*adquietavit*) itself of the King's geld.

765   i, 132v (1-6) <u>Terra Regis; King's Walden</u>: TRE Leofgifu held two hides in King's Walden from Earl Harold and could sell them without his permission. She found cartage and watch and ward for the King's service, but unjustly and through force (*iniuste et per vim*), so the shire testifies. Now King William holds this land. TRW Esger's widow has a hide of this same land from the King. She also held it from Earl Harold in King Edward's time, and she could sell without the Earl's permission. She found cartage and watch and ward for the King's service unjustly and through force (*iniuste per vim*), so the shire testifies. Ilbert put (*apposuit*) these two manors in Hitchin when he was sheriff, by testimony of the hundred.

766   i, 132v (1-9) <u>Terra Regis; Temple Dinsley</u>: TRW King William holds seven hides in Temple Dinsley. TRE two sokemen held them as two manors from Earl Harold and could sell. Each of them, however, found two cartages and two watches and wards in Hitchin, but through force and unjustly (*per vim et iniuste*), so the hundred testifies. Ilbert held these two manors as one, and was seised of them through the King's writ (*fuit saisitus per breve regis*) for as long as he was sheriff, so the shire testifies. After he handed over (*dimisit*) the sheriffdom, Peter de Valognes and Ralph Taillebois took this manor away (*abstulerunt*) from him and put (*posuerunt*) it in Hitchin, because Ilbert refused (*nolebat*) to find cartage for the sheriff. Geoffrey de Bec, Ilbert's successor, claims (*reclamat*) the King's mercy (*misericordiam regis*) for this manor.

767   i, 133r (1-12) <u>Terra Regis; Wellbury</u>: TRE Leofgifu held a hide in Wellbury and could sell. TRW a sokeman held it from the King. Ilbert put (*apposuit*) this land in his manor of Lilley while he was sheriff. After he lost (*perdidit*) the sheriffdom, Peter de Valognes and Ralph Taillebois took it away (*tulerunt*) from him and put it in Hitchin, so the whole shire testifies. It did not lie there TRE, nor did it pay any customs.

768   i, 133r (1-13) <u>Terra Regis; Wain Wood</u>: TRE Godwine, a man of Earl Harold, held a hide in Wain Wood and could sell it. Now a sokeman holds it from the King. Peter the Sheriff put (*posuit*) this land in Hitchin at farm, where it did not belong in the time of King Edward, nor did it pay customs there. Ilbert had given (*dederat*) this land to one of his knights when he was sheriff. Geoffrey de Bec, however, claims (*reclamat*) the King's mercy (*misericordam regis*) for it. Also in Wain Wood, there is a woodland at fifty pigs attached to this land, which Osmund de Vaubadon annexed (*invasit*) against the King. It lay in the soke of Hitchin, so the shire testifies.

769   i, 133r (1-17) <u>Terra Regis; Hexton</u>: TRW a sokeman of the King holds a virgate in Hexton. This sokemen also held it in King Edward's time. He was the Abbot of St. Albans's man and could sell. Earl Harold put (*apposuit*) this land in Hitchin through force and unjustly (*per vim et iniuste*), so the shire testifies.

770   i, 133r (1-18) <u>Terra Regis; Bayford</u>: [The information on TRE holders for this entry hints at Earl Tosti's dispossession. It reads: "Earl Tosti held this manor, but King Edward had it in his demesne on the day he died."]

771 i, 133r (2-1) Archbishop of Canterbury; Datchworth: TRE Ælfric the Black held a hide in Datchworth from the Abbot of Westminster. He could not separate it from the Church, so the hundred testifies. But, for his other lands, Ælfric was Archbishop Stigand's man. Now Ansketil holds this hide from Archbishop Lanfranc.

772 i, 133r (2-2) Archbishop of Canterbury; Watton: TRW Ansketil holds two and a half hides in Watton from the Archbishop of Canterbury. TRE Ælfric the Black held two of them from the Abbot of Westminster, and he could not separate them from the Church. Almær, Ælfric's man held the remaining half hide and could sell.

773 i, 133r (2-3) Archbishop of Canterbury; Shephall: TRW Ansketil holds two hides in Shephall from the archbishop. TRE Ælfric, a man of Archbishop Stigand, held them. They were in the demesne of St. Albans Abbey, and Ælfric could neither sell nor separate them from that Church.

774 i, 133r (2-4) Archbishop of Canterbury; Libury: TRW an Englishman holds two acres in Libury from the archbishop. TRE the same man held them in mortgage (*in vadimonio*). He could sell.

775 i, 133v (4-1) Bishop of London; Throcking: TRW Humphrey holds a hide and a half from the Bishop of London in Throcking. TRE two brothers, Bishop William's men, held this land. A virgate of this land was and is in mortgage (*in vadimonio*). Humphrey acquits (*adquietat*) it of the King's geld, yet he does not have it. The bishop's men say that this land is from Bishop William's purchase (*de emptione*), but the men of the shire do not attest to this.

776 i, 134r (4-21) Bishop of London: The Bishop of London and his knights hold thirty-six hides [presumably described in all the entries above this statement]. Along with these, he claims (*reclamat*) four hides in Hadham, which the Abbot of Ely holds.

777 i, 134r (4-22) Bishop of London; Bishop's Stortford: TRE Eadgifu the Fair held six hides in Bishop's Stortford: TRW the Bishop of London holds them. It is part of the fee which he bought (*emit*).

778 i, 134r (5-6) Bishop of London; Wymondley: TRW Adam holds a hide and a virgate from the Bishop of London in Wymondley. TRE Alflæd held this land from Robert fitz Wimarc. She could not sell it without Robert's permission, so the shire testifies.

779 i, 134v (5-16) Bishop of Bayeux; Reed: TRW Osbern holds a hide in Reed from the Bishop of Bayeux. TRE the girl Eadgifu, by the testimony of the shire, held this land. She was Archbishop Stigand's man.

780 i, 135r (8-3) Abbot of Ely; Much Hadham: TRW the Abbot of Ely holds four hides in Much Hadham. It lay there on the day King Edward was alive and dead, so the whole shire testifies.

781 i, 135r (9-9) Westminster Abbey; Ayot St. Lawrence: TRE the King's thegn Ælfwine held two and a half hides in Ayot St. Lawrence. TRW Geoffrey holds them from the Abbot of Westminster. The abbot vouches (*revocat*) King William to have granted (*concessisse*) this land.

782   i, 135v (10-6) <u>St. Albans Abbey; Codicote, Oxwick</u>: TRE the eight hides in Codicote and Oxwick were two manors. Five hides were held by the Abbot of St. Albans; Ælfwine of Gotton held the other three hides under the abbot, and he could not separate them from the abbey. Now the abbey holds these two manors. The Count of Mortain's men annexed (*invaserunt*) fifteen acres of this land against the abbot, so the men of the hundred testify.

783   i, 135v (10-9) <u>St. Albans Abbey; Abbots Langley</u>: TRE and TRW the Abbot of St. Albans holds Abbots Langley. It was assessed at five and a half hides TRE; now for three. In the time of the Bishop of Bayeux, Herbert fitz Ivo took away (*tulit*) and seized (*occupavit*) a hide of scrub land and fields. It lay in St. Albans on the day King Edward was alive and dead. Now the Count of Mortain holds it.

784   i, 135v (10-12) <u>St. Albans Abbey; Windridge</u>: TRW Geoffrey de Bec holds a hide and a half in Windridge from the abbot. TRE Osbern the Monk and his man Goding held it. They could not separate it from the abbey, so the hundred testifies.

785   i, 136v (15-4) <u>Count of Mortain; Pendley</u>: TRE Eadgifu the Nun held two hides in Pendley from Ingelric and could not grant them. Now the Count of Mortain holds them. They are two of the seven hides that the count took (*sumpsit*) from Tring.

786   i, 136v (15-5) <u>Count of Mortain; Wigginton</u>: TRW Humphrey holds seven and a half hides and the third part of half a hide in Wigginton from the Count of Mortain. Of these, Beorhtric, Queen Edith's man, held three and a half hides; and Godwine, Ingelric's man, held three hides and the third part of half a hide. He could not grant or sell them outside of Tring. These are of the seven hides which the Count of Mortain took (*sumpsit*) from Tring.

787   i, 136v (15-6) <u>Count of Mortain; Gubblecote</u>: TRW Fulcold holds a hide and a half in Gubblecote from the Count. TRE Eadgifu held it from Ingelric. She could not put it outside (*non potuit mittere extra*) Tring. This land is of the seven hides which the Count of Mortain took (*sumpsit*) from Tring.

788   i, 136v (15-9) <u>Count of Mortain; Dunsley</u>: TRW a widow holds the third part of half a hide in Dunsley from the Count of Mortain. TRE Ingelric held this land. It is of the seven hides which the Count took (*sumpsit*) from Tring.

789   i, 136v–137r (16-1) <u>Count Alan; Watton</u>: TRW Godwine holds a hide and a half in Watton from Count Alan. TRE Godwine held it from Westminster Abbey and could not sell it. Instead, after his death, it ought to have returned to the Church (*post mortem eius debebat ad aecclesiam redire*), so the hundred testifies. His wife, however, turned herself (*vertit se*) with this land to Eadgifu the Fair through force (*per vim*), and held it on the day King Edward was alive and dead. Sixteen acres of this land were taken (*sumptae sunt*) after the coming of King William. They are now held by Ansketil de Rots, who holds them under the archbishop. Count Alan, however, acquits (*adquietat*) them of the King's geld.

790   i, 137r (16-2) <u>Count Alan; Munden</u>: TRE Eadgifu the Fair held seven and a half hides and a virgate in Munden. Now Count Alan holds them. There is a woodland there at 150 pigs. After Earl Ralph's forfeiture (*forisfecit*), Roger de Mussegros took away (*abstulit*) a second woodland from the manor, which had pasturage for 200 pigs, so the whole shire testifies

791   i, 137r (17-1) <u>Count Eustace; Tring</u>: TRW Eustace count of Boulogne holds Tring. TRE Ingelric held it. It was assessed for thirty-nine hides, now for five hides and a virgate. Two sokemen, Oswulf son of Frani's men, were there. They had two hides and could sell. Ingelric put (*apposuit*) them in this manor after the coming of King William, so the men of the hundred testify. Similarly, a man of the Abbot of Ramsey had five hides of this manor in the same way – that is, he could not grant or sell his land outside the abbey. Ingelric also put (*apposuit*) him in this manor after the coming of King William. He was not there TRE, so the hundred testifies.

792   i, 137v (17-15) <u>Count Eustace; Braughing</u>: TRW Count Eustace holds five hides in Braughing. TRE two thegns held this manor: one held four hides and was a man of King Edward, and the other, Esger the Staller's man, had a hide. Neither of them could sell because their lands always lay in alms in the time of King Edward and all of his antecessors, so the shire testifies.

793   i, 137v (19-1) <u>Robert d'Oilly; Tiscot</u>: TRW Ralph Bassett holds Tiscot from Robert d'Oilly. TRE it was assessed at four hides; now for two. Five sokemen held this manor. Two of them held a hide and half and were Beorhtric's men. Two others, Oswulf son of Frani's men, held another hide and a half. The fifth, Eadmær Atre's man, held a hide. None of these men belonged to Wigot, Robert d'Oilly's antecessor, but each of them could sell his land. One of them bought (*emit*) his land from King William for nine ounces of gold, so the men of the hundred testify. Later he turned himself to Wigot for protection (*ad Wigotum se vertit pro protectione*).

794   i, 137v (20-2) <u>Robert Gernon; Ayot St. Peter</u>: TRE two thegns, King Edward's men, held two and a half hides of land in Ayot St. Peter and could sell. TRW William holds it from Robert Gernon. This William, who is Robert's man, annexed (*invasit*) it against the King, but he claims (*reclamat*) his lord to warranty (*ad protectorem*). [An "A" has been written in the margin opposite this entry.]

795   i, 138r (21-1) <u>Robert de Tosny; Miswell</u>: TRW Ralph holds Miswell from Robert de Tosny. Oswulf son of Frani, a thegn of King Edward and Robert de Tosny's antecessor, held it in the time of King Edward. TRE it was assessed at fourteen hides, now for three hides and two and a half virgates.

796   i, 138r (22-2) <u>Ralph de Tosny; Westmill</u>: TRW Roger holds four hides and three virgates from Ralph de Tosny in Westmill. TRE Saxi, a housecarl of King Edward, held them. There, a sokeman of Eskil of Ware had a virgate and could sell. After the coming of King William it was sold and put (*vendita fuit et apposita*) in this manor, where it did not lie TRE.

797   i, 138v (24-2) <u>Ralph Baynard; Little Hormead</u>: TRW William holds a virgate in Little Hormead from Ralph Baynard. TRE Wulfweard, Esger the Staller's

man, held it. Count Eustace's men claim (*reclamant*) this land, of which they had been seised (*fuerunt saisiti*) for two years after the Count came into this honor (*ad hunc honorem venit*), so the men of the hundred testify.

798 i, 138v (25-2) <u>Ranulf brother of Ilger; Stanstead Abbotts</u>: TRE Ranulf brother of Ilger holds seventeen hides and half a virgate in Stanstead Abbotts. TRE Ælfwine of Gotton held eleven hides and half a virgate of this manor. Of these Ralph Taillebois gave (*dedit*) ten hides and a half virgate to Ranulf with his niece, as a marriage portion (*in maritagio*). He put (*posuit*) the eleventh hide in Hunsdon.

799 i, 138v (26-1) <u>Hugh de Grandmesnil; Ware</u>: TRW Hugh de Grandmesnil holds twenty-four hides in Ware. TRE Eskil of Ware held this manor. One of his sokemen held two hides there; another sokeman, a man of Earl Gyrth, held half a hide. Both could sell. These two sokemen were put (*appositi fuerunt*) in this manor after the coming of King William. They did not belong there TRE, so the shire testifies.

800 i, 138v (28-1) <u>William d'Eu; Graveley</u>: TRW William d'Eu holds a virgate and a half in Graveley and Peter holds from him. TRE Ælfstan of Boscombe held a virgate of this land. It lay in Weston. Leofsige, a sokeman of King Edward, held the other half virgate and could sell. Eight acres and a toft of this land lay in Stevenage, which King Edward gave (*dedit*) to Westminster. Now Roger, Peter de Valognes's official (*minister*), holds the toft and eight acres.

801 i, 139r (31-8) <u>Eudo Dapifer; land in Hertford Hundred</u>: TRW Humphrey holds half a hide in Hertford Hundred from Eudo Dapifer. TRE Leofsige, King Edward's reeve, held this land and could sell. The Bishop of Bayeux took it away (*abstulit*) from Leofsige and gave (*dedit*) it to Eudo. It has been seized (*occupata est*) against the King. When Humphrey took (*sumpsit*) it from Eudo, he got with it 68 oxen, 350 sheep, 150 pigs, 50 goats, a mare, and 13s. 4d. of the King's rent (*de censu regis*). Between cloth and vessels, 20s.

802 i, 139r (32-1) <u>Edward the Sheriff; Great Gaddesden</u>: TRW Edward of Salisbury holds three hides in Great Gaddesden. TRE Wulfwynn held this manor from the Abbot of St. Albans. She could not put this land outside (*non poterat mittere extra*) the abbey; after her death it ought to have returned to the Church (*post mortem suam redire debebat ad aecclesiam*), so the hundred testifies.

803 i, 140r (33-18) <u>Geoffrey de Mandeville; Thorley</u>: TRW Geoffrey de Mandeville holds four hides in Thorley. TRE Godgyth, Esger the Staller's man, held this manor and could sell. William bishop of London bought (*emit*) it from King William through a grant (*per concessionem*) of Godgyth. The bishop now claims (*reclamat*) it.

804 i, 140r (34-13) <u>Geoffrey de Bec; Hailey</u>: TRW Geoffrey de Bec holds two hides in Hailey. TRE Wulfwine, a man of Earl Harold, held this land. Of this land, Ralph de Limesy claims (*reclamat*) as much woodland as belongs to three hides of Amwell, along with two villeins with a virgate, a bordar with ten acres, and another twenty-four acres of land. Ilbert of Hertford took (*sumpsit*)

these and put (*apposuit*) them in this manor, so the men of the shire testify. The canons of Waltham Holy Cross claim (*reclamant*) as much woodland as belongs to a hide.

805   i, 140v (35-3) <u>Gosbert de Beauvais; Wallington</u>: TRW Fulk holds three hides and forty acres from Gosbert de Beauvais in Wallington. TRE Eadric, a man of Earl Ælfgar, held this manor and could sell. A sokeman of Eadgifu the Fair held twenty-four acres of this land and could sell. Earl Ralph had been seised (*fuit saisitus*) of them, but on the day on which he forfeited he was not seised of them (*sed die qua forisfecit non erat saisitus*), by the testimony of the hundred.

806   i, 141r (36-9) <u>Peter de Valognes; Libury</u>: TRW Peter de Valognes holds half a virgate and ten acres in Libury. A sokeman of King Edward held it TRE and could sell. He paid through custom the fourth of a cartage or a penny for the King's sheriff each year. Peter the Sheriff took (*sumpsit*) the land of this sokeman of King William. It is in the King's hand through forfeiture (*pro forisfactura*) for not paying the King's geld, so Peter's men say. But the men of the shire do not bear (*portant*) testimony for the sheriff, because this land was quit from geld and from other King's dues as long as the sokeman held it, by testimony of the hundred.

807   i, 141r (36-11) <u>Peter de Valognes; Sacombe</u>: TRW Peter de Valognes holds nine hides less a virgate in Sacombe. TRE Ælmær held four of these hides as a manor, by testimony of the hundred. In the same manor a woman held five virgates under Eskil of Ware. She could sell all, except one virgate, which she put in mortgage (*posuit in vadimonio*) with Almær of Benington for 10s.

808   i, 141r (36-13) <u>Peter de Valognes; Stonebury</u>: TRW Peter de Valognes holds a hide and a half in Stonebury. Four sokemen held this land. One of them was a reeve of the King. He had half a hide. He seized (*occupavit*) the lands of the other three sokemen against King William, so the whole shire testifies.

809   i, 141r–v (36-19) <u>Peter de Valognes; Tewin</u>: TRW Healfdene holds five and a half hides from Peter de Valognes in Tewin. This same Healfdene held this land TRE. He was a thegn of King Edward and could sell. But King William gave (*dedit*) this manor to Healfdene and his mother for the soul of his son Richard, so he himself says, and shows this through his writ (*pro anima Ricardi filii sui, ut ipsemet dicit et per breve suum ostendit*). Now Peter says that he holds this manor by gift of the King (*ex dono regis*).

810   i, 141v (37-9) <u>Hardwin de Scales; Ashwell</u>: TRW Theobald holds half a hide in Ashwell from Hardwin de Scales. TRE Uhtræd held it under Robert fitz Wimarc. He could not sell without Robert's permission, so the men of the hundred testify.

811   i, 141v–142r (37-19) <u>Hardwin de Scales; Berkesdon</u>: TRW Peter and Theobald hold a virgate from Hardwin de Scales in Berkesdon. TRE three sokemen held this land. One was a man of Eadgifu the Fair and held a quarter of a virgate. The second was Ælfgar's man, and he similarly held a quarter of a virgate. The third was Gyrth's man. He had half a virgate. All of them could sell. Count Alan claims (*reclamat*) that he ought, in justice (*iuste*), to have

three-quarters of this virgate, because he was seised (*erat saisitus*) of it when he recently crossed the sea, so the men of the hundred bear (*portant*) testimony for him. But Hardwin claims (*reclamat*) Peter the Sheriff to warranty and for livery (*ad protectorem et liberatorem*), by order (*iussu*) of the Bishop of Bayeux, because he delivered it in exchange for (*liberavit pro excambio*) Libury.

812 i, 142r (37-21) Hardwin de Scales; Little Berkhamsted: TRW Hardwin de Scales holds five hides in Little Berkhamsted. TRE Sæmær the Priest held two hides of this manor, the widow Leofgifu two hides, and Wulfric Werden one hide. These lands were from King Edward's alms and the alms of all of the Kings, his antecessors, so the shire testifies.

813 i, 142r (38-2) Edgar the Ætheling; Great Hormead: TRW Godwine holds six hides and three virgates from Edgar the Ætheling in Great Hormead. Alnoth, a thegn of Archbishop Stigand, held one and a half hides of this land as a manor TRE. Wulfwine, Esger the Staller's man held a hide. Alweard, a man of Almær of Benington, held a hide; and seven sokemen of King Edward held three hides and a virgate. All of these men could sell their land. Ilbert the Sheriff put (*apposuit*) them in this manor in the time of King William. They were not there TRE, so the hundred testifies.

814 i, 142r (39-1) Mainou the Breton; Dunsley: TRW Mainou the Breton holds the third part of half a hide in Dunsley. TRE Ingelric held it. It lay in Tring, and is of the seven hides which the Count of Mortain took (*assumpsit*).

815 i, 142r (42-6) King's thegns; Wormley: TRE Alwine Doddason holds two and a half hides from the King in Wormley. TRE Wulfweard, a man of Esger the Staller, held them and could sell. This manor was sold (*fuit venditum*) for three marks of gold after the coming of King William.

816 i, 142r–v (42-11) King's thegns; Welwyn: TRW a priest holds a hide in Welwyn in alms from the King. He held it himself from King Edward in alms. It lies in the church of this vill. William the Black, a man of the Bishop of Bayeux, annexed (*invasit*) twelve acres of this alms land against the King, so the hundred testifies.

Huntingdonshire

817 i, 203r (B-1) Borough of Huntingdon: TRW there are 116 burgesses in Huntingdon. They pay all customs and the King's geld. Ramsey Abbey had ten of these burgesses TRE with sake and soke and all customs except geld. In the time of King William, Eustace the Sheriff took these ten burgesses away (*abstulit*) from the abbey through force (*per vim*), and they are now in the King's hand with the others.

818 i, 203r (B-10) Borough of Huntingdon: TRE Ælfric the Sheriff had a messuage in Huntingdon, which King William later granted (*concessit*) to Ælfric's wife and sons. Eustace the Sheriff now holds it, but the impoverished son claims it with his mother (*pauper cum matre reclamat*).

819 i, 203r (B-12) <u>Borough of Huntingdon</u>: TRE Burgræd the Priest and Thorkil the Priest had a church with two hides of land and twenty-two burgesses with their houses. All of this belonged to Burgræd's and Thorkil's church along with sake and soke. Eustace the Sheriff now has all of this. The two priests claim the King's mercy (*reclamant miscericordiam regis*).

820 i, 203r (B-13) <u>Borough of Huntingdon</u>: TRW Geoffrey bishop of Coutances has a church and a house in Huntingdon, which Eustace took away (*abstulit*) from Ramsey Abbey. Ramsey still claims (*reclamat*) them.

821 i, 203r (B-14) <u>Borough of Huntingdon</u>: TRE Gos and Hunæf had sixteen houses with sake and soke and toll and team (*thol et them*). Countess Judith now has them.

822 i, 203r (B-18) <u>Borough of Huntingdon</u>: TRW there are two carucates and forty acres of land and ten acres of meadow, which lie in Huntingdon. The King has two-thirds, and the earl a third, and they divide the rent from this (*unde partiuntur censum*). The burgesses cultivate this land and lease (*locant*) it through the King's officials (*ministros*) and the earl.

823 i, 203r (B-21) <u>Borough of Huntingdon</u>: TRW in Hurstingstone Hundred the demesne plows are exempt from the King's geld. The villeins and the sokemen pay geld according to the hides written in the returns (*in brevi scriptas*), except in Broughton, where the Abbot of Ramsey pays geld for one hide with the other men.

824 i, 203v (1-2) <u>Terra Regis; Botolph Bridge</u>: King Edward held five hides in Botolph Bridge. TRW Ranulf brother of Ilger has custody of it. In this manor and in others the Abbot of Thorney's dam has killed (*necat exclusa*) 300 acres of meadow.

825 i, 203v (2-2) <u>Bishop of Lincoln; Great Staughton</u>: TRW Remigius bishop of Lincoln holds six hides in Great Staughton, and Eustace the Sheriff holds from him. The Abbot of Ramsey claims (*clamat*) this manor against the bishop.

826 i, 203v (2-6) <u>Bishop of Lincoln; Orton Longueville</u>: TRE Leofric had three hides and a virgate of land in Orton Longueville. TRW John holds it from Bishop Remigius. The King claims (*clamat*) the soke of this land. [A "k" for *klamor* appears in the margin of the entry next to this last statement.]

827 i, 203v (2-7) <u>Bishop of Lincoln; Stilton</u>: Tovi held two hides of land in Stilton, but it was given (*fuit data*) to Wulfwig bishop of Dorchester in the time of King Edward. Now John holds it from the Bishop of Lincoln.

828 i, 203v (2-8) <u>Bishop of Lincoln; Leighton Bromswold</u>: TRE Thorkil the Dane held fifteen hides in Leighton Bromswold. Earl Waltheof gave (*dedit*) this manor to St. Mary's, Stow in alms. Now the Bishop of Lincoln holds it.

829 i, 203v (2-9) <u>Bishop of Lincoln; Pertenhall [Beds.]</u>: TRE Alwine held a virgate in Pertenhall. TRW William holds it from Bishop Remigius of Lincoln. This land is located in Bedfordshire, but it pays geld and service in Huntingdonshire. The King's officials (*ministri*) claim (*clamant*) it for the King's use. [A "k" for *klamor* appears in the margin next to this statement.]

830 i, 204r (6-3) <u>Ramsey Abbey; Broughton</u>: TRE and TRW the Abbot of Ramsey holds four hides in Broughton. There are also five hides of sokemen's land there. These sokemen say that they had the forfeitures from adultery (*legreuuitam*), bloodshed (*blodeuuitam*), and their fines for theft (*latrocinium suum*) up to 4d. The Abbot of Ramsey had the forfeiture for robbery (*forisfacturam latrocinii*) over 4d. Eustace the Sheriff claims (*calumniatur*) five of these hides. [There is a "k" for *klamor* written in the margin next to the notice about Eustace's claim.]

831 i, 204v (6-7) <u>Ramsey Abbey; St. Ives</u>: TRE and TRW the Abbot of Ramsey holds twenty hides in St. Ives. Eustace the Sheriff claims (*calumniatur*) two and a half of these hides. [A "k" for *klamor* is written in the margin next to the notice of Eustace's claim.]

832 i, 204v (6-8) <u>Ramsey Abbey; Houghton</u>: TRE and TRW the Abbot of Ramsey held seven hides in Houghton. Eustace claims (*calumniatur*) one of these hides. [A "k" for *klamor* is written in the margin next to the notice of Eustace's claim.]

833 i, 204v (6-17) <u>Ramsey Abbey; Hemingford Abbots</u>: TRE Godric held a hide in Hemingford Abbots from the Abbot of Ramsey. TRW Ralph fitz Osmund holds it, but the men of the hundred do not know through whom.

834 i, 205r (7-8) <u>Thorney Abbey; Whittlesey Mere</u>: Æthelsige abbot of Ramsey has one boat, Thurold abbot of Peterborough another, and Gunter of Le Mans abbot of Thorney has two boats. Of these two, the Abbot of Peterborough holds one from the Abbot of Thorney along with two fisheries, two fishermen, and a virgate of land. For these he gives (*dat*) pasture sufficient for 120 pigs; if the pasture is deficient (*deficit*), he feeds and fattens sixty with grain. He also finds timber for a house of sixty feet and poles for the court around the house. He also repairs the house and court if they weaken. This agreement (*conventio*) was made between them in King Edward's time.

835 i, 205r (8-4) <u>Peterborough Abbey; Orton Waterville</u>: TRE Godwine held three and a half hides in Orton Waterville. King Edward had soke over this land. It did not belong to Peterborough TRE. In the time of King William, however, it was given (*data est*) to the abbey.

836 i, 206r (19-13) <u>Eustace the Sheriff; Hargrave [Northants.]</u>: TRE Langfer held a virgate of land in Hargrave. TRW Herbert, a man of Eustace the Sheriff, holds it. Tovi claims (*clamat*) that this land was unjustly taken away (*iniuste ablatam*) from him by Eustace.

837 i, 206r (19-15) <u>Eustace the Sheriff; Great Gidding</u>: TRE six sokemen – Alweald and his five brothers – held four and a half hides in Great Gidding. TRW Eustace the Sheriff holds them. Alweald and his brothers claim (*clamant*) Eustace to have unjustly taken away (*iniuste abstulisse*) this land from them. William Inganie claims (*calumniatur*) half a virgate and eighteen acres of this land, by the testimony of the whole hundred.

838 i, 206r (19-18) <u>Eustace the Sheriff; Thurning</u>: TRW Alvred and Jocelyn hold five hides in Thurning from Eustace the Sheriff. Robert Dispensator claims (*clamat*) a hide and a virgate of this land.

839 i, 206v (19-27) Eustace the Sheriff; Hail Weston: TRE Algeat held one and a half hides in Hail Weston: TRW Countess Judith claims (*clamat*) it against Eustace the Sheriff, who holds it.

840 i, 206v (20-1) Countess Judith; Conington: TRE Thorkil held nine hides in Conington. Now Countess Judith holds them. Six of these hides belonged to Thorney Abbey TRE. Thorkil held them from the Abbot and paid a payment (*karitatem*) from it, but the men of the hundred do not know how much this payment was.

841 i, 206v (20-3) Countess Judith; Stukeley: TRE Hungifu held three hides of land in Stukeley. TRW Countess Judith holds it. Eustace the Sheriff claims (*calumniatur*) it. [A "d" appears in the margin opposite this statement.]

842 i, 206v (20-6) Countess Judith; Eynesbury: King Edward held nine hides of land in Eynesbury. TRW Countess Judith holds it. She gave (*dedit*) the Church of St. Helen's, Elstow a sheep fold, 662 sheep, and 60 acres of meadow there.

843 i, 207r (22-1, 2) Aubrey de Vere; Yelling, Hemingford Abbots: TRE Ælfric held five hides in Yelling and eleven hides in Hemingford Abbots from the Abbot of Ramsey. Now Aubrey de Vere holds them from the King. Ralph fitz Osmund holds them from Aubrey.

844 i, 208r (D-1) Clamores: The sworn men of Huntingdon (*homines qui iuraverunt in Huntedune*) say that the Church of St. Mary in Huntingdon and the land that belongs to it belonged to Thorney, and that the abbot mortgaged (*invadiavit*) it to the burgesses. King Edward, however, gave (*dedit*) it to his priests Vitalis and Bernard. They sold (*vendiderunt*) it to Hugh, King Edward's chamberlain. Hugh, in turn, sold (*vendidit*) it to two priests of Huntingdon, for which they have King Edward's seal (*inde sigillum regis Edwardi*). Eustace now has it without livery, writ, or seisor (*sine liberatore et sine brevi et sine saisitore*).

845 i, 208r (D-2) Clamores: Eustace the Sheriff took away (*abstulit*) Leofgifu's house through force (*per vim*) and gave (*dedit*) it to Ogier of London.

846 i, 208r (D-3) Clamores: They testify that the land of Hunæf and Gos was in King Edward's hand on the day he was alive and dead, and that they held it from the King and not the earl. They also say, however, that they heard that King William was said to give it (*sed dicunt se audisse quod rex Willelmi debuerit eam dare*) to Waltheof.

847 i, 208r (D-4) Clamores: Concerning the five hides in Broughton, they say that they were sokemen's land TRE, but that the King gave (*dedit*) the land and the soke over them to Ramsey Abbey, for the service which Alwine abbot of Ramsey did for him in Saxony. The abbey has had it ever since.

848 i, 208r (D-5) Clamores: The county testifies that the land of Beorhtmær Belehorne was reeveland (*revelande*) TRE and belonged to the farm.

849 i, 208r (D-6) <u>Clamores</u>: They testify that the land of Alwine the Priest was the abbot's. Both his holdings were priest-land and reeveland (*terram presbyteri et præfecti*).

850 i, 208r (D-7) <u>Clamores</u>: They testify that the land of Ælfric at Yelling and Hemingford Abbots belonged to Ramsey Abbey. It had been granted (*fuisse concessas*) to Ælfric for his life on the condition that after his death, the land should return to the Church (*in vita sua tali ratione quod post mortem suam debuerunt redire ad aecclesiam*). Boxted [Essex], too, was with Yelling and Hemingford. This Ælfric was killed at the Battle of Hastings, and the abbot took (*recepit*) his land until Aubrey de Vere disseised (*desaisiuit*) him.

851 i, 208r (D-8) <u>Clamores</u>: Concerning the two hides which Ralph fitz Osmund holds in Hemingford Abbots, they say that one of these hides was in the demesne of Ramsey Abbey in King Edward's day, and that Ralph holds it against the abbot's wishes (*contra voluntatem*). They also say that Godric held the other hide from the abbot, but that when the abbot was in Denmark, Osmund, Ralph's father, seized (*rapuit*) it from Sæwine the Falconer, to whom the abbot had given (*dederat*) the land because of his love of the King (*ob amorem regis*).

852 i, 208r (D-9) <u>Clamores</u>: Concerning Sumarlithr, they say that he held his land from Thorulf, who gave (*dedit*) it to him. Afterwards, he held it from Thorulf's sons. They had sake and soke over him.

853 i, 208r (D-10) <u>Clamores</u>: They say that the land of Wulfwine Chit of Hail Weston was itself a manor, and that it did not belong to Kimbolton. He was, nonetheless, Earl Harold's man.

854 i, 208r (D-11) <u>Clamores</u>: Concerning Algeat's hide and a half, the sworn men (*homines qui iuraverunt*) say that Algeat held this land from Earl Tosti with sake and soke; and that afterward, he held it from Earl Waltheof.

855 i, 208r (D-12) <u>Clamores</u>: Godric the Priest similarly held a hide of land from Earl Waltheof TRE. Count Eustace now holds it.

856 i, 208r (D-13) <u>Clamores</u>: They say that Godwine's land in Hail Weston did not belong to Saxi, Fafiton's antecessor.

857 i, 208r (D-14) <u>Clamores</u>: The men of the county testify that King Edward gave (*dedit*) Swineshead [Beds.] to Earl Siward with sake and soke, and so Earl Harold had it, except that its men paid geld in the hundred and went with them against the host.

858 i, 208r (D-15) <u>Clamores</u>: Concerning Fursa's land, it was in the King's soke.

859 i, 208r (D-16) <u>Clamores</u>: Concerning Alwine Deule's virgate in Pertenhall [Beds.], King Edward had the soke.

860 i, 208r (D-17) <u>Clamores</u>: They say that Wulfwine Chit's hide in Catworth was in the King's soke, and that Earl Harold did not have it.

861 i, 208r (D-18) <u>Clamores</u>: Wulfwine Chit had another hide in Little Catworth, over which King Edward always had sake and soke. Nonetheless, Wulfwine could grant or sell the land to whom he wished. Countess Judith's men say that the King was to have given (*dedisse*) this land to Earl Waltheof.

862   i, 208r (D-19) <u>Clamores</u>: The county testifies that a third part of half a hide which lies in Easton and pays geld in Bedfordshire belongs to the Abbot of Ely's manor of Spaldwick. The abbot held this land in the time of King Edward and for five years after the coming of King William. Eustace seized it from the Church and kept it back (*rapuit et retinuit*).

863   i, 208r (D-20) <u>Clamores</u>: They say that Keyston was in King Edward's farm, and still is. Although Ælfric the Sheriff settled (*sedisset*) in the vill, he always paid farm to the King for it, and so too did his sons, until Eustace took (*accepit*) the sheriffdom. They have neither seen nor heard of a seal of King Edward, which put the land outside the King's farm (*nec unquam viderunt vel audierunt sigillum regis Edwardi quod eam foris misisset de firma sua*).

864   i, 208r (D-21) <u>Clamores</u>: Alweald and his brothers claim (*clamant*) Eustace to have unjustly (*iniuste*) taken away (*abstulisse*) their land. The county denies that they have seen a seal or seisor who seised him of this land (*negat se vidisse sigillum vel saisitorem qui eum inde saisisset*).

865   i, 208r (D-22) <u>Clamores</u>: On the day King Edward was alive and dead Great Gidding was a berewick of Alconbury, in the King's farm.

866   i, 208r (D-23) <u>Clamores</u>: The county testifies that Buckworth was a berewick of Paxton in the time of King Edward.

867   i, 208r (D-24) <u>Clamores</u>: They say that thirty-six hides of land in Brampton, which Richard Inganie claims (*clamat*) belong to the forest, were of the King's demesne farm and did not belong to the forest.

868   i, 208r (D-25) <u>Clamores</u>: They say that Grafham is and was soke of the King. They have seen neither a writ nor a seisor who delivered it (*nec brevem nec saisitorem vidisse qui liberasset eam*) to Eustace.

869   i, 208r–v (D-26) <u>Clamores</u>: Concerning the six hides in Conington, they say that they had heard that these hides used to lie in Thorney Abbey, and that they had been granted to Thorkil on the condition that after his death they ought to return to the Church (*concesse fuerunt Turchillo tali ratione, quod post mortem suam debent ad aecclesiam redire*) along with three other hides in this vill. They said that they had heard but not seen this, and had not been there (*se audisse sed non vidisse neque inter fuisse*).

870   i, 208v (D-27) <u>Clamores</u>: Concerning the land of Tosti of Sawtry, they say that Tosti's brother Erik designated Sawtry to Ramsey Abbey after his death, and the deaths of his brother and sister (*denominavit eam aecclesiae de Ramesy post mortem suam et fratris et sororis suae*).

871   i, 208v (D-28) <u>Clamores</u>: Concerning Fletton, they say that in King Edward's day all of Fletton lay in Peterborough Abbey, and it ought to lie there still.

872   i, 208v (D-29) <u>Clamores</u>: Concerning Leofric's land, they say that it was in the King's soke. Bishop Remigius, however, shows a writ (*ostendit brevem*) of King Edward, through which the King gave (*dederit*) Leofric with all his land to the bishopric of Dorchester, with sake and soke.

Kent

873 i, 1r (D-2) <u>Dover</u>: The burgesses of Dover gave (*dederunt*) twenty ships with twenty-one men in each to the King once each year for fifteen days. They did this because the King had pardoned (*perdonaverat*) the sake and soke over to them.

874 i, 1r (D-4) <u>Dover</u>: The King's truce or peace (*treuua vel pax*) was in the town from the feast of St. Michael to the feast of St. Andrew. If anyone broke (*infregisset*) it, the King's reeve took the common fine (*accipiebat communem emendationem*).

875 i, 1r (D-8) <u>Dover</u>: There are twenty-nine messuages in Dover over which the King has lost (*perdidit*) customs. Of these Robert of Romney has two, Ralph de Courbépine three, William fitz Theodwald one, William fitz Ogier one, William fitz Theodwald and Robert the Black six, William fitz Geoffrey three including the burgesses' guildhall (*gihalla burgensium*), Hugh de Montfort one house, Durand one, Ranulf de Colombières one, Wadard six, and Modbert's son one. All these men vouch (*revocant*) the Bishop of Bayeux as protector and warrantor or donor (*ad protectorem et liberatorem vel datorem*).

876 i, 1r (D-9) <u>Dover</u>: Concerning the messuage which Ranulf de Colombières holds, which was an exile's – that is, an outlaw's (*exulis vel utlage*) – they agree (*concordant*) that half the land is the King's. Ranulf, however, has both halves himself.

877 i, 1r (D-9) <u>Dover</u>: Humphrey Loripes holds a messuage, half of which was forfeited (*erat forisfactura*) to the King.

878 i, 1r (D-9) <u>Dover</u>: Roger of Westerham built a house on the King's waterway (*super aquam regis*) and until now has had the King's customs. The house was not there TRE.

879 i, 1r (D-10) <u>Dover</u>: There is a mill in the entrance of Dover's port, which ruins (*confringit*) almost all the ships through its great disturbance of the sea. It does the greatest of harm to the King and his men, and was not there TRE. Concerning this mill, Herbert's nephew says that the Bishop of Bayeux granted (*concessit*) his uncle, Herbert fitz Ivo, permission to make it.

880 i, 1r (D-11) <u>Dover</u>: The men of four lathes – that is, the borough Lathe, Eastry Lathe, Lympne Lathe, and Wye Lathe – agree (*concordant*) upon the King's laws (*leges regis*) written below:

881 i, 1r (D-12, 13) <u>Dover</u>: If anyone builds a fence or a foss which narrows the public road of the King (*publica via regis*) or if anyone fells a tree that stood outside the road and has carried off a branch or foliage from it, for each of these forfeitures (*forisfacturas*) he shall pay (*solvet*) 100s. to the King. And if he goes away from home without being apprehended or distrained (*non appraehensus vel divadiatus*), the King's official (*minister regis*) shall follow him, and he shall pay a fine (*emendabit*) of 100s.

882 i, 1r (D-14, 15) <u>Dover</u>: Concerning breach of peace (*girbrige*), if anyone breaches the peace and is charged on the road (*calumniatus in calle*) or has been distrained (*divadiatus fuerit*), he shall pay a fine (*emendabit*) of £8 to the King. If, however, he is quit from the King, he shall not be quit from the lord whose man he is. Other forfeitures (*forisfacturis*) are like breach of peace (*gribrige*), except that he shall pay a fine (*emendabit*) of 100s.

883 i, 1r (D-16, 17) <u>Dover</u>: The King has these forfeitures (*forisfacturas*) over all alodiaries in the whole county of Kent, and over their men: when an alodiary dies the King has relief (*relevationem*) for his land, except for the land of Christ Church, St. Augustine's, and St. Martin's, and with these exceptions: Godric of Bourne, Godric Karlison, Æthelnoth Cild, Esbiorn Bigge, Sigeræd of Chilham, Thorgisl, Northmann, and Azur. Even now, however, the King has the forfeiture of these men's heads (*forisfacturam de capitibus*), and he has relief (*relevamen*) on the lands of those who have sake and soke.

884 i, 1r (D-18) <u>Dover</u>: Over these lands – "Goslahes," the three Bucklands, Hurst, a yoke of Oare, a yoke of Harty, "Schildricheham," Macknade, Arnolton, "Oslachintone," the two Perrys, Throwley, Ospringe, and Horton – the King has the following forfeitures (*forisfacturas*): housebreaking (*handsocam*), breach of peace (*gribrige*), and robbery (*foristel*).

885 i, 1r (D-19) <u>Dover</u>: Concerning adultery (*adulterio*), throughout all of Kent the King has the forfeiture of the man and the archbishop of the woman, except for the land of Christ Church, St. Augustine's, and St. Martin's, from which the King has nothing.

886 i, 1r (D-20) <u>Dover</u>: Concerning theft (*latrone*), the King has half the property (*pecuniae*) of whomever has been judged to die (*qui iudicatus est ad mortem*).

887 i, 1r (D-21) <u>Dover</u>: The King has the forfeiture (*forisfacturam*) from whoever takes in an outlaw (*exulem receperit*) without permission of the King.

888 i, 1r (D-22, 23) <u>Dover</u>: From the aforementioned land of Æthelnoth Cild and others like him, the King has ward and watch (*custodiam*) for six days at Canterbury or at Sandwich, and they have food and drink from the King. If they have not had food and drink, they can withdraw without forfeiture (*sine forisfactura recedunt*). If they are summoned (*fuerint præmoniti*) for a meeting of the shire (*conveniant ad sciram*), they go as far as Penenden, but no further. If they do not come, the King has 100s. for this forfeiture (*forisfactura*) and for all others, except for breach of peace (*gribrige*), for which the payment (*emendatur*) is £8. And from forfeitures of the roads the payment is as written above.

889 i, 1v (D-25) <u>Dover</u>: These men had sake and soke in the Lathe of Sutton and in the Lathe of Aylesford: Beorhtsige Cild, Æthelweald of Eltham, Eskil of Beckenham, Azur of Lessness, Alwine Horne, Wulfweard White, Ording of Horton Kirby, Esbiorn of Chelsfield, Leofnoth of Sutton, Edward of Stone, Wulfstan and Leofric of Wateringbury, Osweard of Norton, Edith of Asholt, and Athelræd of Yalding.

890 i, 1v (M-3) <u>Canons of St. Martin's Dover; Charlton (near Dover)</u>: TRW William fitz Ogier holds a minster-church from the Bishop of Bayeux in Dover, which pays 11s. to him. The canons of St. Martin's claim (*calumniantur*) it. TRE Sigeræd held it.

891 i, 1v (M-13) <u>Canons of St. Martin's Dover; land in Cornilo Hundred</u>: Edwin holds eighty-five acres in Cornilo Hundred TRW and held it TRE. The Bishop of Bayeux took (*sumpsit*) eight acres from this prebend and gave (*dedit*) them to Alan his clerk. Now Wulfric of Oxford has it.

892 i, 1v (M-14) <u>Canons of St. Martin's Dover; Deal</u>: TRW Ansketil the Archdeacon holds a sulung of land in Deal, which Archbishop Stigand held TRE. The Bishop of Bayeux also gave (*dedit*) Ansketil fifty acres of land in Deal and another fifty acres at St. Margaret's Cliffe. These hundred acres were from prebends, so they testify.

893 i, 1v (M-18) <u>Canons of St. Martin's, Dover; Deal</u>: TRW the Abbot of St. Augustine's holds a sulung in Deal. His antecessor held it similarly in prebend.

894 i, 2r (C-1) <u>Canterbury</u>: The Abbot of St. Augustine's has fourteen burgesses in an exchange (*pro excambio*) for the castle.

895 i, 2r (C-2) <u>Canterbury</u>: A monk of Christ Church took two houses away (*abstulit*) from two burgesses – one outside and the other inside Canterbury. They were located on the King's road.

896 i, 2r (C-3) <u>Canterbury</u>: The burgesses had forty-five *messuages* outside Canterbury, from which they had rent (*gablum*) and customs. The King, however, had the sake and soke. The burgesses also had thirty-three acres of land from the King in their guild (*in gildam suam*). Ranulf de Colombières holds these houses and this land. He also has eighty more acres of land which the burgesses held from the King in alod. He also holds five hides which in justice (*iuste*) belong to a church. Concerning all this land, Ranulf vouches (*revocat*) the Bishop of Bayeux to warranty (*ad protectorem*).

897 i, 2r (C-4) <u>Canterbury</u>: Ralph de Courbépine has four messuages in Canterbury which Harold's concubine held. The King has the sake and soke over them, but until now he has had nothing.

898 i, 2r (C-6) <u>Canterbury</u>: The King has sake and soke throughout the whole of the city of Canterbury, except for the land of Christ Church, St. Augustine's, Queen Edith, Æthelnoth Cild, Esbiorn Bigge, and Sigeræd of Chilham. Concerning the straight roads which have entry and exit through the city, it is agreed (*concordatum est*) that whosoever makes a forfeiture on them (*in illis forisfecerit*) shall pay a fine (*emendabit*) to the King. The same is true of the straight roads outside the city as far as one league, three perches, and three feet. If anyone digs or fixes a post within these public roads (*publicas vias*), inside the city or outside of it, the King's reeve shall pursue him wherever he has gone and take a fine (*emendam accipiet*) for the King's use.

899 i, 2r (C-7) <u>Canterbury</u>: The archbishop claims (*calumniatur*) the forfeiture (*forisfacturam*) on roads outside the city on each side, where the land is his.

900 i, 2r (C-8) <u>Canterbury</u>: TRE a reeve named Brunmann took (*cepit*) customs from foreign (*extraneis*) merchants on the land of Christ Church and St. Augustine's. Afterward, in the time of King William, Brunmann acknowledged (*recognouit*), before (*ante*) Archbishop Lanfranc and the Bishop of

Bayeux, that he had unjustly taken (*iniuste accepisse*) these customs. He swore on the sacrament (*sacramento facto iuravit*) that in the time of King Edward, Christ Church and St. Augustine's had their customs quit. From this time on, both Christ Church and St. Augustine's had customs on their land, by judgment of the King's barons, who held the plea (*iudicio baronum regis placitum tenuerunt*).

901   i, 2r (P-19) <u>Possession of St. Martin's</u>: Ranulf de Colombières takes away (*aufert*) a meadow from the canons of St. Martin's, and Robert of Romney takes away (*aufert*) 20d. each year from them as well as a salthouse and a fishery. Herbert fitz Ivo gave (*dedit*) the Bishop of Bayeux a mark of gold for one of the canons' mills, against their refusals (*nolentibus illis*). Lambert, too, has a mill, as has Wadard and Ralph de Courbépine.

902   i, 2r (P-20) <u>Possession of St. Martin's</u>: TRE Æthelnoth Cild, through Harold's violence (*per violentiam*), took away (*abstulit*) Merclesham and Hawkhurst from St. Martin's, and he gave (*dedit*) the canons an unfair exchange (*iniquam commutationem*) for this land. Now Robert of Romney holds them. The canons have always claimed (*calumniantur*) it from him.

903   i, 2v (1-1) <u>Terra Regis; Dartford</u>: TRW King William holds a sulung and a half in Dartford. It is assessed by the English at £60, but the French reeve who holds it at farm says that the value is £90. Nonetheless, he pays £70 by weight from the manor, along with 111s. of pence at 20d. to the *ora*, and £7 and 26d. by tale. The men of the hundred testify that a meadow, an aldergrove, a mill, and twenty acres of land have been taken away (*ablatum est*) from the manor, as well as as much meadow as belongs to ten acres of land. All of these were in King Edward's farm while he lived. Their value is 20s. They also say that Osweard the Sheriff leased (*praestitit*) them to Alstan the reeve of London. Now Helto the Steward and his nephew hold them. They also testify that half a sulung in Hawley has been taken away (*ablata est*) from this manor. TRE the sheriff [presumably Osweard] held this land. When he lost the sheriffdom (*vicecomitatum amittebat*), it remained in the King's farm, even after King Edward's death. Now Hugh de Port holds it with another fifty-four acres of land. From this same manor six acres of land and a wood have been taken away (*sunt ablatae*), which Osweard the Sheriff put outside (*posuit extra*) the manor through a mortgage (*per . . . vadimonium*) of 40s.

904   i, 2v (1-2) <u>Terra Regis; Aylesford</u>: TRW King William holds a sulung in Aylesford. The Bishop of Rochester holds as much of this land as is valued at 17s. 4d. in an exchange (*pro excambio*) for the land on which the castle in Rochester sits.

905   i, 2v (1-3) <u>Terra Regis; Milton Regis</u>: Hugh de Port holds eight sulungs and a yoke of Milton Regis, a manor of King William's, assessed at eighty sulungs. TRE they were with the other sulungs in paying customs. In this same manor Wadard has as much of the King's woodland as pays 16d. a year. He holds half a dene which a villein held TRE. Æthelnoth Cild took away two-thirds from a villein through force (*per vim abstulit*).

906 i, 3r (2-2) <u>Archbishop of Canterbury; Sandwich</u>: The Archbishop of Canterbury holds Sandwich. The men of the borough testify that before King Edward gave (*dedisset*) Sandwich to Christ Church, it paid £15 to the King. At the time of King Edward's death it was not at farm. When the archbishop acquired (*recepit*) it, it paid £40 in farm and 40,000 herring for the victualing of the monks. In the year in which this survey has been made (*in anno quo facta est haec descriptio*) Sandwich paid £50 in farm and the same amount of herring as before.

907 i, 4v (2-43) <u>Archbishop's knights; Langport (near Romney)</u>: TRW Robert of Romney holds a sulung and a half in Langport from the archbishop. Twenty-one burgesses of Romney belong to this manor, from whom the archbishop has the three forfeitures (*forisfacturas*): theft (*latrocinium*), breach of peace (*pacem fractam*), and robbery (*foristellum*). The King, however, has all their service. The burgesses themselves have all the customs and other forfeitures (*forisfacturas*) in return for service at sea. They are in the King's hand.

908 i, 5v (4-16) <u>Bishop of Rochester; Stoke</u>: TRW Gundulf bishop of Rochester holds five sulungs in Stoke. TRE this manor was the bishopric of Rochester's, but Earl Godwine bought (*emit*) it from two men who held it from the bishop. This sale was made without the bishop's knowledge (*eo ignorante facta est haec venditio*). Afterwards, in the reign of King William, Archbishop Lanfranc established his title (*diratiocinavit*) to it against the Bishop of Bayeux, and so Rochester is now seised of it (*inde est modo saisita*).

909 i, 6r (5-1) <u>Bishop of Bayeux; Hawley</u>: TRW Hugh de Port holds half a sulung in Hawley from the Bishop of Bayeux. In this manor a man named Wulfræd holds twenty acres of land. He does not belong to this manor, nor could he have any lord except the King.

910 i, 6r (5-4) <u>Bishop of Bayeux; "Eddintone"</u>: TRW Ralph holds half a sulung from the Bishop of Bayeux in "Eddintone." TRE Leofstan held it from King Edward. After the King's death, Leofstan turned himself (*vertit se*) to Æthelnoth Cild. Now the land is in dispute (*in calumpnia*).

911 i, 6r (5-12) <u>Bishop of Bayeux; Lullingstone</u>: TRE Osbern Paisforiere holds half a sulung in Lullingstone from the Bishop of Bayeux. Sæweard Sot held it TRE and could go where he wished with the land. The King has woodland here as a new gift (*pro novo dono*) from the Bishop of Bayeux.

912 i, 6r (5-13) <u>Bishop of Bayeux; Farningham</u>: TRW Wadard holds half a sulung from the Bishop of Bayeux in Farningham. Apart from this half sulung, Wadard holds half a yoke in the same vill, which has never acquitted itself to the King (*se quietavit apud regem*).

913 i, 6r (5-16) <u>Bishop of Bayeux; Darenth</u>: TRW Ansketil de Rots holds half a sulung in Darenth from the Bishop of Bayeux. TRE Ælfric held it from the King. From this manor, King William has what is valued at 10d. as a new gift (*pro novo dono*) from the Bishop of Bayeux.

914 i, 6r–v (5-18) <u>Bishop of Bayeux; Horton Kirby</u>: TRW Ansketil holds a sulung from the Bishop of Bayeux in Horton Kirby. TRE Godel held it from

Beorhtsige and could turn where he wished with the land. The King has a new gift (*pro novo dono*) from the Bishop of Bayeux of as much of this manor's woodland as is valued at 5s.

915   i, 7r (5-40) <u>Bishop of Bayeux; Leybourne</u>: TRW Adam holds two sulungs in Leybourne from the Bishop of Bayeux. The King holds what is valued at 24s. 2d. as a new gift (*pro novo dono*) from the bishop.

916   i, 7r (5-44) <u>Bishop of Bayeux; Eccles</u>: TRW Ralph son of Thurold holds three yokes from the Bishop in Eccles. The King holds 8s. 5d. as a new gift (*pro novo dono*) from the bishop. Furthermore the bishop had three houses in Rochester at 31d., which the King took (*cepit*) into his hand from the manor.

917   i, 7r (5-49) <u>Bishop of Bayeux; Tottington</u>: TRW Robert Latimer holds Tottington at farm from the King. This is part of the new gift (*de novo dono*) of the Bishop of Bayeux. It is valued at 40s. TRE Godwine held it from King Edward.

918   i, 7r (5-50) <u>Bishop of Bayeux; Tottington</u>: TRW Robert Latimer holds a yoke in Tottington at farm from the King. This is part of a new gift (*de novo dono*) of the Bishop of Bayeux.

919   i, 7v (5-67) <u>Bishop of Bayeux; Leeds</u>: TRW Æthelwulf holds three sulungs from the Bishop of Bayeux in Leeds. The Abbot of St. Augustine's has half a sulung from this manor in exchange (*pro excambio*) for the Bishop of Bayeux's park.

920   i, 8v (5-93) <u>Bishop of Bayeux; Hoo</u>: TRE Earl Godwine held Hoo, which was assessed at fifty sulungs. TRW the Bishop of Bayeux holds it for thirty-three sulungs. Nine houses in Rochester belonged to this manor. Now they have been taken away (*ablatae sunt*).

921   i, 8v–9r (5-104) <u>Bishop of Bayeux; Chalk</u>: TRW Adam holds three sulungs from the Bishop of Bayeux in Chalk. The King has in his hand what is valued at 7s. from a new gift (*de novo dono*) of the bishop.

922   i, 9r (5-118) <u>Bishop of Bayeux; Tonge</u>: TRW Hugh de Port holds two sulungs from the Bishop of Bayeux. Of these sulungs, Osweard held five. He took away (*abstulit*) the remaining three sulungs and one and a half yokes from the King's villeins.

923   i, 9r (5-119) <u>Bishop of Bayeux; Patrixbourne</u>: TRW Richard fitz William holds Patrixbourne from the Bishop of Bayeux. There is a pasture there, from which men from elsewhere (*extranei homines*) have ploughed six acres of land.

924   i, 9v (5-125, 126, 127) <u>Bishop of Bayeux; Canterbury, Nackington, and unnamed land in Canterbury Hundred</u>: TRW in the hundred in the city of Canterbury, Adam fitz Hubert has four houses. Outside the city he has another two houses. Haimo the Sheriff holds half a sulung in Nackington and another half sulung elsewhere. Adam and Haimo hold this land from the Bishop of Bayeux. TRE the burgesses of Canterbury held it. They held it up until the Bishop of Bayeux's time. He took (*cepit*) these things from them.

925   i, 9v (5-128) <u>Bishop of Bayeux; Folkestone</u>: TRE Earl Godwine held forty sulungs in Folkestone. Now William d'Arques holds them from the Bishop of Bayeux. Bernard of St. Ouen holds four sulungs of this land. From a dene and from the land which has been given (*data est*) from these sulungs come £3 at farm.

926   i, 9v (5-133) <u>Bishop of Bayeux; unnamed land in Eastry Hundred</u>: TRW Ranulf de Colombières holds a yoke from the Bishop of Bayeux, which paid scot (*escotavit*) in Hardres. It has not yet, however, paid scot to the King (*scotum regis non scotavit*).

927   i, 9v (5-138) <u>Bishop of Bayeux; Barham</u>: TRE Archbishop Stigand held six sulungs in Barham. It was not of the archbishopric, but was from the demesne farm of King Edward. TRW Fulbert holds it from the Bishop of Bayeux. The Bishop, however, gave (*dedit*) Herbert fitz Ivo Hougham, which is a berewick of this manor. He also gave (*dedit*) Osbern Paisforiere a sulung of this manor's land and two mills.

928   i, 10r (5-149) <u>Bishop of Bayeux; Badlesmere</u>: TRW Ansfrid holds soke in Badlesmere from the Bishop of Bayeux. The Abbot of St. Augustine's claims (*reclamat*) this manor because he had it TRE. The hundred testifies for him, but the son of the man says that his father could turn where he wished. The monks do not assent (*non annuunt*) to this.

929   i, 10v (5-159) <u>Bishop of Bayeux; Eastling</u>: TRE Sigeræd held Eastling from the King. TRW Fulbert holds it from the bishop. It answered for five sulungs TRE, and now for two, and did so after the bishop gave (*dedit*) the manor to Hugh fitz Fulbert.

930   i, 10v (5-178) <u>Bishop of Bayeux; Romney</u>: TRW Robert of Romney has fifty burgesses in the borough of Romney. The King has all the service from them. They are quit from all customs because of service at sea, except for three – theft (*latrocinium*), breach of peace (*pace infracta*), and robbery (*forstel*).

931   i, 11v (5-205) <u>Bishop of Bayeux; land in Eastry Hundred</u>: TRW Wibert holds half a yoke from the Bishop of Bayeux, which lay in the guild (*gildam*) of Dover. It is now assessed with the land of Osbern fitz Ledhard.

932   i, 11v (5-209) <u>Bishop of Bayeux; unnamed land in Summerdene Hundred</u>: TRW Robert Latimer holds six acres of land. He has it as a new gift (*de novo dono*) of the bishop in the hand of the King from Richard fitz Gilbert.

933   i, 11v (5-223) <u>Bishop of Bayeux; Hemsted</u>: TRW Ranulf de Vaubadon holds half a yoke in Hemsted, which two freemen held from King Edward in Buckland (near Dover). Now Ranulf says that the Bishop of Bayeux gave (*dedit*) it to his brother.

934   i, 11v (6-1) <u>Battle Abbey; Wye</u>: TRW The Abbot of Battle holds a seven-sulung manor called Wye. Its value TRE was £80 and 106s. and 8d. When he acquired (*recepit*) it, it was valued at £125 10s. at twenty pence to the *ora*. TRW it is valued at £100 by tale. If the abbot had had sake and soke, it would be assessed at £20 more. TRW the sake and soke and all forfeitures (*forisfactura*) of twenty-two hundreds, which belong to the manor of Wye, belong in justice (*iuste*) to the King.

935   i, 12r (7-6) <u>St. Augustine's Abbey; Garrington</u>: TRE Eadric held half a

sulung and forty-two acres in Garrington from Esbiorn Bigge. Now the Abbot of St. Augustine's holds it, and Ralph holds from him. The Bishop of Bayeux gave (*dedit*) it to him in exchange (*pro excambio*) for his park.

936   i, 12r (7-10) <u>St. Augustine's Abbey; Fordwich</u>: TRW the Abbot of St. Augustine's holds the small borough of Fordwich. King Edward gave (*dedit*) two-thirds to St. Augustine's. The remaining third belonged Earl Godwine, but the Bishop of Bayeux granted (*concessit*), by allowance (*annuente*) of King William, this third to the abbey.

937   i, 12r (7-17) <u>St. Augustine's Abbey; Ripton</u>: TRW Ansered holds two yokes in Ripton. The Abbot of St. Augustine's gave (*dedit*) it to him from his demesne.

938   i, 12v (7-30) <u>St. Augustine's Abbey; Badlesmere</u>: The shire testifies that Badlesmere was St. Augustine's TRE, and that the abbot had sake and soke over he who held it.

939   i, 13r (9-9) <u>Hugh de Montfort; Atterton</u>: The hundred and the burgesses of Dover, along with the Abbot of St. Augustine's men and the men of Eastry Lathe, testify that the land of Atterton, which the canons of St. Martin's of Dover claim (*calumniantur*) against Hugh de Montfort, was held by Wulfwile Wilde in alod TRE, and is assessed at one yoke.

940   i, 14r (11-1) <u>Richard fitz Gilbert; Yalding</u>: TRW Richard fitz Gilbert holds two sulungs in Yalding. TRE Ealdræd held them from King Edward, and it was valued, both in the time of King Edward and after, at £30. TRW it is valued at £20 because the land has been despoiled of its stock (*vastata est a pecunia*).

941   i, 14v (13-1) <u>Albert the Chaplain; Newington (near Milton Regis)</u>: TRW Albert the Chaplain holds Newington from the King. TRE Sigar held it from Queen Edith. The Bishop of Bayeux has three denes valued at 40s. They were part of this manor TRE, so the hundred testifies, but have been separated (*sunt foris*) from it.

Leicestershire

942   i, 230r (C-5) <u>City of Leicester</u>: King William has £20 at 20d. to the *ora* each year from the moneyers. Hugh de Grandmesnil has the third penny from this £20.

943   i, 230r (C-11) <u>City of Leicester</u>: TRW Hugh de Grandmesnil has three houses in Leicester which belong to "Legham." He bought (*emit*) them from Osbern.

944   i, 230r (C-12) <u>City of Leicester</u>: Hugh de Grandmesnil has two churches and six houses, four of which are waste. Hugh de Gouville holds another five houses from Hugh de Grandmesnil in Leicester with sake and soke. They are part of the exchange (*de mutatione*) for Watford.

945   i, 230v (1-4) <u>Terra Regis; Great Bowden</u>: King Edward held Great Bowden along with its numerous appurtenances. TRW King William holds it. Included among Great Bowden's appurtenances are two carucates of soke in Blaston. These carucates belong to Great Bowden, but Robert de Tosny holds them.

946   i, 230v (1-10) <u>Terra Regis; Shepshed</u>: TRW Godwine holds two and a half hides and four carucates in Shepshed from the King in fee. TRE Asgot held them with sake and soke. £6 came from this land from farm, by order (*praecepto*) of the Bishop of Bayeux, for the service (*pro servitio*) of the Isle of Wight.

947   i, 231r (5-2) <u>Peterborough Abbey; Great Easton</u>: TRW Peterborough Abbey holds twelve carucates in Great Easton. Earl Ralph gave (*dedit*) them to the abbey TRE.

948   i, 232r (13-3) <u>Hugh de Grandmesnil; Sharnford</u>: TRE Alwine held two carucates in Sharnford with sake and soke. TRW Hugh de Grandmesnil holds them from the Queen's fee, so he says.

949   i, 232r (13-21) <u>Hugh de Grandmesnil; Birstall</u>: TRE Alwine Buxton held six carucates of land in Birstall. TRW Hugh de Grandmsnil holds it and says that the King gave (*dedit*) it to him.

950   i, 232r (13-23) <u>Hugh de Grandmesnil; Thurmaston</u>: TRW Hugh de Grandmesnil holds ten carucates of land in Thurmaston. He holds them as one manor, but the shire denies (*negat*) this.

951   i, 232v (13-33) <u>Hugh de Grandmesnil; Shearsby</u>: TRW Howard holds a carucate in Shearsby from the King's alms, which he has in mortgage (*in vadimonio*).

952   i, 232v–3r (13-63) <u>Hugh de Grandmesnil; Wymeswold</u>: TRW Robert and Serlo hold nine carucates and five bovates of land in Wymeswold from Hugh de Grandmesnil. TRE two brothers held this land as two manors. Later, but still in the time of King Edward, one bought (*emit*) the other's share and made one manor from the two.

953   i, 233r (14-3) <u>Henry de Ferrers; Worthington</u>: TRW Henry de Ferrers holds four carucates in Worthington. Alwine claims (*calumniatur*) the soke of one carucate of this land, saying that it belonged to the King's manor of Shepshed.

954   i, 233r (14-16) <u>Henry de Ferrers; Houghton on the Hill</u>: TRW Godric holds nine carucates from Henry de Ferrers in Houghton on the Hill. TRE Earl Waltheof held it. Countess Judith claims (*calumniatur*) it.

955   i, 233v (14-23) <u>Henry de Ferrers; Swepstone</u>: TRW Nigel holds ten carucates in Swepstone from Henry de Ferrers. TRE Esbiorn held two carucates of this land and could go where he wished. The remaining land was held by Leofric, whose land Osmund bishop of Salisbury holds from the King.

956   i, 234v (19-6) <u>Robert Dispensator; Shackerstone</u>: TRW Robert Dispensator holds a carucate and a half in Shackerstone. Robert was seised (*saisiuit*) of a carucate and a half of land there, which Henry de Ferrers claims (*calumniatur*) against him.

957   i, 234v (19-9) <u>Robert Dispensator; Odstone</u>: TRW Robert Dispensator holds a carucate of land in Odstone. Henry de Ferrers claims (*calumniatur*) it. The soke of these two carucates belongs to Snarestone.

958   i, 235r (23-2, 3, 4) <u>Guy de Raimbeaucourt; Stormesworth, Misterton,</u> <u>Husbands Bosworth</u>: TRW Benedict abbot of Selby holds nine carucates in Stormesworth (which belongs to Stanford in Northamptonshire), one carucate in Misterton, and two carucates and two bovates in Husbands Bosworth from Guy de Raimbeaucourt. He bought (*emit*) them from Guy.

959   i, 235v (29-1, 2) <u>Geoffrey de la Guerche; Stanton under Bardon, East</u> <u>Norton</u>: TRE Alwine and Ulf held three carucates in Stanton and four and a half carucates in East Norton freely. TRW Geoffrey de la Guerche holds them. King William gave (*dedit*) this land to Geoffrey in exchange (*pro commutatione*) for the vill of Thurcaston.

960   i, 235v (29-15) <u>Geoffrey de la Guerche; Cold Newton</u>: TRW Aubrey holds six carucates in Cold Newton from Geoffrey. This land is from the exchange (*de commutatione*) for Thurcaston.

961   i, 235v (29-19, 20) <u>Geoffrey de la Guerche; Little Dalby, Withcote</u>: TRE Alweald held four and a half carucates in Little Dalby and one and a half carucates in Withcote freely. TRW the first of these holdings is held by Robert from Geoffrey de la Guerche and the second by Alweald from Geoffrey. This land is part of the exchange (*de commutatione*) for Thurcaston, so Geoffrey's men say.

962   i, 236v (42-5) <u>King's officials; Hoton</u>: TRW Robert de Jort holds five carucates of land in Hoton from the King. There, he holds a meadow, which he possesses through force (*vi possidet*).

963   i, 237r (43-4) <u>Earl Hugh; Burton on the Wolds</u>: TRW Godric holds two carucates from Earl Hugh in Burton on the Wolds. Hugh de Grandmesnil claims (*reclamat*) the soke of this land.

964   i, 237r (43-5) <u>Earl Hugh; Theddingworth</u>: TRE Earl Harold held five carucates in Theddingworth. TRW Roger holds them from Earl Hugh. This land is in the King's claim (*est in calumnia regis*).

Lincolnshire

965   i, 336r (C-2, 3) <u>Lincoln</u>: TRE there were twelve lawmen (*lageman*) in Lincoln, that is men having sake and soke: Harthacnut; Swærting son of Grimbald; Ulf's son Svartbrandr, who had toll and team (*thol et theim*); Wælhræfn; Alweald; Beorhtric; Gyrth; Wulfberht; Godric son of Eadgifu; Siward the Priest; Leofwine the Priest; and Healfdene the Priest. Now there are as many men in Lincolnshire who similarly have sake and soke: Swærting in the place of his father Harthacnut; Swærting; Svartbrandr in place of his father Ulf; Aghmund in place of his father Wælhræfn; Alweald; Godwine son of Beorhtric; Norman Crassus in place of Gyrth; Wulfberht brother of Ulf, who is still living; Peter de Valognes in place of Godric son of Eadgifu;

Wulfnoth the Priest in place of Siward the Priest; Burgweald in place of his father Leofwine, who is now a monk; and Leodwine son of Rawn in place of Healfdene the Priest.

966 i, 336r (C-4) <u>Lincoln</u>: Toki son of Auti had thirty messuages in Lincoln, a hall, and two and a half churches. He had thirty other messuages through a lease (*locationem*). The King had toll and forfeitures (*theloneum et forisfacturam*) over these thirty messuages, so the burgesses swore (*iuraverunt*). Wulfgeat the Priest, however, disputes their swearings and offers to bear the ordeal that it is not as they say (*iurantibus contradicit Vluiet presbyter, et offert se portaturum iudicium quod non ita est sicuti dicunt*). Geoffrey Alselin and his nephew Ralph hold this hall. Bishop Remigius holds these thirty messuages in the Church of St. Mary, Lincoln, so that Geoffrey Alselin has nothing from them, either by exchange or by any other payment (*neque scangium neque aliam redditionem*).

967 i, 336r (C-6) <u>Lincoln</u>: Earnwine the Priest has one of Earl Morcar's messuages with sake and soke. Earnwine holds it from the King in the same way that Morcar had it, so he himself says.

968 i, 336r (C-10) <u>Lincoln</u>: Countess Judith has one of Stori's messuages without sake and soke. Ivo Taillebois claims (*calumniatur*) it through the burgesses.

969 i, 336r (C-12) <u>Lincoln</u>: Outside the city, in the fields of Lincoln, there are twelve and a half carucates of land besides the Bishop of Lincoln's city carucate. The King and the earl have eight of these carucates in demesne. King William gave (*dedit*) one of these to Ulfkil for a ship, which he bought (*emit*) from him. But the man who sold (*vendidit*) the ship is dead, and no one has this carucate unless by the King's consent (*concedente*).

970 i, 336r (C-14) <u>Lincoln</u>: TRE Siward the Priest and Auti had another of these carucates outside the city along with six acres of land, which Wulfgeat the Priest holds. Now Ælfnoth has half of this carucate, and Northmann son of Siward the Priest has the other half. But Olaf the Priest annexed (*invasit*) half of this land along with the wife of Siward the Priest, while it was in the King's seisin (*in saisitione regis*), because of 40s., which the King had imposed (*imposuerat*) against Siward the Priest.

971 i, 336r (C-16) <u>Lincoln</u>: Another of the carucates outside the city was attached to the Church of All Saints, Lincoln TRE, along with twelve tofts and four crofts. Godric son of Garwine had this church and all that belonged to it. But now he has become a monk, and the Abbot of Peterborough possesses (*obtinet*) it. All the burgesses of Lincoln, however, say that the abbot holds it unjustly (*iniuste*), because neither Garwine nor his son Godric could give (*dare potuerunt*) it outside the city nor outside their kindred (*extra civitatem nec extra parentes eorum*) without the King's consent (*nisi concessu regis*). Earnwine the Priest claims (*clamat*) this church and all that belongs there by inheritance from his kinsman Godric (*hereditate Godrici consanguinei sui*).

972 i, 336r (C-20) <u>Lincoln</u>: Those written below have not given the King geld, as they ought: the land of St. Mary's, Lincoln, where Theodberht lives on the

Great Way, has not given geld; nor has the bishop's land situated at St. Lawrence's given geld on one house. The Abbot of Peterborough has not given geld for one house and three tofts. Earl Hugh has not given geld on any of his land, nor has Thurold of Greetwell, nor Losuard, nor Ketilbert. Hugh fitz Baldric has not given geld on two tofts, nor, similarly, has Geoffrey Alselin on two tofts. Nor has Gilbert given geld on three houses; nor has Peter de Valognes on his house; nor Countess Judith on her house; nor Ralph Pagnell on one house; nor Ralph de Bapaume on his house; nor Hertald on his house.

973 i, 336r–v (C-21) <u>Lincoln</u>: Norman Crassus claims (*clamat*) the Abbot of Peterborough's house from the King's fee, which has not, so it has been said, given geld. This is because Guthrøthr, his antecessor, had it in mortgage (*in vadimonio*) for three and a half marks of silver.

974 i, 336v (C-22) <u>Lincoln</u>: Outside Lincoln, Kolsveinn has thirty-six houses and two churches, to which nothing is attached. He settled (*hospitavit*) them on waste land that the King gave (*dedit*) him, which had never been settled before. Now the King has all customs from them.

975 i, 336v (C-23) <u>Lincoln</u>: Alvred nephew of Thurold has three tofts from Sibbi's land, which the King gave (*dedit*) him. He has all customs except the King's geld from mintage.

976 i, 336v (C-25) <u>Lincoln</u>: Hugh fitz Baldric has two tofts which the King gave (*dedit*) him.

977 i, 336v (C-26) <u>Lincoln</u>: There are seventy-four messuages outside the precinct of the castle which are waste – not because of the oppression (*oppressionem*) of the sheriff or officials (*ministrorum*), but because of misfortune, poverty, and the conflagration of the fire.

978 i, 336v (C-27) <u>Lincoln</u>: TRE the city of Lincoln paid £20 to the King and £10 to the earl. Now it pays £100 by tale between the King and the earl.

979 i, 336v (C-28, 29, 30, 31) <u>Lincoln</u>: The customs of the King and the earl in South Lincolnshire pay £28. The customs of the King and the earl in the North Riding pay £24. The customs of the King and the earl in the West Riding pay £12. The customs of the King and the earl in the South Riding pay £15.

980 i, 336v (C-32) <u>Lincoln</u>: If the peace, given by the King's hand or his seal, shall be broken (*pax manu regis vel sigillo eius data si fuerit infracta*), a fine is paid (*emendatur*) throughout eighteen hundreds. Each hundred pays (*soluit*) £8. Twelve hundreds pay a fine (*emendant*) to the King and six to the earl.

981 i, 336v (C-33) <u>Lincoln</u>: If any one for any crime (*reatu*) shall be outlawed (*exulatus fuerit*) by the King and by the earl and by the men of the shrievalty, no one but the King can give him peace (*dare pacem poterit*).

982 i, 336v (S-1, 4) <u>Stamford</u>: There were and are six wards (*custodie*) in Stamford, five in Lincolnshire, and the sixth in Northamptonshire. In the five wards in Lincolnshire there are seventy-seven sokemen's messuages. These sokemen have their land in demesne and can seek (*petunt*) lords where they wish. The

King has nothing over them except for the fine of their forfeitures (*emendationem forisfacturae eorum*), heriot (*heriete*), and toll.

983 i, 336v (S-4) <u>Stamford</u>: There is a mill in Stamford at 30s., which Eustace of Huntingdon took away (*abstulit*). It was a sokeman's.

984 i, 336v (S-5) <u>Stamford</u>: There were twelve lawmen (*lagemanni*) in Stamford TRE who had sake and soke within their houses and over their men (*infra domos suas sacam et socam et super homines suos*), except for geld, heriot (*heriete*), and forfeitures of their bodies (*forisfacturam corporum suorum*) of 40 *ora* of silver, and except for theft (*latronem*). They also have these rights now, but there are only nine lawmen. The ninth of these lawmen has three messuages, but Hugh Musard has taken two away (*abstulit*) from him.

985 i, 336v (S-6) <u>Stamford</u>: TRW Eudo Dapifer has twenty-three messuages – twenty-two were held by Earnwine the Priest TRE, and one was held by Eadsige. The King had all customs over them. Now he does not.

986 i, 337r (T-1) <u>Torksey</u>: In Torksey there were 213 burgesses TRE. All of them had the same customs as the people of Lincoln. In addition, any of them who had a messuage in Torksey gave neither toll nor custom when entering or leaving town (*neque intrans neque exiens theoloneum dabat nec consuetudinem*).

987 i, 337r (T-1) <u>Torksey</u>: If a burgess wished to go elsewhere and to sell his house, he could do so if he wished, without the knowledge or permission of the reeve (*sine scientia et licentia praepositi*).

988 i, 337r (T-3) <u>Torksey</u>: TRE Earl Morcar had the third penny of all customs from Torksey.

989 i, 337r (T-5) <u>Rubric</u>: [This list notes those who have sake and soke and toll and team (*tol et thiam*) in Lincolnshire: the Bishop of Lincoln, Queen Edith, the Abbot of Peterborough, the Abbot of Ramsey, the Abbot of Croyland, Earl Harold, Earl Morcar, Earl Waltheof, Earl Ralph, Ulf Fenisc, Merlesveinn, Thorgot Lag, Toki son of Auti, Stori, Ralph the Staller, Siward Barn, Harold the Staller, Fiacc, Rolf son of Skialdvor, Godric son of Thorfridh, Aki son of Siward and Vighlak his brother concerning their father's land, Leofwine son of Alwine, Azur son of Svala, Æthelric son of Mærgeat, Auti son of Azur, Æthelstan son of Godram, Thorir son of Roald, Toli son of Alsige, Azur son of Burg, Wulfweard White, Ulf, Hemming, Barthi, and Swein son of Svavi.]

990 i, 337v (1-9) <u>Terra Regis; Grantham Winnibrigs</u>: TRE Queen Edith had twelve carucates in Grantham Winnibrigs. No one had sake and soke there except Alswith the Nun, who gave (*dedit*) them to Peterborough Abbey. Now Kolgrimr has this with sake and soke. There are seventy-seven tofts there. The Bishop of Durham claims (*calumniatur*) the seven, which Earnwine the Priest has. The hundred bears (*portat*) testimony for the bishop.

991 i, 338v (1-65) <u>Terra Regis; Caistor, Hundon</u>: Earl Morcar had three carucates of land in the manor and berewick of Caistor and Hundon. The Bishop of Lincoln claims (*clamat*) the church and the priest there.

992 i, 340v (3-7) <u>Bishop of Durham; Wold Newton</u>: TRE Grimkel held eleven bovates in Wold Newton; now Walbert, the Bishop of Durham's man, holds them. Norman d'Arcy unjustly (*iniuste*) holds a mill in Thorganby, which belongs to this holding.

993 i, 340v (3-13, 15) Bishop of Durham; Kirkby on Bain, Tattershall Thorpe: TRE Harold had ten bovates of land in Kirkby on Bain. Now the Bishop of Durham has them. There is inland and soke of this manor in Tattershall Thorpe. Eudo claims (*calumniatur*) them. [There is a "k" for *klamor* written in the margin of this entry.]

994 i, 340v (3-22) Bishop of Durham; Spilsby, Eresby, Thorpe St. Peter: TRE Eskil had six carucates in Spilsby, Eresby, and Thorpe St. Peter. Now the Bishop of Durham has them. Eudo claims (*clamat*) this land. [There is a "k" for *klamor*, written in the margin of this entry.]

995 i, 340v (3-25) Bishop of Durham; East Keal: TRE Alnoth had six bovates in East Keal. Now the Bishop of Durham holds them. Eudo claims (*clamat*) the soke. [There is a "k" for *klamor* written in the margin of this entry.]

996 i, 341r (3-32) Bishop of Durham; Newton (near Folkingham): TRE Wulfric the Wild had seven bovates in Newton. Now the Bishop of Durham has half and Wulfgeat and his wife have the other half from the King. All of this land was his wife's mother's. The Bishop claims (*clamat*) Wulfgeat's part.

997 i, 342r (4-1) Bishop of Bayeux; South Carlton: TRE Ealdormann had a carucate of land in South Carlton. Now Ralph the Steward and Gilbert of Ghent have this land through the Bishop of Bayeux's seal (*per sigillum*). Earnwine the Priest says that it ought to be the King's.

998 i, 342v (4-42) Bishop of Bayeux; North Thoresby, Audby: TRE Thorfridh had four carucates, three and a sixth bovates in North Thoresby and Audby. Edward exchanged (*cambiavit*) this land with the Bishop of Bayeux.

999 i, 345r (7-55) Bishop of Lincoln; Hougham: Robert the Priest had a carucate of land in Hougham from the King in alms. Now he has become a monk at St. Mary's, Stow with this land. No one, however, is permitted (*licet*) to have this land without the King's consent (*concessu*).

1000 i, 346v (11-9) Croyland Abbey; Bucknall: TRE Gamal had ten bovates of land in Bucknall and ten bovates of soke in Belchford. Now Croyland Abbey has them. Thorald the Sheriff gave (*dedit*) this to St. Guthlac's for his soul (*pro anima sua*).

1001 i, 347v (12-29) Count Alan; Beesby (in Hawerby): TRE Ingimund, Øne, Eadric, and Ecgwulf had three carucates and three and three-quarter bovates and a third of a bovate in Beesby. Now Count Alan has them. William Blunt had Ecgwulf's land – that is five and a half bovates – on the day Earnwine the Priest was captured (*captus fuit*) and before.

1002 i, 348r (12-59) Count Alan; Drayton: TRE Bishop Wulfwig had a carucate of land in Drayton. This land was Ramsey Abbey's, according to the testimony of the men of the wapentake, who says that they do not know through whom the bishop held it. Now Count Alan holds it.

1003 i, 348v (12-83) Count Alan; Holbeach, Whaplode: TRE Earl Ælfgar had a carucate of land in Fleet's berewick of Holbeach and Whaplode. Now Count Alan has it, but the King's officials (*ministri*) claim (*clamant*) it for the use of the King.

1004   i, 348v (12-84) <u>Count Alan; Holbeach, Whaplode</u>: TRE Earl Ælfgar had thirteen carucates and six bovates of Gedney's soke in Holbeach and Whaplode. Now Count Alan holds them, and Landric holds from him. This land has been adjudged (*deratiocinata est*) for the King's use.

1005   i, 348v (12-90) <u>Count Alan; Quadring</u>: TRE Thorkil had a carucate of land in Quadring. Gyrth, Count Alan's man, holds this land, but the men of the wapentake do not know through whom.

1006   i, 348v (12-92) <u>Count Alan; North Hykeham Hundred</u>: TRE Siward had four carucates of land in North Hykeham Hundred. Now Kolgrimr, a man of Count Alan, has them. [A "k" for *klamor* is written in the margin of this entry, as are the words "Svartbrandr claims" (*calumniatur*).]

1007   i, 352r (16-3) <u>Roger the Poitevin; Middle Rasen</u>: TRW Mainard, a man of Roger the Poitevin, holds three bovates in Middle Rasen. [A "k" for *klamor* is written in the margin of this entry.]

1008   i, 352r (16-6) <u>Roger the Poitevin; Thornton le Moor</u>: TRW Roger the Poitevin has eleven bovates in Thornton le Moor. [A "k" for *klamor* is written in the margin of this entry.]

1009   i, 352r (16-8) <u>Roger the Poitevin; Owersby (North or South)</u>: TRE Earnwig had a carucate and a half in Owersby, which lies in the church of Winghale. Roger the Poitevin now has it. [A "k" for *klamor* is written in the margin of this entry.]

1010   i, 352r (16-28) <u>Roger the Poitevin; Laughton (near Blyton)</u>: TRE Swein had a carucate and a half of land in Laughton. Now Blancard, Roger the Poitevin's man, has it. [A "k" for *klamor* is written in the margin of this entry.]

1011   i, 353v (22-5) <u>William de Percy; Thornton le Moor</u>: TRE Alwine had two carucates and six bovates in Thornton le Moor. Besides these eleven bovates [*sic*] of land, Roger the Poitevin similarly has eleven bovates, which William de Percy ought to have, by testimony of the men of the wapentake.

1012   i, 354r (22-19) <u>William de Percy; Apley</u>: TRE Tonni had seven bovates of land in Apley. The soke is in Barlings. Now William de Percy has it. [A "k" for *klamor* is written in the margin of this entry.]

1013   i, 354r (22-20) <u>William de Percy; Apley</u>: TRE Ælfric had two bovates of land in Apley. The soke is in Bullington. Now William de Percy has it. [A "k" for *klamor* is written in the margin of this entry.]

1014   i, 354r (22-26) <u>William de Percy; Covenham St. Bartholomew</u>: TRE Alsige, Ketil, and Thorfridh had three and a half carucates of land in Covenham St. Bartholomew as three manors. Ketil and Thorfridh were brothers. After the death of their father they divided (*diviserunt*) the land in such a way that Ketil, when doing the King's service, should have the aid (*haberet adiutorium*) of his brother Thorfridh. William de Percy had Ketil's and Alsige's land from the

King. William de Percy, however, bought (*emit*) Thorfridh's land from Ansketil the Cook in the time of King William.

1015   i, 356r (25-10) Hugh fitz Baldric; Cuxwold: TRW Hugh fitz Baldric has three bovates in Cuxwold, a berewick of Cabourne. [There is a "k" for *klamor* written in the margin of this entry.]

1016   i, 356v (26-6) Kolsveinn; Scothern, Holme (in Sudbrooke), Sudbrooke: TRW Kolsveinn has a carucate of land from the King, so he says, from which he pays customs in Fiskerton to Peterborough Abbey.

1017   i, 358r (27-25) Alvred of Lincoln; Cockerington: TRE Eadric and Maccus had seven bovates in Cockerington as three manors. TRW Alvred of Lincoln and Jocelyn his man have them. [There is a "k" for *klamor* written in the margin of this entry.]

1018   i, 358v (27-64) Alvred of Lincoln; Brocklesby: TRW Alvred of Lincoln has a bovate and a half of land in Brocklesby. The soke is in Newsham. [A "k" for *klamor* has been written in the margin of this entry.]

1019   i, 359v (29-6, 7) Eudo son of Spearhavoc; Waddingworth, Wispington: TRW there are six carucates in Waddingworth. The soke is in Little Sturton and Kirkby on Bain. Half is the Bishop of Durham's and half is Eudo son of Spearhavoc's. [A "k" for *klamor* has been written in the margin of this entry.] TRW there are also four carucates in Wispington, the soke of which is similarly divided in two between the bishop and Eudo in Little Sturton and Kirkby on Bain. Eudo claims (*clamat*) against the bishop's half of both lands.

1020   i, 360r (30-14) Drogo de la Beuvrière; Great Grimsby: TRW Drogo de la Beuvrière has a berewick in Great Grimsby at one bovate. [The following statement is written in the margin of this entry: "Inquire concerning the arable land of Roger de Mortimer and the Bishop of Bayeux."]

1021   i, 360v (30-32) Drogo de la Beuvrière; Witham on the Hill: TRE Ulf has five bovates in Witham on the Hill. Now Drogo de la Beuvrière has them. The Abbot of Peterborough claims (*clamat*) a bovate in the soke of Gilbert.

1022   i, 361r (31-3) Walter d'Aincourt; Old Somerby: TRW Reginald, a man of Walter d'Aincourt, holds two carucates and two bovates in Old Somerby. TRE Thorir held this manor. Northmann held it after him in the same time, but the men of the country and wapentake do not know by what pact (*quo pacto*) he had it, because they have not seen him do any service for it.

1023   i, 362v (35-12) Ralph Pagnell; Swinstead: TRE Merle-sveinn had five carucates in Swinstead. King Edward gave (*dedit*) a thegn there to Merle-sveinn, so the men of the hundred testify. Now Ralph Pagnell holds this land.

1024   i, 364r (40-8) Rainer de Brimeux; South Willingham: TRW Rainer de Brimeux has ten bovates in South Willingham. [A "k" for *klamor* is written in the margin of this entry.]

1025   i, 364r (40-26) Rainer de Brimeux; Withcall: TRE Iolfr had fifteen and a third bovates in Withcall. Now Rainer de Brimeux has them. He also has a third of a church there, and claims (*clamat*) the other two-thirds by testimony of the wapentake.

1026 i, 366r (51-12) Godfrey de Cambrai; Wilsford: TRE Siward had nine carucates of land in Wilsford, and his brother Azur had six bovates of this land and a mill. TRW Bishop Remigius bought (*emit*) this manor from Godfrey de Cambrai for the Church of St. Mary, Lincoln.

1027 i, 366v (56-4) Countess Judith; Uffington: TRE Leofric abbot of Peterborough had sixty acres of land in Uffington. Now Countess Judith has them. She has no livestock (*pecunie*) there, but she cultivates it in the manor of Belmesthorpe [Rutland].

1028 i, 367r (57-12) Guy de Craon; Dowsby: TRE Osfram had three carucates in mortgage (*in vadimonio*) in Dowsby. Hernald fitz Ansgot redeemed (*disvadiavit*) this land before Guy de Craon was seised (*fuit saisitus*) of Osfram's land. Afterwards Guy always had the service.

1029 i, 367r–v (57-14) Guy de Craon; Scottlethorpe: TRE Æthelstan had a carucate of land in Scottlethorpe. Guy has had it in soke until now. Now it has been adjudged (*est deratiocinatum*) a caput manor for the use of the King.

1030 i, 367v (57-18) Guy de Craon; Haceby: TRE Ælfric had eleven bovates of land in Haceby. Now Godwine, Guy de Craon's man, has them. Waldin claims (*clamat*) this land from the King's gift (*de dono regis*). Guy de Craon has the soke over eleven bovates of Waldin's land: this the wapentake testifies.

1031 i, 368r (57-56) Guy de Craon; Drayton: TRE Æthelstan had a half carucate of land in Drayton. It was delivered (*fuit liberata*) to Guy de Craon as a manor.

1032 i, 369r (61-5) Heppo the Balistarius; Surfleet: TRE Alsige had four and a half carucates in Surfleet. Now Heppo the Balistarius holds it. [A "k" for *klamor* is written in the margin of this entry.]

1033 i, 369r (62-2) Ralph fitz Hubert; Gunby (near North Witham): TRE Wulfwine had a carucate in Gunby. Ansfrid, Ralph fitz Hubert's priest, annexed (*invasit*) this land.

1034 i, 370r (65-1, 2, 3, 4, 5) Baldwin the Fleming; Haddington, Whisby, South Hykeham, Skellingthorpe, North Hykeham: TRW Baldwin the Fleming holds eight and a half carucates in Haddington, six carucates in Whisby, four carucates in South Hykeham, twelve carucates in Skellingthorpe, and eight carucates in North Hykeham. All of this land belongs to Doddington, a manor of Westminster Abbey. Baldwin holds this land from the King, but the abbot claims (*clamat*) it for the use of Westminster, by testimony of the men of the whole county.

1035 i, 371r (68-31) Svartbrandr and other thegns; Fillingham: TRE Godric the Deacon had two bovates of land in Fillingham. Later Earnwine the Priest held it from the Queen. Now it is the King's. Roger the Poitevin took it without livery (*accepit sine liberatore*). Ansketil holds it.

1036 i, 371r (68-37) Svartbrandr and other thegns; Yaddlethorpe: TRE Ketil had a carucate of land in Yaddlethorpe. Waldin had it, but the King returned (*reddidit*) it to an Englishman.

1037   i, 375r (CS) <u>Rubric</u>: [The rubric heading the claims of the South Riding reads: "Claims (*clamores*) which are in the South Riding of Lincoln and their settlement through sworn men (*concordia eorum per homines qui iuraverunt*)."]

1038   i, 375r (CS-1) <u>Clamores; South Riding</u>: The Bishop of Bayeux's men claim (*clamant*) a carucate of land in Tathwell Hundred against Robert Dispensator, and the men of the wapentake say that the bishop himself ought by law (*iure*) to have it.

1039   i, 375r (CS-2) <u>Clamores; South Riding</u>: The Bishop of Bayeux's men claim (*clamant*) three bovates in Tathwell Hundred against Earl Hugh, and the wapentake says that the bishop himself ought to have them.

1040   i, 375r (CS-3) <u>Clamores; South Riding</u>: The wapentake says that Robert Dispensator ought to have the mill in Tathwell Hundred, which was Aghmund's and then afterwards was held by Lambert and his son Jocelyn.

1041   i, 375r (CS-4) <u>Clamores; South Riding</u>: The Bishop of Lincoln claims (*clamat*) a mill in Louth Hundred against Count Alan, and the wapentake testifies that it ought to be the Bishop's.

1042   i, 375r (CS-5) <u>Clamores; South Riding</u>: Alsige and Ulfgrimr put (*posuerunt*) the lands they held in Lindsey in the Church of St. Mary, Lincoln in the mercy (*misericordia*) of Bishop Wulfwig. Because these men had £160 for these lands in the time of King Edward, Bishop Remigius claims (*clamat*) them.

1043   i, 375r (CS-6) <u>Clamores; South Riding</u>: The King's officials (*ministri*) claim (*clamant*) the lands of two brothers – Godric and Eadric – in Burwell Hundred in Haugham and Maidenwell against Earl Hugh. The men of the wapentake have adjudged (*deratiocinaverunt*) them for the King's use.

1044   i, 375r (CS-7) <u>Clamores; South Riding</u>: William de Percy claims (*clamat*) a half carucate of land in Little Carlton Hundred against Kolsveinn. The wapentake testifies for him.

1045   i, 375r (CS-8) <u>Clamores; South Riding</u>: Alvred of Lincoln claims (*clamat*) a half carucate of land in Somercotes Hundred in Yarburgh against the King, but the riding says that he has nothing there except nine and half acres and a toft, the soke of which lies in the King's manor of Gayton le Wold.

1046   i, 375r (CS-9) <u>Clamores; South Riding</u>: Siward Buss claims (*clamat*) a mill in Somercotes Hundred against Alvred. The men of the riding say that Alvred has half, which belongs to Rainer de Brimeux's holding in Keddington; and that the Bishop of Durham has the other half as a soke in Keddington.

1047   i, 375r (CS-10) <u>Clamores; South Riding</u>: Alvred claims (*clamat*) three bovates of land in Skidbrooke Hundred in Stewton against Ilbert. The men of the riding say that Alvred ought to have them.

1048   i, 375r (CS-11) <u>Clamores; South Riding</u>: Rainer claims (*clamat*) the whole minster-church in Withcall Hundred, and the men of the riding say that it was his antecessor's. So too was a third of the soke. Ilbert de Lacy has the other two-thirds of the soke over the church and over the land that lies in it.

1049   i, 375r (CS-12) <u>Clamores; South Riding</u>: Robert Dispensator claims (*clamat*) a carucate of land in Swaby Hundred in Claythorpe against Earl Hugh. The men of the riding say that the soke lies in Greetham and was Vighlak's, and that he himself left the land (*terram exiuit*) and forfeited it (*forisfecit*). They say that Robert Dispensator has nothing there.

1050   i, 375r (CS-13) <u>Clamores; South Riding</u>: Losuard claims (*clamat*) a carucate of land in Rigsby Hundred in Well against Gilbert of Ghent. The men of the riding say that TRE Thorulf had it with sake and soke, and that afterwards Tonni had it, and that this land was delivered (*fuit deliberata*) to Bishop Odo through a charter (*per cartam*), but they have not seen the King's writ (*brevem*) for it. He had it himself on the day on which he was captured (*fuit captus*). Afterwards he was disseised (*fuit dissaisitus*).

1051   i, 375r (CS-14) <u>Clamores; South Riding</u>: Rainer de Brimeux claims (*clamat*) two bovates of land in Rigsby Hundred in Ulceby (near Well) against Earl Hugh. The men of the riding say that he ought to have nothing but the soke in Cumberworth, and that the earl ought to have the land.

1052   i, 375r (CS-15) <u>Clamores; South Riding</u>: The Bishop of Durham claims (*clamat*) two bovates in Theddlethorpe Hundred in Mablethorpe against Earl Hugh. The men of the riding say that he has nothing there except a bovate which was Bærghthor's, and that the soke is Earl Hugh's in Greetham. There also William Blunt has three bovates which were Sumarlithr's, Godric's, and Siward's, and the soke is in Greetham, by testimony of the whole riding.

1053   i, 375r (CS-16) <u>Clamores; South Riding</u>: Alvred claims (*clamat*) two bovates of land in Huttoft Hundred, and the men of the riding say that he ought to have one of them with sake and soke. Similarly the other is his, but Earl Hugh has the soke in Greetham.

1054   i, 375r (CS-17) <u>Clamores; South Riding</u>: The riding says that Alvred ought to have the soke of one bovate in Huttoft Hundred in Sutton on Sea, which he claims (*clamat*) against Ketilbiørn.

1055   i, 375r (CS-18) <u>Clamores; South Riding</u>: Count Alan claims (*clamat*) two bovates of land in Mumby Hundred against Gilbert of Ghent. But the riding says that Gilbert's antecessor had sake and soke of it in the time of King Edward, and that it ought to be his.

1056   i, 375r (CS-19) <u>Clamores; South Riding</u>: The Bishop of Durham claims (*clamat*) the land of Alnoth the Priest in Willoughby Hundred against Gilbert of Ghent. The men of the riding say that they never saw the bishop's antecessor seised (*fuisse saisitum*) of it, either through writ or through legate (*neque per brevem neque per legatum*). They testify that it is for Gilbert's use.

1057   i, 375r (CS-20) <u>Clamores; South Riding</u>: The men of the riding testify that Ketilbiørn ought to have twenty acres of woodland in Willoughby Hundred in Hanby (in Welton le Marsh), and that Ivo Taillebois ought to have the soke.

1058   i, 375r (CS-21, 22) <u>Clamores; South Riding</u>: Concerning the claim (*calumnia*) between the Bishop of Durham and Eudo son of Spearhavoc, the men of Horncastle Wapentake have borne testimony (*portaverunt testimonium*), with the assent (*annuente*) of the whole riding, that three brothers – Harold, Guthfrith, and Ælfric – divided (*diviserunt*) their father's demesne land equally and in parage (*aequaliter et pariliter*), and that only Harold and Guthfrith divided (*diviserunt*) their father's soke, without the third brother. These two held the soke equally and in parage (*equaliter et pariliter*) TRE. Concerning the six bovates of soke which are claimed (*est calumnia*) between the Bishop of Durham and Eudo in Langton by Wragby and "Torp," the men of Wraggoe Wapentake say that TRE the two brothers – Harold and Guthfrith – held the soke equally and in parage (*equaliter et pariliter*), but in the year in which King Edward died, Guthfrith's sons had all of the soke, but they do not know for what reason they had it – whether through force or by the gift of their uncle (*nesciunt qua ratione eam habebant, utrum vi vel dono patrui sui*).

1059 i, 375r (CS-23) <u>Clamores; South Riding</u>: Concerning the claim (*calumnia*) which Robert Dispensator makes against Gilbert of Ghent over the woodland in Low Langton, Wraggoe Wapentake says that Tonni had it TRE with sake and soke in Baumber, and because of this Gilbert of Ghent has it by law (*iure*). The whole riding assents (*annuente*) to this.

1060 i, 375r (CS-24) <u>Clamores; South Riding</u>: Concerning the underwood in Hainton which Robert Dispensator claims (*clamat*) against the King and the underwood in Wragby which he claims against Erneis de Buron, he has nothing there, by testimony of the wapentake. But he does have soke over Earl Hugh's twelve acres and the Bishop of Bayeux's eight acres, through the testimony of the men of the wapentake and riding.

1061 i, 375r (CS-25) <u>Clamores; South Riding</u>: Concerning the claim (*clamorem*) which Rainer de Brimeux made against Alvred of Lincoln about the soke of three and a half bovates, Rainer ought to have nothing there, so the men of the wapentake and riding testify. But Roger the Poitevin ought to have it in Hainton in the house of his antecessor Klac.

1062 i, 375r–v (CS-26) <u>Clamores; South Riding</u>: Concerning the claim (*calumnia*) which Erneis de Buron makes against William de Percy about the soke of four bovates in Legsby, the wapentake says that Erneis ought by law (*iure*) to have it.

1063 i, 375v (CS-27) <u>Clamores; South Riding</u>: Concerning the claim (*calumnia*) which Archbishop Thomas made, that is, that he ought to have soke over the land of Siward, the antecessor of Ivo Taillebois, the wapentake and the riding say that Siward held his land as fully with sake and soke as Godwine, the antecessor of the archbishop, held his. He does not, therefore, rightly claim (*non recte clamat*) it.

1064 i, 375v (CS-28) <u>Clamores; South Riding</u>: Archbishop Thomas ought to have soke over the land of Eskil, which the Bishop of Bayeux has in South Willingham. This is because – so the whole county testifies – the archbishop's antecessor had sake and soke over the same land. The bishop's men unjustly took away (*iniuste auferunt*) the soke from the archbishop.

1065 i, 375v (CS-29) <u>Clamores; South Riding</u>: TRE Almær, antecessor of

Archbishop Thomas, was seised (*fuit saisitus*) of the soke of ten bovates in South Willingham. This land was Koddi's and is now Rainer de Brimeux's. It was mortgaged (*fuit invadiata*) for £3 TRE. Now the men of the riding affirm (*affirmant*) that the archbishop ought by law (*iure*) to have this soke until the £3 are repaid to him.

1066 i, 375v (CS-30, 31) <u>Clamores</u>; <u>South Riding</u>: Gilbert of Ghent and Norman d'Arcy claim (*calumniantur*) the soke of twelve bovates in Stainfield against William de Percy. It belongs to Barlings and was Tonni's. But the wapentake and the county say that Gilbert and not Norman ought to have it. But William de Percy holds it by the King's gift (*dono regis*), as Robert son of Stigand held it. They testify, for the same reason (*eandem rationem*) concerning the soke of seven bovates in Apley, because it lies in Barlings and Tonni held it TRE.

1067 i, 375v (CS-32) <u>Clamores</u>; <u>South Riding</u>: The Bishop of Durham claims (*calumniatur*) the soke of two bovates in Apley against William de Percy, and the wapentake says that the same antecessor of the bishop had it, and that the bishop himself ought to have it in Bullington.

1068 i, 375v (CS-33) <u>Clamores</u>; <u>South Riding</u>: The Wapentake of Horncastle says that Robert Dispensator unjustly makes a claim (*iniuste facit calumniam*) against Gilbert of Ghent concerning a half carucate of land in Baumber and about another half carucate in Edlington. TRE Tonni had this land.

1069 i, 375v (CS-34) <u>Clamores</u>; <u>South Riding</u>: Robert Dispensator ought to have soke over the fishery and toft which Ketilbiørn holds in Coningsby, because Aki, Robert's antecessor, had it TRE.

1070 i, 375v (CS-35) <u>Clamores</u>; <u>South Riding</u>: Candleshoe Wapentake says that Ivo Taillebois ought to have what he claims (*clamat*) against Earl Hugh in Ashby by Partney – that is, a mill and a bovate of land. But the soke belongs to Greetham.

1071 i, 375v (CS-36) <u>Clamores</u>; <u>South Riding</u>: Concerning two carucates of land which Robert Dispensator claims (*calumniatur*) against Gilbert of Ghent in Scremby through Vighlak his antecessor, the wapentake says that Vighlak only had one carucate, and that the soke of that carucate was in Bardney. Vighlak, however, forfeited (*forisfecit*) that land to the loss of (*contra*) his lord Gilbert. Robert, therefore, has nothing there, by testimony of the riding.

1072 i, 375v (CS-37) <u>Clamores</u>; <u>South Riding</u>: Ketilbiørn claims (*clamat*) a carucate in Scremby against Gilbert of Ghent through Godric, but they say that he only had a half carucate, and that its soke was in Bardney. Ketilbiørn unjustly claims (*iniuste clamat*) this, so the wapentake says, because his antecessor forfeited (*forisfecit*) it.

1073 i, 375v (CS-38) <u>Clamores</u>; <u>South Riding</u>: The men of Candleshoe Wapentake testify, with the consent (*consentiente*) of the whole riding, that Sighwat, Alnoth, Fenkell, and Eskil equally and in parage divided (*equaliter et pariliter diviserunt*) their father's land between themselves TRE, and held it so that if they were needed for the King's expedition, and Sighwat could go, the other brothers aided (*iuuerunt*) him. After him, the next one went and Sighwat, with the rest, aided (*iuuit*) him, and so on with all of them. Sighwat, however, was the King's man. Bolingbroke Wapentake testifies to the same concerning the aforementioned men, and the South Riding also assents (*annuente*).

1074 i, 375v (CS-39) <u>Clamores; South Riding</u>: In Saltfleet, Mare, and Swine a new toll has been established (*est novum theloneum assuefactum*), and Ansgar of Skidbrook took (*accepit*) it, as has Rainald, Humphrey, and Geoffrey. Louthesk Wapentake and the whole South Riding say that this toll was not there TRE. Godric gave (*dedit*) a toll of 1d., by testimony of Ulfkil of Asterby, who saw it. Arnketil of Withern testifies that he himself saw Ansgar take (*recipere*) the toll from twenty-four ships from Hastings.

1075 i, 375v (CS-40) <u>Clamores; South Riding</u>: In Saltfleet Hugh the Sergeant takes the customs of the ships which come there freely or under compulsion (*gratis et ingratis*). These customs were not there TRE. They began this new custom, and the men of the riding say that they saw a claim made (*clamorem fieri*) for it.

1076 i, 375v (CN-1, 2) <u>Clamores; North Riding</u>: Gilbert of Ghent's men take (*accipiunt*) another toll on bread, fish, and skins in Barton-upon-Humber and in South Ferriby than the one they took (*acceperunt*) TRE, and they take a toll on many other things for which nothing was ever given. In Caistor the King's men do likewise.

1077 i, 375v (CN-3) <u>Clamores; North Riding</u>: Ivo Taillebois claims (*clamat*) six bovates of land against the King in Limber (Great or Little). The men of the county say that he ought to have the land, and the King ought to have the soke.

1078 i, 375v (CN-4) <u>Clamores; North Riding</u>: For the thirty acres of meadow which Alvred claims (*clamat*) in Ulceby (near Wootton), he ought to have a field of land in the same vill.

1079 i, 375v (CN-5) <u>Clamores; North Riding</u>: Yarborough Wapentake testifies that Morcar gave (*dedit*) Hugh four bovates of land with sake and soke in Goxhill, which Drogo de la Beuvrière claims (*clamat*). Alvred claims (*clamat*) a bovate of this land. The wapentake says that the land is Hugh's, and the soke is Alvred's.

1080 i, 375v (CN-6) <u>Clamores; North Riding</u>: The wapentake testifies that King William gave (*dedit*) the church of Caistor in alms to St. Mary's, Lincoln. Two bovates belong to this church in demesne, along with two villeins, a mill, and the soke of one carucate in Hundon.

1081 i, 375v (CN-7) <u>Clamores; North Riding</u>: Jocelyn claims (*clamat*) three bovates of land in Searby against Count Alan. The county says that Jocelyn, and not Alan, ought to have it.

1082 i, 375v (CN-8) <u>Clamores; North Riding</u>: Hugh fitz Baldric claims (*clamat*) a half bovate of land in Brocklesby. The men of the riding say that the land ought to be his, and the soke Norman's, through their antecessors.

1083 i, 375v (CN-9) <u>Clamores; North Riding</u>: The wapentake says that Rainer the Deacon held Elaf's two manors in Stallingborough on the day on which he left this country (*exiuit de hac patria*).

1084 i, 375v (CN-10) <u>Clamores; North Riding</u>: Rainer de Brimeux ought to have the soke of half a bovate of land in Great Limber, which Archbishop Thomas has in Stallingborough.

1085 i, 375v (CN-11) <u>Clamores; North Riding</u>: Concerning one of Elaf's manors, which Archbishop Thomas now has in Keelby, Rainer the Deacon was seised (*erat saisitus*) of it on the day on which he left (*exiuit*) this land.

1086 i, 375v (CN-12) <u>Clamores; North Riding</u>: Alvred ought to have the land of two bovates in Great Coates, and Durand Malet ought to have the soke, along with three villeins who belong to it.

1087 i, 375v–376r (CN-13) <u>Clamores; North Riding</u>: Rainer the Deacon was seised (*fuit . . . saisitus*) of a carucate of land in Swallow when he left (*exiit*) this land. Similarly he was seised (*erat saisitus*) of Erik's land in Grimsby Hundred. Now the Bishop of Bayeux has it.

1088 i, 376r (CN-14) <u>Clamores; North Riding</u>: Ralph de Mortimer's and Losuard's men take (*accipiunt*) a new toll in Great Grimsby, which was not there TRE. Losuard, however, denies that his men made the toll through him (*negat suos homines fecisse per eum*).

1089 i, 376r (CN-15) <u>Clamores; North Riding</u>: The Bishop of Bayeux and the Bishop of Lincoln ought to have soke over two and a half bovates of land which lie in the Church of Winghale.

1090 i, 376r (CN-16) <u>Clamores; North Riding</u>: The Bishop of Bayeux has soke over a half carucate of land in Owersby Hundred, which was Earnwine the Priest's. Now it is Siward the Priest's.

1091 i, 376r (CN-17) <u>Clamores; North Riding</u>: Jocelyn fitz Lambert ought to have soke over half a bovate of land in Osgodby (near West Rasen).

1092 i, 376r (CN-18) <u>Clamores; North Riding</u>: Rainer the Deacon had Erik's land in Tealby Hundred with all that belongs there. Jocelyn holds it and Rainer claims (*calumniatur*) it. The riding testifies that Count Alan's antecessor had the soke, but they do not know what kind (*nesciunt qualem*).

1093 i, 376r (CN-19) <u>Clamores; North Riding</u>: Jocelyn fitz Lambert ought to have a mill in Claxby (near Walesby) which Geoffrey, Ivo Taillebois's man, annexed (*invasit*) against him.

1094 i, 376r (CN-20) <u>Clamores; North Riding</u>: William Blunt ought to have a garden in Croxby on Ivo Taillebois's land, but he is impeded (*impeditur*) on account of a mill, which was not there TRE.

1095 i, 376r (CN-21) <u>Clamores; North Riding</u>: The Bishop of Durham ought to have forty acres of land – meadow – and four tofts in Fulstow, and Count Alan ought to have soke over them, so the wapentake says.

1096 i, 376r (CN-22) <u>Clamores; North Riding</u>: They judge (*iudicant*) that Count Alan has soke over a carucate of land in Fulstow in Robert Dispensator's land; and that Drogo ought to have the salthouse there which he claims (*clamat*), and Count Alan ought to have soke over it.

1097 i, 376r (CN-23) <u>Clamores; North Riding</u>: Rainer the Deacon was seised (*fuit saisitus*) of Fulcric's land in Cuxwold when he left (*exiuit*) this land. Now Archbishop Thomas holds it. It is claimed by (*calumniatur*) Rainer de Brimeux.

1098 i, 376r (CN-24) <u>Clamores; North Riding</u>: William de Percy ought to have two bovates of land in Cuxwold, which he claims (*clamat*), in Hugh fitz Baldric's land. The wapentake testifies for him.

1099 i, 376r (CN-25) <u>Clamores; North Riding</u>: The wapentake says that Count Alan ought to have soke over the hall of Grimkel, whose land the Bishop of Durham has in Wold Newton.

1100 i, 376r (CN-26) <u>Clamores; North Riding</u>: Kolsveinn did not deliver (*liberavit*) the land of Ingimund and his brothers to Count Alan, but the same Ingimund made it subject (*subiugavit*) to the count because of the other land which he held from him.

1101 i, 376r (CN-27) <u>Clamores; North Riding</u>: The North Riding and all the county testify that the land of Ulf of North Ormsby – that is, four and a half carucates – was sold (*fuit vendundata*) to St. Mary's, Stow TRE, and it lay there on the day on which King Edward died. Later Bishop Remigius was seised (*fuit saisitus*) of it.

1102 i, 376r (CN-28) <u>Clamores; North Riding</u>: Drogo claims (*clamat*) three messuages in Scemund (North Ormsby), in Ivo Taillebois's land, which he ought to have with sake and soke, by testimony of the wapentake.

1103 i, 376r (CN-29) <u>Clamores; North Riding</u>: In Fotherby, in the land of Berenger de Tosny, the Bishop of Durham ought to have five bovates of land and Berenger de Tosny the soke over it.

1104 i, 376r (CN-30) <u>Clamores; North Riding</u>: The wapentake and the whole county testify that the Bishop of Durham ought to have the land of three brothers with sake and soke, and that Eudo son of Spearhavoc ought to have the land of the fourth brother, similarly with sake and soke. The brother's names are Sighwat or Godwine, Alnoth, Fenkell, and Eskil.

1105 i, 376r (CW-1) <u>Clamores; West Riding</u>: Lawress Wapentake testifies that Alnoth had sake and soke over his land – three carucates in Burton. Now Svartbrandr has it after him.

1106 i, 376r (CW-2) <u>Clamores; West Riding</u>: The Abbot of Peterborough claims (*clamat*) four bovates of land in Riseholme, Kolsveinn's land. The wapentake testifies that in the time of King Edward these bovates lay in the Church of All Saints in Lincoln.

1107 i, 376r (CW-3) <u>Clamores; West Riding</u>: Three burgesses of Lincoln – Guthrøthr, Leofwine, and Sigewine – held land in mortgage (*invadiaverunt*) from Aghmund, which Jocelyn fitz Lambert claims (*clamat*) in Middle Carlton against Norman Crassus.

1108 i, 376r (CW-4) <u>Clamores; West Riding</u>: Norman Crassus added £3 and one gold mark in Scampton, and he mortgaged (*vadiavit*) this to Ivo the Sheriff.

1109 i, 376r (CW-5) <u>Clamores; West Riding</u>: TRE Godric, Norman's antecessor, had four and a half bovates in Scothern Hundred, so the wapentake testifies.

1110 i, 376r (CW-6) <u>Clamores; West Riding</u>: Gilbert of Ghent claims (*clamat*) a carucate of land in Scothern Hundred against the Abbot of Peterborough. But the wapentake testifies that Peterborough had this land with its soke on the day when King Edward was alive and dead.

1111 i, 376r (CW-7) <u>Clamores; West Riding</u>: Bishop Remigius claims (*clamat*) two bovates of land in Nettleham Hundred, and the wapentake testifies that he ought to have it.

1112 i, 376r (CW-8) <u>Clamores; West Riding</u>: The wapentake says that Peterborough Abbey ought to have the fourth part of the woodland in Reepham, which Ranulf and Kolsveinn claim (*calumniantur*).

1113 i, 376r (CW-9) <u>Clamores; West Riding</u>: The wapentake testifies that Ulfkil, Asfrith, Restelf, and Wulfmær had sake and soke over their lands and over their men in Sturton by Stow Hundred. St. Mary's, Stow had two-thirds of the soke of the forfeiture (*forisfacturam*) in the wapentake, and the earl one-third. Now the King has it. Similarly with heriot (*heriete*): if they forfeited (*forisfecissent*) their land, St. Mary's used to have two-thirds, and the earl a third.

1114 i, 376r (CW-10) <u>Clamores; West Riding</u>: The shire testifies that the land of Gunnhvati – a manor with a carucate in demesne – was forfeited (*fuit forisfacta*). Two-thirds went to St. Mary's, Stow and a third went for the earl's use. The soke which belongs to Gate Burton or Broughton was similarly divided. So too was Steingrimr's eighteen bovates of land.

1115 i, 376r (CW-11) <u>Clamores; West Riding</u>: Concerning all the thegns who have land in Well Wapentake, St. Mary's, Stow has two-thirds of their forfeitures (*forisfactura*), and the earl has a third. It is the same with heriot (*heriet*). Similarly, if one of these thegns had forfeited (*forisfecissent*) his land, two-thirds went to St. Mary's, and a third was in the earl's hand. Now the King has it. Gilbert of Ghent is not in this custom (*in hac consuetudine*), nor are Roger de Tosny and Ralph de Mortimer, through their antecessors.

1116 i, 376r (CW-12) <u>Clamores; West Riding</u>: TRE Grimkel had sake and soke over his land, but in the year in which King Edward died, Grimkel forfeited (*fuit ipse forisfactus*) and gave (*dedit*) it to Merle-sveinn the Sheriff, because of his crime against the King, and made Merle-sveinn heir to it (*pro reatu regis et de illo fecit heredem*).

1117 i, 376r (CW-13) <u>Clamores; West Riding</u>: Jocelyn has nine bovates of Aghmund's land in Ownby-by-Spital, and Ivo has one bovate. Bishop Remigius ought to have the soke over this land.

1118 i, 376v (CW-14) <u>Clamores; West Riding</u>: TRE Siward Rufus had a carucate of land in Northorpe Hundred with sake and soke. Ralph de Neville recently held it from Abbot Thurold, but he did not have livery (*liberatorem*) for it. Now it is adjudged (*est deratiocinata*) for the King's use.

1119 i, 376v (CW-15) <u>Clamores; West Riding</u>: Guy de Craon, through his antecessor Wilgrim, claims (*clamat*) soke over Swein's land in Northorpe

Hundred in the vill of Laughton (near Blyton). The wapentake testifies that
Wilgrim had sake and soke over Swein in the time of King Edward.

1120   i, 376v (CW-16) <u>Clamores; West Riding</u>: The shire testifies that Eskil, on
the day King Edward was alive and dead and afterwards, had three manors
from the King – Scotton, Scotter, and Raventhorpe (in Broughton) in his
own franchise (*in propria libertate*). Similarly, he had North Muskham in
Nottinghamshire. He also held the manor of Manton on lease (*in presto*) from
his brother Brand the Monk.

1121   i, 376v (CW-17) <u>Clamores; West Riding</u>: The West Riding testifies that the
claims (*calumniae*) which are in Epworth Wapentake have been rightly made
(*recte factae sunt*): Norman Crassus claims (*clamat*) seven bovates of land against
Geoffrey de la Guerche in Haxey. Gilbert of Ghent claims (*clamat*) four
carucates of land and six bovates against Geoffrey de la Guerche. This is Ulf
Fenisc's land in Belton (near Epworth). Henry de Ferrers claims (*clamat*) three
bovates of land against Geoffrey de la Guerche. This is Siward Barn's land in
Amcotts. Gilbert of Ghent also claims (*clamat*) a half carucate of soke in
Belton (near Epworth) against Geoffrey de la Guerche, which was Ulf
Fenisc's.

1122   i, 376v (CW-18) <u>Clamores; West Riding</u>: The wapentake testifies that Erneis
de Buron ought to have Wege's land in Winteringham Hundred – that is, six
bovates of land and a toft in Gilbert of Ghent's soke. He ought to have
another toft with sake and soke.

1123   i, 376v (CW-19) <u>Clamores; West Riding</u>: Ralph Pagnell claims (*clamat*) a toft
in Thealby Hundred. The wapentake says that he ought to have it, and that
the King ought to have its soke in Kirton in Lindsey.

1124   i, 376v (CW-20) <u>Clamores; West Riding</u>: Norman d'Arcy claims (*clamat*)
three bovates of land in Normanby against Drogo. The wapentake says that
the land ought to be his, and the soke ought to be Drogo's.

1125   i, 376v (CK-1) <u>Clamores; Kesteven</u>: Ness Wapentake and all the riding have
testified that the land of Wulfgeat and his mother Wulfflæd was not
Arnbiorn's, his sister's kinsman (*sororii sui*). He only had custody (*habuisse nisi
in custodia*) of it until Wulfgeat could hold the land. This land is made up of
seven carucates in Uffington, six and a half carucates in Tallington, six
bovates in Casewick, and four bovates in Deeping.

1126   i, 376v (CK-2) <u>Clamores; Kesteven</u>: The wapentake says that Peterborough
Abbey had sixty acres of land TRE, which Countess Judith has and cultivates
with plows from Belmesthorpe [Rutland]. The warnode of these sixty acres
of land and forty-eight acres of meadow lies in Uffington, which belongs to
Alvred of Lincoln. It has been kept back by force (*vi est retenta*).

1127   i, 376v (CK-3) <u>Clamores; Kesteven</u>: The wapentake says that Azur's half
carucate of land in Barholm ought to be Gunfrid de Chocques's.

1128   i, 376v (CK-4) <u>Clamores; Kesteven</u>: The wapentake says that Hereweard did
not have Asfrith's land in Barholm Hundred on the day on which he fled
(*aufugiit*).

1129 i, 376v (CK–5) <u>Clamores; Kesteven</u>: Ralph Pagnell has six bovates of Morcar's land in Burton-le-Coggles Hundred, but Merle-sveinn did not have it TRE.

1130 i, 376v (CK–6) <u>Clamores; Kesteven</u>: The Abbot of Peterborough claims (*clamat*) a bovate of land in Witham on the Hill Hundred against Drogo. The wapentake says that the land ought to be Peterborough's and the soke ought to be Gilbert of Ghent's in Edenham.

1131 i, 376v (CK–7) <u>Clamores; Kesteven</u>: Ratbod ought to have a carucate of land in Little Bytham Hundred, which he claims (*clamat*), but the soke is Peterborough's.

1132 i, 376v (CK–8) <u>Clamores; Kesteven</u>: They say that the warnode of 4d. from sixty acres of woodland in Skillington belongs in Castle Bytham.

1133 i, 376v (CK–9) <u>Clamores; Kesteven</u>: They say that Arnbiorn had thirteen acres of woodland and twenty-five acres of arable in Irnham, and that it belongs to Aslackby, which Robert de Tosny has.

1134 i, 376v (CK–10) <u>Clamores; Kesteven</u>: Archbishop Ealdræd acquired (*adquisiuit*) Lenton and Skillington with the berewick of Hardwick [Northants.], from Ulf son of Topi with his own money, which he gave in the sight (*per pecuniam suam quam ei dedit vidente*) of the wapentake. Later, they saw the King's seal through which he has been reseised of these lands (*sigillum regis per quod resaisitus est de ipsis terris*), because Ilbold had disseised (*dissaisierat*) him of them.

1135 i, 376v (CK–11) <u>Clamores; Kesteven</u>: The wapentake says that Eskil was a King's thegn, and never had his land under Merle-sveinn.

1136 i, 376v (CK–12) <u>Clamores; Kesteven</u>: Robert of Stafford unjustly (*iniuste*) held six bovates of soke of Arnketil's land in Rauceby Hundred, thus says the wapentake.

1137 i, 376v (CK–13) <u>Clamores; Kesteven</u>: They say that Bishop Remigius' claim (*calumniam*), which he makes concerning Arnketil's soke in Rauceby Hundred, is unjust (*iniustam esse*) because he had only ten bovates from the demesne of Arnketil's land in exchange (*in escangio*). All the other land has been delivered (*liberata est*) to the Bishop of Durham.

1138 i, 376v (CK–14) <u>Clamores; Kesteven</u>: The wapentake says that the nine bovates of land which Walter d'Aincourt claims (*clamat*) are a soke of Branston, the land of Alsige the Deacon, which Walter now has. Thus he claims it justly (*iuste calumniatur*).

1139 i, 376v (CK–15) <u>Clamores; Kesteven</u>: The men of Navenby keep back 16s. through force (*detinent per vim*) from the customs of pasturage which are in Scopwick and Kirkby Green. They did not give them TRE.

1140 i, 376v (CK–16) <u>Clamores; Kesteven</u>: Robert of Stafford claims (*clamat*) that the land of Auti, Archbishop Thomas's man, ought to lie in the soke of his antecessor Leofsige. The wapentake, however, says that they never saw Auti give the soke to Leofsige.

1141 i, 376v (CK–17) <u>Clamores; Kesteven</u>: Concerning Earl Hugh's claim (*clamore*), they say that Øthin had the land TRE, and that the soke lay in Potterhanworth.

1142 i, 377r (CK-18) <u>Clamores; Kesteven</u>: Svartbrandr claims (*clamat*) 140 acres in Canwick. The wapentake bears testimony for him (*fert ei testimonium*), because his father Ulf gave (*dedit*) a gold mark in mortgage (*in vadimonium*) for this land.

1143 i, 377r (CK-19) <u>Clamores; Kesteven</u>: Countess Judith holds two manors in Ponton (Great and Little). They were Almær's and his brothers'. Robert de Tosny claims (*calumniatur*) them, and the wapentake bears testimony for him (*portat ei testimonium*) that they were delivered to him in exchange (*deliberata sunt ei in escangio*) for Marston.

1144 i, 377r (CK-20) <u>Clamores; Kesteven</u>: Robert de Tosny claims (*clamat*) two bovates and two tofts against Robert Malet. The wapentake says that they ought to lie in Woolsthorpe. They say that a garden in the same vill ought to lie in Robert of Stafford's manor of Casthorpe (in Barrowby).

1145 i, 377r (CK-21) <u>Clamores; Kesteven</u>: They say that Northmann son of Merewine had seven gardens in Grantham, and that the soke of these gardens belongs there. The gardens themselves, however, belong to Gonerby. Similarly, they say that the soke of two bovates of land which belong to Gonerby lies in Grantham.

1146 i, 377r (CK-22) <u>Clamores; Kesteven</u>: Ivo Taillebois claims (*calumniatur*) two carucates less thirty acres in Stenwith against Robert de Tosny, for which Ivo gives geld. Concerning this, they say that it is right that they themselves should go over to this land and divide it rightly in proportion to the geld they give (*rectum esse ut ipsi eant super ipsam terram et partiantur eam recte sicut dant geldum*).

1147 i, 377r (CK-23) <u>Clamores; Kesteven</u>: Robert of Stafford claims (*clamat*) Karli's three carucates of land in Stoke Rochford Half-Hundred. The wapentake says that this land was Ralph the Staller's, and that Robert has nothing there.

1148 i, 377r (CK-24) <u>Clamores; Kesteven</u>: They say that the tithes and church customs from Winnibriggs and Threo Wapentakes, from all the sokes and inlands which the King has there, belong to the church of Grantham.

1149 i, 377r (CK-25) <u>Clamores; Kesteven</u>: Osbern, the King's legate (*legatus*), claims (*clamat*) one carucate of land in Thurlby (near Norton Disney) which, by testimony of the wapentake, he ought to have and to render soke in Countess Judith's manor of Eagle.

1150 i, 377r (CK-26) <u>Clamores; Kesteven</u>: Drogo de la Beuvrière claims (*clamat*) ten bovates of soke in Thurlby (near Norton Disney) against Osbern d'Arques. But the wapentake says that he claims them unjustly (*clamat iniuste*).

1151 i, 377r (CK-27) <u>Clamores; Kesteven</u>: Concerning the claim (*calumnia*) which the Abbot of Westminster makes against Baldwin about the land and soke of Æthelric son of Mærgeat, they say that they heard that Æthelric gave (*dedit*) it to Westminster Abbey, but they do not know whether he gave all or half.

They say, however, that there are eight and a half carucates of land in Haddington, which are a soke and inland of Doddington; four carucates of land in South Hykeham, which are a soke of Doddington; twelve carucates in Skellingthorpe, which are a soke in Doddington; and six carucates in Whisby, which are inland and soke in Doddington. The Abbot of Westminster claims (*clamat*) all of this, because the head manor was given to St. Peter's. All the county bears (*fert*) testimony for St. Peter.

1152 i, 377r (CK-28) <u>Clamores; Kesteven</u>: The wapentake says that Kofse had ten bovates of land and a church in the soke of Thorpe on the Hill.

1153 i, 377r (CK-29) <u>Clamores; Kesteven</u>: The wapentake says that Siward, not Ulf father of Svartbrandr, had a manor of four carucates in North Hykeham. His claim, therefore, is not right (*clamor eius non est rectus*).

1154 i, 377r (CK-30) <u>Clamores; Kesteven</u>: They say that the six bovates of land in Ewerby Thorpe, which were Godric's and now are Martin's, ought to be inland of Ewerby.

1155 i, 377r (CK-31) <u>Clamores; Kesteven</u>: Ralph Pagnell claims (*clamat*) six bovates in Heckington against Kolsveinn, which were Algar the Deacon's. The wapentake says that Merle-sveinn, Ralph's antecessor, did not have this land.

1156 i, 377r (CK-32) <u>Clamores; Kesteven</u>: Waldin the Breton claims (*clamat*) fourteen bovates of land in Quarrington against the Abbot of Ramsey. The wapentake, however, says that he does not rightly claim them (*non recte clamat*).

1157 i, 377r (CK-33) <u>Clamores; Kesteven</u>: Bishop Remigius claims (*clamat*) to have mortgaged (*invadiasse*) Arnketil's land in Quarrington, but Arnketil denies (*negat*) this and holds from the King.

1158 i, 377r (CK-34) <u>Clamores; Kesteven</u>: Kolsveinn claims (*calumniatur*) two bovates of land and a garden in Kirkby la Thorpe from Earl Morcar's land, which Thorkil held against the King. The wapentake says that not only was the soke Earl Morcar's, but also that this land does not lie in another manor.

1159 i, 377r (CK-35) <u>Clamores; Kesteven</u>: Robert Malet claims (*clamat*) soke over four bovates of land in Ingoldsby, which Gilbert of Ghent has. The wapentake says that Robert himself ought to have it through Azur, his antecessor.

1160 i, 377r (CK-36) <u>Clamores; Kesteven</u>: Gilbert of Ghent claims (*clamat*) the meadow in Caythorpe Hundred, which was his antecessor Æthelric's, against Robert de Vessey. The wapentake, however, says that Æthelric had all the meadow and that Gilbert's antecessor did not have anything from it, except through leasing it for money (*per locationem mercedis*).

1161 i, 377r (CK-37) <u>Clamores; Kesteven</u>: The wapentake testifies that the tithe and other customs of Carlton Scroop lie in the church of the same vill.

1162 i, 377r (CK-38) <u>Clamores; Kesteven</u>: Count Alan claims (*clamat*) ten bovates of land in Long Bennington, but the wapentake says that they belong to Carlton Scroop, William de Warenne's manor. Earl Harold, his antecessor, held them thus.

1163 i, 377r (CK-39) <u>Clamores; Kesteven</u>: The Bishop of Durham claims (*clamat*) two bovates of land in Marston from Thorfridh's land. Concerning this, they say that Northmann gave (*dedit*) Throfridh three gold marks for this land TRE, and after the King's death, he gave him a fourth mark.

1164 i, 377r (CK-40) <u>Clamores; Kesteven</u>: The men of Aveland Wapentake testify that the manor of Bourne was Earl Morcar's TRE. Now Ogier has it from the King. Drogo claims (*calumniatur*) it, but unjustly (*iniuste*).

1165 i, 377r (CK-41) <u>Clamores; Kesteven</u>: The wapentake says that three and a half bovates, which Ogier has in Dyke, lie in Haconby and are by right (*per rectum*) Heppo the Balistarius's.

1166 i, 377r (CK-42) <u>Clamores; Kesteven</u>: They say that a carucate of inland in Morton (near Hanthorpe) and a bovate and a half of soke in Hanthorpe belong to Haconby, and were there TRE. Leofric had them.

1167 i, 377r (CK-43) <u>Clamores; Kesteven</u>: They say that Ramsey Abbey ought to have a half carucate of land in Morton (near Hanthorpe) with sake and soke. Ogier holds it unjustly (*iniuste*).

1168 i, 377r (CK-44) <u>Clamores; Kesteven</u>: They say that Ogier unjustly (*iniuste*) holds nine bovates of land in Haconby, because Gilbert of Ghent ought to have them through his antecessor Ulf Fenisc, who held them TRE.

1169 i, 377r (CK-45) <u>Clamores; Kesteven</u>: The wapentake says that Healfdene's land in Dunsby (near Bourne), which Bishop Remigius holds and the Abbot of Peterborough claims (*calumniatur*), was not Peterborough's in the time of King Edward.

1170 i, 377r (CK-46) <u>Clamores; Kesteven</u>: Ogier holds a carucate of land in Rippingale, which the wapentake says belonged to Robert de Tosny's antecessor.

1171 i, 377r (CK-47) <u>Clamores; Kesteven</u>: They say that Osfram's land in Kirkby Underwood was not in Arnbiorn's soke.

1172 i, 377r–v (CK-48) <u>Clamores; Kesteven</u>: They say that St. Guthlac's land in Rippingale, which Ogier holds, was in the monks' demesne farm, and that Abbot Ulfkil loaned (*commendasse*) it to Hereweard at farm, as might be agreed between them (*sicut inter eos conveniret*) each year. But the abbot reseised (*resaisiuit*) it before Hereweard fled the country (*de patria fugeret*), because he had not held to the agreement (*conventionem non tenuisset*).

1173 i, 377v (CK-49) <u>Clamores; Kesteven</u>: They say that the soke of three carucates of land in Dowsby, which Osfram had in mortgage (*in vadimonio*), and which was afterwards redeemed (*devadiata fuit*), ought to lie in Croyland Abbey's manor of Rippingale. They say that it was so TRE and afterwards, until Guy de Craon seised (*saisiuit*) it.

1174 i, 377v (CK-50) <u>Clamores; Kesteven</u>: Concerning the claims (*clamores*) which Drogo de la Beuvrière makes on Morcar's land, they hand them over for the King's judgment (*dimittunt in iudicio regis*).

1175 i, 377v (CK-51) <u>Clamores; Kesteven</u>: They say that Robert of Stafford unjustly claims (*iniuste clamat*) Karli's land in Billingborough, because Karli held it from Ralph the Staller.

1176 i, 377v (CK-52) <u>Clamores; Kesteven</u>: They say that Wulfric the Wild's land in Walcot (near Folkingham) Hundred ought to belong half to the Bishop of Durham and half to Wulfgeat, who has it through the alms of the King.

1177 i, 377v (CK-53) <u>Clamores; Kesteven</u>: Ralph Pagnell claims (*clamat*) sake and soke over Ælfric's land, which Guy de Craon has in Osbournby. The wapentake says that Ralph ought to have a horse from this land whenever he goes on expedition.

1178 i, 377v (CK-54) <u>Clamores; Kesteven</u>: There are two carucates of land in Pickworth which were Auti's. Now they are Kolsveinn's. They are not in the count of any hundred, and they do not have their like in Lincolnshire.

1179 i, 377v (CK-55) <u>Clamores; Kesteven</u>: Concerning Thorir's land in Old Somerby, which Walter d'Aincourt has, they say that TRE they saw the same Thorir have it. But in the year in which King Edward died, Northmann took it in mortgage (*est invadiavit*). The men of the wapentake do not know through what pact (*pacto*), because they have not seen him do any service for it.

1180 i, 377v (CK-56) <u>Clamores; Kesteven</u>: They say that the tithe and other church customs from Thorir's land in Ropsley Hundred belong to Peterborough Abbey.

1181 i, 377v (CK-57) <u>Clamores; Kesteven</u>: Walter d'Aincourt claims (*clamat*) the service of Guy de Raimbeaucourt's men in the manor of Syston. He does not, however, have a right claim (*rectum clamorem*).

1182 i, 377v (CK-58) <u>Clamores; Kesteven</u>: Drogo claims (*clamat*) four carucates of land in Welby Hundred against Guy de Craon, but the wapentake bears testimony (*portat Widoni testimonium*) for Guy, that by law (*iure*) they are his.

1183 i, 377v (CK-59) <u>Clamores; Kesteven</u>: They say that Walter d'Aincourt ought not to have a half carucate of land in Belton (near Grantham), which he claims (*clamat*) against the King. The King ought to have it.

1184 i, 377v (CK-60) <u>Clamores; Kesteven</u>: Kolgrimr ought to have a bovate of Algar's land in Belton (near Grantham), which Guy de Craon has. The soke, however, belongs to Guy in Towthorpe (in Londonthorpe).

1185 i, 377v (CK-61) <u>Clamores; Kesteven</u>: They say that TRE Leofric Cild kept back (*detinuit*) the warnode from ten acres of meadow in Belton (near Grantham). Kolgrimr claims (*clamat*) the soke of these ten acres.

1186 i, 377v (CK-62) <u>Clamores; Kesteven</u>: They say that all the church customs and tithes from Westhorpe (in Old Somerby) belong to the church of Grantham, just as Bishop Osmund claims (*clamat*).

1187 i, 377v (CK-63) <u>Clamores; Kesteven</u>: Gilbert claims (*clamat*) the soke of two and a half carucates of land in Honington Hundred through his antecessor Ulf. But the wapentake says that Ivo ought to have the soke just as Azur, his antecessor, had it from Ulf.

1188 i, 377v (CK-64) <u>Clamores; Kesteven</u>: Robert of Stafford claims (*clamat*) two mills in Barkston. Kolsveinn also claims (*clamat*) them. The wapentake says that the mills lie in Marston, and their soke lies in Grantham.

1189   i, 377v (CK-65) <u>Clamores; Kesteven</u>: Count Alan has a carucate of land in Drayton Hundred from Ramsey Abbey. Bishop Remigius claims (*clamat*) it. The wapentake bears testimony for him (*portat ei testimonium*), because his antecessor Wulfwig held it from Ramsey TRE.

1190   i, 377v (CK-66) <u>Clamores; Kesteven</u>: Guy de Craon holds four bovates of land in Drayton and ten bovates in Bicker Hundred from the land of Æthelstan son of Godram. Count Alan claims (*calumniatur*) these bovates, and his man Algar has given the King's barons a pledge to confirm through ordeal or through battle (*dedit vadimonium baronibus regis ad confirmandum per iudicium aut per bellum*) that Æthelstan was not seised (*saisitus non fuit*) of these fourteen bovates in the time of King Edward. Against this (*e contra*), Ælfstan of Frampton, Guy's man, has given his pledge to prove that he had been seised of this land (*dedit suum vadimonium ad convincendum quod inde saisitus erat*) with sake and soke, and that Guy was seised (*fuit saisitus*) of them from the time of Ralph the Staller until now, and that he holds them now.

1191   i, 377v (CK-67) <u>Clamores; Kesteven</u>: The men of Holland testify that Healfdene, the antecessor of Bishop Remigius, had three carucates in Stenning (in Swineshead) quit. Count Alan now has them unjustly (*iniuste*), because the bishop was seised (*saisitus fuit*) of them.

1192   i, 377v (CK-68) <u>Clamores; Kesteven</u>: Alvred of Lincoln claims (*clamat*) a carucate of land in Quadring against Count Alan. The men of Holland agree (*concordant*) with Alvred, because it was his antecessor's, and because he was seised of it (*saisitus inde fuit*) in the time of Earl Ralph.

1193   i, 377v (CK-69) <u>Clamores; Kesteven</u>: Gyrth, a man of Count Alan, gave a pledge to affirm (*dedit vadimonium ad affirmandum*) that Count Alan's antecessor had six bovates of land in Gosberton with sake and soke. Guy de Craon, therefore, does not claim them rightly (*non recte eas clamat*).

1194   i, 377v (CK-70) <u>Clamores; Kesteven</u>: The men of Holland testify that the soke of Ketil's church of Long Sutton lies in the King's manor of Tydd St. Mary.

1195   i, 377v (CK-71) <u>Clamores; Kesteven</u>: Six carucates of land in Holbeach, which the King's officials (*ministri*) claim (*clamant*), lay in the King's manor of Gedney. Now Count Alan has one of these carucates as a manor by the King's gift (*regis dono*).

Middlesex

1196   i, 128v (4-11) <u>Westminster Abbey; Kingsbury</u>: TRW William the Chamberlain holds two and a half hides in Kingsbury under the Abbot of Westminster. TRE Alwine Horne, a thegn of King Edward, held this land in mortgage (*in vadimonio*) from one of Westminster Abbey's men.

1197   i, 129r (7-1) <u>Roger of Montgomery; Hatton</u>: TRW Earl Roger holds five hides in Hatton. TRE two sokemen held them. They were men of Albert of

Lorraine and could grant or sell their land. Now Hatton has been put (*apposita est*) in Colham, where it did not lie TRE.

1198 i, 129r (7-3) <u>Roger of Montgomery; Harmondsworth</u>: TRW Earl Roger holds one hide in Harmondsworth. TRE Alwine, a man of Wigot, held this land and could do what he wished with it. Now Harmondsworth lies in Colham, where it did not lie TRE.

1199 i, 129r (7-7) <u>Roger of Montgomery; Dawley</u>: TRW Alnoth holds three hides in Dawley from Earl Roger. TRE it was held by Godwine Ælfgyth, Wigot's man. He could do what he wished with it. The manor now lies in Colham, where it did not lie TRE.

1200 i, 129r (7-8) <u>Roger of Montgomery; Ickenham</u>: TRW three knights and an Englishman hold nine and a half hides in Ickenham from Earl Roger. TRE this land was held by a number of Englishmen; Toki, a housecarl of King Edward, two sokemen who were men of Wulfweard, and Alwine a man of Wulfsige son of Manni. These men could all sell their land to whom they wished. Now the whole of Ickenham is in Colham, where it did not lie TRE.

1201 i, 129r (8-1) <u>Count of Mortain; Laleham [Surrey]</u>: TRW the Count of Mortain holds two hides in Laleham, and the Abbot of Fécamp holds from him. TRE the reeve of Staines [Surrey] held this land under the Abbot of Westminster. He could not grant or sell it outside of Staines, except with permission of the abbot.

1202 i, 129r (8-2) <u>Count of Mortain; Ashford [Surrey]</u>: TRW the Count of Mortain holds a hide in Ashford. TRE Ælfric, a man of the Abbot of Chertsey, held it and could do what he wished with it. Now it has been put (*apposita est*) in the count's manor of Kempton [Surrey], where it did not lie TRE. The soke was in Staines [Surrey].

1203 i, 129v (9-1) <u>Geoffrey de Mandeville; Ebury</u>: TRW Geoffrey de Mandeville holds ten hides in Ebury. TRE Harold son of Earl Ralph held it. Queen Edith had charge of him (*custodiebat*) along with the manor. Afterwards, William the Chamberlain held it from the Queen in fee for £3 from the farm each year. After the death of the Queen, he held it the same way from the King. Now, it has been four years since William has lost (*amisit*) the manor. Since that time it has not paid the King's farm, that is, £12.

1204 i, 130r (11-2) <u>Walter fitz Othere; East Bedfont</u>; TRW Richard holds ten hides in East Bedfont from Walter fitz Othere. TRE Azur held eight and a half hides of this manor, which were a berewick of Stanwell. Three sokemen had the other one and a half hides. One of them was King Edward's man, another Leofwine's, and the third Azur's. TRE all could grant or sell their land, and none of the three belonged to this manor.

1205 i, 130r (15-1) <u>Robert Fafiton; Stepney</u>: TRW Robert Fafiton holds four hides in Stepney from the King. TRE Sigeræd, a canon of St. Paul's, held this manor and could sell to whom he wished. The Bishop of London claims (*reclamat*) that he ought to have this land. Along with these four hides, there are now fifty-three acres of land which were not there TRE. Hugh de Bernières seized (*occupavit*) them from the canons of St. Paul's, and put (*apposuit*) them in this manor, so the hundred testifies.

1206 i, 130v (16-1) <u>Robert fitz Roscelin; Stepney</u>: TRW Robert fitz Roscelin holds three and a half hides in Stepney from the King. Æthelwine Stichehare, a man of King Edward, held this land as a manor TRE and could sell to whom he wished. The Bishop of London claims (*reclamat*) this land.

1207 i, 130v (17-1) <u>Robert Blunt; Laleham [Surrey]</u>: TRW Robert Blunt holds eight hides in Laleham from the King, and Estrild the Nun holds from him. TRE Aki, a housecarl of King Edward, held it and could sell to whom he wished. The soke lay in Staines [Surrey].

1208 i, 130v (18-1) <u>Roger de Raismes; Charlton [Surrey]</u>: TRW Roger de Raismes holds five hides in Charlton from the King. TRW two brothers held it. One was a man of Archbishop Stigand and the other a man of Earl Leofwine. They could sell to whom they wished. The soke, however, belonged to Staines [Surrey].

1209 i, 130v (25-2) <u>Land in alms; land in Spelthorne Hundred</u>: TRW Ælfgifu wife of Hwætmann of London holds a half hide and the third part of a half hide of land in Spelthorne Hundred. TRE it was held by Alwine the White, a man of Earl Leofwine. He could sell. Geoffrey de Mandeville was seised (*erat saisitus*) of this land when he went across the sea in the service of the King, so his men and the whole hundred say.

Northamptonshire

1210 i, 219r (B-14) <u>Northampton</u>: TRW Ansgar, the King's chaplain, has a house from which the King ought to have soke.

1211 i, 219v (1-5) <u>Terra Regis; Portland (in Stamford)</u>: TRW the King has two and two-thirds carucates of land and twelve acres of meadow in the demesne of Portland. TRE Portland, with its meadow, paid 48s. along with 10s. for blankets for the King's packhorses. In addition, the King ought to have £9 12s. from the other income of the borough (*aliis exitibus burgi*).

1212 i, 219v (1-10) <u>Terra Regis; Hardingstone</u>: TRW the King holds five hides in Hardingstone. William Peverel and Gunfrid de Chocques, so they themselves say, have two of these hides and sixty acres of meadow by the King's gift (*dono regis*).

1213 i, 220r (1-21) <u>Terra Regis; Barford</u>: TRE Oslac the White held a hide in Barford alongside two sokemen over whom he had soke. King William granted (*concessit*) Barford to Godwine.

1214 i, 220r (1-27) <u>Terra Regis; Rockingham</u>: TRE Bovi held a hide in Rockingham with sake and soke. Now the King holds it. It was waste when King William ordered (*iussit*) a castle to be made there.

1215 i, 220r (2-2) <u>Bishop of Bayeux; Great Houghton</u>: TRE Ulf son of Azur held one hide and a half virgate in Great Houghton with sake and soke. Now William Peverel holds it from the fee of the Bishop of Bayeux. Countess Judith claims (*calumniatur*) it.

1216 i, 220r (2-3) Bishop of Bayeux; Brafield-on-the-Green: TRE Ulf son of Azur held three virgates in Brafield-on-the-Green. TRW William Peverel holds it from the fee of the Bishop of Bayeux. Nigel claims (*calumniatur*) it for the use of Countess Judith.

1217 i, 220r (2-9) Bishop of Bayeux; Roade: TRW Stephen holds one hide from the Bishop of Bayeux. It is in the King's hand.

1218 i, 220v (4-1) Bishop of Coutances; Raunds: TRE Burgræd held six hides and one and a half virgates in Raunds with sake and soke. Now the Bishop of Coutances holds it from the King. William claims (*calumniatur*) one hide and a half virgate of this land against the Bishop.

1219 i, 220v (4-23) Bishop of Coutances; Woodford (near Denford): TRW Ralph holds a hide and a virgate in Woodford. TRE Burgræd held it, but the soke belonged to Peterborough Abbey.

1220 i, 222r (6a-27) The men of Peterborough Abbey; Aldwincle St. Peter: TRE there were three hides in Aldwincle St. Peter for the victualing of the monks. Ferron holds them by the King's order (*per iussum*), against the wishes (*contra voluntatem*) of the abbot.

1221 i, 222r (8-4) Bury St. Edmund's; Scaldwell: TRE Earl Ælfgar held one hide and three virgates in Scaldwell. King William gave (*dedit*) this land to Bury St. Edmund's for the soul (*pro anima*) of Queen Mathilda.

1222 i, 223r (18-1) Count of Mortain; Sywell: TRE Osmund son of Leofric held four hides in Sywell with sake and soke. Now the Count of Mortain holds them. Countess Judith claims (*calumniatur*) the soke of a virgate and a half of this land.

1223 i, 223r (18-31) Count of Mortain; Hanging Houghton: TRE Fredegis held two hides less a virgate freely in Hanging Houghton. Now Ralph holds them from the Count of Mortain. The Abbot of Bury St. Edmund's claims (*calumniatur*) the soke of two and a half virgate of this land.

1224 i, 224v (23-3) Hugh de Grandmesnil; Weedon Bec: TRW Hugh de Grandmesnil holds three and a half hides in Weedon Bec in exchange (*pro excambitio*) for Watford.

1225 i, 225r (30-7) Robert de Bucy; Weldon: TRW Robert de Bucy holds a virgate of land in Weldon. The King claims (*calumniatur*) it.

1226 i, 225v (35-1e) William Peverel; Higham Ferrers: TRW William Peverel holds one hide and three virgates of land of soke [*sic*] in Irchester. It is a berewick of Higham Ferrers. There is a mill there, which is in dispute (*calumniosum*) between the King and William.

1227 i, 225v (35-1j) William Peverel; Higham Ferrers: TRE the sokemen of Higham Ferrers' berewicks of Rushden, Irchester, and Raunds were Burgræd's men. For this reason Geoffrey bishop of Coutances claims their homage (*clamat hominationem*).

1228 i, 226v (40-2) <u>Winemar the Fleming; land in Higham Hundred</u>: TRW Winemar the Fleming holds two hides and three virgates in Higham Hundred. TRE six freemen held them. One of them was called Asgot. Countess Judith claims (*calumniatur*) this Asgot's land.

1229 i, 226v (41-3) <u>Guy de Raimbeaucourt; Stanford on Avon</u>: TRE Leofric held two hides less a half virgate of land freely in Stanford on Avon. TRW Guy de Raimbeaucourt holds it. Benedict abbot of Selby bought (*emit*) this land from him.

1230 i, 226v (41-5) <u>Guy de Raimbeaucourt; Isham</u>: TRE Alwine son of Ulf held one hide and two and a half virgates in Isham freely. Now Ralph holds them from Guy de Raimbeaucourt. The Bishop of Coutances claims (*calumniatur*) a virgate and a half of this land and three little gardens.

1231 i, 227r (42-2) <u>Eudo Dapifer; Easton on the Hill</u>: TRW Roland holds one and a half hides from Eudo Dapifer in Easton on the Hill. This land is of Peterborough Abbey.

1232 i, 227v (46-5) <u>Gilbert of Ghent; Empingham [Rutland]</u>: TRW Gilbert of Ghent holds seven and a half hides and a bovate in Empringham from the King's soke of Rutland, and he says that the King is his warrantor (*regem suum advocatum esse*).

1233 i, 227v (46-6) <u>Gilbert of Ghent; Easton on the Hill</u>: TRE Tonni held a half hide in Easton on the Hill with sake and soke. In the time of King William Gilbert of Ghent gave (*dedit*) it to Saint-Pierre-sur-Dives.

1234 i, 227v (48-12) <u>Gunfrid de Chocques; Knuston</u>: TRE Wulfgeat held one hide and three virgates in Knuston. Now Winemar holds this land from Gunfrid de Chocques. Eustace claims (*calumniatur*) it.

1235 i, 228r (53-1) <u>Drogo de la Beuvrière; Chadstone</u>: TRE Ulf, Earl Waltheof's man, held one hide and three virgates in Chadstone. Now Drogo de la Beuvrière holds it from the King. Countess Judith claims (*calumniatur*) it.

1236 i, 228r (55-1) <u>Eustace of Huntingdon; Isham</u>: TRW Eustace of Huntingdon holds one hide and two and a half virgates of land from the King in Isham. He seized it by force (*vi occupavit*) against Ramsey Abbey.

1237 i, 229r (56-51) <u>Countess Judith; Wollaston</u>: TRE Strikr held two hides in Wollaston freely. TRW Corbelin holds it from Countess Judith. Winemar of Hanslip claims (*calumniatur*) it.

1238 i, 229r (56-61) <u>Countess Judith; Boughton (near Northampton)</u>: TRE two thegns held three hides less a half virgate in Boughton. In the time of King William Countess Judith gave (*dedit*) it to St. Wandrille with the King's consent (*concessu*).

1239 i, 229r (56-65) <u>Countess Judith; Piddington</u>: TRE two of Burgræd's men held one hide and three virgates in Piddington, and they could go where they wished. Now Gilbert holds this land from Countess Judith. Geoffrey bishop of Coutances claims (*calumniatur*) it, as does Winemar of Hanslip.

Nottinghamshire

1240   i, 280r (B-2) <u>Borough of Nottingham</u>: TRE Earl Tosti had a carucate of land in Nottingham. King Edward had two pennies from its soke, and the earl had the third penny.

1241   i, 280r (B-6) <u>Borough of Nottingham</u>: It was customary (*soliti erant*) for the burgesses of Nottingham to fish in the River Trent, but they now make a plea (*querelam faciunt*) because they are prohibited (*prohibentur*) from fishing.

1242   i, 280r (B-20) <u>Borough of Nottingham</u>: In Nottingham the River Trent, the foss, and the road to York are so protected (*custodiuntur*) that if anyone impedes (*impedierit*) the passage of ships on the river, or plows, or makes a dyke within two perches of the King's road, he has to pay a fine (*emendare habet*) of £8.

1243   i, 280v (S-1) <u>Nottinghamshire and Derbyshire</u>: In Nottinghamshire and Derbyshire, when the King's peace is broken, which has been given by his hand or his seal (*pax regis manu vel sigillo data si fuerit infracta*), a fine is paid (*emendatur*) throughout eighteen hundreds, with each hundred paying £8. The King has two-thirds of this fine (*emendationis*) and the earl a third; that is twelve hundreds pay the King a fine (*emendant*) and six the earl.

1244   i, 280v (S-2) <u>Nottinghamshire and Derbyshire</u>: If any man is outlawed according to the law (*legem exulatus fuerit*) for any crime (*reatu*), no one but the King can restore peace (*regem pacem reddere potest*) to him.

1245   i, 280v (S-3) <u>Nottinghamshire and Derbyshire</u>: A thegn with more than six manors does not give relief (*relevationem*) on his land to anyone but the King, to whom he gives £8. If, however, he has six or less manors, whether he lives inside the borough or outside it, he gives the sheriff a relief (*relevationem*) of three marks of silver.

1246   i, 280v (S-4) <u>Nottinghamshire and Derbyshire</u>: If a thegn who has sake and soke should forfeit (*forisfecerit*) his land, the King and the earl between them have half his land and half his goods (*pecuniae*). His lawful wife along with his legitimate heirs (*legalis uxor cum legitimis hæredibus*), if he has any, get the other half.

1247   i, 280v (S-5) <u>Nottinghamshire and Derbyshire</u>: Here is noted those who had soke and sake and toll and team (*tol et thaim*) and the King's custom of two pennies: the Archbishop of York over his manors; and Countess Godgifu over Newark Wapentake; Ulf Fenisc over his land; the Abbot of Peterborough over Collingham; the Abbot of Burton; Earl Hugh over Markeaton [Derby.]; the Bishop of Chester; Toki; Swein son of Svavi; Siward Barn; Azur son of Svala; Wulfric Cild; Alsige of Illing; Leofwine son of Alwine; Countess Ælfgifu; Countess Gode; Alsige son of Karski over Worksop; Henry de Ferrers over Ednaston [Derby.], Doveridge [Derby.] and Brailsford [Derby.]; Walter d'Aincourt over Granby, Morton [Derby.], and Pilsley (in North Wingfield) [Derby.]. Of these, none could have the earl's third penny TRE, unless by his consent (*concessu*), and that for as long as he should live (*quamdiu viveret*), except for the Archbishop of York, Ulf Fenisc, and Countess Godgifu.

1248 i, 280v (S-6) <u>Nottinghamshire and Derbyshire</u>: Over the soke which lies in Clifton, the earl ought to have the third part of all customs and services (*operum*).

1249 i, 282v (2-10) <u>Count Alan; Leverton</u>: TRE Godric and Wulfmær had seven bovates and a fifth of a bovate in Leverton. Count Alan and Roger de Bully have held this land until now.

1250 i, 283v (6-1) <u>Bishop of Lincoln; Newark-on-Trent</u>: TRE Countess Godgifu held seven carucates and two bovates in Newark-on-Trent. Now it is held by the Bishop of Lincoln. All customs of the King and the earl from the wapentake of Newark are attached to this manor.

1251 i, 291r (18-5) <u>Gilbert Tison; Winkburn</u>: TRW Gilbert Tison holds twelve bovates in Winkburn. TRE Swein held them. Two bovates of this land, however, were held by five thegns, one senior to the others (*erat senior aliorum*). This land did not belong to Swein.

1252 i, 291r (20-3, 4) <u>Ilbert de Lacy; Elston, East Stoke</u>: TRE Thorkil held five bovates in East Stoke. Now they are held by Ilbert de Lacy, and Manfred holds from him. In Elston Ilbert has three messuages in which there are two sokemen and a bordar. These men belong to East Stoke and have no land. Ilbert claims (*calumniatur*) a priest's land against Bishop Remigius in Elston, and in East Stoke he claims (*calumniatur*) the fourth part of the vill.

1253 i, 291r (20-7) <u>Ilbert de Lacy; Cropwell Butler</u>: TRE Wulfgeat and Godric held four bovates in Cropwell Butler. Ilbert de Lacy was seised (*fuit saisitus*) of this land. When Roger the Poitevin, however, took (*accepit*) land, he was seised (*saisiuit*) of this manor against Ilbert. The wapentake bears (*portant*) testimony that Ilbert was seised (*fuisse saisitus*) of it. It is now in the hand of the King, except for a third of the manor and a thegn, which are in the head of the manor, which Ilbert now holds.

1254 i, 292v (30-22) <u>King's thegns; Kingston on Soar</u>: TRE Ulfkil had one and a half bovates in Kingston on Soar. Now Godric holds it, but the men of the country do not know through whom or how he holds it.

Oxfordshire

1255 i, 154r (B-9) <u>Oxford</u>: TRW Walter Giffard holds seventeen messuages which pay 22s. Seven are waste. Walter's antecessor had one of these by King Edward's gift (*dono regis Edwardi*).

1256 i, 154r (B-10) <u>Oxford</u>: If the wall is not repaired, when the work is needed by he who ought to repair it, he shall either pay the King a fine (*emendabit*) of 40s. or loose (*perdit*) his house.

1257 i, 154v (1-1) <u>Terra Regis; Benson</u>: King William holds twelve hides less a virgate in Benson. The soke of four and a half hundreds belongs to this manor.

1258 i, 154v (1–2) <u>Terra Regis; Headington</u>: King William holds ten hides in Headington. The soke of two hundreds belongs to this manor. Richard de Courcy withdraws (*retrahit*) sixteen hides for himself.

1259 i, 154v (1–3) <u>Terra Regis; Kirtlington</u>: King William holds eleven and a half hides in Kirtlington. The soke of two and a half hundreds belongs to this manor. One and a half hides in Launton lay in Kirtlington in the time of King Edward, but the King gave (*dedit*) it to Westminster Abbey and to Baldwin his godson (*filiolus*).

1260 i, 154v (1–4) <u>Terra Regis; Wootton</u>: King William holds five hides in Wootton. The soke of three hundreds belongs to this manor.

1261 i, 154v (1–5) <u>Terra Regis; Shipton-under-Wychwood</u>: King William holds thirty-three hides and three virgates in Shipton-under-Wychwood. The soke of three hundreds belongs to this manor.

1262 i, 154v (1–6) <u>Terra Regis; Bampton</u>: King William holds twenty-seven and a half hides in Bampton. The soke of two hundreds belongs to this manor. Ilbert de Lacy holds a half hide of this land by gift (*dono*) of the Bishop of Bayeux. Walter fitz Poyntz holds a small piece of land, and Henry de Ferrers holds a woodland which Bondi the Forester held. All this land belongs to the King's demesne: this the county testifies. TRE Joseph had sixty acres of land in Stockley from the King's demesne, but later Earl Harold took (*accepit*) it into his demesne. It was in the King's demesne when King William crossed the sea.

1263 i, 154v (1–7a, 7b) <u>Terra Regis; Bloxham, Adderbury</u>: TRE Earl Edwin held thirty-four and a half hides in Bloxham and Adderbury. Now King William holds them. The soke of two hundreds belongs to this manor. From the time of Earl Tosti, a thegn named Sægeat has lived in Bloxham, and he used to serve as a freeman. Earl Edwin gave (*dedit*) him to Ralph d'Oilly. R. d'Oilly brought him back (*retraxit*) into the demesne of the King.

1264 i, 154v (1–11) <u>Terra Regis; "Verneveld"</u>: TRW the King has a half hide of waste in "Verneveld." Hervey unjustly (*iniuste*) had the profit (*prosicuum*) from this land.

1265 i, 154v (1–13) <u>Terra Regis</u>: If anyone breaks the King's peace given through his hand or seal, so that he kills a man to whom the peace has been given, his life and limbs shall be in the judgment of the King, if he is captured. (*Pax regis manu vel sigillo data siquis infregerit, ita ut hominem cui pax ipsa data fuerit occidat et membra et vita eius in arbitrio regis erunt si captus fuerit.*) If he cannot be captured, he shall be an outlaw to all men (*si capi non potuerit, ad omnibus exul habebitur*). If anyone prevails to kill (*occidere praevaluerit*) him, he will have license to the killer's spoils (*spolia eius licenter habebit*).

1266 i, 154v (1–13) <u>Terra Regis</u>: If a stranger (*extraneus*) chooses to live in Oxford and has a house but is without kinsmen (*sine parentibus*), and finishes his life there, the King shall have all that he leaves (*reliquerit*).

1267 i, 154v (1–13) <u>Terra Regis</u>: If anyone violently breaks into or enters a hall or a house, with the result that he kills, wounds, or assaults a man (*curiam vel* *domum violenter effregerit vel intraverit ut hominem occidat vel vulneret vel assaliat*), he shall pay a fine (*emendat*) of 100s. to the King.

1268   i, 154v (1–13) <u>Terra Regis</u>: Similarly, if anyone is called to go on an expedition, but does not go, he owes the King 100s.

1269   i, 154v (1–13) <u>Terra Regis</u>: If anyone kills anyone within his hall or house (*interfecerit intra curiam vel domum suam*), his body and all his property (*substantia*) shall be in the power of the King (*in potestate regis*), except for the dowry (*dotem*) of his wife, if he had her with a dowry (*si dotatam habuerit*).

1270   i, 155v (6–14) <u>Bishop of Lincoln; Yarnton</u>: TRW Roger d'Ivry holds Yarnton from the Bishop of Lincoln. This land is of Eynsham Abbey.

1271   i, 156v (9–7) <u>Abingdon Abbey; Garsington</u>: TRW Gilbert holds seven and a half hides in Garsington from the Abbot of Abingdon. There is a hide of inland there that was never gelded. It lies dispersed among the King's land.

1272   i, 157r (13–1) <u>Abbey of St. Denis; Taynton</u>: TRW the Abbey of St. Denis holds ten hides in Taynton from the King. King Edward gave (*dedit*) it to the abbey.

1273   i, 157v (24–5) <u>Henry de Ferrers; Dean, Chalford</u>: TRW Henry de Ferrers holds eight hides in Dean and Chalford, and Robert holds them from him. Henry holds five of these hides from the King, and he bought (*emit*) three hides from Edwin the Sheriff. Bondi held this land freely TRE.

1274   i, 157v (24–6) <u>Henry de Ferrers; "Asce"</u>: TRE Cynewig held two hides in "Asce." Henry de Ferrers holds them TRW. He has given neither geld nor any other renders that he ought to the King's officials (*ministris*). He has joined these hides to his land in Gloucestershire.

1275   i, 157v (24–7) <u>Henry de Ferrers; Chastleton</u>: TRW Henry de Ferrers holds a hide in Chastleton from the fee of Winchcombe Abbey. It is waste.

1276   i, 158r (28–16) <u>Robert d'Oilly; Hardwick</u>: TRW Drogo holds seven and a half hides in Hardwick from Robert d'Oilly. Robert exchanged (*excambiuit*) this land with Walter Giffard.

1277   i, 158v (28–19) <u>Robert d'Oilly; Bletchingdon</u>: TRW Gilbert holds eight hides from Robert d'Oilly in Bletchingdon. Robert redeemed (*redemit*) this land from the King.

1278   i, 158v (28–23) <u>Robert d'Oilly; Rousham</u>: TRW Reginald holds three hides and a virgate less three acres from Robert d'Oilly in Rousham. Robert redeemed (*redemit*) this land from the King.

1279   i, 158v (28–24) <u>Robert d'Oilly; Ludwell</u>: TRW Reginald holds one and a half hides in Ludwell from Robert d'Oilly. King William gave (*dedit*) it to Robert at the siege of Sainte-Susanne.

1280   i, 158v (29–13) <u>Roger d'Ivry; Brookhampton</u>: TRW Reginald holds three hides in Brookhampton from Roger d'Ivry. In addition to these three hides there are another two which have been adjudged (*sint diratiocinatae*) to stand in the King's demesne. Reginald keeps back (*retinet*) this land against the King's seisin (*saisionem*).

1281   i, 159r (29–18) <u>Roger d'Ivry; Clanfield</u>: TRW Payne holds seven hides less a virgate from Roger d'Ivry in Clanfield. This land is from the first fee of the King (*de primo feudo regis*).

1282   i, 159v (35-22) <u>Miles Crispin; Britwell Salome</u>: TRE Wulfstan held five hides in Britwell Salome freely. Now Almalric holds them from Miles Crispin. Concerning the fifth hide of this land, Almalric has paid neither geld nor anything else.

1283   i, 159v (35-24, 25) <u>Miles Crispin; Berrick Salome, Gangsdown</u>: TRW Ordgar holds four hides in Berrick Salome from Miles Crispin and a hide in Gangsdown from the same man. He ought, however, to hold them from the King, because he, his father, and his uncle held them freely TRE.

1284   i, 160v (58-27) <u>Richard and the King's officials; Bletchingdon</u>: TRW Alwig the Sheriff holds two and a half hides in Bletchingdon from the King. Manasseh bought (*emit*) this land from him, without the King's permission.

1285   i, 160v (58-33) <u>Richard and the King's officials; Little Minster</u>: TRE Sæweald held three hides in Little Minster. TRW the same Sæweald holds it, and Robert d'Oilly holds from him in mortgage (*in vadimonio*).

1286   i, 160v (58-34) <u>Richard and the King's officials; two mills in or near Oxford</u>: TRW Sæweald holds two mills next to the wall of Oxford from the King, which the King granted (*concessit*) to him with his wife.

Lands between the Ribble and the Mersey

1287   i, 269v (R1-39) <u>Roger the Poitevin; West Derby</u>: The manor of West Derby with its attached hides paid King Edward a farm of £26 2s. Three of its hides were free, because the King pardoned (*perdonavit*) the thegns who held them from tax (*censum*). These hides paid £4 14s. 8d.

1288   i, 269v (R1-40a) <u>Roger the Poitevin; West Derby</u>: All the thegns associated with West Derby in the time of King Edward paid two *ora* of pence for each carucate of land. Through custom (*per consuetudinem*), these thegns used to build the King's houses, fisheries, haies, stagbeats, and whatever belonged to them, as if they were villeins. Any man who did not do this when he ought, paid a fine (*emendabat*) of 2s., and afterward came and labored until the work was done. Each of these thegns sent his reapers to cut the King's corn for a day in August. If he did not, he paid a fine (*emendabat*) of 2s.

1289   i, 269v (R1-40b) <u>Roger the Poitevin; West Derby</u>: If any freeman committed theft (*faceret furtum*), robbery (*forestel*), housebreaking (*heinfara*), or breach of the King's peace (*pacem regis infringebat*), he paid a fine (*emendabat*) of 40s.

1290   i, 269v (R1-40c) <u>Roger the Poitevin; West Derby</u>: If anyone drew blood (*faciebat sanguinem*), raped a woman (*raptum de femina*), or stayed away from the shiremoot without a reasonable excuse (*remanebat de siremot sine rationabili excusatione*), he paid a fine (*emendabat*) of 10s.

1291   i, 269v (R1-40d) <u>Roger the Poitevin; West Derby</u>: If anyone stayed away from the hundred or did not go to the pleas when the reeve ordered (*non ibat ad placitum ubi praepositus iubebat*), he paid a fine (*emendabat*) of 5s.

1292 i, 269v (R1-40e) Roger the Poitevin; West Derby: If the reeve ordered (*iubebat*) a man to go on his service, but that man did not go, he paid a fine (*emendabat*) of 4s.

1293 i, 269v (R1-40f) Roger the Poitevin; West Derby: Anyone who wished to withdraw from the King's land gave (*dabat*) 40s. and could go where he wished.

1294 i, 269v (R1-40g) Roger the Poitevin; West Derby: He who wished to have his dead father's land gave 40s. relief (*relevabat*). If he did not wish to, the King had the father's land and all his goods (*omniem pecuniam*).

1295 i, 269v (R1-41) Roger the Poitevin; West Derby: TRE Uhtræd held Crosby and Kirkdale as a hide. This land was quit of all customs except these six: breach of peace (*pace infracta*), robbery (*forestel*), housebreaking (*heinfara*), a fight which persisted after an oath has been made (*pugna quae post sacramentum factum remanebat*), if one constrained by the judgment of the reeve (*constrictus iusticia praepositi*) did not pay his debt (*debitum soluebat*) or did not pay attention to a due-date given by the reeve (*terminum a praeposito*). If he committed any of these acts, he paid a fine (*emendabat*) of 40s.

1296 i, 269v (R1-42) Roger the Poitevin; West Derby: Three hides in North Meols, Halsall, and Hurlston were quit from geld, and from forfeitures of bloodshed (*forisfactura sanguinis*) and the violation of a woman (*femine violentia*), but these lands paid all other customs.

1297 i, 269v (R1-43) Roger the Poitevin; West Derby: The following men now hold land in West Derby by gift (*dono*) of Roger the Poitevin: Geoffrey holds two hides and a half carucate; Roger holds one and a half hides; William has one and a half hides; Warin a half hide; Geoffrey a hide; Theobald one and a half hides; Robert two carucates; and Gilbert one carucate.

1298 i, 269v (R2-2) Roger the Poitevin; Newton-le-Willows: TRE all but two of the freemen in the hundred of Newton-le-Willows were under the same customs as the men of West Derby, except in addition they reaped the King's fields for two more days in August. The aforementioned two men had five carucates of land and the forfeitures of bloodshed (*forisfacturam sanguinis*) and violence towards women (*feminae violentiam passae*). They also had the pannage of their men. The King had the other forfeitures.

1299 i, 270r (R4-1) Roger the Poitevin; Blackburn: King Edward held Blackburn. Twenty-eight freemen were attached to this hundred. They held five and a half hides and forty carucates as twenty-eight manors. They were under the aforementioned customs.

1300 i, 270r (R4-2) Roger the Poitevin; Blackburn: TRE, in the same hundred, King Edward had two carucates in Huncoat, two carucates in Walton-le-Dale, and a half hide in Pendleton. The whole manor with the hundred paid £32 2s. in farm to the King. Roger the Poitevin gave (*dedit*) all this land to Roger de Bully and Albert Grelley. There are as many men as have eleven and a half plows, to whom Roger and Albert granted to be quit (*quos ipsi concesserant esse quietos*) for three years. It is not, therefore, assessed.

1301   i, 270r (R5-1, 3) <u>Roger the Poitevin; Salford</u>: King Edward held Salford. Twenty-one berewicks belonged to this manor or hundred, in which there were eleven and a half hides and ten and a half carucates of land. Twenty-one thegns held them for twenty-one manors. One of these thegns, Gamal, held two hides in Rochdale. He had his customs quit (*consuetudines quietas*), except for these six: theft (*furtum*), housebreaking (*heinfare*), robbery (*forestel*), breach of the King's peace (*pacem regis infractam*), breach of a due-date fixed by a reeve (*terminum fractum a praeposito stabilitum*), and a fight after an oath has been made (*pugnam post sacramentum factum remanentem*). For these he paid a fine (*emendabat*) of 40s.

1302   i, 270r (R5-6) <u>Roger the Poitevin; Salford</u>: The following knights hold land in the manor of Salford by gift (*dono*) of Roger the Poitevin: Nigel holds three hides and a half carucate; Warin two carucates; another Warin one and a half carucates; Geoffrey one carucate; and Gamal two carucates.

1303   i, 270r (R6-1, 2) <u>Roger the Poitevin; Leyland</u>: King Edward held Leyland. Twelve freemen held twelve carucates as twelve manors, which belonged to Leyland. These men and the men of Salford did not work, through custom, at the King's hall, nor did they reap in August. However, they made a haie in the woodland. They had the forfeiture for bloodshed (*sanguinis forisfacturam*) and violence against women (*feminae passae violentiam*). They shared the other customs of the other manors, as noted above.

1304   i, 270r (R7-1) <u>Roger the Poitevin</u>: There are 188 manors of 79 hides in the six hundreds of West Derby, Newton, Warrington, Blackburn, Salford, and Leyland. The value of what Roger the Poitevin gave (*dedit*) to his knights in these hundreds is assessed at £20 11s.

Rutland

1305   i, 293v (2-7) <u>Countess Judith; Market Overton</u>: In the time of King Edward, Earl Waltheof had three and a half carucates in Market Overton and its berewick Stretton. Now Countess Judith holds them. Alvred of Lincoln, however, claims (*calumniatur*) the fourth part in Stretton.

1306   i, 293v (1-17, 19, 20) <u>Terra Regis; Oakham, Hambleton, Ridlington</u>: TRE Queen Edith held manors in Oakham, Hambleton, and Ridlington. They were assessed at four carucates apiece. TRW they are held by King William, but all are described, nonetheless, as "church soke."

Shropshire

1307   i, 252r (C-1, 2) <u>City of Shrewsbury</u>: King Edward had the following customs: if anyone knowingly broke the King's peace given by his own hand, he was made an outlaw (*pacem regis manu propria datam scienter infringebat utlagus fiebat*). But a man who broke the King's peace given by the sheriff (*pacem regis a vicecomite datam infringebat*) paid a fine (*emendabat*) of 100s. He who committed robbery or housebreaking (*forestel vel heinfare faciebat*) owed the same amount. King Edward had these three forfeitures (*forisfacturas*) in his demesne over all England in addition to the farms.

1308 i, 252r (C-4) <u>City of Shrewsbury</u>: When the sheriff wished to continue into Wales, if a man commanded (*edictus*) by him did not go, he owed a forfeiture (*forisfactura*) of 40s.

1309 i, 252r (C-5) <u>City of Shrewsbury</u>: If a woman, who was a widow, took a husband in any way, she owed 20s. to the King. If she was a girl, she owed 10s., whatever way she took a man.

1310 i, 252r (C-6) <u>City of Shrewsbury</u>: If any burgess's house burned through misfortune, accident, or negligence (*casu vel eventu sive negligentia*), he owed 40s. as a forfeiture (*forisfactura*) to the King, and 2s. each to his two nearest neighbors (*propinquioribus vicinis suis*).

1311 i, 252r (C-7) <u>City of Shrewsbury</u>: When a burgess in the King's demesne died, the King had 10s. in relief (*de relevamento*).

1312 i, 252r (C-8) <u>City of Shrewsbury</u>: If a burgess broke a time-limit, which the sheriff had imposed on him (*frangebat terminum quem vicecomes imponebat ei*), he paid a fine (*emendabat*) of 10s.

1313 i, 252r (C-9) <u>City of Shrewsbury</u>: He who shed blood (*sanguinem fundebat*) paid a fine (*emendabat*) of 40s.

1314 i, 252r (C-12) <u>City of Shrewsbury</u>: In the year preceding this survey (*descriptionis*), Shrewsbury paid £40 to Earl Roger.

1315 i, 252r (C-14) <u>City of Shrewsbury</u>: The English burgesses of Shrewsbury say that it is very hard (*multum grave*) for them to pay as much geld now as they paid in the time of King Edward, because the earl's castle has seized (*occupaverit*) fifty-one messuages, and fifty other messuages are waste. Also forty-three French burgesses hold messuages which were gelded TRE. The earl, moreover, has given (*dederit*) the abbey, which he is building in Shrewsbury, thirty-nine burgesses who once paid geld like the others. In total, there are 193 messuages which are not gelded.

1316 i, 252v (3b-1) <u>Shrewsbury Abbey; Shrewsbury</u>: Earl Roger is building an abbey in the city of Shrewsbury, and has given (*dedit*) the new abbey St. Peter's Minster, where the parochial church of the city was.

1317 i, 252v (3b-2) <u>Shrewsbury Abbey; Eyton on Severn</u>: TRE Earl Leofric held eight and a half hides in Eyton on Severn. Now Shrewsbury Abbey holds them. TRE this land was valued at £21. When the earl gave (*dedit*) it to the abbey, it paid £14.

1318 i, 252v (3c-9) <u>Wenlock Abbey; Stoke St. Milborough</u>: TRW the Church of St. Milburgh holds twenty hides in Stoke St. Milborough. Earl Roger gave (*dedit*) this land to his chaplains, but the Church ought to have it.

1319 i, 252v (3d-6, 7) <u>Church of St. Mary, Bromfield; Bromfield</u>: TRW the

Church of St. Mary, Bromfield holds ten hides in Bromfield. In the time of King Edward there were twenty hides in this manor, which twelve canons of the Church held. One alone – Spirites – held ten hides, but after he had been outlawed (*fuisset exulatus*) from England, King Edward gave (*dedit*) these hides to Robert fitz Wimarc, as if he were a canon (*sicut canonico*). But Robert gave (*dedit*) this same land to his son-in-law. When the canons informed (*indicassent*) the King of this, he immediately ordered (*praecepit*) that the land ought to be returned (*reverti*) to the Church, only waiting until, at the imminent Christmas court (*curiam instantis natalis*), he could order (*iuberet*) Robert to provide (*provideret*) other land for his son-in-law. The King, however, died during those feast days, and from then until now, the Church has lost (*perdit*) the land.

1320 i, 253r (3g-7) <u>Church of St. Alkmund's, Shrewsbury; Albrightlee</u>: TRW St. Alkmund's Church holds a hide in Albrightlee. There is a league of woodland there, but Earl Roger took it away (*abstulit*) from the Church.

1321 i, 253r (4,1-1) <u>Roger of Montgomery; Wrockwardine</u>: TRW Earl Roger holds five hides in Wrockwardine. King Edward held them. Two pennies belonged to this manor from Wrockwardine Hundred TRE. The earl had the third penny.

1322 i, 253r (4,1-2) <u>Roger of Montgomery; Condover</u>: TRW Earl Roger holds thirteen hides in Condover. King Edward held them. TRE two pennies belonged to this manor from Condover Hundred.

1323 i, 253r (4,1-5) <u>Roger of Montgomery; Morville</u>: TRW Earl Roger holds twelve hides in Morville. King Edward held them. The whole of Alnothstree Hundred belonged to this manor. Two pennies were King Edward's, and the third penny was the earl's.

1324 i, 253v (4,1-6) <u>Roger of Montgomery; Corfham</u>: King Edward held four hides in Corfham. Now Earl Roger holds them. The whole of Culvestone Hundred and Patton Hundred belong to this manor. TRE it paid £10 at farm with the two pennies from the hundreds. Now, with the hundreds, it pays £6 to the earl.

1325 i, 254r (4,1-37) <u>Roger of Montgomery; Shrewsbury</u>: TRW Earl Roger holds the King's city of Shrewsbury. In total, Shrewsbury, the hundreds, and the pleas of the county (*placita comitatus*) pay £300 and 115s. in farm.

1326 i, 254r (4,3-8) <u>Roger of Montgomery; Tugford</u>: TRE Alwine held three and a half hides in Tugford. He was free with the land. In the time of King William, Reginald the Sheriff, who held this land from Earl Roger, gave (*dedit*) it to Shrewsbury Abbey for the soul of his antecessor Warin (*pro anima Warini antecessoris sui*).

1327 i, 255v (4,3-71) <u>Roger of Montgomery; Albrighton</u>: TRE Geri held three hides in Albrighton. Afterwards, Ealhhere held them from Warin, Reginald the Sheriff's antecessor. Now Reginald the Sheriff holds this land from Earl Roger.

1328 i, 255v (4,4-23) <u>Roger of Montgomery; Montford</u>: TRE Almær held three hides in Montford. Now Roger fitz Corbet holds it from Earl Roger. Bishop R. claims (*calumniatur*) this land.

1329 i, 257r (4,14-12) Roger of Montgomery; Bayston: TRW William Pandolf holds a hide in Bayston. TRE Eadric held it from the Bishop of Hereford. The bishop, however, could not alienate (*divertere*) it to him because it was for his victualing, and he had leased (*prestiterat*) it to Eadric for his life only (*tantum in vita sua*). [There is a "k" for "*klamor*" written in the margin of this entry.]

1330 i, 258r (4,20-19) Roger of Montgomery; "Cavrtune": TRE the Church of St. Alkmund held a half hide in "Cavrtune" in alms. Now Picot holds it unjustly (*iniuste*).

1331 i, 259r (4,26-2) Roger of Montgomery; Broom: A hide in Broom lies in Baschurch Hundred. It belongs to Albert's vill of Welshampton. The earl's men are litigating (*litigant*) over it.

1332 i, 259r (4,26-3) Roger of Montgomery; Wrentnall: TRE Earnwig and Ketil held two hides in Wrentnall as two manors. Now Roger the Huntsman holds them from Earl Roger. The Church of St. Chad [i.e. the bishopric of Chester] claims (*calumniatur*) one and a half hides of this land. The county testifies that they were in the Church before the time of King Edward, but they are ignorant as to how they were lost (*ignorant quomodo exierunt*).

1333 i, 260r (6-3) Ralph de Mortimer; Mawley, "Lel," "Fech": TRW Ralph de Mortimer holds a hide in Mawley, a virgate in "Lel," and a virgate in "Fech." TRE three thegns held this land as three manors and were free men. When Thurstan of Wigmore took (*recepit*) them from Earl William, he joined them to Cleobury Mortimer.

1334 i, 260r (6-11) Ralph de Mortimer; Leintwardine [Hereford]: King Edward held four hides and a virgate in Leintwardine. Now Ralph de Mortimer holds them. There are two men there who pay 4s. for the lease (*de locatione*) of the land.

1335 i, 260v (9-1) Nigel the Physician; Wistanstow: TRW Nigel the Physician holds Wistanstow from the King. TRE Spirites the Priest held it from the Church of St. Alkmund. It was for the victualing of the canons.

Somerset

1336 i, 86r (1-1) Terra Regis; Somerton: King Edward held Somerton; now King William holds it. Three lands, assessed at five and a half hides, have been added to this manor. Three thegns – Beorhtnoth, Ælfric, and Sæwine – held them TRE. A half hide at Deadman's Well has been taken away (*est ablata*) from this manor. It was from King Edward's demesne farm, but now Alvred d'Epaignes holds it.

1337 i, 86r (1-2) Terra Regis; Cheddar: King Edward held Cheddar; now King William holds it. Giso bishop of Wells holds Wedmore, one of this manor's berewicks, which he also held from King Edward. William the Sheriff, however, accounts (*computat*) £12 for it from the King's farm each year. Also, a half virgate has been taken away (*est ablata*) from this manor, which was part of King Edward's demesne farm. Robert d'Auberville now holds it.

1338 i, 86r (1-4) <u>Terra Regis; South Petherton</u>: King Edward held South Petherton; now King William holds it. A half hide has been taken away (*ablata est*) from this manor. Norman holds it from Roger de Courseulles. TRE Cricket St. Thomas paid a customary due to the manor of South Petherton of six sheep, six lambs, and a bloom of iron from every freeman. TRW Thurstan holds Cricket St. Thomas from Robert count of Mortain, but he has not paid these dues since the count has had the land.

1339 i, 86r (1-5) <u>Terra Regis; Curry Rivel</u>: King Edward held Curry Rivel; now King William holds it. A virgate has been taken away (*est ablata*) from this manor, which Bretel holds from the Count of Mortain.

1340 i, 86v (1-6) <u>Terra Regis; Williton, Cannington, Carhampton</u>: King Edward held Williton, Cannington, and Carhampton. Now King William holds them. A half hide has been added to Williton. Særic held it TRE as two manors. Another half hide has been added to Williton at Westowe, which Alwine held TRE. Another half hide has been added to Williton. [No information is given about its TRE holder.] A customary due of eighteen sheep a year has been added to Williton from Alvred d'Epaignes's manor of Monksilver. It did not belong to Williton in the time of King Edward.

1341 i, 86v (1-9) <u>Terra Regis; Bruton</u>: King Edward held Bruton; now King William holds it. Nine acres have been taken away (*sunt ablati*) from Bruton, which Bretel holds from the Count of Mortain. Another half hide in Kilmington [Wilts.] has also been taken away (*est ablata*) from this manor. TRE it was in the demesne farm, but Serlo de Burcy now holds it. Another hide has been taken away (*est ablata*) from this manor. Jocelyn holds it from Robert fitz Gerald.

1342 i, 86v (1-11) <u>Terra Regis; Brompton Regis</u>: TRE Countess Gytha held ten hides in Brompton Regis; and when she held Brompton Regis, the third penny of Milverton was paid there. In the time of King William it has been taken away (*ablatus est*). Now King William holds this land. One hide of this manor is in Preston Bowyer. TRE it was part of the demesne farm, but now it is held by the Count of Mortain.

1343 i, 86v (1-12) <u>Terra Regis; Dulverton</u>: TRE Earl Harold held two and a half hides in Dulverton. Now they are held by King William. Two hides less a half furlong have been added to this manor. Thirteen thegns held them TRE. The customs of the Count of Mortain's manor of Brushford, that is, twenty-four sheep a year, have been taken away (*est ablata*) from this manor. These were paid to Dulverton TRE, when Earl Harold held it. Mauger keeps them back through the count.

1344 i, 86v (1-13) <u>Terra Regis; Old Cleeve</u>: TRE, when Earl Harold held this manor, the third penny of the borough-dues (*burgherist*) of Carhampton, Williton, Cannington, and North Petherton were attached to Old Cleeve.

1345   i, 86v (1-17) <u>Terra Regis; Winsford</u>. TRE Winsford was held by Earl Tosti, and it paid geld for three and a half hides. Now it is held by King William. A half hide has been added to this manor. Three thegns held it TRE and served the reeve of the manor through custom, without giving farm.

1346   i, 86v (1-19) <u>Terra Regis; North Curry</u>: TRE Earl Harold held North Curry, and it paid geld for twenty hides. King William holds it, but Ansgar holds one of this manor's hides from the Count of Mortain.

1347   i, 86v–87r (1-20) <u>Terra Regis; Crewkerne</u>: TRE Queen Edith held Crewkerne, and it did not pay geld. Easthams has been taken away (*est ablata*) from this manor. TRE it was of Crewkerne's farm and could not be separated from it. Now Thurstan holds it from the Count of Mortain.

1348   i, 87r (1-21) <u>Terra Regis; Congresbury</u>: TRE Earl Harold held Congresbury, and it paid geld for twenty hides. Now King William holds it. Two hides, which lay in this manor TRE, have been taken away (*ablatae sunt*). Giso bishop of Wells holds one, and Serlo de Burcy and Gilbert fitz Thurold hold the other.

1349   i, 87r (1-27) <u>Terra Regis; Martock</u>: King William holds thirty-eight hides in Martock. TRE they were held by Queen Edith. The value of this manor is given as follows: "It pays £70 by tale and 100s. more if Bishop Walkelin were to testify." Three hides have been added to this manor. Three thegns held them TRE. A hide and a virgate of land in Compton Durville has been taken away (*est ablata*) from this manor. Ansgar the Cook holds it. Another hide and a half has been taken away (*est ablata*) from this manor. Ælfric the Small holds it.

1350   i, 87r (1-28) <u>Terra Regis; Keynsham</u>: TRE Queen Edith held Keynsham, which paid geld for fifty hides. Now it is held by King William. Of these fifty hides Eustace of Boulogne holds four hides in Belluton, and Alvred holds from him. Tovi held them as a manor TRE.

1351   i, 87r (1-31) <u>Terra Regis; Bath</u>: Edward of Salisbury pays £11 from the third penny of this borough.

1352   i, 87r (1-31) <u>Terra Regis; information following the description of Bath</u>: Concerning the third penny of Ilchester, William de Mohun pays £6 at twenty pence to the *ora*; from Milborne Port 20s.; from Bruton 20s.; from Langport 10s.; from Axbridge 10s.; from Frome 5s.

1353   i, 87r (1-35) <u>Terra Regis; Mudford</u>: TRW Warmund holds Mudford in mortgage (*in vadimonio*) from Wulfweard White, by the testimony of the King's writ (*testimonio brevis regis*).

1354   i, 87v (2-2, 3, 4) <u>Bishop of Winchester; Taunton</u>: These are the customs which belong to Taunton: borough-dues (*burgheristh*), thieves (*latrones*), breaking the peace (*pacis infractio*), housebreaking (*hainfare*), hundred-penny (*denarii de hundret*), Peter's pence, churchscot, three times a year the bishop's pleas without summons (*ter in anno teneri placita episcopi sine ammonitione*), and setting out on military expedition with the bishop's men. These customs are paid in Taunton by Tolland, Oake, Holford, Upper Cheddon, Cheddon Fitzpaine, Maidenbrook, Ford, Hillfarrance, Hele (in Bradford-on-Tone), Nynehead, Norton Fitzwarren, Bradford-on-Tone, Halse, Heathfield, Shopnoller, and Stoke St. Mary. The last two lands do not owe military expedition, and those of Bagborough owe all of these customs except military expedition and burial. From all these lands, those who have to make an oath or bear the ordeal (*facturi sacramentum vel iudicium portaturi*) come to Taunton. When the lords of these lands die, they are buried in Taunton.

1355   i, 87v (2-9) <u>Bishop of Winchester; Taunton</u>: To the manor of Taunton has been added land in Lydeard St. Lawrence and Leigh (in Lydeard St. Lawrence), which a thegn held in parage TRE. This thegn could go to whatever lord he wished. TRW these lands are held by Wulfweard and Alweard, who hold them from the Bishop of Winchester through a grant (*concessionem*) of King William. King William granted (*concessit*) these lands to St. Peter and Bishop Walkelin, as he himself acknowledged at Salisbury in the hearing of the Bishop of Durham, whom he ordered to write down this grant of his in the returns (*recognovit apud Sarisberiam audiente episcopo Dunelmensi, cui praecepit, ut hanc ipsam concessionem suam in brevibus scriberet*).

1356   i, 87v (3-1) <u>Bishop of Salisbury; Seaborough [Dorset]</u>: TRW the Bishop of Salisbury holds Seaborough. Alweard held it TRE. Another Seaborough has been added to this manor. Alfred held it TRE. These two lands are not of the bishopric of Salisbury. Bishop Osmund holds them as a manor, and Walter holds from him. TRE they lay in the King's manor of Crewkerne, from which Alweard and Alfred could not be separated. Through custom they paid twelve sheep with their lambs and a bloom of iron from every freeman.

1357   i, 87v (4-1) <u>Bishop of Bayeux; Temple Combe</u>: TRE Earl Leofwine held Temple Combe, which paid geld for eight hides. TRW the Bishop of Bayeux holds it, and Sampson holds from him. To this manor have been added three virgates of land in Thorent. Alweard held them as a manor TRE.

1358   i, 87v (5-1) <u>Bishop of Coutances; Dowlish</u>: TRE Alweard held Dowlish, and it paid geld for two hides and a virgate. TRW Geoffrey bishop of Coutances holds it, and William holds from him. Seven hides have been added to Dowlish. TRE three thegns held them as three manors.

1359   i, 87v (5-2) <u>Bishop of Coutances; Chaffcombe</u>: TRE two thegns held three and a half hides in Chaffcombe. TRW the Bishop of Coutances holds them, and Ralph holds from him. A hide and three virgates have been added to this manor. TRE two thegns held them as two manors.

1360   i, 87v (5-5) <u>Bishop of Coutances; Exton</u>: TRE Edwin held Exton, and it paid geld for three hides and a furlong. TRW the Bishop of Coutances holds it, and Drogo holds from him. Of this land, three virgates lay in the King's manor of Nettlecombe TRE.

1361   i, 88r (5-10, 11, 12) <u>Bishop of Coutances; Hutton, Elborough, Winterhead</u>: TRW Hutton, Elborough, and Winterhead are held by the Bishop of

Coutances. These three manors, however, belonged to Glastonbury Abbey
TRE, and the men who held them – two unnamed thegns and Alweard and
Beorhtric – could not be separated from the abbey.

1362 i, 88r (5-15) <u>Bishop of Coutances; Timsbury</u>: TRE Api held Timsbury, and
it paid geld for three hides. Now the Bishop of Coutances holds it, and
William holds from him. Two hides have been added to this manor, which
Sibbi held as a manor TRE.

1363 i, 88r (5-18) <u>Bishop of Coutances; Farmborough</u>: TRE Eadric held Farm-
borough, and it paid geld for five hides. Now the Bishop of Coutances holds
it, and William holds from him. Five hides have been added to this manor.
TRE Ælfric held them as a manor.

1364 i, 88v (5-37) <u>Bishop of Coutances; Bathwick</u>: TRE Ælfric held Bathwick,
and it paid geld for four hides. TRW the Bishop of Coutances holds it. A
hide in Woolley has been added to Bathwick, which Ælfric held as a manor
TRE.

1365 i, 88v (5-40) <u>Bishop of Coutances; Wraxall</u>: TRE Ælfric held twenty hides in
Wraxall. TRW the Bishop of Coutances holds them. A hide has been added
to this manor, which a thegn held TRE.

1366 i, 88v (5-41) <u>Bishop of Coutances; Winford</u>: TRE Alweald held Winford,
and it paid geld for ten hides. TRW the Bishop of Coutances holds it. A hide
has been added to this manor, which Ælfric held TRE. Now Kolsveinn holds
it from the bishop.

1367 i, 88v (5-43) <u>Bishop of Coutances; Stratton-on-the-Fosse</u>: TRW the Bishop
of Coutances holds Stratton-on-the-Fosse and William holds from him. TRE
Alweald held it from Glastonbury, and he could not be separated from the
Church. [That the Bishop of Coutances's tenancy is not legal is suggested by
the marginal cross written next to the beginning of this entry. These crosses
occur occasionally in Somerset in the margins of some, but not all entries
dealing with land taken illegally from a church.] One and a half hides in
Pitcote have been added to this manor. Wulfmær held it TRE, and he could
go where he wished.

1368 i, 88v (5-46) <u>Bishop of Coutances; Twerton</u>: TRE Alfred held Twerton
from Queen Edith. Now the Bishop of Coutances holds it from the King, so
he says.

1369 i, 88v (5-50) <u>Bishop of Coutances; "Millescote" (lost in Mells)</u>: TRE two
thegns held "Millescote" from Glastonbury Abbey, and they could not
separate themselves from the Church. TRW Azelin holds this land from the
Bishop of Coutances. [The marginal cross, drawn beside the beginning of this
entry, suggests that the TRW tenancy is not legal.]

1370 i, 88v (5-53) <u>Bishop of Coutances; Tellisford</u>: TRE Edward held Tellisford,
and it paid geld for two hides. TRW the Bishop of Coutances holds it, and
Moses holds from him. Three hides have been added to this manor. Ælfgeat
held them TRE.

1371 i, 89r (5-57) <u>Bishop of Coutances; Newton St. Loe</u>: TRE Ælfric held

Newton St. Loe, and it paid geld for three hides. TRW the Bishop of Coutances holds it. Seven hides have been added to this manor, which two thegns held TRE.

1372   i, 89r (6-1) Bishop of Wells; Wells: TRE and TRW the Bishop of Wells holds Wells, and it paid geld for fifty hides. Manasseh's wife holds two of these fifty hides, but not from the bishop.

1373   i, 89r (6-7) Bishop of Wells; Wellington: TRE and TRW the Bishop of Wells holds Wellington, which paid geld for fourteen hides. A hide has been added to this manor. TRE Ælfgifu held it as a manor.

1374   i, 89v (6-14) Bishop of Wells; Yatton: TRE John the Dane held twenty hides in Yatton. TRW the Bishop of Wells holds them. There is a pasture there, called Wemberham, which belonged to the King's manor of Congresbury.

1375   i, 89v (6-19) Bishop of Wells; Ash Priors: TRE Ash Priors was held by Giso bishop of Wells, and it lay in his manor of Bishops Lydeard. TRW Roger Arundel holds it from the King unjustly (*iniuste*).

1376   i, 90r (8-2) Glastonbury Abbey; Winscombe: TRE and TRW Glastonbury Abbey holds Winscombe, and it paid geld for fifteen hides. The Bishop of Coutances holds one of this manor's hides from the King. Beorhtric held it freely TRE, but he could not be separated from the Church.

1377   i, 90r (8-19) Glastonbury Abbey; Lattiford: TRE Ælfric held two hides in Lattiford, and he could not be separated from Glastonbury. Now Humphrey the Chamberlain holds them from the King.

1378   i, 90r (8-20) Glastonbury Abbey; Pilton: TRE and TRW Glastonbury holds Pilton, which paid geld for twenty hides. Of this land, Alnoth the Monk holds a hide freely from the abbot by consent (*concessu*) of the King.

1379   i, 90v (8-25) Glastonbury Abbey; Mells: TRW Azelin holds five and a half hides from the Bishop of Coutances, who holds from the King. They belong to Glastonbury's twenty-hide estate at Mells. Two thegns held them TRE, but they could not be separated from Glastonbury.

1380   i, 90v (8-30) Glastonbury Abbey; Ditcheat: TRE and TRW Glastonbury holds Ditcheat, which paid geld for thirty hides. Of these thirty hides Ælfric and Everard hold a hide from the King, and the Count of Mortain holds a further seven hides from him. TRE the thegns who held this land could not be separated from the abbey.

1381   i, 90v (8-31) Glastonbury Abbey; Camerton: TRE Eadmær Atre held ten hides in Camerton. Now Glastonbury holds them. The Count of Mortain gave (*dedit*) them to the abbot in exchange (*pro excambio*) for Tintinhull.

1382   i, 91r (8-37) Glastonbury Abbey; Ilchester: Maurice bishop of London holds the Church of St. Andrew in Ilchester from the King, along with three hides of land. TRE Beorhtric held the church and the hides from Glastonbury and could not be separated from it.

1383   i, 91r (8-38) Glastonbury Abbey; Hutton, Elborough, Hiscombe, Stratton-on-the-Fosse: TRW the Bishop of Coutances holds Hutton, Elborough, Hiscombe, and Stratton-on-the-Fosse from King William. These lands, however, were thegnland TRE, and they could not be alienated from Glastonbury. TRW, moreover, Glastonbury does not have service for them.

1384 i, 91r (8-39) Glastonbury Abbey; Kingstone, Stoke sub Hamdon, Stoke sub Hamdon, Draycott (in Limington): The Count of Mortain holds these manors from the King: Kingstone, Stoke sub Hamdon, and Draycott. These lands were thegnland TRE and could not be separated from Glastonbury.

1385 i, 91r (8-40) Glastonbury Abbey; Butleigh: Robert Count of Mortain holds a woodland, two furlongs in length and one in breadth, in the manor of Butleigh. TRE it was Glastonbury's.

1386 i, 91r (8-41) Glastonbury Abbey; Limington: TRW Roger de Courseulles has a manor in Limington, which his father gave (*dedit*) in exchange (*in excambio*) for five hides that he held from Glastonbury Abbey. TRE these hides could not be separated from the Church. Glastonbury has lost the service (*servitium perdit*) from these hides.

1387 i, 91r (10-1) Athelney Abbey; Ilton: TRE and TRW Athelney Abbey held eight hides in Ilton. Robert count of Mortain holds two of these hides, which were in the Church TRE.

1388 i, 91r (10-2) Athelney Abbey; Long Sutton: TRW Athelney Abbey holds ten hides in Long Sutton. Roger de Courseulles holds two hides of this manor against the Abbot's wishes (*invito*). TRE two thegns held them from the abbey and could not be separated from it.

1389 i, 91r (10-6) Athelney Abbey; Ashill, Long Sutton, Bossington: TRW the Count of Mortain holds two hides in Ashill. Roger de Courseulles holds two hides from the manor of Long Sutton, and Ralph de Limesy holds one hide from Bossington. All of this land, however, lay in Athelney Abbey TRE and could not be separated from it.

1390 i, 91r (13-1) St. Mary's, Montebourg; five unidentified hides: TRE Spirites the Priest held five hides. TRW the Church of St. Mary, Montebourg holds them from King William, by gift (*dono*) of Nigel the Physician.

1391 i, 91v (19-7) Count of Mortain; Crowcombe: TRW Robert holds Crowcombe from the Count of Mortain. TRE Old Minster, Winchester held it. [That Robert's tenancy is illegal is suggested by the marginal cross, drawn next to the beginning of this entry.]

1392 i, 91v (19-9) Count of Mortain; Tintinhull: TRW the Count of Mortain holds Tintinhull. Glastonbury Abbey held it TRE. [That Robert's tenancy is illegal is suggested by the marginal cross, drawn next to the beginning of this entry.]

1393 i, 92r (19-10, 11, 12, 13) Count of Mortain; Kingstone, Stoke sub Hamdon, Draycott (in Limington), Stoke sub Hamdon: TRW Hubert holds Kingstone from the Count of Mortain. TRE Glastonbury Abbey held it. Furthermore, the abbey no longer has service from this land. [That Robert's tenancy is illegal is suggested by the marginal cross, found at the beginning of this entry.]

1394 Exon (for 19-15) Count of Mortain; Swell: TRW Bretel holds Swell from the Count of Mortain. TRE Alweald held it, and it paid geld for three hides. TRE a virgate of this manor lay in Curry Rivel, the King's manor. It paid 10s. 8d. in the King's farm, but since Bretel received the land from the Count of Mortain, this customary due has not been paid to the King's manor [fo. 268a].

1395   i, 92r (19-18) Count of Mortain; Ashill: Two thegns held Ashill TRE. TRW Mauger holds from the Count of Mortain. It ought to pay 30d. to the King's manor of Curry Rivel.

1396   i, 92r (19-20) Count of Mortain; Ashbrittle: TRE Wada held Ashbrittle, and it paid geld for four hides. TRW the Count of Mortain holds it, and Bretel holds from him. One hide has been added, which two thegns held TRE.

1397   i, 92r (19-25) Count of Mortain; South Bradon: Drogo holds South Bradon from the Count of Mortain. It ought to render two sheep with lambs as a customary due to the King's manor of Curry Rivel.

1398   i, 92r (19-33) Count of Mortain; Easthams: TRW the Count of Mortain holds Easthams, and Thurstan holds from him. TRE it was held by Godwine the King's reeve. It was held with the King's manor of Crewkerne. Easthams could not be separated from the farm.

1399   i, 92r (19-35) Count of Mortain; Preston Bowyer: TRE Earl Harold held Preston Bowyer. TRW the Count of Mortain holds it, and Robert holds from him. This land lay in the King's manor of Brompton Regis TRE, with the farm.

1400   i, 92v (19-40) Count of Mortain; Hele (in Bradford-on-Tone): Ealdræd held Hele TRE. It could not be separated from Taunton, the Bishop of Winchester's manor. TRW Alvred holds it from Robert count of Mortain. [That this tenancy is illegal is suggested by the marginal cross, drawn beside this entry.]

1401   i, 92v (19-57) Count of Mortain; Shepton Montague: TRE Toli held Shepton Montague, and it paid geld for five hides. TRW the Count of Mortain holds it, and Drogo holds from him. Stoney Stoke has been added to this manor. Robert fitz Wimarc held it TRE.

1402   i, 93r (19-86) Count of Mortain; "Biscopestone" (lost in Montacute): The Count of Mortain holds "Biscopestone" in demesne, and his castle, Montacute, is there. TRE it belonged to Athelney Abbey. The Count gave (*dedit*) Purse Caundle [Dorset] to Athelney for this land.

1403   i, 93r (21-6) Roger de Courseulles; Waldron: TRE Alwig held Waldron, and it paid geld for a hide and a furlong. TRW Roger de Courseulles holds it, and William holds from him. A hide in Perry has been added to this manor. TRE Alweard held it.

1404   i, 93v (21-35) Roger de Courseulles; Blackmore: TRE Ælfric held a virgate in Blackmore. TRW Roger de Courseulles holds it, and Ansketil holds from him. An acre has been added to this manor, which a thegn held TRE.

1405   i, 93v (21-37) Roger de Courseulles; Knowle St. Giles: TRE Godric and Ælfric held Knowle St. Giles, and it paid geld for a hide and a virgate. TRW

Roger de Courseulles holds it, and William holds from him. Three virgates in Eleigh have been added to this manor, which Bruning held as a manor TRE.

1406 i, 93v (21-47) <u>Roger de Courseulles; Kilve</u>: TRE Beorhtric held Kilve, and it paid geld for two and a half hides. TRW Roger de Courseulles holds it. Two hides in Hill have been added to this manor, which Eadweald held as a manor TRE. Another half hide has been added in Pardlestone. TRE Perlo held it.

1407 i, 93v (21-54) <u>Roger de Courseulles; Puckington</u>: TRE two thegns, Lyfing and Alweard, held land in Puckington from Muchelney Abbey, and they could not be separated from it. TRW William holds this land from Roger de Courseulles. [That this tenancy is illegal is suggested by the marginal cross, drawn beside this entry.]

1408 i, 94r (21-55) <u>Roger de Courseulles; Moortown</u>: TRE Swet held Moortown from Muchelney Abbey, and he could not be separated from the Church. TRW Ogis holds this land from Roger de Courseulles. It is part of Drayton, and it is thegnland. [That this tenancy is illegal is suggested by the marginal cross, drawn beside this entry.]

1409 Exon (for 21-65) <u>Holnicote</u>: TRW Roger de Courseulles holds Holnicote, and William holds from him. From this manor has been taken away (*est ablata*) a furlong of land, which Odo fitz Gamelin holds. Roger pays geld on it unjustly (*iniuste*) [fo. 431a].

1410 i, 94r (21-90) <u>Roger de Courseulles; Witham Friary</u>: TRE Herlebald held two hides in Witham Friary. TRW Roger de Courseulles holds them, and William holds from him. TRE this land lay in William de Mohun's manor of Brewham, and it could not be separated from it.

1411 i, 94r (21-92) <u>Roger de Courseulles; Barton St. David</u>: TRE Alstan held Barton St. David, and it paid geld from one and a half hides. TRW Roger de Courseulles holds it, and Norman holds from him. Keinton Mandeville lay in this manor TRE. The Count of Mortain now holds it.

1412 i, 94v (21-98) <u>Roger de Courseulles; Long Sutton</u>: TRE two thegns held Long Sutton from Athelney Abbey, and they could not be separated from it. TRW Dodeman and Warmund hold it from Roger de Courseulles. [That this tenancy is illegal is suggested by the marginal cross, drawn beside this entry.]

1413 i, 94v (22-14) <u>Roger Arundel; Timberscombe</u>: TRE Æthelfrith held Timberscombe, and it paid geld for one and a half hides. TRW Roger Arundel holds it, and Drogo holds from him. A furlong has been added to this manor. Algar held it TRE.

1414 Exon (for 22-19) <u>Charlton Mackrell</u>: Half a hide has been added to Roger Arundel's manor of Charlton Mackrell, which a thegn held in parage TRE. Warmund held it from Roger and still vouches him to warranty, but Roger has failed him entirely in this, from the day on which King William made him put Warmund once again in possession again of this land [fo. 516a].

1415 i, 94v (22-20) <u>Roger Arundel; Ash Priors</u>: TRE Alric held Ash Priors, and it paid geld for two hides. TRW Roger Arundel holds it from King William and Givold holds from him. A hide and a virgate in Ash Priors have been added to this land. TRE Sæwine held it from the Bishop of Wells and could not be separated from him. [That this tenancy is illegal is suggested by the marginal cross, drawn beside this entry.]

1416 i, 95r (24-6) Walter de Douai; Dunwear: TRE Algar held a virgate of land called Dunwear. TRW Walter de Douai holds it. It is part of the land which King William gave (*dedit*) him between the two waters.

1417 i, 95r (24-8) Walter de Douai; West Bower: TRE Særic held West Bower, which paid geld for a half hide. TRW Walter de Douai holds it, and Rædmær holds from him. TRE this land belonged to Melcombe, which Robert d'Auberville now holds.

1418 i, 95r (24-11) Walter de Douai; Chapel Allerton: TRE Wulfnoth held Chapel Allerton, and it paid geld for five hides. TRW Walter de Douai holds it, and Ralph holds from him. Six hides have been added to Chapel Allerton, which two thegns held TRE as two manors.

1419 i, 95r (24-16) Walter de Douai; Wincanton: TRE Alsige held Wincanton, and it paid geld for three and a half hides. TRW Walter de Douai holds it and Rainward holds from him. A half hide has been added to this manor, which Beorhtmær the Priest held TRE.

1420 i, 95v (24-30) Walter de Douai; Chilcompton: TRE Everwacer held four hides in Chilcompton. TRW Walter de Douai holds them, and Ralph holds from him. A hide called Chilcompton has been added to this manor, which Alric held as a manor TRE.

1421 i, 95v (25-1) William de Mohun; Stockland: TRE Algar held Stockland, and it paid geld for four hides and a virgate. TRW William de Mohun holds it from the King. Three virgates in Seavington (in Stogursey) have been added to this manor. TRE Ælfric held it as a manor.

1422 i, 95v (25-7) William de Mohun; Brompton Ralph: TRE Beorhtric held Brompton Ralph, but it belonged to Glastonbury Abbey, and it could not be separated from it. TRW Thorgisl holds from William de Mohun. [That this tenancy is illegal is suggested by the marginal cross, drawn beside this entry.]

1423 i, 95v (25-8) William de Mohun; Clatworthy: TRE Ælfgeat held Clatworthy, which was thegnland and could not be separated from Glastonbury Abbey. TRW Ogis holds it from William de Mohun. [That this tenancy is illegal is suggested by the marginal cross, drawn beside this entry.]

1424 i, 95v (25-18) William de Mohun; Staunton: TRE Walo held three virgates in Staunton. TRW William de Mohun holds them. A virgate has been added to this manor, which a thegn held TRE as a manor.

1425 i, 96r (25-46) William de Mohun; Poleshill: TRE Wulfric held Poleshill, and it paid geld for a half hide. TRW William de Mohun holds it, and Dodeman holds from him. A hide has been added to this manor, which a thegn held freely TRE.

1426 i, 96v (25-55) William de Mohun; Brewham: TRE Robert fitz Wimarc held

twelve hides in Brewham. TRW William de Mohun holds them. Three
virgates of land have been added to this manor, which Almær held TRE.
Three hides have been taken away (*sunt ablate*) from this manor, which
Herlebald held from Robert TRE. He could not be separated from the
manor. Roger de Courseulles now holds these three hides.

1427 i, 96v (26-3) William d'Eu; Yeovilton: TRE Ælfstan of Boscombe held
Yeovilton, and it paid geld for eight hides. TRW William d'Eu holds it, and
Ralph holds from him. Two hides have been added to this manor, which five
thegns held in parage TRE.

1428 i, 96v (26-6) William d'Eu; Yeovil: TRE Ælfstan of Boscombe held Yeovil,
and it paid geld for six hides. TRW William d'Eu holds it, and Hugh holds
from him. Twenty-two messuages have been added to this manor, which
twenty-two men held in parage TRE.

1429 i, 96v (27-1) William de Falaise; Stogursey: TRE Beorhtsige held Stogursey,
and it paid geld for four and a half hides. TRW William de Falaise holds it
from the King. A half hide has been added to this manor, which a thegn held
in parage TRE, and he could go where he wished.

1430 i, 96v (27-3) William de Falaise; Woodspring: TRE Woodspring was held by
Everwacer. TRW William de Falaise holds it by consent of the King (*concessu
regis*). Serlo de Burcy gave it to him with his daughter (*dedit ei cum sua filia*).
Three hides have been added to this manor, which Alweard and Cola held
TRE as two manors.

1431 i, 96v (28-2) William fitz Guy; Cheriton: TRE Alweald held six hides in
Cheriton. He bought (*emit*) five of them from Cerne Abbey, for his life only.
After his death the land ought to have returned to the abbey (*in vita sua
tantummodo et post mortem eius terra debebat redire ad aecclesiam*). William fitz
Guy, however, holds this land TRW, and Bernard holds from him.

1432 i, 96v (30-2) Ralph de la Pommeraye; Oare: TRE Oare paid twelve sheep a
year in customs to the King's manor of Carhampton. Ralph de la Pommeraye
keeps back (*retinet*) this customary due.

1433 i, 97r (32-4) Ralph de Limesy; Allerford: TRE this manor paid twelve sheep
each year as a customary due to the King's manor of Carhampton. Ralph de
Limesy has kept back (*detinuit*) these dues until now.

1434 i, 97r (32-5) Ralph de Limesy; Bossington: TRE Bossington was held by
Athelney Abbey for the victualing of the monks. TRW Ralph de Limesy
holds it, but when King William gave (*dedit*) his land to Ralph, the Church
was seised (*erat aecclesia saisita*) of it. [That this tenancy is illegal is further
suggested by the marginal cross, drawn beside this entry.]

1435 i, 97r (35-1) Alvred d'Epaignes; Woolmersdon: TRE Alwig held Woolmersdon, and it paid geld for a half hide. TRW Alvred d'Epaignes holds it,
and Walter holds from him. A virgate and a half have been added to this
manor. Alwig the Reeve leased (*praestitit*) it TRE. It was of the King's manor
of North Petherton.

1436 i, 97r (35-2) Alvred d'Epaignes; East Bower: TRE Alwig held a half hide in

East Bower. TRW Alvred d'Epaignes holds it. A virgate of land, which is of the King's farm in North Petherton, has been added to this manor.

1437 i, 97r (35-4) <u>Alvred d'Epaignes; Stringston</u>: TRE Alwig held Stringston, and it paid geld for a hide. TRW Alvred d'Epaignes holds it, and Ranulf holds from him. A half virgate has been added to this manor, which Beorhtgifu held freely TRE.

1438 i, 97r (35-12) <u>Alvred d'Epaignes; Nether Stowey</u>: TRE Osweard and Æthelweard held Nether Stowey, and they hold it TRW from Alvred d'Epaignes. This land has been added to Alwig Bannasuna's lands, which Alvred holds.

1439 i, 97r (35-14) <u>Alvred d'Epaignes; Woodcocks Ley</u>: TRE Dunna held Woodcocks Ley. TRW Hugh holds it from Alvred d'Epaignes. This land has been added to the lands of Alwig, which Alvred holds.

1440 i, 97v (35-24) <u>Alvred d'Epaignes; Oakley</u>: Alwig held Oakley TRE. TRW Alvred d'Epaignes had Oakley, but it has been added to the King's manor of Martock.

1441 i, 97v (36-2) <u>Thurstan fitz Rolf; Witham Friary</u>: TRE Ketil held Witham Friary, and it paid geld for one hide. TRW Thurstan fitz Rolf holds it, and Botolph holds from him. A hide in "Wltune" has been added to this manor, which Ketil held as a manor TRE. This land has been added to Alweald's land, which Thurstan holds.

1442 i, 97v (36-5) <u>Thurstan fitz Rolf; North Cadbury</u>: TRE Alweald the Bald held North Cadbury, and it paid geld for twelve hides. Weston Bampfylde has been added to this manor. TRE Alwig held it as a manor and could go where he wished.

1443 i, 97v (36-7) <u>Thurstan fitz Rolf; South Cadbury</u>: TRE Alweald the Bald held South Cadbury, and it paid geld for three virgates. TRW Thurstan fitz Rolf holds it, and Bernard holds from him. Two hides and a virgate of land have been added to this manor, which were held freely by four thegns TRE. Another hide in Woolston (in North Cadbury) has been added to this manor, which Alnoth held freely TRE. Another two hides have also been added at Clapton (in Maperton). Alnoth held them freely TRE. All these lands have been added to Alweald's lands, which Thurstan holds.

1444 i, 97v (36-13) <u>Thurstan fitz Rolf; Dunkerton</u>: TRE Alweald the Bald held Dunkerton, and it paid geld for three hides. TRW Thurstan fitz Rolf holds it, and Bernard holds from him. A virgate of land has been added to this manor, which Eadwig held freely TRE.

1445 i, 97v (37-4) <u>Serlo de Burcy; Chillyhill</u>: TRE Everwacer held three virgates in Chillyhill. TRW Serlo de Burcy holds them. Chew Stoke has been added to Chillyhill. TRE Ælfric held it as a manor.

1446 i, 98r (37-6) <u>Serlo de Burcy; Ridgehill</u>: TRE four thegns held land in Ridgehill. TRW Guntard and Walter hold it from Serlo. This land, however, did not belong to Everwacer. A hide and a virgate of land have been added to Ridgehill. TRE a thegn held this land freely.

1447 i, 98r (37-7) Serlo de Burcy; Kilmington: TRW Shaftesbury Abbey holds Kilmington [Wilts.] from Serlo de Burcy for his daughter, who is there.

1448 i, 98r (37-9) Serlo de Burcy; Wheathill: TRE Almær held three hides in Wheathill from Glastonbury Abbey, and he could not be separated from the Church. TRW Serlo de Burcy holds this land. [That this tenancy is illegal is suggested by the marginal cross, drawn beside this entry.]

1449 i, 98r (37-12) Serlo de Burcy; Mudford: TRE Almær held Mudford, which paid geld for three hides. TRW Serlo de Burcy holds it, and Reginald holds from him. Stone (in Mudford) has been added to this manor. TRE Særæd held it freely as a manor.

1450 i, 98r (40-2) Edward of Salisbury; Norton St. Philip: TRW Edward of Salisbury holds land in Norton St. Philip. TRE Iuing held it, and it paid geld for ten hides. King Edward gave (*dedit*) two carucates of this land to Iuing.

1451 i, 98r (44-2) Matthiew de Mortagne; Chelvey: TRE Thorkil the Dane held Chelvey, and it paid geld for a hide. TRW Matthew de Mortagne holds it, and Rumold holds from him. A virgate, which Thorkil held with this land TRE, has been taken away (*est ablata*). The Bishop of Coutances holds it.

1452 i, 98v (45-1,2) Humphrey the Chamberlain; Lyte's Cary: TRE Lyte's Cary was held by Ordric and Lyfing. TRW Humphrey the Chamberlain holds it from the King. This land has been joined to Beorhtric's land, but Ordric and Lyfing could go where they wished.

1453 i, 98v (46-2) Robert d'Auberville and other of the King's officials; an unnamed virgate: Robert d'Auberville holds a virgate of land, which Dodda held freely TRE. This land has been added to the King's manor of Dulverton. Now it has been adjudged thegnland (*diiudicata est esse tainland*).

1454 i, 98v (46-3) Robert d'Auberville and other of the King's officials; Withypool: Three foresters held a half hide in Withypool TRE. TRW Robert d'Auberville holds it, and he pays 20s. from it into the King's farm at Winsford. It has now been adjudged thegnland (*diratiocinata est in tainland*).

1455 i, 98v (46-4) Robert d'Auberville and other of the King's officials; Wellisford: TRE two thegns held a hide in Wellisford. TRW Robert d'Auberville holds it. Of this hide, the Count of Mortain holds a virgate, and Bretel holds from him.

1456 i, 98v (46-5) Robert d'Auberville and other of the King's officials; Melcombe: TRE Særic held Melcombe, and it paid geld for a virgate and a half. TRW Robert d'Auberville holds it. A half hide has been taken away (*est ablata*) from this manor, which belonged to it TRE. Walter de Douai holds it with his manor of West Bower.

1457 i, 98v (46-11) Robert d'Auberville and other of the King's officials; Huntstile: TRE Alweard held Huntstile, and it paid geld for a virgate. TRW John holds it. A half virgate and a furlong of this land belonged to Somerton TRE.

1458 i, 98v (46-21) Robert d'Auberville and other of the King's officials; Barton St. David: TRE Eadwulf held Barton St. David, and it paid geld for three and a half hides. TRW Edmund fitz Payne holds it from the King. A hide has been taken away (*est ablata*) from this manor, which Mauger de Carteret holds.

1459 i, 98v (47-1) <u>King's thegns; Buckland St. Mary</u>: TRE and TRW Beorhtric and Wulfweard hold Buckland St. Mary. They held this land from Peter bishop of [Lichfield and Chester] while he lived, and paid 10s. to him; but since the bishop's death, the King has had nothing from it.

1460 i, 98v (47-5) <u>King's thegns; Capland</u>: TRE Tovi held a hide in Capland. TRW Hearding holds it. A half hide has been added to this manor, which was of the King's manor of Curry Rivel.

1461 i, 99r (47-25) <u>King's thegns; Otterhampton</u>: TRW Osmær holds a virgate of land in Otterhampton, which his father held TRE. Two-thirds have been taken away (*sunt . . . ablatae*) and put (*sunt . . . positae*) in the King's manor of Cannington.

1462 i, 99r (45-3) <u>Humphrey the Chamberlain and others; Babcary</u>: TRE Brun held Babcary. TRW Humphrey the Chamberlain holds it. This has been added to Beorhtric's land.

1463 i, 99r (45-12) <u>Humphrey the Chamberlain and others; Knowle (in Shepton Montague)</u>: TRE Alnoth held Knowle, and it paid geld for one and a half hides. TRW Drogo of Montacute holds it. A hide has been taken away (*est ablata*) from this land which was there TRE. Thurstan fitz Rolf holds it.

1464 i, 99r (45-14) <u>Humphrey the Chamberlain and others; Rode</u>: TRW Richard holds Rode. He held it himself from Regenbald the Priest, with the permission of the King, so Richard says, and indeed Regenbald held it TRE.

Staffordshire

1465 i, 246r (B-12) <u>Borough of Stafford</u>: TRE the borough of Stafford paid £9 of pence from all customs. Two-thirds were the King's and a third the earl's. Now King William has £7 from the payments of the borough, both for his share and for the earl's. Robert has half of the King's own share, by his gift (*dono*), so Robert says.

1466 i, 247v (5-1, 2) <u>Abbey of St. Remigius, Rheims; Meaford, Hamstall Ridware</u>: TRW the Abbey of St. Remigius, Rheims holds a half hide in Meaford and a virgate in Hamstall Ridware. TRE Earl Ælfgar gave (*dedit*) this land to the Church.

1467 i, 247v (7-2) <u>Clerks of Wolverhampton; Upper Arley [Worcs.]</u>: TRW the canons of Wolverhampton hold two hides in Upper Arley. A half hide of land in Lower Arley belongs to this land, which Osbern fitz Richard took away (*tollit*) from the canons by force (*vi*).

1468 i, 248r (8-5) <u>Roger of Montgomery; Sheriff Hales [Salop]</u>: TRE Earl Ælfgar held two hides in Sheriff Hales. TRW Reginald holds them from Earl Roger. The sheriff, however, claims (*calumniatur*) this manor for the King's farm, and the county attests (*attestatur*) that Earl Edwin may have held it (*tenuerit*).

1469 i, 248v (10-6, 7) <u>Henry de Ferrers; Fauld</u>: TRW Henry de Ferrers holds a hide in Fauld. Hubert holds a half hide there from him, and Roger holds the other half. TRE the Church of St. Werburgh, Chester held it.

1470 i, 248v (10-9) <u>Henry de Ferrers; Chebsey</u>: TRW Henry de Ferrers holds five hides in Chebsey, and Humphrey holds from him. Land in the borough of Stafford, upon which the King ordered (*praecepit*) a castle to be built, belonged to this manor. The castle is now destroyed (*est destructum*).

1471 i, 248v (11-8) <u>Robert of Stafford; Walton (in Stone)</u>: TRW Robert of Stafford holds three hides in Walton, and Arnold holds from him. TRE Aki, a freeman, held it. He gave (*dedit*) a carucate of this land to his sister.

1472 i, 249r (11-37) <u>Robert of Stafford; Madeley (in Checkley)</u>: TRW Robert of Stafford holds a half hide in Madeley, and Wulfheah holds from him. Godgifu held it TRE. She even (*etiam*) held it after the coming of King William into England, but she could not withdraw with her land.

1473 i, 249r (11-38) <u>Robert of Stafford; Bramshall</u>: TRW Robert of Stafford holds a virgate of land in Bramshall. Half of this virgate is the King's, because the road divides it (*sicut via eam dividit*). But Robert annexed (*invasit*) the King's part, and makes himself answerable for it (*se defensorem facit*). [An "A" is written in the margin opposite this statement, perhaps an abbreviation for *adiudicate*.]

1474 i, 249v (12-1) <u>William fitz Ansculf; Sedgley</u>: TRE Earl Ælfgar held six hides in Sedgley. TRW William fitz Ansculf holds them from the King. The priests of Wolverhampton claim (*calumniantur*) part of the woodland of this manor.

1475 i, 250v (16-1) <u>Nigel of Stafford; Thorpe Constantine</u>: TRE Wulfwine held three hides in Thorpe Constantine. Now Nigel of Stafford holds them. Nicholas claims (*calumniatur*) them for the King's farm in Clifton Campville.

Surrey

1476 30r (1-1b) <u>Terra Regis; Guildford</u>: TRW Ranulf the Clerk has three urban tenements where six men live, and from them Ranulf has sake and soke except when the common geld comes to the town, from which no one can escape (*nisi commune geldum in villa venerit unde nullus evadat*). If one of Ranulf's men has done wrong in Guildford and is distrained there but escapes (*delinquit et divadiatus evadat*), the King's reeve has nothing from him. If, however, he should be accused and distrained (*calumniatus ibi fuerit et divadiatus*) there, then the King has the fine (*emendam*). Archbishop Stigand held these *hagae* in the same way.

1477 i, 30r (1-1c) <u>Terra Regis; Guildford</u>: TRW Ranulf the Sheriff holds one urban tenement in Guildford, which he used to hold from the Bishop of Bayeux. The men, however, testify that it is not included in any manor, but that the man who held it TRE granted (*concessit*) it to Tovi, the reeve of the vill, as a fine for one of his forfeitures (*pro emendatione unius suae forisfacturae*).

1478 i, 30r (1-1d) <u>Terra Regis</u>; Guildford: There is a house in Guildford which the reeve of the Bishop of Bayeux holds from the manor of Bramley. The men of the county say that he has no other right (*rectitudinem*) to this house, but that the reeve of the vill took (*accepit*) a widow, whose house it was, and that the bishop put (*misit*) the house in his manor. From it, the King has lost customs (*perdidit rex consuetudines*). These the bishop has.

1479 i, 30r (1-1e) <u>Terra Regis</u>; Guildford: The sworn men (*homines qui iuraverunt*) say that there is a house in Guildford which belongs to Bramley. It is there only because the reeve of this vill was a friend (*amicus*) of the man who had this house, and on that man's death, the reeve transferred (*convertit*) it to the manor of Bramley.

1480 i, 30r (1-1f) <u>Terra Regis</u>; Guildford: Waleran disseised (*desaisiuit*) a man of a house in Guildford, from which King Edward had customs (*consuetudinem*). Now Odbert holds it with customs, through King William, so Odbert says.

1481 i, 30r (1-1g) <u>Terra Regis</u>; Guildford: Robert de Watteville holds a house in Guildford which paid all customs TRE. Now it pays nothing.

1482 i, 30r (1-2) <u>Terra Regis</u>; Woking: King William holds Woking. King Edward held it, and it was assessed at fifteen and a half hides. Of this land a forester held three virgates, which Walter fitz Othere now holds. They were put outside (*fuit posita extra*) the manor through King Edward.

1483 i, 30r (1-5) <u>Terra Regis</u>; Merton: King William holds Merton, which is assessed at twenty hides. TRE Earl Harold held it. The Bishop of Lisieux holds two sulungs in Kent which were attached to this manor TRE and TRW, so the men of the hundred testify. The bishop claims (*reclamat*) the Bishop of Bayeux as warrantor (*advocatus*), but his reeve has refused to plead on that (*inde noluit placitare*).

1484 i, 30r (1-6) <u>Terra Regis</u>; Wallington: King William holds Wallington, which is assessed at eleven hides. Richard of Tonbridge holds a virgate of this manor with woodland, from which he took away (*abstulit*) a peasant (*rusticum*) who lived there.

1485 i, 30v (1-8) <u>Terra Regis</u>; Kingston upon Thames: King William holds Kingston upon Thames. TRE it was of King Edward's farm. Humphrey the Chamberlain had and has one of the villeins of this vill in his care (*in custodia*) to collect the Queen's wool. Humphrey also took (*accepit*) 20s. in relief (*in relevamm*) from this villein when his father died.

1486 i, 30v (1-9) <u>Terra Regis</u>; Ewell: King William holds Ewell, which was assessed at sixteen hides less a virgate, and now for thirteen and a half hides. The men of the hundred testify that two hides and a virgate have been subtracted (*subtractae sunt*) from this manor. They were there TRE, but the reeves lent them to their friends (*accomodaverunt eas suis amicis*), along with a dene and a croft.

1487 i, 30v (1-11) <u>Terra Regis</u>; Gomshall: King William holds Gomshall, which was assessed at twenty hides, and now for nothing. Earl Harold held it. Odo bishop of Bayeux has unjustly (*iniuste*) put (*posuit*) a half hide of this manor's land in his manor of Bramley, and holds it. It was in Gomshall TRE and in the time of King William as well.

1488   i, 30v (1-13) <u>Terra Regis; Dorking</u>: King William holds Dorking. Queen Edith held it TRE, and it was assessed at ten and a half hides. [The description of this manor ends with the following information: a certain Eadric, who held this manor, gave (*dedit*) two hides to his daughters, who could go where they wished with their lands. Of these, Richard of Tonbridge has one, which does not belong to any manor, and Herfrid holds the other from the Bishop of Bayeux.]

1489   i, 30v–31r (2-3) <u>Archbishop of Canterbury; Mortlake</u>: TRW the Archbishop of Canterbury holds eighty hides in Mortlake, and the canons of St. Paul's hold eight of these hides. In Mortlake there is a fishery without dues. TRE Earl Harold had this fishery, but they say that in the time of King Edward, Harold built it through force (*vi*) on the land of Kingston upon Thames and on the land of St. Paul's. Archbishop Stigand had the fishery for a while in the time of King William.

1490   i, 31r (4-2) <u>Bishop of Exeter; Tyting</u>: TRW Bishop Osbern holds a hide in Tyting. Almær the Huntsman held it TRE. The men of the hundred testify, however, that this manor was leased (*prestitum fuit*) through the sheriff outside King Edward's farm, and that Bishop Osbern did not have this manor TRE.

1491   i, 31r (5-1a) <u>Bishop of Bayeux; Bramley</u>: The Bishop of Bayeux holds Bramley. TRE Æthelnoth Cild held it from King Edward. It was then assessed at thirty-four hides. Four of these hides belonged to freemen who could withdraw from Æthelnoth. Beyond these, there is land for two plows in the manor which never paid geld. Now all of this land is in the farm of Bramley. Since the bishop was seised (*saisiuit*) of this land, it has not paid geld.

1492   i, 31r (5-1b-1h) <u>Bishop of Bayeux; Chilworth, Bramley, and land in Wotton and Blackheath Hundreds</u>: Eleven and a half hides in Chilworth, Bramley, and elsewhere belong to Bramley TRW, and none of it has paid geld since the Bishop took (*recepit*) it.

1493   i, 31r–v (5-2, 3) <u>Bishop of Bayeux; Rodsall, Farncombe</u>: TRE Tovi held five hides in Rodsall, and Asgot held three and a half hides in Farncombe. Now Odo of Bayeux holds them all. A king's reeve named Lufa, however, claims (*calumniatur*) Farncombe. The men of the hundred testify that Lufa held it when King William was in Wales, and until Odo came into Kent. Odo himself transferred (*convertit*) both Rodsall and Farncombe to the farm of Bramley.

1494   i, 31v (5-6) <u>Bishop of Bayeux; Mitcham</u>: TRE Beorhtric held six and a half hides in Mitcham from King Edward. Now the canons of Bayeux hold this land from the bishop. Of this land, however, Odbert holds one hide, which his antecessor held in pledge (*in vadio*) from Beorhtric for half a gold mark.

1495   i, 31v (5-13) <u>Bishop of Bayeux; Peckham</u>: TRW the Bishop of Lisieux holds two hides in Peckham from the Bishop of Bayeux. TRE Alflæd held them from Earl Harold. They lay in Battersea.

1496 i, 32r (5-25) <u>Bishop of Bayeux; Esher</u>: TRW Hugh de Port holds a hide in Esher from the Bishop of Bayeux, and a woman holds them from him. When Hugh was seised (*saisiuit*) of this land, however, he had neither livery nor the King's writ (*liberatorem vel brevem regis*) for it, so the hundred testifies.

1497 i, 32r (5-26) <u>Bishop of Bayeux; Weybridge</u>: TRE two sisters held four hides in Weybridge. TRW Herfrid holds it from the Bishop of Bayeux. Nonetheless, when the bishop was seised (*saisiuit*) of this land, they had neither livery nor the King's writ (*liberatorem vel brevem regis*) for it, so the hundred testifies.

1498 i, 32r (5-27) <u>Bishop of Bayeux; Thames Ditton</u>: TRE Leofgar held six hides in Thames Ditton from Earl Harold and served him, but he could go where he wished with the land. When he died TRE, he divided (*dispertiuit*) this land between his three sons. Now Wadard holds it from the Bishop of Bayeux.

1499 i, 32r (5-28) <u>Bishop of Bayeux; Southwark</u>: TRW the Bishop of Bayeux has a minster in Southwark and a tidal waterway. King Edward held them on the day he died, and whoever had the church, held it from the King. The King had two-thirds of the exactions (*de exitu*) from the shore where the ships moored, and Earl Godwine had the remaining third. But the men of the hundred, both French and English, testify that the Bishop of Bayeux began a plea (*placitum inierit*) with Ranulf the Sheriff, but when he realized that the plea was not being rightfully conducted to the King's advantage, he withdrew it (*sed ille intelligens placitum non duci per rectitudinem ad prosicuum regis placitum deferuit*). The bishop, however, gave (*dedit*) the church and the waterway first to Æthelwold and then to Ralph in exchange (*pro excambio*) for a house. The sheriff denies (*negat*) that he ever received an order from the King or his seal (*praeceptum vel sigillum regis*) for this matter.

1500 i, 32r (5-28) <u>Bishop of Bayeux; Southwark</u>: The men of Southwark testify that TRE no one took (*capiebat*) toll on the strand or on the waterfront except the King. If anyone who incurred a forfeiture was charged there (*forisfaciens ibi calumpniatus fuisset*), he paid a fine (*emendabat*) to the King. But if he was not charged (*non calumpniatus*) and went elsewhere, to the man who had sake and soke, then that man had the criminal's fine (*ille emendam de reo haberet*). The men of Southwark have been adjudged (*deratiocinati sunt*) one urban tenement and its tolls which belong to the farm of Kingston upon Thames. Eustace of Boulogne held it.

1501 i, 32r (6-1) <u>Westminster Abbey; Battersea</u>: TRE Earl Harold held Battersea. TRW Westminster Abbey holds it. King William gave (*dedit*) this manor to St. Peter's in exchange (*pro excambio*) for Windsor [Berks.]. The Count of Mortain holds one and a half hides of this manor, which was there TRE and for some time afterward. Gilbert the Priest holds three hides. They were there in the same way. The Bishop of Lisieux holds two hides with which

Westminster Abbey was seised (*fuit aecclesia saisita*) in the time of King William. But afterward, the Bishop of Bayeux disseised (*desaisiuit*) the abbey. The Abbot of Chertsey holds a hide of Battersea, which the reeve of the vill took away (*abstulit*) from the manor because of a feud (*inimicitiam*). He put (*misit*) it in Chertsey.

1502   i, 32r (6-4) Westminster Abbey; Upper Tooting: TRE Swein held four hides in Upper Tooting from the King. TRW it is held by Westminster Abbey. Odbert holds it from St. Peter's, but has given nothing for geld. Earl Waltheof took (*accepit*) this land from Swein after the death of King Edward and mortgaged (*invadiavit*) it to Æthelnoth of London for two marks of gold. Æthelnoth then granted (*concessit*) it to St. Peter's for his soul.

1503   i, 32r (6-5) Westminster Abbey; Pyrford: TRE Earl Harold held Pyrford. It was assessed at twenty-seven hides, but after Harold had it, it was assessed at sixteen at his pleasure (*ad libitum Heraldi*). The men of the hundred, however, have never heard nor seen a writ on the King's behalf (*nunquam audierunt nec viderunt brevem ex parte regis*), which put (*posuisset*) it at sixteen hides. Now Westminster Abbey holds it.

1504   i, 32v (8-4) Chertsey Abbey; land in Tandridge Hundred: TRW Chertsey Abbey holds two hides in Tandridge Hundred, and William holds from the abbot. The men of the hundred, however, testify that it was Alwine's demesne land TRE, and that Alwine could go where he wished.

1505   i, 32v (8-7) Chertsey Abbey; land in Elmbridge Hundred: TRW Chertsey Abbey holds two hides, and William de Watteville holds from Chertsey. TRE an Englishman held them, and while King Edward lived, he gave (*dedit*) this land to Chertsey in alms. The land belongs to the manor of Esher.

1506   i, 32v (8-12) Chertsey Abbey; land in Kingston Hundred: Chertsey Abbey held a half hide two years before the death of King Edward. Before this, three men held it from the King, but they could not withdraw without an order from the King (*sine praecepto regis*), because they were beadles in Kingston upon Thames.

1507   i, 32v (8-16) Chertsey Abbey; Esher: TRW Chertsey Abbey holds a hide in Esher, and Reginald holds from Chertsey. A woman held it TRE. She could go where she wished, but she put herself under the abbey for her protection (*pro defensione sub abbatia se misit*).

1508   i, 32v (8-18) Chertsey Abbey; Chertsey: TRE and TRW Chertsey Abbey held five hides in the vill of Chertsey. TRW, however, two and a half of these hides are held by Richard Sturmid under King William. The hundred testifies, however, that Richard's antecessor held this land from the abbey, and could not go elsewhere without the abbot's permission.

1509   i, 34r (8-29) Chertsey Abbey; East Clandon: Chertsey Abbey holds ten hides in East Clandon TRE and TRW. TRE, moreover, the Abbot of Chertsey bought (*emit*) two hides in East Clandon and put (*misit*) them in this manor. Eskil held them from the King. The Bishop of Bayeux unjustly (*iniuste*) put (*misit*) them in Bramley, so the men of the hundred testify.

1510 i, 34r (8-30) <u>Chertsey Abbey; Henley</u>: Azur held eight hides in Henley until he died. He gave (*dedit*) them to Chertsey for his soul (*pro anima sua*) in the time of King William, so the monks say, and they have the King's writ for it.

1511 i, 34r (10-1) <u>Abbey of St. Leufroy; Esher</u>: TRE seven hides and three virgates of land in Esher were held by Tovi from King Edward. TRW the Abbot of St. Leufroy holds it by gift (*de dono*) of King William. Since St. Leufroy has held it, it has never given geld.

1512 i, 34r (11-1) <u>Battle Abbey; Limpsfield</u>: Earl Harold held twenty-five hides in Limpsfield TRE; now the Abbot of Battle holds them. TRE 'Brameselle' belonged to this manor, so the men of the hundred say.

1513 i, 34r (14-1) <u>Church of St. Mary, Lambeth; Lambeth</u>: TRE Countess Gode, King Edward's sister, held ten hides in Lambeth. TRW the Church of St. Mary, Lambeth holds it. The Bishop of Bayeux, however, has a field belonging to this manor, which belonged to the Church of Lambeth before and after Gode's death.

1514 i, 34v (19-10) <u>Richard fitz Gilbert; Tooting Bec</u>: TRE Starcher held eleven hides in Tooting Bec from King Edward. TRW the Abbey of Bec holds this land by gift (*de dono*) of Richard fitz Gilbert.

1515 i, 35r (19-18) <u>Richard fitz Gilbert; land in Elmbridge Hundred</u>: TRW Richard fitz Gilbert holds a hide from the King in Elmbridge Hundred, which Almær held from King Edward TRE and could go with it where he wished. Since Richard had it, it has never given geld.

1516 i, 35r (19-25) <u>Richard fitz Gilbert; Malden</u>: The hide in Malden which Robert de Watteville holds TRW, remains in dispute (*remansit in calengio*). The men of the hundred say that Edward of Salisbury and Robert d'Oilly established their title to it against Richard of Tonbridge (*diratiocinaverunt eam Ricardo de Tonebrige*). It remains quit, in the hand of the King.

1517 i, 35r (19-27) <u>Richard fitz Gilbert; Apps</u>: TRW Richard fitz Gilbert has six hides in Apps, which Wulfweald abbot of Chertsey delivered to him in compensation (*deliberavit ei in emendatione*) for Walton-on-Thames, so Richard's men say. But the men of the hundred say that they have seen neither a writ of the King nor livery, which had seised him of it (*vidisse brevem vel liberatorem regis qui eum inde saisisset*).

1518 i, 35r (19-28) <u>Richard fitz Gilbert; Apps</u>: A villein holds a half hide in Apps, from which he has given 30d. rent (*gablo*) to Richard's men. Now it remains quit in the hand of the King. Picot also holds a half hide in Apps, which Almær held without the King's gift (*sine dono regis*), because his antecessor Almær held it.

1519 i, 35r (19-30) <u>Richard fitz Gilbert; East Molesey</u>: TRW John holds a hide from Richard fitz Gilbert in East Molesey, which was given in compensation (*in emendatione*) for Walton-on-Thames.

1520 i, 35v (19-35) <u>Richard fitz Gilbert; Dirtham</u>: There are one and a half hides in Dirtham which Ælfric held from King Edward as a manor TRE. Later he gave (*dedit*) this land to his wife and daughter for Chertsey Abbey, so the men of the hundred testify. Richard fitz Gilbert, however, claims (*calumniatur*) this land. It does not lie in any manor, nor does he hold it as a manor, but it was delivered (*liberata fuit*) to him.

1521 i, 35v (19-44) Richard fitz Gilbert; Effingham: TRW Osweald holds Effingham from Richard fitz Gilbert. TRE Azur held it from King Edward, and it was assessed at six hides. With these six hides Osweald holds a hide and a virgate of land which a freeman held under King Edward. But in the time of King William he sold it to Azur for a certain need of his (*pro quandam necessitate sua vendidit*).

1522 i, 35v (19-48) Richard fitz Gilbert; Hartshurst: TRE Almær held two hides in Hartshurst from King Edward. He was a free man, and he could go where he wished with the land. TRW Richard fitz Gilbert holds it, but it does not belong to any of Richard's manors.

1523 i, 35v–6r (21-3) William fitz Ansculf; Wandsworth: TRE six sokemen held twelve hides in Wandsworth. TRW William fitz Ansculf holds this land. Ansculf had this land after he took (*recepit*) the sheriffdom, but the men of the hundred say that they have seen neither a seal nor livery (*non vidisse sigillum nec liberatorem*).

1524 i, 36r (22-4) Walter fitz Othere; a man in Kingston Hundred: Walter fitz Othere holds a man from the soke of Kingston upon Thames, to whom he has commended (*commendavit*) the keeping of the King's wild mares, but we do not know how. This man holds two hides, but he has no right (*non habet rectum*) in the land itself.

1525 i, 36r (23-1) Walter de Douai; land in Wallington Hundred: TRW Walter de Douai holds two hides from the King, so he says, but the men of the hundred say they have never seen a writ nor a sergeant of the King (*nunquam vidisse brevem vel nuncium regis*) who had seised him (*saisisset*) of it. They testify, however, that a certain freeman who held this land and who could go where he wished, put himself in Walter's hand for his own protection (*summisit se in manu Walterii pro defensione sui*).

1526 i, 36r (25-1) Geoffrey de Mandeville; Clapham: TRE ten hides in Clapham were held by Thorbiorn from King Edward. TRW Geoffrey de Mandeville holds this land. The men say that Geoffrey de Mandeville holds this manor unjustly (*iniuste*) because it does not belong to Esger's land.

1527 i, 36r (25-2) Geoffrey de Mandeville; Carshalton: TRE five freemen held twenty-six hides as five manors in Carshalton and could go where they wished. TRW Geoffrey de Mandeville holds this land. The men of the county and the hundred say that they have never seen a writ nor livery (*brevem vel liberatorem*) which seised (*saisisset*) Geoffrey de Mandeville of this manor on behalf of the King (*ex parte regis*). From these hides Wesman holds six hides from Geoffrey son of Count Eustace. Geoffrey de Mandeville gave (*dedit*) Geoffrey this land with his daughter. From the same hides, a smith of the King has a half hide, which he took (*accepit*) with his wife TRE. But he has never done service for it.

1528 i, 36r (25-3) <u>Geoffrey de Mandeville; Wanborough</u>: Geoffrey de Mandeville holds Wanborough, but it is not from Esger's land. The brothers Swein and Leofwine held it from King Edward. It was assessed at seven hides; now it is at three.

1529 i, 36r (26-1) <u>Geoffrey Orlateile; Balham</u>: TRE Eskil held Balham from Earl Harold. TRW Geoffrey Orlateile holds it without the King's gift and without warrantor (*sine dono regis et sine warant*).

1530 i, 36v (28-1) <u>Robert Malet; Sutton (in Woking)</u>: TRE Wynsige held five hides in Sutton from King Edward. TRW Robert Malet holds this land. [At the end of the description of this land, it is noted that Durand was seised (*saisiuit*) of this land, and that the men of the hundred say that he has it unjustly (*iniuste*), because none of them has seen the King's writ nor livery (*brevem regis vel liberatorem*).]

1531 i, 36v (29-1) <u>Miles Crispin; Beddington</u>: TRW Miles Crispin holds Beddington, and William fitz Thurold holds from him. TRE Ulf held it from King Edward, and it was assessed at twenty-five hides. Thirteen messuages in London and eight in Southwark have been taken away (*ablatae sunt*) from this manor. Roger of Montgomery holds them, and they pay 12s.

1532 i, 36v (29-2) <u>Miles Crispin; Chessington</u>: TRW Miles Crispin holds Chessington. Magni the Black held it TRE, and it was assessed at five hides. When King William came to England, Wigot did not hold it.

1533 i, 36v (31-1) <u>Humphrey the Chamberlain; Coombe</u>: Humphrey the Chamberlain holds Coombe from the Queen's fee. In the time of King William, the woman who held this land put herself and the land in the hand of Queen Mathilda (*misit se cum ea in manu reginae*).

1534 i, 36v (36-1) <u>Osweald and other thegns; "Pechingeorde"</u>: Osweald held "Pechingeorde" from the King TRE, as he does now. The men of the Bishop of Bayeux claim (*calumniantur*) two marks of gold or two hawks against this land for the King's use each year: this through the grant (*per concessionem*) of the Abbot of Chertsey, Osweald's brother, namely for battle (*pro bello*) which he ought to have fought against Geoffrey the Small.

1535 i, 36v (36-2) <u>Osweald and other thegns; land in Copthorne Hundred</u>: TRW Sæmann holds a virgate in Copthorne Hundred. He also held it from King Edward and could turn to whom he wished. But since King William came to England, he has served Osweald and paid him 20d.

1536 i, 36v (36-4) <u>Osweald and other thegns; Wotton</u>: Osweald holds Wotton TRW. It was assessed at six hides, now at five hides. Harold held it TRE, but the men of the hundred say that they do not know how Harold held it.

Sussex

1537 i, 16v (3-2) <u>Bishop of Chichester; Henfield</u>: TRW the Bishop of Chichester holds Henfield. TRE it was assessed at fifteen hides, now for eleven hides and a virgate. The mill and the fishery belonging to this manor are missing through the encroachment (*desunt pro superfacto*) of William de Braose.

1538 i, 17r (3-10) <u>Bishop of Chichester; unidentified land</u>: The canons of Chichester hold sixteen hides in common, which were never gelded, so they say.

1539 i, 17r–v (6-1) <u>Bishop of Exeter; Bosham</u>: TRE and TRW Bishop Osbern held and holds the church of Bosham from the King. A hundred and twelve hides belonged to this church. Now forty-seven are outside of it. Hugh fitz Ranulf holds thirty of these hides, and Ralph de Quesnay holds seventeen. TRE a hide in West Itchenor also belonged to this manor. Now Warin, Earl Roger's man, holds it.

1540 i, 17v (7-1) <u>New Minster, Winchester; Southease</u>: The Abbot of New Minster holds Southease. From the villeins' forfeitures (*forisfactura*) come £9 and three *summae* of peas.

1541 i, 18r (9-11) <u>Count of Eu; Bexhill</u>: TRW Osbern holds Bexhill from the Count of Eu. TRE Bishop Æthelric held it, because it was in the bishopric of Selsey. He held it until King William gave (*dedit*) the castlery of Hastings to the count.

1542 i, 20r (9-120) <u>Count of Eu; Ewhurst</u>: TRW the Count of Eu holds Ewhurst in demesne. Ælfhere held it from King Edward. It was then assessed for six hides, now for four hides and three virgates. Five virgates are in arrears (*sunt retro*) because one hide is in the Count of Mortain's rape.

1543 i, 20r (9-121) <u>Count of Eu; Higham</u>: TRW the Count of Eu holds Higham. TRE Earl Godwine held it. There were two and a half hides there, but it answered for two, so they say.

1544 i, 21v (10-44) <u>Count of Mortain; Frog Firle</u>: TRW the Abbot of Grestain holds Frog Firle from the Count of Mortain. Queen Edith held it, and in the time of King Edward she gave (*dedit*) it to St. John's. It then answered for eight hides; now for five.

1545 i, 21v (10-63) <u>Count of Mortain; Parrock</u>: TRW the Count of Mortain holds a half hide in Parrock, which never paid geld. TRE Queen Edith held it. There, in Parrock, is a virgate where the count has his hall. Earl Harold similarly had it. He took it away (*abstulit*) from St. John's.

1546 i, 22r (10-82) <u>Count of Mortain; Hankham</u>: TRW the Count of Mortain holds one hide and a half virgate in Hankham. King Edward held it. There is no response from there (*inde nullum responsum*).

1547 i, 22r (10-85) <u>Count of Mortain; "Lodiutone"</u>: Thirteen shillings ought to be put (*mitti*) in "Lodiutone," from the pasture which the Count of Mortain gave (*dedit*) to William.

1548 i, 22v (10-99) <u>Count of Mortain; Burleigh</u>: TRW William holds one and a half hides in Burleigh from the Count of Mortain. TRE Ælfhere held it from Christ Church in the manor of Wootton (in East Chittington), so the hundred testifies.

1549 i, 22v (10-116) <u>Count of Mortain; Lode</u>: TRW Alan holds a virgate in Lode from the Count of Mortain. It lay in New Minster TRE, and was never gelded. Almær held it as a manor from King Edward.

1550 i, 23r (11-8) Roger of Montgomery; Treyford: TRW Robert fitz Theobald holds Treyford from Earl Roger. TRE Æthelheard held it from Earl Godwine. It is and was assessed at eleven hides. In this manor there are two hides in prebend of the Church of Chichester. Robert holds them from the bishop. Offa held them from the bishop in fee as a manor. The Abbot of New Minster claims (*calumniatur*) this manor. The hundred testifies that the man who held Treyford TRE, held it from the abbot for his life only (*vitae suae*).

1551 i, 23v–4r (11-30) Roger of Montgomery; Westbourne: TRW Roger of Montgomery holds Westbourne. TRE Earl Godwine held it. There are thirty-six hides there, but then and now it is assessed at twelve hides. Payne holds four hides of this land. Alric held if from the minster.

1552 i, 24r (11-42) Roger of Montgomery; ploughland in Stockbridge Hundred: TRW Ketil holds land for one plow, which was never hidated. King William granted (*concessit*) it to him.

1553 i, 26r (12-1) William de Warenne; Lewes: Whoever sells a horse in the borough of Lewes gives a penny to the reeve, and the buyer gives another penny. Whoever buys an ox gives a half penny. Whoever buys a man gives 4d., wherever the purchaser buys him within the rape.

1554 i, 26r (12-1) William de Warenne; Lewes: He who sheds blood (*sanguinem fundens*) pays a fine (*emendat*) of 7s. 4d.

1555 i, 26r (12-1) William de Warenne; Lewes: A man who commits adultery or rape (*adulterium vel raptum faciens*) pays a fine (*emendat*) of 8s. 4d., and the woman gives the same. The King has money from the adulterous man, the archbishop from the woman.

1556 i, 26r (12-1) William de Warenne; Lewes: From a fugitive, if he is captured (*fugitivo si recuperatus fuerit*), comes 8s. 4d.

1557 i, 26r (12-1) William de Warenne; Lewes: From all the payments of Lewes, two-thirds were the King's and one-third was the earl's.

1558 i, 26r (12-7) William de Warenne; Falmer: TRW the Church of St. Pancras holds Falmer from William de Warenne. Wilton Abbey held it TRE and was seised of it (*fuit saisita*) on the day King Edward died. Then it answered for twenty-one hides; now for eighteen.

1559 i, 26v (12-13) William de Warenne; Brighton: TRW Ralph holds five and a half hides in Brighton from William de Warenne. TRE Beorhtric held them by gift (*de dono*) of Earl Godwine.

1560 i, 27r (12-30) William de Warenne; Poynings: TRW William fitz Reginald holds Poynings from William de Warenne. TRE Cola held it from Earl Godwine, because he gave (*dedit*) it to him. It was at eight hides, but was never gelded.

1561 i, 27r (12-41) William de Warenne; Westmeston: TRW Robert holds twelve hides in Westmeston from William de Warenne. Countess Gytha held them

TRE, and the villeins held it under her. There was no hall there, nor, so they say, did this land pay geld.

1562   i, 27v (12-48) <u>William de Warenne; Barcombe</u>: TRW William de Watteville holds Barcombe from William de Warenne. TRE Azur held it from Earl Godwine. It was then assessed at thirteen hides; now for ten and a half. The other hides are in the Count of Mortain's rape, and were never gelded, so they say.

1563   i, 28r (13-9) <u>William de Braose; Washington</u>: TRW William de Braose holds Washington, which is the site of Bramber Castle. TRE Earl Gyrth held it, and it answered for fifty-nine hides. Now it does not give geld. Leofwine holds a half hide of this land. He could withdraw with his land, and gave geld to his lord. His lord gave nothing.

Warwickshire

1564   i, 238r (B-4) <u>Borough of Warwick</u>: Between them, the farm of the royal manors and the county pleas (*placita comitatus*) pay £145 each year by weight, £23 for the customs of the dogs, 20s. for a packhorse, £10 for a hawk and 100s. for the Queen's gift (*gersumma*).

1565   i, 238r (B-6) <u>Borough of Warwick</u>: It was the custom of Warwick that when the King went on an expedition by land ten of Warwick's burgesses went on behalf of all the others. Whosoever was instructed (*monitus*) to go, but did not, paid the King a fine (*emendabat*) of 100s.

1566   i, 238r (1-6) <u>Terra Regis; Coton</u>: King William holds one hide in Coton. TRE Earl Edwin held it, and, along with the borough of Warwick and the third penny of the pleas of the shire (*tercio denario placitorum sirae*), it paid £17.

1567   i, 238v (3-4) <u>Bishop of Worcester; Alveston</u>: TRW the Bishop of Worcester holds fifteen hides in Alveston. In the time of King Edward, Beorhtwine held seven and a half hides there. Archbishop Ealdræd had the sake and soke, and toll and team (*tol et teim*), and churchscot, and all other forfeitures (*forsfacturas*) from this land except those four which the King has throughout his whole kingdom. Beorhtwine's sons, Leofwine and Eadmær, and four others testify to this, but they do not know from whom Beorhtwine held this land – perhaps the Church or Earl Leofric, whom he served. They say, however, that they themselves held it from Earl Leofric and could turn where they wished with the land. Beorhtnoth and Alwig held the remaining seven and a half hides in the vill, but the county does not know from whom they held. Bishop Wulfstan, however, says that he established his claim (*deplacitasse*) to this land before (*coram*) Queen Mathilda in the presence (*in praesentia*) of four sheriffdoms, and he has King William's writs (*breves*) for it and also the testimony of the county of Warwick.

1568   i, 238v (6-5) <u>Coventry Abbey; Binley</u>: TRE Ealdgyth wife of Gruffydd held three hides in Binley. Now Coventry Abbey holds them. The Abbot bought (*emit*) this land from Osbern fitz Richard.

1569 i, 238v (6-9) Coventry Abbey; Clifton upon Dunsmore: TRE Æthelwine the Sheriff gave (*dedit*) Clifton upon Dunsmore to Coventry Abbey with the consent (*concessu*) of King Edward, his sons and for his soul (*pro anima sua*), by testimony of the county. Earl Aubrey annexed it unjustly (*iniuste invasit*), and took it away (*abstulit*) from the Church.

1570 i, 239r (7-1) Abingdon Abbey; Hill: TRW Abingdon Abbey has two hides in Hill, which the abbot bought (*emit*) from the fee of Thorkil. Warin holds it from the abbot.

1571 i, 239r (8-1) Burton Abbey; Austrey: TRW Burton Abbey holds two and a half hides in Austrey. Earl Leofric gave (*dedit*) this land to the Church.

1572 i, 239r (9-1) Malmesbury Abbey; Newbold Comyn: TRW Malmesbury Abbey holds three hides in Newbold Comyn. Wulfwine the Monk held them and gave (*dedit*) them to Malmesbury when he was made a monk.

1573 i, 239v (14-2) Earl Aubrey; Clifton upon Dunsmore: TRE Æthelwine the Sheriff held five hides in Clifton upon Dunsmore. He gave (*dedit*) them to Coventry for his soul (*pro anima sua*). TRW Earl Aubrey took them away (*abstulit*).

1574 i, 241r (17-15) Thorkil of Arden; Barston: TRW Robert d'Oilly holds nine hides in Barston in mortgage (*in vadimonio*). Æthelmær held them TRE, and with the King's permission, sold (*vendidit*) them to Thorkil's father, Æthelwine the Sheriff.

1575 i, 241r (17-16) Thorkil of Arden; Baddesley Ensor: TRW William holds two hides in Baddesley Ensor from Thorkil of Arden. William encroached upon (*praeoccupavit*) a fifth of this land against King William. Beorhtric, who held this land TRE, lives there. The remaining four-fifths of this land were held by Thorkil's men Arnketil and Ceolræd.

1576 i, 241v (17-56) Thorkil of Arden; Radford Semele: TRE Edwin held five hides in Radford Semele freely. Now Ermenfrid holds them from Thorkil of Arden. Ermenfrid bought (*emit*) this land from Ketilbert with permission and holds it in fee from the King, so the King's writ testifies (*ut testatur brevis regis*).

1577 i, 241v (17-60) Thorkil of Arden; Myton: TRW the Count of Meulan holds two hides in Myton from the fee of Thorkil of Arden. TRE Earl Edwin held this land. R. Halebold bought (*emit*) it.

1578 i, 242r (20-1) Roger d'Ivry; Cubbington: TRE Thorbiorn held five hides in Cubbington freely. Now Roger d'Ivry, so he says, holds them from the King. This land is from the fee of the Bishop of Bayeux.

1579 i, 242r (21-1) Robert d'Oilly; Marston (in Lea Marston): TRW Robert d'Oilly holds two hides in Marston and Robert the Huntsman holds from him. TRE Ælfric held them freely. Robert bought (*emit*) this land from Ælfric with the permission of King William.

1580 i, 242v (23-4) Robert Dispensator; Barston: TRW Robert Dispensator holds ten hides in Barston. Æthelmær held them freely TRE, and sold (*vendidit*) them to Æthelwine the Sheriff with King William's permission.

1581 i, 243r (28-1) <u>William fitz Corbucion; Amington</u>: TRE Thorkil Batock held four hides in Amington freely. Now William fitz Corbucion holds them from the King, and Robert holds from William in mortgage (*in vadimonio*).

1582 i, 243r (28-19) <u>William fitz Corbucion; Chillington [Staffs.]</u>: TRE William fitz Corbucion holds three hides in Chillington. The Bishop of Chester claims (*calumniatur*) this land.

1583 i, 244r (42-3) <u>Christina; Long Itchington</u>: TRW Christina holds twenty-four hides in Long Itchington. When the King gave (*dedit*) them to Christina, they paid £36.

1584 i, 244v (44-11, 12) <u>Richard and other thegns and officials of the King; Flecknoe</u>: TRW Leofwine holds one and a half hides in Flecknoe from the King. He bought (*emit*) this land from his brother Alwine. The same Leofwine also holds another two hides and a half virgate there. He said that he himself holds this land from Bishop Wulfstan, but the bishop failed him in the plea (*defecit in placito*). For this, he is in the King's mercy (*in misericordia regis*).

Wiltshire

1585 i, 64v (M-2) <u>Borough of Malmesbury</u>: There is a half messuage in Malmesbury in the Bishop of Bayeux's fee, which is waste. It pays no service.

1586 i, 64v (M-16) <u>Borough of Malmesbury</u>: Roger of Berkeley and Arnulf d'Hesdin each hold a messuage in Malmesbury from the King's farm. Arnulf took his illegally (*incaute accepit*). Neither messuage pays service.

1587 i, 64v (B-4) <u>Boroughs</u>: TRW the King has £6 from the third penny of Salisbury, £4 from the third penny of Marlborough, £5 from the third penny of Cricklade, £11 from the third penny of Bath, and £6 from the third penny of Malmesbury.

1588 i, 64v (B-5) <u>Boroughs</u>: TRE the pleas (*placita*) of Chedglow and Startley Hundreds were in the King's farm of Malmesbury.

1589 i, 64v (1-1) <u>Terra Regis; Calne</u>: King Edward held Calne. Now King William holds it. Nigel holds the church of this manor from the King with six hides of land. Alvred d'Epaignes holds five hides of land, which Nigel claims. They belonged TRE, by the testimony of the shire, to the church of this manor.

1590 i, 64v (1-2) <u>Terra Regis; Bedwyn</u>: King Edward held Bedwyn. Now King William holds it. There was a wood there TRE in the King's demesne. Now Henry de Ferrers holds it.

1591 i, 64v (1-3) <u>Terra Regis; Amesbury</u>: King William holds Amesbury. King Edward held it. The lands of three thegns are accounted for (*numerantur*) in this manor, which they themselves held TRE. This land – "Quintone,"

Swindon, and Cheverell was thegnland. Earl William gave (*dedit*) it to Amesbury in exchange (*pro mutuatione*) for Bowcombe, on the Isle of Wight. This land belonged to Amesbury's farm. In his illness, King Edward gave (*dedit*) two hides of this manor to the Abbess of Wilton. She had never had this land before, but she held it afterward.

1592 i, 64v (1-5) <u>Terra Regis; Chippenham</u>: King William holds Chippenham. King Edward held it. A land belongs to this manor, which King Edward had given (*dederat*) to his huntsman Wulfgeat. This land was from the King's demesne. Now it is in his farm.

1593 i, 65r (1-10) <u>Terra Regis; Aldbourne</u>: TRE Countess Gytha held forty hides in Aldbourne. Now King William holds them. This manor pays £70 by weight, but the English assess it at only £60 by tale.

1594 i, 65r (1-11) <u>Terra Regis; Corsham</u>: TRE Earl Tosti held thirty-four hides in Corsham. Now King William holds them. With its appendages Corsham pays £30 by weight: the English, however, assess it at £31 by tale.

1595 i, 65r (1-12) <u>Terra Regis; Melksham</u>: TRE Earl Harold held eighty-four hides in Melksham with its appendages. This manor pays £111 11s. by weight. The English, however, assess it at £111 11s. by tale.

1596 i, 65v (2-1) <u>Bishop of Winchester; Downton</u>: TRW the Bishop of Winchester holds Downton. TRE it paid geld for ninety-seven hides. Two of these hides were not the bishop's because they had been taken away (*ablatae fuerunt*) from the Church and from the hand of the bishop, along with three other hides, in the time of King Cnut.

1597 i, 66r (3-1) <u>Bishop of Salisbury; Potterne</u>: TRW the Bishop of Salisbury holds Potterne. TRE it paid geld for fifty-two hides. Two Englishmen hold six hides and a virgate of this land. One of them is a knight, by order of the King (*iussu regis*). He was the nephew of Herman bishop of Ramesbury. Alweard holds another three hides of this land, which Wulfweard White bought (*emit*) from Bishop Herman TRE for his life only (*in vita sua tantum*). Afterwards they ought to have returned (*redirent*) to the bishop's farm, because they were from his demesne. From this same land, Arnulf d'Hesdin holds three hides and a virgate from the King. The Bishop of Salisbury, however, claims (*calumniatur*) them, since the person who held this land TRE could not be separated from the bishop.

1598 i, 66r (3-5) <u>Bishop of Salisbury; Charnage</u>: TRE Algar held five hides in Charnage. TRW the Bishop of Salisbury holds them, and Hugh holds from him. This is from the exchange (*de excambio*) of "Scepeleia."

1599 i, 66r (5-6) <u>Bishop of Coutances; Littleton Drew</u>: TRW Robert holds five hides in Littleton Drew from the Bishop of Coutances. TRE Alweard held them from the Abbot of Glastonbury, and he could not be separated from the Church.

1600 i, 66v (7-1) <u>Glastonbury Abbey; Damerham [Hants.]</u>: TRW Glastonbury Abbey holds fifty-two hides in Damerham. TRE the value of this manor was £36. Now it pays £61, but it is not assessed by the men at more than £45 because of the ruin of the land, and because of the farm, which is too high (*propter confusionem terrae et propter firmam que nimis est alta*).

1601   i, 66v (7-2) <u>Glastonbury Abbey; Hannington</u>: TRW Robert holds fifteen hides from the Abbot of Glastonbury in Hannington. TRE the abbot had sold (*vendiderat*) three hides of this land to a thegn for the lives of three men (*ad aetatem trium hominum*). The abbot himself had the service from these hides. Afterwards they were to return (*redire*) to his demesne and are thus now with the other twelve hides.

1602   i, 66v (7-5) <u>Glastonbury Abbey; Stanton St. Quinton, Littleton Drew</u>: TRE the Abbot of Glastonbury leased (*praestitit*) six acres of meadow in Stanton St. Quinton to Beorhtric. Osbern Giffard now holds them. Similarly, the abbot leased (*prestitit*) four acres of meadow to Alweard in Littleton Drew. Bishop Geoffrey now holds them. These ten acres of meadow ought to lie in Christian Malford.

1603   i, 66v (7-13) <u>Glastonbury Abbey; Little Langford</u>: TRW Edward holds a hide in Little Langford from the King, which by law (*iure*) belongs to Glastonbury Abbey as thegnland.

1604   i, 66v (7-15) <u>Glastonbury Abbey; Gomeldon</u>: TRW Glastonbury Abbey holds five hides in Gomeldon. Waleran holds a virgate of this land. The thegns testify that it ought to belong to the Church, and the abbot claims (*calumniatur*) it.

1605   i, 67r (8-8) <u>Malmesbury Abbey; Long Newnton [Glos.]</u>: TRW Malmesbury Abbey holds thirty hides in Long Newnton. The abbot gave (*dedit*) one of his knights a hide of the villeins' land.

1606   i, 67r (8-12) <u>Malmesbury Abbey; Bremhill</u>: TRW Malmesbury Abbey holds thirty-eight hides in Bremhill. Theodric holds a hide of the villeins' land, which the abbot gave (*dedit*) him. Edward holds two of these hides from the King, and Gilbert holds from him. An English abbot took these hides away (*abstulit*) from the Church's demesne and gave (*dedit*) them to a reeve. Later on he gave (*dedit*) them to a thegn, who could on no account separate himself from the Church. William d'Eu also holds a hide of this land. TRE the abbot leased (*prestitit*) it to Ælfstan.

1607   i, 67r (9-1) <u>Westminster Abbey; Cricklade</u>: Westminster Abbey holds the third penny of Cricklade.

1608   i, 67v (10-3) <u>New Minster, Winchester; Pewsey</u>: TRW New Minster, Winchester holds thirty hides in Pewsey. Arnulf d'Hesdin holds two of these hides from the King, which the abbot, in the time of King Edward, gave (*dedit*) to a thegn, who could not be separated from the Church.

1609   i, 67v (12-1) <u>Shaftesbury Abbey; Beechingstoke</u>: TRW Thurstan holds five hides in Beechingstoke from the Abbess of Shaftesbury. Hearding, who through an agreement (*per conventio*) ought to have held it for his life (*in vita sua*), returned it voluntarily to the Church (*reddidit sponte sua*).

1610   i, 67v (13-2) <u>Wilton Abbey; North Newnton</u>: TRW Wilton Abbey holds thirteen and a half hides and a half virgate in North Newnton. The abbess gave (*dedit*) three and a half hides and a half virgate of this land to a knight. Ælfric the Huntsman also held one hide and one and a half virgates of this land from the Abbess of Wilton, on condition that after his death it should return to the Church (*ea conditione ut post mortem eius rediret ad aecclesiam*), because it was from its demesne farm. Now Richard Sturmid holds it.

1611 i, 68r (13-9) <u>Wilton Abbey; Chalke</u>: TRW Wilton Abbey holds seventy-seven hides in Chalke. Richard Poynant holds seven and a half hides of this land from the King. Of these Æthelgifu held two TRE, and the men of the Church serving as villeins held the others. The abbess claims (*calumniatur*) these hides.

1612 i, 68r (13-21) <u>Wilton Abbey; two unidentified hides</u>: TRE Wilton Abbey held two hides which Thorth had given (*dederat*) there with his two daughters. They were clothed from these hides until the Bishop of Bayeux unjustly took them away (*iniuste abstulit*) from the Church.

1613 i, 68r (14-1) <u>Nunminster, Winchester; Urchfont</u>: TRW Nunminster holds Urchfont. TRE it was gelded for thirty hides. Six hides are in demesne. The abbess's reeve held two of these demesne hides TRE. Afterwards he returned (*reddidit*) the land with all his stock (*pecunia sua*) to the Church. They have been in demesne since that time.

1614 i, 68v (16-5) <u>Amesbury Abbey; Winterslow</u>: Amesbury Abbey held two hides in Winterslow both in the time of Kings Edward and William. They are for the victualing of the nuns. The Count of Mortain holds them unjustly (*iniuste*).

1615 i, 68v (17-1) <u>Bec Abbey; Brixton Deverill</u>: TRE Beorhtric held ten hides in Brixton Deverill. Now Bec Abbey holds them from the King. Queen Mathilda gave (*dedit*) them to the Church.

1616 i, 69r (23-7) <u>Earl Aubrey; Allington (near Amesbury)</u>: TRE Earl Harold held four hides in Allington. Afterward Earl Aubrey held them. There are another four hides of land in this vill which Earl Harold unjustly removed (*iniuste abstraxit*) from Amesbury Abbey, according to the testimony of the thegns of the shire. Now the Church has them.

1617 i, 69r (24-14) <u>Edward of Salisbury; North Tidworth</u>: Edward of Salisbury holds four hides in North Tidworth. Alweard held them TRE. There is a virgate of land in North Tidworth which Croc established (*diratiocinavit*) ought to belong to him. Edward of Salisbury, however, holds it.

1618 i, 69v (24-19) <u>Edward of Salisbury; Bradenstoke</u>: TRE Strami held Bradenstoke. It was gelded for sixteen hides and a virgate. Now Edward of Salisbury holds it. A hide and a virgate of land are attached to this manor, so it was adjudged by the English (*sicut diratiocinati sunt angli*). William de Picquigny, however, holds this land.

1619 i, 69v (24-42) <u>Edward of Salisbury; Little Langford</u>: TRE Azur held a hide in Little Langford. TRW Ledhard holds it from Edward of Salisbury. The thegns adjudged (*diratiocinantur*) this land to be Glastonbury Abbey's.

1620 i, 69v (25-2) <u>Arnulf d'Hesdin; Potterne</u>: TRW Robert holds three hides and a virgate in Potterne from Arnulf d'Hesdin, which paid geld TRE with the Bishop of Salisbury's manor of Potterne. Bishop Osmund claims (*clamat*) this land. Algar, who held it TRE, could not be separated from the Church.

1621   i, 70r (25-21) Arnulf d'Hesdin; Chedglow: TRW a thegn holds two and a half virgates in Chedglow from Arnulf d'Hesdin. TRE this thegn could go to whichever lord he wished. In the time of King William he turned himself to Arnulf voluntarily (*sponte se vertit*).

1622   i, 70r (25-23) Arnulf d'Hesdin; Upton Scudamore: TRE Tous held two and a half hides in Upton Scudamore. TRW Regenbald holds them from Arnulf d'Hesdin. Included in this land is a half hide that paid geld TRE, but which has not done so since King William came into England. Also within this land, Arnulf holds a half hide from William d'Eu, and as much land as is valued at one hide from the King's demesne land.

1623   i, 70v (26-19) Alvred of Marlborough; Chedglow: TRW Edward holds a hide and a virgate in Chedglow from Alvred of Marlborough. Beside this land, Durand of Gloucester has a half virgate which this Edward also held TRE. Almaric de Dreux took it away from him unjustly (*ei abstulit iniuste*), so all the thegns of the shire testify.

1624   i, 71r (28-10) Miles Crispin; Chedglow: TRE two thegns held one hide and one and a half virgates in Chedglow, and could go where they wished. Now the thegn Siward holds this land from Miles Crispin. Besides this land, Durand has a half virgate of land which Siward held TRE. Almaric de Dreux took it away from him unjustly (*abstulit ei iniuste*), so the thegns of the shire say.

1625   i, 71v (30-5) Durand of Gloucester; Ashley [Glos.]: TRE Ealdræd held five hides less a virgate in Ashley. Now Durand of Gloucester holds them. One of Miles Crispin's knights claims (*calumniatur*) a virgate of land in this vill.

1626   i, 71v (32-2) William d'Eu; Littleton Pannell: TRW William d'Audrieu holds six hides and a virgate in Littleton Pannell. TRE this land was thegnland of the Church of Salisbury. Ælfstan held it.

1627   i, 71v (32-11) William d'Eu; Ditteridge: TRW Warner holds one hide and three virgates from William d'Eu in Ditteridge. An abbot of Malmesbury leased (*prestitit*) a hide of this land to Ælfstan.

1628   i, 71v (32-17) William d'Eu; Upton Scudamore: TRE Toli held three hides in Upton Scudamore. TRW Ansfrid holds them from William d'Eu. This land did not pay geld for a half hide after King William came into England. Arnulf d'Hesdin unjustly (*iniuste*) holds another half hide in this vill.

1629   i, 72r (41-4) Ralph de Mortimer; Highway: TRW Ralph de Mortimer holds a hide in Highway. TRE Toti bought (*emit*) it from Malmesbury Abbey for the lives of three men (*ad etatem trium hominum*). Within this term (*terminum*) he could go with it to whichever lord he wished.

1630   i, 72v (41-8) Ralph de Mortimer; Kington St. Michael: TRW Roger holds one and a half hides in Kington St. Michael from Ralph de Mortimer. TRE Alwine held this land from Glastonbury Abbey. He could not be separated from the Church, and he served the abbot from it.

1631 i, 72v (45-2) <u>Roger of Berkeley; Chippenham</u>: TRW Roger of Berkeley holds a hide less a half virgate from the demesne farm of Chippenham. Ceolwine held it TRE on lease (*per prestum*) from Eadric the Sheriff.

1632 i, 72v (48-12) <u>Osbern Giffard; Ugford</u>: TRE Eadnoth held two and a half hides in Ugford. TRW Gundwine holds it from Osbern Giffard. Earl Godwine took this land away (*abstulit*) from Wilton Abbey, and Eadnoth recovered (*recuperavit*) it.

1633 i, 73r (50-5) <u>Hugh the Ass; Kennett</u>: TRE Hunwine held a hide and three virgates in Kennett. Now Nunminster, Winchester holds it from Hugh for his daughter.

1634 i, 73r (58-2) <u>Richard Poynant; Trow</u>: TRW Richard Poynant holds seven and a half hides in Trow. Wilton Abbey held it in the time of King Edward, and it could not be separated from the Church.

1635 i, 73v (67-11) <u>Oda and other King's Thegns; Potterne</u>: TRW Alweard holds three hides in Potterne. TRE they were gelded with the Bishop's manor. Bishop Osmund claims (*calumniatur*) it. [An "r," for "require" is written in the margin opposite this entry.]

1636 i, 73v (67-15) <u>Oda and other King's Thegns; Wilsford (near Pewsey)</u>: TRE Beorhtmær held five hides in Wilsford. TRW Ælfric of Melksham holds it from the King. Edward holds it in mortgage (*in vadimonio*).

1637 i, 74v (68-23) <u>Officials of the King; near Thornhill</u>: TRW William fitz Ansculf holds two hides near Thornhill. According to the testimony of the thegns, one of them belongs to Edward the Sheriff's manor of Bradenstoke, and the other to Gilbert de Breteuil's manor of Clyffe Pypard.

1638 i, 74v (68-25) <u>Officials of the King; Swindon</u>: TRE Thorbert held twelve hides in Swindon. Now Odin the Chamberlain holds them. Miles Crispin holds two hides of this land. Odin claims (*calumniatur*) them.

Worcestershire

1639 i, 172r (C-2, 3) <u>City of Worcester</u>: TRW the sheriff pays £17 by weight and £16 by tale to the King for the pleas of the county and hundreds (*de placitis comitatus et hundretis*). If he does not receive (*accipit*) this money from the pleas, he pays it from his own money (*de suo propio reddit*). In the county there are twelve hundreds. Seven of them, so the shire says, are so quit that the sheriff has nothing in them. Therefore, the sheriff, so he says, loses (*perdit*) much in farm.

1640 i, 172r (C-4) <u>City of Worcester</u>: If anyone shall knowingly breach the peace which the King shall give with his own hand, he is judged an outlaw (*scienter fregerit pacem quam rex manu sua dederit utlaghe iudicatur*). If anyone shall knowingly breach (*sciens fregerit*) the King's peace which the sheriff gives, he shall be fined (*emendabit*) 100s. He who commits robbery (*forestellum*) shall pay a fine of (*emendabit*) 100s.; he who commits housebreaking (*heinfaram*)

100s.; he who rapes (*raptum*) let there be no fine but corporal punishment (*non fit emendatio alia nisi de corpore iusticia*). The King has all these forfeitures (*forisfacturas*) in this county, except in the lands of Westminster Abbey, because King Edward, so the county says, donated (*donavit*) whatever he had there to the abbey.

1641 i, 172r (C-5) <u>City of Worcester</u>: When the King goes against the host, if a man, when called by the King's edict (*edictu eius vocatus*), remains behind, if he is so free a man that he has sake and soke and can go where he wishes with his land, he is in the King's mercy with all his land (*de omni terra sua est in misericordia regis*). If, however, a freeman of another lord has remained behind from the host, and his lord led another man in his place, he who was called shall pay a fine (*emendabit*) of 40s. to his lord. But if no one at all has gone for him, he himself shall give (*dabit*) 40s. to his lord, and his lord shall pay a fine (*emendabit*) of 40s. to the King.

1642 i, 172r–v (1–3a–b) <u>Terra Regis; Droitwich</u>: From all that he held in Droitwich, King Edward had £52 in farm. In the brine-pits in Droitwich Earl Edwin had fifty-one and a half salthouses, as well as 6s. 8d. from the *hocci*. All this paid £24 at farm. Now King William has in demesne what King Edward and Earl Edwin had. From this the sheriff paid £65 by weight and two mits of salt, as long as he had woodland. If, however, so he says, he does not have woodland, in no way can he pay this.

1643 i, 172v (2-1) <u>Bishopric of Worcester; Oswaldslow</u>: The Church of Worcester has a hundred called Oswaldslow, in which 300 hides lie. The bishop of this Church, by an arrangement of ancient times (*constitutione antiquorum temporum*), has all the payments of justice (*redditiones socharum*) from them, and all customs there which belong to the demesne victualing – both the King's service and his own – so that no sheriff can have a lawsuit there, neither in any plea nor in any other case whatsoever (*querelam nec in aliquo placito nec in alia qualibet causa*). All the county attests to this. These 300 hides were from the demesne of the Church, and if any of them was subject to or leased to (*attributum vel prestitum fuisset*) any man in any way, the man who held such land on lease (*prestitam*), in order to serve the bishop from it, could not keep back any customs for himself, except through the bishop, nor could he keep the land beyond the completed time (*impletum tempus*) arranged (*constituerant*) between the bishop and himself, nor could he turn elsewhere with his land.

1644 i, 172v (2-4) <u>Bishopric of Worcester; Lower Wolverton</u>: TRW Roger de Lacy holds two hides of the manor of Kempsey at Lower Wolverton, and Æthelwulf holds from him. In the time of King Edward these hides were in demesne, and Alric still held them in the time of King William. He paid all customs of the farm from them, just as his antecessors had paid, except for rustic's work (*rustico opere*), on terms that he could bargain (*deprecari poterat*) from the reeve.

1645 i, 173r (2-20) <u>Bishopric of Worcester; Bradley</u>: TRW Æthelric the Archdeacon holds a hide of the manor of Fladbury in Bradley. TRE Archbishop

Ealdræd leased (*præstitit*) this land to his reeve, and when he wished, he justly took it away from him (*quando voluit iuste ei abstulit*).

1646 i, 173r (2-21) <u>Bishopric of Worcester; Bishampton</u>: TRW Roger de Lacy holds ten hides of the manor of Fladbury in Bishampton, and two Frenchmen hold from him. Four freemen held this land from the bishop TRE, and paid all soke and sake and churchscot, burial, expeditions, naval expeditions, and pleas (*socam et sacam et circset et sepultura et expeditiones et navigia et placita*) at the Hundred of Oswaldslow. Those who now hold this land do the same.

1647 i, 173r (2-24) <u>Bishopric of Worcester; Cutsdean [Glos.]</u>: TRW Æthelric the Archdeacon holds two hides of the manor of Bredon in Cutsdean. Bishop Beorhtheah had leased (*prestiterat*) this land to Dodda, but Archbishop Ealdræd established title (*deratiocinavit*) to it against Dodda's son, in the time of King William.

1648 i, 173r (2-27) <u>Bishopric of Worcester; Little Washbourne [Glos.]</u>: TRW Urso holds three hides of the manor of Bredon in Little Washbourne. TRE Almær held it, and afterwards became a monk. Thus the bishop took (*recepit*) his land.

1649 i, 173r (2-30) <u>Bishopric of Worcester; Bushley</u>: TRE Beorhtric Algarson held a hide of the manor of Bredon in Bushley from the bishop. He paid farm (*firmabat*) to the bishop each year, as well as whatever he owed to the King's service to the soke of the bishop. Now it is in King William's hand.

1650 i, 173r (2-32) <u>Bishopric of Worcester; Earl's Croome</u>: TRW Ordric holds a hide of the bishop's manor of Ripple in Earl's Croome. TRE Godric held it and served the bishop from it. Archbishop Ealdræd took it from him by law (*iure accepit*).

1651 i, 173r (2-33) <u>Bishopric of Worcester; Croome</u>: TRW Siward holds five hides of the bishop's manor of Ripple in Croome. TRE Sigrefr held them from the bishop. When he died, the bishop gave his daughter with this land to one of his knights, who fed her mother and served the bishop from it (*quo mortuo dedit episcopus filiam eius cum hac terra cuidam suo militi, qui et matrem pasceret et episcopo inde serviret*).

1652 i, 173r (2-36) <u>Bishopric of Worcester; Queenhill</u>: Ralph de Bernay had a hide of the bishop's manor of Ripple in Queenhill. Æthelric held it TRE and served the bishop from it. Now it is in the hand of the King.

1653 i, 173r (2-37) <u>Bishopric of Worcester; Barley</u>: TRE Beorhtric Algarson held a hide of the bishop's manor of Ripple in Barley and served the bishop from it. Now it is in the King's hand.

1654 i, 173r (2-40) <u>Bishopric of Worcester; unidentified hides</u>: TRW Ansgot holds one and a half hides of the bishop's manor of Blockley [Glos.]. It is properly villeins' land (*propria terra villanorum*).

1655 i, 173r (2-43, 44) <u>Bishopric of Worcester; Evenlode [Glos.], Daylesford [Glos.]</u>: TRW Stephen fitz Fulcred holds three hides in Daylesford, and Hereweard holds five hides in Evenlode. The Abbot of Evesham held these two lands from the Bishop of Worcester until the Bishop of Bayeux took (*accepit*) them from the abbey. These lands were for the victualing of the monks.

1656 i, 173v (2-48, 49) Bishopric of Worcester; Northwick: TRW ninety houses in Worcester belong to Northwick, a manor of the Bishop of Worcester. TRE the bishop had the third penny of the borough of Worcester. Now he has it with the King and the earl.

1657 i, 173v (2-63) Bishopric of Worcester; Sedgeberrow: TRW the Church of Worcester has four hides in Sedgeberrow. Dodda holds it, and it is for the victualing of the monks. Archbishop Ealdræd has established title to it (*diratiocinatus est*) against Dodda's son Beorhtric.

1658 i, 173v (2-66, 67) Bishopric of Worcester; Grimley, Knightwick: TRW the Church of Worcester holds three hides. Robert Dispensator holds one of these hides in Knightwick. In the time of King Edward this hide paid sake and soke and all the King's service to Grimley. It is for the demesne victualing of the monks. Nonetheless, it was leased (*praestita fuit*) to Edith the Nun so that she might have it and do service (*deserviret*) for it as long as the brothers were willing (*voluissent*) and could be without the land. But, in King William's time, as the congregation grew, she returned (*reddidit*) it. She is still living, and this is her testimony (*ipsa adhuc vivens inde est testis*).

1659 i, 174r (2-74) Bishopric of Worcester; Hampton: TRW the Abbot of Evesham holds five hides of the manor of Cropthorne in Hampton. TRE the Bishop of Worcester only had the geld of Hampton in his hundred of Oswaldslow. It is quit of all other dues at Evesham Abbey, so the county says.

1660 i, 174r (2-80) Bishopric of Worcester: In all of the Church of Worcester's manors in Oswaldslow, there cannot be more plows than the number stated (*dictum est*). The shrievalty says that the Bishop of Worcester ought to have a *summa* of the better corn which grows there on the feast of St. Martin from each and every hide of its land, whether free land or villein's land. If St. Martin's Day has passed, and the corn has not been paid, he who keeps it back shall pay (*persolvet*) it eleven fold. In addition, the bishop shall take a forfeiture (*forisfacturam episcopus accipiet*), just as he ought from his own land.

1661 i, 174r (3-3) Bishop of Hereford; Inkberrow: TRE Earl Harold held fifteen and a half hides of land in Inkberrow unjustly (*iniuste*). King William, however, returned (*reddidit*) it to Bishop Walter, because it was from the bishopric.

1662 i, 174r (6-1) Cormeilles Abbey; Tenbury Wells: Earl William gave (*dedit*) Cormeilles Abbey a half hide in Tenbury Wells.

1663 i, 174v (8-1) Westminster Abbey; Pershore: King Edward, by testimony of the whole county, held 200 hides in Pershore and gave (*dedit*) them to Westminster, as quit and free from all claims (*quietum et liberum ab omni calumnia*) as he himself had held them in his demesne.

1664 i, 175r (8-25) Westminster Abbey; Nafford: TRW Robert Parler holds a bit of land called Nafford from Gilbert fitz Thurold. This land is not gelded, nor does it owe (*pergit*) service at the hundred.

1665 i, 175r (8-28) <u>Westminster Abbey; Pershore</u>: TRE Pershore paid £83 and fifty sesters of honey with all the pleas of the free men (*placitis francorum hominum*).

1666 i, 175r (9-1b) <u>Pershore Abbey; Pershore</u>: TRW Urso d'Abetot holds one and a half hides of Pershore. Azur held it TRE and served the Church from it. As an acknowledgment of this (*pro recognitione*), he gave (*dabat*) the monks a farm or 20s. each year. There was an agreement (*conventio*) that after his death and the death of his wife, this land was to return (*rediret*) to the demesne of the Church. Azur was alive on the day King Edward died, and was holding the land thus. Afterwards, when his wife was dead, he was made an outlaw (*factus est utlagh*).

1667 i, 175r (9-1c) <u>Pershore Abbey; Drake's Broughton</u>: TRW Urso holds a hide of Pershore in Drake's Broughton. He says that King William gave (*dedit*) it to him, and that he ought to pay service to the Church from it.

1668 i, 175r (9-1e) <u>Pershore Abbey; Wadborough</u>: There is a hide of land in Wadborough in which there was a cow pasture of the monks. Godric, a thegn of King Edward, bought (*emit*) it for the life of three heirs (*vita trium haeredum*). He gave (*dabat*) the monks a farm each year in acknowledgment of this (*pro recognitione*). Now Urso, the third heir (*tercius heres*), holds the land. After Urso's death, it ought to return (*redire*) to Pershore Abbey.

1669 i, 175r–v (9-4) <u>Pershore Abbey; Broadway</u>: TRW Pershore Abbey holds thirty hides in Broadway. A freeman held two and a half hides of this land TRE, which he bought (*emit*) from Abbot Edmund. It was from the demesne. Urso claims (*reclamat*) this land by the King's gift (*de dono regis*), and says that he exchanged (*excambiavit*) it himself with (*contra*) the abbot for a manor which was from the demesne.

1670 i, 175v (9-5c) <u>Pershore Abbey; Bransford</u>: TRW Pershore Abbey holds three hides in Leigh. Urso holds one of these hides in Bransford. The county says that this land was of Pershore Abbey TRE. The Abbot of Evesham, however, held it on the day King Edward died, but the county does not know how.

1671 i, 175v (9-6a) <u>Pershore Abbey; Mathon [Hereford]</u>: TRW Pershore Abbey holds five hides in Mathon and two radmen hold them from the abbey. One of the hides lies in Herefordshire, in Radlow Hundred. The county of Worcester adjudged (*diratiocinavit*) it for the use of Pershore Abbey, [and established] that it belongs to the abbey's manor of Leigh.

1672 i, 175v (9-7) <u>Pershore Abbey</u>: The county says that Pershore Abbey ought to have churchscot from all 300 hides – that is, it ought to have a *summa* of corn on the feast of St. Martin's from each hide where a freeman lives. If he has more hides, they should be free. If the date is broken (*si dies ille fractus fuerit*), he who has kept back (*retinuit*) the corn shall pay (*persolvet*) eleven fold. First, however, he shall pay what he owes. The Abbot of Pershore himself has the forfeitures (*forisfacturam*) of his 100 hides, just as he ought to have from his own land. From the other 200 hides, the abbot has *summae* of corn and payments (*persolutionem*). The Abbot of Westminster has the forfeitures (*forisfacturam*) of these 200 hides because they are his land. The Abbot of Evesham, similarly, has forfeitures from his own land, and all other men similarly have forfeitures from their lands.

1673 i, 175v (10-10) Evesham Abbey; Ombersley: TRW Evesham Abbey holds Ombersley. In ancient times (*antiquitus*) there were three free hides, so the charters of the Church (*cartae de aecclesia*) say, but in the time of King Edward it was reckoned at (*fuit numerata pro*) fifteen hides between woodland and fields.

1674 i, 175v (10-12) Evesham Abbey; Bengeworth: TRW Evesham Abbey holds four hides in Bengeworth and Urso holds a fifth hide. Abbot Walter established his title (*diratiocinavit*) to these five hides at "Ildeberga" (in Evenlode) [Glos.] in four shires in front of (*in iiii sciris coram*) the Bishop of Bayeux and all the King's barons.

1675 i, 175v (10-13) Evesham Abbey; Abbots Morton: TRW Evesham Abbey holds Abbots Morton and Ranulf holds from the abbot. There were five hides TRE, but the greater part of them had been leased outside this manor (*prestita fuit foris*).

1676 i, 176r (11-1) Bishop of Bayeux; Acton Beauchamp [Hereford]: TRE Evesham Abbey held six hides in Acton Beauchamp. Afterwards Urso took (*recepit*) them from the Abbot of Evesham in exchange (*per excambitionem*) for another land. Now Urso holds this land from the fee of the Bishop of Bayeux.

1677 i, 176r (11-2) Bishop of Bayeux; Sheriff's Lench: TRE two thegns held two hides in Sheriff's Lench and Ælfgifu held two. Now the Bishop of Bayeux holds this land and Urso holds it from him. Gilbert fitz Thurold gave (*dedit*) two hides of this land to Evesham Abbey for the soul of Earl William with the consent of King William (*pro anima Willelmi comitis concessu regis Willelmi*). Consequently, one monk was put (*est . . . positus*) in the Church. Abbot Æthelwig gave (*dedit*) a gold mark to King William for the other two hides. The King granted (*concessit*) this land to the Church for his soul (*pro anima sua*), by testimony (*teste*) of Gilbert fitz Thurold, who took (*recepit*) the gold for the King's use. Evesham Abbey was seised (*fuit . . . saisita*) of these four hides for many years, until the Bishop of Bayeux took them away (*abstulit*) from the Church and gave (*dedit*) them to Urso.

1678 i, 176r (15-9) Ralph de Tosny; Astley: TRE Earnsige held six hides in Astley and could go where he wished. TRW St. Taurin's Abbey holds these hides from Ralph, four of which are quit and exempt (*quietas et solutas*) from all customs belonging to the King, just as King William granted (*concessit*), when Ralph gave (*dedit*) it to the saint.

1679 i, 176v (19-13) Osbern fitz Richard; Elmbridge: TRE Ealdgyth held eight hides in Elmbridge; now Osbern fitz Richard holds them. Three of these hides, by testimony of the county, are quit from geld.

1680 i, 177r (23-1) William fitz Ansculf; Selly Oak [War.]: TRW William fitz Ansculf holds four hides in Selly Oak from the King, and Wibert holds them from him. TRE Wulfwine held them. He bought (*emit*) this manor from the Bishop of Chester for the lives of three men (*aetatem trium hominum*). When he was ill and had come to the end of his life (*Qui cum infirmatus ad finem vitae venisset*), he called his son, the Bishop of Lichfield, his wife, and his many friends and said: "Hear me, my friends. I wish that my wife, while she lives, hold this land, which I bought (*emit*) from the Church. And after her death, the Church from which I took (*recipiat*) it, should take it back (*accepit*). Let he who takes it away from the Church be excommunicated (*qui inde abstulerit, excommunicatus sit*)." The better men of the whole county testify that this was so (*Hoc ita fuisse testificantur meliores homines totius comitatus*).

1681   i, 177r (23-8) William fitz Ansculf; Bell: TRE Leofnoth, a thegn of King Edward, held three hides in Bell. Now Robert holds them from William fitz Ansculf. Ralph fitz Hubert held this manor for more than five years, but William fitz Osbern unjustly took it away from him (*iniuste ei abstulit*).

1682   i, 177v (26-15) Urso d'Abetot; Upton Warren: TRW Herlebald holds three hides in Upton Warren from Urso d'Abetot. TRE Æthelwig abbot of Evesham held it, and it ought, by right (*recte*), to be in the abbey, by testimony of the county.

1683   i, 177v (26-16) Urso d'Abetot; Witton in Droitwich: TRW Urso d'Abetot holds a half hide in Witton. TRE Evesham Abbey held it. Wulfgeat donated (*donavit*) this land to Evesham Abbey, and put his gift on the altar (*posuit donum super altare*) when his son Ælfgeat was made a monk there. This was done in the fifth year of King Edward's reign. Afterward Abbot Æthelwig leased (*praestitit*) this land to his uncle for as long as the uncle should live. This man later died in Harold's battle against the Norse, and the abbey again took (*recepit*) his land before King William came into England. The abbot held it as long as he lived. His successor, Abbot Walter, similarly held it for more than seven years.

1684   i, 177v (26-17) Urso d'Abetot; Hampton Lovett: TRE the Abbot of Evesham held four hides in Hampton Lovett. TRW Urso d'Abetot holds them, and Robert holds from him. The Abbot of Evesham bought (*emit*) this manor from a thegn who, by right (*recte*), could sell his land to whom he wished. He donated his purchase (*emptum donavit*) to the abbey through the Gospels put on the altar (*per unum textum positum super altare*), by testimony of the county.

1685   i, 178r (28-1) Eadgifu; Chaddesley Corbett: TRE and TRW Eadgifu holds Chaddesley Corbett. There are twenty-five hides with eight berewicks there. Of these, ten hides were quit from geld, by testimony of the county.

1686   i, 178r (X-2) Feckenham, Hollow: Ten hides in Feckenham and three hides in Hollow lie in Esch Hundred. They are written in the returns for Hereford (*scriptae sunt in brevi de Hereford*).

1687   i, 178r (X-3) Martley, Suckley: Thirteen hides in Martley and five hides in Suckley lie in Doddingtree Hundred. They plead (*placitant*) there and are gelded there. They pay their farm at Hereford and are written in the King's return (*sunt scriptae in breve regis*).

Yorkshire

1688   i, 298r (C-1a) <u>City of York</u>: In the city of York there were six shires (*scyrae*) besides the archbishop's shire. The archbishop still has a third of one of these. In them no one else had customs, unless as a burgess, with these exceptions: Merle-sveinn in a house which is now below the castle; the canons wherever they lived; and the four judges (*iudices*), to whom the King gave this gift through his writ for as long as they lived (*dabat hoc donum per suum brevem, et quamdiu vivebant*).

1689   i, 298r (C-2) <u>City of York</u>: The Church of St. Cuthbert, Durham has and always had a house, which, so many say, was quit of all customs. The burgesses, however, say that it was not quit TRE, unless it was quit like one of the burgesses' houses, and in so far as, on account of that house, St. Cuthbert's had its own toll and the toll of the canons.

1690   i, 298r (C-2) <u>City of York</u>: Besides this house, the Bishop of Durham has, by the King's gift (*de dono regis*), the Church of All Saints and all that belongs to it, along with the whole of Uhtræd's and Earnwine's land, which [Earl] Hugh the Sheriff delivered (*deliberavit*) to Bishop Walcher through the King's writ (*per brevem regis*). The burgesses who live in the house say that they hold it under the King.

1691   i, 298r (C-3) <u>City of York</u>: The Count of Mortain has fourteen messuages in York, along with two stalls in the meat market [the Shambles] and the Church of St. Cross. Osbern fitz Boso took (*recepit*) these and all that belongs to them. These messuages had belonged to the following men: one to Sunulf the Priest; one to Morulf; one to Sterri; one to Snarri; one to Gamal with four drengs; five to Arnketil; two to Lyfing the Priest; one to Thorfin; and one to Ligulf.

1692   i, 298r (C-6) <u>City of York</u>: Waldin stole (*intercepit*) two of Ketil the Priest's messuages for one of Sterri's.

1693   i, 298r (C-9) <u>City of York</u>: Nigel Fossard stole (*intercepit*) two messuages, but he said that he had returned (*reddidisse*) them to the Bishop of Coutances.

1694   i, 298r (C-10) <u>City of York</u>: William de Percy has two messuages which belonged to two of Earl Harold's reeves. But the burgesses say that one of these had not been the Earl's, and that the other had been forfeited (*esse forisfactam*) to him. William also calls (*advocat*) Earl Hugh for the Church of St. Cuthbert and seven little messuages, measuring fifty feet in width. Concerning the messuage of Uhtræd, the burgesses say that William de Percy carried it off (*asportasse*) into his castle, after he returned from Scotland. William, however, denies (*negat*) that he had had the land of this Uhtræd, but he says that he had taken away (*tulisse*) Uhtræd's house into the castle, through Hugh the Sheriff, in the first year after the destruction (*destructionem*) of the castle.

1695   i, 298r (C-11) <u>City of York</u>: Hugh fitz Baldric has the Church of St. Andrew, which he bought (*emit*).

1696   i, 298r (C-20) <u>City of York</u>: Landric the Carpenter has ten and a half messuages which the sheriff leased (*prestitit*) him.

1697   i, 298r (C-25) <u>City of York</u>: Ralph Pagnell holds three carucates in Sandburn. The canons say that they held it in the time of King Edward.

1698   i, 298v (C-36) <u>City of York</u>: In the time of King Edward these men held sake and soke and toll and team (*tol et thaim*) and all customs: Earl Harold; Merlesveinn; Ulf Fenisc; Thorgot Lag; Toki son of Auti; Edwin and Morcar over Ingeld's land only; Gamal son of Osbert over Cottingham only; Kofse over Coxwold only; and Cnut. Of these men, anyone who forfeited (*forisfecit*) paid no one a fine (*emendavit*) but the King and the earl.

1699   i, 298v (C-37) <u>City of York</u>: The earl had nothing at all in the demesne manors, and the King had nothing in the earl's manors except what belongs to the *christianitatem*, which belongs to the archbishop. Neither the King, the earl, nor anyone else had any customs in all the land of the Churches of St. Peter, York, St. John, St. Wilfrid, St. Cuthbert, and Holy Trinity.

1700   i, 298v (C-37) <u>City of York</u>: In the city of York the King has three roads by land and a fourth by water. All forfeitures (*forisfactum*) on all of these roads are the King's and the earl's, wherever the roads go, whether through the King's land, the archbishop's, or the earl's.

1701   i, 298v (C-38) <u>City of York</u>: If the peace, given by the King's hand or his seal, shall be broken (*pax data manu regis vel sigillo eius si fuerit infracta*), only the King is paid a fine (*emendatur*) throughout twelve hundreds – each hundred paying £8.

1702   i, 298v (C-38) <u>City of York</u>: When peace is given by the earl and broken (*pax a comite data et infracta*) by anyone, the earl is paid a fine (*emendatur*) throughout six hundreds – each hundred paying £8.

1703   i, 298v (C-39) <u>City of York</u>: If anyone shall be outlawed according to the law, no one but the King shall give him peace (*secundum legem exulatus fuerit, nullus nisi rex ei pacem dabit*). Nonetheless, if the earl or sheriff should have expelled anyone from the realm (*de regione foras miserint*), they can recall him and give him peace if they wish (*eum revocare et pacem ei dare possunt si voluerint*).

1704   i, 298v (C-40) <u>City of York</u>: Those thegns who have more than six manors only give (*dant*) the King relief (*relevationem*) for their lands. The relief is £8. If a man has six manors or less, however, he gives (*dat*) three marks of silver to the sheriff for relief. The burgesses of the city of York do not give relief (*dant relevationem*).

1705   i, 299v (1Y-15) <u>Terra Regis; Wakefield</u>: King Edward held Wakefield with its nine berewicks. Now it is King William's, and there are sixty carucates and three and a third bovates of land. Besides this land and extensive sokes, there are two carucates in Holme (near Holmfirth), Yateholm, Austonley, and Upper Thong. Some say this is thegnland, and others say that it is soke in Wakefield.

1706   i, 301v (1W-53) <u>Terra Regis; Castley</u>: TRE Alwine had a carucate in Castley and Biarni and Alflæd had a carucate there. Now Everard, William de Percy's man, cultivates it, but William de Percy does not vouch (*advocat*) for it.

1707 i, 303r (2N-5) <u>Archbishop of York; East Newton</u>: TRW the Archbishop of York has four carucates in East Newton. Gamal gave (*dedit*) it to St. Peter's TRE.

1708 i, 303r (2N-15) <u>Archbishop of York; Stonegrave</u>: TRW the Archbishop of York has six bovates in Stonegrave. TRE Ulf held them. He gave (*dedit*) them to St. Peter's.

1709 i, 304r (2E-26) <u>Archbishop of York; Ottringham</u>: The Archbishop of York has six and a half carucates in Ottringham, which is a berewick and lies in Holderness. A knight leases (*locat*) it and pays 10s.

1710 i, 304r (2E-33) <u>Archbishop of York; Routh</u>: The Archbishop of York has fifteen bovates of land in Routh, which is a berewick and lies in Holderness. In the same vill, Drogo takes away (*aufert*) two carucates of waste land from St. John's.

1711 i, 306v (5E-27) <u>Count of Mortain; Middleton-on-the-Wolds</u>: TRE Edith had a manor of three carucates and five bovates in Middleton-on-the-Wolds. Now Richard has it from the Count of Mortain, but the count's antecessor did not have it.

1712 i, 306v (5E-28) <u>Count of Mortain; Middleton-on-the-Wolds</u>: There are six bovates in Middleton-on-the-Wolds, which are a soke of the King's manor of Great Driffield. The King, however, does not have the soke.

1713 i, 307r (5E-37) <u>Count of Mortain; Cherry Burton</u>: There is a carucate in Cherry Burton, which is a soke of Welton. Nigel held it, but he is now handing it over (*dimittit*).

1714 i, 315v (9W-26) <u>Ilbert de Lacy; Birkin</u>: TRE Ælfric had a carucate of land in Birkin. Now Gamal has it under Ilbert de Lacy. This land is said to belong to Snaith.

1715 i, 329r (36W-14) <u>Osbern d'Arques; Nether Poppleton</u>: TRE Oda the Deacon had two and a half carucates in Nether Poppleton. This was St. Everild's land. Now Osbern d'Arques holds it.

1716 i, 373r (CN-1) <u>Clamores; North Riding</u>: Earl Hugh claims (*calumpniatur*) a carucate of land against William de Percy in Fyling, saying that it belongs to Whitby. But he does not have testimony (*testimonium*).

1717 i, 373r (CN-2) <u>Clamores; North Riding</u>: Ralph Pagnell claims (*calumniatur*) six bovates of Ulf's land in Stonegrave, but the sworn men (*homines qui iuraverunt*) say that it is the Church of St. Peter, York.

1718 i, 373r (CN-3) <u>Clamores; North Riding</u>: They testify that William Malet held Havarth's land in Yorkshire before the castle was captured.

1719 i, 373r (CN-4) <u>Clamores; North Riding</u>: They say that William Malet bought (*emit*) seven carucates of Sprot's land in Sand Hutton for ten marks of silver.

1720 i, 373r (CN-5) <u>Clamores; North Riding</u>: Nigel Fossard unjustly (*iniuste*) held the land of Thorulf, Thorkil, and Thorsten in Sheriff Hutton – that is, three manors of four carucates. Nigel, however, has handed this land over (*dimisit*), and it is in the hand of the King.

1721 i, 373r (CE-1) <u>Clamores; East Riding</u>: Nigel Fossard has relinquished (*reliquit*) two carucates of land, a manor, in South Cliffe. They were Basinc's.

1722 i, 373r (CE-2) <u>Clamores; East Riding</u>: Nigel Fossard has relinquished (*reliquit*) two carucates of land in Ellerton (near Bubwith) which were Barn's and Ulf's.

1723 i, 373r (CE-3) <u>Clamores; East Riding</u>: Nigel Fossard held a carucate of land in Middleton-on-the-Wolds, which was Mylnugrimr's. He has now handed it over (*dimisit*).

1724 i, 373r (CE-4) <u>Clamores; East Riding</u>: Nigel Fossard has, until now, kept back through force (*per vim retinuit*) the soke of a half carucate as well as the third of a bovate of land in Middleton-on-the-Wolds. They belong to the King's manor of Great Driffield.

1725 i, 373r (CE-5) <u>Clamores; East Riding</u>: Hamelin has, until now, kept back through force (*detinuit . . . per vim*) two carucates and five bovates of land in Middleton-on-the-Wolds. The soke belongs to Great Driffield.

1726 i, 373r (CE-6) <u>Clamores; East Riding</u>: Richard de Sourdeval holds three carucates and five bovates of land in Middleton-on-the-Wolds. They were Ealdgyth's, whose land was not delivered (*non fuit deliberata*) to Count Robert.

1727 i, 373r (CE-7) <u>Clamores; East Riding</u>: Richard de Sourdeval holds six bovates of land in Middleton-on-the-Wolds. Its soke belongs to Great Driffield, but until now, it has not been returned (*reddita . . . non est*).

1728 i, 373r (CE-8) <u>Clamores; East Riding</u>: Nigel Fossard held two carucates and a bovate of land in North Dalton, which were Northmann's. He has now handed them over (*dimittit*).

1729 i, 373r (CE-9) <u>Clamores; East Riding</u>: Robert Malet has handed over (*dimisit*) two carucates of land in Naburn, which were Thorkil's. Geoffrey de Beauchamps held them from Robert Malet.

1730 i, 373r (CE-10) <u>Clamores; East Riding</u>: Nigel Fossard has handed over (*dimisit*) two carucates of land in Croome which were Mylnugrimr's. They are in Thorshowe Wapentake. Now this land is in the King's hand.

1731 i, 373r (CE-11) <u>Clamores; East Riding</u>: Nigel Fossard held a carucate of Morcar's land in Cherry Burton, a manor of St. John's, Beverley. Its soke is in Welton. He now relinquishes (*reliquit*) it.

1732 i, 373r (CE-12) <u>Clamores; East Riding</u>: TRE Orm and Basinc held four bovates of land in Belby. They had halls there. Afterwards, until now, the Bishop of Durham held them. Now, however, no one – neither the sheriff nor the bishop – claims (*clamat*) this land.

1733 i, 373r (CE-13) <u>Clamores; East Riding</u>: The sworn men (*homines qui iuraverunt*) say that William Malet had the land of Northmann son of Ulf in Brantingham in demesne. Nigel Fossard now has it. Similarly, they say that Nigel has the land of Ulf the Deacon in North Cave, but that William Malet had it.

1734 i, 373r (CE-14) <u>Clamores</u>; <u>East Riding</u>: By the testimony of the sworn men (*hominum qui iuraverunt*), the three and a half bovates of land which Ralph de Mortimer claims (*clamat*) in Lund were Alwine's, who was Gilbert Tison's antecessor, and not Eadgifu's, whose land Ralph de Mortimer has.

1735 i, 373r (CE-15) <u>Clamores</u>; <u>East Riding</u>: They testify that all of Asa's land ought to be Robert Malet's, because she had her land separate and free from the lordship and power of her husband Beornwulf (*separatam et liberam a dominatu et potestate Bernulfi mariti sui*), even when they were together, so that he could make neither a donation nor a sale of her land, nor a forfeiture (*nec donationem nec venditionem facere nec forisfacere posset*). After their separation (*separationem*), she withdrew (*recessit*) with all of her land and possessed it as a lord (*ut domina possedit*). All the men of the county, moreover, saw William Malet seised (*saisitum*) of all of her land until the castle was attacked (*invasum est*). This is attested for all of Asa's land which she had in Yorkshire.

1736 i, 373r (CE-16) <u>Clamores</u>; <u>East Riding</u>: They say that the soke, which Gilbert Tison claims (*clamat*) in Burland, ought to be the Bishop of Durham's in Howden.

1737 i, 373r (CE-17) <u>Clamores</u>; <u>East Riding</u>: They say that the fourteen bovates of land, which the Bishop of Durham claims (*clamat*) against Robert Malet in Belby, belonged to Muli, Ecgbrand, Basinc, and Orm with sake and soke. William Malet had this land.

1738 i, 373r (CE-18) <u>Clamores</u>; <u>East Riding</u>: They say that the land which Earnwine the Priest claims (*clamat*) in Aughton (near Bubwith), ought to be his. Nigel Fossard, however, claims the King as warrantor (*clamat regem advocatum*) for this land for the use of Count Robert.

1739 i, 373r (CE-19) <u>Clamores</u>; <u>East Riding</u>: They say that William Malet was seised (*fuisse saisitum*) of seven carucates of land in North Duffield, which Nigel Fossard has, and that William Malet had the land and service until the castle was destroyed (*fractum est*).

1740 i, 373r (CE-20) <u>Clamores</u>; <u>East Riding</u>: They say that the two carucates of land which Nigel Fossard has in South Duffield belong to the King's demesne in Pocklington. William Malet, however, had the remaining six carucates of land in South Duffield, as long as he held the castle of York, and men paid service to him.

1741 i, 373r (CE-21) <u>Clamores</u>; <u>East Riding</u>: Nigel Fossard holds three carucates of land in Cliffe and three carucates in Osgodby. Those who have sworn (*qui iuraverunt*) say that William Malet had these carucates in demesne for as long as he held land in Yorkshire.

1742 i, 373r (CE-22) <u>Clamores</u>; <u>East Riding</u>: They testify that William Malet had Sancton in demesne, and was seised (*saisitum fuisse*) of seven and a half carucates of land there – that is, half of the vill.

1743 i, 373r (CE-23) <u>Clamores</u>; <u>East Riding</u>: The whole county testifies that as long as he held land in Yorkshire, William Malet held in his demesne all the land that Northmann son of Mælcolumban held in the East Riding.

1744   i, 373r (CE-24) <u>Clamores; East Riding</u>: They say that the soke of five carucates and two bovates of land, which the Bishop of Durham claims (*clamat*), in truth (*vere*) lay in Welton. But the canons of Beverley claim (*clamant*) this land by King William's gift and confirmation (*donum regis Willelmi et confirmationem*). Similarly, they say that the soke of a carucate of land in "Neutone," which the Bishop of Durham claims (*clamat*) for Welton, was so TRE, but the clerks now claim (*clamant*) this in the same way from the King.

1745   i, 373r (CE-25) <u>Clamores; East Riding</u>: They say that the soke of two bovates in "Ianulfestorp," which William de Percy has, ought to be the archbishop's.

1746   i, 373r (CE-26) <u>Clamores; East Riding</u>: They testify that the whole vill of Scoreby – that is, six carucates of land – was William Malet's, and that he possessed (*possedisse*) it in demesne. Similarly, they testify that the fourteen bovates of land in "Ianulfestorp" and Dunnington, which were Northmann's and Healfdene's, were William Malet's, and he held them in demesne.

1747   i, 373r (CE-27) <u>Clamores; East Riding</u>: Concerning Sunulf's land in Grimston, which Nigel Fossard holds and William de Percy claims (*clamat*), they do not know which of them ought to have it. Earnwine the Priest also claims (*clamat*) the same land.

1748   i, 373v (CE-28) <u>Clamores; East Riding</u>: They testify that the six bovates of land in Thorpe le Street, which the Archbishop of York claims (*clamat*), ought to be Gilbert Tison's.

1749   i, 373v (CE-29) <u>Clamores; East Riding</u>: They testify that Ulfkil's six carucates of land in Elvington, which William de Percy has, is for Robert Malet's use, because his father had them, just as he had the abovementioned lands.

1750   i, 373v (CE-30) <u>Clamores; East Riding</u>: Those who have sworn (*qui iuraverunt*) testify that the four carucates of land in Wheldrake, which William de Percy holds and of which the soke belongs in Clifton, were held in William Malet's demesne. And he was seised (*saisitum fuisse*) not only of these four carucates, but of the whole vill of Wheldrake.

1751   i, 373v (CE-31) <u>Clamores; East Riding</u>: Richard de Sourdeval claims (*clamat*) the land of Northmann and Asa, but the sworn men (*qui iuraverunt*) say that it ought to be the King's.

1752   i, 373v (CE-32) <u>Clamores; East Riding</u>: Odo the Balistarius has the land of Orm and Bondi in Skirpenbeck and "Scardiztorp" (in Skirpenbeck), but the sworn men (*qui iuraverunt*) testify that it ought to be the King's.

1753   i, 373v (CE-33) <u>Clamores; East Riding</u>: Gamal had four carucates of land in Risby, which he sold (*vendidit*) to Archbishop Ealdræd in the time of King William. The soke of this land used to lie in Welton, but Archbishop Thomas has King William's writ (*brevem*) through which the King granted (*per quem concessit*) this soke quit to the Church of St. John, Beverley. Similarly the soke of four carucates of land in Walkington belonged to Welton, but King William donated (*donavit*) it quit to Archbishop Ealdræd, by testimony of the wapentake, which saw and heard the King's writ for this (*qui brevem regis inde vidit et audiuit*).

1754 i, 373v (CW-1) <u>Clamores; West Riding</u>: The men of Barkston Wapentake and Skyrack Wapentake produce (*perhibent*) testimony for Osbern d'Arques that his antecessor Wulfberht had all of Thorner – that is, four manors of eight carucates of land. They do not know by whose gift (*dono*). But all of Thorner sits within the boundary of Ilbert's castle, according to the first measurement (*secundum primam mensuram*). But it sits outside it according to the newest measurement (*secundum novissimam mensuram*).

1755 i, 373v (CW-2) <u>Clamores; West Riding</u>: They produce (*perhibent*) [testimony] that William Malet had these lands: Gamal's land – a manor of two carucates – in Yeadon; Grim's and Esger's land – two manors of a carucate – in Oglethorpe, the soke, however, lay in Bramham; Gamal son of Osmund's land – three manors of twelve bovates – in Hazelwood; and a carucate of Arnketil's and his brother's land in the same vill. Hazelwood is within Ilbert's boundary (*sedet infra metam*), according to the first measurement (*secundum primam mensuram*), and it is outside of it according to the newest measurement (*secundum novissimam*).

1756 i, 373v (CW-3) <u>Clamores; West Riding</u>: William Malet, so they say, had the whole of Stutton – that is, three manors, of three carucates of land and a mill; Thorkil's land in Tadcaster – that is, two manors of two carucates and two bovates and a field; Wulfstan's land in North Milford – that is, a manor of two carucates – this vill is within Ilbert's boundary (*est infra metam Ilberti*), as has been said above of the others. William Malet also had Ketil's land in "Neuhuse" – that is, a manor of two carucates; Thorkil's land in Toulston – that is, a carucate – similarly within Ilbert's territory (*infra fines*). He had Ketil's and his brother's land in Ryther – that is, two manors of two carucates. This is within Ilbert's boundary (*infra metam*), as is said above of the others. He had Ketil's land in "Saxehale" – that is, a manor of two carucates within the castle boundary (*infra metam castelli*). He had two carucates in Lead, the soke of which lies in Hazelwood. He had Ligulf's and Thorn's land in Newton Kyme, that is, a manor of two carucates. They say that William Malet was seised (*fuisse . . . saisitum*) of all of this.

1757 i, 373v (CW-4) <u>Clamores; West Riding</u>: According to their testimony, Gilbert of Ghent has a carucate of Ulf's land in Birkin.

1758 i, 373v (CW-5) <u>Clamores; West Riding</u>: They say that Dunstan did not have Thorkil's land in Tadcaster in the time of King Edward.

1759 i, 373v (CW-6) <u>Clamores; West Riding</u>: They say that Ligulf's land lay in Weardley and East Rigton, and that Richard de Sourdeval's land lay in Compton.

1760 i, 373v (CW-7) <u>Clamores; West Riding</u>: The men of Strafforth Wapentake testify that two carucates of Siward's land in Clifton, which Roger de Bully claimed (*clamabat*), are for William de Warenne's use.

1761   i, 373v (CW-8) <u>Clamores; West Riding</u>: They testify that four bovates of Brun's land in Clifton, which William de Warenne had, is in demesne and for the King's use.

1762   i, 373v (CW-9) <u>Clamores; West Riding</u>: They testify that six carucates of land in Barnburgh, which belong to Conisbrough, are for the use of William de Warenne.

1763   i, 373v (CW-10) <u>Clamores; West Riding</u>: They testify that fifteen acres of land in Wilsic are for the use of William de Warenne. They lie in Barnburgh and all that belongs to it.

1764   i, 373v (CW-11) <u>Clamores; West Riding</u>: They say that Nigel Fossard ought to have seven bovates of Alwine's land in Kirk Sandall. Its soke belongs to Conisbrough. He also ought to have Skotkollr's church, which lies in the same vill, and which soke lies in Conisbrough.

1765   i, 373v (CW-12) <u>Clamores; West Riding</u>: They say that Nigel Fossard ought to have three bovates of Ulfkil's land, the soke of which is in Conisbrough. He also ought to have a bovate of Ulfkil's land in Kirk Bramwith. Its soke is similarly in Conisbrough.

1766   i, 373v (CW-13) <u>Clamores; West Riding</u>: Nigel Fossard has a bovate of land and three tofts of Ulfkil's land in Tudworth and Stainforth. The soke lies in Conisbrough. He also has a toft and a quarter of a bovate of Northmann's land in Fishlake. The soke is in Conisbrough.

1767   i, 373v (CW-14) <u>Clamores; West Riding</u>: Fulk de Lisors has two bovates of Wulfmær's land in Loversall. The soke lies in Nigel's land in Hexthorpe. Fulk also has a carucate of Swein's land in Edenthorpe. It's soke lies in Conisbrough.

1768   i, 373v (CW-15) <u>Clamores; West Riding</u>: Roger de Bully has a carucate of Alsige's land in Cantley.

1769   i, 373v (CW-16) <u>Clamores; West Riding</u>: Geoffrey Alselin has four bovates of Toki's land in Loversall. The soke lies in Hexthorpe.

1770   i, 373v (CW-17) <u>Clamores; West Riding</u>: Two marshals seised (*saisierunt*) Northmann's land and held it. The men of the wapentake do not know how or for whose use, but they saw them holding it.

1771   i, 373v (CW-18) <u>Clamores; West Riding</u>: Nigel Fossard has a manor of fourteen bovates of Siward's land in Wadworth, and a manor of a carucate of Siward's land in Stancil.

1772   i, 373v (CW-19) <u>Clamores; West Riding</u>: Geoffrey Alselin ought to have ten and a half carucates of Toki's land in Wadworth, but Roger de Bully holds it. They do not know in what way.

1773   i, 373v (CW-20) <u>Clamores; West Riding</u>: The King has a manor of six bovates of Godhyse's land in Great Houghton.

1774   i, 373v (CW-21) <u>Clamores; West Riding</u>: Concerning Nigel Fossard's claims (*calumniis*) in Hexthorpe, they say that it is now as it was in King Edward's day.

1775 i, 373v (CW-22) <u>Clamores; West Riding</u>: They say that Archbishop Ealdræd bought (*emisse*) Swein of Adwick le Street's land after King Edward's death, and that he had it quit.

1776 i, 373v (CW-23) <u>Clamores; West Riding</u>: Concerning St. Mary's Church, which is in Morley, the King has half of the alms of the three feasts of St. Mary, because it lies in Wakefield. Ilbert and the priest who serves the church have the other half, by judgment (*iudicio*) of the men of Morley Wapentake.

1777 i, 373v (CW-24) <u>Clamores; West Riding</u>: The men of Ainsty Wapentake testify to William Malet's use of Arnketil son of Wulfstan's land in Steeton, Colton and Catterton – that is, two manors of three carucates and five bovates. Osbern d'Arques holds this land.

1778 i, 374r (CW-25) <u>Clamores; West Riding</u>: They say that William Malet had three carucates of Arnketil son of Ulf's land in Haggenby, which William de Percy holds. One of those carucates lies in the soke of Healaugh.

1779 i, 374r (CW-26) <u>Clamores; West Riding</u>: They testify that four and a half carucates of Northmann son of Mælcolumban's land, which Osbern d'Arques holds, are for William Malet's use.

1780 i, 374r (CW-27) <u>Clamores; West Riding</u>: They testify that thirteen bovates of Godwine son of Eadric's land in Colton and Steeton, which Osbern d'Arques holds, are for William Malet's use.

1781 i, 374r (CW-28) <u>Clamores; West Riding</u>: They say that William Malet ought to have a carucate of land in Askham Richard, which was Ulf the Deacon's, and which Osbern d'Arques holds.

1782 i, 374r (CW-29) <u>Clamores; West Riding</u>: They say that William Malet ought to have the seven bovates of Wulfstan the Priest's land in Colton, which Osbern d'Arques holds.

1783 i, 374r (CW-30) <u>Clamores; West Riding</u>: They testify that a carucate of Northmann's land in Pallathorpe and a half carucate in "Mulehale," which Landric holds, ought to be William Malet's.

1784 i, 374r (CW-31) <u>Clamores; West Riding</u>: There are ten bovates of Healfdene's land and five bovates of Oda's and Alwine's land in Hornington. William de Percy holds this land, but the men of the wapentake say that Malet ought to have it.

1785 i, 374r (CW-32) <u>Clamores; West Riding</u>: There is a manor in Scagglethorpe and another in the two Poppletons (Nether and Upper) of six and a half carucates of land. This was Earnwine Catenase's land, and Osbern d'Arques holds it. But they testify to the use of Malet, and furthermore, they say that Earnwine the Priest ought to have this land from Robert Malet. They testify thus: that they saw William Malet seised (*saisitum*) and holding this land, and that the men of the land did service to him and were his men (*servitium sibi fecerunt et homines eius fuerunt*). But they do not know how he had them.

1786 i, 374r (CW-33) <u>Clamores; West Riding</u>: William de Percy has five carucates of Ligulfr's land in Bolton Percy. The soke belongs to Healaugh, Geoffrey Alselin's land.

1787   i, 374r (CW-34) <u>Clamores; West Riding</u>: Concerning twelve bovates of Godwine's land in Bolton Percy, the soke belongs to Healaugh, Geoffrey Alselin's land.

1788   i, 374r (CW-35) <u>Clamores; West Riding</u>: William de Percy calls on his equals to witness (*advocat pares suos in testimonium*) that while William Malet was alive and held the sheriffdom in York, William de Percy was seised (*fuit ipse saisitus*) of Bolton Percy and held it.

1789   i, 374r (CW-36) <u>Clamores; West Riding</u>: Osbern d'Arques confirms (*confirmat*) that his antecessor Wulfberht had Appleton Roebuck and all the other lands quit.

1790   i, 374r (CW-37) <u>Clamores; West Riding</u>: Ulfkil brother of Swein held two carucates in Steeton, a half carucate in Hornington, a carucate in Oxton, six bovates in Pallathorpe, and seven bovates in Colton. Count Robert now has them. Nigel Fossard holds from him.

1791   i, 374r (CW-38) <u>Clamores; West Riding</u>: The men of Burghshire Wapentake testify that Ralph Pagnell has the use of four bovates of Merle-sveinn's land in Nun Monkton, which Osbern d'Arques holds.

1792   i, 374r (CW-39) <u>Clamores; West Riding</u>: Concerning all the land which Drogo claimed (*calumniabatur*) against the Church of St. John, Beverley, the men of the riding testified that this land is for the use of St. John's, by gift of King William (*per donum regis Willelmi*). He gave (*dedit*) it to St. John's in Archbishop Ealdræd's time, and the canons have the seal (*sigillum*) of King Edward and King William for this.

1793   i, 374r (CW-40-52) <u>Clamores; Holderness</u>: The sworn men of Holderness (*homines de Heldernesse qui iuraverunt*) have testified that William Malet had the use of the lands noted below, because they saw him seised (*saisire*) and the lands in his hand, and saw him having and holding them until the Danes captured him. But concerning this land, they have seen neither the King's writ nor his seal (*breve regis vel sigillum*): four manors of eleven carucates of land in Brandesburton, which were Ealdwif's, Ulf's, and Ulf's brother Ulfkil's; a manor of one carucate of land in "Luuetotholm," which was Luvetote's; a manor of "Chenuthesholm," which was Cnut's; a manor of six carucates of land in Catfoss, which was Cnut's; a manor of seven and a half carucates of land in Rise, which was Cnut's; a berewick of four carucates of land in Catwick, which was Ealdwif's; a manor of four carucates of land in Ellerby, which was Frani son of Thor's; a manor of one carucate of land in Langthorpe, which was Ecgfrith's; a manor of six carucates in Sproatley, which was Thorsten's; a manor of eight carucates in Keyingham, which was Thorfridh's; seven manors of sixteen carucates of land in Preston, which were Frani's and his brother's; a manor of two carucates in "Andrebi," which was Ramkel's; a manor of five carucates in Waxholme, which was Brandulfr's; a manor of one carucate in Redmere, which was Ramkel's; five manors of eight carucates in Holmpton, which were Oda the Priest's, Æthelstan's, and Siward's; a manor of two carucates in Rysome Garth, which was Thorgot's; a manor of three carucates of land in Northorpe, which was Grimkel's; and a manor of one carucate of land in Southcoates, which was Oda the Deacon's. Drogo has this land.

1794 i, 374r (CW-40, 41, 42) <u>Clamores; Healaugh</u>: This land lies in Healaugh: five carucates of land in Bolton Percy; a carucate of land in Haggenby; a bovate in Acaster Selby; two and a half carucates of inland and four bovates of soke in Ouston. William de Percy holds these. There are twelve bovates of land in Walton and a carucate in Rufforth. Osbern d'Arques holds these. There is a carucate of land in Askam Bryam. Count Alan holds it.

Little Domesday Book

Essex

1795 ii, 1b (1-1) <u>Terra Regis; Benfleet (North or South)</u>: TRE Earl Harold held eight hides of land in Benfleet. Now it is in the custody of Ranulf brother of Ilger and is in the King's hand. TRE there was a freeman in this manor with half a hide. Now he has become (*effectus est*) one of the villeins. Half a hide of this manor was given (*data fuit*) TRE to the church of another manor, but after Benfleet came into the King's demesne, it was taken away (*ablata fuit*) from the church, and it lies once again in this manor.

1796 ii, 1b–2a (1-2) <u>Terra Regis; Witham</u>: TRE Earl Harold held five hides of land in Witham. Now it is in Peter the Sheriff's custody, in the hand of the King. TRE there were eighteen men's plows there, now seven. This loss (*perditio*) was in the time of Sheriff Swein and Sheriff Baynard, and caused by a mortality of beasts. TRE its value was £10, now £20; but the sheriff takes (*recepit*) £34 from it between his customs and the pleas (*placita*) of the half-hundred of Witham, and a £4 gift (*de gersuma*). TRE thirty-four freemen were attached to this manor, and they paid 10s. and 11d. of customs. Ilbold holds two of these men with forty-five acres of land: they pay their customs to the manor. Theodric Pointel holds eight of these men with a half hide and twenty-two and a half acres of land: they pay customs. Ranulf Peverel holds ten of these men with two hides and forty-five acres of land: they do not pay customs. William fitz Gross holds five men with a hide and fifteen acres of land: only one of them pays customs. Ralph Baynard holds six men with half a hide and thirty-five acres of land: only one pays customs. Haimo Dapifer holds one man with half a hide of land: he pays customs. Jocelyn Lorimer has the land of one of these men, that is, one hide, and he does not pay customs. The monks of Ely claim (*calumpniantur*) this hide. The hundred testifies for Ely concerning half this hide, but it knows nothing about the other half.

1797 ii, 2a–b (1-3) <u>Terra Regis; Hatfield Broad Oak</u>: TRE Earl Harold held twenty hides of land in Hatfield Broad Oak. Now King William holds it. TRE there were forty men's plows there, now thirty-one and a half. This loss (*perditio*) was in the time of all the sheriffs and because of a mortality of beasts. A hide and thirty acres of land belonged to the church of this manor, and used to pay customs to the manor. Swein, however, took it away (*abstulit*) after he lost (*perdidit*) the sheriffdom. A sokeman with half a hide of land also belonged to the manor TRE. Geoffrey de Mandeville took this away (*abstulit*). Attached to this manor is a villein with one acre, which Count Eustace holds. There are also thirty acres there, which a smith held TRE. He was killed on account of theft (*latrocinium interfectus fuit*), and the King's reeve added this land to the manor. There were forty acres of woodland in this manor, which were held by King Edward's reeve. Osmund d'Anjou, however, disseised (*desaisiuit*) the King's reeve and this manor of the land and woodland. Robert Gernon now holds the forty acres and the woodland. TRW Robert Gernon also holds half a hide, which a sokeman held TRE. Three berewicks were attached to this manor as well TRE – Hertford, Amwell, and Hoddesdon – which lie in Hertfordshire, and which Ralph de Limesy now holds. Later we recovered (*recuperavimus*) half a hide, which a sokeman of Harold held TRE. Now Ralph de Marcey holds it in the fee of Haimo.

1798   ii, 2b–3a (1-4) <u>Terra Regis; Havering-atte-Bower</u>: TRE Earl Harold held ten hides of land in Havering-atte-Bower. Four freemen were attached to this manor with four hides of land, and they paid customs. Now Robert fitz Corbucion holds three of these hides and Hugh de Montfort the fourth hide. They have not paid customs from these hides since Robert and Hugh have held them. Robert fitz Corbucion also holds four and a half hides which a freeman held in this manor in the time of King Edward. A sokeman was also attached to Havering-atte-Bower with thirty acres, and he paid customs. Now John fitz Waleran holds.

1799   ii, 3a (1-6) <u>Terra Regis; Latchingdon</u>: TRE Alwine, a freeman, held half a hide and thirty acres of land in Latchingdon. Afterwards Theodric Pointel annexed (*invasit*) it. Now the King has this.

1800   ii, 3a (1-8) <u>Terra Regis; White Roding</u>: Goldstan, a sokeman of King William, holds a hide of land in White Roding. He has never paid service nor customs for it. For this he has given a pledge (*dedit vadem*).

1801   ii, 3b (1-9) <u>Terra Regis; Great Chesterford</u>: TRE Earl Ælfgar held ten hides of land in Great Chesterford. Now Picot the Sheriff holds it in the King's hand. TRE another one and a half hides of land were attached to this manor in Cambridgeshire. Hardwin de Scales now holds it, but the hundred does not know how. The half hide, on which a man lived, was in demesne. The hide was held by a sokeman, who paid soke in the King's manor. And Picot holds another half hide, which a sokeman held TRE.

1802   ii, 3b (1-11) <u>Terra Regis; Shalford</u>: TRE Earl Ælfgar held five hides and thirty acres of land in Shalford. Afterwards the Queen held it. Now Otto the Goldsmith holds it at rent in the King's hand (*ad censum in manu regis*). Thirty acres of woodland are missing (*desunt*), which the Queen gave (*dedit*) to Richard fitz Gilbert. TRE half a hide of soke lay Shalford: now Walter fitz Gilbert holds it.

1803   ii, 4a (1-13) <u>Terra Regis; Wethersfield</u>: TRE Earl Ælfgar held two hides less fifteen acres of land in Wethersfield. Now Picot holds it in the King's hand. Thirty acres of land lay in this manor TRE, which were held in alms by a priest and paid soke. Another eight and half acres belonged to another church. Gilbert fitz Warin now holds these two lands. Another seven and half acres belonged to this manor, which Count Alan now holds. There are also forty-five acres of demesne which Swein holds from the fee (*ad feudum*) of Richard fitz Gilbert.

1804 ii, 4b (1-16) Terra Regis; "Vluuinescherham": TRE four freemen held one hide less six acres of land in "Vluuinescherham." Now they are not there. Theodric Pointel claims (*calumpniatur*) this land in exchange (*pro escangio*).

1805 ii, 4b (1-16a) Terra Regis; unidentified land: Freemen hold fifty-one acres of land that are not in the King's farm. A servant (*famulus*) of the King holds it and does not pay tax.

1806 ii, 4b (1-17a) Terra Regis; unidentified land: TRE two freemen held six acres and lay in the King's hundred. Now Baynard holds them.

1807 ii, 4b–5a (1-19) Terra Regis; Stanway: TRE Earl Harold held five and a half hides in Stanway. Now King William holds them. Raymond Gerald took away (*tulit*) a villein with half a hide of land, which paid customs. Northmann used to hold it, and he paid customs, but Raymond took it away (*abstulit*) and Roger similarly. Also Roger the Poitevin has taken (*accepit*) a villein who holds an acre; and Ingelric took away (*abstulit*) Beorhtgifu – she held eighteen acres of land and paid 32d. each year to the manor.

1808 ii, 5a–b (1-24) Terra Regis; Writtle: TRE Earl Harold held sixteen hides of land in Writtle. Now King William holds this for fourteen hides. After the King came into England, Ingelric encroached upon (*praeoccupavit*) two hides of Harold's reeve, which had paid all customs to this manor; that is, £12. Count Eustace now holds this, because his antecessor was seised (*fuit saisitus*) of it. In Harold's time there was also a swineherd who lived on a virgate and fifteen acres of this land, and he paid customs to the manor. After King William came, Robert Gernon took (*accepit*) the swineherd from the manor and made him a forester in the King's woodland. TRE Harold gave (*dedit*) a hide in Writtle to one of his priests, but the hundred does not know if he gave (*dederit*) it freely or in alms. Now Robert bishop of Hereford holds it. There is also half a hide there, which a sokeman held freely. He paid soke in the manor, although he could go where he wished with the land. Count Eustace attached (*adiunxit*) this man to his land.

1809 ii, 5b–6a (1-25) Terra Regis; Maldon: Sixteen pence have always come from two of Eudo Dapifer's houses in Maldon, but the King has not had them since he came into this land.

1810 ii, 5b–6a (1-25) Terra Regis; Maldon: There is a sokeman in Maldon with forty-nine acres of land, valued at 5s. Ranulf Peverel had a custom of 3s. each year from the sokeman. In the time of King Edward, however, Ranulf's antecessor had nothing except the sokeman's commendation.

1811 ii, 6a–b (1-27) Terra Regis; Lawford: TRE Earl Harold held ten hides of land in Lawford. Now King William holds it. In the time of King Edward seventeen sokemen with a hide of land lay in this manor, and they paid all customs. After King William came into this land, and while Baynard was sheriff, Theodric Pointel seized (*occupavit*) this land. Now it is in the King's hand, and thirteen men hold it. Peter de Valognes received (*recepit*) twenty-one oxen in the demesne of this manor, 4 rounceys, 45 swine, and 190 sheep. TRE a berewick of four hides also belonged to this manor. Ingelric annexed (*invasit*) it. Now Count Eustace holds it. TRE twenty-one sokemen who held a hide, two virgates, and five acres also belonged to this manor. Roger de Raismes has them in exchange (*per escangio*), so he says, and for this he vouches Swein to warranty (*vocat liberatorem*). TRE there were also four sokemen in this manor, who held half a hide and fifteen acres of land and paid all customs. Richard fitz Gilbert annexed (*invasit*) them in the time when Swein was sheriff. They are now in the King's hand, because there was no one on Richard's behalf who could say how he came to have them (*nullus fuit ex parte eius qui dixisset quomodo eos habuerit*). TRE this was valued at 13s., and until now, Richard has had this rent (*censum*). Waleran annexed (*invasit*) a sokeman with thirty acres of land here. The value is 10s., and until now Waleran has had this rent (*censum*). Hagebeorht holds another thirty acres in Lawford, which a sokeman held TRE, and for this Hagebeorht vouches Swein to warranty (*revocat liberatorem*). Count Eustace also holds one and a half hides and forty-five acres of land in Lawford, which Ingelric annexed (*invasit*). Also there, the Bishop of Bayeux holds half a hide, which Ralph son of Thurold holds under him; Ranulf brother of Ilger holds fifteen acres; Hugh de Montfort thirty acres; Ralph Baynard half a hide and thirty-five acres; Eudo Dapifer thirty-seven and half acres; Roger, a man of the Bishop of London, a hide and thirty acres; Walter the Deacon five acres. All of this land paid customs to Lawford in the time of King Edward.

1812   ii, 7a (1-28) <u>Terra Regis; Newport</u>: TRE Earl Harold held eight and a half hides of land in Newport. Now King William holds it. Robert Gernon holds two sokemen with two and a half hides of land, who belong to this manor and pay all customs. He took (*accepit*) them when Swein was sheriff. The hundred does not know how he came to have them, because neither a writ nor a legate came into the hundred on the King's behalf (*neque breve neque legatus ex parte regis in hundredo*) [saying] that the King had given (*dedisset*) this land to him. A clerk of Count Eustace had annexed (*invaserat*) another forty-two acres of this land and was holding them in Count Eustace's fee. The hundred testifies that these forty-two acres are in Newport, and because of this the King now has them. The clerk has been judged to be in the King's mercy concerning his body and his property (*iudicatus est esse in misericordia regis et de omni cessu suo et de corpore suo*).

1813   ii, 9b (3-2) <u>Bishop of London; Orsett</u>: TRE and TRW the Bishop of London holds thirteen hides of land in Orsett, but Count Eustace holds one of these hides, which is not one of his 100 manors.

1814   ii, 10a (3-6, 7) <u>Bishop of London; Layer Marney</u>: TRE two freemen held three hides of land in Layer Marney, and a free woman held three hides there. Now Roger holds this land from the Bishop of London. Bishop William established title (*deratiocinavit*) to these two manors, for the use of his church after the death of King Edward, by King William's order (*iussu*).

1815   ii, 10a (3-8) <u>Bishop of London; Rayne</u>: TRE Bishop William held four hides and thirty acres of land in Rayne. In the time of King William fifteen acres were added to this manor. A freeman held them TRE, so the hundred testifies.

1816 ii, 10a–b (3-9) Bishop of London; Southminster: TRW the Bishop of London holds thirty hides of land in Southminster in demesne. King Cnut took away (*tulit*) this land, but Bishop William recovered (*recuperavit*) it in the time of King William.

1817 ii, 10b (3-10) Bishop of London; Copford: TRW the Bishop of London holds one and a half hides of land and eighteen acres of land in Copford in demesne. TRE twelve sokemen belonged to this manor – now ten – holding one hide and two and half acres of land. They could not withdraw, so the hundred testifies. TRE the bishop held seventeen acres in this manor. Now Robert Gernon holds them by gift (*de dono*) of the King. Robert also holds a virgate of land which the bishop held. A freeman held it from him on condition that he could go where he wished, but the soke remained in the manor.

1818 ii, 10b (3-11) Bishop of London; Little Warley: TRE Earl Gyrth held four hides less fifteen acres of land in Little Warley. Now Humphrey holds it from the Bishop of London. After he crossed the sea, King William gave (*dedit*) this manor to Bishop William, because in ancient times (*in antiquo tempore*) it was the Church of St. Paul.

1819 ii, 11b (4-8) Fee of Bishop of London; Little Burstead: TRE Godwine held three hides of land in Little Burstead. Now Walter holds it from the Bishop of London. A woodland for sixty swine along with another thirty acres are claimed from the time of King Edward (*calumpniantur de tempore regis Edwardi*).

1820 ii, 11b–12a (4-9) Fee of Bishop of London; Corringham: TRE Sigar, a freeman, held four hides and ten acres of land in Corringham. Now William holds it from the Bishop of London. There are now three and a half hides and ten acres there. A half hide was taken away from there (*est inde ablata*). The Bishop of Bayeux holds it.

1821 ii, 12a (4-10) Fee of Bishop of London; Horndon on the Hill: TRE Godwine, a free man, held one and a half hides of land in Horndon on the Hill. Now William holds it from the Bishop of London. A half hide has been taken away (*ablata est*) from this manor, which the Bishop of Bayeux holds.

1822 ii, 12b (5-1) Canons of the Bishopric of London; Lee Chapel: TRE Eadgifu held half a hide and thirty acres of land in Lee Chapel freely. The canons of St. Paul's now hold it. This land has been claimed (*calumpniata est*) for the King's use.

1823 ii, 12b (5-2) Canons of the Bishopric of London; Chingford: TRE the Church of St. Paul held six hides of land in Chingford. From this manor Peter de Valognes took away (*abstulit*) a hide of land, eight acres of meadow, and a woodland for fifty swine. They belonged there in the time of King Edward. Geoffrey de Mandeville also took away (*tulit*) ten acres of meadow from the same manor.

1824 ii, 13a (5-5) <u>Canons of the Bishopric of London; Tillingham</u>: TRE the Church of St. Paul, London held twenty hides and six acres of land in Tillingham. Besides this land, ten acres, which lie in this manor, were given (*datae fuerunt*) to the Church.

1825 ii, 13a (5-6) <u>Canons of the Bishopric of London; Norton Mandeville</u>: TRE Godgyth held half a hide of land in Norton Mandeville. Now St. Paul's, London holds it. Godgyth gave (*dedit*) this land to St. Paul's after King William came into England, but St. Paul's shows neither a writ nor the consent of the King (*non ostendit brevem neque concessum regis*) for it.

1826 ii, 13a–b (5-7, 8) <u>Canons of the Bishopric of London; Navestock</u>: TRE two freemen, Howard and Wulfsige, held five hides less twenty acres of land in Navestock as two manors. Since King William came into this land, St. Paul's, London has held it. The canons say they had it by the King's gift (*ex dono regis*). TRE Thurstan the Red held one hide and forty acres in the other Navestock. Now St. Paul's has annexed (*invasit*) it, and it is with the their other land in Navestock. A priest holds another half hide and twenty acres of land in Navestock, but the hundred bears (*fert*) testimony that it is from St. Paul's. Now it is in the King's hand.

1827 ii, 13b (5-10) <u>Canons of the Bishopric of London; Heybridge</u>: The Church of St. Paul's, London has always held eight hides of land in Heybridge as a manor, but Ralph Baynard now holds half a hide of this land. The hundred does not know how he came to have it.

1828 ii, 13b–14a (5-12) <u>Canons of the Bishopric of London; Barling</u>: The Church of St. Paul's, London has always held two and a half hides less fifteen acres of land in Barling. TRE a freeman held another half hide and ten acres there. Now St. Paul's holds this land as well. The canons seized (*occupaverunt*) this land after the King came into England.

1829 ii, 14a (6-1) <u>Westminster Abbey; South Benfleet</u>: TRW Westminster Abbey has seven hides and thirty acres of land in South Benfleet: TRE it lay in the Church of St. Mary, South Benfleet. But King William gave (*dedit*) the church with the land to Westminster Abbey. Ingelric gave (*dedit*) an eighth hide of the same Church of St. Mary to the Church of St. Martin le Grand and it is still there, so the county (*consulatus*) testifies, without the King's order (*sine iussu regis*).

1830 ii, 14a (6-4) <u>Westminster Abbey; Fanton</u>: TRE Æthelstan Stric held a hide of land in Fanton. It has been claimed (*calumpniata est*) for the King's use, because it came to Westminster Abbey through a false writ (*per falsum brevem*).

1831 ii, 14b (6-8) <u>Westminster Abbey; Feering</u>: TRE Harold held four hides and thirty acres of land in Feering. Now Westminster Abbey holds it. Mauger, a man of the Archbishop of Canterbury, annexed (*invasit*) a freeman there against the King, who was from St. Peter's manor TRE, and who held half a virgate of land. Now this is in the King's hand.

1832 ii, 14b–15a (6-9) <u>Westminster Abbey; Kelvedon Hatch</u>: TRE Æthelric held two hides of land in Kelvedon Hatch. Now Westminster Abbey holds it. This Æthelric departed for a naval battle against King William, and when he returned he fell ill (*cecidit in infirmitate*). He then gave (*dedit*) St. Peter's this manor, but only one man from the county knows this (*sed nullus hominum ex comitatu scit hoc nisi unus*). St. Peter's has held Kelvedon Hatch in this way until now. The monks have had neither a writ nor a servant of the King on their behalf (*neque brevem neque famulum regis ex parte habuerunt*) since King William came into this land.

1833 ii, 15a (6-11) <u>Westminster Abbey; North Ockendon</u>: TRE Harold held two hides less forty acres of land in North Ockendon. Now Westminster Abbey holds it. This land is in exchange (*pro escangio*), since the King crossed the sea.

1834 ii, 15a (6-12) <u>Westminster Abbey; Wennington</u>: Westminster Abbey has always held two and a half hides of land in Wennington. A freeman put (*misit*) half a hide in Westminster Abbey, but Robert the Lascivious, a man of Robert Gernon, encroached upon (*praeocupavit*) it.

1835 ii, 15a (6-15) <u>Westminster Abbey; Paglesham</u>: TRW Westminster Abbey holds one and a half hides of land in Paglesham. A thegn gave (*dedit*) the abbey this land when he went with Harold to the battle in York.

1836 ii, 15b (7-1) <u>Bishop of Durham; Waltham</u>: TRE Earl Harold held forty hides of land in Waltham. Now it is in the lands of the Bishop of Durham. Two sokemen belong to this manor. They held six hides TRE, now five. Waltham Holy Cross has half of the sixth hide; William de Warenne took away (*tulit*) the other half. William de Warenne also took away (*tulit*) another hide less fifteen acres, which still belonged to this manor. And Ranulf brother of Ilger [has taken away] thirty acres of land and four of meadow. The Bishop's men assessed what Earl Harold held at £63 5s. 4d.; but now the value, so the other men of the hundred testify, is £100. A gate in London belongs to the manor, which the King gave (*dedit*) to the bishop's antecessor.

1837 ii, 16a–b (8-8) <u>Canons of Waltham Holy Cross; Debden (in Loughton)</u>: Waltham Holy Cross has always held three hides and forty acres of land in Debden. A freeman held forty acres there, which the Church annexed (*invasit*) after the King came into this land, and it still holds them.

1838 ii, 16b (8-9) <u>Canons of Waltham Holy Cross; South Weald</u>: Waltham Holy Cross has always held South Weald. TRE there were two hides; now one and a half. Geoffrey de Mandeville has the other half hide, but the hundred does not know why he has it. Geoffrey says that he has it in exchange (*pro escangio*). A sokeman, who held a carucate of land, lay in this manor, but Robert Gernon now has this by the King's gift (*ex dono regis*), so he himself says.

1839 ii, 17b (9-1) <u>Barking Abbey; Mucking</u>: TRW Barking Abbey holds seven hides of land in Mucking. Thurold of Rochester took away (*abstulit*) thirty acres of this land, and they now lie in the fee of the Bishop of Bayeux.

1840 ii, 17b (9-2) <u>Barking Abbey: Bulphan</u>: TRW Barking Abbey holds seven hides of land in Bulphan. Ravengar took away (*tulit*) twenty-four acres of this land.

1841 ii, 17b (9-5) <u>Barking Abbey; 6 freemen in Barstable Hundred</u>: TRW six freemen in Barstable Hundred hold two hides and fifty acres of land. These men existed freely (*libere exstiterunt*) at Barking, but the King can now do what he pleases with them (*quod sibi placuerit*).

1842 ii, 17b–18a (9-7) <u>Barking Abbey; Barking</u>: Barking Abbey has always held thirty hides of land in Barking. TRE it was valued at £80; now the same, so the Englishmen say, but the Frenchmen assess it at £100. In London half a church belongs to this manor, which paid 6s. 8d. TRE, but now pays nothing. TRE twenty-four acres also belonged to this manor, which Jocelyn Lorimer has taken away (*tulit*).

1843 ii, 18a (9-10) <u>Barking Abbey; Stifford</u>: TRW Barking Abbey has forty acres of land in Stifford. There were another thirty acres there, which William de Warenne, so he himself says, now has in exchange (*pro escangio*).

1844 ii, 18b (9-14) <u>Barking Abbey; Tollesbury</u>: Barking Abbey has always held eight hides of land in Tollesbury. Ranulf Peverel holds a hide there as well, which Siward held from the abbey, and Ranulf wants to do such service (*ipse vult facere tale servitium*) as did his antecessor. The abbess, however, does not want it, because this land was for the victualing of the abbey. Oda, a man of Swein, took (*accepit*) another ten acres there, which were from the abbey: this is testified by the hundred. But Oda calls his lord as warrantor for this (*inde vocat dominum suum ad tutorem*).

1845 ii, 18b (10-1) <u>Ely Abbey; Broxted</u>: Ely Abbey has always held three hides of land in Broxted. Nine acres were taken away (*ablatae sunt*) from this manor in the time of King William, and Eudo Dapifer holds them. There are also two carucates of land of Broxted's demesne, which Eudo holds.

1846 ii, 19a (10-2) <u>Ely Abbey; Aythorp Roding</u>: Ely has always held Aythorp Roding. TRE there were three hides and forty-five acres of land there; now there are two hides and forty-five acres. William de Warenne took away (*tulit*) the third hide, which lay in demesne TRE.

1847 ii, 19a (10-3) <u>Ely Abbey; Rettendon</u>: TRE Ely Abbey held Rettendon as twenty hides. The abbey now holds it for sixteen and a half hides. TRE Siward held a hide and thirty acres of land there from Ely; now Ranulf Peverel holds it from the King, but the hundred testifies that it is the abbey's. TRE the abbey also held two hides and thirty acres of land in Rettendon, and Leofsunu held this from Ely Abbey. Eudo now holds it from the abbot, because his antecessor held. The hundred, however, testifies that Leofsunu could not sell it without the abbot's permission.

1848 ii, 19a–b (10-5) <u>Ely Abbey; Littlebury</u>: Ely Abbey has always held twenty-five hides of land in Littlebury. William Cardon, a man of Geoffrey de Mandeville, unjustly took (*accepit . . . iniuste*) twenty-four acres of this land's woodland when Swein was sheriff, so the hundred testifies.

1849 ii, 19b (11-2) <u>Bury St. Edmund's; Harlow</u>: Bury St. Edmund's has always held one and a half hides of land in Harlow. Three hides were added to this manor in the time of King William, which five freemen held TRE.

1850 ii, 20a (11-7) Bury St. Edmund's; Little Waltham: TRE Stanheard held two hides of land less fifteen acres in Little Waltham. Bury St. Edmund's holds it by gift of the King (*de dono regis*).

1851 ii, 20b (12-1) Church of St. Martin le Grand; Good Easter: TRE Æthelmær, a thegn of King Edward, held four hides and fifty acres of land in Good Easter. Count Eustace gave (*dedit*) it to the Church of St. Martin le Grand. TRE a berewick was also attached to this manor with half a hide and twenty acres of land, but Count Eustace kept it back for himself (*sibi retinuit*).

1852 ii, 21b (15-1) Holy Trinity, Caen; Felsted: TRE Earl Ælfgar held five hides of land in Felsted. Now the Abbey of Holy Trinity, Caen holds Felsted for four hides. The fifth hide is not in the manor, because King William gave (*dedit*) three virgates to Roger God-Save-the-Ladies, and the fourth virgate to Gilbert fitz Solomon.

1853 ii, 22a (17-1, 2) St. Ouen's Abbey; West Mersea: TRE and TRW St. Ouen's Abbey holds twenty hides of land in West Mersea. A house in Colchester belonged to this manor, but Waleran took it away (*abstulit*). TRW in the Hundred of Winstree there are eight sokemen of the King, who hold 107 acres of land. St. Ouen's Abbey has two-thirds of this. Ingelric took away (*tulit*) two sokemen with half a hide and thirty acres of land. Count Eustace now has them. Two sokemen, furthermore, have been added to the King's manor at Layer, in another hundred. Of all this soke, St. Ouen's has two-thirds, and always two-thirds, of the forfeitures of the hundred (*de forisfacturis de hundret*). The King has the remaining third.

1854 ii, 22b (18-1) Bishop of Bayeux; Vange: TRE two freemen held five and a half hides of land in Vange. TRW Ralph son of Thurold of Rochester holds it from the Bishop of Bayeux. A freeman held thirty acres of this land, which were added to this manor in the time of King William, but it is not known how.

1855 ii, 22b (18-2) Bishop of Bayeux; Great Burstead: TRE Ingvar, a thegn, held ten hides of land in Great Burstead. Now the Bishop of Bayeux holds it in demesne. Twenty-eight freemen were added to this manor in the time of King William with twenty-eight hides and five acres of land.

1856 ii, 22b–23a (18-5) Bishop of Bayeux; Ingrave: TRE a freeman held two hides of land in Ingrave. Now Ralph son of Thurold of Rochester holds it from the Bishop of Bayeux. Seven freemen with three hides of land were added to this manor in the time of King William.

1857 ii, 23a (18-6) Bishop of Bayeux; Ramsden Cray: TRE two freemen held three hides of land in Ramsden Cray. Now two knights hold it from the Bishop of Bayeux. Ravengar, so the English say, took land away (*abstulit*) from one of these freemen, and Robert fitz Wimarc [took] land away from the other one, but they do not know how it has come to the Bishop of Bayeux.

1858 ii, 23a (18-7) Bishop of Bayeux; Wheatley, Wickford: TRW Pointel and Osbern hold two hides of land in Wheatley and Wickford from the Bishop of

Bayeux. Two freemen held it in the time of King Edward, but Ravengar took it away (*abstulit*) from them. Now the English do not know how it has come into the hand of the Bishop of Bayeux.

1859 ii, 23a–b (18-11) Bishop of Bayeux; Chadwell: TRW Ralph son of Thurold of Rochester holds Chadwell from the Bishop of Bayeux. TRE King Edward's reeve Eadweald held it for one and a half hides. Thirty acres of this land were part of another manor TRE.

1860 ii, 24a (18-22) Bishop of Bayeux; Dengie: TRW a knight of the Bishop of Bayeux holds Dengie. TRE Sigeric held it for two and a half hides. TRE two freemen were in this manor with forty-seven acres of land. The same knight seized (*occupavit*) this.

1861 ii, 24a (18-23) Bishop of Bayeux; Bradwell Quay (formerly Hackfleet): TRW a knight of the Bishop of Bayeux holds Bradwell Quay. TRE Alweard, a freeman, held it for two hides and thirty acres. There was a freeman in this vill with thirty acres of land. He was outlawed (*udlagavit*). Now Swein's men have taken (*acceperunt*) the land and still hold it.

1862 ii, 24b (18-32) Bishop of Bayeux; Stifford: TRE Ælfric, a freeman, held a hide and thirty acres of land in Stifford. Now Hugh holds it from the Bishop of Bayeux. Fifteen acres of this manor are in William Peverel's soke in Grays Thurrock, so the county testifies. Thirty acres of land, which the neighbors gave (*vicini dederunt*) in alms, lie in the church of this manor.

1863 ii, 24b–25a (18-34) Bishop of Bayeux; Stifford: Gilbert, the Bishop of Bayeux's man, used to hold one and a half hides of land in Stifford. Now Ralph son of Thurold of Rochester holds it from the Bishop of Bayeux. Except for ten acres, this land lay in William Peverel's manor of Grays Thurrock TRE: this is testified by the hundred.

1864 ii, 25a (18-36) Bishop of Bayeux; South Hanningfield: TRE Frithebert held nine hides of land in South Hanningfield. Now Ralph son of Thurold holds it from the Bishop of Bayeux. Twenty-three freemen in South Hanningfield held another fourteen hides of land and could withdraw without the permission of the lord of South Hanningfield. The bishop now holds them, but the county does not know how he has them. Thurold of Rochester encroached upon (*praeoccupavit*) these hides. Ely Abbey claims (*calumpniatur*) two hides and three virgates of this land, which two men held TRE. The hundred testifies that these men held their land freely, but were commended only to the Abbot of Ely.

1865 ii, 25b (18-43, 44) Bishop of Bayeux; Thorrington, Alresford: TRE Æthelstan held four hides of land in Thorrington. Thurold of Rochester annexed (*invasit*) this land. Now Ralph son of Thurold holds it from the Bishop of Bayeux. TRE a freeman held half a hide in Alresford, which Thurold also annexed (*invasit*). The hundred does not know how he had this land, because neither a legate nor any other man came on his behalf, who might have established title (*neque legatus neque alius homo venit ex parte sua qui derationasset*) to this land. Now it is in the King's hand with the other land.

1866 ii, 26a (20-1) <u>Count Eustace; Fobbing</u>: TRE Beorhtmaer, a thegn of King Edward, held five hides of land in Fobbing. Now Count Eustace holds it in demesne. Thurold took away (*tulit*) thirty acres of this manor, which are now in the Bishop of Bayeux's fee. Besides this, Ingelric added twenty-two freemen to this manor, who hold fifteen and a half hides and fifteen and half acres of land.

1867 ii, 26b (20-4) <u>Count Eustace; Orsett</u>: TRE the Bishop of London held a hide of land in Orsett, and Ingelric held it from the bishopric. Now Count Eustace holds it. It does not lie in the count's one hundred manors.

1868 ii, 26b (20-5) <u>Count Eustace; "Gravesandam" (lost in Tilbury)</u>: TRE Harold held a hide of land in "Gravesandam," and Ingelric held from him. Now Count Eustace holds it. This hide does not lie in the count's one hundred manors.

1869 ii, 26b (20-6) <u>Count Eustace; White Notley</u>: TRE Harold held White Notley. Now the thegn Ælfric holds it from Count Eustace. Ralph de Marcy took away (*tulit*) thirty acres from this manor. They lie in the fee of Haimo Dapifer's son.

1870 ii, 26b–27a (20-7) <u>Count Eustace; Coggeshall</u>: TRW Count Eustace holds three and a half hides and thirty-three acres of land in Coggeshall in demesne. TRE Cola, a freeman, held it. Thirty-eight acres of land have been added to this manor, which a freeman holds from the King.

1871 ii, 27a (20-8) <u>Count Eustace; Rivenhall</u>: TRE Queen Edith held two and a half hides of land in Rivenhall. Now Count Eustace holds it in demesne. Richard de Sackville took half a mill away (*abstulit*) from this manor.

1872 ii, 27b (20-17) <u>Count Eustace: Purleigh</u>: TRE Eadgifu held a hide and thirty acres of land in Purleigh. Count Eustace now holds it, but it was not from Ingelric's fee.

1873 ii, 27b–28a (20-19) <u>Count Eustace; Langenhoe</u>: TRW Count Eustace holds seven hides of land in Langenhoe. TRE Ingelric held it. In King William's time Ingelric added two hides that a freeman held TRE, and half a hide that three freemen held.

1874 ii, 28a (20-22) <u>Count Eustace; Shortgrove</u>: TRE a freeman held a hide and thirty acres of land in Shortgrove. Now Æthelwulf holds it from Count Eustace. Ingelric seized (*occupavit*) this land in King William's time.

1875 ii, 28b (20-25) <u>Count Eustace; Claret</u>: TRE Leodmær, a free man, held one and a half hides and thirty-five acres of land in Claret. Now Count Eustace holds it in demesne. In the time of King William, Ingelric added a freeman to this manor, who had fifteen acres of land.

1876 ii, 28b (20-26) <u>Count Eustace; Belchamp Otten</u>: TRE Leodmær, a freeman, held a hide and forty-five acres of land in Belchamp Otten. Now Wulfmær holds it from Count Eustace. Five sokemen lie in this manor, two of whom Ingelric seized (*occupavit*) in the time of King William. They were freemen.

1877 ii, 28b (20-27) <u>Count Eustace; Steeple Bumpstead</u>: TRW Æthelwulf de Marck holds half a hide of land in Steeple Bumpstead from Count Eustace. A freeman held it TRE. Ingelric added a freeman to this manor with three and half acres of land.

1878   ii, 29a–b (20-34) <u>Count Eustace; Maldon</u>: TRW the Church of St. Martin le Grand holds Maldon from the Count of Boulogne. TRE a freeman held it for one and a half hides and thirty acres. Afterwards Ingelric held it. TRE a freeman also held thirty acres of land in Maldon, which Ingelric seized (*occupavit*). Now St. Martin's le Grand holds all of this land from Count Eustace, as well as another freeman with thirty acres of land. Ingelric put (*posuit*) these men in his hall.

1879   ii, 29b (20-36) <u>Count Eustace; Tey (Great, Little, or Marks)</u>: TRE a freeman held three and a half hides of land in Tey. Now Count Eustace holds it. Five freemen, who were not in this manor TRE, held eighty-eight acres of land there. The count now has them because his antecessor was seised (*saisitus fuit*).

1880   ii, 30a (20-38) <u>Count Eustace; East Donyland</u>: TRE Eadric held one and a half hides of land in East Donyland. Now Count Eustace holds it in demesne. A freeman held another half hide there, which the count now holds. Ingelric had it, but the hundred does not know how he should have it.

1881   ii, 30a (20-41) <u>Count Eustace; Colne</u>: TRE Ælfric Bigga held a virgate and ten acres of land in Colne. Now Robert holds it from Count Eustace. Ælfric held the land freely, but Ingelric had it after King William came. The hundred does not know how.

1882   ii, 30b (20-43) <u>Count Eustace; Stanford Rivers</u>: TRE Leofwine held nine hides of land in Stanford Rivers. Afterwards Ingelric held it, and now Count Eustace holds it in demesne. A freeman held forty acres in the same place, but Ingelric took (*accepit*) him, joining him to this manor. TRE Beorhtwine also held twenty acres of land in Stanford Rivers, which Ingelric attached to his manor.

1883   ii, 30b (20-45) <u>Count Eustace; Laver</u>: TRE Leofwine held a hide and forty acres of land in Laver. Alwine held the other half of this manor, also assessed at one hide and forty acres. But Ingelric joined them to his manor. Now Count Eustace holds all of this in demesne. TRE another freeman held forty acres of land in the same place, which Ingelric added to this manor. Now Ralph holds this from Count Eustace.

1884   ii, 30b–31a (20-46) <u>Count Eustace; Chipping Ongar</u>: TRE Æthelgyth held a hide in Chipping Ongar. Now Count Eustace holds it in demesne. In the same place a freeman held a half hide, which was from this manor. Now Ralph Baynard holds it.

1885   ii, 31a (20-49) <u>Count Eustace; Fyfield</u>: TRW Richard holds forty acres of land in Fyfield from the Count of Boulogne. TRE Beorhtmær held it. A freeman held another ten acres there, but Ingelric annexed (*invasit*) them.

1886   ii, 31a (20-51) <u>Count Eustace; Newland</u>: TRE Harold held three hides of land in Newland. Now Mauger holds it from Count Eustace. Ingelric annexed (*invasit*) this manor. The hundred testifies that it lay in Writtle TRE, and that the count now holds it.

1887 ii, 31a–b (20-52) <u>Count Eustace; Little Baddow</u>: TRE Leofwine held five hides of land in Little Baddow. Now Lambert holds it from Count Eustace. Ingelric annexed (*invasit*) this land after King William came.

1888 ii, 31b (20-53) <u>Count Eustace; Runwell</u>: TRE Leofstan held a hide of land in Runwell. Now Lambert holds it from Count Eustace. Ingelric annexed (*invasit*) it.

1889 ii, 31b (20-54) <u>Count Eustace; Runwell</u>: TRE Eadgifu held four hides of land in Runwell. Now Æthelwulf holds it from Count Eustace. Ingelric annexed (*invasit*) it.

1890 ii, 31b (20-55) <u>Count Eustace; Little Waltham</u>: TRE Leofstan held two hides and a virgate of land in Little Waltham. Now Lambert holds it from Count Eustace. Ingelric annexed (*invasit*) it.

1891 ii, 31b–32a (20-56) <u>Count Eustace; Boreham</u>: TRE fourteen freemen held eight hides and twenty-three acres of land in Boreham. Now Lambert holds it from Count Eustace. Ingelric annexed (*invasit*) this after King William came into this land. Ranulf Peverel claims (*calumpniatur*) half a hide and eighteen acres, that lie in the church of this manor, along with half the church. Ingelric was not seised of this (*non fuit saisitus*). Count Eustace, however, gave (*dedit*) it to one of his knights, who vouches him to warranty (*revocat eam ad defensorem*) for it. There are also thirty acres there, which, so the hundred testifies, paid 12d. a year to Ranulf Peverel's antecessor.

1892 ii, 32b–33a (20-67) <u>Count Eustace; Birch (in Kirby-le-Soken)</u>: TRW Robert holds three hides in Birch from Count Eustace. Ingelric held them from the bishopric of London.

1893 ii, 33a (20-69) <u>Count Eustace; Lawford</u>: TRE Ælfric, a freeman, held two hides of land in Lawford. Later Ingelric held it as a manor. In the same place three sokemen held a half hide and thirty acres of land, which Ingelric annexed (*invasit*). Now Æthelwulf holds all of this from Count Eustace.

1894 ii, 33a–b (20-71) <u>Count Eustace; Chrishall</u>: TRE Ingvar held six hides of land in Chrishall. Now Count Eustace holds it in demesne from Ingelric's fee. Two sokemen belong to this manor with eight acres of land, along with another sokeman with eight acres. Ingelric seized (*occupavit*) them in the time of King William. TRE another sokeman with three virgates was attached to this manor, but William Cardon now holds from the fee of Geoffrey de Mandeville. He was paying 2d. per year.

1895 ii, 33b (20-73) <u>Count Eustace; Chishill (Great or Little)</u>: TRE Godric, a freeman, held two and a half hides of land in Chishill. Now Guy holds it from Count Eustace. A freeman was also there, who held half a hide of land. Ingelric seized (*occupavit*) it in the time of King William. Now Anselm holds it from the count.

1896 ii, 33b (20-74) <u>Count Eustace; Elmdon</u>: TRW Roger de Sommery holds fourteen hides of land in Elmdon from Count Eustace. TRE Almær, a freeman, held it. Ingelric seized (*occupavit*) this manor in the time of King William.

1897 ii, 34a (20-76) Count Eustace; Crawleybury: TRW Roger de Sommery holds thirty acres of land in Crawleybury from Count Eustace. TRE Leofsige, a freeman, held it. Ingelric seized (*occupavit*) this land in the time of King William.

1898 ii, 34a (20-77) Count Eustace; Bendysh: TRE Leodmær the Priest held four and a half hides of land in Bendysh. Now Count Eustace holds it in demesne. TRE a sokeman held another acre and a perch of land there, who Ingelric annexed (*invasit*). Now the count holds it.

1899 ii, 34a–b (20-79) Count Eustace; Little Bardfield: TRW Æthelwulf holds two hides and a virgate of land in Little Bardfield from Count Eustace. Northmann held it TRE. Afterwards Ingelric annexed him (*invasit eum*).

1900 ii, 34b (20-80) Count Eustace; Shopland: TRE a freeman held five hides of land in Shopland. Afterwards Ingelric held it, and now Count Eustace holds it in demesne. In the same place a freeman held a half hide and thirty acres of land, which Ingelric seized (*occupavit*).

1901 ii, 36a (22-3) William de Warenne; Housham: TRE Holefest, a freeman, held a hide and three virgates of land in Housham. Now Richard holds it from William de Warenne. A virgate was added to this manor in the time of King William, which Wulfric, a freeman, held TRE.

1902 ii, 36b (22-7) William de Warenne; High Roding: TRE the Abbot of Ely held two and a half hides of land in High Roding. Now William de Watteville holds them from William de Warenne.

1903 ii, 36b (22-8) William de Warenne; Leaden Roding: TRW Walter holds Leaden Roding from William de Warenne. TRE a free woman held it for two and a half hides. Now there are three and a half hides there. The third hide, so the hundred testifies, lay in Ely in the time of King Edward.

1904 ii, 37a–b (22-13) William de Warenne; Hunt's Hall (formerly Pooley): TRE twenty-three men held three and a half hides and thirteen acres of land in Hunt's Hall. Now William de Warenne holds it. Of this land, Richard holds twenty-five acres, and Gladiou holds three virgates. William claims (*reclamat*) these lands in exchange (*pro escangio*).

1905 ii, 37b (22-14) William de Warenne; Kenningtons: TRE three freemen held four hides of land in Kenningtons. Now William de Warenne holds it in exchange (*pro escangio*), so he says; and Wulfberht holds from him.

1906 ii, 37b (22-15) William de Warenne; West Hanningfield: TRE three freemen held four hides and twenty-seven acres of land in West Hanningfield as three manors. Now William holds this land through his exchange (*pro suo escangio*).

1907 ii, 38a (22-19) William de Warenne; Wendens Ambo: TRW Richard holds one and a half hides and thirty acres of land in Wendens Ambo from William de Warenne. TRE Wulfmær held it. This is in exchange (*pro escangio*).

1908 ii, 38a (22-21) William de Warenne; Great Chishill: TRE eight freemen held a hide and forty-five acres of land in Great Chishill. Now William de Warenne has it in exchange (*pro escangio*), and Richard holds from him.

1909 ii, 38a (22-23) William de Warenne; Plumberow: TRE a freeman held thirty acres of land in Plumberow. Now Ranulf holds it from William de Warenne. William claims (*reclamat*) these manors for an exchange in Normandy (*pro escangio de normannia*).

1910 ii, 38a (22-24) <u>William de Warenne; Fordham</u>: TRE Ælfric held twenty-five acres of land in Fordham freely. Now William de Warenne holds it by the same exchange (*pro eodem escangio*).

1911 ii, 38b (23-2) <u>Richard fitz Gilbert; Thaxted</u>: TRE Wihtgar held nine and a half hides in Thaxted. Now Richard fitz Gilbert holds them in demesne. The value is now £50, so the French and the Englishmen say, but Richard has given (*dedit*) this land to an Englishman for a rent (*ad censum*) of £60, but each year they are deficient (*deficiunt*) at least £10. TRE a sokeman of King Edward held seven and half acres of land in Thaxted, which were added to this manor in the time of King William. They have not paid the King's customs.

1912 ii, 38b–39a (23-3) <u>Richard fitz Gilbert; Great Dunmow</u>: TRE Wihtgar held two hides and thirty acres in Great Dunmow. Now Arnold holds them from Richard fitz Gilbert. Vitalis, a knight, claims (*calumpniatur*) this land, which, so he testifies, was held by a freeman TRE.

1913 ii, 40a–b (23-28, 29) <u>Richard fitz Gilbert; Boyton, Bures</u>: TRE Colseg, a freeman, held half a hide and ten acres of land in Boyton. Now Richard fitz Gilbert holds it. Forty-five acres were added to this manor TRW, which used to lie in the King's manor of Wethersfield. TRE Leofgifu, a free woman, held forty acres of land in Bures. Now Richard fitz Gilbert, so his men say, has both Boyton and Bures in exchange (*pro escangio*).

1914 ii, 40b (23-30) <u>Richard fitz Gilbert; Morrell Roding</u>: TRW Richard fitz Gilbert holds three virgates of land in Morrell Roding in demesne. TRE Coleman held it, and he was so free that he could go where he wished with sake and soke, although he was a man of Wihtgar, Richard's antecessor.

1915 ii, 40b (23-33) <u>Richard fitz Gilbert; Alresford</u>: TRE Algar held thirty-seven acres of land in Alresford. He now holds it from Richard fitz Gilbert. This land, so the hundred testifies, is from the King's soke of Lawford.

1916 ii, 41b (23-42) <u>Richard fitz Gilbert; Bardfield (Great or Little)</u>: TRW Widelard holds a hide of land in Bardfield from Richard fitz Gilbert. TRE two of Wihtgar's servants (*servientes*) held it. They paid neither customs nor the King's geld, nor could they go elsewhere, so the hundred testifies, without their lord's order (*sine iussu domini sui*).

1917 ii, 42a (24-1) <u>Swein of Essex; West Horndon</u>: TRE Alwine, a thegn of King Edward, held five hides and fifteen acres of land in West Horndon. King William gave (*dedit*) this land to Robert fitz Wimarc. Now Swein of Essex holds it, and Sigeric holds from him.

1918 ii, 42a (24-4) <u>Swein of Essex; Childerditch</u>: TRW Osbern holds a hide and forty acres of land in Childerditch from Swein of Essex. TRE Alwynn, a free woman, held this land. It is not known how it came to Robert fitz Wimarc.

1919 ii, 42a–b (24-5) <u>Swein of Essex; Horndon on the Hill</u>: TRE Ælfric the Priest, a freeman, held two hides and thirty acres of land in Horndon on the Hill. He gave (*dedit*) half a hide and thirty acres of this land to a church, but Swein of Essex took it away (*abstulit*) from the church. Payne now holds it from Swein.

1920 ii, 42b (24-9) <u>Swein of Essex; Wickford</u>: TRW Thorkil holds a half hide and thirty-five acres of land in Wickford from Swein of Essex. TRE Leofstan held it freely. Swein added a half hide and fifteen acres of land to this manor, which were held TRE by the free woman Beorhtgifu. He also added three freemen with forty-five acres of land, and one freeman with nine acres.

1921 ii, 44a (24-22) <u>Swein of Essex; Prittlewell</u>: TRW Swein of Essex holds seven and a half hides of land in Prittlewell in demesne. Two men have added thirty acres from another manor to the church of this manor.

1922 ii, 45b (24-41a) <u>Swein of Essex; Rochford Hundred</u>: TRW Swein of Essex has 100s. from the pleas (*de placitis*) of Rochford Hundred.

1923 ii, 46b (24-48) <u>Swein of Essex; Dunmow (Great or Little)</u>: TRE a freeman held thirty acres of land in Dunmow. Seven acres were added after the coming of King William: they belonged to another freeman. Now Eadmær holds these thirty-seven acres from Swein of Essex.

1924 ii, 46b (24-52) <u>Swein of Essex; Clavering Half-Hundred</u>: The half-hundred of Clavering is Swein of Essex's. Its pleas (*placita*) pay him 25s. a year.

1925 ii, 47b (24-59) <u>Swein of Essex; Stapleford Tawney</u>: TRW Sigeric holds five hides of land in Stapleford Tawney from Swein of Essex. TRE Godric held it. Of these five hides, Godric gave (*dedit*) four freely to ten of his freemen, and kept back (*retinuit*) one in demesne. After the King came, Robert fitz Wimarc held one hide by the King's gift (*dono regis*). Swein, his son, attached the four hides to this one, after his father's death.

1926 ii, 47b (24-60) <u>Swein of Essex; Theydon Mount</u>: TRW Robert holds three hides and eighty acres of land in Theydon Mount from Swein of Essex. Godric held it TRE. Swein holds this manor by gift of the King (*dono regis*), who gave (*dedit*) it to Robert fitz Wimarc, Swein's father.

1927 ii, 48a (24-65) <u>Swein of Essex; Foulton</u>: TRW Odard holds a hide less ten acres of land in Foulton from Swein of Essex. TRE Beorhtsige held it freely. When the King came into this land, Beorhtsige was outlawed (*utlagavit*), and Robert fitz Wimarc took (*accepit*) his land. Afterwards, Swein of Essex had it.

1928 ii, 49a (25-2) <u>Eudo Dapifer; Harlow</u>: TRW Thorgisl holds a hide and three virgates of land in Harlow from Eudo Dapifer. TRE Godwine, a freeman, held it. Fifty acres of this land were added in the time of King William by Lisois.

1929 ii, 49a (25-3) <u>Eudo Dapifer; Morrell Roding</u>: TRW Thorgisl holds one and a half hides and forty-five acres of land in Morrell Roding from Eudo Dapifer. Sæmær, a freeman, held it TRE. The Abbot of Ely claims (*calumpniatur*) this manor, by testimony (*teste*) of the hundred.

1930 ii, 49b (25-5) <u>Eudo Dapifer; Mundon</u>: TRE Godwine, the King's thegn, held ten hides of land in Mundon. Now Eudo Dapifer holds it in demesne.

Two freemen (*franci homines*) had half a hide there, which Lisois seized (*occupavit*), because one of them was outlawed (*utllagavit*).

1931 ii, 50a (25-12) <u>Eudo Dapifer; Broxted</u>: TRW Richard holds nine acres of land in Broxted from Eudo Dapifer, which two sokemen held from the Abbot of Ely TRE.

1932 ii, 50b (25-16) <u>Eudo Dapifer; Pledgdon</u>: TRW Richard holds five hides less twenty acres in Pledgdon from Eudo Dapifer. TRE two freemen held them. Geoffrey de Mandeville claims (*calumpniatur*) two hides of this land less twenty acres. The hundred testifies for him (*testatur ei*).

1933 ii, 51a (25-20) <u>Eudo Dapifer; Rettendon</u>: TRW Richard holds two hides and thirty acres of land in Rettendon from Eudo Dapifer. TRE Leofsunu held it. Ely Abbey claims (*calumpniatur*) this land, and the hundred bears (*fert*) testimony.

1934 ii, 52a (26-3) <u>Roger d'Auberville; Arkesden</u>: TRE Leofwine held a hide of land in Arkesden freely. Now Roger d'Auberville holds it in his exchange (*in suo escangio*).

1935 ii, 52a (26-4) <u>Roger d'Auberville; Arkesden</u>: TRE Wulfa held a hide of land in Arkesden freely. Now Roger d'Auberville holds it in exchange (*pro escangio*).

1936 ii, 52b–53a (27-3) <u>Hugh de Montfort; Leyton</u>: TRW Hugh de Montfort holds three hides and thirty acres of land in Leyton in demesne. TRE Alsige held it. In the time of King Edward one of these hides paid customs to the King's manor of Havering-atte-Bower. Now it does not.

1937 ii, 53a (27-6) <u>Hugh de Montfort; Purleigh</u>: TRE ten freemen held seven hides of land in Purleigh. Hugh de Montfort took (*recepit*) this land as two manors, but the hundred does not know this.

1938 ii, 54a (27-14) <u>Hugh de Montfort; Bensted</u>: TRW Robert holds four hides of land in Bensted from Hugh de Montfort. TRE Guthmund held it. The monks of Ely claim (*calumpniantur*) this manor, which was in the demesne of the abbey in the time of King Edward: this is testified by the hundred.

1939 ii, 54a (27-15) <u>Hugh de Montfort; Wix</u>: TRE Queen Edith held a hide of land in Wix along with the soke. Now Roger holds it from Hugh de Montfort. The hundred does not know how.

1940 ii, 54a–b (27-17) <u>Hugh de Montfort; Goldhanger</u>: TRW Hugh fitz Mauger, a knight of Hugh de Montfort, holds Goldhanger from Hugh. TRE Leofwine held it, and later Hager did, as a manor for one hide and fifteen acres. Hugh fitz Mauger took (*accepit*) fifteen acres from a free thegn, and put (*misit*) them with his manor. He did not, so the hundred testifies, have livery (*non habuit liberatorem*). Thus, it is in the King's hand.

1941 ii, 55a (28-6) <u>Haimo Dapifer; Ryes</u>: TRE Ralph holds half a hide of land in Ryes from Haimo Dapifer. TRE Earl Harold held it with the manor of Hatfield Broad Oak.

1942 ii, 55a (28-7) <u>Haimo Dapifer; Dunmow (Great or Little)</u>: TRE a freeman held thirty acres of land in Dunmow. Now Serlo holds it from Haimo

Dapifer. Seven and a half acres were added there in the time of King William.

1943 ii, 55a–b (28-8) <u>Haimo Dapifer; Roding</u>: TRW Serlo holds a hide and fifteen acres of land in Roding from Haimo Dapifer. TRE Vithi held it from Harold as one and a half hides. Eudo Dapifer holds forty-five acres of this land, which Haimo claims (*calumpniatur*).

1944 ii, 55b (28-9) <u>Haimo Dapifer; Little Wigborough</u>: TRW Vitalis holds seven hides of land and a hide of woodland in Little Wigborough from Haimo Dapifer. Gauti, a freeman, held this TRE. Bernard took away (*tulit*) the hide of woodland, and holds it from Baynard's fee. Ingelric took away (*tulit*) another half hide of land, which Count Eustace holds.

1945 ii, 56a (28-15) <u>Haimo Dapifer; Kelvedon Hatch</u>: TRW Ralph holds a hide and forty-five acres of land in Kelvedon Hatch from Haimo Dapifer. TRE Leofgifu held it. Haimo says that he has this land in his fee.

1946 ii, 57b (30-1) <u>Geoffrey de Mandeville; Marks Tey</u>: TRW Geoffrey de Mandeville holds one and a half hides and twenty acres of land in Marks Tey. TRE Wulfric held it. There were three freemen there, who held twelve acres of land, but they were not of this manor, which Geoffrey holds. Geoffrey, however, vouches himself to livery (*ipse revocat liberatorem*).

1947 ii, 57b (30-2) <u>Geoffrey de Mandeville; Shelley</u>: TRW Reginald holds eighty acres of land in Shelley from Geoffrey de Mandeville. TRE Leofdæg held it. This land was not from Esger's fee. Leofdæg was only Esger's man.

1948 ii, 57b (30-3) <u>Geoffrey de Mandeville; Abbess Roding</u>: TRW Geoffrey Martel holds three virgates of land in Abbess Roding from Geoffrey de Mandeville. TRE Leofhild held it. This land, which Geoffrey now holds, was in Barking Abbey, so the hundred testifies. Leofhild was only a man of Geoffrey's antecessor, and she could not put (*potuit . . . mittere*) this land anywhere except the abbey.

1949 ii, 57b–58a (30-4) <u>Geoffrey de Mandeville; Ockendon (North or South)</u>: TRE the thegn Frithebert held ten and a half hides and twenty acres of land freely in Ockendon. Now Thurold holds it from Geoffrey de Mandeville. Geoffrey, so he says, has this in exchange (*pro escangio*).

1950 ii, 59a (30-15) <u>Geoffrey de Mandeville; Chignall</u>: TRE Sæwine the Priest held fifteen acres of land in Chignall. Now Richard holds it from Geoffrey de Mandeville. In the same vill Eadsige also held fifteen acres. Richard also holds them from Geoffrey. Both Sæwine and Eadsige were so free, so the hundred testifies, that they could sell their land with sake and soke wherever they wished.

1951 ii, 59a (30-16) <u>Geoffrey de Mandeville; Leighs (Great or Little)</u>: In the time of King Edward, Esger held two and a half hides and fifteen acres of land in Leighs. Now W. holds it from Geoffrey de Mandeville. Esger gave (*dedit*) this manor to Harold, and Harold then gave (*dedit*) it to Skalpi, his housecarl. Skalpi then gave (*dedit*) it to his wife in dower (*in dote*), in the sight (*videntibus*) of two men – Roger the Marshal and an Englishman. The hundred testifies that they heard these men acknowledge (*recognoscere*) Skalpi. Skalpi himself held it after King William came into this land, until he went to York, where he died in outlawry (*in utlageria*).

1952 ii, 59a (30-17) <u>Geoffrey de Mandeville; Cuton</u>: TRE Toli held two hides and a virgate of land in Cuton. Now Osbert holds it from Geoffrey de Mandeville, in his exchange (*in suo escangio*), so he says.

1953 ii, 59a–b (30-18) <u>Geoffrey de Mandeville; Moze</u>: TRE Leofsunu held four hides of land in Moze. Now Geoffrey de Mandeville holds it in demesne. The King gave (*dedit*) this manor to Geoffrey when he stayed (*remansit*) in London.

1954 ii, 59b (30-21) <u>Geoffrey de Mandeville; freemen in Barstable Hundred</u>: TRE six freemen were in Barstable Hundred, and Geoffrey de Mandeville annexed (*invasit*) them against the King. They held twelve hides of land, which five knights now hold from Geoffrey. Of these twelve hides, Ravengar took away (*tulit*) twelve acres and put (*apposuit*) them in his fee. Swein took away (*tulit*) another thirty acres, and put (*posuit*) them in his manor of West Tilbury.

1955 ii, 59b–60a (30-22) <u>Geoffrey de Mandeville; Black Notley</u>: TRW Walter holds one and a half hides and forty-five acres in Black Notley from Geoffrey de Mandeville. TRE Esger held this land. There are two freemen there with forty acres. Geoffrey claims the King as warrantor (*clamat regem ad warant*) for them.

1956 ii, 60a (30-23) <u>Geoffrey de Mandeville; Ridley</u>: TRW Walter holds a hide of land in Ridley from Geoffrey de Mandeville, which Esger held TRE. Thirty acres were attached to this manor TRE. Of these Geoffrey has twenty, and Richard fitz Gilbert has ten. But the hundred testifies that all this, by right (*recte*), is from Geoffrey's manor.

1957 ii, 60a (30-24) <u>Geoffrey de Mandeville; Little Hallingbury</u>: TRE Esger held a hide of land in Little Hallingbury. Now Martel holds it from Geoffrey de Mandeville. A priest and a villein with twenty acres of land were attached to the church, but now they are not.

1958 ii, 60a–b (30-27) <u>Geoffrey de Mandeville; High Easter</u>: TRE Esger held two hides of land in High Easter. Now Geoffrey de Mandeville holds it in demesne. TRE half a hide belonged to this manor's church. Now Guthbert holds it from Geoffrey. The Abbot of Ely claims (*calumpniatur*) this manor, and the hundred testifies that it was in the abbey in the time of King Edward, although Esger held it on the day King Edward was alive and dead.

1959 ii, 60b–61a (30-28, 29, 30) <u>Geoffrey de Mandeville; Newton, Barnston, Berners Roding</u>: TRW Hugh de Bernières holds two hides and a virgate of land in Newton from Geoffrey de Mandeville, which Wulfric Cavva held TRE. Hugh also holds two hides and thirty acres from Geoffrey in Barnston, which Wulfwine held; and two and a half hides in Berners Roding, which Wulfric held. The King ordered (*praecepit*), through Robert d'Oilly, that Hugh should hold these three manors from Geoffrey de Mandeville, if

Geoffrey could establish (*deratiocinari*) that they were part of his fee. Before Geoffrey established title (*derationaret*), Hugh held them from Geoffrey.

1960 ii, 61b (30-39) <u>Geoffrey de Mandeville; Roding</u>: TRE Esger held two hides less ten acres in Roding. Now Rainalm holds them from Geoffrey de Mandeville. Ten acres have been added to this manor, which were held by a freeman in King Edward's time. Now the whole hundred testifies that they are from King William's demesne.

1961 ii, 61b–62a (30-40) <u>Geoffrey de Mandeville; Roding</u>: TRW William holds a hide and three virgates of land in Roding from Geoffrey de Mandeville. TRE a freeman held it. Half of this land paid soke to Esger and the other half was free, which the King gave (*dedit*) to Geoffrey, so his men say.

1962 ii, 62a (30-41) <u>Geoffrey de Mandeville; Shellow Bowells</u>: TRW William holds thirty-five acres in Shellow Bowells from Geoffrey de Mandeville, which a freeman held TRE. In King Edward's time this land lay in Eudo Dapifer's manor of Morrell Roding. The Abbot of Ely claims (*calumpniatur*) both this land and the manor of Morrell Roding, by testimony (*teste*) of the hundred.

1963 ii, 62b (30-46) <u>Geoffrey de Mandeville; Great Chishill</u>: TRE Wulfheah, a freeman, held two and a half hides of land in Great Chishill. Now William Cardon holds it from Geoffrey de Mandeville. He also holds three hides and seventeen acres of land in the same vill, which five freemen held TRE. Geoffrey claims (*reclamat*) these lands in exchange (*pro escangio*).

1964 ii, 62b (30-47) <u>Geoffrey de Mandeville; Emanuel Wood</u>: TRW an Englishman holds three virgates of land in Emanuel Wood from Geoffrey de Mandeville, which a freeman held TRE. In the time of King William this freeman became (*effectus est*) Geoffrey's man of his own accord (*sponte sua*). Geoffrey's men say that after this, the King granted (*concessit*) this land to Geoffrey in exchange (*pro escangio*), but neither the man himself nor the hundred produce testimony for Geoffrey (*neque ipse homo nec hundret testimonium Goisfrido perhibent*).

1965 ii, 64a (32-8) <u>Robert Gernon; West Ham</u>: TRW Robert Gernon holds eight hides and thirty acres of land in West Ham in demesne. TRE Æthelstan, a freeman, held it. King William [gave] this manor to Ranulf Peverel and Robert Gernon. Ranulf Peverel has half of it.

1966 ii, 64a–b (32-9) <u>Robert Gernon; East Ham</u>: TRE Leofræd, a freeman, held seven hides of land in East Ham. Now Robert Gernon holds it in demesne. In the time of King William three virgates were added to this manor, which Edwin, a free priest, held TRE.

1967 ii, 66a (32-24) <u>Robert Gernon; Wormingford</u>: TRW Ilger holds one and a half hides and ten acres in Wormingford from Robert Gernon. TRE Godwine held them. There were nineteen sokemen there in the time of King Edward, holding two and a half hides less six acres. Robert, so he says, has them in his exchange (*in suo escangio*), and Ilger holds them from him. These sokemen, so the county testifies, could not remove (*removere*) themselves from this manor. Raymond Gerald took away (*abstulit*) a villein, of whom Robert Gernon was seised (*de quo fuit Robertus saisitus*). Roger the Poitevin still has him.

1968 ii, 66a (32-25) <u>Robert Gernon; Wivenhoe</u>: TRW Nigel holds five hides less fifteen acres in Wivenhoe from Robert Gernon. TRE Ælfric held them. A freeman held twenty acres there, which Robert holds by the King's gift (*de dono regis*), and Nigel holds from him. Another freeman held twenty acres there, which the hundred warden (*custos hundret*) has. Nigel holds all of this.

1969 ii, 66b (32-28) <u>Robert Gernon; Rainham</u>: TRW Robert holds three and a half hides of land in Rainham from Robert Gernon. TRE Alweard held it. A freeman held another hide there. Afterwards he forfeited (*forisfecit*) it, because he had stolen (*quia furtus est*), and it was in the King's hand. Robert the Lascivious, however, annexed (*invasit*) it, so the hundred testifies.

1970 ii, 66b (32-29) <u>Robert Gernon; South Weald</u>: TRE Sprot held a hide in South Weald. Now Ralph holds it from Robert Gernon. Robert has this land, so he says, in exchange (*pro escangio*), through (*per*) Hubert de Port. It has never paid geld, nor did it render the last geld (*neque reddidit geltum et neque ultimum*).

1971 ii, 67a (32-31) <u>Robert Gernon; Fryerning</u>: TRE Edwin Grut held a hide and thirty-three acres of land in Fryerning. Now Ilger holds it from Robert Gernon. Robert had it in his exchange (*in suo escangio*).

1972 ii, 67a (32-34) <u>Robert Gernon; Fryerning</u>: TRW William holds two and a half hides and thirty-one acres of land in Fryerning from Robert Gernon. TRE Sylvi and Topi held it. Robert has this land in exchange (*in escangio*).

1973 ii, 67a (32-35) <u>Robert Gernon; Patching</u>: TRW Picot holds two and a half hides of land in Patching from Robert Gernon. TRE Brorda held it. Robert has this land in exchange (*in escangio*).

1974 ii, 67b (32-38a) <u>Robert Gernon; Tendring</u>: TRW Walter holds one hide less fifteen acres of land in Tendring from Robert Gernon. TRE a freeman held it. Robert took it in his exchange (*recepit Robertus in suo escangio*).

1975 ii, 68a (32-41) <u>Robert Gernon; Widdington</u>: TRW Robert holds three hides and a virgate of land in Widdington from Robert Gernon. TRE Ingulf held it. Robert, so he says, has it in exchange (*in escangio*).

1976 ii, 68a (32-42) <u>Robert Gernon; Shortgrove</u>: TRW Robert holds two hides of land in Shortgrove from Robert Gernon. TRE Wulfwine and Grimkel held it. Robert has this in exchange (*in escangio*).

1977 ii, 68a (32-43) <u>Robert Gernon; Arkesden</u>: TRW Picot holds a hide less eight acres of land in Arkesden from Robert Gernon. TRE Grimkel held it. Robert has it in exchange (*pro escangio*).

1978 ii, 68a (32-44) <u>Robert Gernon; Elsenham</u>: TRW Peter holds a hide of land in Elsenham from Robert Gernon, which Leofstan held TRE. Robert has it in exchange (*in escangio*).

1979 ii, 68a–b (32-45) <u>Robert Gernon; Tolleshunt D'Arcy</u>: TRW Robert de Verly holds five and a half hides of land in Tolleshunt D'Arcy from Robert

Gernon. TRE Gauti held it. Robert says that he has this land in his exchange (*in suo escangio*).

1980 ii, 68b (33-1) <u>Ralph Baynard; Ulting</u>: TRE Hakun held a hide and forty acres of land in Ulting. Now Gerard holds it from Ralph Baynard. Five acres of land were added in the time of King William, and are of his customs.

1981 ii, 68b–69a (33-2) <u>Ralph Baynard; Langford</u>: TRW Geoffrey holds five freemen from Ralph Baynard with three virgates and an acre of land in Langford. They paid the King 15d. in customs TRE.

1982 ii, 69a (33-3) <u>Ralph Baynard; Cold Norton</u>: TRW Ralph Baynard holds eight hides in Cold Norton in demesne. TRE Wulfric, a freeman, held them. Ralph also has three hides and forty-five acres there, which six freemen have always held. This was delivered in exchange (*liberatum est pro escangio*).

1983 ii, 69a (33-5) <u>Ralph Baynard; Curling Tye Green</u>: TRW Pointel holds a hide of land in Curling Tye Green from Ralph Baynard. TRE Grim held it. Godric also holds a half hide there from Ralph, which Ralph, so he says, has in exchange (*pro escangio*). But the hundred does not know this.

1984 ii, 69a–b (33-6) <u>Ralph Baynard; Little Dunmow</u>: TRW Ralph Baynard holds four and a half hides in Little Dunmow in demesne, which Æthelgyth, a free woman, held TRE. Another hide was added to this manor, which a freeman held TRE. Yet another half hide is attached to this manor, which a sokeman of Baynard's antecessor held and still holds.

1985 ii, 70a (33-12) <u>Ralph Baynard; Burnham</u>: TRW Ralph Baynard holds four hides and twelve acres of land in Burnham in demesne. TRE Alweard, a freeman, held it. In the same vill ten freemen had eight hides and twenty-eight acres of land TRE. Ralph now holds it in demesne. Ralph claims (*reclamat*) this land in exchange (*pro escangio*).

1986 ii, 70b–71a (33-17) <u>Ralph Baynard; Michaelstow</u>: TRW Bernard holds two and a half hides of land in Michaelstow from Ralph Baynard. TRE Alric held it. Ralph also holds two sokemen there in his exchange (*in suo escangio*), so his men say, but others do not testify, except only those from the manor (*sed alii non testantur nisi ipsi soli de manerio*) of Lawford. Roger also holds a hide in "Witelebroc" from Ralph, which Alric held TRE. This land did not lie in the other lands.

1987 ii, 71a (33-18) <u>Ralph Baynard; Wenden Lofts</u>: TRW Amalfrid holds one and a half hides and thirty acres of land in Wenden Lofts from Ralph Baynard. TRE a freeman, Alwine Stille held it. Ralph has it in exchange (*in escangio*).

1988 ii, 71a (33-20) <u>Ralph Baynard; Ashdon</u>: TRW Ralph Baynard holds two hides of land in Ashdon in demesne. TRE Æthelgyth held it. There were two sokemen there, who held fifteen acres freely. Ralph took (*accepit*) them in exchange (*in escangio*).

1989 ii, 71a (33-21) <u>Ralph Baynard; Paglesham</u>: TRW Theodric Pointel holds a half hide and fifteen acres of land in Paglesham, which a freeman held TRE. Ralph Baynard claims (*reclamat*) this in exchange (*pro escangio*).

1990 ii, 71a–b (33-22) <u>Ralph Baynard; Langford</u>: TRE Cola and Æthelmær held three and a half hides in Langford. Æthelmær held the half hide from the bishopric of London at rent (*ad censum*), but Ralph Baynard is now seised (*est saisitus*) of it, and Geoffrey holds all of this land from him.

1991 ii, 71b (33-23) <u>Ralph Baynard; Tolleshunt (D'Arcy, Knights or Major)</u>: TRW Bernard holds three hides and eight acres of land in Tolleshunt from Ralph Baynard. TRE Æthelmær held it. In the same vill there are eight freemen with one and a half hides and fourteen acres of land. Ralph Baynard has this in exchange (*pro escangio*).

1992 ii, 71b–72a (34-2) <u>Ranulf Peverel; Vange</u>: TRW Serlo holds a hide of land in Vange from Ranulf Peverel, which a freeman, who became a man of Ranulf Peverel's antecessor (*effectus est homo antecessoris Ranulfi Piperelli*), held as a manor. But the freeman did not give (*non dedit*) Ranulf his land. When the King gave (*dedit*) land to Ranulf, however, he was seised (*saisiuit*) of it with the other land.

1993 ii, 72a–b (34-6) <u>Ranulf Peverel; Terling</u>: TRE Æthelmær, a thegn of the King, held two and a half hides and thirty acres of land in Terling. Now Richard holds it from Ranulf Peverel. A freeman with five acres there paid 10d. to Ranulf's antecessor. He now pays Ranulf the same.

1994 ii, 72b (34-7) <u>Ranulf Peverel; Fairstead</u>: TRW Thurold holds fifty-five acres of land in Fairstead from Ranulf Peverel. Beorhtmær held it TRE. Another fifteen acres lay there TRE, of which Saswalo disseised (*desaisiuit*) him. They now lie in the fee of Geoffrey de Mandeville.

1995 ii, 72b (34-8) <u>Ranulf Peverel; West Ham</u>: TRE Æthelstan, a free man, held eight hides and thirty acres of land in West Ham. Now Ranulf Peverel holds it in demesne. King William gave (*dedit*) this manor to Ranulf Peverel and Robert Gernon, and Robert Gernon has half of it.

1996 ii, 73a (34-10) <u>Ranulf Peverel; Willingale Doe</u>: TRW Ravenot holds one hide and one and a half virgates of land in Willingale Doe from Ranulf Peverel. TRE Siward held it. A sokeman, whom Ranulf Peverel's antecessor held, has been added to this manor. Ranulf still holds him, and Ravenot holds from him. Another thirty acres were added to this manor in the time of King William, which a freeman held TRE.

1997 ii, 73b–74a (34-19) <u>Ranulf Peverel; Amberden</u>: TRW Ranulf Peverel holds five hides of land in Amberden in demesne. TRE Siward held it. The Abbot of Ely claims (*calumpniatur*) this vill, and the hundred testifies that it lay in the abbey.

1998 ii, 74a–b (34-22) <u>Ranulf Peverel; Lamarsh</u>: TRW Thurold holds three and a half hides of land in Lamarsh from Ranulf Peverel. TRE Algar held it as a manor. TRE Alweard also held another one and a half hides in Lamarsh as a manor. Thurold also holds this land from Ranulf. In the time of King Edward, these two manors were divided between two brothers in this way (*erant sic divisae*). Afterwards they were given (*data sunt*) to Ranulf as one manor, so his men say.

1999 ii, 74b–75a (34-27) <u>Ranulf Peverel; Prested</u>: TRW Ranulf Peverel holds one and a half hides in Prested, which Beorhtmær held TRE. A freeman always held five acres of land there, and was commended to Ranulf's antecessor. Nonetheless he could go where he wished with his land. Now Ranulf has this.

2000   ii, 75a (34-28) Ranulf Peverel; Plunker's Green: TRW Ravenot holds fourteen acres of land in Plunker's Green from Ranulf Peverel. TRE Wulfric, a priest of Harold, held it freely. Now Ranulf has it because his antecessor was seised (*fuit saisitus*) of the priest. But it did not belong to him, so the county testifies.

2001   ii, 75a (34-30) Ranulf Peverel; Rettendon: TRW Ralph fitz Brian holds one hide and thirty acres of land in Rettendon from Ranulf Peverel. TRE Siward held it. Ely Abbey claims (*calumpniatur*) it.

2002   ii, 75a–b (34-32) Ranulf Peverel; Tendring: TRW Ranulf Peverel holds a half hide and thirty acres of land in Tendring in demesne. TRE Wulfwig held it freely. Ranulf has it in exchange (*in escangio*).

2003   ii, 76a–b (35-2) Aubrey de Vere; "Udecheshale": TRE Wulfwine held a hide of land in "Udecheshale." Now Aubrey de Vere holds it in demesne. A virgate and eight acres of land, which a freeman held TRE, has been added to this manor. Now Ralph holds it from Aubrey.

2004   ii, 77a (35-7) Aubrey de Vere; Horseham: TRW Æthelhelm holds forty-five acres of land in Horseham from Aubrey de Vere, which two sokemen of Aubrey's antecessor held on condition that they could not withdraw without his permission.

2005   ii, 77b (35-11) Aubrey de Vere; Beaumont: TRE Wulfwine held two hides of land in Beaumont. Now Edward holds it from Aubrey de Vere. A sokeman belongs to this manor, who could not withdraw without the permission of Aubrey's antecessor. He holds two hides less fifteen acres of land.

2006   ii, 78a (35-13) Aubrey de Vere; Radwinter: TRW Demiblanc holds a half hide and fifteen acres of land in Radwinter from Aubrey de Vere. TRE the sokeman Ælfric held it. He could sell his land, but the soke and sake remained with Aubrey's antecessor.

2007   ii, 78a (35-14) Aubrey de Vere; Stevington End: TRW Reginald holds forty-five acres in Stevington End from Aubrey de Vere. Alwine held thirty of them and Ordric held fifteen. These two men were in King William's soke, but he gave (*dedit*) them to Aubrey.

2008   ii, 78b (36-3) Peter de Valognes; Little Parndon: TRE a freeman held three hides of land in Little Parndon. Now Roger holds it from Peter de Valognes. Five acres of land have been added, which a freeman held TRE.

2009   ii, 78b (36-5) Peter de Valognes; Leyton: TRE Swein the Black held three hides of land in Leyton. Now Peter de Valognes holds it in demesne. There was a mill there, but now there is none, because it was taken away (*ablatus est*) in the time of King William. When Peter took the manor, there was nothing there except land (*recepit non erat ibi praeter sola terra*).

2010 ii, 78b–79a (36-6) <u>Peter de Valognes; Higham</u>: TRW Peter de Valognes holds five hides of land in Higham. Healfdene, a freeman, held it in the time of King Edward. When Peter took (*recepit*) this manor, he found nothing there except an ox and a sown acre. TRE two freemen held one of these hides, which I have spoken of (*dixi*) above. It was added to this manor in the time of King William. William holds it from Peter.

2011 ii, 79a (36-9) <u>Peter de Valognes; Binsley</u>: TRE Wulfwine held one hide of land in Binsley. Now Peter de Valognes holds it. He has it in mortgage by the King's order (*in vadimonio iussu regis*), on condition that the King did not lose (*perdidit*) his customs, by testimony (*teste*) of the Bishop of Bayeux.

2012 ii, 79a–b (36-11) <u>Peter de Valognes; Theydon Bois</u>: TRE Hakun held three and a half hides and eighty acres of land in Theydon Bois. Now Peter de Valognes holds it in demesne. This is in exchange (*pro escangio*), so Peter himself says. Walter also holds a half hide and forty acres there from Peter, which Wulfwine held. Peter de Valognes holds this land in mortgage (*in vadimonio*), so he himself says, with the King's consent (*concessu regis*).

2013 ii, 79b (36-12) <u>Peter de Valognes; North Weald Bassett</u>: TRW Ralph Fatatus holds two hides and forty acres of land in North Weald Bassett from Peter de Valognes. TRE two freemen held it. Peter has it in exchange (*in escangio*). A man also held forty acres there freely, which Peter now has in exchange (*in escangio*).

2014 ii, 80a (37-3) <u>Ranulf brother of Ilger; Roydon</u>: TRW Ranulf holds six hides in Roydon in demesne, which Ingvar, a freeman, held TRE. Four hides have been added to this manor, which five freemen held TRE.

2015 ii, 80b (37-9) <u>Ranulf brother of Ilger; Nazeing, Epping</u>: TRE two freemen held four and a half hides less fifteen acres of land in Nazeing and Epping. Besides this, a hide of land was added to this manor, which a freeman held TRE, and he still holds it. Another virgate of land is there, which was added in the time of King William. It belonged to Waltham Holy Cross TRE. Ranulf brother of Ilger took it away (*tulit*) from Waltham, so the hundred testifies. Now Ranulf holds all of this in demesne.

2016 ii, 81a–b (37-17) <u>Ranulf brother of Ilger; Mountnessing</u>: TRE Ælfheah and Algar held two hides and twenty-six acres of land in Mountnessing. TRW William de Bosc-le-Hard holds it from Ranulf brother of Ilger. Ranulf has it in his exchange (*in suo escangio*).

2017 ii, 81b (37-19) <u>Ranulf brother of Ilger; Fouchers</u>: TRE two free girls held eighty acres of land in Fouchers. Now Ranulf brother of Ilger holds it in his exchange (*in suo escangio*), and William holds from him.

2018 ii, 81b (37-20) <u>Ranulf brother of Ilger; Derleigh</u>: TRE Eadric of Easthope held two and a half hides of land in Derleigh. Now Ranulf brother of Ilger holds it, and Roger holds from him. Ranulf has this land in exchange (*pro escangio*).

2019 ii, 81b (38-1) <u>Tihel the Breton; Yardley</u>: TRE two freemen held a hide of land in Yardley. Now Serlo holds it from Tihel the Breton. Tihel claims (*reclamat*) this land by the King's gift (*de dono regis*).

2020 ii, 82a (38-3) <u>Tihel the Breton; Radwinter</u>: TRE Leofsige held half a hide and a half virgate of land in Radwinter. Now Guthøthr holds it from Tihel, who claims (*reclamat*) it by the King's gift (*de dono regis*).

2021 ii, 83a (39-4) <u>Roger de Raismes; Messing</u>: TRE Ordmær, a freeman, held a half hide of land in Messing. Now Roger de Raismes holds it in demesne. Three sokemen belong to this manor, who hold eighteen acres freely. Gerald holds them from Roger, and Roger says that he has them in exchange (*in escangio*).

2022 ii, 83b (39-12) <u>Roger de Raismes; Ardleigh</u>: TRW Roger de Raismes holds six freemen with a hide of land in Ardleigh in demesne. This is in exchange (*pro escangio*).

2023 ii, 84a (40-3) <u>John fitz Waleran; Little Maplestead</u>: TRE Grim, a freeman, held half a hide of land in Little Maplestead. TRW Osmund holds it from John fitz Waleran. There is a mill there, which William de Warenne holds in mortgage (*pro vadimonio*).

2024 ii, 84b–85a (40-9) <u>John fitz Waleran; Aveley</u>: TRE Swein held three and a half hides in Aveley. Now John fitz Waleran holds them in demesne. A freeman, Wulfsige, held half a hide of land, which he could sell, but Waleran, John's father, added him to this manor.

2025 ii, 85b (41-8) <u>Robert fitz Corbucion; Waltham</u>: TRW Ranulf holds a freeman with thirty acres of land in Waltham from Robert fitz Corbucion, which Robert annexed (*invasit*).

2026 ii, 85b (41-9) <u>Robert fitz Corbucion; Bensted</u>: TRE Starcher held three and a half hides in Bensted. Now Nigel holds them from Robert fitz Corbucion. In the same place a freeman, whom Robert fitz Corbucion annexed (*invasit*), held half a hide of land. Now Godfrey holds this from Robert.

2027 ii, 86a (41-12) <u>Robert fitz Corbucion; Tolleshunt Major</u>: TRE Starcher held a hide in Tolleshunt Major. Now Mauger holds it from Robert fitz Corbucion. In the same place eight freemen, whom Robert annexed (*invasit*), held four hides and two acres of land, and could go where they wished. Now four knights hold it from Robert.

2028 ii, 86a–b (42-1) <u>Walter the Deacon; Bowers Gifford</u>: TRW Walter the Deacon holds two hides of land in Bowers Gifford, which were from his brother Theodric's land. Forty acres, which were held by a freeman TRE, were added to this manor in the time of King William. Theodric had them.

2029 ii, 87a (42-7) <u>Walter the Deacon; Wix</u>: TRE Queen Edith held four hides of land in Wix. Now Walter the Deacon holds it in demesne. Queen Edith gave (*dedit*) this land to Walter after the coming of King William.

2030 ii, 87b (43-1) <u>Roger Bigot; Sible Hedingham</u>: TRE fifteen freemen held twenty-five acres of land in Sible Hedingham, and three freemen held another forty-eight and half acres in the same vill. Now Werengar holds these two manors from Roger Bigot. Concerning the forty-eight acres, the hundred does not testify for Roger Bigot, that he was seised of them on the

King's behalf (*inde de parte regis esset saisitus*). Roger de Raismes claims (*calumpniatur*) these two manors, but the hundred does not testify for him.

2031   ii, 88b–89a (45-1) <u>William d'Ecouis; Moreton</u>: TRE Saxi held one hide and twenty acres in Moreton. Now William d'Ecouis holds them in demesne. A freeman held another forty-three and a half acres there. Now William has annexed (*invasit*) this. It did not belong to this manor, which Ralph holds from him.

2032   ii, 89b (47-3) <u>Hugh de Gournai; Fordham</u>: TRE Esbiorn held two hides of land in Fordham. Now Geoffrey holds it from Hugh de Gournai. Roger the Poitevin took away (*abstulit*) ten acres from this manor, so the hundred testifies.

2033   ii, 90a (48-1) <u>William Peverel; East Horndon</u>: TRE Æthelmær, a freeman, held one and a half hides in East Horndon. Now Drogo holds them from William Peverel. Then and now four sokemen hold two and a half hides and twenty-one acres of this land. Fifty-six acres have been taken away (*ablate sunt*) from this.

2034   ii, 90a (48-2) <u>William Peverel; Grays Thurrock</u>: TRE Æthelmær held three hides and forty-two acres in Grays Thurrock. Now William Peverel holds them. Nine sokemen also lay in this manor TRE, and they held three hides of land. Now there are five sokemen there, and they hold one and a half hides. Gilbert, a man of the Bishop of Bayeux, holds one and a half hides less ten acres of land. The hundred does not know how. Also Eskil, the Bishop of London's man, holds twenty acres which lay in this manor. Similarly, the hundred does not know how.

2035   ii, 90a–b (49-1) <u>Ralph de Limesy; Brundon</u>: TRE a freeman held two and a half hides less fifteen acres in Brundon. Now Ralph de Limesy holds them in demesne. Hardwin added twenty acres of land to this manor in the time of King William.

2036   ii, 90b (49-3) <u>Ralph de Limesy; Chigwell</u>: TRE Harold held seven hides in Chigwell from King Edward. Now Ralph de Limesy holds them in demesne. Six freemen lived there on two hides and fifteen acres of land. Robert Gernon, so he himself says, has this by the King's gift (*ex dono regis*). Also there is a freeman, whom Peter the Sheriff now has, who held and holds thirty acres. Peter had livery of this land with his fee (*liberatorem cum suo feudo*).

2037   ii, 90b (49-6) <u>Ralph de Limesy; Chigwell</u>: TRW Ralph de Limesy holds six acres of the King's soke in Chigwell, but his antecessor annexed (*invasit*) this.

2038   ii, 91a (52-1) <u>Walter de Douai; Upminster</u>: TRW Walter de Douai holds six and a half hides and thirty acres of land in Upminster in demesne. Swein the Black held it TRE. Ten acres used to lie in this manor, which Geoffrey de Mandeville, so he says, now holds in his exchange (*in suo escangio*).

2039   ii, 91a (52-2) <u>Walter de Douai; Rainham</u>: TRE Leofstan the Reeve held eight hides of land in Rainham. Now Walter de Douai holds it in demesne. A half hide of land, which three freemen held TRE, was added to this manor.

After King William came, Walter added them to his manor, to which they were not attached TRE, so the county testifies.

2040 ii, 92b–93a (57-5) <u>Sasselin; Childerditch</u>: TRW Sasselin holds one and a half hides and thirty acres in Childerditch. Ordgar, a freeman, held them TRE. A sokeman with fifteen acres of land was also in this manor. He could sell his land, but the soke lay in Little Warley, in the bishopric of London's land.

2041 ii, 93a (60-1) <u>Hugh de St. Quentin; Horndon on the Hill</u>: TRE Winge held one and a half hides of land in Horndon on the Hill. Now Hugh de St. Quentin holds them. Godwine took away (*abstulit*) two *mansiones* from this manor.

2042 ii, 93b (60-3) <u>Hugh de St. Quentin; Little Birch</u>: TRE Wulfweard held a half hide and fifteen acres of land in Little Birch. Now Hugh de St. Quentin holds it by the Queen's gift (*de dono reginae*).

2043 ii, 94b (66-1) <u>William the Deacon; Peldon</u>: TRE Thorkil, a freeman, held five hides of land in Peldon. Now William the Deacon holds it. Haimo Dapifer took away (*tulit*) 80 acres of arable land and 200 acres of marsh from this manor. It was attached there, so the hundred testifies, both in the time of King Edward and after the coming of King William. We have ordered this seizure into the King's hand (*hanc occupationem percepimus in manu regis*). The value of what was taken away (*ablatum est*) from this manor is 20s.

2044 ii, 95a (68-2) <u>Modwin; Witham</u>: TRW Modwin holds a hide of land in Witham, which Harold held TRE. There were eight acres of meadow there, now four. Geoffrey Baynard took away (*tulit*) the others.

2045 ii, 96a (71-3) <u>Theodric Pointel; unidentified land in Wibertsherne Hundred</u>: TRW Theodric Pointel holds one and a half hides of land in exchange (*pro escangio*) for Coggeshall, which Tesselin held.

2046 ii, 97a–b (77-1) <u>Ralph Pinel; Great Bromley, "Westnanetunam"</u>: TRE Beorhtmær held four and a half hides of land in Great Bromley and "Westnanetunam," and there were two halls there. Now Ralph Pinel holds this. Ralph did service (*deserviuit*) for this land to Geoffrey de Mandeville, because this same Geoffrey told him how the King had given (*dederat*) him the service of this land. But twice Ralph gave his rent to the King's servants (*per duas vices dedit de suo censu ministris regis*), when the King sent his legates into this land (*misit legatos suos in hac terram*).

2047 ii, 97b (79-1) <u>Reginald the Balistarius; South Fambridge</u>: TRW Reginald the Balistarius holds three and a half hides of land in South Fambridge. The monks of Ely claim (*calumpniantur*) this land, and the hundred testifies for them. Reginald was also seised (*saisiuit*) of a half hide of land next to South Fambridge after the coming of King William, which is valued at 30s. a year.

2048 ii, 97b–98a (81-1) <u>Otto the Goldsmith; Gestingthorpe</u>: TRE Earl Ælfgar held half a hide of land in Gestingthorpe. Now Otto the Goldsmith holds it. Then it was valued at £10, now at £12. When the King gave (*dedit*) it, it was valued at £15.

2049 ii, 98a (82-1) <u>Gilbert the Priest; Middleton</u>: TRE nine sokemen of Earl

Ælfgar held one and a half hides and twenty-eight acres of land in Middleton. Now Gilbert the Priest holds it. He claims this land by the Queen's gift (*reclamat ex dono reginae*).

2050 ii, 98a (83-1) Grim the Reeve; Bowers Gifford: TRW Grim the Reeve has two hides of land in Bowers Gifford. One of these two hides is from men forfeited to the King, which after the coming of King William, Grim added to his other land (*de hominibus forisfactis erga regem, quam post adventum regis addidit Grim ad suam aliam terram*) through (*per*) Robert fitz Wimarc the sheriff, so Grim himself says.

2051 ii, 98a (83-2) Grim the Reeve; Chadwell: TRE Godmann, a freeman, held twenty acres of land in Chadwell. He made a forfeiture, and could not pay it (*forisfactus non potuit emendare*). Grim the Reeve, however, gave (*dedit*) 30s. to the King in his place (*pro eo*), and holds it through the permission (*per licentiam*) of Hubert de Port.

2052 ii, 98a–b (84-1) Wulfgifu wife of Fin; Pitsea: There were three hides of land in Pitsea TRE, which Wulfgifu wife of Fin now holds. Three other hides have been added to this land, along with thirty acres of woodland, on which eight freemen live. These three hides remain (*remanent*) the King's.

2053 ii, 99a (89-1) King's freemen; freemen in Lexden Hundred: The King has seven freemen, who hold a half hide of land. The hundred reeve has them.

2054 ii, 99a (89-2) King's freemen; unidentified land in Lexden Hundred: TRE a freeman held three and half acres of land. When Robert de Montbegon annexed (*invasit*) it, it was valued at 10s.; now nothing.

2055 ii, 99a (89-3) King's freemen; unidentified land in Lexden Hundred: TRE a freeman held thirteen acres of land. Richard, a man of Haimo Dapifer, annexed (*invasit*) it, and until now he has had the spoils (*spolia*) from it.

2056 ii, 99a (90-1) Annexations (*invasiones*) against the King; Hordon on the Hill: Godwine Gudhen annexed (*invasit*) two *mansiones* in Horndon on the Hill, which are from the land which Hugh de St. Quentin holds from the King. Godwine has given a pledge (*dedit vadem*) for this.

2057 ii, 99a (90-2) Annexations (*invasiones*) against the King; Hordon on the Hill: Godwine Gudhen annexed (*invasit*) three virgates of land in Hordon on the Hill against the King, from the land of a freeman. It remains (*remanet*) with the King through a judgment (*per iudicium*) of the hundred. Again Godwine has given a pledge (*dedit vadem*).

2058 ii, 99a (90-3) Annexations (*invasiones*) against the King; Dunton: There are fifteen acres of land in Dunton which Wulfwine held, and they remain the King's in peace (*remanent regi quietae*).

2059 ii, 99a (90-4) Annexations (*invasiones*) against the King; Little Thurrock: Concerning the annexation (*invasio*) of Theodric Pointel: TRE eleven freemen held one and a half hides and forty-two acres in Little Thurrock. Theodric Pointel annexed (*invasit*) this land, and it is in the King's hand.

2060 ii, 99b (90-5) Annexations (*invasiones*) against the King; Layer (Breton, de la Haye, or Marney): TRE Wulfric, a freeman, held two hides of land in Layer.

Theodric Pointel annexed (*invasit*) it. There were two plows there, now none; nor were there any when Theodric took (*recepit*) it.

2061 ii, 99b (90-6) <u>Annexations (*invasiones*) against the King; Burnham</u>: Theodric Pointel annexed (*invasit*) fifteen and a half acres in Burnham. These acres, however, were in the King's hand before these pleas were made (*hec placita fierent*).

2062 ii, 99b (90-7, 8) <u>Annexations (*invasiones*) against the King; Little Stambridge, Paglesham</u>: TRE a freeman held one and a half hides and twenty acres in Little Stambridge. Theodric Pointel annexed (*invasit*) this land, and three knights now hold from him. TRE two freemen held a half hide and fifteen acres of land in Paglesham. Theodric Pointel annexed (*invasit*) it, and Robert holds from him. Theodric has held these two manors in exchange (*pro escangio*) for Coggeshall. They are now in the King's hand.

2063 ii, 99b (90-9) <u>Annexations (*invasiones*) against the King; "Midebroc"</u>: Theodric Pointel annexed (*invasit*) twenty acres of land in "Midebroc." Its soke, so the hundred testifies, lies in Christ Church, Canterbury. Theodric has this by exchange (*pro escangio*), and it is in the King's hand.

2064 ii, 99b (90-10) <u>Annexations (*invasiones*) against the King; Terling</u>: Concerning the annexation (*invasio*) of Ranulf Peverel: Ranulf Peverel annexed (*invasit*) five freemen who held three hides less fifteen acres of land in Terling in the time of King Edward. Roger holds two hides and eighty acres of this land from Ranulf, and Ranulf holds the remaining thirty acres.

2065 ii, 99b (90-11) <u>Annexations (*invasiones*) against the King; Widdington</u>: Ranulf Peverel annexed (*invasit*) thirty acres of land in Widdington, which he holds in demesne.

2066 ii, 99b (90-12) <u>Annexations (*invasiones*) against the King; Stansgate</u>: Ranulf Peverel annexed (*invasit*) a hide and thirty acres of land in Stansgate, which Ralph fitz Brian holds from him. Two freemen held it TRE.

2067 ii, 99b (90-13) <u>Annexations (*invasiones*) against the King; Great Henny</u>: TRE twelve freemen held twenty and a half acres in Great Henny. Now Thurold holds them from Ranulf Peverel.

2068 ii, 99b (90-14) <u>Annexations (*invasiones*) against the King; Lamarsh</u>: Ranulf Peverel holds two acres of free land in Lamarsh.

2069 ii, 100a (90-15, 16) <u>Annexations (*invasiones*) against the King; freeman</u>: Concerning the annexation (*invasio*) of Hugh de Montfort: Hugh de Montfort annexed (*invasit*) a freeman against the King, and William fitz Gross ten freemen. These men held three hides and nine acres TRE. Hugh also annexed (*invasit*) another four freemen there with two hides and twenty acres of land.

2070 ii, 100a (90-17) <u>Annexations (*invasiones*) against the King; freemen</u>: Hugh de Montfort annexed (*invasit*) three freemen who held one hide and thirty acres in Lexden Hundred. One of these men lies in the fee of Westminster Abbey at Feering. This is by testimony (*est testimonio*) of the hundred. But it was delivered (*fuit liberatus*) to Hugh, so his men say, in the numeration of his manors (*in numero suorum maneriorum*).

2071 ii, 100a (90-18) <u>Annexations (*invasiones*) against the King</u>; Bockingham: TRE a freeman held fifteen acres of land in Bockingham. Now William fitz Gross holds it from Hugh de Montfort.

2072 ii, 100a (90-19) <u>Annexations (*invasiones*) against the King</u>; Havering-atte-<u>Bower</u>: There is a freeman with forty acres of land, who belonged to Havering-atte-Bower in the time of King William. Westminster Abbey now has him, because he came of his own accord (*sua sponte venit*) to the abbey. He does not pay customs at Havering-atte-Bower.

2073 ii, 100a (90-20) <u>Annexations (*invasiones*) against the King</u>; Mashbury: Concerning the annexation (*invasio*) of Geoffrey de Mandeville: TRE Ælfgifu, a free woman, held a hide in Mashbury. Geoffrey de Mandeville annexed (*invasit*) it against the King. Now Wulfric holds it by the King's gift (*ex dono regis*).

2074 ii, 100a (90-21) <u>Annexations (*invasiones*) against the King</u>; Canfield: Geoffrey de Mandeville annexed (*invasit*) eight acres of land against the King in Canfield. Richard holds it from Geoffrey.

2075 ii, 100a–b (90-22, 23) <u>Annexations (*invasiones*) against the King</u>; Rockells <u>(formerly Wyggepet)</u>: TRE Bosi, a freeman, held two and a half hides in Rockells. Another freeman held three hides there. Now Geoffrey de Mandeville holds all of this.

2076 ii, 100b (90-24) <u>Annexations (*invasiones*) against the King</u>; Wendens (Ambo <u>or Lofts)</u>: TRE a freeman held six and a half acres of land in Wendens. Now Geoffrey de Mandeville holds it.

2077 ii, 100b (90-25) <u>Annexations (*invasiones*) against the King</u>; Farnham: TRE four freemen held three hides and three virgates of land in Farnham. Now four knights hold this from Geoffrey de Mandeville.

2078 ii, 100b (90-26) <u>Annexations (*invasiones*) against the King</u>; Stambourne: TRE a freeman held a half hide in Stambourne. Now Geoffrey de Mandeville holds it.

2079 ii, 100b (90-27) <u>Annexations (*invasiones*) against the King</u>; "Wesuunic": TRE six freemen held one hide and forty-six acres of land in "Wesuunic." Now Geoffrey de Mandeville holds it.

2080 ii, 100b (90-28) <u>Annexations (*invasiones*) against the King</u>; Arkesden: TRE Godwine Fech held a hide less eight acres in Arkesden. Geoffrey de Mandeville held this land, and Wulfmær held fifteen acres of Esger's fee under Geoffrey. The county does not testify (*comitatus non testatur*).

2081 ii, 100b (90-29) <u>Annexations (*invasiones*) against the King</u>; unidentified land: Hugh de Bernières was holding thirty-seven acres of land from the King, which he has denied (*negavit*). Afterwards, it was adjudged (*fuit derationata*) for the use of the King, and Hugh has given a pledge (*dedit vadem*).

2082 ii, 100b (90-30) <u>Annexations (*invasiones*) against the King</u>; "Plesinchou": TRE a freeman held one hide in "Plesinchou." Humphrey Golden Balls annexed against (*invasit super*) the King.

2083 ii, 100b (90-31) <u>Annexations (*invasiones*) against the King</u>; Little Wigborough:

Haimo Dapifer added two of the King's sokemen with thirty acres of land to Little Wigborough. He annexed them against (*invasit super*) the King.

2084   ii, 100b (90-32) Annexations (*invasiones*) against the King; Northey Island: TRW Haimo Dapifer holds eight acres of land in Northey Island.

2085   ii, 100b (90-33) Annexations (*invasiones*) against the King; Stambourne: TRE Æthelstan, a freeman, and twelve other freemen held forty acres of land in Stambourne. They still have it.

2086   ii, 100b (90-34) Annexations (*invasiones*) against the King; sokeman: William Cardon seized (*occupavit*) a sokeman with eight acres of land. He lies in Great Chishill, in Geoffrey de Mandeville's fee.

2087   ii, 101a (90-35) Annexations (*invasiones*) against the King; Bollington, "Bertuna": Concerning the annexation (*invasio*) of Swein: TRE Godwine, a freeman, held four and a half hides of land in Bollington and "Bertuna" from Harold. Now Alvred holds it from Swein. Robert fitz Wimarc annexed (*invasit*) this land in the time of King William, and Swein holds it still.

2088   ii, 101a (90-36) Annexations (*invasiones*) against the King; Manuden: Aubrey de Vere annexed (*invasit*) one and a half hides and fifteen acres of land in Manuden, which three freemen held TRE.

2089   ii, 101a (90-37) Annexations (*invasiones*) against the King; Smalton: Aubrey de Vere holds fifteen acres of land in Smalton, which a freeman held TRE.

2090   ii, 101a (90-38) Annexations (*invasiones*) against the King; Little Maplestead, Pebmarsh: Aubrey de Vere's wife annexed (*invasit*) five freemen with an acre and a quarter of land in Little Maplestead and Pebmarsh. Theobald held under her.

2091   ii, 101a (90-39) Annexations (*invasiones*) against the King; Henham: Ralph Baynard annexed (*invasit*) a half hide and ten acres in Henham, which two freemen held TRE.

2092   ii, 101a (90-40) Annexations (*invasiones*) against the King; Coupals (formerly Chelveston): Ralph Baynard holds one hide and forty-three acres in Coupals, which six freemen held TRE.

2093   ii, 101a (90-41) Annexations (*invasiones*) against the King; Bollington: TRE a freeman held twenty acres of land in Bollington. He holds it still, but has concealed (*celavit*) it. He has, therefore, given a pledge (*dedit vadem*).

2094   ii, 101a (90-42) Annexations (*invasiones*) against the King; Farnham: TRE a freeman held thirty acres of land in Farnham. Now Ralph Latimer holds it, but has concealed (*celavit*) it. He has, therefore, given a pledge (*dedit vadem*).

2095   ii, 101a (90-43) Annexations (*invasiones*) against the King; "Liffildeuuella": A freeman held and still holds thirty acres in "Liffildeuuella."

2096   ii, 101a (90-44) Annexations (*invasiones*) against the King; Great Henny: Concerning the annexation (*invasio*) of Thurold: TRE four freemen held eighteen acres of land in Great Henny. They hold it still.

2097   ii, 101b (90-45) Annexations (*invasiones*) against the King; Lamarsh: Thurold annexed (*invasit*) forty-seven acres of land in Lamarsh, which eight freemen held TRE. They hold it still.

2098 ii, 101b (90-46) <u>Annexations (*invasiones*) against the King</u>; Henny (Great or Little): Concerning the annexation (*invasio*) of Waleran: TRE seven freemen held a half hide and ten and a half acres of land in Henny. Now Roger holds from John fitz Waleran.

2099 ii, 101b (90-47) <u>Annexations (*invasiones*) against the King</u>; Halstead: TRE Wulfwine held ten acres in Halstead, which Waleran annexed (*invasit*).

2100 ii, 101b (90-48) <u>Annexations (*invasiones*) against the King</u>; Braintree: TRE three freemen held thirty acres of land in Braintree. Leodmær of Hempstead annexed (*invasit*) this land, and held it from Richard fitz Gilbert's fee. Richard is not his warrantor for this (*non est inde sibi tutor*).

2101 ii, 101b (90-49) <u>Annexations (*invasiones*) against the King</u>; unidentified land: Concerning the annexation (*invasio*) of Richard fitz Gilbert: Almær of Borley, Goldstan, Ælfric of Alderford, and Wulfric of Brundon hold half a hide and six acres of land. They also held it TRE. Now Goismer holds from Richard fitz Gilbert.

2102 ii, 101b (90-50) <u>Annexations (*invasiones*) against the King</u>; Finchingfield: TRE Beorhtric, a freeman, held eighty acres in Finchingfield. Now Arnold holds these from Richard fitz Gilbert.

2103 ii, 101b (90-51) <u>Annexations (*invasiones*) against the King</u>; Lashley: TRE Grim, a freeman, held a half hide of land in Lashley. Now Arnold holds it from Richard fitz Gilbert.

2104 ii, 101b (90-52) <u>Annexations (*invasiones*) against the King</u>; Horseham: TRE Beorhtmær, a freeman, held a hide in Horseham. Now Walard holds it from Richard fitz Gilbert.

2105 ii, 101b–102a (90-53) <u>Annexations (*invasiones*) against the King</u>; Howe: TRE Coleman, a freeman, held thirty-seven and a half acres of land in Howe. Now Germund holds it from Richard fitz Gilbert.

2106 ii, 102a (90-54) <u>Annexations (*invasiones*) against the King</u>; Yeldham: TRE Godwine, a freeman, held forty acres of land in Yeldham. Now Bernard holds it from Richard fitz Gilbert.

2107 ii, 102a (90-55) <u>Annexations (*invasiones*) against the King</u>; Borley: TRE Grim and Godgifu, both freemen, held half a hide and twenty-three acres of land in Borley. Now Ansketil holds it from Richard fitz Gilbert.

2108 ii, 102a (90-56) <u>Annexations (*invasiones*) against the King</u>; Toppesfield: TRE Æthelstan, a freeman, held fifteen acres of land in Toppesfield. Now Ralph holds it from Richard fitz Gilbert.

2109 ii, 102a (90-57) <u>Annexations (*invasiones*) against the King</u>; Toppesfield: TRE Dufe held fifteen acres of land in Toppesfield. Now G. holds it from Richard fitz Gilbert.

2110 ii, 102a (90-58) <u>Annexations (*invasiones*) against the King</u>; Cornish Hall (formerly Norton): TRE Beorhtric, a freeman, held fifty-five acres of land in Cornish Hall. Now Mascerel holds it from Richard fitz Gilbert.

2111 ii, 102a (90-59, 60, 61, 62, 63) <u>Annexations (*invasiones*) against the King</u>; Pebmarsh, Alphamstone, Steeple Bumpstead, Great Saling, Ovington: TRE

Leofcild, a freeman, held three acres in Pebmarsh. He still holds them from Richard fitz Gilbert. Deorwulf held four acres in Alphamstone; and Hold, a freeman, held one acre there. Leofwine and Leofmær held five acres in Steeple Bumpstead; Algar held twenty acres in Great Saling; and Beorhtwulf held thirty acres in Ovington. Wihtgar had the commendation only of all of these men. Now Richard fitz Gilbert holds.

2112   ii, 102b (90-64) <u>Annexations (*invasiones*) against the King; Bendysh</u>: Wihtgar, Richard fitz Gilbert's antecessor, annexed (*invasit*) thirty acres of land in Bendysh after King William came into this land. Afterwards, Ingelric held it. The hundred testifies that it belonged to the fee of Ingelric, but until now Richard fitz Gilbert has held.

2113   ii, 102b (90-65) <u>Annexations (*invasiones*) against the King; Great Bardfield</u>: TRE Fælaghi held one hide and thirty acres of land in Great Bardfield from Earl Ælfgar. After King William came into this land, Richard fitz Gilbert annexed (*invasit*) it. But his antecessor, so the hundred testifies, did not hold it.

2114   ii, 102b (90-66) <u>Annexations (*invasiones*) against the King; "Hocsenga"</u>: TRE Fælaghi held a half hide in "Hocsenga," Now Richard fitz Gilbert holds it, as he does the abovementioned land, and Walter holds from him.

2115   ii, 102b (90-67) <u>Annexations (*invasiones*) against the King; "Hasingham"</u>: TRE a freeman held two and a half acres of land in "Hasingham" in Lexden Hundred. He was, however, commended only to Richard fitz Gilbert's antecessor. Now Richard holds it.

2116   ii, 102b (90-68) <u>Annexations (*invasiones*) against the King; Colne</u>: TRE Lutting held forty acres in Colne. Now Richard fitz Gilbert holds them. His antecessor had no customs except (*nisi*) commendation from this land.

2117   ii, 102b (90-69) <u>Annexations (*invasiones*) against the King; Crepping</u>: TRE Alweard held sixty-eight and a half acres of land freely in Crepping, which Richard fitz Gilbert now holds, as he does the other land.

2118   ii, 102b (90-70) <u>Annexations (*invasiones*) against the King; West Bergholt</u>: TRE Alwig the Huntsman held one half hide and twenty-six and a half acres freely. Now Richard fitz Gilbert holds them in West Bergholt, as he does the other land.

2119   ii, 102b (90-71) <u>Annexations (*invasiones*) against the King; Colne</u>: TRE Wulfric held five acres of land freely in Colne. Now Richard fitz Gilbert holds it, as he does the other land.

2120   ii, 102b (90-72) <u>Annexations (*invasiones*) against the King; Fordham</u>: TRE Tofa-Hildr held three acres of land in Fordham. Now Richard fitz Gilbert holds it, as he does the other land.

2121   ii, 102b (90-73) <u>Annexations (*invasiones*) against the King; West Bergholt</u>: TRE Goding held six acres of land in West Bergholt. Now Richard fitz Gilbert holds it.

2122   ii, 103a (90-74) <u>Annexations (*invasiones*) against the King; Halstead</u>: TRE a freeman held two and a half acres of land in Halstead. The value is 30d.

Alfred, Richard fitz Gilbert's reeve, has taken these pence (*istos denarios recepit*) and has given a pledge for this (*inde dedit vadem*).

2123 ii, 103a (90-75) Annexations (*invasiones*) against the King; Horseham: TRE a free woman held thirty acres of land in Horseham. Now Widelard holds it from the King, so he says, but the hundred does not testify. Richard fitz Gilbert has had the service.

2124 ii, 103a (90-76) Annexations (*invasiones*) against the King; Braintree: Three freemen held thirty acres of land in Braintree TRE, which Leodmær the Reeve claimed from the fee (*reclamavit ad feudum*) of Richard fitz Gilbert. Richard's men, however, do not testify, and the reeve has given a pledge concerning this (*inde dedit vadem*).

2125 ii, 103a (90-77) Annexations (*invasiones*) against the King; Chaureth: TRE Wulfric, a freeman, held thirty acres of land in Chaureth. Now Warner, Richard fitz Gilbert's man, holds it. He called (*vocavit*) Ilbold as warrantor (*ad tutorem*), and afterwards he did not bring a warrantor (*non adduxit tutorem*).

2126 ii, 103a (90-78) Annexations (*invasiones*) against the King; Chaureth: TRE two freemen held half a hide of land in Chaureth. Æthelmær, Richard fitz Gilbert's reeve, annexed (*invasit*) this land, and vouched Richard to warranty (*revocavit eum ad tutorem*); but Richard failed (*defuit*) him, and Æthelmær has given a pledge concerning this (*ex hoc dedit ille vadem*).

2127 ii, 103a (90-79) Annexations (*invasiones*) against the King; Lawling: TRW the monks of Canterbury hold a hide in Lawling, which three freemen held in the time of King Edward. This land was added to the manor TRW.

2128 ii, 103a (90-80) Annexations (*invasiones*) against the King; Colne: TRW Thorbiorn holds twenty-two acres in Colne without the King's gift (*sine dono regis*). He has paid no customs.

2129 ii, 103a (90-81) Annexations (*invasiones*) against the King; Steeple: Henry de Ferrers annexed (*invasit*) a freeman with sixteen acres of land in Steeple.

2130 ii, 103a (90-82) Annexations (*invasiones*) against the King; "Sciddeham": William Leofric annexed (*invasit*) a freeman with six acres of land in "Sciddeham."

2131 ii, 103a (90-83) Annexations (*invasiones*) against the King; Helions Bumpstead: Robert Blunt annexed (*invasit*) ten acres in Helions Bumpstead, which Eadwig, a freeman held.

2132 ii, 103b (90-84) Annexations (*invasiones*) against the King; Middleton: Robert Malet annexed (*invasit*) fifteen acres in Middleton, which a freeman held TRE.

2133 ii, 103b (90-85) Annexations (*invasiones*) against the King; Stevington End: Until now Frodo, the Abbot of Bury St. Edmunds's brother, has held two freemen in Stevington End, whom Ordgar, Frodo's antecessor, annexed (*invasit*), and who lived in the King's soke.

2134 ii, 103b (90-86) Annexations (*invasiones*) against the King; Chishill: TRE Leofwine held five acres of land in Chishill. Now Roger d'Auberville holds it, because his antecessor was seised (*fuit saisitus*).

2135 ii, 103b (90-87) <u>Annexations (*invasiones*) against the King; Ongar</u>: Fifteen acres of Ongar lie in Rochford Hundred, which Berenger, a man of Eustace of Boulogne, holds.

2136 ii, 104a (B-1, 2) <u>Colchester</u>: TRE Godric, a freeman, held four *mansiones* of land and a church in Colchester, along with four hides of land in Greenstead. When he died, his sons divided (*dimiserunt*) this land into four parts. The King has two of them, to which belong two houses in the borough which have always paid and still pay the King customs. Eustace of Boulogne and John fitz Waleran each hold a hide from the other two parts. The King has not had customs from these two parts. The burgesses of Colchester claim (*calumpniantur*) five hides of land in Lexden, which lay in the aforementioned manor of Godric, and which were in the custom and the tax (*ad consuetudinem et cootum*) of Colchester.

2137 ii, 104b (B-3a) <u>Colchester</u>: TRW Leofwine, a King's burgess, holds a house in Colchester and ten acres of land by agreement (*consilio*).

2138 ii, 104b (B-3a) <u>Colchester</u>: TRW Godwine also holds two houses in Colchester and six acres of land by agreement (*consilio*).

2139 ii, 106a (B-3a) <u>Colchester</u>: TRW Tesco holds two houses in Colchester and twenty acres of land, and he owes customs to the King, but never pays.

2140 ii, 106a (B-3a) <u>Colchester</u>: TRW Ralph Pinel holds four houses below the walls of Colchester and five acres of land. He has not paid customs and has given a pledge (*indedit vadem*).

2141 ii, 106a (B-3b) <u>Colchester</u>: TRW Haimo Dapifer holds a house, a court (*curiam*), a hide of land, and fifteen burgesses in Colchester. Thorbiorn, his antecessor, held all of this in the time of King Edward. Everything except his hall paid customs TRE, and the burgesses still pay on their heads (*de suis capitibus*). Customs, however, have been paid neither from their land nor from the hide they now hold from Haimo.

2142 ii, 106a–b (B-3d) <u>Colchester</u>: TRW Eudo Dapifer holds five houses and forty acres of land in Colchester, which burgesses held TRE. They paid all burgal customs (*omnes consuetudines burgensium*). Now, however, they do not pay customs, except on their heads (*nisi de suis capitibus*).

2143 ii, 106b (B-3e) <u>Colchester</u>: TRW Hugh de Montfort holds a house in Colchester, which his antecessor Godric held in the time of King Edward. At that time, it paid the King's customs, but afterwards and now it does not pay them – not since Hugh has had it.

2144 ii, 106b (B-3f) <u>Colchester</u>: TRW Roger the Poitevin holds a house in Colchester, which his antecessor Alflæd held TRE. It paid the King's customs. Now it does not pay them, nor has it paid since Roger has had it.

2145 ii, 106b (B-3g) <u>Colchester</u>: TRW Count Eustace holds twelve houses in Colchester along with one that Ingelric seized (*occupavit*). These houses paid the King's custom TRE, but now they do not, nor have they paid since Eustace has had them.

2146 ii, 106b (B-3j) <u>Colchester</u>: TRW Otto the Goldsmith holds three houses in Colchester, which lie in Shalford. Countess Ælfgifu held them, and they paid the King's customs. Now they do not. This is from the Queen's land.

2147 ii, 106b (B-3k) <u>Colchester</u>: TRW the Abbot of Westminster holds four houses in Colchester, which Earl Harold held in Feering in the time of King Edward. Then they paid customs; now they do not.

2148 ii, 106b (B-3l) <u>Colchester</u>: TRW Geoffrey de Mandeville holds two houses in Colchester, which Ginni held in Ardleigh TRE. Then they paid customs; now they do not.

2149 ii, 106b (B-3m) <u>Colchester</u>: TRW Swein holds a house in Colchester, which Goda held in Elmstead TRE. It used to pay the King's customs; now it only pays on the men's head (*nisi caput hominis*).

2150 ii, 106b (B-3n) <u>Colchester</u>: TRW William de Watteville holds a house in Colchester from Swein, which Robert fitz Wimarc held TRE. Then it paid customs; now it does not.

2151 ii, 106b–107a (B-3p) <u>Colchester</u>: TRW Thurstan Wiscart holds three houses in Colchester and half a hide of land from John fitz Waleran. Two burgesses held all of this TRE. Then it paid customs; now it does not.

2152 ii, 107a (B-3q) <u>Colchester</u>: TRW Ranulf Peverel holds five houses in Colchester (one outside the walls), which Æthelmær held in Terling TRE. Then they paid customs; now they do not.

2153 ii, 107a (B-3r) <u>Colchester</u>: TRW Ralph Baynard holds a house in Colchester, which Æthelmær Melk held in Tolleshunt TRE. Then it paid customs; now it does not.

2154 ii, 107a (B-3s) <u>Colchester</u>: TRE the Abbess of Barking held three houses in Colchester. Then they paid customs; now they do not.

2155 ii, 107a (B-3t) <u>Colchester</u>: TRW Aubrey de Vere holds two houses in Colchester and three acres of land, which his antecessor Wulfwine held TRE. Then they paid customs; now they do not.

2156 ii, 107a (B-5) <u>Colchester</u>: In the burgal commune (*in commune burgensum*) there are eighty acres of land and eight perches around the wall. The burgesses have 60s. each year from the whole of this, for the service of the King (*ad servitium regis*), if it should be needed for his use (*si opus fuerit*). If, however, it is not, they are divided in common (*in commune dividunt*).

2157 ii, 107a (B-6) <u>Colchester</u>: In Colchester there is the custom that once each year, on the fifteenth day after Easter, the burgesses pay two marks of silver to the King: this belongs to the King's farm. Beyond this, once a year from each house that can pay, comes 6d. for the victualing of the King's soldiers (*soldariorum*), either for an expedition by land or by sea. This is to be paid if the King either has soldiers (*soldarios*) or makes an expedition (*expetitionem facerit*). This is not of the King's farm. Beyond this custom of 6d., each year in the time of King Edward the whole city used to pay, from all that was owed, £15 5s. 3d. The moneyers paid £4 of this £15 5s. 3d. in the time of King Edward. Now Colchester pays £80 and four sesters of honey, or 40s. 4d.

Beyond this, the sheriff has 100s. as a gift (*de gersuma*) and 10s. 8d. are paid for the feeding of the prebends (*ad prebendarios pascendos*).

2158   ii, 107b (B-6) <u>Colchester</u>: Beyond this, the burgesses of Colchester and Maldon pay £20 for the mint: this was arranged (*constituit*) by Waleran, and the burgesses vouch the King to warranty that he pardoned them (*advocant regem ad turtorem, quod condonavit*) for £10. Bishop Walkelin holds this, and he asks (*querit*) £40 from them.

2159   ii, 107b (B-7) <u>Colchester</u>: Two priests held the Church of St. Peter, Colchester, along with two hides of land, in the King's alms TRE. Concerning these alms, Robert son of Ralph of Hastings claims (*reclamat*) three-quarters, and Eudo Dapifer holds a quarter. In the time of King Edward, all of this paid customs; now it does not.

Norfolk

2160   ii, 109b (1-1) <u>Terra Regis; Great Massingham</u>: TRE Earl Harold held three carucates of land in Great Massingham. Now King William holds it. Twenty-five sokemen were present (*aderant*) in this manor TRE, with all customs. Now Guy d'Anjou holds twenty of them, and they have two carucates and fifty-eight and a quarter acres of land. William de Warenne has three, who have 120 and a half acres of land. Roger Bigot has one, who has fifteen acres; and William d'Ecouis has one with ten acres. Similarly, fourteen freemen and twelve villeins, whom Ralph Baynard now holds, have been taken away (*sunt . . . ablati*) from this manor.

2161   ii, 109b–110a (1-2) <u>Terra Regis; Southmere</u>: TRE Earl Harold held Southmere. Now King William holds it. There were four sokemen and four acres of land there both in the time of King Edward and after the coming of King William. Afterwards Roger Bigot took (*recepit*) this manor, and Brun his reeve took these men away (*tulit*) from the manor. Now Roger holds them.

2162   ii, 110a (1-4, 5, 6) <u>Terra Regis; Saham Toney</u>: King Edward held three carucates and forty-five acres of land in Saham Toney. Now King William holds it. TRE forty-six sokemen with three carucates and twenty-seven acres of land lay in this manor with all customs. Now there are thirty-one. Rainald fitz Ivo has fifteen of them, and Berner the Balistarius has two. Four of Harold's freemen in Caston, with 204 acres of land, were added to Saham Toney after the coming of King William, by his order (*suo praecepto*). And eight freemen in Breckles with two carucates of land, who were in Harold's soke TRE, were also added to Saham Toney in the time of King William. The value of Harold's freemen was 53s. TRE. Now they are in the farm for £20.

2163   ii, 110b (1-7) <u>Terra Regis; Saham Toney</u>: There are five sokemen in Saham Toney, whom the reeve of Saham sold (*vendidit*) for a bridle to Eudo, a man of Earl Ralph. They lay in Little Ellingham at farm. Earl Ralph held them on the day he forfeited (*forisfecit*). Then Robert Blunt had 10s. 8d. from them, as long as he held his office (*habuit ministerium*). Now they are again in Saham Toney, and they do not pay rent (*censum*) to Godric.

2164 ii, 110b (1-10) Terra Regis; Saham Toney: In Breckles, in the time of King Edward, there was a quarter acre and customs in pasture, which lay in Saham Toney. Now the same. But Godric vouches (*revocat*) this to the fee of Earl Ralph in Stow Bedon, saying that he held it himself for two years before Earl Ralph forfeited (*forisfaceret*), and for two years after. A servant of the King at Stow Bedon has offered to bear the ordeal concerning this (*ex hoc offert quidam famulus regis de Stou portare iudicum*).

2165 ii, 110b–111a (1-11) Terra Regis; Hingham: King Edward held two carucates and twenty-five acres in Hingham: now King William holds them. There were forty-three sokemen there, now twenty. Of those who remain, William de Warenne has twelve; Count Alan three; and Eudo fitz Clamahoc took (*accepit*) eight of them, whom Ralph de Beaufort now holds.

2166 ii, 111b–112a (1-19) Terra Regis; Holt: King Edward held two carucates in Holt. Now King William holds them. TRE eight freemen belonged to this manor with three and a half carucates of land. Now Walter Giffard, so his men say, holds them through the King's livery (*per liberationem regis*). Another freeman with twenty-three acres belonged to this manor. Now Earl Hugh holds.

2167 ii, 112b (1-28) Terra Regis; Gunthorpe: There is a half carucate of land in Gunthorpe, which Alwine held TRE. This has been added to the manor of Holt from the land of Bishop Æthelmær.

2168 ii, 112b (1-29) Terra Regis; Holt: Ketil, a freeman in Morston, Earl Gyrth's manor, who held thirty acres of land, was added to Holt after King Edward's death.

2169 ii, 113b (1-44) Terra Regis; Walsham Hundred: Walsham Hundred pays 40s. to the King and 20s. to the earl.

2170 ii, 114a (1-51) Terra Regis; Burston: TRE there were six sokemen with forty acres of land in Burston. This land is appended to Diss, in Suffolk, and is assessed there. All the soke and sake of the half hundred of Diss was there TRE, except for the land of Bury St. Edmund's (and of this Bury has half and the King has half), Wulfgeat's land, and Stigand's land. Concerning the land of all the others, the soke was in the hundred TRE.

2171 ii, 114a–b (1-52) Terra Regis; Foulsham: King Edward held twelve carucates and three acres of land in Foulsham. Now King William holds it. TRE there were thirty sokemen there, now twenty-four, and Walter Giffard holds six of them. In the time of King William two more freemen were attached to this manor through (*per*) Ralph Taillebois: this is testified by the hundred.

2172 ii, 114b–115a (1-57) Terra Regis; Cawston: TRE Earl Harold held eleven carucates and forty acres of land in Cawston. Now King William holds it. There were ten sokemen there TRE. Now Rainald fitz Ivo has two; William bishop of Norwich two; Count Alan one. Godric holds two from the fee of the King, who were held by Earl Ralph when he forfeited (*forisfecit*). William de Warenne has two, and Roger Bigot has one. Earl Harold also held Marsham and Blickling in Cawston along with twenty-three sokemen. Bishop Herfast held these two manors, and now William bishop of Norwich holds them. Walter Giffard also holds twenty-six sokemen there, whom his antecessor Bodin held. Earl Harold also held five sokemen in Cawston, whom Earl Ralph held: now Godric holds them from the fee of the King. There is a berewick in Oulton of one carucate, which has always lain in Cawston. There are four and a half sokemen there. Earl Ralph held half of the half sokeman with 110 acres of land when he forfeited (*forisfecit*). The reeve of Cawston sold (*vendidit*) another of these sokemen with thirteen acres of land for 10s. Ralph held this sokeman when he forfeited (*forisfecit*). Ralph had also been seised (*erat saisitus*), when he forfeited (*forisfecit*), of another of these sokemen with five acres of land. TRE there was a freeman of St. Benedict's there with eighty-four acres of land. He has been added to this manor.

2173   ii, 114a–115b (1-57) <u>Terra Regis; Wickmere</u>: TRE a freeman of Harold's held thirty acres in Wickmere. Drogo de la Beuvrière claims (*calumpniatur*) this land as part of his fee, because Humphrey held it.

2174   ii, 115b–116a (1-59) <u>Terra Regis; Ormesby (St. Margaret or St. Michael)</u>: TRE Gyrth held three carucates and thirty acres of land in Ormesby from Ramsey Abbey. There are eighty sokemen there with four carucates and forty-six acres of land. Richard holds three of these sokemen with half a carucate of land, by gift (*de dono*) of Bishop Herfast.

2175   ii, 116a (1-61) <u>Terra Regis; Norwich</u>: TRE there were 1,320 burgesses in Norwich. One of them was so much in the demesne of the King that he could neither withdraw nor do homage without the King's permission (*unus erat ita dominicus regis, ut non posset recedere nec homagium facere sine licentia ipsius*). His name was Eadstan. He had eighteen acres of land and twelve of meadow, two churches, and the sixth part of a third church in Norwich. A messuage in the borough belonged to one of these churches along with six acres of meadow. Now Roger Bigot holds all of this by gift of the King (*de dono regis*).

2176   ii, 116a–b (1-61) <u>Terra Regis; Norwich</u>: The King and the earl had the soke and sake and customs of 1,238 burgesses. Archbishop Stigand had the soke, sake, and commendation of fifty. Harold had the soke, sake, and commendation of thirty-two. One of these men was so much in Harold's demesne that he could neither withdraw, nor could he do homage without his permission (*ita ei dominicus ut non posset recederae nec homagium facere sine licentia ipsius*). All of these burgesses had twelve and a half acres of meadow, which Wihenoc took away (*tulit*) from them. Now Rainald fitz Ivo has this. These burgesses, moreover, had two acres of meadow which lay in the Church of All Saints: Wihenoc took them away (*tulit*), and now Rainald has them.

2177   ii, 116b (1-61) <u>Terra Regis; Norwich</u>: The Church of St. Martin is in the borough of Norwich. Archbishop Stigand held it TRE along with twelve acres of land. Now William de Noyers has it from Stigand's fee. Stigand also held the Church of St. Michael, Norwich with 112 acres of land, six acres of meadow, and a plow. William bishop of Norwich holds this, but not from his bishopric.

2178 ii, 116b (1-61) <u>Terra Regis; Norwich</u>: TRE twelve burgesses of Norwich held the Church of the Holy Trinity. Now Bishop William holds it by gift of the King (*de dono regis*).

2179 ii, 116b (1-61) <u>Terra Regis; Norwich</u>: TRW there are 665 English burgesses in Norwich who pay customs, and 480 bordars who do not because of their poverty.

2180 ii, 116b (1-61) <u>Terra Regis; Norwich</u>: On the land in Norwich over which Earl Harold had soke, there are fifteen burgesses and seventeen empty messuages, which have been seized for the castle (*sunt in occupatione castelli*). There are 190 empty messuages in the borough as well, that used to be in the soke of the King and the earl. Eighty-one have been seized for the castle (*in occupatione castelli*).

2181 ii, 116b–117a (1-61) <u>Terra Regis; Norwich</u>: King William does not have his customs from fifty houses in Norwich. Of these Rainald, Roger Bigot's man, has two houses and two messuages; Robert Baro has two houses; Abba one house; Rabel two houses and two messuages, and two messuages which are held by two women; Ansculf the Englishman has one house; Theobald, the Abbot of Bury St. Edmunds's man, one house; Burgheard one house; Walo one house; William, Hervey de Vere's man, one house; Mainard the Watchman one house; the lesser burgesses one house; Hervey de Vere one house; Ralph the Balistarius two houses and one messuage; Herbert the Fosarius three houses; Roger the Poitevin two houses; Mainard, the Abbot of Ramsey man, one house; Peter, the Abbot of Bury St. Edmund's man, one messuage; Everwine the Burgess one house; Baldwin one house; Willelm the Englishman one house; Gerard the Watchman one house; Robert Lorimer one messuage; Hildebrand Lorimer one house; Godwine the Burgess one house; William, Hermer's man, one house; Gilbert the Watchman one house; Fulbert, the priest of Hermer, one house; Walter one house; Rainald fitz Ivo one house; Richard de Saint-Claire one house; Hugh, William d'Ecouis's man, one house. Also the Bishop of Norwich's men have ten houses, and in the bishop's own court (*in propria curia*) there are fourteen messuage which King William gave (*dedit*) to Bishop Herfast for the principal seat of the bishopric (*ad principalem sedem episcopatus*). Gilbert the Balistarius has one house and two messuages; William d'Ecouis one house; Mainard one house; the Abbot of Ely one messuage. The whole of the borough paid £20 to the King TRE and £10 to the earl, along with 21s. 4d. to the prebendaries, six sesters of honey, a bear, and six dogs for the bear. Now it pays £70 by weight, and 100s. *ad numerum*, and a goshawk as a gift (*gersuma*) to the Queen, and £20 blanched to the earl, and 20s. *ad numerum* as a gift (*gersuma*) to Godric.

2182 ii, 117b (1-61) <u>Terra Regis; Norwich</u>: TRE Bishop Æthelmær held the Churches of St. Simon and St. Jude in Norwich. Afterwards Bishop Herfast held them, and now Bishop William does. Three-quarters of a mill, half an acre of meadow, and a messuage lie in these churches. This is not from the bishopric, but rather from Bishop Æthelmær's patrimony (*de patrimonio*).

2183 ii, 117b (1-63) <u>Terra Regis; Norwich</u>: In the time of King William twenty-two of the burgesses who lived in Norwich left, and they now live in Beccles [Suffolk], the Abbot of Bury St. Edmunds's vill. Six others have left the borough and live in Humbleyard Hundred. One lives in Thorpe St. Andrew, the King's vill; one on the land of Roger Bigot; one under William de Noyers; and one under Richard de Saint-Claire. Those fleeing (*fugientes*) and the others remaining have been totally devastated (*sunt vastati*), partly because of Earl Ralph's forfeitures (*forisfacturas*), partly because of a fire, partly because of the King's geld (*geltum regis*), and partly through (*per*) Waleran.

2184 ii, 117b (1-64) <u>Terra Regis; Norwich</u>: Ranulf fitz Walter took (*accepit*) a waste house in Norwich by gift of the King (*de dono regis*).

2185 ii, 117b (1-64) <u>Terra Regis; Norwich</u>: Walter the Deacon has a house in the borough, but it was not there TRE.

2186 ii, 117b (1-64) <u>Terra Regis; Norwich</u>: Two of Earl Ralph's men took away (*abstulerunt*) two acres of meadow from the Church of the Holy Sepulchre, Norwich. The priest later had it back (*rehabuit*) with the consent (*concessu*) of the sheriff.

2187 ii, 118a (1-66) <u>Terra Regis; Norwich</u>: In the new borough there are thirty-six burgesses and six Englishmen, and each paid an annual custom of one penny besides forfeitures (*forisfacturas*). The King had two-thirds of this, and the earl a third. All of the land of these burgesses was in Earl Ralph's demesne, and he granted (*concessit*) it to the King in common (*in commune*) for the making of the new borough between himself and the King, so the sheriffs testify. All the lands of both the knights and the burgesses pay customs to the King. In the new borough, Earl Ralph also made a new church and gave (*dedit*) it to his chaplains. Now Walo, a priest of the sheriff, holds it by gift of the King (*de dono regis*). As long as Robert Blunt held the county, he had an ounce of gold from the new borough once each year.

2188 ii, 118a–b (1-67) <u>Terra Regis; Yarmouth</u>: King Edward held Yarmouth. Now King William holds it. The value TRE, with two-thirds of the soke of three hundreds, was £18 *ad numerum*. The earl's third was £9 *ad numerum*. Now the King's two-thirds are valued at £17 16s. 4d. blanched, and the earl's third is valued at £10 blanched. The sheriff has £4 and an English hawk as a gift (*de gersumma*). The burgesses give (*dant*) these £4 freely and with friendship (*dant burgenses gratis et amicitia*).

2189 ii, 118b–119a (1-69, 70) <u>Terra Regis; Thetford</u>: Archbishop Stigand held the Church of St. Mary, Thetford. Now the sons of Bishop Herfast hold it. Four churches are attached to this church – the Churches of St. Peter, St. John, St. Martin, and St. Margaret. Concerning the King's land in Thetford beyond the water towards Norfolk: the King has two-thirds of a league of land in length and half a league in width. A third of this two-thirds lies in the county (*in consulatu*). Roger Bigot has the other third. There are also two mills there. The King has two-thirds and the earl (*consul*) a third. The King also has two-thirds of another mill, and of these two-thirds, the earl has a third. The other part of this land is towards Suffolk. There is a half league of land there in length and a half in width. A third of this is in the county (*est ad comitatum*).

2190 ii, 118b–119a (1-70) <u>Terra Regis; Thetford</u>: TRE there were 943 burgesses in Thetford. King Edward had all their customs. Thirty-six of these burgesses were so much in the demesne of the King, that they could not be anyone else's men without his permission (*sine licentia regis*). All the others could be anyone else's men, but their customs always remained with the King, except for heriot (*herigete*).

2191 ii, 119b (1-71) <u>Terra Regis (in Godric's service); Sporle</u>: King William holds Sporle, and Godric has custody of it. TRE it was a royal manor, but King Edward gave (*dedit*) it to Ralph the Staller.

2192 ii, 120a (1-75) <u>Terra Regis (in Godric's service); Pickenham (North or South)</u>: TRE a freeman in Pickenham held sixty acres of land. After King William came into the country (*patria*), Earl Ralph gave (*dedit*) it to the reeve of the hundred (*praeposito hundret*), and the reeve still holds this land through (*per*) the King's sheriffs.

2193 ii, 120b (1-77) <u>Terra Regis (in Godric's service); Horningtoft</u>: TRE Ælfric, a freeman, held three carucates of land in Horningtoft. Now King William holds it, and Godric has custody. TRE there were nine sokemen and two bordars there, with a carucate of land. Stigand had the soke of the nine sokemen, but Earl Ralph annexed (*invasit*) it: thus Godric has it.

2194 ii, 120b (1-77) <u>Terra Regis (in Godric's service); Kipton</u>: TRE Ælfric and Ælfhere held three carucates of land in Kipton. There are nine sokemen there with half a carucate of land. TRE Stigand had the soke of these nine sokemen. Then Earl Ralph, before he could forfeit (*forisfeceret*), annexed (*invasit*) it and held it: thus Godric holds it.

2195 ii, 121a (1-81) <u>Terra Regis (in Godric's service); Kimberley</u>: TRE Hagne held two carucates of land in Kimberley. Now it is King William's, and Godric has custody of it. Sixteen freemen in Carleton Forehoe lay in this manor with sixty acres of land. In the time of King Edward, nine of them were Stigand's sokemen, but Earl Ralph had them all before he could forfeit (*forisfaceret*).

2196 ii, 122a (1-87) <u>Terra Regis (in Godric's service); Cranworth, Shipdham</u>: TRE a sokeman of Stow Bedon held thirty acres of land in Cranworth and Shipdham. Robert Blunt had them, but Godric never did.

2197 ii, 123a (1-95, 96) <u>Terra Regis (in Godric's service); Limpenhoe, Hassingham</u>: TRE Alsige had sixteen freemen and a carucate of land in Limpenhoe under Ralph the Staller. There were also six freemen of Ralph the Staller in Hassingham with seventy acres of land. TRE the soke of these two vills was the King's, by testimony (*testimonio*) of the hundred. But Ralph held the soke from the time he was earl. Now Godric holds it in the King's hand.

2198 ii, 123a (1-97) Terra Regis (in Godric's service); Freethorpe: There are nine freemen in Freethorpe with sixty acres of land. In the time of King Edward, Ralph the Staller had soke over five of these men and the King over four. But from the time Ralph was earl, he had all of these men's soke.

2199 ii, 123b (1-101) Terra Regis (in Godric's service); Witton (near Norwich): There are four freemen with sixty acres of land in Witton. The soke is in the hundred of Blofield at the third penny and pays 8s.

2200 ii, 123b–124a (1-106) Terra Regis (in Godric's service); Shotesham: TRE Alnoth held a carucate of land in Shotesham. Now King William holds it, and Godric has custody. Alnoth also held two freemen in Shotesham and had half the commendation of another four. Between them all they held thirty-two acres of land. When Earl Ralph forfeited (*se forisfecit*), he held three of these men and twelve and a half acres of land. Now Aitard, a man of Roger Bigot, holds them, and claims (*reclamat*) them from the fee of the Bishop of Bayeux. Aitard, however, has nothing from his antecessor there except the commendation of half of one of these men, by testimony (*teste*) of the hundred.

2201 ii, 124a (1-107, 108, 109, 110, 111, 112, 113) Terra Regis, (in Godric's service); Stoke Holy Cross, Surlingham, Rockland St. Mary, the other Shotesham (All Saints), Yelverton, Poringland, Shotesham (St. Mary): TRE there was a freeman commended to Alnoth with five acres of land in Stoke Holy Cross, and another three and a half freemen in Surlingham with forty-five acres of land. In Rockland St. Mary there were two freemen commended to Alnoth with twenty-four acres of land. In the other Shotesham, there was a freeman and two half freemen commended to Alnoth with forty acres of land. In Yelverton there were two freemen, one and a half commended to Alnoth and half commended to Alfred, with thirty-three acres of land. Earl Ralph held these two men when he forfeited (*se forisfecit*). Later Godric held them in the King's hand. Now Aitard, a man of Roger Bigot, holds half of one of these men and fifteen acres of land. He claims (*reclamat*) this from the fee of the Bishop of Bayeux. In Poringland there were also two freemen commended to Alnoth with thirteen acres of land. In Shotesham there was a freeman with ten acres of land. The value of all of these freemen is 40s., but in the time of King Edward they were not in the rent (*in censu*) of Shotesham. Robert Blunt has rented (*adcensavit*) them.

2202 ii, 124b (1-120) Terra Regis (in Godric's service); Whitlingham, Bramerton, Rockland St. Mary: TRE there was a freeman in Whitlingham commended to Eadric, three in Bramerton, and one in Rockland St. Mary. Eadric had the commendation of four and a half of these men; Ulfkil of one and a half; and Alfred had the commendation only of half a freeman when King William conquered (*conquisiuit*) England. Earl Ralph held all of these freemen when he forfeited (*se forisfecit*), and afterwards Godric held them in the service of the King (*in ministerium regis*). This is testified by the hundred. Now Aitard de Vaux holds them, and he vouches (*revocat*) them from the fee of the Bishop of Bayeux, from the tenancy (*de tenetura*) of his antecessor Alfred. The hundred fails (*deficit*) him, because these men did not belong to his antecessor.

2203   ii, 124a–125b (1-121, 124) Terra Regis (in Godric's service); Trowse: TRE there was a sokeman of Archbishop Stigand in Trowse with ten and a half acres of land. When Earl Ralph forfeited (*se forisfecit*), he held him. Now Aitard de Vaux claims (*reclamat*) him from the fee of the Bishop of Bayeux, by (*ab*) his antecessor Alfred, under whose commendation only the sokeman was after King William came to England. There are another six sokemen there, who belong to this manor, with fifty-six acres of land. This manor was at rent in the custody (*ad censum in ministerium*) of Godric for 30s. But Godric did not have them because she (?) herself vouches the King to warranty (*revocat ipsa regem ad defensorem*).

2204   ii, 124b–125a (1-122) Terra Regis (in Godric's service); Holverston: There are six men and six half men in Holverston, whom Aitard claims (*reclamat*) from the fee of the Bishop of Bayeux. Their value TRE was 10s. When Godric took custody (*recepti ministerium*) 36s. Now Aitard has 13s. 8d.

2205   ii, 125a (1-127) Terra Regis (in Godric's service); Saxlingham (Nethergate or Thorpe): TRE a freeman commended to Harold held thirty acres of land in Saxlingham. Godric Dapifer had custody (*servavit*) of this land in the hand of the King, but the land does not pay rent to him (*ei censum*).

2206   ii, 125a–b (1-128) Terra Regis (in Godric's service); Rendenhall: TRE Rada held a freeman in Redenhall with two carucates of land, who was commended to Eadric. Now the King holds this, and Godric has custody. There are also two freemen there, with one hundred acres of land. William bishop of Norwich claims (*calumpniatur*) twenty of these acres, and the hundred testifies for ten of them.

2207   ii, 125b (1-131) Terra Regis (in Godric's service); Rendenhall: TRE there were twenty freemen in Rendenhall, who were commended to Rada, with eighty acres of land. Earl Ralph rented (*adcensavit*) them; afterwards Ivo Taillebois did the same. In the same place a freeman commended to Eadric held a carucate of land. In the time of Earl Ralph, his men and Iudhael paid 30s. for this. But Iudhael had been made quit from the hall (*erat quietus de aula*), because he was the earl's falconer. After Ralph forfeited (*se forisfecit*), and Iudhael was in the hand of the King under Godric, he paid nothing, and claims the King as warrantor (*reclamat regem defensorem*).

2208   ii, 126a (1-135) Terra Regis (in Godric's service); Stow Bedon: TRE Ælfhere held Stow Bedon. Now King William holds it, and Godric has custody. TRE its value was £10. When taken (*recepit*) it was valued at £12 13s. 4d. Godric gave (*dedit*) it for £13 13s. 4d. and a gift (*gersumma*) of 20s., as long as he had the soke. Now, after he has lost (*amisit*) the soke, Stow Bedon pays £7, and against (*super*) the sokemen, whom he lost (*amisit*), are £7.

2209   ii, 126b (1-136) <u>Terra Regis (in Godric's service); Little Ellingham</u>: TRE Ælfric, a freeman, held two carucates of land in Little Ellingham. Now King William holds it, and Godric has custody. Six sokemen lay in this manor on the day Earl Ralph forfeited (*forisfecit*): then they paid Robert Blunt 16s. Now they are in Saham Toney, by testimony (*teste*) of the hundred.

2210   ii, 126b–127a (1-139, 142) <u>Terra Regis (in Godric's service); Buckenham (near Attleborough)</u>: TRE Ralph the Staller held three carucates of land in Buckenham, which is in Shropham Hundred. Now King William holds it, and Godric has custody. There are forty-three sokemen there with ten carucates of land. Other men had their commendation, but Ralph added them all to Buckenham in the time of King William. The whole hundred pays 40s. and belongs to the custody (*pertinet ad ministerium*) of Godric.

2211   ii, 127b (1-144) <u>Terra Regis (in Godric's service); Quidenham</u>: TRE Goding, a freeman, held a carucate of land in Quidenham. The Abbot of Bury St. Edmund's had his commendation only. Godric held this land from the Abbot of Bury for three years after the coming of King William, but Godwine, Earl Ralph's uncle, took this land away (*abstulit*) from him unjustly (*iniuste*). Now King William holds it, and Godric has custody.

2212   ii, 128a (1-149) <u>Terra Regis (in Godric's service); East Beckham</u>: TRE Siward Barn held a freeman with thirty acres of land in East Beckham, which lies in North Erpingham Hundred. Earl Ralph added him to Aylsham. There is also a villein there, who has always belonged to Aylsham, as well as a sokeman with an acre of land. They are assessed in Aylsham. Now King William holds this, and Godric has custody. The King has the soke and sake of North Erpingham Hundred except for the land of Siward Barn.

2213   ii, 129b (1-161) <u>Terra Regis (in Godric's service); Wickhampton</u>: TRE there was a sokeman in Wickhampton with a carucate of land. King Edward had the soke, as did Earl Ralph when he forfeited (*se forisfecit*). Now King William holds it, and Godric has custody.

2214   ii, 129b (1-163) <u>Terra Regis (in Godric's service); Moulton St. Mary, Wickhampton</u>: TRW there are seven freemen in Moulton St. Mary and a sokeman in Wickhampton with fifty-six acres of land. They are in the soke of Walsham Hundred. All of these men, with other men who are in another hundred, pay £8 blanched, 100s. in customs *ad numerum*, and a gift (*gersumma*) of 20s. The earl had soke and sake over all of those who were seeking (*requirebant*) his fold; the King and the earl over all the others.

2215   ii, 130a (1-172) <u>Terra Regis (in Godric's service); Shimpling</u>: TRE one of Eadric's freemen held twelve acres of land in Shimpling; and another two sokemen held sixteen acres of land there. Bury St. Edmund's claims (*calumpniatur*) fourteen of these acres, and this is testified by the hundred. But Earl Ralph held it when he forfeited (*se forisfecit*).

2216   ii, 130a–b (1-174, 181) <u>Terra Regis (in Godric's service); Winfarthing, Fersfield</u>: All of the men described under Winfarthing were free with soke (*liberi cum soco*), when Godric took (*recepit*) Winfarthing. Now they pay £7, but they can no longer (*amplius*) pay so much. TRE the soke and sake of all of those men who had less than thirty acres lay in Fersfield. The soke and sake of those men who had thirty acres of land lay in Winfarthing Hundred. When Earl Ralph forfeited (*foresfecit*), he had it.

2217 ii, 130b–131a (1-182) Terra Regis (in Godric's service); Bedingham: TRE Hagne, a King's thegn commended to Stigand, held two carucates of land in Bedingham. Now the King holds it, and Godric has custody. TRE six sokemen lay in this manor with all customs. Afterwards and now there are twenty-six sokemen, twenty of whom Earl Ralph added with soke-fold. They have eighty acres of land. There were another five freemen in Bedingham; three were commended to Hagne and two to Algar. There was also a freeman commended to Godwine in Woodton. Between all of these men, they had one and a half carucates of land. King Edward had the soke over all these freemen, but Earl Ralph unjustly (*iniuste*) held it when he forfeited (*se foresfecit*).

2218 ii, 132a–b (1-192) Terra Regis (in Godric's service); Aylsham: TRE Gyrth held sixteen carucates of land in Aylsham. Now King William holds it, and Godric has custody. Thirty acres in Brundall also lie in this manor. Humphrey nephew of Ranulf brother of Ilger held them, but the hundred has adjudged (*derationavit*) this land to the King. Humphrey has given a pledge (*dedit vadem*) for this. His antecessor, however, held it.

2219 ii, 132b–133a (1-194) Terra Regis (in Godric's service); Belaugh, Little Barningham, Scottow: There are two sokemen of Ramsey Abbey in Belaugh with thirty-four acres of land. Ramsey Abbey had another sokeman with sixteen acres of land in Little Barningham. Earl Ralph held these sokemen when he forfeited (*forisfecit*). Now Godric has them from the King's fee. There is another sokeman of Ramsey Abbey in Scottow with forty-three acres of land. He is held in the same way as the others.

2220 ii, 133a (1-195) Terra Regis (in Godric's service); Hevingham: TRW a priest, who is a freeman, holds forty acres of land in Hevingham in alms, and he sings three masses each week. There is also a sokeman there with eight acres of land. Leofstan, the antecessor of Tihel, held this sokeman TRE, and Earl Ralph held him when he forfeited (*forisfecit*). Now Godric holds him, and he is in the soke of Cawston. But Thurold, William de Warenne's man, seised him against the King (*saisiuit super regem*), and held him for three years. Now it has been adjudged against (*derationatus est super*) Thurold, and Thurold pays 5s. to the King as compensation for stolen goods, and he has given a pledge to do justice (*de catallo regis, et dedit vadem de iusticia facienda*).

2221 ii, 133a–b (1-196) Terra Regis (in Godric's service); Witton (near North Walsham): TRW there is a priest in Witton who holds thirty acres in alms. He sings three masses for the King and the Queen for this land. TRE he paid 2s.

2222 ii, 133b (1-197) Terra Regis (in Godric's service); Happisburgh: TRE Eadric held thirteen carucates of land in Happisburgh. Now King William holds it, and Godric has custody. There are twelve freemen there, over whom Eadric had commendation only. They had four carucates of land. Eadric, a man of Count Alan, annexed (*invasit*) half a carucate of this land, and he has given a pledge (*dedit vadem*). Earl Ralph added these freemen to this manor, and they are now rented (*sunt adcensati*) in the same manor. He held them when he forfeited (*forisfecit*). Robert Malet claims (*calumpniatur*) Happisburgh, and says that his father held it when he went into the marsh. This is testified by the hundred. Yet William Malet did not hold it on the day on which he died.

2223   ii, 134a–b (1-201) <u>Terra Regis (in Godric's service)</u>; <u>Caister</u>: TRE and TRW there are eighty freemen in Caister with four carucates of land. Earl Ralph made this a manor. Its value was £8; afterwards £10. Now it is valued at £14. The Abbot of St. Benet of Holme, however, has £6 from this manor. This land, so Godric says, was delivered with all customs in exchange (*liberatum est pro escangio*) for land in Cornwall.

2224   ii, 134b (1-202) <u>Terra Regis (in Godric's service)</u>; <u>Mautby</u>: TRE Wynstan, a freeman of Ralph the Staller, held one and a half carucates of land in Mautby. Now King William holds it, and Godric has custody. Earl Ralph added fourteen freemen there with two carucates and fifty acres of land.

2225   ii, 135a (1-205) <u>Terra Regis (in Godric's service)</u>; <u>Eaton</u>: TRE Eadric of Laxfield, Robert Malet's antecessor, held a carucate of land in Eaton. Now King William holds it, and Godric has custody.

2226   ii, 135b (1-208) <u>Terra Regis (in Godric's service)</u>; <u>Raveningham</u>: TRE Ulf, a man of the antecessor of Robert Malet, held three carucates of land in Raveningham. Now the King holds it, and Godric has custody.

2227   ii, 135b–136a (1-209) <u>Terra Regis (in William de Noyers's custody)</u>; <u>Hunstanton</u>: TRE Archbishop Stigand held Hunstanton. Now King William holds it, and William de Noyers has custody. TRE a free woman with thirty acres of land lay in this manor. Afterwards Earl Ralph held it when he forfeited (*forisfaceret*) and for three years before. After this, Robert Blunt held it. Godric had it at farm for 30s. with other land. Siward has once again made it lie in this manor, and it does not pay farm to Godric. William de Noyers added three of Ramsey Abbey's sokemen to Hunstanton, with four acres of land.

2228   ii, 136a–b (1-210) <u>Terra Regis (in William de Noyers's custody)</u>; <u>Methwold</u>: TRE Archbishop Stigand held twenty carucates of land in Methwold. Now King William holds it, and William de Noyers has custody. Four freemen lay in this manor TRE. Now William de Warenne has them.

2229   ii, 136b (1-211) <u>Terra Regis (in William de Noyers's custody)</u>; <u>Croxton (near Thetford)</u>: TRE Archbishop Stigand held five carucates of land in Croxton. Now King William holds it, and William de Noyers has custody. There was a mill there TRE, which Earl Ralph took (*cepit*) in the time of King William. Seventeen sokemen lay there TRE. Now William de Warenne has sixteen of them, and Ralph de Tosny has one.

2230   ii, 137a (1-213) <u>Terra Regis (in William de Noyers's custody)</u>; <u>Bittering</u>:

There are seven acres of woodland and one acre of land in Bittering. Godric vouches (*revocat*) this from the fee of Earl Ralph, and Siward holds it in mortgage (*in vadimonio*). The woman who held this land in the time of King Edward wishes to bear the ordeal (*vult ferre iudicium*) that it has been released of its mortgage (*dissolutum est a vadimonio*).

2231   ii, 137b (1-215) Terra Regis (in William de Noyers's custody); Wymondham: TRE Archbishop Stigand held four carucates of land in Wymondham. Now King William holds it, and William de Noyers has custody. The men there had sixty plows, but now there are only twenty-four. Ralph Wader caused this ruin (*hanc confusionem fecit*) before he could forfeit (*forisfaceret*). These plows could all be restored (*possent restaurari*). Eighty-seven sokemen lay in this manor TRE. Now only eighteen are there with thirty acres of land. There was another sokeman there with a carucate of land. Among the sokemen who have been taken away (*ablati sunt*), William de Warenne has fifty-five with five carucates of land; Ralph de Beaufour has ten with two carucates; Count Alan has one with one and a half carucates; and Roger Bigot has two with forty-five acres of land.

2232   ii, 137b–138a (1-216) Terra Regis (in William de Noyers's custody); Thorpe St. Andrew: TRE Archbishop Stigand held three carucates of land in Thorpe St. Andrew. Now King William holds it, and William de Noyers has custody. There have always been twenty-six sokemen with two carucates of land in Thorpe St. Andrew. Earl Ralph had half of one of them with thirty acres of land along with the soke of Archbishop Stigand. When Ralph forfeited (*se forisfecit*), he had the man and the soke. Afterwards, Robert Blunt had this man at rent (*ad censum*). Now William de Noyers has him in the rent (*in censum*) of Thorpe St. Andrew. There are another three and a half sokemen there with soke and sake and thirty-two acres of land. Now Godwine Healfdene holds them by gift (*ex dono*) of Earl Ralph: this is testified by the hundred, but they belong in Thorpe St. Andrew with customs.

2233   ii, 138a (1-217) Terra Regis (in William de Noyers's custody); Somerton (East or West): TRE Archbishop Stigand held a freeman with a carucate of land in Somerton, who could sell without his permission. William de Noyers holds this land in the farm of Mileham, and the soke is in the hundred. Richard Poynant has rented it (*adcensavit*).

2234   ii, 138a–b (1-218) Terra Regis (in William de Noyers's custody); Arminghall: In Arminghall there is a berewick of one carucate, belonging to Thorpe St. Andrew. Now King William holds it, and William de Noyers has custody. There was a mill in Arminghall. Afterwards and now there is not one, because Eudo fitz Clamahoc took it away (*abstulit*) in the time of King William. Now Ralph de Beaufour, his successor (*successor*) holds it, by testimony (*teste*) of the hundred.

2235   ii, 138b (1-220) Terra Regis (in William de Noyers's custody); Denton: TRE there were twelve sokemen in Denton. Archbishop Stigand had the soke of nine of them in Earsham: they had sixty acres of land. Bury St. Edmund's had the soke of four of them with forty acres of land, and they could neither grant nor sell their land outside the abbey. Roger Bigot added these men to Earsham because of their customs and because their soke was in the hundred. Now King William holds this, and William de Noyers has custody.

2236 ii, 138b–139a (1-221) <u>Terra Regis (in William de Noyers's custody); Alburgh</u>: TRE there were fifteen sokemen in Alburgh. The antecessor of Eudo son of Spearhavoc had the commendation of thirteen of them; Bury St. Edmund's had the commendation of two. Together, they had eighty acres of land. Now King William holds it, and William de Noyers has custody.

2237 ii, 139a (1-223) <u>Terra Regis (in William de Noyers's custody); Starston</u>: TRE fifteen of Archbishop Stigand's sokemen in Starston belonged to Earsham with soke. They held eighty acres of land. In the same place there were fifteen sokemen with sixty acres of land, who were commended to Bury St. Edmund's. All of their land was in the abbey, but the soke and sake were in Earsham. Thus, Roger Bigot added all of these men when he held the manor of Earsham, in the time of Archbishop Stigand. Now King William holds it, and William de Noyers has custody.

2238 ii, 139a (1-225) <u>Terra Regis (in William de Noyers's custody); Thorpe Abbots</u>: TRE there were twenty freemen in Thorpe Abbots. Two were commended to Stigand, and they held 100 acres of land. Eighteen were commended to Bury St. Edmund's, and they could not give up their land without the permission (*non poterant reddere sine licentia*) of the saint. The soke and sake, however, were in Earsham.

2239 ii, 139a–b (1-226) <u>Terra Regis (in William de Noyers's custody); Brockdish</u>: TRE there were twenty-eight freemen in Brockdish. Five of them, with half a carucate of land, were Archbishop Stigand's. The remaining twenty-three were Bury St. Edmund's. They had 140 acres of land, but they could neither grant nor sell without permission of Archbishop Stigand, who had their soke, and they paid him 40s. If they did not pay, they forfeited (*non redderent essent forefacti*) £4. Now they pay £16 *ad numerum* in Earsham, where Richard Poynant has rented them (*eos adcensavit*).

2240 ii, 139b (1-226) <u>Terra Regis (in William de Noyers's custody); Earsham Half-Hundred</u>: TRE Archbishop Stigand had the soke and sake of Earsham Half-Hundred, except for Thorpe Abbots, which was Bury St. Edmund's, and Pulham, which lay in Earsham and was Ely Abbey's. When Earl Ralph forfeited (*se forefecit*), he had the soke and sake of Redenhall and of those men commended to him. When Raymond Gerald departed (*discessit*) he had the soke of his land. Later, his successor (*successor*) Roger the Poitevin had it. Bury St. Edmund's held the soke of the lands of Bury in this half-hundred. In Billingford (near Diss), Werengar has kept back (*detinuit*) land from the fee of Roger de Raismes.

2241 ii, 140a (1-229) <u>Terra Regis (in William de Noyers's custody); Mundham</u>: There are seven freemen who belong to Mundham, a berewick of Earsham, which King William holds and William de Noyers has custody. TRE three of these men were commended to Archbishop Stigand, two to Edwin, one to Algar, and one to Toli the Sheriff. Between them all, they had sixty acres of land. Robert fitz Corbucion claims (*calumniatur*) four of them along with twenty-four acres of land, by livery (*ex liberatione*) of the King and by testimony (*teste*) of the hundred. But afterwards Roger Bigot added these men to Earsham, and he has fifty-two acres.

2242   ii, 140a (1-230) <u>Terra Regis (in William de Noyers's custody)</u>; Seething: TRE a freeman held a carucate of land in Seething under Archbishop Stigand. After King William came into England, Stigand added it to Toft Monks as a berewick. Now King William holds it, and William de Noyers has custody.

2243   ii, 140a–b (1-231) <u>Terra Regis (in William de Noyers's custody)</u>; Horstead: TRE Archbishop Stigand held four carucates of land in Horstead. Now King William holds it, and William de Noyers has the custody. In the time of King Edward eighteen sokemen with three carucates of land lay in to this manor. They were delivered (*fuerunt liberati*) to Robert Blanchard. Now they are in the fee of Roger the Poitevin.

2244   ii, 141a–b (1-239) <u>Terra Regis (in William de Noyers's custody)</u>; Stockton: TRE Archbishop Stigand held two carucates of land in Stockton as a berewick of Earsham. Now King William holds it, and William de Noyers has custody. Eight freemen in Stockton with twelve acres of land were added to this manor. There are also twelve freemen in Gillingham with three carucates of land. Nine of them were commended to the antecessor of Ralph de Beaufour TRE; one to Æthelwig of Thetford; one and a half to the Abbot of St. Edmund's; and half to Archbishop Stigand. Another four freemen in Gillingham have fifteen acres of land. TRE Archbishop Stigand had the soke. All of this has been added in the rent (*in censu*) of Earsham.

2245   ii, 141b (1-240) <u>Terra Regis (in William de Noyers's custody)</u>; Raveningham: TRE there was a freeman in Raveningham with sixty acres of land, which he had in pledge (*habebat in wadiatas*) from many men. Now King William holds it, and William de Noyers has custody.

2246   ii, 141b (1-241) <u>Terra Regis (in William de Noyers's custody)</u>; Thurlton: TRW there is a freeman with eight acres of land in Thurlton. He was a freeman of the antecessor of Ralph de Beaufour. Now King William holds him, and William de Noyers has custody.

2247   ii, 142a (2-1) <u>Bishop of Bayeux</u>; Gayton Thorpe: TRE there were two sokemen in Gayton Thorpe with sixty acres of land. Now Odo of Bayeux holds it. One of these men was commended only to the antecessor of Roger Bigot.

2248   ii, 143b (3-1) <u>Count of Mortain</u>; rubric: [An "f," for "*fecit retornam*," appears in the margin, opposite the rubric which marks the beginning of the Count of Mortain's holdings, indicating that he made a return.]

2249   ii, 144a (4-1) <u>Count Alan</u>; Swaffham: TRE Swaffham belonged to the realm (*ad regionem*), and King Edward gave (*dedit*) it to Ralph the Staller. Now Count Alan holds it.

2250 ii, 144b (4-3) <u>Count Alan; Foulden</u>: TRE Æthelstan held half a carucate of land in Foulden. Now Ribald holds it from Count Alan. It has been measured (*mensurata est*) with the land of William de Warenne.

2251 ii, 145a (4-10) <u>Count Alan; Wramplingham</u>: TRE a sokeman of Gyrth held fifteen acres of land in Wramplingham. Now Count Alan holds it. Godric claims (*calumpniatur*) half a house there from the King's fee, and this is testified by the hundred.

2252 ii, 145b (4-14) <u>Count Alan; "Toketorp"</u>: TRW Enisant Musard holds thirty acres of land in "Toketorp" from Count Alan, which were added to the manor of Costessey.

2253 ii, 145b (4-16) <u>Count Alan; Westfield</u>: TRW Faeicon holds a carucate of land in Westfield from Count Alan, which Ely Abbey held TRE.

2254 ii, 146a (4-20) <u>Count Alan; Warham, Holkham, Wells next the Sea</u>: TRW Ribald holds eleven sokemen with two carucates of land in Warham, Holkham, and Wells next the Sea from Count Alan. Eadwig the King's reeve claims (*calumpniatur*) one of these men with thirty acres of land. This is testified by the hundred.

2255 ii, 146b (4-25) <u>Count Alan; Matlask</u>: TRW Ribald holds sixteen acres of land in Matlask from Count Alan. A man of the King claims (*calumpniatur*) this land by offering ordeal or battle against (*offerendo iudicium vel bellum contra*) the hundred, which testifies that they were the count's. But a man of Count Alan wishes to prove that the hundred testified the truth either by ordeal or by battle (*vult probare quod hundret verum testatur vel iudicio vel bello*).

2256 ii, 146b (4-26) <u>Count Alan; Somerton (East or West)</u>: TRE Ælfric, a man of Harold, held three carucates of land in Somerton. Now Wimarc holds it from Count Alan. There are also nine freemen there with two carucates of land. Two halves of these men were St. Benet of Holme's. Godram annexed (*invasit*) them in the time of Earl Ralph.

2257 ii, 147a (4-28) <u>Count Alan; Weston Longville</u>: TRW there are twenty sokemen in Weston Longville with a carucate of land. They are valued in Costessey. TRE their soke was in the King's manor of Foulsham. Now Count Alan holds them because Earl Ralph did.

2258 ii, 148a–b (4-38, 39) <u>Count Alan; Hickling, Ingham</u>: TRE Godwine, a freeman of Eadric of Laxfield, held three and a half carucates of land in Hickling. Now Wimarc holds it from Count Alan. TRE Eadric, a man of Eadric of Laxfield, held three carucates of land in Ingham. Now Count Alan holds it. Robert Malet claims (*calumpniatur*) these two manors because in the time of King Edward his antecessor Eadric had the commendation only of those who held this land. He says that his father was seised of them (*ex eis saisitus fuit*). This is testified by Roger Bigot.

2259 ii, 149a (4-42) <u>Count Alan; Waxham</u>: TRE Eadric, a freeman, held eighty acres of land in Waxham. Now Count Alan holds it. In the time of Earl

Ralph, Eadric added two of Ramsey Abbey's sokemen with three and a half acres of land. There were also eight freemen there with eighty acres of land, who were commended only. Eadric held all of this when Earl Ralph forfeited (*forisfecit*).

2260   ii, 149a (4-44) <u>Count Alan; Islington</u>: TRE Rolf, a freeman, held a carucate of land in Islington. The Bishop of Bayeux had this land on the day Earl Ralph forfeited (*forisfecit*). Now Count Alan has half in his share (*in sua parte*). Ivo Taillebois delivered (*liberavit*) it.

2261   ii, 150a (4-51) <u>Count Alan; Happisburgh</u>: TRE two freemen held one hundred acres of land in Happisburgh. Now Count Alan holds it. Sixty of these acres were in the demesne of Happisburgh when Earl Ralph forfeited (*forisfecit*), but Eadric annexed them and vouches Ivo Taillebois and his companions as warrantor and has given a pledge concerning this (*eas invasit et revocat warant Ivonem Tailesbosc et suos socios et ex hoc dedit vadem*).

2262   ii, 150a (4-51) <u>Count Alan; Ludham</u>: TRE nineteen sokemen of Ramsey Abbey held a carucate of land in Ludham. In the time of Earl Ralph, Eadric, Count Alan's man, annexed (*invasit*) this land, and he was seised when the division of lands was made between the King and the earl (*erat inde seisitus quando facta est divisio terrarum inter regem et comitem*).

2263   ii, 150a (4-51) <u>Count Alan; Palling</u>: Eadric, Count Alan's man, annexed (*invasit*) thirty acres of land in Palling in the time of Earl Ralph.

2264   ii, 150b (4-53) <u>Count Alan; Earlham</u>: TRE a freeman of Eadric, the antecessor of Robert Malet, held thirty acres of land in Earlham. Now Count Alan holds it.

2265   ii, 150b (4-56) <u>Count Alan; Tasburgh</u>: TRW Count Alan has six sokemen with twenty-one acres of land in Tasburgh. One of them was a man of Roger Bigot's antecessor, and Earl Ralph held him when he forfeited (*forisfecit*).

2266   ii, 151a (5-1) <u>Count Eustace; Great Massingham</u>: TRE Ordgar, a freeman, held four carucates of land in Great Massingham. Now Count Eustace holds it, and Guy d'Anjou holds from him. There are also twenty of Harold's sokemen in Massingham with two and a half carucates of land. These men were delivered just as Harold had held them (*fuerunt liberati sicut tenebat eos Heroldus*).

2267   ii, 151a–b (5-2) <u>Count Eustace; Anmer</u>: TRE Ordgar, a freeman, held two carucates of land in Anmer. Now Count Eustace holds it. There are also six freemen there with a carucate of land. Eustace claims them by gift of the King (*reclamat de dono regis*). There are another three sokemen there with thirty acres of land, which Osmund holds by livery (*de liberatione*).

2268   ii, 152a (6-1) <u>Earl of Chester; Shropham</u>: TRE Anund, a freeman, held two carucates of land in Shropham. Now Richard de Vernon holds it from Earl Hugh. TRE the soke was the King's, in Buckenham (near Attleborough). This was so, so Godric says, until Walter de Dol had it by gift (*de dono*) of Earl Ralph.

2269   ii, 152b (6-5) <u>Earl of Chester; Seething</u>: TRE there were nine freemen and four half-freemen of Archbishop Stigand in Seething. Walter de Dol took them away (*abstulit*) and added them to Hedenham. They had half a carucate of land. Now Earl Hugh holds.

2270 ii, 152b–153a (6-6) <u>Earl of Chester; Fundenhall</u>: TRE Burgheard, a thegn, held two carucates of land in Fundenhall. Now Roger Bigot holds it from Earl Hugh. Walter de Dol added two freemen in Hampton with ninety acres to this manor. One was Archbishop Stigand's and the other was Gyrth's. He also added another three freemen with eight acres. From all of this, Walter de Dol made a manor (*fecit . . . i manerium*).

2271 ii, 153a (6-7) <u>Earl of Chester; Kirby Cane</u>: TRE Osmund, a thegn of Archbishop Stigand and the antecessor of Ralph de Beaufour, held a carucate of land in Kirby Cane. Waring now holds it from Earl Hugh.

2272 ii, 153b–154a (7-3) <u>Robert Malet; Kilverstone</u>: TRE Eadric held two carucates of land in Kilverstone. Now Robert Malet holds it, and Walter de Caen holds from him. A sokeman of the King lies there with sixty acres of land. Robert's antecessor had his commendation only, and Robert claims the land by gift of the King (*clamat de dono regis*).

2273 ii, 154a (7-4) <u>Robert Malet; Saxlingham (Nethergate or Thorpe)</u>: TRE Eadric, the antecessor of Robert Malet, held two and a half sokemen with sixty-six acres of land in Saxlingham. Now Walter holds this from Robert Malet.

2274 ii, 154b (7-9) <u>Robert Malet; Thorpe Parva</u>: TRE Eadric, a sokeman under Eadric, antecessor of Malet, held eighty acres of land in Thorpe Parva. Now Hubert holds it from Robert Malet.

2275 ii, 155a (7-14) <u>Robert Malet; Burston</u>: TRE a freeman commended to Leofric of Thorndon held twenty acres of land in Burston. Now Robert Malet holds it by the Queen's gift (*ex dono regine*), and Robert's mother holds from him.

2276 ii, 155a–b (7-16) <u>Robert Malet; Horsford</u>: TRE Eadric, a freeman, held two and a half carucates of land in Horsford. Now Robert Malet holds it. There were twenty-two sokemen there, now twenty-one, with a carucate of land. The King and the earl have the soke of two sokemen there, and they have the six forfeitures over the others (*super alios vi forisfacturas*).

2277 ii, 155b (7-17) <u>Robert Malet; Horsham St. Faith</u>: TRE Eadric, a freeman, held three carucates of land in Horsham St. Faith. Now Robert Malet holds it. There are nineteen sokemen there with a carucate of land. The King and the earl have the soke of three of these men. They have the six forfeitures over the others (*super alios vi forisfacturas*).

2278 ii, 156b (7-20) <u>Robert Malet; Fritton</u>: TRE a freeman commended to Robert Malet's antecessor had thirty acres of land in Fritton. Now Warin the Cook holds it from Robert Malet.

2279 ii, 156b (7-21) <u>Robert Malet; Fritton</u>: TRW Robert Malet has a freeman with fifteen acres of land in Fritton. His antecessor had commendation only.

2280 ii, 157a (8-1) <u>William de Warenne; Stinton</u>: TRE Withar, a freeman, held three carucates of land in Stinton. There are fourteen sokemen there with eighty acres of land. Earl Ralph held two of these men with twelve acres when he forfeited (*forisfecit*). Now William de Warenne holds all of this.

2281   ii, 157a (8-2) <u>William de Warenne; Kerdiston</u>: TRE Godwine, a freeman, held two carucates of land in Kerdiston. Now Randolph holds it from William de Warenne. A freeman with forty-five acres of land was added to this manor in the time of King William. All of this is in exchange (*pro escangio*) for the two manors of Lewes [Sussex].

2282   ii, 157b (8-3) <u>William de Warenne; Hackford (near Reepham)</u>: TRE Withar, a freeman, held one and a half carucates in Hackford. Now Thurold holds it from William de Warenne. It is in exchange (*pro escangio*) for Lewes [Sussex].

2283   ii, 157b (8-4, 5) <u>William de Warenne; Wood Dalling, Thurning</u>: TRW William de Warenne holds five freemen in Wood Dalling and a freeman in Thurning with a carucate of land. This is in exchange (*pro escangio*) for Lewes [Sussex]. The man from Thurning was in the rent (*in censu*) of the King's manor of Sall in the time of Earl Ralph, as well as under Robert Blunt, and for a year under Godric. Now he is held by William de Warenne. This is testified by the hundred: that he was a freeman in the time of King Edward.

2284   ii, 158a–b (8-8) <u>William de Warenne; Coltishall</u>: TRW Thurold holds what sixteen sokemen of Stigand and Ralph the Staller held, that is, 110 acres of land in Coltishall. He holds this from William de Warenne. Ralph, along with his wife, gave (*dedit*) his half of the soke to Ramsey Abbey, so the abbot says.

2285   ii, 158a–b (8-8) <u>William de Warenne; Coltishall</u>: There were two freemen in Mortoft in demesne with half a carucate of land; a freeman of Harold in Itteringham with fifteen acres; a free woman of Harold in Wickmere with twenty-four acres; two freemen of Harold in Little Barningham with thirty acres; two freemen of Ralph the Staller in Mannington with seventeen acres; a freeman of Thurold in Irmingland with eight acres; two freeman in Corpusty with fourteen acres; two freemen of Gyrth in Tuttington with sixteen acres; Thurold holds ten acres in Crackford which a freeman of Gyrth held in Aylsham, and he holds three sokemen of Harold in Brampton with six acres. Humphrey de St. Omer held all of these sokemen from the fee of his antecessor. This is testified by the hundred, and Drogo claims them (*Drogo eos calumpniantur*). Humphrey held this land when he forfeited (*forisfecit*), and Drogo held afterward. But William de Warenne had this before him, and now similarly has it.

2286   ii, 158b (8-10) <u>William de Warenne; Hautbois</u>: TRE a sokeman of Ralph the Staller held 160 acres of land in Hautbois. It lies in Hoveton (St. Peter or St. John), which Earl Ralph, along with his wife, gave (*dedit*) to Ramsey Abbey, so the abbot says, with the consent (*concedente*) of the King. There were also two of Ramsey Abbey's sokemen there with 175 acres of land. This was delivered (*fuit liberatum*) for a carucate of land. All of this is in exchange (*pro escangio*) for Lewes [Sussex].

2287 ii, 159a (8-12) <u>William de Warenne; Witton (near North Walsham)</u>: TRW William de Warenne holds a freeman in Witton with thirty acres of land. TRE and TRW Bishop Æthelmær had half. William Malet had the other half.

2288 ii, 159a (8-12) <u>William de Warenne; Sco Ruston, Barton Turf</u>: TRE there were four sokemen of Stigand in Sco Ruston with ten acres of land. William de Warenne now holds this. It is in the value of Coltishall and is in exchange (*de escangio*) for Lewes [Sussex]. There is another sokeman with sixteen acres in Barton Turf. Ramsey Abbey had the soke TRE. Now William de Warenne holds it. It is in the same exchange (*pro eodem scangio*). All of this was in the soke of Ramsey Abbey. Now William holds the soke with the land.

2289 ii, 159a (8-13) <u>William de Warenne; Filby</u>: TRW William de Warenne holds a freeman, who was Esger's man TRE, with a carucate and nine acres of land in Filby, and Thurold holds from him. This is in exchange (*de escangio*) for Lewes [Sussex].

2290 ii, 159b (8-14) <u>William de Warenne; Carleton Rode</u>: TRE Almær, a freeman, held thirty acres of land in Carleton Rode under Stigand. Now William de Warenne holds it. This is by gift of the King (*de dono regis*).

2291 ii, 159b (8-17) <u>William de Warenne; Hilgay</u>: TRE eight men held twenty-two acres of land in Hilgay. Now William de Warenne holds it, but the hundred testifies that this was for the victualing of the monks of Ramsey Abbey.

2292 ii, 160a (8-18) <u>William de Warenne; Denver</u>: TRE Ælfric, a freeman, held two carucates and three acres of land in Denver. Now Hugh holds it from William de Warenne. William claims it in exchange (*reclamat pro escangio*). William also holds four freemen with seventy-one acres there, which Osmund held TRE. Hermer's antecessor had the commendation only.

2293 ii, 160a (8-19) <u>William de Warenne; Downham Market</u>: TRW William de Warenne holds nine freemen in Downham Market with thirty acres of land. Ramsey Abbey has the commendation and soke of these nine men, but William de Warenne claims them in exchange (*reclamat pro escangio*).

2294 ii, 160b (8-23) <u>William de Warenne; Gayton</u>: TRW William de Warenne has sixteen freemen in Gayton with two carucates of land. He has this in exchange (*pro escangio*).

2295 ii, 161a (8-26) <u>William de Warenne; Congham</u>: TRW William de Warenne holds a freeman with a carucate of land in Congham. There are also twelve freemen there with fifteen acres of land. All of this is in exchange (*pro escangio*) for Lewes [Sussex].

2296 ii, 161a (8-28) <u>William de Warenne; Hillington</u>: TRE two freemen held two carucates of land in Hillington. Now William de Warenne holds it. This is in exchange (*pro escagio*).

2297 ii, 161a–b (8-29) <u>William de Warenne; Massingham (Great or Little)</u>: TRE Alflæd, a free woman, held a carucate of land in Massingham. Now William de Warenne holds it. His antecessor had the commendation only, and Harold had the soke. Rainald fitz Ivo claims (*calumpniatur*) this from his fee. Wihenoc had been seised of it (*inde fuit saisitus*), as were Rainald's father and Rainald himself: this is testified by the hundred.

2298 ii, 161b (8-31) <u>William de Warenne; Anmer</u>: TRE a freeman held half a carucate of land in Anmer. Now William de Warenne holds it. His antecessor had nothing from this except commendation only. Guy vouches (*revocat*) this land, because it had been delivered (*fuit liberata*) to his uncle Osmund and to Count Eustace. William de Warenne's men have disseised (*disaiserunt*) them.

2299 ii, 161b (8-32) <u>William de Warenne; Flitcham</u>: TRE four freemen held a carucate of land in Flitcham. Now William de Warenne holds it. He claims it in exchange (*reclamat pro escangio*).

2300 ii, 161b (8-33) <u>William de Warenne; Barwick</u>: TRE two freemen held a carucate of land in Barwick. One was Harold's man and the other was commended only to the antecessor of Frederick. Now Simon holds from William de Warenne.

2301 ii, 161b (8-37) <u>William de Warenne; Feltwell</u>: TRW William de Warenne holds forty sokemen in Feltwell with three carucates and forty acres of land. Godric claims (*calumpniatur*) this from the fee of Earl Ralph, which lay in Stow Bedon. Concerning this, a man of Godric wishes to bear the ordeal (*vult . . . portare iudicium*). Ely Abbey had the soke, customs, and commendation over all of these men. Seven of them were free with their lands, but the soke and commendation remained with Ely Abbey. All of this was delivered (*fuit liberatum*) to William in exchange (*pro escangio*).

2302 ii, 162a (8-38) <u>William de Warenne; Methwold</u>: TRW William de Warenne holds four freemen with three carucates of land in Methwold. Stigand had the soke. These men were delivered in exchange (*fuerunt liberati pro escangio*).

2303 ii, 162b (8-40) <u>William de Warenne; Mundford</u>: TRE seven sokemen of Ely Abbey (which had all customs) had half a carucate of land in Mundford. Now William de Warenne has this in exchange (*pro escangio*). Also in Mundford there was a freeman of Harold TRE, with half a carucate of land. William de Warenne holds it in exchange (*pro escangio*).

2304 ii, 162b (8-40) <u>William de Warenne; Colveston</u>: TRE a freeman of Harold held a carucate of land in Colveston, which William de Warenne now holds. This is for the castlery (*pro castellatione*) of Lewes [Sussex].

2305 ii, 162b–163a (8-41, 42, 43, 44, 45) <u>William de Warenne; Ickburgh, Santon, Ottering Hithe, Weeting</u>: TRW Roger holds two freemen with half a carucate and six acres of land from William de Warenne in Ickburgh. Walter also holds half of five freemen with two carucates of land in Santon from William de Warenne, and half of three freemen with a carucate of land in Ottering Hithe. Wascelin and Osweard hold a third of nine freemen with five and a half carucates of land from William in Weeting. The commendation of eight of these men were in Ely Abbey. The whole of this is for the castlery (*est de castaellatione*) of Lewes [Sussex].

2306 ii, 163a (8-46) <u>William de Warenne; Cranwich</u>: TRE a freeman of Harold held Cranwich. Now William de Warenne holds it. In the same place William also holds a freeman with two carucates of land. Ely Abbey had the soke and commendation. All of this is for the castlery (*de castellatione*) of Lewes [Sussex].

2307 ii, 163b (8-48) <u>William de Warenne; Snettisham</u>: TRE seven sokemen of Stigand held two carucates of land in Snettisham, and another eleven of his sokemen held twenty acres there. Now William de Warenne holds all of this. This is in exchange (*pro escangio*).

2308 ii, 163b (8-49) <u>William de Warenne; Fring</u>: TRW William de Warenne has a freeman with twenty acres of land in Fring. His antecessor had the commendation only. Archbishop Stigand had the soke.

2309 ii, 163b (8-50) <u>William de Warenne; Threxton</u>: TRW Hugh holds a carucate of land in Threxton from William de Warenne. It belongs to Lewes [Sussex].

2310 ii, 163b (8-51) <u>William de Warenne; Caston</u>: TRW William de Warenne holds three freemen with a carucate of land in Caston. The King and the earl had soke over two of these men, and the antecessor of John, nephew of Waleran, had soke over the third. This belongs to the castle (*ad castellum*) of Lewes [Sussex].

2311 ii, 163b (8-52) <u>William de Warenne; Rockland St. Peter</u>: TRW William de Warenne has four freemen with one and a half carucates of land in Rockland St. Peter. This is in exchange (*pro escangio*).

2312 ii, 164a (8-53) <u>William de Warenne; Little Ellingham, Scoulton, Thompson</u>: TRW William de Warenne has six freemen with eighty acres of land in Little Ellingham. He has six freemen with thirty acres of land in Scoulton and six freemen with a carucate of land in Thompson. This is in exchange (*pro escangio*).

2313 ii, 164a (8-54) <u>William de Warenne; Larling</u>: TRW Hugh holds one and a half carucates of land in Larling from William de Warenne, but it was delivered (*fuit liberata*) for a carucate, which a freeman held TRE.

2314 ii, 164a (8-55, 56) <u>William de Warenne; Rockland (All Saints or St. Andrew)</u>: TRE Brodde, a freeman, held three carucates of land in Rockland. Now Simon holds it from William de Warenne. Simon also holds six and a half freemen with seventy acres of land in Rockland, of whom Brodde had commendation only. The soke of these men was in the King's manor of Buckenham in the time of King Edward and afterwards, until William de Warenne had it. Nine and a half freemen were also added to this land with a carucate and fifty-four acres of land. This is in demesne. The soke and commendation of four and a half of these men were in the King's manor of Buckenham (near Attleborough) TRE and later, until William de Warenne had it. The whole was delivered (*fuit liberatum*) in the time of Earl Ralph. All of this is for the one manor of Lewes [Sussex].

2315 ii, 164b (8-57) <u>William de Warenne; Roudham</u>: TRW William de Warenne has two freemen in Roudham with a carucate of land. TRE the soke was in the King's manor of Buckenham (near Attleborough), and it was delivered (*liberatum est*) in the time of Earl Ralph. Afterwards, he kept back (*retinuit*) the soke.

2316   ii, 164b (8-58) William de Warenne; Illington: TRW William de Warenne holds a freeman in Illington with one and a half carucates of land. The soke is in Buckenham (near Attleborough). It is for the castle (*de castello*) of Lewes [Sussex].

2317   ii, 164b (8-59) William de Warenne; Blo Norton: TRE a freeman held a carucate of land in Blo Norton. Now Fulcher holds it from William de Warenne. This is for the castle (*de castello*) of Lewes [Sussex]. Until William had it, the soke was always in the King's manor of Kenninghall.

2318   ii, 164b (8-60) William de Warenne; Wick: TRW William de Warenne holds a carucate of land in Wick, which a freeman held TRE. There are also eight sokemen there with thirty-two acres of land. All of this was delivered (*fuit liberatum*) for a carucate of land and is for the castle (*de castello*) of Lewes [Sussex]. The soke was in Kenninghall until William de Warenne had it.

2319   ii, 164b–165a (8-61) William de Warenne; Banham: TRE Leofsige, a freeman, held a carucate of land in Banham. He also held five sokemen with thirty-one acres of land. Now William de Warenne holds this. All of this is for the castle (*de castello*) of Lewes [Sussex].

2320   ii, 165a–b (8-64) William de Warenne; Weasenham: TRE twelve of Stigand's sokemen held two carucates of land in Weasenham. Now there are six more sokemen. William de Warenne holds this, and Wimarc holds from him. This is in exchange for new land (*de escagio de nova terra*).

2321   ii, 165b (8-66) William de Warenne; Fransham (Great or Little): TRE two freemen held one and a half carucates of land in Fransham. Frederick's antecessor, and later Frederick, had the commendation only. Afterwards Frederick held it. Now William de Warenne holds, and Gilbert holds from him.

2322   ii, 165b (8-67) William de Warenne; Scarning: TRE Fredegis, a freeman, held one and a half carucates of land in Scarning. Now William de Warenne holds it. It is from the fee of Frederick. Frederick's antecessor had the commendation only, and his antecessors themselves had the soke.

2323   ii, 165b (8-68) William de Warenne; Rougham, Fransham (Great or Little): TRE Toki, a freeman, held two carucates of land in Rougham and Fransham. Now William de Warenne holds it. This is in exchange (*pro escagio*) for Lewes [Sussex].

2324   ii, 165b–166a (8-69) William de Warenne; Tittleshall: TRE five freemen held a carucate of land in Tittleshall. Now Wimarc holds it from William de Warenne. This is in exchange (*pro escagio*) for Lewes [Sussex].

2325   ii, 166a (8-70) William de Warenne; Stanfield: TRE thirty-three freemen under Stigand's soke and commendation held two carucates of land in Stanfield. Now William de Warenne holds it. This is in exchange (*de escagio*) for Lewes [Sussex].

2326 ii, 166a (8-71) <u>William de Warenne; Griston</u>: There is a church in Griston with ten acres of land. Godric claims (*calumpniatur*) that it lay in Stow Bedon in the time of Earl Ralph. One of the King's men wishes to bear the ordeal (*vult ferre iudicium*) that it lay in Stow Bedon when Earl Ralph forfeited (*forisfecit se*) and for a year before and a year after. The men of the hundred, however, testify that it is from the fee of William de Warenne.

2327 ii, 166b (8-80) <u>William de Warenne; Wymondham</u>: There were thirty freemen in Wymondham when William de Warenne took (*recepit*) it. Now there are forty-three. There has always been a carucate of land there. All of this is in exchange for Lewes [Sussex] from the land of the saints (*de escagio de laquis de terra sanctorum*).

2328 ii, 166b–167a (8-83, 84) <u>William de Warenne; Letton, Shipdham</u>: TRE there were nine freemen with a half carucate of land in Letton and eleven freemen in Shipdham with a carucate of land. William de Warenne now holds all of this in exchange (*pro escagio*) for Lewes [Sussex]. There are also nine acres in "Turestuna." This is from the same exchange (*de eodem scangio*).

2329 ii, 167a (8-88) <u>William de Warenne; Yelverton</u>: TRE there was a freeman commended to Harold in Yelverton with thirty acres of land. Now William de Warenne holds it. It is assessed in Acre and is from the exchange (*de escangio*).

2330 ii, 167a–b (8-90) <u>William de Warenne; Foulden</u>: Twenty-four freemen held six carucates of land in Foulden, and they still hold under William de Warenne. He says that he has this in the exchanges (*pro escangiis*) for Lewes [Sussex].

2331 ii, 167b (8-91) <u>William de Warenne; Hilborough</u>: TRE Osmund held Hilborough. Now William de Warenne holds it by gift of the King (*de dono regis*), and William holds from him.

2332 ii, 168a (8-98) <u>William de Warenne; Sculthorpe</u>: TRE Toki held three carucates of land in Sculthorpe. Now William de Warenne holds it. It is from Frederick's fee. Its value was £6; later and now £10. It was at farm for £15 but could not pay it.

2333 ii, 168a–b (8-99) <u>William de Warenne; Barsham (East or West)</u>: TRE Toki held four carucates of land in Barsham. Now Hugh holds it from William de Warenne. There was also a freeman there with a carucate of land, and he lived in two halls. This was delivered as a manor (*fuit liberata pro terra*).

2334 ii, 169b (8-109) <u>William de Warenne; Rudham</u>: TRE a freeman held a carucate of land in Rudham. Now Lambert holds it from William de Warenne. Eighteen freemen also lie in this same manor, in the same carucate. All of this was delivered to him as a manor (*fuit sibi liberata pro terra*).

2335 ii, 170a (8-112) <u>William de Warenne; Shereford</u>: TRE six freemen held a carucate of land in Shereford. Now William de Warenne holds it. It is in exchange (*pro escangio*) for Lewes [Sussex].

2336 ii, 170b (8-117) <u>William de Warenne; Egmere</u>: TRE Alweald, a freeman, held a half carucate of land in Egmere. Now William de Warenne holds it. It was delivered to Frederick as a manor to make (*fuit liberata pro terra ad perficiendum*) his manors.

2337   ii, 170b (8-118) <u>William de Warenne; Holkham</u>: TRW Walter holds half a carucate from William de Warenne in Holkham. It belongs to Burnham and is from Frederick's fee.

2338   ii, 170b–171a (8-119, 120, 121) <u>William de Warenne; Gimingham, Side-strand, Knapton</u>: TRE Rathi, a freeman, held two carucates of land in Gimingham. Now William de Warenne holds it. Another freeman held a carucate of land in Sidestrand as a manor from Archbishop Stigand. Now William de Warenne holds it. Waleran delivered this to make (*hoc liberavit Waleramus ad perficiendum*) the manor of Gimingham. Yet another freeman held a carucate of land in Knapton, which William de Warenne now holds. It was delivered to make (*fuit liberatum ad perficiendum*) the manor of Gimingham. All of this was delivered (*hoc totum fuit liberatum*) as a manor of four carucates.

2339   ii, 171a–b (8-122, 123, 124, 125, 126, 127, 128) <u>William de Warenne; Thorpe Market, Mundesley, Trunch, Repps, Northrepps, Sidestrand, South-repps, Northrepps</u>: TRE a freeman held two carucates of land from Stigand in Thorpe Market, and five sokemen held thirty-two acres of land there. Grimkel, a freeman, held thirty acres in Mundesley; and three of Eadric's freemen held ten acres there. In Trunch a freeman of Harold, one of Ralph the Staller and one of Ketil held ninety acres of land; and six of Eadric's freemen held thirty-four acres. In Repps two freemen of Eadric held thirty acres. In Northrepps a freeman of Ketil held thirty acres. In Sidestrand a freeman of Eadric and a freeman of Almær held sixty acres. In Southrepps and Northrepps two freemen of Alweald abbot of St. Benet of Holme, five of Rathi of Gimingham, and a freeman of Osbert held sixteen acres of land. All of this land was delivered (*fuit liberata*) to William de Warenne as a manor of five carucates in Thorpe Market.

2340   ii, 171b (8-129) <u>William de Warenne; Mundesley, Trunch</u>: In Mundesley and Trunch Robert Malet claims (*calumpniatur*) the commendation of three freemen along with sixteen freemen with all customs. William de Warenne holds them.

2341   ii, 172a (8-134) <u>William de Warenne; Plumstead (near Holt)</u>: TRW Thurold holds a freeman with twelve acres of land in Plumstead from William de Warenne. Drogo de la Beuvrière claims (*calumpniatur*) this for homage only (*pro homagio tantum*).

2342   ii, 172a–b (8-137) <u>William de Warenne; Helhoughton</u>: TRE William de Warenne holds Helhoughton from Frederick's fee. He holds a freeman there in the same way as his antecessor held him (*ita tenuit*) – that is, this man could not withdraw from his land without his permission. This is testified by the hundred. A man of Drogo de la Beuvrière named Frank claims (*calumpniatur*) Helhoughton from the fee of his lord, by gift of the King by livery (*ad feudum domini sui de dono regis de liberatione*), saying that his antecessor Humphrey held it in the time of Frederick, and that, after Frederick, Drogo held it. This is testified by the hundred: that these men held it, but it has not seen this in a writ nor has it seen livery (*in brevem nec liberatorem*).

2343   ii, 172b (8-138) William de Warenne; North Barsham: TRE Earl Harold held two freemen in North Barsham with a carucate of land belonging to Fakenham. Now William de Warenne holds it, but his men do not know (*nesciunt*) how. The hundred testifies that they are William's, because he was seised of them (*ex eis est saisitus*). But a man of the King offers the ordeal (*offert iudicium*) because they belonged to the King's manor of Fakenham TRE.

2344   ii, 173a (9-1) Roger Bigot; Thetford: TRW Roger Bigot has two carucates of land in demesne in Thetford, which are quit from all customs. There are twenty bordars there. The King only has the head tax (*scotum de suo capite tantum*) of these bordars. Roger also has thirty-three men in Thetford commended to him, which were held by his antecessor, who had nothing but commendation (*nichil praeter commendationem*). He also has a mill there, which Thurstan, a burgess, holds. Roger claims it by gift of the King (*reclamat de dono regis*), but the hundred does not know how.

2345   ii, 173a (9-5) Roger Bigot; Great Massingham: TRW there is a freeman in Great Massingham with thirty acres. Humphrey de Culey holds this from Roger Bigot. Æthelwig annexed (*invasit*) this land after the King came into this country. The soke lies in Great Massingham, the King's manor.

2346   ii, 173a–b (9-6) Roger Bigot; Flitcham: TRE Algar held two carucates of land in Flitcham from Archbishop Stigand. Now Ranulf fitz Walter holds it from Roger Bigot. TRE Stigand had the soke over this manor and over all the men who were in it. This was delivered to Roger for his lifetime (*fuit liberatum Rogero vivente eo*).

2347   ii, 173b (9-8) Roger Bigot; Ringstead: TRE Tovi, a freeman, held land in Ringstead. A sokeman of Ramsey Abbey with two acres of land was added in the time of King William. TRE Alstan also held a carucate of land in Ringstead under Stigand. There was another sokeman there with six acres; two sokemen of Ramsey Abbey with sixteen acres; and a freeman with twenty-four acres. All of this was delivered to Roger Bigot to make the manors (*hoc fuit sibi liberatum pro perficiendis manerii*).

2348   ii, 174a–b (9-13) Roger Bigot; Sutton (near Stalham): TRW seven freemen with a carucate of land lie in Sutton. They are in Repps (near Acle) and Rollesby. The hundred testifies that half of one of these freemen, with his six acres of land, is St. Benet of Holme's. A man of Earl Ralph annexed (*invasit*) him. Now Roger Bigot holds.

2349   ii, 174b (9-14) Roger Bigot; Oby: TRE Hringwulf, a freeman, held thirty acres of land in Oby. Now Stanheard holds it from Roger Bigot. There are six freemen there under him with thirty acres of land. Roger Bigot claims (*reclamat*) these men by gift of the King (*ex dono regis*). They are from the fee of his antecessor Æthelwig of Thetford.

2350   ii, 174b (9-15) Roger Bigot; Oby: TRE Godwine, a freeman, held thirty acres of land in Oby. There were also three freemen there under him with fifteen acres of land. Roger Bigot has these men from the fee of his antecessor Æthelwig.

2351 ii, 174b (9-16) <u>Roger Bigot; Clippesby, Ormesby (St. Margaret or St. Michael)</u>: TRE there was one freemen of St. Benet of Holme's in Clippesby and two in Ormesby commended to St. Benet's. Afterwards Æthelwig held them. Now Roger Bigot holds them by gift of the King (*ex dono regis*) with thirty-three acres of land.

2352 ii, 174b (9-17, 18, 19, 20, 21, 22, 23) <u>Roger Bigot; Thurne, Burgh St. Margaret, Billockby, Repps (near Acle), Bastwick, Oby, Somerton (East or West)</u>: TRE there was half a freeman with twenty-one acres of land in Thurne. Ulfkil, a freeman commended to Eadric, held thirty acres of land in Burgh St. Margaret; and three freemen commended to Æthelwig held forty-five acres of land there. A freeman commended to Æthelwig held twenty acres in Billockby; four freemen commended to St. Benet of Holme, two commended to Æthelwig, and one commended to Bishop Æthelmær held eighty acres in Repps; two free women commended to Eadric and Hringwulf held thirteen acres in Bastwick; a freeman held six acres of land in Oby; and a freeman held twenty-one acres in Somerton. The King, so Roger Bigot claims (*reclamat*), gave (*dedit*) these freemen, with their land, to Æthelwig of Thetford.

2353 ii, 175a (9-25) <u>Roger Bigot; Stoke Holy Cross</u>: [Following this entry is a rubric stating that "This is from the exchange (*de escangio*) of Isaac's land." It is unclear to which entries this refers.]

2354 ii, 175b (9-30) <u>Roger Bigot; Framingham Pigot</u>: TRE there was a freeman in Framingham Pigot commended to Edwin. Afterwards he was under Godric Dapifer, Edwin's successor (*successoris sui*), under Earl Ralph. When Earl Ralph forfeited (*se forefecit*), Bishop Æthelmær held him. Now Roger Bigot holds him.

2355 ii, 176a (9-32) <u>Roger Bigot; Bixley</u>: [This entry is preceded by the rubric "from the exchange (*de escangio*) of Isaac's land." It is unclear to which entries this refers.]

2356 ii, 176a–b (9-42) <u>Roger Bigot; Bixley</u>: TRE a freeman commended to Ulfkil and half a freeman under him held seventeen acres in Bixley. Godric Dapifer claims (*calumpniatur*) this land through his man Ralph, by ordeal or by battle (*per hominem suum iudicio vel bello*), that he held this land from the fee of Earl Ralph. It is testified by the hundred to the fee of Roger Bigot, but Godric claims this land with the half that is in the King's return (*reclamat istam cum medietate quae est in breve regis*). Godric took (*recepit*) it for half a carucate.

2357 ii, 176b (9-43, 44, 45) <u>Roger Bigot; Surlingham, Rockland St. Mary, Bramerton</u>: TRE two and a half of Godwine's freemen, who were under Stigand, held twenty acres of land in Surlingham. In Rockland St. Mary there was a freeman and two half freemen of Godwine under Stigand with twenty acres of land. And in Bramerton there were three freemen and another two half freemen of Godwine with twenty acres of land. These men were delivered to make (*fuerunt liberati ad perficiendum*) the manor of Bixley.

2358 ii, 176b (9-46) Roger Bigot; Shimpling: TRE Thorbert, a freeman of Stigand, held forty acres of land in Shimpling. Now Robert de Vaux holds it from Roger Bigot. Four freemen with sixteen acres of land were delivered to make this manor (*liberati ad hoc manerium perficiendum*).

2359 ii, 176b (9-48) Roger Bigot; Osmondiston: TRE Algar Trec held half a carucate of land in Osmondiston under Eadric. Now Hugh de Corbon holds it from Roger Bigot. Another one and a half freemen were delivered to make this manor (*fuit liberatus ad hoc manerium perficiendum*).

2360 ii, 176b–177a (9-49) Roger Bigot; Mundham: TRE Ælfric, a freeman under Stigand, held thirty acres of land in Mundham. Ælfric was outlawed (*utlagavit*), and Ulfkil the King's reeve seised (*saisiuit*) this land into the hand of the King. Roger Bigot asked (*rogavit*) the King for it, and he granted (*concessit*) it to him. Count Alan, however, claims (*calumpniatur*) this land, because Earl Ralph had it in his manor of Rumburgh [Suffolk]. The men of the hundred heard Ulfkil acknowledge (*cognoscenterat*) that one time for one year before Ralph forfeited (*forefecisset*), and one time after that, that he, Ulfkil, was doing service (*deserviebat*) in Rumburgh. The hundred also heard Ulfkil say that he was doing service (*deserviebat*) to Roger Bigot. Count Alan's men have had 10s. each year from this land, except for the last four years, and wish to prove it any way they can (*volunt probare quolibet*). Ulfkil now holds.

2361 ii, 177a (9-50) Roger Bigot; Mundham: TRE eight freemen of Ulfkil held sixty acres of land in Mundham. Roger Bigot now has this in the five carucates which the King gave (*dedit*) him.

2362 ii, 177a–b (9-59) Roger Bigot; Carleton St. Peter: TRE a freeman of Swetmann held five acres of land in Carleton St. Peter. Now Roger Bigot holds it by the King's livery (*de liberatum regis*).

2363 ii, 178a–b (9-75) Roger Bigot; Little Snarehill: TRE Æthelwig held a carucate and sixty acres of land in Little Snarehill. Now Æthelstan the Englishman holds from Roger Bigot. There are six sokemen there with all customs, but each one has always paid 4d. for cartage (*ex summagio*) in the King's manor of Kenninghall, and the King has the six forfeitures (*vi forisfacturas*) from them.

2364 ii, 178b (9-78) Roger Bigot; Blo Norton: TRE Æthelwig, a freeman, held a carucate of land in Blo Norton. Now Alfred the Englishman holds it from Roger Bigot. Æthelwig added this land to Lopham (North or South) as a berewick in the time of King William. He had had this as a manor in the time of King Edward.

2365 ii, 178b (9-79) Roger Bigot; Banham: TRE there was a sokeman with ten acres of land in Banham, all of whose customs were in Ely Abbey. After King William came to England, Roger Bigot's antecessor had the sokeman's commendation only. Now Bernard holds from Roger Bigot.

2366 ii, 179a–b (9-86) Roger Bigot; Field Dalling: TRE Alsige, Leofstan,

Godwine, and Robert held a freeman in Field Dalling with two carucates of land. Now Roger the Sheriff holds. Roger Bigot vouches (*revocat*) this land from the exchange (*pro mutuo*) of land which the King gave (*dedit*) to Isaac.

2367 ii, 179b (9-87) <u>Roger Bigot; Hanworth</u>: TRE Wihtric, a freeman, held four carucates of land in Hanworth. Now Roger Bigot holds it. There is a villein in Ingworth, whom Toki of Winterton held, and who was added to this manor by Roger's antecessor. A bordar in Aldborough held by Wulfstan was similarly added, as was a villein of Godwine of Scottow in Calthorpe. These three men hold thirty-six acres of land. Wihtric had sake and soke over Hanworth, and the King and the earl had the six forfeitures (*vi forisfacturas*).

2368 ii, 179b–180a (9-88) <u>Roger Bigot; Sutton (near Stalham)</u>: TRE Eadric of Laxfield held three and a half carucates of land in Sutton. Sutton was one of Earl Ralph's manors, and it had been rented (*erat adcensatum*) for £10. The King gave it thus (*sic dedit*) to Roger Bigot, so Roger himself says, when his brother William came from Apulia with Geoffrey Ridel.

2369 ii, 180a (9-92) <u>Roger Bigot; Ness</u>: There was a freeman with fifteen acres of land in Ness, which Æthelwig annexed (*invasit*) in the time of King William. Roger Bigot vouches this to his fee by gift of the King (*revocat ad suum feudum de dono regis*).

2370 ii, 181a–b (9-99) <u>Roger Bigot; Tharston</u>: TRE Wulfric held two carucates of land in Tharston under Stigand. Now Robert de Vaux holds it from Roger Bigot. Robert has added seven and a half freemen to this manor with eighty-two acres of land. His antecessor had the commendation only of all of these men except for one, who was a sokeman of Archbishop Stigand.

2371 ii, 181b (9-100) <u>Roger Bigot; Hudeston</u>: TRE Æthelwig of Thetford held two carucates of land in Hudeston. Now Robert de Courson holds it from Roger Bigot. There are also five freemen there with forty-two acres of land. Æthelwig had the commendation only of two of them; the third was a man of Robert Malet's antecessor; the fourth of Ralph Berlant's antecessor; and the fifth Eudo son of Spearhavoc's antecessor.

2372 ii, 181b (9-102) <u>Roger Bigot; Swanton (in Forncett)</u>: TRE Hardekin, a freeman, held thirty acres of land in Swanton. Now Walter holds it from Roger Bigot. Roger claims this by gift of the King (*reclamat de dono regis*).

2373 ii, 181b–182a (9-104) <u>Roger Bigot; Hales</u>: TRE Æthelstan, a thegn of Harold, held a carucate and forty acres of land in Hales. Now Roger Bigot holds it. This Æthelstan commended himself to Æthelwig of Thetford in the time of King William, and Æthelwig was seised of this (*ex hoc erat saisitus*) when King William gave (*dedit*) his land to Roger Bigot. But the hundred has seen neither a writ nor livery (*brevem vel liberatorem*) which gave (*daret*) this to Æthelwig.

2374 ii, 182a (9-105) <u>Roger Bigot; Haddiscoe</u>: TRE a sokeman of Eadric of Laxfield held thirty acres of land in Haddiscoe. This sokemen commended himself to Æthelwig in the time of King William, and Æthelwig was seised of this (*erat inde saisitus*) when King William gave (*dedit*) the land to Roger Bigot.

2375 ii, 182a (9-108) <u>Roger Bigot; Raveningham</u>: TRE a freeman held twelve acres of land in Raveningham. Æthelwig was seised (*erat saisitus*) of him when Roger Bigot took (*recepit*) his land.

2376 ii, 182b (9-111) <u>Roger Bigot; Heckingham</u>: TRE Bondi, a freeman, held thirty acres of land in Heckingham. Now Roger Bigot holds him from the fee of Ulfkil. But Ulfkil himself had had half of this man's commendation, and the whole commendation of his wife in the time of King Edward. Godric Dapifer claims (*calumpniatur*) him, because he held Bondi when Earl Ralph forfeited (*forisfecit*). The hundred testifies that Bondi served (*serviebat*) Godric, but they do not know how.

2377 ii, 184b (9-147) <u>Roger Bigot; Runton</u>: TRE Bondi held a freeman with thirty acres of land in Runton. This was delivered (*liberatus fuit*) as one freeman, but now it is held by two freemen, and Roger Bigot holds. Then and after its value was 8s. It was 20s., but it could not pay. For this reason, it is now at 15s.

2378 ii, 184b (9-148) <u>Roger Bigot; Roughton</u>: TRE Wihtric held two freemen with thirty acres of land in Roughton. Eadric held another freeman there with three acres of land. These men could not withdraw without Eadric's permission, and Robert Malet claims (*calumpniatur*) them. Now Roger Bigot holds this.

2379 ii, 185b (9-160) <u>Roger Bigot; Stoke Holy Cross</u>: TRE a freeman commended to Gyrth held twenty-four acres of land in Stoke Holy Cross. Earl Ralph held him when he forfeited (*se foresfecit*) with half his land, and Ralph Baynard had the other half, by testimony (*teste*) of the hundred. Now Roger Bigot holds all of this, and vouches it from the fee of his freemen, by gift of the King (*revocat ad feudum suorum liberorum ex dono regis*). Roger Bigot acknowledges (*cognoscit*) having taken (*suscepisse*) the land in custody in the King's hand after Earl Ralph forfeited (*se forefecit*), and he has custody still. Aitard contradicts (*contradicit*) the hundred, which testifies this; but Mainard affirms this with the hundred (*affirmat cum hundreto*).

2380 ii, 186a (9-167) <u>Roger Bigot; Starston</u>: TRE a freeman of Ely Abbey held half a carucate of land in Starston. Although the soke and sake was Stigand's in Earsham, the freeman could not grant or sell his land without permission of both Ely Abbey and Stigand. Now Roger Bigot vouches this from the fee of his freemen, by gift of the King (*revocat ad feudum liberorum suorum ex dono regis*), and Godwine holds from him. But the hundred testifies that it belonged in Earsham when Richard Poynant was the reeve there. But the man who holds it now, who was then Richard's under-reeve (*sub praepositus*) in Earsham, took it away (*abstulit*). By testimony (*teste*) of the hundred, he gave a rent (*dedit censum*) in Earsham, namely for this and other land of 20s. 6d. every year, but he has not paid it this year. William de Noyers has had the rent (*censum*) until now.

2381 ii, 187a (9-179) <u>Roger Bigot; Felmingham</u>: TRW Roger Bigot holds a carucate of land in Felmingham, which belongs to four men in Suffield. One of these men was a man of Robert Malet's antecessor.

2382 ii, 187a (9-180) <u>Roger Bigot; Smallburgh</u>: TRW Roger Bigot holds three freemen with a carucate of land in Smallburgh. One of them was the man of Robert Malet's antecessor. The others were in the soke of Ramsey Abbey.

2383 ii, 187a (9-182) <u>Roger Bigot; Palling</u>: TRE a freeman of Gyrth held a carucate of land in Palling. Now Roger Bigot holds it. There are also five men there with twenty-three acres of land, whom Hugh d'Houdain holds from Roger. Four of them were free, but they could not withdraw unless they were to give (*dando*) 2s.

2384 ii, 187b (9-183) <u>Roger Bigot; Stalham, Brumstead, Horsey</u>: TRW Roger Bigot holds a freeman in Stalham with fifteen acres; a freeman in Brumstead with fifteen acres; and a freeman in Horsey with twelve acres. His antecessor Æthelwig did not have their commendation in the time of King Edward. But Roger vouches them from Æthelwig's fee, by gift of the King (*eos revocat ad suum feudum ex dono regis*), because Æthelwig had their commendation in the time of King William.

2385 ii, 187b (9-184) <u>Roger Bigot; East Carleton</u>: TRW Roger Bigot has twenty-seven and a half freemen with one and a half carucates and ten acres of land in East Carleton, commended only under Ulf and with fold-soke. He has another four freemen there with fifty acres of land – Ranulf Peverel's antecessor had the commendation of two, and half of the commendation of the third; and Eudo Dapifer's antecessor had the commendation of one, and half the commendation of the other. Roger Bigot's antecessor had nothing from these men.

2386 ii, 187b (9-187) <u>Roger Bigot; Nayland, Wreningham</u>: TRW Roger Bigot has nine freemen in Nayland and Wreningham. Roger's antecessor had the commendation only of eight and a half of these men along with fold-soke. Hermer's antecessor had the commendation only and fold-soke over the remaining half man.

2387 ii, 187b (9-188) <u>Roger Bigot; Walsingham (Great or Little)</u>: TRW Roger Bigot holds six freemen in Walsingham with 130 acres of land. They were under Roger's antecessor in fold-soke and commendation only.

2388 ii, 187b (9-189) <u>Roger Bigot; Bracon Ash</u>: TRW Roger Bigot holds five freemen in Bracon Ash with 150 acres of land. Roger's antecessor had half the commendation of four of these men and all the commendation of the fifth. Ranulf Peverel's antecessor had half the commendation over four of them.

2389 ii, 187b–188a (9-190) <u>Roger Bigot; Flordon</u>: TRW Roger Bigot has five freemen in Flordon with a carucate and thirty acres of land. His antecessor had half their commendation only. Godric Dapifer's antecessor had the other half.

2390 ii, 188a (9-191) <u>Roger Bigot; Nayland</u>: TRW Roger Bigot has four freemen with a carucate of land in Nayland. Roger Bigot's antecessor had the commendation of two and a half of these men TRE, Stigand of one, and Hermer's antecessor of the remaining half.

2391 ii, 188a (9-193) <u>Roger Bigot; Mangreen</u>: TRW Roger Bigot has one and a half freemen in Mangreen with thirty-three acres of land. His antecessor had half their commendation and Godric's antecessor had half.

2392 ii, 188a (9-194) <u>Roger Bigot; Swardeston</u>: TRW Roger Bigot has eight freemen with forty-five acres in Swardeston. His antecessor had the commendation only of three and a half of these men, Godric's antecessor of four, and Ranulf Peverel's antecessor of half.

2393 ii, 188a–b (9-196) <u>Roger Bigot; Mulbarton</u>: TRE a freeman commended only to Godric's antecessor had thirty acres of land in Mulbarton. There was also a free woman there commended only to Godric's antecessor, who held thirty acres of land. Godric had been seised (*erat . . . saisitus*) of all of this when Earl Ralph forfeited (*forisfecit*), and the woman paid a 5s. debt to him (*ex debito reddebat ei*). This woman's son, a man commended only to Roger Bigot, lived on this land with his mother, so Roger vouches (*revocat*) that half this land [is his]. This man's father had other free land in another place, under Roger's antecessor. He was commended only. Now Roger Bigot holds this land as well.

2394 ii, 188b (9-197) <u>Roger Bigot; Ketteringham</u>. TRE five freemen had a carucate and sixteen acres of land in Ketteringham. They were half commended to Roger Bigot's antecessor, and half commended only to Godric's antecessor. Now Ranulf fitz Walter holds it from Roger Bigot.

2395 ii, 188b (9-198) <u>Roger Bigot; Keswick</u>: TRW Aitard holds fourteen freemen with sixty acres of land in Keswick from Roger Bigot. Four of these men were under Roger Bigot's antecessor in commendation only; five were commended to and in the fold-soke of Godric's antecessor; and five were under the commendation of Godric's antecessor. There are also another four freemen there with a carucate of land. Two were commended only to Godric's antecessor, one was under Godric's antecessor, and one under Stigand. Godric had been seised (*saisitus erat*) of thirty acres of this land when Earl Ralph forfeited (*forisfecit*), and two of his women were living there. Now Aitard holds this from Roger Bigot.

2396 ii, 188b–189a (9-200) <u>Roger Bigot; Flordon</u>: TRW Roger Bigot has five freemen with fifteen acres of land in Flordon. Roger's antecessor had the commendation only of four of these men, and Roger de Raismes's antecessor had commendation only of the fifth. There are also another two freemen with thirty acres of land in Flordon. Stigand had the commendation of one and a half of these men, and Roger Bigot's antecessor had the commendation only of half. Godric had been seised (*erat . . . saisitus*) of half this land as his fee (*ad suum feudum*), when Earl Ralph forfeited (*forisfecit*).

2397 ii, 189a (9-204) <u>Roger Bigot; Flordon</u>: TRW Roger Bigot holds a freeman with thirty acres of land in Flordon. In the time of King Edward, Godric's antecessor had his commendation.

2398 ii, 189a (9-211) <u>Roger Bigot; Aslacton</u>: TRW Roger Bigot holds eleven freemen with fifty-four acres of land in Aslacton, and Hugh holds from him. Robert Malet's antecessor had the commendation of three of these men TRE. On the day William Malet died he was seised (*fuit saisitus*) of two.

2399 ii, 189b–190a (9-219, 227) <u>Roger Bigot; Tasburgh</u>: TRE there were seven freemen with 110 acres of land in Tasburgh. Now Berard and Azelin hold them from Roger Bigot. Hermer claims (*calumpniatur*) one of these men. An Englishman, Hermer's man, offers [to undertake] the ordeal concerning this (*ex hoc offert iudicium*), that Hermer's antecessor had been seised of him (*erat ex eo saisitus*) on the day King Edward was alive and dead. The whole hundred contradicts (*contradicit*) this, [offering] either battle or ordeal (*vel bello vel iudico*). The Englishman has given a pledge concerning this (*ex hoc dedit ille anglicus vadem*).

2400 ii, 190a (9-228) <u>Roger Bigot; Haddiscoe</u>: TRW Roger Bigot holds a freemen with forty acres in Haddiscoe and Thurold holds from him. He was a freeman of King Edward. Roger's antecessor Æthelwig had this man's commendation after King William came.

2401 ii, 190a–b (9-232) <u>Roger Bigot; West Dereham</u>: TRW Roger Bigot holds six freemen with nine acres of land in West Dereham. He also has a freeman there with sixteen acres. His antecessor had the commendation only of this man. Roger also holds sixty acres in West Dereham which Godric, a freeman, held TRE. This same man holds TRW. Roger Bigot's and Baynard's antecessors had the commendation only of this man.

2402 ii, 190b (9-233) <u>Roger Bigot; Beechamwell</u>: TRE Ælfheah, a freeman, held two carucates of land in Beechamwell. Now Robert de Vaux holds this from Roger Bigot. Wihenoc took away (*tulit*) thirty acres of this manor's demesne. He claims them by gift of the King (*istos reclamat de dono regis*).

2403 ii, 193a (10-19) <u>Bishop of Norwich; Stratton (St. Mary or St. Michael)</u>: TRW Walter the Deacon holds two carucates and thirty acres of land in Stratton from William bishop of Norwich. Bishop Æthelmær held it TRE. Ranulf and Walter the Deacon also hold twenty-six sokemen there with eighty-three acres of land. One of Count Alan's men claims (*calumpniatur*) half of one of these men, saying that Earl Ralph held him before he could forfeit (*forisfaceret*). He offers the ordeal concerning this (*ex hoc offert iudicium*).

2404 ii, 193b (10-20) <u>Bishop of Norwich; Sedgeford</u>: TRE Gyrth held fifteen acres of land in Sedgeford. Now the Bishop of Norwich holds it. TRE there was a mill there. Anand, the antecessor of Peter de Valognes, took it away (*tulit*).

2405 ii, 194a (10-21) <u>Bishop of Norwich; Eccles (near Attleborough)</u>: TRE Ralph the Staller held four carucates of land in Eccles. Later Earl Ralph, his son, held it. After this, Bishop Æthelmær held it from both of them. The hundred does not know how he held it. Later it was Bishop Herefast's. Now Bishop William holds it. It was never part of the bishopric, by testimony (*teste*) of the hundred.

2406 ii, 194a (10-22) <u>Bishop of Norwich; Langham</u>: TRE Gyrth held four carucates of land in Langham. Now the Bishop of Norwich holds it. Sixty acres were taken away (*ablate sunt*) from this manor. Peter de Valognes holds them.

2407 ii, 194a (10-23) <u>Bishop of Norwich; Gunton</u>: TRE Bishop Æthelmær bought (*emit*) two carucates of land for the bishopric in Gunton, and he held this land on the day he died. Now the Bishop of Norwich holds it.

2408 ii, 194b (10-25) <u>Bishop of Norwich; Beighton</u>: TRE Bishop Æthelmær held three carucates of land in Beighton along with the soke and sake of the bordars and those seeking the fold. He held this through purchase (*per emptionem*) from Earl Ælfgar. Now the Bishop of Norwich holds.

2409 ii, 194b (10-27) <u>Bishop of Norwich; South Walsham</u>: There is a freeman with eighteen acres of land in South Walsham, which that freeman gave (*dedit*) to St. Benet of Holme. But Bishop Herfast took it away (*abstulit*). Now Bishop William holds.

2410 ii, 194b–195a (10-28) <u>Bishop of Norwich; Blofield</u>: TRE Bishop Æthelmær held two carucates of land in Blofield. Bishop Æthelmær took (*accepit*) this manor with his wife, before he was bishop. Afterwards he held it in the bishopric. Now Bishop William holds it. Bishop William also holds five [*sic*] sokemen there – Rainald, Baldwin, Helius. TRE Bishop Æthelmær had the six forfeitures (*vi forisfacturas*) over them, but the hundred has seen neither a writ nor a seal nor the consent of the King (*nec vidit breve nec sigillum nec concessum regis*) concerning this.

2411 ii, 195a (10-29) <u>Bishop of Norwich; Plumstead (Great or Little)</u>: TRW a sokeman was added by Herfast to Plumstead with three acres of land, but he was Stigand's. Now the Bishop of Norwich holds him.

2412 ii, 195a–b (10-30) <u>Bishop of Norwich; Hemsby</u>: In the time of King Edward, Earl Ælfgar held three carucates in Hemsby, and Alwig bought (*emit*) them. Stigand took them away (*abstulit*) and gave (*dedit*) them to his brother Æthelmær. The hundred does not know how. Afterwards they were held in the bishopric.

2413 ii, 195b–196a (10-33) <u>Bishop of Norwich; Langley</u>: TRE Anand, a freeman, held three carucates of land in Langley under King Edward. In the time of King Edward, Bishop Æthelmær had the land of this Anand, and they were companions (*socii fuerunt*), and Anand suddenly died (*subita morte fuit morteus*). Now Bishop William holds this land.

2414 ii, 196b (10-39) <u>Bishop of Norwich; Little Barningham</u>: TRW Bishop William holds a carucate and fifty acres of land in Little Barningham. They lie in Blickling. There was a mill there. Godric now holds it from the King's fee.

2415 ii, 197a (10-43) <u>Bishop of Norwich; Scratby</u>: In Scratby TRW there are seven sokemen with twenty acres of land and ten freemen with two carucates and five acres of land. Bishop Æthelmær held the commendation of the ten freemen. Bishop Æthelmær held all of this TRE, then Herfast, and now Bishop William. The Abbot of St. Benet of Holme, however, had the commendation only of one of these men TRE.

2416   ii, 197b (10-48) Bishop of Norwich; Great Cressingham: Concerning the annexations (*de invasionibus*) of the same fee: Ralph, the Bishop of Thetford's man, annexed (*invasit*) a freeman with a carucate of land, who was in the King's soke of Great Cressingham. He keeps back (*detenet*) the soke of two men.

2417   ii, 197b (10-50) Bishop of Norwich; Mintlyn: TRW the Bishop of Norwich holds fifteen freemen with forty acres of land in Mintlyn. His antecessor had their commendation only, and Stigand had the soke.

2418   ii, 197b (10-52) Bishop of Norwich; Stanford: TRW there is a freeman with sixty acres of land in Stanford. The antecessor of Bishop William had this man's commendation only, and the King had his soke. Bishop William now holds him.

2419   ii, 197b (10-53) Bishop of Norwich; Gateley: TRW there is a freeman with six acres in Gateley. Bondi, a freeman and the antecessor of Hugh de Montfort, held him TRE. Afterwards he became a man (*ea effectus est homo*) of Bishop Herfast, and thus Bishop William holds him.

2420   ii, 197b (10-54) Bishop of Norwich; Colkirk: TRW Bishop Herfast annexed (*invasit*) a woodland in Colkirk from Fakenham. It is sixty acres long.

2421   ii, 198a (10-59) Bishop of Norwich; Briningham: TRW Roger Longsword holds six acres of land in Briningham from Bishop William, which Earl Ralph held. Afterwards Count Alan held it. This is testified by the hundred.

2422   ii, 198b (10-61) Bishop of Norwich; Hindringham: Drogo de la Beuvrière held a man and an acre of land in Hindringham, as did his antecessor. Afterwards one of Bishop William's reeves, Sæwulf, seised (*saisiuit*) him and holds him now.

2423   ii, 199a (10-66) Bishop of Norwich; Hemblington: TRW there are two freemen with sixty acres of land in Hemblington. TRE Ralph the Staller held them with sake and soke, but Bishop Æthelmær had the commendation only of one of these men. Now Bishop William holds one, and Earl Ralph the other.

2424   ii, 199a (10-67) Bishop of Norwich; Plumstead (Great or Little): TRE Godwine held a freeman of Gyrth with a carucate of land in Plumstead. Now Bishop William holds it. After King William came into this land, Bishop Æthelmær annexed (*invasit*) it for a forfeiture, because the woman who held it married within a year of her husband's death (*pro forisfactura quia mulier que tenuit nupsit intra annum post mortem viri*).

2425   ii, 199a (10-69) Bishop of Norwich; Plumstead (Great or Little): TRE there were two freemen of Gyrth and Stigand in Plumstead with fifty acres of land. Bishop Herfast annexed (*invasit*) them. Earl Ralph held them when he forfeited (*se forisfecit*), and Robert Blunt had them at rent (*ad censum*). Now Bishop William holds.

2426   ii, 199a–b (10-71) Bishop of Norwich; Freethorpe: TRE Alsige, a freeman under Earl Ralph, held sixteen acres of land in Freethorpe. Baldwin the Bishop's reeve had his commendation only. Now Alsige is commended to Godric, in the King's hand.

2427 ii, 200a (10-76) Bishop of Norwich; Bradeston: TRE the freeman Eadric, steersman (*rector*) of King Edward's ship, had a carucate of land in Bradeston. Ten and a half freemen were there as well with eighty acres of land. They were commended only to Eadric's antecessor. Now William bishop of Norwich holds all of this.

2428 ii, 200a (10-77) Bishop of Norwich; South Burlingham: TRE Eadric held four and a half acres of land in South Burlingham, which belong to Bradeston. After King William came into England, Eadric was an outlaw (*exlex*) in Denmark, and Bishop Æthelmær annexed (*invasit*) the land. Now William de Noyers holds it from Bishop William.

2429 ii, 200a (10-78) Bishop of Norwich; Catton (in Postwick): TRE a freeman commended only to Gyrth held sixty acres of land in Catton. When Herfast came to the bishopric, he gave (*dedit*) it to his man Rainald. Now Bishop William holds it.

2430 ii, 200b (10-83) Bishop of Norwich; Somerton (East or West): TRE three freemen held 106 acres of land in Somerton. After Earl Tosti left (*exiit*) England, Berard held it. There was a church of St. Benet of Holme there. Now Bishop William holds.

2431 ii, 201a (10-87) Bishop of Norwich; Rollesby: TRE there was a freeman with eighty acres of land in Rollesby commended only to Bishop Æthelmær and Alweald abbot of St. Benet of Holme. This man was in the monastery of St. Benet of Holme in such a way that he could neither grant nor sell his land. Now Bishop William holds.

2432 ii, 201a (10-90) Bishop of Norwich; Billockby: TRE Ketil, a freeman, held fifty-seven acres of land in Billockby. He was half Bishop Æthelmær's commended man, but all of his land was in the monastery of St. Benet of Holme for victualing, and he could neither grant nor sell it. Bishop Herfast annexed (*invasit*) it. Now Berard holds it under Bishop William.

2433 ii, 201b (10-93) Bishop of Norwich; Tivetshall: TRE a freeman held forty acres of land in Tivetshall, by testimony (*teste*) of the hundred. The man's twenty acres belonged to Ely Abbey, and his wife's twenty acres belonged to Bury St. Edmund's. Bishop Herfast annexed (*invasit*) all of this. Now Bishop William holds by (*ab*) antecession, and Rainald de Pierrepont holds under him.

2434 ii, 201b (10a-1) Church of St. Michael, Norwich; rubric: [An "f," for "*fecit retornam*," appears in the margin, opposite the rubric which marks the beginning of St. Michael's holdings, indicating that it had made a return.]

2435 ii, 202a (11-3) Bishop Osbern; Hindringham: TRE three freemen held thirty-two acres of land in Hindringham. Now Bishop Osbern holds it. Drogo's men claim (*calumpniantur*) the three men, whom Berard holds, from the fee of their lord (*ad feudum domini sui*).

2436 ii, 202a–b (12-1) Godric Dapifer; Gooderstone: TRE Asgot held Gooderstone freely. Now Godric Dapifer holds it. Ten freemen lived there, whom King William gave (*dedit*) to Earl Ralph and afterwards to Godric. Archbishop Stigand had the commendation of two of them.

2437 ii, 203a–b (12-17) <u>Godric Dapifer; Alpington</u>: TRE Edwin held two carucates of land in Alpington. There are two freemen there with forty acres of land. They were freemen of Edwin, Godric Dapifer's antecessor. Now Godric Dapifer holds all of this.

2438 ii, 204b (12-32) <u>Godric Dapifer; Little Melton</u>: TRE Edwin held two carucates of land in Little Melton from Ramsey Abbey thus: he had granted it to the abbot after his death (*abbati concesserat post mortem suam*). A freeman who was a thegn held another carucate of land there. Godric held it when Earl Ralph forfeited (*fecit*), and holds it now.

2439 ii, 204b–205a (12-34) <u>Godric Dapifer; Colney</u>: TRW Walter holds one and a half carucates of land in Colney from Godric Dapifer and has the commendation only of eighteen freemen there with thirty acres of land. There is another freeman there as well, who was commended only to the antecessor of Roger Bigot. This freeman holds half an acre of land, which was purchased (*mercatus est*) from Roger's land after Ralph forfeited (*forisfecit*).

2440 ii, 205a (12-38) <u>Godric Dapifer; Flordon</u>: TRE three freemen held nineteen acres of land in Flordon. Roger Bigot's antecessor held the commendation only of two of these men, and Godric Dapifer's antecessor had the commendation only of one. Now Godric holds all of this.

2441 ii, 205a–b (12-42) <u>Godric Dapifer; Heckingham</u>: TRE Hagne held four carucates of land in Heckingham from Stigand. In the time of King William, Earl Ralph added eight freemen with a carucate of land. Now Godric Dapifer holds all of this. Roger Bigot claims (*calumpniatur*) thirty acres of this land from the fee of Æthelstan.

2442 ii, 205b (12-45) <u>Godric Dapifer; Southwood</u>: In Southwood there is a freeman with an acre of land. Roger fitz Rainard's antecessor had his commendation TRE. Godric Dapifer held this when Earl Ralph forfeited (*forisfecit*).

2443 ii, 205b (13-1) <u>Hermer; Marham</u>: TRE Thorkil held twenty acres of the soke of Ely Abbey in Marham. Now Hermer holds it. This land has been measured in the returns (*mansurata est in brevi*) of Ely Abbey.

2444 ii, 206b (13-10) <u>Hermer; Stradsett</u>: TRE Swærting, a freeman, held two carucates of land in Stradsett. Now Fulbert holds it from Hermer. There are also thirteen freemen in Stradsett with 210 acres of land. Baynard's antecessor had the commendation of two of these men. This was delivered (*fuit liberatum*) as one carucate to make (*ad perficiendum*) a manor.

2445 ii, 207a (13-13) <u>Hermer; Islington</u>: TRE Thorkil held one and a half carucates of land in Islington, and now he holds it from Hermer. Fifteen freemen with thirty acres of land lay in this manor TRE and lie there now. Hermer's antecessor had the commendation of these men, and they could withdraw if they gave (*darent*) 2s. Stigand had the soke.

2446 ii, 207a (13-14) <u>Hermer; North Runcton</u>: TRE Thorkil, a freeman, held two carucates of land in North Runcton. Now Hermer holds it. It pays 12d. of a 20s. King's geld (*geto regis*).

2447 ii, 207b–208a (13-19) <u>Hermer; Whinburgh</u>: TRE Thorkil, a freeman, held three carucates and one and a half acres of land in Whinburgh. Now Hermer holds it. There is a berewick in Garveston with a carucate of land. There are also nineteen freemen in Garveston with one hundred acres of land. The hundred testifies that Hermer's antecessor had no customs from these men except commendation and offers the ordeal (*offert iudicium*) concerning this. A man of Hermer, too, offers the ordeal (*offert iudicium*) that Hermer's antecessor had all customs TRE except for the soke of Ely Abbey, and that this man could sell his land. About this, they have given pledges (*dederunt vades*).

2448 ii, 208a (13-21) <u>Hermer; Whinburgh</u>: TRE a sokeman held thirty acres of land in Whinburgh. Now Hermer holds it. The hundred testifies that this freeman could not sell his land, but the sheriff contradicts (*contradicit*) this, [saying] that he could sell without the permission of his lord.

2449 ii, 208a (13-22) <u>Hermer; Yaxham</u>: TRE four sokemen of Hermer's antecessor held twenty acres of land in Yaxham. Now Hermer holds it.

2450 ii, 209b–210a (14-14) <u>Bury St. Edmund's; Buckenham (near Acle)</u>: TRE Bury St. Edmund's held a carucate of land in Buckenham for its victualing. Now Roger Bigot holds it from Bury St. Edmund's.

2451 ii, 210a (14-15) <u>Bury St. Edmund's; Caistor St. Edmunds</u>: Bury St. Edmund's has always held three carucates of land in Caistor St. Edmunds. There are four sokemen there with twenty-five acres of land with all customs, belonging to the manor, by consent of the King (*concessu regis*), by testimony (*teste*) of the hundred.

2452 ii, 210a (14-16) <u>Bury St. Edmund's; Brooke</u>: TRE Earl Gyrth held four carucates in Brooke. King William gave (*dedit*) this to Bury St. Edmund's when he first came to the abbey.

2453 ii, 210a–b (14-16, 17) <u>Bury St. Edmund's; Shotesham (All Saints or St. Mary), Howe, Poringland</u>: TRW there are sixteen freemen in Shotesham commended to Earl Gyrth with a carucate of land. They belong to Brooke. In Howe there is a freeman of Gyrth with a carucate of land, who belongs to Brooke. In Poringland there is a freeman who was commended to Earl Gyrth. He belongs to Bury St. Edmund's manor of Brooke. King Edward had sake and soke over all these freemen. Afterwards, Gyrth took it by force (*accepit per vim*), but King William gave (*dedit*) Bury the soke and sake of all of Gyrth's freemen, along with the manor of Brooke, just as he held it himself: this the monks claim (*reclamant*).

2454 ii, 211b (14-31) <u>Bury St. Edmund's; Gissing</u>: There are one and a half freemen with thirty-three acres of land in Gissing. Roger, a man of Robert Malet, annexed (*invasit*) this.

2455 ii, 211b (14-32) <u>Bury St. Edmund's; Gissing</u>: When Earl Ralph had power over his men and his lands (*fuit potestatiuus et sui et terrae suae*), his servants exchanged (*seruientes eius cambierunt*) four men in Burston for four in Gissing with the servants (*seruientibus*) of Bury St. Edmund's, so that the earl had four men and the abbot had four.

2456   ii, 211b (14-35) <u>Bury St. Edmund's; Loddon</u>: TRE Bury St. Edmund's holds three carucates and ten acres of land in Loddon. Now Frodo holds it from the Abbot. Frodo also holds a carucate of land in Broome, which Toli the Sheriff held and gave (*dedit*) to Bury St. Edmund's in the time of King Edward. Afterwards Toli held this land from the abbey at two days' farm.

2457   ii, 212b (15-1) <u>Ely Abbey; Marham</u>: TRE and TRW Ely Abbey holds Marham. It is a league and one hundred perches long and half a league and a furlong wide. The measurement in the marsh is not known (*nescit mensuram*). Twenty-seven sokemen lay in this manor TRE with all customs, but after the coming of King William, Hugh de Montfort had all but one. And William de Warenne has a sokeman with six acres of land from the church.

2458   ii, 213a (15-2) <u>Ely Abbey; Fodderstone</u>: TRW Ely Abbey has a carucate of land in Fodderstone. Ulfkil, a man of Hermer, claims this land to be free (*calumpniatur esse liberam*) however it should now be judged – either by battle or ordeal (*quocumque modo iudicetur vel bello vel iudicio*). Another man is ready to prove (*praesto probare*) in the same way that the land lay in Ely Abbey on the day King Edward died. The whole hundred testifies that it was Ely's TRE.

2459   ii, 213a–b (15-7) <u>Ely Abbey; Feltwell</u>: TRE and TRW Ely Abbey holds six carucates of land in Feltwell. TRE thirty-four sokemen lay in this manor with all customs, and they are now held by William de Warenne. There were also six freemen in Ely's soke and commendation only. William has them as well.

2460   ii, 213b (15-10) <u>Ely Abbey; Bridgham</u>: TRE and TRW Ely Abbey holds four carucates of land in Bridgham. There is also a sokeman there with half a carucate of land. He was one of Roger Bigot's freemen, but the Abbot of Ely has established title (*derationavit*) to him, and holds him.

2461   ii, 213b–214a (15-11) <u>Ely Abbey; Banham</u>: TRE Ely Abbey held a sokeman with two carucates of land in Banham. Now William d'Ecouis holds it from the abbey. There are also three freemen in Banham with half a carucate and five acres of land. The Abbot of Ely had nothing from them, except commendation. Their soke was in the King's manor of Kenninghall. Radfrid held these freemen. Afterwards William d'Ecouis held them. The Abbot of Ely was seised of them because of his commendation (*saisiuit eos propter comendationem suam*).

2462   ii, 214a (15-12) <u>Ely Abbey; Rushford</u>: TRE Ely Abbey held one and a half carucates of land in Rushford. Now John, Waleran's nephew, holds it from the abbey. Wulfric, a freeman, held another sixty acres of land in Rushford TRE. Its soke was in Kenninghall. He forfeited £8 against (*forisfactus fuit erga*) King William: thus, this land has remained (*remansit*) in the King's hand. John also holds this from the abbot.

2463   ii, 214a (15-13) <u>Ely Abbey; Blo Norton</u>: There is a sokeman with eighty acres of land in Blo Norton. He was one of Roger Bigot's freemen, but the Abbot of Ely has established title (*derationavit*).

2464 ii, 214a (15-14) <u>Ely Abbey; Oxwick</u>: TRE Ely Abbey held a carucate of land in Oxwick. Rainald fitz Ivo holds this land from the Abbot of Ely, but prior to this, he held from the King.

2465 ii, 214b (15-18) <u>Ely Abbey; Calvely</u>: TRE Ely Abbey held a carucate of land in Calvely. Now Berner holds it from the abbot. Godric claims (*calumpniatur*) this land from the fee of Earl Ralph, because Ralph held it before he could forfeit (*forisfaceret*). This is testified by the hundred.

2466 ii, 214b (15-22) <u>Ely Abbey; Yaxham</u>: TRW there are fourteen sokemen in Yaxham with ninety acres of land. Roger Bigot holds them from the Abbot of Ely, but prior to this he held from the King.

2467 ii, 215a (16-1) <u>Ramsey Abbey; rubric</u>: [An "fr," for "*fecit retornam,*" appears in the margin, opposite the rubric which marks the beginning of Ramsey Abbey's holdings, indicating that the abbey made a return.]

2468 ii, 215a–b (16-1) <u>Ramsey Abbey; Hilgay</u>: TRW Ramsey Abbey holds two carucates of land in Hilgay. William de Warenne took away (*tulit*) eight men with forty-four acres of land, who paid customs to this manor (*consuetudinarios ad hoc manerium*), so the hundred testifies.

2469 ii, 215b (16-5) <u>Ramsey Abbey; Ringstead</u>: TRE and TRW Ramsey Abbey holds Ringstead. Thirty-one freemen, who lay there TRE were taken away (*ablati sunt*) from this manor. Of these, Radfrid had nine, and he has them now; William d'Ecouis and William de Warenne have seven; there are three in the King's manor of Titchwell; William de Noyers has four; and Roger Bigot has five. There is also one in the King's manor of Hunstanton with two acres of land.

2470 ii, 216b (17-9) <u>St. Benet of Holme; Winterton</u>: TRE and TRW the Abbey of St. Benet of Holme holds a carucate of land in Winterton. There is a sokemen there with 100 acres of land. He is so in the monastery (*ita est in monasterio*) that he is unable to sell or forfeit (*forisfacere*) outside the abbey. But his soke is in the hundred.

2471 ii, 217a–b (17-18) <u>St. Benet of Holme; Saxlingham (Nethergate or Thorpe)</u>: TRE Eadric, a freeman of Stigand, held one and a half carucates of land in Saxlingham under Stigand, with soke and sake. After King William came into England this Eadric, so that he might redeem himself from capture by Waleran, mortgaged this land (*ut autem se redimeret a captione Walerami invadiavit eam*) to St. Benet of Holme for a mark of gold and £7. Now John, nephew of Waleran, holds it from St. Benet of Holme in fee. Ten acres lie in the same place, which are in the demesne of St. Benet's. The abbey leased (*praestavit*) them to Eadric, by testimony (*teste*) of the hundred.

2472 ii, 217b (17-21) <u>St. Benet of Holme; Wroxham</u>: TRE Ralph the Staller held four sokemen with a carucate of land in Wroxham, which lie in Hoveton St. John. Ralph gave (*dedit*) this to St. Benet of Holme in the time of King William.

2473 ii, 217b (17-22) <u>St. Benet of Holme; Rackheath</u>: TRE a freeman held thirty acres of land in Rackheath. This land was forfeited (*forisfacta est*) in the time of King William, but a monk gave (*dedit*) half a mark of gold for the forfeiture (*pro forisfactura*) to the reeves, that is to Alwig of Colchester. And so he had the land without permission (*licentia*) of the King.

2474 ii, 217b–218a (17-24) St. Benet of Holme; Easton: TRE Ralph the Staller held a carucate of land in Easton. TRW he and his wife gave (*dedit*) it to St. Benet of Holme, by grant (*concessione*) of the King.

2475 ii, 218a (17-30) St. Benet of Holme; Tuttington: TRE St. Benet of Holme held a carucate of land in Tuttington. Earl Ralph had been seised (*erat saisitus*) of half this land when he forfeited (*forisfecit*), along with the commendation of the women who held it.

2476 ii, 219a (17-43) St. Benet of Holme; Worstead: TRE and TRW St. Benet of Holme holds two and a half carucates of land in Worstead. TRE this land was for the victualing of the monks. Now Robert the Balistarius has it from the abbot.

2477 ii, 219b (17-49) St. Benet of Holme; Smallburgh: TRE a sokeman of St. Benet of Holme held a carucate of free land in Smallburgh. He gave (*dedit*) it to the abbey TRE, and still holds it from the abbot.

2478 ii, 219b (17-51) St. Benet of Holme; Honing: TRE St. Benet of Holme held two carucates of land in Honing, and Eadric held from the abbot thus: that the Abbot had given (*dederat*) him half his demesne, and he had granted (*concesserat*) the Abbot the other half of his fee, so that he held it all from the abbot and was doing service (*deserviebat*). Now Robert Malet holds this, and Robert de Glanville holds from him.

2479 ii, 220a (17-55) St. Benet of Holme; Whimpwell: TRE and TRW St. Benet of Holme holds one and a half carucates of land at Whimpwell. The value of the manor is 30s., but when Godric was holding it from the fee of Earl Ralph, he was paying £4.

2480 ii, 221a (17-63) St. Benet of Holme; Caister: TRE and TRW St. Benet of Holme holds a carucate of land in Caister. There are fourteen freemen there, over whom the abbot has established title against (*derationavit super*) Godric.

2481 ii, 221b (18-1) St. Stephen's Abbey, Caen; rubric: [An "f," for "*fecit retornam*," appears in the margin, opposite the rubric which marks the beginning of the holdings of St. Stephen's, Caen, indicating that the abbey had made a return.]

2482 ii, 221b (19-2) William d'Ecouis; Clenchwarton: TRW there are forty acres of land in Clenchwarton. Radfrid held this land, and Earl Ralph established title (*derationavit*) to half of it. He held it on the day he forfeited (*forisfecit*). Now Wulfwig, Radfrid's man, holds it from William d'Ecouis's fee. He vouches the King to warranty (*revocat regem ad tutorem*).

2483 ii, 222a (19-6) William d'Ecouis; Middleton (near King's Lynn): TRW William d'Ecouis holds six freemen in demesne with a carucate of land in Middleton. TRE Stigand had the soke of two of these men, and it was delivered (*fuit liberata*) to Radfrid as a carucate of land.

2484 ii, 222a (19-8) William d'Ecouis; Great Massingham: TRE Godwine, a freeman, held a carucate of land in Great Massingham. Now Ralph fitz

Herluin holds it from William d'Ecouis. William de Warenne's antecessor had the commendation only. The soke is in the King's manor of Great Massingham.

2485 ii, 222a–b (19-9) <u>William d'Ecouis; Great Bircham</u>: TRE Biorn held a carucate of land in Great Bircham under King Edward. Now Roger d'Evreux holds it from William d'Ecouis. There were also three freemen there with eighty-five acres of land. And Brunheard, a freeman, is there, and he holds thirty acres of land. Radfrid held all these men. Now, however, they are in the King's hand, because there was no one who establishes title to them (*quia non fuit qui rationarat*).

2486 ii, 223a (19-14) <u>William d'Ecouis; Kenninghall</u>: TRW William d'Ecouis has the soke of six forfeitures (*soca de vi forisfacturis*) in Kenninghall.

2487 ii, 223b (19-20) <u>William d'Ecouis; Repps</u>: TRE Gyrth held a freeman in Repps with thirty acres of land. Later, when Earl Ralph forfeited (*se forisfecit*), Hardwin held him. Now Quentin holds from William d'Ecouis and vouches Robert Blunt to livery (*revocat liberatorem*)

2488 ii, 224a (19-24) <u>William d'Ecouis; Reedham</u>: TRE Beorhtric held two carucates in Reedham. Now Richard holds them from William d'Ecouis. The Abbot of St. Benet of Holme claims (*calumpniatur*) a sokeman there with forty acres of land, and this is testified by the hundred. The abbot also claims (*calumpniatur*) a bordar and an acre of land, by testimony (*testimonio*) of the hundred.

2489 ii, 225a–b (19-36) <u>William d'Ecouis; Stokesby</u>: TRE Edwin, a freeman of Gyrth, held three carucates of land in Stokesby. Now William d'Ecouis holds it. There are three freemen of William's there with one hundred acres of land, whom Hardwin added in the time of King Edward. William's antecessor had their commendation TRE.

2490 ii, 225b (19-40) <u>William d'Ecouis; Thurlton</u>: TRW Odard holds seven and a half freemen with forty-five acres of land in Thurlton from William d'Ecouis. TRE the antecessor of Ralph de Beaufour had the commendation only of these men.

2491 ii, 225b–226a (20-1) <u>Ralph de Beaufour; Bircham Newton</u>: TRE Tovi, a freeman, held two carucates in Bircham Newton. Now Ralph de Beaufour holds them. Eleven freemen lie there with one and a half carucates and eleven and a half acres. Eudo fitz Clamahoc, Ralph's antecessor, had these freemen. Stigand had the soke.

2492 ii, 226b (20-7) <u>Ralph de Beaufour; Swanton Morley</u>: TRE Godwine, a freeman, held eight carucates of land in Swanton Morley. Now Ralph de Beaufour holds it. There is also a freeman there with twelve acres of land. TRE Ralph's antecessor had his commendation only, and his soke was in Mileham. Eudo fitz Clamahoc held him, and now Ralph holds him by gift of the King (*dono regis*). The value of all of this then and later was £8. Now it is £12, but after Ralph had it, he gave (*dedit*) it at farm for £25.

2493 ii, 227a–b (20-10) <u>Ralph de Beaufour; Deopham</u>: TRE Leofwine, a freeman, held a carucate and eighty acres of land in Deopham. Besides this, six freemen, whom Eudo held, were added to the manor TRW. They have 120 acres of land. There are another six freemen there. The hundred testifies that three of them were Stigand's sokemen, and their soke was in the King's manor of Hingham. Ralph de Beaufour gave (*dedit*) the whole of this at farm for £12, but now it pays only £6.

2494 ii, 227b (20-11) <u>Ralph de Beaufour; Morley</u>: TRE Leofwine, a freeman, held a carucate of land in Morley. Now Hugh holds it from Ralph de Beaufour. Fourteen freemen were added to this manor with sixty acres of land. They were Stigand's men, and their soke was in Hingham. Another two freemen were added TRW with thirty acres of land. One was Stigand's man, and the other was the King's. Their soke was in Hingham.

2495 ii, 227b (20-13) <u>Ralph de Beaufour; Crownthorpe</u>: TRW Ralph de Beaufour holds thirty acres of land in Crownthorpe, which Coleman, a freeman, held under Stigand's soke and commendation. Ralph Baynard claims (*calumpniatur*) a half man there with three acres of land.

2496 ii, 228a (20-17) <u>Ralph de Beaufour; East Tuddenham</u>: TRW Ralph de Beaufour holds six freemen in East Tuddenham with a half carucate and three acres of land. All of this was delivered to him (*fuit sibi liberatum*) and his antecessor as a manor.

2497 ii, 229a–b (20-29) <u>Ralph de Beaufour; Buxton</u>: TRE five brothers, who were freemen, held seven carucates of land in Buxton. One of these brothers was commended to the antecessor of Robert Malet, but Robert was not seised of this (*non fuit inde saisitus*). Now Ralph de Beaufour holds this land.

2498 ii, 229b (20-31) <u>Ralph de Beaufour; Belaugh</u>: TRE a freeman of Harold's held a carucate and eleven acres of land in Belaugh. TRE there was also a sokeman of Ralph the Staller in Belaugh with fifteen acres of land. Ralph the Staller gave (*dedit*) this man to Ramsey Abbey. Then Eudo fitz Clamahoc took him away (*tulit*). Now Ralph de Beaufour has him. There are another twenty-two acres of land in Belaugh. Ralph the Staller and Stigand had the soke. Ralph gave (*dedit*) his half to Ramsey Abbey.

2499 ii, 229b (20-31) <u>Ralph de Beaufour; Skeyton</u>: TRE a sokeman of Ramsey Abbey held eleven and a half acres of land in Skeyton. Radbodo, Ralph de Beaufour's reeve, took this away (*tulit*) from the abbey under Ralph's antecessor Eudo fitz Clamahoc.

2500 ii, 229b (20-32) <u>Ralph de Beaufour; Hautbois</u>: TRE a sokeman of Ramsey Abbey held half a carucate of land in Hautbois. Eudo fitz Clamahoc had this land by livery (*de liberatione*), so Ralph de Beaufour says. Now Ralph holds it.

2501 ii, 230a (20-36) <u>Ralph de Beaufour; "Thurketeliart" (lost in Aldeby)</u>: TRE one of Stigand's freemen held two carucates of land in "Thurketeliart." Now Ralph de Beaufour holds it. Eleven freemen lie in this manor with two and a half carucates and thirty acres of land. Ralph's antecessor had the commendation only of seven of these men TRE, and Stigand of four. This was delivered to Ralph's antecessor as a manor (*fuit suo antecessori liberatum pro terra*).

2502 ii, 230a (21-1) Rainald fitz Ivo; Fincham: TRE a freeman held sixteen acres of land in Fincham. Wihenoc annexed (*invasit*) it. Now Rainald fitz Ivo holds it.

2503 ii, 230b–231a (21-5) Rainald fitz Ivo; Upwell: TRE Toli, a freeman, held a carucate of land in Upwell. Now Rainald fitz Ivo holds it. Seventeen freemen with sixty-four acres of land also lay in this manor. Wihenoc annexed (*invasit*) them.

2504 ii, 231a (21-7) Rainald fitz Ivo; Shouldham (All Saints or St. Margaret): TRE Thorkil held a carucate and six acres of land in Shouldham. Now Ranulf holds it from Rainald fitz Ivo. Ten freemen, commended only, also lay there TRE with thirty acres of land, which he also holds. Wihenoc annexed (*invasit*) them.

2505 ii, 231a–b (21-8) Rainald fitz Ivo; Beechamwell: TRE a freeman held twenty-four acres of land in Beechamwell. Now Rainald fitz Ivo holds it. Wihenoc annexed (*invasit*) it. Herman, his antecessor, had the commendation only.

2506 ii, 231b (21-8) Rainald fitz Ivo; Fodderstone: TRE there was half a carucate of land in Fodderstone. Now Ranulf holds it from Rainald fitz Ivo. Wihenoc annexed (*invasit*) it.

2507 ii, 231b (21-12) Rainald fitz Ivo; Stanford: TRE two freemen held fourteen acres of land in Stanford. They were delivered (*fuerunt liberati*) to Wihenoc. Now Ralph holds from Rainald fitz Ivo.

2508 ii, 231b–232a (21-13) Rainald fitz Ivo; Caldecote: TRE a freeman held a half carucate of land in Caldecote. After King William came into this land Wihenoc seized (*occupant*) it. For this reason, Rainald fitz Ivo holds it, and the King has soke and sake. In the same way Rainald also holds three freemen in Caldecote with fifty acres.

2509 ii, 232a (21-14) Rainald fitz Ivo; Pickenham (North or South): TRE a freeman held thirty acres of land in Pickenham. After King William came into that country, Earl Ralph held it. But a man of Wihenoc loved a woman in that manor and married (*duxit*) her. Afterwards he held this land from Wihenoc's fee without the King's gift and without livery (*sine dono regis et sine liberatione*). It is held by his successors (*successoribus suis*).

2510 ii, 232a (21-15) Rainald fitz Ivo; Houghton on the Hill: TRW Herluin holds a freeman with sixteen acres of land in Houghton on the Hill from Rainald fitz Ivo. Wihenoc annexed (*invasit*) it.

2511 ii, 232a (21-15) Rainald fitz Ivo; Pickenham (North or South): Wihenoc annexed (*invasit*) fifteen acres in Pickenham, and Rainald fitz Ivo now holds them. Ralph de Tosny claims (*calumpniatur*) this. The hundred testifies.

2512 ii, 232b (21-18) Rainald fitz Ivo; Threxton: TRE eight freemen held three carucates and twenty-eight acres of land in Threxton. Now Ranulf holds it from Rainald fitz Ivo. It was delivered (*liberatum est*) for a carucate of land.

2513 ii, 233a (21-22) Rainald fitz Ivo; Raynham: TRE Bondi held four freemen in Raynham, which Boteric now holds. Harold held one man; now Rainald fitz

Ivo holds him with half a carucate of land. The sheriff claims (*calumpniatur*) that Harold's man is in Fakenham, and this is testified by the hundred.

2514 ii, 233a–b (21-25) Rainald fitz Ivo; Stiffkey: TRE Ketil held two carucates of land in Stiffkey. Now Ranulf holds it from Rainald fitz Ivo. Four sokemen were added to this manor with one and a half carucates of land. Rainald fitz Ivo holds this through the King's livery (*per liberationem regis*).

2515 ii, 233b (21-26) Rainald fitz Ivo; Carleton St. Peter: TRE Ælfric, a freeman under King Edward, held thirty acres of land in Carleton St. Peter. Now Rainald fitz Ivo holds it. There were also fourteen freemen there commended to Wulfsige. They were delivered with sixty acres to make (*liberati ad perficiendum*) this manor.

2516 ii, 234a–b (21-32) Rainald fitz Ivo; Scottow: TRE Ketil held two and a half carucates of land in Scottow. Now Roger holds it from Rainald fitz Ivo. Wihenoc added two of Ramsey Abbey's sokemen to this manor with eighteen acres of land. Roger also holds this from Rainald.

2517 ii, 234b (21-35) Rainald fitz Ivo; Banningham: TRW Rainald fitz Ivo holds a villein of Cawston in Banningham, with sixteen acres of land, and Roger holds from him. This villein used to pay 5s. in Cawston. Wihenoc annexed (*invasit*) this.

2518 ii, 235b (22-11) Ralph de Tosny; Fransham (Great or Little): TRE there were sixteen of Harold's sokemen with three carucates of land in Fransham. Eudo fitz Clamahoc had a carucate of this land, held by three of them, by livery, as long as he lived (*liberatione quam diu vixit*). Afterwards Ralph de Beaufour held. Now Ralph de Tosny has it in Necton, where it lay in the time of King Edward.

2519 ii, 235b–236a (22-13) Ralph de Tosny; Godwick: TRE a freeman of King Edward held a carucate of land in Godwick. Now Ralph de Tosny holds it in Necton, but it did not lie there TRE, nor in the time of Harold. Roger Bigot claims it by gift of the King and vouches livery (*revocat de dono regis et revocat liberatorem*).

2520 ii, 238a (23-9) Hugh de Montfort; Marham: TRW there are twenty-six sokemen in Marham whom Walter holds from Hugh de Montfort. TRE Ely Abbey held them at soke. Hugh took this land in exchange (*recepit pro escangio*), and it is measured in the returns (*est in mensurata in brevi*) of Ely Abbey.

2521 ii, 238b (23-14) Hugh de Montfort; Stanford: TRE a freeman held a carucate of land in Stanford. Hugh de Montfort's antecessor had this man's commendation only, and King Edward had the soke. Now Hugh de Montfort holds.

2522 ii, 239b (24-1) Eudo Dapifer; Rockland (All Saints or St. Andrew): TRW Richard holds ten freemen with a carucate of land in Rockland from Eudo Dapifer. TRE and after, until Lisois had the land, the soke lay in the King's manor of Buckenham (near Attleborough). This is testified by the hundred.

2523 ii, 239b (24-2) Eudo Dapifer; Shropham: TRE there were eight freemen with one and a half carucates of land in Shropham. Now Roland holds this from Eudo Dapifer. The soke was in the King's manor of Buckenham (near Attleborough), but Lisois kept it back (*retinuit*), and so too does Eudo.

2524   ii, 239b (24-3) <u>Eudo Dapifer; Roudham</u>: TRW Ralph holds eight freemen with a carucate and ten acres of land in Roudham from Eudo Dapifer. The soke was in Buckenham (near Attleborough), but Lisois kept it back (*retinuit*), and so too does Eudo.

2525   ii, 239b (24-4) <u>Eudo Dapifer; Brettenham</u>: TRE Thorgisl held seven freemen with one and a half carucates of land in Brettenham. Now Eudo Dapifer holds it. The soke of six of these men was in the King's manor of Buckenham (near Attleborough), and Ely Abbey had the soke and commendation of the seventh. But Lisois kept back (*retinuit*) all of this, and now Eudo keeps it back (*retinet*).

2526   ii, 240a (24-6) <u>Eudo Dapifer; Postwick</u>: TRE Skuli, a freeman, held two carucates of land in Postwick. Now Eudo Dapifer holds it. In the same place Rathi, a freeman, held a carucate of land TRE, and the freeman Skalpi held a carucate there. Lisois held all of this as a manor. Now Eudo Dapifer, his successor (*successor*), holds it. TRE its soke and sake were in the hundred, but now Eudo holds it.

2527   ii, 240a–b (24-7) <u>Eudo Dapifer; Intwood</u>: TRE Coleman, a freeman of Stigand, held one and a half carucates of land in Intwood. Now Ralph holds it from Eudo Dapifer. There is also a berewick in Swainsthorpe with sixty acres of land. There were fifteen sokemen there with forty acres of land and five freemen with twenty acres of land. Eudo's antecessor had their commendation only TRE.

2528   ii, 241a (25-6) <u>Walter Giffard; Swannington</u>: TRE seven freemen held one and a half carucates and sixteen acres of land in Swannington. Now Walter Giffard holds it. The soke was in the King's manor of Foulsham TRE. Now Walter holds it.

2529   ii, 241b (25-8) <u>Walter Giffard; Ringland</u>: TRE three freemen held sixty acres of land in Ringland. Now Walter Giffard holds it. The soke was in the King's manor of Foulsham TRE. Now Walter holds it.

2530   ii, 241b (25-9) <u>Walter Giffard; Attlebridge, Felthorpe</u>: TRE three and a half freemen held five acres of land in Attlebridge, and another freeman held thirty acres of land in Felthorpe. Now Walter Giffard holds this. The King and the earl had the soke of all of them TRE. Now Walter has it.

2531   ii, 242a (25-15) <u>Walter Giffard; Lynford, Ickburgh</u>: TRW Walter Giffard has fourteen freemen with four carucates and thirty-five acres of land in Lynford and Ickburgh. TRE these men were commended to Ralph Wader's antecessor. Afterwards they were delivered (*liberati sunt*) to Bodin de Vere on the King's behalf (*ex parte regis*). Later still, Ralph established title (*derationavit*) to them from his fee (*ad suum feudum*), and when he forfeited (*forisfecit*) Hervey de Vere was holding them from him. This is testified by the hundred.

2532   ii, 242b (25-24) <u>Walter Giffard; North Barningham</u>: TRE Kee, a freeman, held twenty acres of land in North Barningham. Now Walter Giffard holds it. It was delivered to make (*fuit liberata ad perficiendum*) Letheringsett.

2533 ii, 242b–243a (25-25) Walter Giffard; Shotesham (All Saints or St. Mary): TRE there were three freemen commended to the Abbey of St. Benet of Holme and five sokemen with all customs in Shotesham. Now Walter Giffard holds them by (*ab*) his antecessor Bodin de Vere. Between them, they have ninety acres of land.

2534 ii, 243b–244a (26-3) Roger the Poitevin; Spixworth: TRE Swærting, a freeman, held two carucates of land in Spixworth under Harold. Now Albert holds it. It was Roger the Poitevin's. TRE six freemen of Stigand also held a carucate of land in Spixworth, and Robert Blanchard added them to this manor in the time of King William.

2535 ii, 244a–b (26-5) Roger the Poitevin; Tunstead: TRW Roger the Poitevin held five and a half carucates of land in Tunstead. TRE Ælfhere, a thegn of Harold, held it. There are twenty-four sokemen there with a carucate of land. They were added in the time of King William. Earl Ralph added another six freemen there with one and a half carucates of land. Ramsey Abbey has the soke of these men and the commendation of one of them. The abbey also has the three forfeitures (*tres forisfactaras*) of the twenty-four sokemen. After Earl Ralph forfeited (*forisfecit*) Robert the Balistarius added (so he says, by the order (*iussu*) of Godric, but Godric denies (*negat*) this) a carucate of land which lay in Hoveton (St. John or St. Peter) TRE, and which Earl Ralph, along with his wife, gave (*dedit*) to Ramsey Abbey. Then, there were one and a half plows; when Robert the Balistarius took it away (*tulit*), the same. Now there is one plow.

2536 ii, 244b (27-1) Ivo Taillebois; rubric: [A "*non fr*," for "*fecit non retornam*," appears in the margin, opposite the rubric which marks the beginning of Ivo Taillebois's holdings, indicating that he had not made a return.]

2537 ii, 244b (27-1) Ivo Taillebois; Newton (near Castle Acre): TRW Odo holds Newton from Ivo Taillebois, which Ælfhere, a freeman, held TRE. There are also two freemen living there, whom Ivo's antecessor held, holding a carucate of land.

2538 ii, 244b–245a (27-2) Ivo Taillebois; Shernborne: TRE sixteen freemen whom Harold held, held five carucates of land in Shernborne. Afterwards Earl Ralph held this land when he forfeited (*forisfecit*). Now Ivo Taillebois holds three of these men, and they hold from Ivo. Earl Ralph took away (*tulit*) a carucate of this land for Roger fitz Rainard the year before he could forfeit (*forisfaceret*), by testimony (*teste*) of the hundred.

2539 ii, 245a (28-1) Ralph de Limesy; rubric: [An "*r non f*," for "*fecit non retornam*," appears in the margin, opposite the rubric which marks the beginning of Ralph de Limesy's holdings, indicating that he had not made a return.]

2540 ii, 245a (28-1) Ralph de Limesy; Oxborough: TRE Thorkil held Oxborough. Now Ralph de Limesy holds it. There are eight freemen there holding one hundred acres of land. One of these freemen is claimed (*calumpniatur*) by Ralph de Tosny, because Ralph's antecessor held him with soke and sake, so the hundred testifies.

2541 ii, 245b (29-1) Eudo son of Spearhavoc; rubric: [A "*non*," for "*fecit non retornam*," appears in the margin, opposite the rubric which marks the beginning of Eudo son of Spearhavoc's holdings, indicating that he had not made a return.]

2542 ii, 245b (29-4) Eudo son of Spearhavoc; Dersingham: TRE Skiotr, a freeman, held Dersingham. Now Ricwold holds it from Eudo son of Spearhavoc. There are four freemen there with forty-four acres of land. Eudo took them to make (*recepit pro perficiendum*) his manors.

2543 ii, 246a (29-7) Eudo son of Spearhavoc; Alburgh: TRE Ælfric held Alburgh with its berewick Tibenham as a carucate of land. Now Morvan holds this from Eudo son of Spearhavoc. Ælfric also held a freeman commended to Ely Abbey, who could neither grant nor sell his land outside the abbey. Herfrid had him by livery to make (*ex liberatione ad perficienda*) his manor. Now Eudo son of Spearhavoc, his successor (*successor*), holds him. He has half a carucate of land.

2544 ii, 246a–b (29-8) Eudo son of Spearhavoc; Topcroft: TRE Godwine, a freeman commended only to Gyrth, held three carucates of land in Topcroft. Now Eudo son of Spearhavoc holds it. Under him there are four freemen with a carucate of land, delivered (*liberati*) to his antecessor Herfrid as a manor.

2545 ii, 246b (29-10) Eudo son of Spearhavoc; Tibenham: TRE the thegn Alric held three carucates of land in Tibenham. Now Eudo son of Spearhavoc holds it. There are twenty-six men there with fifty acres of land. They are commended and in fold-soke. They could sell their land, but afterward they offered it to their lord (*obtulissent domino suo*).

2546 ii, 246b (29-11) Eudo son of Spearhavoc; Carleton Rode: TRE a freeman held eight acres of land in Carleton Rode. Now Eudo son of Spearhavoc holds it. Herfrid took (*recepit*) these freemen as a manor.

2547 ii, 247a (30-1) Drogo de la Beuvrière; rubric: [An "fr," for "*fecit retornam*," appears in the margin, opposite the rubric which marks the beginning of Drogo de la Beuvrière's holdings, indicating that he made a return.]

2548 ii, 247a (30-2) Drogo de la Beuvrière; Bessingham: TRE a freeman commended to Eadric held a carucate of land in Bessingham. On the day that Robert Malet's father went on the King's service, he held him. But Drogo de la Beuvrière's man keeps him away (*prohibet*).

2549 ii, 247b (31-1) Ralph Baynard; rubric: [A "*non*," for "*fecit non retornam*," appears in the margin, opposite the rubric which marks the beginning of Ralph Baynard's holdings, indicating that he had not made a return.]

2550 ii, 248a (31-2) Ralph Baynard; Skeyton: TRE Esger, a freeman, held two carucates and twenty-seven acres of land in Skeyton. Now Geoffrey Baynard holds it from Ralph Baynard. There were also three sokemen there with seventy-eight acres of land. Ramsey Abbey held all but four of these acres in the time of King Edward.

2551 ii, 248a (31-4) <u>Ralph Baynard; Barton Turf</u>: TRW Geoffrey holds three freemen with ninety acres of land in Barton Turf from Ralph Baynard. Ramsey Abbey has the soke. One of these three freemen, with thirty acres of land, was a sokeman of Ramsey Abbey in such a way that he could not withdraw.

2552 ii, 248b–249a (31-6) <u>Ralph Baynard; Hempnall</u>: TRE Thorn held eight carucates of land in Hempnall. Now Ralph Baynard holds it. There is woodland there for two hundred pigs. Ramsey Abbey claims (*calumpniatur*) the part of the woodland called "Schieteshaga," which it held in the time of King Edward.

2553 ii, 249a (31-8) <u>Ralph Baynard; Hudeston</u>: TRE Thorn held four carucates and an acre of land in Hudeston. Now Geoffrey holds it from Ralph Baynard. TRE eighteen freemen (now twelve) lay in this manor in commendation only. They had a carucate and twenty acres of land. These freemen are in exchange (*sunt escangio*).

2554 ii, 249a (31-9) <u>Ralph Baynard; Fritton, Hardwick</u>: TRE a freeman held ten acres of land in Fritton and Hardwick. This has been added to the manor of Hempnall.

2555 ii, 249b (31-11) <u>Ralph Baynard; Southwood</u>: TRW Wimund, a freeman of whom Godric's antecessor had commendation TRE, holds sixty acres of land in Southwood. Now Ralph Baynard holds it. This is in exchange (*pro escangio*). Robert fitz Corbucion claims (*reclamat*) this land by gift of the King (*de dono regis*), and he vouches livery (*revocat liberatorem*). The hundred, however, testifies that Baynard was seised (*saisitus fuit*) of this before him.

2556 ii, 249b (31-12) <u>Ralph Baynard; Kirby Cane</u>: TRE Wulfmær, a freeman of King Edward, held thirty acres of land in Kirby Cane. Now Ralph Baynard holds it. Robert fitz Corbucion claims (*calumpniatur*) this and has livery (*habet liberatorem*). This is in exchange (*pro escangio*).

2557 ii, 249b (31-14) <u>Ralph Baynard; "Ierpstuna"</u>: TRE a freeman held thirty acres of land in "Ierpstuna." Half of this man was commended to the antecessor of Baynard; the other half was Bury St. Edmund's with half the land. Now Ralph Baynard holds all of this.

2558 ii, 249b–250a (31-15) <u>Ralph Baynard; Raveningham</u>: TRE a freeman held thirty acres of land in Raveningham. Now Ralph Baynard holds it. Robert fitz Corbucion claims (*calumpniatur*) this and has livery (*habet liberatorem*).

2559 ii, 250a–b (31-17) <u>Ralph Baynard; Wheatacre</u>: TRE a freeman of Harold held two carucates of land in Wheatacre. Now a Frenchman holds it from Ralph Baynard. Robert fitz Corbucion claims (*calumpniatur*) this and has livery (*habet liberatorem*). It is in exchange (*pro escangio*).

2560 ii, 250b (31-18) <u>Ralph Baynard; Haddiscoe</u>: TRE a freeman of Stigand held fifteen acres of land in Haddiscoe, and Stigand had the soke. Now Ralph Baynard holds it. It is in exchange (*pro escangio*).

2561 ii, 250b (31-20) <u>Ralph Baynard; Fincham</u>: TRE Æthelgyth, a free woman, held a carucate of land in Fincham. Now Ralph Baynard holds it. Ely Abbey claims (*calumniatur*) this land, and the hundred testifies.

2562   ii, 251a (31-23) Ralph Baynard; Shouldham Thorpe, Tottenhill: TRW twenty-two and a half freemen hold 110 acres of land in Shouldham Thorpe and Tottenhill from Ralph Baynard. TRE Æthelgyth held it. Ralph claims it in exchange (*reclamat pro escangio*).

2563   ii, 251a (31-26) Ralph Baynard; Stoke Ferry: TRW Ralph Baynard has thirteen freemen at soke in Stoke Ferry. He claims this in exchange (*reclamat pro escangio*).

2564   ii, 251a–b (31-28) Ralph Baynard; West Dereham: TRW Lovel holds a carucate of land in West Dereham from Ralph Baynard. TRE St. Benet of Holme had 20s. from this land, by testimony (*teste*) of the hundred.

2565   ii, 251b (31-29) Ralph Baynard; Beechamwell: TRW Ralph Baynard has twelve freemen with a carucate of land in Beechamwell. William de Warenne claims (*relamat*) one of these men with thirty acres of land, and vouches warranty (*revocat liberatorem*). Ralph Baynard, however, claims this in exchange (*reclamat pro escangio*).

2566   ii, 251b (31-32) Ralph Baynard; Lynn (King's, North, South, or West): TRW Ralph Baynard has fifty-eight acres of meadow in Lynn, along with three acres of land and two salthouses. He also has a freeman, over whom Stigand had soke, with three acres of land, eight acres of meadow, and half a salthouse. He has all of this in exchange (*pro escangio*).

2567   ii, 251b (31-33) Ralph Baynard; Sturston: TRE Thorn held six carucates of land in Sturston. Now Lovel holds it from Ralph Baynard. There are sixteen freemen there with two carucates and an acre of land. Ralph has these in exchange (*pro escangio*).

2568   ii, 252b (31-39) Ralph Baynard; Wellingham: TRE Harold held two carucates of land in Wellingham. Now Ralph Baynard holds it. Three sokemen of Stigand are there, whose forty acres of land, with all customs, lay in the King's manor of Mileham in the time of King Edward. But, while Stigand was living, it was delivered (*liberatum est*) to Baynard in exchange (*pro escangio*), so his men say.

2569   ii, 252b (31-40) Ralph Baynard; Scarning: TRE there were two sokemen in Scarning with twelve acres. Now Ralph Baynard holds them. The soke has always, in justice (*iuste*), been in Mileham.

2570   ii, 253a (31-43) Ralph Baynard; Chedgrave: TRE Thorth held two carucates of land in Chedgrave. Now Einbold holds it from Ralph Baynard. There were also thirteen and a half sokemen there, who were freemen of Thorth, with ninety-nine acres of land. Ralph claims these men in exchange (*reclamat pro escangio*).

2571   ii, 253a–b (31-44) Ralph Baynard; Chedgrave: TRE Leofric, a freeman commended to Harold, held two carucates of land in Chedgrave. Now Geoffrey holds it from Ralph Baynard. This is in exchange (*pro escangio*). Robert fitz Corbucion claims this land by livery (*calumpniatur hanc terram ex* *liberatione*), but Baynard was seised first (*primum fuit saisitus*), and afterwards Robert was, but the hundred does not know how.

2572   ii, 253b (31-45) Ralph Baynard; Carleton St. Peter: TRE a freeman under Thorth held thirty acres of land in Carleton St. Peter. Now Nigel holds it from Ralph Baynard. This is in exchange (*pro escangio*).

2573   ii, 254a (32-1) Ranulf Peverel; rubric: [A "*non*," for "*fecit non retornam*," appears in the margin, opposite the rubric which marks the beginning of Ranulf Peverel's holdings, indicating that he had not made a return.]

2574   ii, 254a (32-1) Ranulf Peverel; Billingford (near East Dereham): TRE Thorth, a freeman, held three carucates of land in Billingford. Now Humphrey holds it from Ranulf Peverel. Six sokemen belonged there TRE with forty-eight acres of land. Earl Ralph took them away (*abstulit*), and now Count Alan holds them.

2575   ii, 254b (32-4, 6) Ranulf Peverel; Great Melton: TRE Ketil held two carucates of land in Great Melton. Now Warin holds it from Ranulf Peverel. TRW Warin also holds a freeman from Ranulf Peverel in Great Melton with six acres of meadow. Ranulf Peverel annexed (*invasit*) this.

2576   ii, 254b–255a (32-7) Ranulf Peverel; Rushall: TRW Warin holds one and a half carucates of land in Rushall from Ranulf Peverel. Henry held it from Bury St. Edmund's, completely in the abbey TRE. Ranulf now holds this land from the King's fee.

2577   ii, 255a (33-1) Robert Gernon; rubric: [An "*fr*," for "*fecit retornam*," appears in the margin, opposite the rubric which marks the beginning of Robert Gernon's holdings, indicating that he had made a return.]

2578   ii, 256a (34-1) Peter de Valognes; rubric: [A "*non*," for "*fecit non retornam*," appears in the margin, opposite the rubric which marks the beginning of Peter de Valognes's holdings, indicating that he had not made a return.]

2579   ii, 256b (34-4) Peter de Valognes; Ingoldisthorpe: TRE Thorbert, a freeman, held three carucates of land in Ingoldisthorpe in demesne. Now Peter de Valognes holds it. There are also three freemen there with thirty-eight acres of land. Peter's antecessor had the fold-soke and commendation of these men, and Archbishop Stigand had the other soke.

2580   ii, 256b–257a (34-6) Peter de Valognes; Gateley: TRW Ralph holds two sokemen in Gateley from Peter de Valognes with thirty-four acres of land. The antecessor of Hugh de Montfort had the fold-soke and commendation of these men. The other soke was in the King's manor in Mileham. Now Peter holds them by livery (*de liberationem*).

2581   ii, 257b (34-13) Peter de Valognes; Gunthorpe: TRE a freeman of Harold held half a carucate of land in Gunthorpe. Now Peter de Valognes holds it. It was delivered to him to make (*fuit sibi liberata ad perficiendum*) the manor of Barney.

2582   ii, 258a (34-17) Peter de Valognes; Barney: TRE Thorkil held two carucates of land in Barney. Now William holds it from Peter de Valognes. There are also seventeen freemen there with eighty acres of land. Peter claims them through livery to make this manor (*hos reclamat ex deliberationem ad perficiendum hoc manerium*). One of the King's servants, however, claims (*calumpniatur*), by whatever manner of judgment he be judged (*quocumque iudicio iudicatur*), thirteen and a half of these men from the fee of Earl Ralph, who held them when he forfeited (*se forisfecit*). This is testified by the hundred.

2583 ii, 258a (34-18) Peter de Valognes; Great Walsingham: TRE Bondi, a thegn, held one and a half carucates of land in Great Walsingham. Now Humphrey holds it from Peter de Valognes. This land was delivered to make (*fuit liberata ad perficiendum*) a manor, but Peter's men do not know which one.

2584 ii, 258a (34-19) Peter de Valognes; Holkham: TRE Toki, a freeman, held thirty-three acres of land in Holkham. Peter de Valognes now holds this in the same way as the manor spoken of above.

2585 ii, 258b (35-1) Robert fitz Corbucion; rubric: [A "*non*," for "*fecit non retornam*," appears in the margin, opposite the rubric which marks the beginning of Robert fitz Corbucion's holdings, indicating that he had not made a return.]

2586 ii, 259a–b (35-8) Robert fitz Corbucion; Mundham: TRE Godwine, a freeman commended to Edwin, antecessor of Godric Dapifer, held thirty acres of land in Mundham. Now Nigel holds it from Robert fitz Corbucion.

2587 ii, 259b (35-11) Robert fitz Corbucion; Loddon: TRW Humphrey holds half an acre of land in Loddon under Robert fitz Corbucion, which St. Benet of Holme claims (*calumniatur*). The hundred testifies that it was in St. Benet's demesne.

2588 ii, 260a (35-15) Robert fitz Corbucion; Stratton (St. Mary or St. Michael): TRE a thegn held two carucates of land in Stratton. Now Humphrey holds it from Robert fitz Corbucion. There are seven freemen there with seventeen acres of land. Robert's antecessor had their commendation TRE, but Robert has them as a manor.

2589 ii, 260a (35-16) Robert fitz Corbucion; Fritton: TRE Ulfkil, a freeman of Eadric of Laxfield, antecessor of Robert Malet, held thirty acres of land in Fritton. Now Giffard holds it from Robert fitz Corbucion. William Malet was seised (*erat saisitus*) of this when he went into the marsh.

2590 ii, 260b (36-1) Ranulf brother of Ilger; rubric: [An "*fr*," for "*fecit retornam*," appears in the margin, opposite the rubric which marks the beginning of Ranulf brother of Ilger's holdings, indicating that he had made a return.]

2591 ii, 260b–261a (36-5) Ranulf brother of Ilger; Walcott: TRE Eadric, a thegn, held four carucates and six acres of land in Walcott. Now Humphrey holds it from Ranulf brother of Ilger. He also holds four freemen there with ninety acres of land, who were added to this manor in the time of King William. Ranulf brother of Ilger added them, and Humphrey holds them. Ranulf's antecessor had the commendation only of two of these men, and Robert Malet's antecessor of one.

2592 ii, 261b (37-1) Tihel the Breton; rubric: [An "*f*," for "*fecit retornam*," appears in the margin, opposite the rubric which marks the beginning of Tihel's holdings, indicating that he had made a return.]

2593 ii, 261b (37-3) <u>Tihel the Breton; Booton</u>: TRE a sokeman of Harold held a carucate of land in Booton. Now Tihel holds it. All of this was delivered for a manor (*fuit liberatum pro uno manerio*).

2594 ii, 262a (38-1) <u>Robert de Verly; rubric</u>: [An "f," for "*fecit retornam,*" appears in the margin, opposite the rubric which marks the beginning of Robert de Verly's holdings, indicating that he had made a return.]

2595 ii, 262a (38-2) <u>Robert de Verly; Burnham Thorpe</u>: TRE Godwine held a carucate of land in Burnham Thorpe. Afterwards, Earl Ralph held when he forfeited (*se forisfecit*). Now Robert de Verly holds it.

2596 ii, 262a (38-3) <u>Robert de Verly; Field Dalling</u>: TRE Godwine, uncle of Ralph, held eleven sokemen in Field Dalling with a carucate of land. Now Robert de Verly holds this, saying that he holds in exchange (*pro mutuo*) for Roding [Essex]. He vouches (*revocat*) Robert Blunt for livery (*liberatorem*).

2597 ii, 262a (39-1) <u>Humphrey fitz Aubrey; rubric</u>: [An "f," for "*fecit retornam,*" appears in the margin, opposite the rubric which marks the beginning of Humphrey fitz Aubrey's holdings, indicating that he had made a return.]

2598 ii, 262b (39-2) <u>Humphrey fitz Aubrey; Billingford (near Dereham)</u>: TRE a free woman held a carucate of land in Billingford. Now Humphrey fitz Aubrey holds it. TRE the soke was in the King's manor of Foulsham. Now Humphrey holds it.

2599 ii, 262b (40-1) <u>Humphrey de Bohun; rubric</u>: [An "f," for "*fecit retornam,*" appears in the margin, opposite the rubric which marks the beginning of Humphrey de Bohun's holdings, indicating that he had made a return.]

2600 ii, 262b (40-1) <u>Humphrey de Bohun; Tatterford</u>: TRE Wulfnoth held a carucate of land in Tatterford from Bishop Stigand. Now Humphrey de Bohun holds it. Four sokemen and forty acres have been taken away (*sunt ablati*) from this manor. William de Warenne holds them.

2601 ii, 263a (41-1) <u>Ralph de Fougères; rubric</u>: [An "f," for "*fecit retornam,*" appears in the margin, opposite the rubric which marks the beginning of Ralph de Fougère's holdings, indicating that he had made a return.]

2602 ii, 263a (42-1) <u>Gilbert fitz Richere; rubric</u>: [A "*nichil*" appears in the margin, opposite the rubric which marks the beginning of Gilbert fitz Richere's holdings, indicating that he had not made a return.]

2603 ii, 263a–b (43-2, 3) <u>Roger de Raismes; Billingford; Starston (near Diss)</u>: TRW Werengar holds twenty-four acres of land in Billingford from Roger de Raismes. This land was in the hall of Bury St. Edmund's in the time of King Edward. There were also twelve freemen of Bury there, who could neither grant nor sell their land without the permission of both Bury and Stigand, who had the soke and sake in Earsham. Werengar also holds them. Werengar holds another forty acres of land in Billingford, which Bury St. Edmund's held TRE, by testimony (*teste*) of the hundred, but the hundred does not know how Werengar holds it. Werengar also holds sixteen acres of land in Starston under Roger de Raismes, which two of Stigand's freemen held TRE, and which belonged in Earsham.

2604 ii, 263b (44-1) <u>Iudhael the Priest; rubric</u>: [An "f," for "*fecit retornam*," appears in the margin, opposite the rubric which marks the beginning of Iudhael the Priest's holdings, indicating that he had made a return.]

2605 ii, 263b (44-1) <u>Iudhael the Priest; Hethel</u>: TRE Algar held half a carucate of land in Hethel under Eadric, antecessor of Robert Malet, to whom he was commended only. Now Iudhael the Priest holds it.

2606 ii, 263b (45-1) <u>Colebern the Priest; rubric</u>: [A "*non*" appears in the margin, opposite the rubric which marks the beginning of Colebern the Priest's holdings, indicating that he had not made a return.]

2607 ii, 263b (45-1) <u>Colebern the Priest; church in Humbleyard Hundred</u>: Colebern the Priest built the Church of St. Nicholas, Norwich with the consent (*concessu*) of the King. And if the King grants (*concedit*), Colebern will give (*dabit*) twenty acres of land. For this reason (*ideo*) he sings mass and the psalms each week for the King.

2608 ii, 264a (46-1) <u>Edmund son of Payne; rubric</u>: [An "f," for "*fecit retornam*," appears in the margin, opposite the rubric which marks the beginning of Edmund son of Payne's holdings, indicating that he had made a return.]

2609 ii, 264a (46-1) <u>Edmund fitz Payne; Dunham (Great or Little)</u>: TRE Payne held four carucates of land in Dunham. Now Edmund fitz Payne holds it, and Rainald the Priest holds from him with the daughter of Payne.

2610 ii, 264a (47-1) <u>Isaac; Thompson</u>: TRE a freeman held a carucate of land in Thompson. Now Isaac holds it. This is from Earl Ralph's fee of Stow Bedon. Robert Blunt delivered (*liberavit*) it.

2611 ii, 264a (47-3) <u>Isaac; Woodton</u>: Two freemen in Woodton, commended only to Godwine in the time of King Edward, were delivered (*liberati*) for sixty acres of land. Now Isaac holds.

2612 ii, 264b (47-7) <u>Isaac; Seething</u>: TRW an impoverished nun claims (*calumpniatur*) four acres of land in Seething, which she held under Ralph both before and after he forfeited (*se forefecisse*): this the hundred testifies. But Isaac vouches it to his fee, by gift of the King (*revocat ex dono regis ad feudum suum*).

2613 ii, 264b (48-1) <u>Tovi; rubric</u>: [The words "*non fecit*," signifying that Tovi did not make a return, are written in the margin opposite the rubric which begins Tovi's chapter.]

2614 ii, 264b (48-2) <u>Tovi; Holkham</u>: TRE Ketil, a freeman, held three carucates of land in Holkham. Now Tovi holds it. Three freemen with one and a half carucates of land have been added to this manor. Two of them were commended to Harold and one to Gyrth. Tovi's antecessor held them.

2615 ii, 264b–265a (48-3) <u>Tovi; Stoke Holy Cross</u>: TRE the thegn Ingeld held sixty acres of land in Stoke Holy Cross. Now Tovi holds it. There are six acres of meadow there. St. Benet of Holme claims (*calumpniatur*) four of these acres, which it held TRE.

2616 ii, 265a (48-4) <u>Tovi; Swainsthorpe</u>: TRE fifteen freemen held 155 acres of land in Swainsthorpe. Ralph the Staller had the commendation of eleven and a half of these men; Stigand of three; and the antecessor of Godric Dapifer of half. Now Tovi holds this.

2617   ii, 265a (48-5) <u>Tovi; Newton Flotman</u>: TRE two freemen held thirty acres of land in Newton Flotman. Roger Bigot's antecessor had the commendation of one and a half of these men, and the antecessor of Ralph de Beaufour had the commendation of half. Now Tovi holds this.

2618   ii, 265a (48-6) <u>Tovi; Kenningham</u>: TRE three freemen held seventy-five acres of land in Kenningham. The antecessor of Roger Bigot had the commendation of two of these men, and the antecessor of Ralph de Beaufour of the one. Now Tovi holds this.

2619   ii, 265b (49-1) <u>John fitz Waleran; rubric</u>: [An "fr," for "*fecit retornam*," appears in the margin, opposite the rubric which marks the beginning of John fitz Waleran's holdings, indicating that he had made a return.]

2620   ii, 265b-266a (49-5) <u>John fitz Waleran; West Carbrooke</u>: TRE a freeman held forty acres of land in West Carbrooke. Roger Bigot's antecessor had his commendation only. Now John fitz Waleran holds it.

2621   ii, 266b (50-1) <u>Roger fitz Rainard; rubric</u>: [An "fr," for "*fecit retornam*," appears in the margin, opposite the rubric which marks the beginning of Roger fitz Rainard's holdings, indicating that he had made a return.]

2622   ii, 266b (50-1) <u>Roger fitz Rainard; Stanford</u>: TRE Alstan held two carucates of land in Stanford. There are also eight freemen there with two carucates and thirty-six acres of land. Now Roger fitz Rainard holds all of this, and claims it by gift of the King (*reclamat de dono regis*).

2623   ii, 267b (50-13) <u>Roger fitz Rainard; Thurlton</u>: TRE a freeman commended only to Ralph de Beaufour's antecessor held twenty acres of land in Thurlton. Now Roger fitz Rainard holds it.

2624   ii, 267b (51-1) <u>Berner the Balistarius; rubric</u>: [An "f," for "*fecit retornam*," appears in the margin, opposite the rubric which marks the beginning of Berner the Balistarius's holdings, indicating that he had made a return.]

2625   ii, 267b (51-2) <u>Berner the Balistarius; Congham</u>: TRE a freeman held sixty acres of land in Congham. There were also four freemen there with three acres of land. Now Berner the Balistarius holds this. He vouches all these free men by gift of the King (*revocat de dono regis*).

2626   ii, 268a (51-5) <u>Berner the Balistarius; Ashill</u>: TRE Ælfric, a thegn of Harold, held two carucates of land in Ashill. Now Berner the Balistarius holds it. This is in exchange (*pro escangio*), and was one of Earl Ralph's manors.

2627   ii, 268b (51-9) <u>Berner the Balistarius; Pickenham (North or South)</u>: TRE a freeman held twelve acres of land and a house in Pickenham. This is from Earl Ralph's fee. Now Berner the Balistarius holds this. Robert Blunt delivered (*liberavit*) it.

2628   ii, 268b (52-1) <u>Gilbert the Balistarius; rubric</u>: [An "f," for "*fecit retornam*," appears in the margin, opposite the rubric which marks the beginning of Gilbert the Balistarius's holdings, indicating that he had made a return.]

2629 ii, 268b (52-1) <u>Gilbert the Balistarius; Shropham</u>: TRE Ælfric held a carucate of land in Shropham. Now Gilbert the Balistarius holds it. A freeman with thirty acres of land has been added there in exchange (*pro escangio*).

2630 ii, 268b–269a (52-3) <u>Gilbert the Balistarius; Brundall</u>: TRE Godwine, a freeman commended to Gyrth, held a carucate of land in Brundall. After the King came, Earl Ralph took (*accepit*) it. Now Gilbert the Balistarius holds it.

2631 ii, 269a (53-1) <u>Ralph the Balistarius; Plumstead (Great or Little)</u>: TRE Tovi, a freeman of Gyrth, held a carucate of land in Plumstead. Now Ralph the Balistarius holds it. There are six and a half freemen living in this manor with twenty acres of land. Ralph claims them through livery (*reclamat ex liberatione*).

2632 ii, 269b (55-1) <u>Rabel the Artificer; rubric</u>: [An "f," for "*fecit retornam*," appears in the margin, opposite the rubric which marks the beginning of Rabel the Artificer's holdings, indicating that he had made a return.]

2633 ii, 270a (56-6) <u>Hagne; Sparham</u>: TRE a freeman held thirty acres of land in Sparham. Now Hagne the King's reeve holds it. His antecessor had the commendation only of this man.

2634 ii, 270a (57-2) <u>Ralph son of Hagne; Mundham</u>: TRE Ely Abbey held twenty acres of land in demesne in Mundham. Now Ralph son of Hagne holds it.

2635 ii, 270b (58-1) <u>Ulfkil; rubric</u>: [An "f," for "*fecit retornam*," appears in the margin, opposite the rubric which marks the beginning of Ulfkil's holdings, indicating that he had made a return.]

2636 ii, 270b (58-2) <u>Ulfkil; Rushford</u>: TRE Bondi, a freeman, held two carucates of land in Rushford. Now Ulfkil holds it. There is also a freeman there with fourteen acres of land, which Ulfkil vouches by gift of the King (*revocat de dono regis*).

2637 ii, 270b (58-3) <u>Ulfkil; Witton (near Norwich)</u>: TRE two freemen of Gyrth held 140 acres in Witton. Now Ulfkil holds them. When Earl Ralph forfeited (*se forisfecit*), he was holding this in his hand. Later Robert Blunt held. Afterwards this was reseised in the King's hand, through a writ of the King (*per breve regis fuit resaitus in manu regis*).

2638 ii, 271a (61-1) <u>Godwine Healfdene; rubric</u>: [An "f," for "*fecit retornam*," appears in the margin, opposite the rubric which marks the beginning of Godwine Healfdene's holdings, indicating that he had made a return.]

2639 ii, 272a–b (64-1, 2, 3, 4, 5, 6, 7, 8, 9) <u>Freemen; Burgh St. Margaret, Rollesby, Repps (near Acle), Clippesby, Bastwick, Billockby, Somerton (East or West), Winterton, Martham</u>: These are the freemen who belonged to no farm TRE, over whom Almær has the service, and who were added to the farm TRW: TRE Gyrth held sixty acres of land freely in Burgh St. Margaret; eight and a half freemen under Gyrth held fifty-five acres of land in soke in Rollesby; seven freemen held twenty acres of land in Repps; five freemen held forty-six acres of land in Clippesby; two freemen held twenty-five acres of land in Bastwick; four freemen held thirty acres of land in Billockby; five freemen held twenty acres of land in demesne in Somerton; eight freemen held fifty-four acres of land in Winterton; and one freeman held ten acres of land in Martham. Furthermore, the value of the land in Burgh St. Margaret is 20s. in the farm of Cawston, to which this land did not belong TRE. Roger Bigot made (*fecit*) a reeve there. And the value of Rollesby is 8s. in the farm of Cawston, to which this land did not belong TRE, but has been added.

2640 ii, 273a (65-10) <u>King's freemen; Scratby</u>: TRW a freeman holds ten acres of land in Scratby. Æthelwig of Thetford added this to the rent (*ad censum*) of Ormesby (St. Margaret or St. Michael) in the time of King William.

2641 ii, 273a (65-13) <u>King's freemen; Moulton St. Michael</u>: TRW Gauti and Eskil, both freemen, hold two and a half acres of land in Moulton St. Michael. Aski the Priest, a man of the Abbot of St. Benet of Holme, held them, and has given a pledge (*dedit vadem*).

2642 ii, 273a–b (65-16) <u>King's freemen; Thurlton</u>: A freeman of Ralph de Beaufour's antecessor held eight acres of land in Thurlton. H. Evil Hands held this land, by testimony (*teste*) of the hundred, but he conceals (*celat*) it.

2643 ii, 273b (65-17) <u>King's freemen; Raveningham</u>: TRW Ketil Friday, a freeman, holds seven acres of land in Raveningham. This land is from Earl Ralph's fee. It was mensual-land (*erat mensa*) from the same manor when Ralph forfeited (*forisfecit*). Later Ketil held his land so that it paid no service to the King. He has given a pledge (*dedit vadem*) for this.

2644 ii, 273b (66-1) <u>Annexations (*invasiones*) in Norfolk; Fincham</u>: Concerning the annexation (*invasio*) of Hermer de Ferrers: TRE there were twenty freemen in Fincham, who held two carucates of land. Eight of them were responsible to Hermer's antecessor for the customs of the fold. The others, however, were free except for commendation.

2645 ii, 273b (66-2) <u>Annexations (*invasiones*) in Norfolk; Barton Bendish</u>: TRE a freeman held twelve acres of land in Barton Bendish, which W. now holds from Hermer de Ferrers. Hermer's antecessor had nothing from this except commendation.

2646 ii, 273b (66-2) <u>Annexations (*invasiones*) in Norfolk; Barton Bendish</u>: TRE a freeman in Barton Bendish, commended only to Hermer de Ferrers's antecessor, held sixty acres of land.

2647 ii, 273b (66-3) <u>Annexations (*invasiones*) in Norfolk; Wormegay</u>: TRE two freemen held four acres of land in Wormegay, but Hermer de Ferrers's antecessor had all customs.

2648 ii, 273b (66-4) <u>Annexations (*invasiones*) in Norfolk; West Briggs</u>: TRE three freemen held half a carucate of land in West Briggs. Hermer de Ferrers's antecessor had commendation only of these men, and Ramsey Abbey had their soke.

2649 ii, 273b–274a (66-5) <u>Annexations (*invasiones*) in Norfolk; Thorpland (near Downham Market)</u>: TRE eight and a half freemen held twenty acres of land in Thorpland. Eight of them were responsible to Hermer de Ferrers's antecessor for the customs of the fold. There are another thirty acres of land there, which Godwine, a freeman who was later outlawed (*utlagavit*), held.

Hermer has given a pledge for this and for other things (*inde dedit vadem et de aliis rebus*).

2650 ii, 274a (66-6) Annexations (*invasiones*) in Norfolk; Stow Bardolph: TRE a freeman held thirty-four acres of land in Stow Bardolph. Now Hermer de Ferrers holds it.

2651 ii, 274a (66-7) Annexations (*invasiones*) in Norfolk; Hilgay: TRE Bury St. Edmund's held the commendation only of six acres of land in Hilgay. Now Hermer de Ferrers holds it. In the same vill, two freemen held two acres of land. Hermer's antecessor had commendation only.

2652 ii, 274a (66-8) Annexations (*invasiones*) in Norfolk; Wimbotsham; Stow Bardolph: TRE three freemen held forty acres of land in Wimbotsham, and four freemen held forty acres in Stow Bardolph. Now Hermer de Ferrers holds all of this. His antecessor had nothing except commendation and half the soke along with Ramsey Abbey.

2653 ii, 274a (66-9) Annexations (*invasiones*) in Norfolk; Bexwell: TRE seven freemen held a carucate of land in Bexwell. Now Hermer de Ferrers holds it. His antecessor had the commendation only of these men.

2654 ii, 274a (66-10) Annexations (*invasiones*) in Norfolk; Ryston: TRE three freemen, who were commended only, held ninety acres of land in Ryston. Now Hermer de Ferrers holds it.

2655 ii, 274a (66-11) Annexations (*invasiones*) in Norfolk; Fordham: TRE three freemen, who were commendation only, held twenty-four acres of land in Fordham. Now Hermer de Ferrers holds it. His antecessor had nothing except commendation.

2656 ii, 274a (66-12) Annexations (*invasiones*) in Norfolk; West Dereham: TRE thirty-two freemen held 120 acres of land in West Dereham. Now Hermer de Ferrers holds it. His antecessor had the commendation of twenty-five of these men. Bordin holds half of three of these men from Hermer. Another seven were commended to Roger Bigot's antecessor. Hermer's antecessor had nothing from them, and Hermer annexed (*invasit*) these seven.

2657 ii, 274a (66-13) Annexations (*invasiones*) in Norfolk; Downham Market: TRE thirteen freemen held forty acres of land in Downham Market. Now Hermer de Ferrers holds it. His antecessor had nothing except commendation.

2658 ii, 274a (66-14) Annexations (*invasiones*) in Norfolk; Shouldham Thorpe: TRE eleven and a half freemen held eighty acres of land in Shouldham Thorpe. Now Hermer de Ferrers holds it. His antecessor had nothing except commendation.

2659 ii, 274a (66-15) Annexations (*invasiones*) in Norfolk; Fodderstone: TRE six freemen held forty acres of land in Fodderstone. Now Hermer de Ferrers holds it. His antecessor had nothing there except commendation. Because they cannot be without (*non possunt carere*) his pasture, these men pay customs to him.

2660 ii, 274a–b (66-16) Annexations (*invasiones*) in Norfolk; Wallington: TRE Thurstan, a freeman, held one hundred acres of land in Wallington. Now

Hermer de Ferrers holds it. Seven freemen held sixty acres in the same vill. Hermer's antecessor had the commendation of six of these men, and Earl Gyrth the seventh. Hermer annexed (*invasit*) him.

2661 ii, 274b (66-17) <u>Annexations (*invasiones*) in Norfolk; Lynn (King's, North, South, or West)</u>: TRW Hermer de Ferrers holds two freemen in Lynn with twenty-five acres of land, whose commendation only his antecessor had.

2662 ii, 274b (66-18) <u>Annexations (*invasiones*) in Norfolk; West Winch</u>: TRE a freeman held a carucate of land in West Winch. TRW Hermer de Ferrers holds it. His antecessor had nothing except commendation.

2663 ii, 274b (66-19) <u>Annexations (*invasiones*) in Norfolk; Wiggenhall</u>: TRE a freeman held half a carucate of land in Wiggenhall. Now Hermer de Ferrers holds it. His antecessor had nothing except commendation.

2664 ii, 274b (66-20) <u>Annexations (*invasiones*) in Norfolk; East Winch</u>: TRE two freemen held thirty acres of land in East Winch, which Bordin now holds from Hermer de Ferrers. His antecessor had nothing except commendation, and Stigand had the soke.

2665 ii, 274b (66-21) <u>Annexations (*invasiones*) in Norfolk; West Walton</u>: TRE three freemen held ninety-one acres of land in West Walton, which Bordin now holds from Hermer de Ferrers. His antecessor had nothing except commendation.

2666 ii, 274b (66-22) <u>Annexations (*invasiones*) in Norfolk; Gayton Thorpe</u>: TRE Thorkil, a freeman, held a carucate of land in Gayton Thorpe. Now Hermer de Ferrers holds it. His antecessor had the commendation only, and Stigand had the soke.

2667 ii, 274b (66-23) <u>Annexations (*invasiones*) in Norfolk; Gayton</u>: TRE a freeman held sixty acres of land in Gayton, which Bordin now holds from Hermer de Ferrers. His antecessor had nothing but the commendation, and Stigand had the soke.

2668 ii, 274b (66-24) <u>Annexations (*invasiones*) in Norfolk; Great Ellingham</u>: TRE three freemen held 110 acres of land in Great Ellingham, which Warenbold now holds from Hermer de Ferrers. His antecessor had commendation only. The soke is in the King's manor of Buckenham (near Attleborough).

2669 ii, 274b (66-25) <u>Annexations (*invasiones*) in Norfolk; Longham</u>: TRE a freeman held half a carucate of land in Longham. Now Hermer de Ferrers holds it. His antecessor had nothing except commendation. The soke is in the King's manor of Mileham.

2670 ii, 274b (66-26) <u>Annexations (*invasiones*) in Norfolk; Thuxton</u>: TRE seven freemen held 100 acres of land in Thuxton. Now Hermer de Ferrers holds it. His antecessor had nothing except commendation.

2671 ii, 275a (66-27) <u>Annexations (*invasiones*) in Norfolk; Reymerston</u>: TRE five freemen held thirty acres of land in Reymerston. Now Hermer de Ferrers holds it. His antecessor had nothing except commendation.

2672 ii, 275a (66-28) <u>Annexations (*invasiones*) in Norfolk; Yaxham</u>: TRE ten freemen held fifty-three acres of land in Yaxham, which Æthelhelm holds from Hermer de Ferrers. His antecessor had nothing except commendation.

2673 ii, 275a (66–29) Annexations (*invasiones*) in Norfolk; Mattishall: TRE twenty freemen, who were commendation only, held a carucate and thirty-nine acres of land in Mattishall. Now Hermer de Ferrers holds it. His antecessor had nothing except commendation.

2674 ii, 275a (66–30) Annexations (*invasiones*) in Norfolk; North Tuddenham: TRE six freemen held 100 acres of land in North Tuddenham. Now Hermer de Ferrers holds it.

2675 ii, 275a (66–31) Annexations (*invasiones*) in Norfolk; Bickerston: TRE a freeman, who was commended only, held eight acres of land in Bickerston. Now Hermer de Ferrers holds it.

2676 ii, 275a (66–32) Annexations (*invasiones*) in Norfolk; North Tuddenham: TRE three freemen, who were commended only, held thirty-two acres of land in North Tuddenham. Now Hermer de Ferrers holds it.

2677 ii, 275a (66–33) Annexations (*invasiones*) in Norfolk; Letton: TRE two freemen, who were commended only, held twenty-one acres of land in Letton. Now a freeman holds it from Hermer de Ferrers.

2678 ii, 275a (66–34) Annexations (*invasiones*) in Norfolk; Southburgh: TRE half a freeman, who was commended only, held two acres of land in Southburgh. Now Hermer de Ferrers holds it.

2679 ii, 275a (66–35) Annexations (*invasiones*) in Norfolk; Fincham: Concerning the annexation (*invasio*) of Ralph Baynard: six and a half freemen held a carucate of land in Fincham, which Ralph Baynard annexed (*invasit*). Ralph's men claim (*reclamant*) this in exchange (*pro escangio*), but they do not have livery (*liberatorem*).

2680 ii, 275a (66–36) Annexations (*invasiones*) in Norfolk; Barton Bendish: TRE a freeman held thirty acres of land in Barton Bendish, which Ralph Baynard now holds. He gave (*dedit*) four of these acres in mortgage (*in vadimonio*), and Wihenoc of Burley took (*tulit*) away another eight acres.

2681 ii, 275a (66–37) Annexations (*invasiones*) in Norfolk; Stoke Ferry: TRE Ulfkil held one hundred acres of land in Stoke Ferry. Now Ralph Baynard holds it. He claims this in exchange (*reclamat pro escangio*).

2682 ii, 275a (66–38) Annexations (*invasiones*) in Norfolk; Scarning: TRE a freeman, who was commended only, held twenty-four acres of land in Scarning. Now Ralph Baynard holds it. The soke is in the King's manor of Mileham.

2683 ii, 275a (66–39) Annexations (*invasiones*) in Norfolk; Dykebeck: TRE twenty-four freemen held 120 acres in Dykebeck, which Ralph Baynard now holds. His antecessor did not have their commendation. Four of them were in Wymondham, one in the bishopric, three in Kimberley, and seventeen in Hingham.

2684 ii, 275b (66–40) Annexations (*invasiones*) in Norfolk; Runcton (Holme or South): TRE five freemen held 150 acres of land in Runcton. The Abbot of

Bury St. Edmund's now holds it from Ralph Baynard. Ralph claims it by gift of the King (*reclamat ex dono regis*). In the same vill a freeman holds half a carucate of land, and three and a half freemen hold forty-six acres of land. Ralph Baynard holds these as well.

2685 ii, 275b (66-41) Annexations (*invasiones*) in Norfolk; Shelfanger: TRE a freeman in Shelfanger, commended only to Algar, held twelve acres of land in Winfarthing. He was killed (*fuit occisus*) at the Battle of Hastings. Afterwards, the abbot held this land in his manor of Bressingham. Ralph Baynard's steward offers to bear the ordeal that he did not know this (*suus dapifer offert se nescisse sicut iudicium pro portat*).

2686 ii, 275b (66-42) Annexations (*invasiones*) in Norfolk; Winfarthing: TRE a freeman held two acres of land in Winfarthing, which Earl Ralph held when he forfeited (*se forisfecit*). Afterwards Godric held it in the King's hand. Then Godric Herewulf held it in the land of Bury St. Edmund's, by permission of the abbot's reeve, by testimony (*teste*) of the hundred. Now Ralph Baynard holds it.

2687 ii, 275b (66-43) Annexations (*invasiones*) in Norfolk; Shropham: TRE a freeman held thirty acres of land in Shropham. Now Ralph Baynard holds it.

2688 ii, 275b (66-44) Annexations (*invasiones*) in Norfolk; West Dereham: TRW Rainald fitz Ivo holds six freemen with thirty-two acres of land in West Dereham. Wihenoc annexed (*invasit*) them, although they were in the commendation only of his antecessor.

2689 ii, 275b (66-45) Annexations (*invasiones*) in Norfolk; Roxham: TRE a freeman, who was commended only, held nine acres of land in Roxham. Now Rainald fitz Ivo holds.

2690 ii, 275b (66-46) Annexations (*invasiones*) in Norfolk; Fordham: TRE three commended freemen held twenty-five acres of land in Fordham. Ramsey Abbey had the soke. Another freeman held five acres there, and he was commended to Bury St. Edmund's TRE. Now Rainald fitz Ivo holds all of this.

2691 ii, 275b–276a (66-47) Annexations (*invasiones*) in Norfolk; Downham Market: TRE three freemen, who were commended only, held two and a half acres of land in Downham Market. Now Rainald fitz Ivo holds it. Another freemen, commended to the antecessor of William de Warenne, held seven acres there. Now Rainald holds this as well.

2692 ii, 276a (66-48) Annexations (*invasiones*) in Norfolk; Bexwell: TRE a freeman, who was commended to Hermer de Ferrers's antecessor, held fifteen acres of land in Bexwell. Another freeman held three acres there. Now Rainald fitz Ivo holds these men.

2693 ii, 276a (66-49) Annexations (*invasiones*) in Norfolk; Upwell: TRE six freemen held two carucates and fifteen acres of land in Upwell. Three of them were commended to Hermer de Ferrers's antecessor. Wihenoc seized (*occupavit*) them. Now Rainald fitz Ivo holds all of this.

2694 ii, 276a (66-50) Annexations (*invasiones*) in Norfolk; West Winch: TRW

Wihenoc added a freeman with thirty acres to West Winch. Now Rainald
fitz Ivo holds.

2695   ii, 276a (66-51) Annexations (*invasiones*) in Norfolk; Fincham: TRW Herluin
fitz Ivo annexed (*invasit*) a freeman with fifteen acres of land in Fincham.
There is another acre and a half of land there, which Maynard annexed
(*invasit*). Now Rainald fitz Ivo holds all of this.

2696   ii, 276a (66-52) Annexations (*invasiones*) in Norfolk; Pickenham (North or
South): TRE a freeman held ten acres of land in Pickenham. Wihenoc
annexed (*invasit*) it. Now Rainald fitz Ivo holds.

2697   ii, 276a (66-53) Annexations (*invasiones*) in Norfolk; Fordham: TRW the
Abbot of Ely holds thirty acres of land from Ely Abbey in Fordham, which a
freeman held TRE. The Abbot had nothing except commendation.

2698   ii, 276a (66-54) Annexations (*invasiones*) in Norfolk; Ryston: TRE three
freemen held six acres of land in Ryston. Now the Abbot of Ely holds it. He
had nothing except commendation, and Ramsey Abbey had the soke.

2699   ii, 276a (66-55) Annexations (*invasiones*) in Norfolk; Lynn (King's, North,
South or West): TRE a freeman held thirteen acres of land in Lynn. Now the
Abbot of Ely holds it. He held it TRE, and it was in Stigand's soke.

2700   ii, 276a (66-56) Annexations (*invasiones*) in Norfolk; Islington: TRW
William d'Ecouis held two freemen with six acres of land in Islington.

2701   ii, 276b (66-57) Annexations (*invasiones*) in Norfolk; Kilverstone: TRE a
freeman, who was commended only, held eleven acres of land in Kilverstone.
Walter de Caen now holds this man from Robert Malet.

2702   ii, 276b (66-58) Annexations (*invasiones*) in Norfolk; Leziate: TRW Robert
Malet held two freemen with sixty acres of land in Leziate. Roger Bigot's
antecessor had the commendation only.

2703   ii, 276b (66-59) Annexations (*invasiones*) in Norfolk; Gissing: TRW Drogo, a
man of Robert Malet, annexed (*invasit*) ten acres of land in Gissing from
Bury St. Edmund's demesne land.

2704   ii, 276b (66-60) Annexations (*invasiones*) in Norfolk; Fritton: TRE a freeman
of King Edward held fifteen acres of land in Fritton, which William Malet
then held. Robert Malet has been holding him. Because he has now finally
acknowledged that this man was not in the fee of his father, he has handed
him over into the King's hand (*cognouit eum non esse de feudo patris sui, dimisit
eum in manu regis*).

2705   ii, 276b (66-61) Annexations (*invasiones*) in Norfolk; Fersfield: TRE a
freeman commended to Alsige held four acres of land in Fersfield. Later
William fitz Gross held it from Robert Malet. William Malet held it on the
day on which he lived and died. Walter now holds this from Robert Malet,
but Robert contradicts (*contradicit*) him, that he did not know (*se nescisse*) this
until the day in which it was returned (*fuit inbreviatus*).

2706   ii, 276b (66-62) Annexations (*invasiones*) in Norfolk; Diss [Suffolk]: TRE a
freeman held five acres of land in the demesne of the manor of Diss. William

Malet held this, but it did not belong to his fee. In the same way, Robert Malet now offers that he did not know (*offert se nescisse*) this.

2707 ii, 276b (66-63) <u>Annexations (*invasiones*) in Norfolk; Swaffham</u>: TRW Germund, a man of Walter Giffard, annexed (*invasit*) four acres of land in Swaffham from Count Alan's manor.

2708 ii, 276b (66-64) <u>Annexations (*invasiones*) in Norfolk; Bradenham (East or West)</u>: TRW William de Warenne holds half a carucate of land in Bradenham, which Godric held. The value was 10s. Now it is the same, but William's men say that he has had nothing from it. William held this land before Ralph forfeited (*forisfacet*), but, so the hundred testifies, Ralph held it when he forfeited (*forisfecit*). Afterwards Robert Blunt held it at farm from the King, and Godric [answered for it] in the King's treasury in his returns (*in thesauro regis in brevi suo*) for 20s. Later, this land was in the King's hand. The men of the hundred saw neither a writ nor a legate which delivered (*brevem vel legatum qui liberasset*) it to William.

2709 ii, 276b (66-65) <u>Annexations (*invasiones*) in Norfolk; Cockley Cley</u>: TRE two freemen held fourteen acres of land in Cockley Cley. Now William de Warenne holds it.

2710 ii, 276b–277a (66-66) <u>Annexations (*invasiones*) in Norfolk; Wilton</u>: TRE a freeman held forty acres of land in Wilton. Now William de Warenne holds it. His antecessor had nothing except commendation.

2711 ii, 277a (66-67) <u>Annexations (*invasiones*) in Norfolk; Shipdham</u>: TRE Brothir and Alwine held forty-four acres of land in Shipdham from King Edward. Now William de Warenne's men hold it. This was always from the King's manor of Saham Toney, and William's men do not have livery (*non habuerunt liberatorem*), so the hundred testifies.

2712 ii, 277a (66-68) <u>Annexations (*invasiones*) in Norfolk; East Tuddenham</u>: TRE four freemen held half a carucate of land in East Tuddenham from Frederick's fee. They were commended to his antecessor. Now Winemar holds from William de Warenne.

2713 ii, 277a (66-69, 70) <u>Annexations (*invasiones*) in Norfolk; Little Cressingham, Holme Hale</u>: King William has two freemen in demesne in Little Cressingham with a carucate of land. One of them has three villeins, a bordar, and four acres of meadow. He pays 12d., which Ralph de Tosny used to have. TRE another freeman held half a carucate of land in Holme Hale. Its value is 5s. Ralph de Tosny similarly used to have this.

2714 ii, 277a (66-71) <u>Annexations (*invasiones*) in Norfolk; Flitcham</u>: TRW Roger Bigot holds ten freemen in Flitcham with eighty acres of land, and Ranulf fitz Walter holds from him. Roger's antecessor had the commendation only over this, and Stigand had the soke and commendation of one of these men, and the soke of the others.

2715 ii, 277a (66-72) <u>Annexations (*invasiones*) in Norfolk; Griston</u>: TRW four freemen held twenty-six acres of land in Griston. Now Ranulf holds from

Roger Bigot. Roger's antecessor had nothing but commendation, and the King and the earl had the soke.

2716 ii, 277a–b (66-73) <u>Annexations (*invasiones*) in Norfolk; Thompson</u>: TRE a freeman held fifteen acres of land in Thompson. Now Ranulf holds it from Roger Bigot. The King and the earl had the soke.

2717 ii, 277b (66-74) <u>Annexations (*invasiones*) in Norfolk; Hockham</u>: TRE a freeman commended only held eight acres of land in Hockham. Now Roger Bigot holds it. It is in the soke of Buckenham (near Attleborough).

2718 ii, 277b (66-75) <u>Annexations (*invasiones*) in Norfolk; Snetterton</u>: TRE a freeman held five acres and three virgates of land in Snetterton. Now Ralph fitz Herluin holds it from Roger Bigot. His antecessor had commendation only.

2719 ii, 277b (66-76) <u>Annexations (*invasiones*) in Norfolk; Great Snarehill</u>: TRE a freeman held fifteen acres of land in Great Snarehill from the fee of Thurstan of Thetford. Thurstan's antecessor had the commendation only. The soke was in the King's manor of Kenninghall.

2720 ii, 277b (66-77) <u>Annexations (*invasiones*) in Norfolk; Great Snarehill</u>: TRE three freemen who were commended and in fold-soke, held twenty acres of land in Great Snarehill. All other soke was in the King's manor of Kenninghall. Now Thurstan of Thetford holds.

2721 ii, 277b (66-78) <u>Annexations (*invasiones*) in Norfolk; Thurne</u>: TRE a freeman, who was commended only to St. Benet of Holme, held forty-three acres of land in Thurne. He was an outlaw (*fuit ex lex*). Because Æthelwig made him an outlaw (*fecit illegem*), he has half this land in Roger Bigot's fee.

2722 ii, 277b (66-79) <u>Annexations (*invasiones*) in Norfolk; Somerton (East or West)</u>: TRE a freeman of Harold held thirty acres of land in Somerton. Now Roger Bigot's reeve holds this and pays 2 *orae* each year to the King's reeve under Roger Bigot. But this land did not belong to Roger, and Roger did not know (*nesciuit*) this.

2723 ii, 277b (66-80) <u>Annexations (*invasiones*) in Norfolk; Bramerton</u>: TRE a free woman commended to Eadric held sixteen acres of land in Bramerton. Earl Ralph held it when he forfeited (*forisfecit*), by testimony (*teste*) of the hundred. Afterwards Robert Blunt held it in the King's hand, and now Aitard, a man commended to Roger Bigot, has held it from Roger, since Ralph forfeited (*forisfecit*). Thus the hundred testifies, and the woman offers the ordeal that what the hundred testifies is the truth (*offert iudicium quod verum est teste*). Aitard, however, contradicts (*contradicit*) this.

2724 ii, 277b–278a (66-81) <u>Annexations (*invasiones*) in Norfolk; Bixley</u>: TRE one and a half freemen, one of whom was commended to Aslac, held seventeen acres of land in Bixley. Roger Bigot, so he says, had custody (*servavit*) of this in the King's hand, and he pays rent (*censum*) in the hundred. But the hundred testifies that Godric Dapifer held it under the King from the fee of Earl Ralph a year before he could forfeit (*forisfaceret*), and for two years after, by gift of the King (*ex dono regis*). Against (*contra*) this, a man of Roger Bigot contradicts (*contradicit*) this [by offering] ordeal or battle (*iudicio vel bello*). Godric claims (*reclamat*) this with half the land which is in Roger Bigot's return (*que est in breve*). Godric Dapifer took (*recepit*) this land for half a carucate.

2725 ii, 278a (66-82) Annexations (*invasiones*) in Norfolk; Poringland: TRE a freeman commended to Edwin held fifteen acres of land in Poringland. Afterwards Godric held it, and later still, because of a forfeiture (*forisfacturam*), Alvred held it. Alvred had made himself quit of this forfeiture (*de illa forisfactura quietum se fecerat*), by testimony (*teste*) of the hundred. But through the order (*per praeceptum*) of the Bishop of Bayeux, Roger Bigot had custody (*servavit*) in the hand of the King, and he has custody still.

2726 ii, 278a (66-83) Annexations (*invasiones*) in Norfolk; Osmondiston: TRW Hugh de Corbon, under Roger Bigot, annexed (*invasit*) half a freeman with ten acres of land in Osmondiston. Earl Ralph held this land when he forfeited (*forisfecit*). Afterwards, when it was in the King's hand, Hugh de Corbon, who now holds it, annexed (*invasit*) it. Ralph de Fougères holds the manor, but he does not have this part.

2727 ii, 278a (66-84) Annexations (*invasiones*) in Norfolk; Filby: TRE a freeman held fifty-one acres of land in Filby. Afterwards, Æthelwig of Thetford had the commendation only of this man's wife, and the wife had nothing from the land. Earl Ralph was seised (*saisitus erat*) of it when he forfeited (*forifecit*), and then Robert Blunt held it at rent (*ad censum*) in the hand of the King. After this the same Æthelwig, Roger Bigot's antecessor, annexed (*invasit*) it under Godric, and Stanheard his son held it. Concerning this, Roger Bigot has given a pledge (*dedit vadem*), and he does not vouch (*revocat*) this land to his fee. Now Godric has custody (*servat*) of it in the King's hand.

2728 ii, 278a (66-85) Annexations (*invasiones*) in Norfolk; Swardeston: TRE a half freeman, commended only to Godric's antecessor, held fifteen acres of land in Swardeston. This same Godric was seised of this (*erat inde saisitus*) when Earl Ralph forfeited (*forisfecit*). Now Ralph de Noron holds him. This freeman used to pay Godric 10s., and now he has paid Ralph de Noron 12s. Ralph has kept back (*detinuit*) this man and another half man similarly from Godric.

2729 ii, 278a–b (66-86) Annexations (*invasiones*) in Norfolk; Hapton: TRE a freeman held fifteen acres of land in Hapton. Herbert, Roger Bigot's chamberlain, held this man. The men of Count Eustace, however, claim (*calumpniantur*) him from Eustace's fee. Now he is in the King's hand. Concerning this, Herbert has given a pledge (*dedit . . . vadem*) of 16d., which he had.

2730 ii, 278b (66-87) Annexations (*invasiones*) in Norfolk; Dersingham: TRE a freeman held twelve acres of land in Dersingham. Peter de Valognes holds this man. His antecessor had his commendation only, and Stigand had the soke. In the same place there were twenty-one freemen with two carucates and thirty-five acres of land. Peter's antecessor had the commendation only of all of these men. Eighteen of them were to give (*darent*) 2s. apiece if they wished to withdraw. Stigand had the soke of all of them. Also in the same place there were two freemen with two carucates of land.

2731 ii, 278b (66-88) <u>Annexations (*invasiones*) in Norfolk; Shernborne</u>: TRE a sokeman of Harold held sixty acres of land in Shernborne, which lay in Sedgeford. Now William de Parthenay holds from Peter de Valognes and claims him for livery (*reclamat liberatorem*).

2732 ii, 278b (66-89) <u>Annexations (*invasiones*) in Norfolk; Binham</u>: TRW Peter de Valognes holds nine freemen with five carucates of land in Binham, who were the King's and Gyrth's men TRE.

2733 ii, 278b (66-90) <u>Annexations (*invasiones*) in Norfolk; Hargham</u>: TRW Ralph de Beaufour holds two freemen with twenty acres of land in Hargham, and Warin holds from him. Ralph's antecessor had the commendation only of these men TRE, and Eudo fitz Clamahoc held them. The soke is in Buckenham (near Attleborough),

2734 ii, 278b–279a (66-91) <u>Annexations (*invasiones*) in Norfolk; Woodbastwick</u>: TRE Godric, a commended freeman, held thirty acres of land in Woodbastwick. He was Godric of Rossa's man. Now Ralph de Beaufour holds.

2735 ii, 279a (66-92) <u>Annexations (*invasiones*) in Norfolk; Upton</u>: TRE four freemen, who were commended only to Godric, held twenty-six acres of land in Upton. Now Ralph de Beaufour holds.

2736 ii, 279a (66-93) <u>Annexations (*invasiones*) in Norfolk; Woodbastwick</u>: TRW Ulfkil holds four freemen with thirty acres of land in Woodbastwick. They were commended to Harold TRE. The same Ulfkil also holds four freemen there with four acres of land.

2737 ii, 279a (66-94) <u>Annexations (*invasiones*) in Norfolk; Thorpe St. Andrew</u>: TRW there is a sokeman in Thorpe St. Andrew with eight acres of land. Ralph de Beaufour has all the customs of his antecessor Eudo fitz Clamahoc.

2738 ii, 279a (66-95) <u>Annexations (*invasiones*) in Norfolk; Wick</u>: TRW Hugh de Montfort holds a freeman in commendation only with thirty acres of land in Wick. The soke is in Kenninghall.

2739 ii, 279a (66-96) <u>Annexations (*invasiones*) in Norfolk; West Bilney</u>: TRW Hugh de Montfort holds eight freemen in commendation only, with a carucate of land in West Bilney.

2740 ii, 279a (66-97) <u>Annexations (*invasiones*) in Norfolk; Weybourne</u>: TRW Ranulf holds twelve and a half freemen in Weybourne with three carucates and fifteen acres of land. He holds them from Earl Hugh. TRE they were commended to Harold. These men live in Weybourne, Salthouse, Kelling, and Bodham.

2741 ii, 279a (66-98) <u>Annexations (*invasiones*) in Norfolk; Raveningham</u>: TRE a freeman held three acres of land in Raveningham. It was in the rent (*in censu*) of Raveningham when Earl Ralph forfeited (*forisfecit*). This has been kept back (*detinuit*) by Nicholas, Earl Hugh's goldsmith. Now it is in the King's hand.

2742 ii, 279a–b (66-99) <u>Annexations (*invasiones*) in Norfolk; North Barningham</u>: TRE seven freemen of Wulfric held forty acres of land in North Barningham. Now Robert Gernon holds it. In the same vill there were two commended freemen TRE with twenty-eight acres of land. Now Eskil son of Ospak holds this. This is in the King's hand because there was no one who could render account (*nemo fuit qui reddet compotum*) for it.

2743 ii, 279b (66-100) <u>Annexations (*invasiones*) in Norfolk; Postwick</u>: TRE two freemen commended to Skuli held sixty acres of land in Postwick. Now Eudo Dapifer holds it by (*ab*) his antecessor Lisois.

2744 ii, 279b (66-101) <u>Annexations (*invasiones*) in Norfolk; Freethorpe, Limpenhoe</u>: TRE twenty freemen commended to Fincus held a carucate and twenty acres of land in Freethorpe and Limpenhoe. Now Rabel the Artificer holds.

2745 ii, 279b (66-102) <u>Annexations (*invasiones*) in Norfolk; Southwood</u>: TRE a freeman commended to Alsige held four acres of land in Southwood. When Ralph forfeited (*forisfecit*) it was in the rent (*fuit in censu*) of the King's manor. Now Rabel the Artificer holds it.

2746 ii, 279b (66-103) <u>Annexations (*invasiones*) in Norfolk; Erpingham</u>: TRE a freeman held four acres of land in Erpingham. Now Humphrey holds it under Ranulf brother of Ilger.

2747 ii, 279b (66-104) <u>Annexations (*invasiones*) in Norfolk; Walcott</u>: TRE three freemen held ninety acres of land in Walcott.

2748 ii, 279b (66-105) <u>Annexations (*invasiones*) in Norfolk; Great Melton</u>: TRW a freeman, whom Ranulf Peverel annexed (*invasit*), has six acres of land in Great Melton.

2749 ii, 280a (66-106) <u>Annexations (*invasiones*) in Norfolk; Forncett (St. Mary or St. Peter)</u>: TRE Skuli, a freeman, of whom Hermer's antecessor had the commendation, held thirteen acres of land in Forncett. Now it is in the King's hand. There was a house in this land in the time of King Edward, which Ulfkil the Reeve transferred (*transtulit*). He has given a pledge (*dedit vadem*) for this.

2750 ii, 280a (66-107) <u>Annexations (*invasiones*) in Norfolk; Tibenham</u>: TRE a freeman commended to the antecessor of Robert Malet held fifteen acres of land in Tibenham. Walter Cnut held this land because his antecessor had had it in mortgage (*habuit in vadimonio*) for 16s. in the time of King Edward.

2751 ii, 280a (66-108) <u>Annexations (*invasiones*) in Norfolk; East Winch</u>: TRE Rainer held a freeman with an acre of land in East Winch.

Suffolk

2752 ii, 281b (1-1) <u>Terra Regis (which Roger Bigot keeps) Thorney</u>: King Edward held five carucates of land in Thorney. Now King William holds it, and Roger Bigot keeps it. There were forty sokemen in this manor TRE with all customs. After Roger Bigot took (*recepit*) it, however, all but seven were taken away (*fuerunt . . . ablati*). There was a church there TRE with a carucate of free land; but Hugh de Montfort has twenty-three acres of this carucate and vouches (*revocat*) it as a chapel which four brothers, Hugh's freemen, built on their own land, next to the cemetery of the mother church (*matris ecclesiae*). These brothers were inhabitants of the parish of the mother church (*manentes de parrochia matris ecclesiae*), and built the chapel because the church could not hold the whole parish. This mother church had, through purchase (*per emptionem*) half of the burial fees (*sepulture*) for all time and a fourth of the other alms that might be made there. The hundred does not know (*nescit*) if the chapel was dedicated (*fuit dedicata*).

2753 ii, 281b–282a (1-2, 6, 7) <u>Terra Regis (which Roger Bigot keeps); Bramford, Stonham (Earl or Little), Hemingstone</u>: King Edward held twelve carucates of land in Bramford. Now King William holds it, and Roger Bigot keeps it. TRE Alwine, a freeman commended to Gyrth, held thirty acres of land in Hemingstone. Wulfmær the Reeve added this freeman to the King's farm in Bramford, and Roger the Sheriff is his warrantor (*est ei warant*). He pays 5s. each year. TRE another sokeman held twelve acres in Stonham, and he could not withdraw. Now the Bishop of Bayeux holds him, and Roger Bigot holds from him.

2754 ii, 282a (1-10, 12) <u>Terra Regis (which Roger Bigot keeps); Blythburgh, Easton Bavants</u>: King Edward held five carucates of land in Blythburgh. Now King William holds it, and Roger Bigot keeps it. The fourth penny of the rent (*de censu*) of the *haie* of "Riseburc" belongs to this manor and [is divided] between the King and the earl. In Easton Bavants there are two villeins with a carucate of land. Earl Ralph held them, and afterward, in the time of Robert Malet, Fulcred added them to the manor of Blythburgh.

2755 ii, 282b (1-14) <u>Terra Regis (which Roger Bigot keeps); Stickingland</u>: TRE Alwine held a carucate and forty acres of land in Stickingland, and Robert Malet's antecessor had the commendation. Now King William holds it, and Roger Bigot keeps it.

2756 ii, 282b (1-16, 17) <u>Terra Regis (which Roger Bigot keeps); Ringsfield</u>: TRE a freeman of King Edward held one and a half carucates of land in Ringsfield. Now King William holds it, and Roger Bigot keeps it. TRE there were eleven freemen there with a carucate of land, who were commended to Wulfsige. TRW eighty-three freemen were added to Hugh de Montfort's manor from the hundred of Wangford (where Ringsfield lies), twelve [*sic*] of whom have been mentioned above, who did not pay any customs to the manor of Ringsfield in the time of King Edward. The freemen now pay £15. Ælfric the Reeve arranged (*constituit*) this custom in the time of Roger Bigot.

2757 ii, 283a (1-23, 24, 25, 26, 27, 28, 29, 30) <u>Terra Regis (which Roger Bigot keeps); Mutford, "Kislea," Rushmere (near Lowestoft), Gisleham, Pakefield, Kirkley, "Bechetuna," Barnby</u>: TRE Earl Gyrth held three and a half carucates of land in Mutford. Now King William holds it, and Roger Bigot keeps it. Twelve freemen commended to Gyrth also held three carucates in Mutford. Four of these men live in Mutford, two in Rushmere, two in Gisleham, three in Pakefield, and two in Kirkley. Another twenty-six men are in Mutford with two carucates of land. There are twenty freemen in "Kislea" with a carucate and ten acres of land. In Rushmere there are four freemen with thirty-three acres. There are six freemen in Pakefield with thirty acres; six in Kirkley with thirty acres; five in "Bechetuna" with a carucate of land; and eight in Barnby with eighty acres. All of these men paid 13s. 6d. TRE. Now they pay £30. Ælfric the Reeve put (*misit*) this custom on them in the time of King William, under Roger Bigot.

2758 ii, 284b (1-55, 56, 57, 58, 59, 60) Terra Regis (which Roger Bigot keeps); Gapton, Akethorpe, Newton (near Lowestoft), Fritton, Belton, Herringfleet: TRE Ulf, a freeman, held sixty acres of land in Gapton; Æthelstan, a freeman, held sixty acres there; Sprotwulf, a freeman, forty acres; and Wulfnoth, a freeman, held another thirty acres there. In Akethorpe Almær the Priest, a freeman, held eighty acres of land. In Newton a freeman had thirty acres of land. In Fritton two freemen held eighty acres; and Leofric, a freeman, held thirty acres. In Belton three freemen held ninety acres of land. In Herringfleet the freeman Wulfsige held a carucate of land. All of these men paid 20s. at farm in the time of King Edward. Afterwards, in the time of Roger Bigot, Ælfric the Reeve increased (*crescebat*) this to 100s. In the time of Hugh d'Houdain, so the men say, it was increased to £50.

2759 ii, 284b (1-62) Terra Regis (which Godric Dapifer keeps in the King's hand); Thurston (near Bury St. Edmund's): King William has fourteen freemen who hold half a carucate of land in Thurston, and Godric Dapifer keeps it in the King's hand. Bury St. Edmund's had the commendation and all customs over four of these freemen and over four half freemen belonging to Norton (near Bury St. Edmund's). But Earl Ralph held them when he forfeited (*se forefecit*).

2760 ii, 285a (1-66) Terra Regis (which Godric Dapifer keeps in the King's hand); Stonham (Earl or Little): TRW there are five sokemen with eighteen acres of land in Stonham. They belong in Mendlesham. Three freemen in Stonham with twelve acres have been added. They now belong in Mendlesham.

2761 ii, 285a (1-67, 68, 69, 70, 71, 72, 73) Terra Regis (which Godric Dapifer keeps in the King's hand); Blakenham (Great or Little), "Langhedena," Offton, Badley, Darmsden, Sharpstone, Ashbocking: TRE there were five freemen in Blakenham with sixty acres of land. They were in the soke and commendation of Eadgifu the Fair. They have been added to Norton. In "Langhedena" there were three freemen with seventy-two acres of land; in Offton two freemen with fifty acres; in Badley one freeman with thirty acres; in Darmsden one freemen with sixty acres; in Sharpstone one freeman with two acres; and in Ashbocking a freeman, Almær, with ninety-three acres. Eadgifu the Fair had the soke and commendation of all of these men TRE. They pay £4 at farm to Norton (near Bury St. Edmund's), and were added there in the time of Earl Ralph. Now the King holds this, and Godric keeps it in the King's hand.

2762 ii, 285b (1-76, 77) <u>Terra Regis (which Godric Dapifer keeps in the King's hand); Mendlesham, Cotton</u>: TRE Burgheard held seven carucates and forty-two acres of land in Mendlesham. Now the King holds it, and Godric keeps it in the King's hand. TRE there were eighteen freemen in Cotton with a carucate and fifteen acres of land. The Abbot had half the commendation of one of these men – Alwine – with ten acres of land. These men have been added to Mendlesham. The hundred testifies that truly (*vere*) the King and the earl had soke and sake TRE, but the men of the vill testify that Burgheard had the soke of both the freemen and his own villeins. They do not have any other testimony except themselves, but they are willing to prove this by all means (*non habent aliquid testimonium praeter se, et tamen volunt probare omni modo*).

2763 ii, 286a (1-88) <u>Terra Regis (which Godric Dapifer keeps in the King's hand); Norton (near Bury St. Edmund's)</u>: TRE Edith, a free woman, held four carucates of land in Norton. Now King William holds it, and Godric keeps it in the King's hand. This manor was in the demesne of the Abbot of Bury St. Edmund's. Edith held it through a loan (*per accomodationem*) from the Abbot, with a pact that after her death the Abbot should have it back (*tali pacto quod post suum obitum rehaberet abbas*). She held it in this way (*ita*) on the day King Edward died.

2764 ii, 286b (1-97) <u>Terra Regis (which William the Chamberlain and Otto the Goldsmith keep in the King's hand); Sudbury</u>: TRE Earl Morcar's mother held three carucates of land in Sudbury. Now King William holds it, and William the Chamberlain and Otto the Goldsmith keep it in the King's hand. The Church of St. Gregory is there with fifty acres of free land, so the hundred testifies.

2765 ii, 287a (1-100, 101) <u>Terra Regis (which Ælfric Wanz has custody); East Bergholt, Bentley</u>: TRE Earl Harold held thirteen carucates of land in East Bergholt. Now King William holds it, and Ælfric Wanz has custody. TRE Earl Gyrth held two carucates of land in Bentley. Afterwards, in the time of King William, Earl Ralph the Staller added it to the manor of East Bergholt as a berewick.

2766 ii, 287a–b (1-102) <u>Terra Regis (which Ælfric Wanz has custody); Shotley</u>: TRE Earl Gyrth held two and a half carucates and an acre of land in Shotley. Now King William holds it, and Ælfric Wanz has custody. In the time of King Edward 210 sokemen belonged to this manor. Now there are only 119, and they have twenty-two and a half carucates less thirty acres of land. Of these, Earl Harold had the commendation only of four, namely Wulfnoth, Eastmund, Ælfric, and Wihtric. Earl Gyrth, Harold's brother, had the commendation of two, namely Manni and Ælfgeat. All the other sokemen were commended to other barons (*baronibus*) TRE. Robert Malet's antecessor had the commendation of one, and Robert fitz Wimarc had the commendation of four. Harold, however, always had the soke.

2767 ii, 287b (1-103) Terra Regis (which Ælfric Wanz has custody); East Bergholt:
East Bergholt, with all that belonged to it, and with the soke of the hundred
and the half-hundred, paid £24 in the time of King Edward. Bentley and
Shotley, the manors of Earl Gyrth that have been added to this farm, paid £9
TRE. When Robert Malet held all of this, it paid in total £60 by weight and
£8 *ad numerum* as a gift (*gersuma*). The manor also paid this much to Roger
Bigot, so the reeve says. Roger, however, says that it paid 40s. more *ad
numerum* along with a mark of gold, but Ælfric the Reeve contradicts
(*contradicit*) this. Roger wishes to prove this through those men who were at
his agreement (*vult probare per illos homines qui ad suas conventiones fuerunt*).
Now Ælfric the Reeve pays £60 by weight, and holds it from the King with
the agreement (*tali conventione*) that he ought to make the King £60 profit (*de
proficuo*). He vouches the King to warranty for this (*ex hoc revocat regem ad
warant*), so he himself says. He also says that not enough remains in this
manor to make this profit.

2768 ii, 287b (1-105) Terra Regis (which Ælfric Wanz has custody); East Bergholt:
TRE the freemen who belonged to the soke of East Bergholt gave (*dabat*) 4d.
a year freely to the reeve and were rendering soke, just as the law allowed
(*reddebat socam, sicut lex ferebat*). Later, when Roger Bigot had the shrievalty,
his *ministri* decided (*statuerunt*) that these men should pay £15 a year, which
they did not do in the time of King Edward. When Robert Malet had the
shrievalty, his *ministri* increased the payment to £20. When Roger Bigot got
them back (*rehabuit*), they gave (*dederunt*) this £20. Now Ælfric Wanz holds
them with the custom (*tali consuetudine*) as it was in King Edward's time.

2769 ii, 288a (1-110) Terra Regis (which William de Noyers keeps in the King's
hand); Bungay: TRE Stigand held nine carucates of land in Bungay. In the
same place Alwine, a freeman commended to Stigand, held a carucate of
land. Since King William came into this country, two brothers have
partitioned (*habent partiti*) it. One of them, Wulfsige, is in the King's hand
and has sixty acres of land. The other brother, Wulfric, is in Earl Hugh's
hand.

2770 ii, 288b–289a (1-115) Terra Regis (which William de Noyers keeps in the
King's hand); Mildenhall: King Edward gave (*dedit*) twelve carucates of land
in Mildenhall to Bury St. Edmund's. Afterwards, during King Edward's
lifetime, Stigand held it under Bury, as a manor. Now King William holds it,
and William de Noyers keeps it in the King's hand.

2771 ii, 289a (1-116) Terra Regis (which William de Noyers keeps in the King's
hand); Ipswich: TRE Stigand had two burgesses in Ipswich with soke and
sake, and King Edward had their customs. Now they are dead, and King
William has customs, soke, and sake.

2772 ii, 289a–b (1-119) Terra Regis (which William de Noyers keeps in the King's
hand); Bramford: TRE Stigand held ten carucates of land in Bramford. Now
King William holds it, and William de Noyers keeps it in the King's hand. In
the same place Brun, a commended freeman, held thirty acres of land. Earl

Harold had the soke in East Bergholt. This was added to Bramford in the time of Bishop Herfast.

2773   ii, 290a (1-122a) <u>Terra Regis (which Roger Bigot keeps in the King's hand);</u> <u>Ipswich</u>: TRE Queen Edith had two-thirds of the half hundred of Ipswich, and Earl Gyrth had the other third.

2774   ii, 290a (1-122c) <u>Terra Regis (which Roger Bigot keeps in the King's hand);</u> <u>Ipswich</u>: In the time of King Edward there were 538 burgesses in Ipswich, who had forty acres of land and paid their customs to the King. Now, however, there are 110 burgesses who pay customs as well as 100 impoverished burgesses (*pauperes burgenses*), with forty acres of land, who cannot pay anything to the King's geld except a penny a head (*nisi unum denarium de suis capitibus*).

2775   ii, 290b (1-122f) <u>Terra Regis (which Roger Bigot keeps in the King's hand);</u> <u>Ipswich</u>: Thorkil and Eadric have held the Church of St. Lawrence, Ipswich with twelve acres of land for half a year at the feast of St. John. TRE Leofflæd, a free woman, held it. Count Alan claims (*reclamat*) it from Earl Ralph's fee, and he vouches (*revocat*) Ivo Taillebois to warranty (*ad liberatorem*). Thorkil and Eadric, on the other hand, vouch (*revocant*) Roger the Sheriff to warranty (*ad garant*), saying that they had the church through (*per*) him, and that Roger, in justice (*iuste*), was as much a warrantor (*tali gaurant*) as any sheriff could be in the time of King Edward.

2776   ii, 290b (1-122g) <u>Terra Regis (which Roger Bigot keeps in the King's hand);</u> <u>Ipswich</u>: Everything in Ipswich paid £15 and six sesters of honey TRE, 4s. for the honey-customs, and 8s. to the prebendaries. Roger the Sheriff gave (*dedit*) all of this at farm for £40 at the feast of St. Michael. Afterwards, he could not have the rent (*censum*), so he has pardoned (*condonavit*) 60s. Thus, it now pays £37. The moneyers paid £4 for the mint TRE. Now they ought to pay £20, but over the last four years they have only paid a total of £27. The earl has always had a third of this.

2777   ii, 291a (2-1, 2, 3, 4, 5) <u>Count of Mortain; Drinkstone, Rattlesden, Bradfield</u> <u>(Combust, St. Clare, or St. George), Welnetham, Stanningfield</u>: TRE a freeman, commended to Ely Abbey and in the soke of Bury St. Edmund's, held a carucate of land in Drinkstone. In Rattlesden a freeman, commended to Ely and in its soke, held a carucate. In Bradfield a freeman of Bishop Æthelmær, commended and in the soke of Bury St. Edmund's, held twenty acres. In Welnetham a freeman of Bishop Æthelmær, commended and in the soke of Bury St. Edmund's, held forty acres. And in Stanningfield, a freeman commended to Bishop Æthelmær and in Bury St. Edmund's soke, held sixty acres. It was valued at 10s., now at 30s., but it pays this with difficulty (*vix*). All of this land was delivered (*fuit liberatum*) to Count Brian, Robert count of Mortain's antecessor, for two carucates and forty acres of land. Now the Count of Mortain holds it.

2778   ii, 291a–b (2-6, 8) <u>Count of Mortain; Combs, Stowmarket</u>: TRE Wulfnoth, a freeman, held two carucates of land in Combs under King Edward. Now

Robert count of Mortain holds it. Wulfnoth had fifty freemen with eight carucates of land there. Afterwards they belonged, in commendation only, to Count Brian, the Count of Mortain's antecessor. The value of the manor of Combs then and later was £10; now £16, but it pays with difficulty (*vix*). The value of the fifty freemen then and later was £16. Now their value is £31, but they cannot endure this without ruin (*non possunt sufferre sine confusione*). After Count Brian, Robert's antecessor, had this manor, it paid no customs in the hundred. Hugh de Montfort holds half a mill in Combs. It belonged to one of the freemen of the manor in Count Brian's time. Hugh claims livery (*reclamat liberatorem*) from the fee of his antecessor, but the hundred testifies that it never belonged to his antecessor. TRW Nigel, a servant of the Count of Mortain, annexed (*invasit*) eleven acres of land from the church of Stowmarket and added it to the manor of Combs. But Nigel died, and there is now no one to answer for it (*non est qui inde respondeat*). The hundred testifies that this land was in the alms of the church of Stowmarket. Twelve sokemen used to be in the parish of this church, but they are now in the church of Combs. Nigel also took them away (*abstulit*).

2779   ii, 291a (2-7) <u>Count of Mortain; Onehouse</u>: TRE Wihtmær held a carucate of land in Onehouse under King Edward. Now Robert count of Mortain holds it. TRE there was also a freeman there with nine acres of land. Nigel held this under Count Robert, but Frodo was formerly seised (*fuit priorus sesitus*) of it, and he claims livery (*reclamat liberatorem*). But the hundred does not know about this. After Count Brian had Onehouse, it paid no customs in the hundred.

2780   ii, 291b (2-9) <u>Count of Mortain; Creeting St. Peter</u>: TRE Wulfnoth, a freeman of King Edward, held a carucate of land in Creeting St. Peter. He was the antecessor of Count Brian. Now the Abbey of St. Mary, Grestain holds it from the Count of Mortain with soke and sake.

2781   ii, 291b (2-10) <u>Count of Mortain; Creeting St. Olave</u>: TRE Wulfnoth, a freeman, held two carucates of land in Creeting St. Olave. Robert count of Mortain gave (*dedit*) it to the Abbey of St. Mary, Grestain. Twelve and a half sokemen with fifty-eight acres of land were added to this manor TRW. Half a mill belongs to this manor as well, which Hardwin, Earl Ralph's brother, took away (*abstulit*) in the time of King William.

2782   ii, 291b (2-13) <u>Count of Mortain; Brettenham</u>: TRE Wulfnoth held four carucates of land in Brettenham. There are five freemen there with thirty-two acres of land. Count Brian added them. Now Robert count of Mortain holds this.

2783   ii, 292a (2-17) <u>Count of Mortain; Morston</u>: TRW Robert count of Mortain holds fifty acres of land in Morston. TRE five freemen held this land – Godwine, Ælfric the Priest's man; Wulfhere and Beorhtric, men of Roger Bigot's antecessor; Wulfwine, a man of Robert Malet's antecessor; and Godric, a man of Godmann antecessor of Roger Bigot.

2784   ii, 292a (2-18) <u>Count of Mortain; Thorpe (in Trimley)</u>: TRE Brunmær, a freeman, held ten acres of land in Thorpe. Robert Malet's antecessor had his commendation. Now Robert count of Mortain holds this land.

2785 ii, 292a (2-20) <u>Count of Mortain; Grimston</u>: TRE two freemen – Ælfric, a man commended to Harold, and Beorhtnoth, a man commended to Robert Malet's antecessor – held fourteen acres of land in Grimston. Now Eudo fitz Nigel holds this from Robert count of Mortain.

2786 ii, 292b (3-8) <u>Count Alan; Thorpe (in Ashfield)</u>: In the time of King William a freeman with sixty-nine acres of land in Thorpe was delivered (*fuit liberatus*) to Count Alan.

2787 ii, 293b (3-28) <u>Count Alan; Little Charsfield</u>: TRE eight freemen commended to Eadric Grim and one commended to Robert Malet's antecessor held sixteen acres of land in Little Charsfield. Now Count Alan holds it.

2788 ii, 293b–294a (3-39) <u>Count Alan; Rendlesham</u>: TRE five freemen and seven half freemen commended to Eadric Grim held fifty acres of land in Rendlesham. In the same place there was a freeman half commended to Eadric of Laxfield, of whom William Malet was seised (*fuit . . . sesitus*) on the day he died. This freeman was also half commended to Eadric Grim. He held thirty-four acres of land. Now Count Alan holds this.

2789 ii, 294a (3-40) <u>Count Alan; Butley</u>: TRE seven and a half freemen commended to Eadric Grim held thirty-four acres of land in Butley. William Malet was seised (*erat . . . sesitus*) of this when he died, and then Earl Ralph [was seised] when he forfeited (*se forisfecit*). Now Count Alan holds it.

2790 ii, 294a (3-41) <u>Count Alan; "Brodertuna"</u>: TRE seven freemen, half commended to Eadric Grim and half commended to Eadric of Laxfield, held fifty-six acres of land in "Brodertuna." Now Count Alan holds it. Robert Malet was seised (*fuit . . . sesitus*) of half this land on the day Earl Ralph forfeited (*forisfecit*), but Count Alan has it through livery (*habet per liberationem*).

2791 ii, 294a–b (3-55) <u>Count Alan; Ipswich</u>: TRE Earl Gyrth held a grange in Ipswich, to which belonged two carucates of land. Now Count Alan holds it. It was valued at 100s. with the third penny of the borough. It was delivered (*fuit liberatum*) for £20 with the third penny of the borough and the third penny of two hundreds. Now, however, it pays only £15.

2792 ii, 294b (3-56) <u>Count Alan; Nettlestead</u>: TRE Gauti, a freeman, held five carucates of land in Nettlestead. Earl Ralph added thirty-four freemen with two and a half carucates of land. TRE his antecessor had the commendation only of twenty-six of these men. Now Erland holds it from Count Alan.

2793 ii, 294b (3-57) <u>Count Alan; Darmsden</u>: TRE Cyneric, a freeman, held thirty acres of land in Darmsden. Now Nardred holds it from Count Alan. Roger Bigot took away (*tulit*) five acres of the demesne, which William holds from him. He was seised of it (*erat inde saisitus*), however, when Earl Ralph forfeited (*forisfecit*).

2794 ii, 294b (3-59) <u>Count Alan; Earl Stonham</u>: TRW Wulfmær holds five freemen with forty-eight acres of land in Earl Stonham from Count Alan.

These men also hold twelve acres of the Count's demesne. TRE twenty-eight acres of woodland and fields belonged in demesne, and Godmær held them. Now Roger Bigot holds this, and Werengar holds from him. Werengar also held this when Earl Ralph forfeited (*forisfecit*).

2795 ii, 296a (3-86) Count Alan; Wantisden: TRE sixteen freemen, half under the commendation of Robert Malet's antecessor and half commended to the Abbot of Ely and in his soke, held sixty acres of land in Wantisden. Now Count Alan holds this in demesne.

2796 ii, 296b (3-89) Count Alan; Blaxhall: TRE Brothir, a freeman, held twelve acres of land in Blaxhall. Now Count Alan holds it in demesne. In the same place Eadric Grim, a freeman half commended to Robert Malet's antecessor and half to the Abbot of Ely, had twenty acres of land. Now Haimo holds it from Count Alan.

2797 ii, 296b–297a (3-94) Count Alan; Carlton (in Kelsale): TRE Eadric Grim, half commended to the Abbot of Ely and half to Robert Malet's antecessor, held a carucate of land in Carlton. William Malet was seised (*saisitus fuit*) of this. There were also eight freemen there in demesne with sixty acres of land. Two of these men – Sten and Ælfric – were under the commendation of Robert Malet's antecessor; and William Malet was seised (*sesitus fuit*) of them. The other men were commended to the Abbot of Ely. Now Haimo holds all of this from Count Alan.

2798 ii, 297a (3-95) Count Alan; Great Glemham: TRE Eadric Grim held twenty acres of land in Great Glemham, which belongs in Kettleburgh. Its soke is the Abbot of Ely's. In the same place Spearhavoc, a freeman commended to Eadric antecessor of Robert Malet, held sixty acres of land; and William Malet was seised (*saisitus fuit*) of it. Also in Great Glemham, there were eight freemen with sixty acres of land – Leofric, Eadric, Wulfmær, half of Hunepot, Godric, Almær, Leofric, and Wulfmær. All of these men were under the commendation of Robert Malet's antecessor. Now Count Alan holds all of this.

2799 ii, 297a (3-97) Count Alan; Sternfield: TRE Osbern, a freeman, held twenty-four acres of land in Sternfield. Now Count Alan holds it in demesne. Two freemen with eight and a half acres of land in the same place have been added.

2800 ii, 297a–b (3-98) Count Alan; Bruisyard: TRE Ulf held eighty-five acres of land in Bruisyard. Ralph the Staller had the soke. There was also a freeman in Bruisyard named Starling with sixty acres of land. He was half commended to the Abbot and half to Robert Malet's antecessor. Robert's father was seised (*sesitus*) of him. Now Haimo holds from Count Alan.

2801 ii, 297b (3-99) Count Alan; Rendham: TRE Ostula, a freeman, held forty acres of land in Rendham. He was commended to Robert Malet's antecessor. William, Robert's father, was seised (*sesitus fuit*) of this. In the same place there were nine freemen with ninety-one acres of land. They were commended to Robert Malet's antecessor, and William, Robert's father, was seised (*sasitus fuit*) of them. Now Count Alan holds all of this.

2802 ii, 297b (3-100) <u>Count Alan; Swefling</u>: TRE Osmund, a freeman commended to Robert Malet's antecessor, held thirty acres of land in Swefling: William Malet was seised (*sesitus fuit*) of it. In the same place there were five freemen with fifty-four acres of land. Two of them – Ælfric and Dot – were under the commendation of Robert Malet's antecessor and held ten acres of land. Another freeman, Burgric, was commended to and in the soke of Ralph the Staller. He had twenty-four acres of land. In the same place there were fourteen freemen with ninety-four acres of land. Robert Malet's antecessor had the commendation of three and a half of them, and half was under commendation. William Malet was seised (*seisitus fuit*) of this. Now Count Alan holds all of this.

2803 ii, 297b–298a (3-101) <u>Count Alan; Benhall</u>: TRE seven freemen held forty-four acres of land in Benhall. Four of these men – Eadric, Beorhtmær, Tutflet, and Magni – were commended to Robert Malet's antecessor, and Robert's father was seised (*sesitus fuit*) of them. Now Count Alan holds this.

2804 ii, 298a (3-102) <u>Count Alan; Great Glemham</u>: TRE two freemen, Wacra, under the commendation of Robert Malet's antecessor, and Wulfgifu, commended to Robert Malet's antecessor, held twenty acres of land in Great Glemham. Now Haimo holds all of this from Count Alan.

2805 ii, 298b (4-2) <u>Earl Hugh; "Manuuic"</u>: TRE Godric, a freeman commended to Earl Hugh's antecessor, held forty-two acres of land in "Manuuic." In the same place a freeman, similarly commended, held twenty-seven acres of land. Now Earl Hugh holds all of this.

2806 ii, 298b–299a (4-6) <u>Earl Hugh; Thorpe (in Ashfield), Ashfield</u>: TRE twenty-one freemen commended to Earl Hugh's antecessor held a carucate and fourteen acres of land in Thorpe and Ashfield. Now Hugh fitz Norman holds it from the earl.

2807 ii, 299a (4-9) <u>Earl Hugh; Parham</u>: TRE four freemen commended to Earl Hugh's antecessor held twenty acres of land in Parham. Now Roger Bigot holds it from the earl.

2808 ii, 299a–b (4-13) <u>Earl Hugh; Halesworth</u>: TRE Ælfric held two carucates of land in Halesworth. Ulf the Priest held forty acres of land in the same place, and four freemen lay there with sixty acres of land. Now Bigot de Loges holds all of this from Earl Hugh. Count Alan claims (*calumpniatur*) the land of Ulf the Priest and the four freemen through (*per*) his antecessor and through his own seisin (*per suam sesinam*), and the hundred testifies.

2809 ii, 299b (4-15) <u>Earl Hugh; Middleton</u>: TRE Munulf held eighty acres of land in Middleton. Earl Hugh's antecessor had half his commendation, and Robert Malet's antecessor had the other half. There were also six freemen in Middleton with fifty acres of land. Brunwine was Munulf's man TRE; Ælfheah and Leofric were half Munulf's men; Asmoth was the woman of Toli the Sheriff; and Beorhtmær, her son, was the man of Beorhtmær, Robert Malet's reeve. Cyneric and Grim were the men of Eadric son of Ingeld and were commended to Robert Malet's antecessor Eadric. He loaned (*commodavit*) them to Walter de Caen after Walter de Dol forfeited (*se forisfecit*). Now Roger Bigot holds them from Earl Hugh's fee.

2810   ii, 301b (4-32) Earl Hugh; Ilketshall: TRE a freeman held twelve acres of land in Ilketshall, which Ralph, a man of W. the Staller, annexed (*invasit*). Earl Ralph was seised (*erat . . . sesitus*) of this on the day he forfeited (*forisfecit*). In the same place there was another freeman with ten acres of land. Roger Bigot held it, but Burnin annexed (*invasit*) this against him.

2811   ii, 302a (4-36) Earl Hugh; "Rodenhala": TRE a freeman commended to Thorth, antecessor of Ralph Baynard, held thirty acres of land in "Rodenhala." Now Earl Hugh holds it.

2812   ii, 302b (4-42) Earl Hugh; Framlingham: TRE Æthelmær, a thegn, held nine carucates of land in Framlingham. Now Roger Bigot holds it from Earl Hugh. In the same place Munulf held a carucate and forty acres of land. He was half commended to Æthelmær and half to Robert Malet's antecessor. William Malet was seised (*fuit sesitus*) of this. Ely Abbey has the soke of all of this land, but Earl Hugh's antecessor held it from Ely.

2813   ii, 303a (5-1) Eustace of Boulogne; Ousden: TRE Leofric, a thegn, held six carucates of land in Ousden. Now Count Eustace holds it. It was valued at £6, now at £7, but it was given (*datum fuit*) at farm for £14.

2814   ii, 303a (5-2) Eustace of Boulogne; Rattlesden: TRE a freeman held sixty acres of land in Rattlesden. He was commended to and in the soke of Ely Abbey. Now Heldræd holds this under Count Eustace. Heldræd, moreover, annexed (*invasit*) seven acres of Ely's demesne in the same vill for the fee of Count Eustace.

2815   ii, 303a–b (5-4) Eustace of Boulogne; Little Finborough: TRE Engelric, Eustace of Boulogne's antecessor, held two and a half carucates of land in Little Finborough. Now Count Eustace holds it.

2816   ii, 304a (6-2) Robert Malet; Chilton (near Sudbury): TRE Godwine son of Ælfhere held two carucates of land in Chilton with the soke. There were also three freemen there with forty acres of land, who were commended to and in the soke of this same Godwine, Robert Malet's antecessor. Now Walter fitz Aubrey holds this from Robert Malet.

2817   ii, 304a–b (6-3) Robert Malet; Creeting St. Peter: TRW Robert de Glanville holds a carucate of land in Creeting St. Peter from Robert Malet. TRE Leofwine, a freeman of Eadric, Robert Malet's antecessor, held it.

2818   ii, 304b (6-4) Robert Malet; Ipswich: TRW Robert Malet has a burgess in Ipswich. TRE his antecessor had this man's commendation.

2819   ii, 304b–305a (6-8) Robert Malet; Hemingstone: TRW Robert Malet's mother has four acres of land in Hemingstone. TRE Eadmær, a freeman commended to Leofric antecessor of Robert Malet's mother, had it.

2820   ii, 305a–b (6-11) Robert Malet; Debenham: TRE Eadric, a freeman commended to the antecessor of Robert Malet, had a carucate of land in Debenham. Now William Goulafre holds it from Robert Malet. In the same place Saxi, Ranulf Peverel's antecessor, held six acres of land in the time of

King Edward. Now Robert Malet's mother holds it. William Malet, Robert's antecessor, was seised (*sesitus fuit*) of this, as was his antecessor, in the time of King William.

2821 ii, 305b (6-18) <u>Robert Malet; Debenham</u>: Robert Malet has to answer for (*ad defendum*) two-thirds of the Church of St. Mary's, Debenham, with twenty acres of land, as well as a quarter of the Church of St. Andrew's and a fourth of its land.

2822 ii, 306a–b (6-28) <u>Robert Malet; "Brutge"</u>: TRE Eadric of Laxfield held forty acres of land in "Brutge." Now Robert de Risboil holds it from Robert Malet. In the same place five freemen with twenty acres of land have been added with their commendation. The wife of one of them was commended to Northmann.

2823 ii, 307a (6-33) <u>Robert Malet; Blaxhall</u>: TRE two freemen held fourteen acres of land in Blaxhall. One and a half were under the commendation of the Abbot of Ely, and half was under the commendation of Robert Malet's antecessor. Now Robert Malet holds this, and William d'Emalleville holds it from him.

2824 ii, 307a (6-34) <u>Robert Malet; Blaxhall</u>: TRE a freemen held ten acres of land in Blaxhall. He was under Eadric's commendation. Now Gilbert holds it from Robert Malet, and the soke is the Abbot of Ely's. In the same place there is a freeman with twelve acres of land. He was half under the commendation of Robert Malet's antecessor and half under the Abbot of Ely. Because of this half, he was reconciled (*ex hac medietate est conciliatus*) with the abbot. Gilbert also holds this land from Robert Malet.

2825 ii, 307a (6-38) <u>Robert Malet; Wantisden</u>: TRE there were two freemen – Alwine and Alflæd – in Wantisden, under the commendation of Robert Malet's antecessor. They held seven acres of land. Now Robert Malet holds it.

2826 ii, 307a (6-39) <u>Robert Malet; Blaxhall</u>: TRE Huna, a freeman under the commendation of Robert Malet's antecessor, held twelve acres of land in Blaxhall. Now Ranulf holds it from Robert Malet.

2827 ii, 307b (6-42, 43) <u>Robert Malet; "Chiletuna," Rendham</u>: TRW Robert Malet holds four carucates and twenty acres of land in "Chiletuna." Eadric held it TRE. In the same place sixteen and a half freemen, commended only, have been added to this manor with 153 acres of land. TRW Robert also holds a carucate and sixty-nine acres of land in Rendham from Robert Malet. It is a berewick of "Chiletuna." Thirteen freemen with eighty acres have been added to this manor.

2828 ii, 307b–308a (6-44) <u>Robert Malet; Cransford</u>: TRE Cus, a freeman commended to Eadric, held ninety acres of land in Cransford. Now Walter holds this from Robert Malet. Two freemen with fourteen acres of land were added to this manor. Walter also holds this from Robert.

2829 ii, 308a (6-45) <u>Robert Malet; Great Glemham</u>: TRE Huna, half under the commendation of the Abbot of Ely and half under the commendation of

Robert Malet's antecessor, held thirty acres of land in Great Glemham. Now Walter holds it from Robert Malet.

2830　ii, 308a–b (6-46) <u>Robert Malet; Swefling</u>: TRE Esbiorn, a freeman commended to Eadric, held sixty acres of land in Swefling. Now Robert de Claville holds it from Robert Malet. In the same place Æthelwig, who was commended to Robert Malet's antecessor, held sixty acres of land. Now Robert fitz Fulcred holds it from Robert Malet. Also in the same place there were eleven freemen with ninety acres of land. All of them were commended to Robert Malet's antecessor except one, a man named Hardwin, who was commended to the antecessor of Roger Bigot. Robert fitz Fulcred also holds this from Robert Malet.

2831　ii, 308b (6-47) <u>Robert Malet; Benhall</u>: TRE six freemen commended to Robert Malet's antecessor held eighty acres of land in Benhall. Now Robert fitz Fulcred holds this from Robert Malet.

2832　ii, 308b (6-49) <u>Robert Malet; Great Glemham</u>: TRE Wulfmær, a freeman commended to Robert Malet's antecessor, held one hundred acres of land in Great Glemham. Now Robert fitz Fulcred holds it from Robert Malet.

2833　ii, 309a–b (6-57) <u>Robert Malet; Wyverstone</u>: TRE Alwine, a freeman commended to Eadric, held 100 acres of land in Wyverstone. His wife was commended to the Abbot of Bury St. Edmund's. In the same place three brothers, who were freemen, along with their mother, held thirty acres of land. A sixth part of one of these brothers – Ælfric – was commended to Robert Malet's antecessor. Aki, Robert Blunt's antecessor, had five-sixths of Ælfric's commendation. In the same place a freeman, half commended to the abbot and half under the commendation of Robert Malet's antecessor, held sixteen acres of land. In the same place Alflæd, a free woman commended to Robert Malet's antecessor, held three acres of land. Now Hubert holds all of this from Robert Malet.

2834　ii, 310b–311a (6-79) <u>Robert Malet; Fordley</u>: TRE Eadric held sixty acres of land in Fordley. Now Robert Malet holds it. Before King Edward died this Eadric was commended to Eadric of Laxfield, Robert Malet's antecessor. Eadric of Laxfield was outlawed (*udlagavit*), and King Edward seised (*saisiuit*) all of his land. Afterwards, he was reconciled (*conciliatus est*) to King Edward, and the King granted (*concessit*) him his land. The King gave him a writ and seal (*dedit etiam brevem et sigillum*), so that whichever of his commended freemen might wish to return to him (*vellent redire*) could return with the King's consent (*suo concessu redirent*). King Edward was seised (*saisiuit*), in his own hand, of this particular Eadric. Afterwards the hundred did not see Eadric return (*rediret*) to his lord Eadric of Laxfield, but this Eadric himself says that he did, and offers the ordeal (*offert iudicium*) that he returned, as did the freemen whom he has under his commendation. He vouches (*revocat*) Robert Malet as warrantor (*warant*).

2835　ii, 311a (6-82) <u>Robert Malet; Huntingfield</u>: TRE twenty-one freemen held two hundred acres of land in Huntingfield. Now Robert Malet holds it. The soke and sake of all the land of these freemen lies in Blythburgh, for the use of the King and the earl. Eadric, Robert Malet's antecessor, had the commendation of all of these men.

2836 ii, 312a (6-89a) Robert Malet; Dunwich: The King has this custom in Dunwich: that two or three shall go to the hundred from Dunwich if they are rightly warned (*duo vel tres ibunt ad hundret si recte moniti fuerint*). If they do not do this, they shall forfeit (*si hoc non faciant, forisfacti sunt*) two *orae*.

2837 ii, 312a–b (6-89b) Robert Malet; Dunwich: If a thief is captured in Dunwich, he shall be judged there (*si latro ibi fuerit captus, ibi iudicabitur*). Corporal judgment shall be made in Blythburgh, and the man under such judgment's goods shall remain with the lord of Dunwich (*corporal iusticia in Blieburc capietur, et sua pecunia remanserit domino de Duneuuic*).

2838 ii, 312b (6-91) Robert Malet; "Wrabretuna": TRE Asmoth, a free woman, held thirty acres of land in "Wrabretuna," and Northmann the Sheriff had her commendation. Now Robert Malet holds it, and Roger Bigot claims (*reclamat*) it.

2839 ii, 312b–313a (6-92) Robert Malet; Peasenhall: TRE Leofsige, a freeman, held forty acres of land in Peasenhall. In the same place Stanwine, a freeman, held a carucate of land. This Stanwine was commended to Eadric, Robert Malet's antecessor, before Eadric could be outlawed (*utlagisset*). After this, Stanwine was Harold's man, and was so, so the hundred says, on the day King Edward was alive and dead. Stanwine alone says that he was Eadric's man by Harold's consent (*concessu*) on the day King Edward died, and he offers the ordeal (*offert iudicium*). Now Fulcred holds all of this from Robert Malet.

2840 ii, 313a–b (6-94) Robert Malet; Darsham: TRE Blachmann, a freeman commended to Eadric, held thirty acres of land in Darsham. Now Walter fitz Richere holds it from Robert Malet. A freeman with twenty-two acres of land was added to this manor. He was commended to Blachmann TRE.

2841 ii, 313b (6-97) Robert Malet; South Cove: TRW Eadric holds two freemen with sixteen acres of land in South Cove from Robert Malet. They were commended TRE to Eadric, Robert Malet's antecessor.

2842 ii, 314a–b (6-110) Robert Malet; Stratton: TRE Wulfmær, a freeman of Eadric of Laxfield, held a carucate of land in Stratton. Twelve freemen with eighty-seven and a half acres of land were added to this manor in the time of King William – Leofric of Hemley, Brunmann of Burgh, Goda of "Strustuna," Leofstan of Falkenham, Gliwmann of Levington, Wihtric of "Carlewuda," Edwin the smith in "Carlewuda," Ælfric of "Hopewella," Thorir of "Kyluertestuna," Ælfric son of the smith of "Carlewuda," Ordgar in "Kyluertestuna," and Modgifu of Colcarr. All of these men were commended to the same Wulfmær TRE. Now Robert de Claville holds all this from Robert Malet.

2843 ii, 314b–315a (6-112) Robert Malet; Playford: TRE Godwine son of Ælfhere held three carucates of land in Playford under Queen Edith. In the same place there were twelve freemen, all of whom were commended to Godwine except for two – Æthelric and Blachmann – of whom Healfdene, Geoffrey de Mandeville's antecessor, had commendation. Now Humphrey fitz Robert holds all this from Robert Malet.

2844   ii, 317b (6-159) Robert Malet; Alderton: TRE thirty-one freemen held a carucate and eighty acres of land in Alderton. Godric, Swein's antecessor, had the commendation of two and a half of these men, but William Malet was seised (*fuit seisitus*) of them. Now Robert Malet holds this.

2845   ii, 318a (6-165, 169) Robert Malet; Sutton, Bredfield: TRW Walter de Caen hold half a freeman named Godwine from Robert Malet, with twelve acres of land in Sutton. TRE this Godwine was commended to Eadric. Mainard claims (*calumpniatur*) that Earl Ralph was seised (*fuit seisitus*) of Godwine of Sutton a year before he forfeited (*se forisfecit*), and the hundred testifies that Robert Malet was seised (*fuit inde seisitus*) of him.

2846   ii, 318b–319a (6-177) Robert Malet; Ramsholt: TRE three and a half freemen commended to Godric, Swein's antecessor, held twenty-nine acres of land in Ramsholt. In the same place there were five freemen with sixteen acres of land: all but half of one of them were commended to Eadric; this half was commended to Roger Bigot's antecessor. Now Ralph holds all of this from Robert Malet.

2847   ii, 319b–320a (6-191) Robert Malet; Eye: TRE Eadric held twelve carucates of land in Eye. Now Robert Malet holds it. Eadric had the soke and sake of what the bishopric of Elmham had, that is what the Bishop ought to have had.

2848   ii, 321a (6-210) Robert Malet; Westhorpe: TRW Robert Malet has three and a half freemen with thirty acres of land in Westhorpe. The Abbot of Bury St. Edmund's claims (*calumpniatur*) one of these men, Ordric, with ten acres of land. The others were commended to Wulfric, antecessor of Eudo son of Spearhavoc.

2849   ii, 321b (6-211) Robert Malet; Wyverstone: TRE four freemen – Wulfmær, Alflæd, Wulfwine, and Alwine – held sixty-seven acres of land in Wyverstone. Alflæd and Alwine were commended to Robert Malet's antecessor, and the Abbot of Bury St. Edmund's had three-quarters of the commendation of Wulfwine. Now Robert Malet holds this. The King and the earl have the soke over all of this except for the three-quarters of the man who was commended to the Abbot of Bury.

2850   ii, 321b (6-212) Robert Malet; "Caldecota": TRE six freemen commended to Leofwine of Bacton held seventy-four acres of land in "Caldecota." On the day he forfeited (*forisfecit*) Walter de Dol was seised (*fuit sesitus*) of two – Wulfgifu and her son. Now Robert Malet holds this.

2851   ii, 322a (6-215) Robert Malet; Thornham Magna: TRE Beorhtmær, who was commended to Wulfgifu, held twenty-six acres of land in Thornham Magna. In the same place there were four freemen with 108 acres of land. When he forfeited (*forisfecit*), Walter de Dol was seised (*fuit sesitus*) of half of

Brungar, one of these freemen. Wulfgifu had the commendation of two and a half others; the Abbot of Bury had the commendation of half; and Burgheard had the commendation of the fourth freeman. Now Robert Malet holds all of this.

2852 ii, 322a–b (6-216) <u>Robert Malet; Gislingham</u>: TRE Besi, a freeman commended to Alsige nephew of Ralph the Staller, held sixteen acres of land in Gislingham. Aubrey de Vere's antecessor held five acres of this land. TRE Cypping, a freeman commended to Wulfwine antecessor of Aubrey de Vere and in his soke, held another twelve acres of land in Gislingham. He also held an acre and a quarter of Wulfwine's demesne land. Now Robert Malet's mother holds all of this.

2853 ii, 322b (6-217) <u>Robert Malet; Cotton</u>: TRE Esger, a freeman commended to Leofwine of Bacton, held thirty acres of land in Cotton. In the same place Teit, half commended to Eadric the King's reeve and half commended to Robert Malet's antecessor, held eight acres of land. Now Robert Malet holds this.

2854 ii, 322b (6-218) <u>Robert Malet; Thornham Parva</u>: TRE eight freemen commended to Wulfgifu held twenty-eight acres of land in Thornham Parva. In the same place two freemen held fifteen acres of land. One was commended to Wulfgifu and the other was half under the commendation of Robert Malet's antecessor. Robert Malet now holds this.

2855 ii, 323b (6-227) <u>Robert Malet; Mellis</u>: TRE Leofric held sixty acres of land in Mellis. Wulfwine, Aubrey de Vere's antecessor, had half his commendation and half his soke. Wulfgifu had the other half of his commendation, and King Edward had the other half of his soke. Now Robert Malet holds this.

2856 ii, 324b–325a (6-251) <u>Robert Malet; Harpole</u>: TRE Huna, a freeman of Eadric, held one hundred acres in Harpole. There were another twenty-nine acres of land there. Part of it was held by ten freemen in Harpole commended to Eadric. The rest was held by four freemen in Wickham Market. Ely Abbey had half the commendation of two of these men, and Robert Malet's antecessor had the other half. Now Robert Malet's mother holds this.

2857 ii, 327b (6-299) <u>Robert Malet; Walsham Le Willows</u>: TRW Hubert holds a freeman with sixty acres of land in Walsham Le Willows from Robert Malet. TRE Robert's antecessor had this man's commendation.

2858 ii, 327b–328a (6-301) <u>Robert Malet; Stanton</u>: TRE Walter de Caen holds a freeman in Stanton from Robert Malet with ninety acres of land. TRE Robert's antecessor had half this man's commendation, and Bury St. Edmund's had the other half as well as his soke and sake.

2859 ii, 328a (6-302) <u>Robert Malet; Rickinghall Inferior</u>: TRW Hubert holds a freeman in Rickinghall Inferior with thirty acres of land from Robert Malet. TRE Robert Malet's antecessor had his commendation, and Bury St. Edmund's had his soke.

2860 ii, 330a (6-318) <u>Robert Malet; Chickering</u>: TRE three commended freemen held thirty-six acres of land in Chickering. Now Walter fitz Grip holds this from Robert Malet. In the same place there was a commended freeman with sixty acres of land. Walter fitz Grip also holds this from Robert Malet. Robert's antecessor had his commendation, and he had this land in mortgage (*in vadimonio*) for 60s.

2861 ii, 330b (7-1) <u>Roger Bigot</u>; <u>Barnham</u>: TRE Æthelwig of Thetford held a carucate of land in Barnham. Now Stanheard holds it from Roger Bigot. There were five freemen there with forty acres of land, and Roger Bigot's antecessor had their commendation in the time of King Edward. Stanheard holds this as well.

2862 ii, 330b–331a (7-3) <u>Roger Bigot</u>; <u>Kelsale</u>: TRE Northmann held four carucates of land in Kelsale. TRW Roger Bigot holds it. Now there is a market there by gift of the King (*de dono regis*).

2863 ii, 331a (7-4) <u>Roger Bigot</u>; <u>Denham (near Eye)</u>: TRE Archbishop Stigand held one and a half carucates of land in Denham. Bishop Æthelmær held it after King William arrived. Now Aitard holds it from Roger Bigot. It is in exchange (*pro escangio*) for Isaac's land.

2864 ii, 331a (7-5) <u>Roger Bigot</u>; <u>Hinton</u>: TRE Æthelweard, a freeman, held fifty acres of land in Hinton. Now Robert of Blythburgh holds it under Roger Bigot. Twelve of the acres that Robert holds are in the church of Blythburgh in the King's alms: this is testified by the hundred. Six freemen with fifty acres of land were added to this manor, over whom Roger's antecessor had commendation.

2865 ii, 331a–b (7-6) <u>Roger Bigot</u>; <u>Bridge</u>: TRE Wulfsige held one and a half carucates of land in Bridge. Four freemen with sixty acres of land were added to this manor. Robert de Courson holds this from Roger Bigot.

2866 ii, 331b (7-8) <u>Roger Bigot</u>; <u>Uggeshall</u>: TRE Godric held two carucates of land in Uggeshall. Now Robert de Courson holds it under Roger Bigot. William Malet was seised (*fuit . . . sesitus*) of this land.

2867 ii, 332a (7-11) <u>Roger Bigot</u>; <u>"Warabetuna"</u>: TRE a free woman commended to Northmann held 100 acres of land in "Warabetuna." Now Robert Malet holds thirty of these acres, and Northmann holds the other seventy from Roger Bigot as a manor.

2868 ii, 332a (7-13) <u>Roger Bigot</u>; <u>Heveningham</u>: TRE Stanwine, a freeman commended to Harold, held a carucate of land in Heveningham, so the hundred testifies. But Stanwine alone offers the ordeal (*offert iudicium*), saying that he was a man of Eadric, Robert Malet's antecessor. Now Ansketil holds this land from Roger Bigot.

2869 ii, 332a–b (7-15) <u>Roger Bigot</u>; <u>Chediston</u>: TRE Wulfsige, a freeman, held thirteen acres of land in Chediston. A man commended to Robert Malet's antecessor had half of Wulfsige's commendation, and Queen Edith had the other half. In the same place Eadric, a freeman, who was half commended to Robert Malet's antecessor and half to the Abbot of Ely, held 100 acres of land. William Malet was seised (*erat sesitus*) of this when he went on the King's service, where he died. In the same place Leofric, a freeman, held twenty-six acres of land. Baynard's antecessor had his commendation. In the same place Gauti, a freeman, held fifteen acres of land. Robert Malet's antecessor had his commendation, and William Malet was seised (*saisitus fuit*) of this. In the same place Leofwine, a freeman, held fourteen acres of land. Robert Malet's antecessor had his commendation, and William, Robert's father, was seised (*saisitus fuit*). Now Robert de Vaux holds all of this from Roger Bigot.

2870 ii, 333a (7-16) <u>Roger Bigot; Thorpe (in Aldingham)</u>: TRE Wulfmær, a freeman of Robert Malet's antecessor, held twenty acres of land in Thorpe. William Malet, his father, was seised (*saisitus fuit*) of it. Now Robert de Vaux holds it from Roger Bigot.

2871 ii, 333a (7-17) <u>Roger Bigot; Halesworth</u>: TRE Gunnar, a freeman commended to Robert Malet's antecessor, held fifteen acres of land in Halesworth, and Robert's father was seised (*saisitus fuit*) of it. Now Robert de Vaux holds this from Roger Bigot.

2872 ii, 333a (7-18) <u>Roger Bigot; Yoxford</u>: TRE Northmann, a thegn, held 100 acres of land in Yoxford. Five freemen with fourteen acres of land, who were commended to Northmann, were added to this manor. Northmann also had the soke. Another two freemen – Algar and Edwin – were added to this manor with seven acres of land. In the time of King Edward they were commended to Æthelweard the King's reeve. Now Hugh de Corbon holds all of this from Roger Bigot.

2873 ii, 333a (7-19) <u>Roger Bigot; Bulcamp</u>: TRE Ali, a freeman commended to Manni, Robert de Tosny's antecessor, held ninety acres of land in Bulcamp. Earl Ralph held this land on the day he forfeited (*se forisfecit*). Now Roger Bigot holds it by gift of the King (*de dono regis*), so he says, and Robert de Vaux holds from him.

2874 ii, 333b (7-24) <u>Roger Bigot; Cookley</u>: TRE Godric, a freeman, held thirty acres of land in Cookley. Wulfsige, the antecessor of Roger Bigot, had a third of Godric's commendation and Wulfsige's two brothers had the other two-thirds. Robert de Vaux now holds this from Roger Bigot.

2875 ii, 333b (7-25) <u>Roger Bigot; Covehithe</u>: TRE Hearding, a freeman commended to Ulfkil antecessor of William de Warenne, held twenty acres of land in Covehithe. Now Roger Bigot holds it.

2876 ii, 333b–334a (7-26) <u>Roger Bigot; Thorpe (in Aldingham)</u>: TRE Wulfmær, a freeman commended to William Malet's antecessor, held fifty acres of land in Thorpe, and William Malet was seised (*fuit saisitus*). Now Roger Bigot holds it.

2877 ii, 334a (7-30) <u>Roger Bigot; Fordley</u>: TRE fifteen freemen held 115 acres of land in Fordley. Northmann had the commendation of thirteen of these men. Robert Malet's antecessor had half the commendation of the other two, and Northmann had the other half. Now Roger Bigot holds this.

2878 ii, 334a–b (7-33) <u>Roger Bigot; Knoddishall</u>: TRE Bote, a freeman of King Edward, held thirty acres of land in Knoddishall. Robert Malet has the soke.

William Malet was seised of this (*fuit saisitus*) on the day he died. Now Roger Bigot holds it.

2879   ii, 334b (7-36) <u>Roger Bigot; Darsham</u>: TRE Eskil the Priest held a carucate of land in Darsham, which was held by seven freemen. One of these men was Toli's man. Æthelweard the King's reeve had half the commendation of Leofric Cob and Thorkil; Alnoth was a man of Northmann the Sheriff; Brunmann Beard was half Northmann's man and half Brunmær's; Wulfric the Deacon was the man of Godwine son of Algar; Osmund was the man of Eadric of Laxfield. Ælfgifu, a free woman, was commended to Northmann; Blachmann was the man of Eadric of Laxfield. William Malet was seised (*saisitus fuit*) of all this on the day he died. Now Eskil, Roger Bigot's chaplain, holds it. Robert Malet claims (*reclamat*) six acres of this land, which one of his men gave (*dedit*) with his daughter, who married (*duxit*) a man of Roger Bigot in the time of King William.

2880   ii, 335a–b (7-42, 43, 44) <u>Roger Bigot; Willingham, Weston, Ellough</u>: TRE Gunnulf, a man commended to Burgheard, held thirty acres of land in Willingham. In the same place five freemen commended to the same Gunnulf held eighty acres of land. Five freemen commended to Burgheard held eighteen acres of land in Weston, and two freemen commended to Burgheard held seven acres of land in Ellough. Earl Ralph had been seised (*erat . . . sesitus*) of all of this when he forfeited (*forisfecit*), but now Roger Bigot holds by the King's gift (*de dono regis*), and Robert de Vaux holds from him.

2881   ii, 336a (7-55) <u>Roger Bigot; Buxhall</u>: TRE a freeman commended only to Ely and in the soke of the hundred, held forty acres of land in Buxhall. Roger took this land to make (*recepit . . . ad perficiendum*) Baylham in another hundred. But the hundred has seen neither writ nor livery (*nec vidit brevem nec liberatorem*).

2882   ii, 336a–b (7-56) <u>Roger Bigot; Ringshall</u>: TRE Leofwine, a freemen commended to the Abbot of Ely, held a carucate and eighty acres of land in Ringshall. In the same place four freemen held fifty acres of land. Leofwine, Roger Bigot's antecessor, had the commendation of two of these men – Frothi and Leofric. He did not have the commendation of the other two – Lustwine and Eadric. Now William de Bourneville holds all of this from Roger Bigot.

2883   ii, 336b–337a (7-58) <u>Roger Bigot; Baylham</u>: TRE Munding, a freeman commended to the Abbot of Ely, held a carucate of land in Baylham. In the same place Wulfric, a freeman commended to Eadric, Robert Malet's antecessor, held sixty acres of land as a manor. And another twenty freemen held ninety-two acres there. None of these men were commended to Roger Bigot's antecessor. Now William de Bourneville holds all of this from Roger Bigot.

2884   ii, 337a (7-59) <u>Roger Bigot; Somersham</u>: TRE Leofsunu, a freeman commended to Leofric Hobbeson, Roger Bigot's antecessor, held thirty acres of land in Somersham. Now William de Bourneville holds it from Roger Bigot.

2885 ii, 337a (7-60) <u>Roger Bigot; Offton</u>: TRE Leofcild, a freeman commended to Archbishop Stigand, held two carucates of land in Offton. Now Hugh d'Houdain holds it from Roger Bigot. Hugh also holds another carucate and five and a half acres of land there from Roger Bigot. TRE it belonged to ten freemen. Of these, the whole of Blæcsunu and half of Ealdwine were commended to Roger Bigot's antecessor, but he had nothing from the others.

2886 ii, 337b (7-64) <u>Roger Bigot; Stonham (Earl or Little)</u>: TRE Brun, the reeve of Ipswich, held sixty acres of land in Stonham. In the same place five freemen commended to Brun held sixteen acres of land. Now Werengar holds all of this from Roger Bigot. In the same place seventeen freemen were added to this manor TRW with sixty-nine acres of land. Five of them were commended to Saxi, Ranulf Peverel's antecessor. Roger de Raismes claims (*calumpniatur*) to have held these freemen in his fee before Roger Bigot could take (*recepisset*) land in Suffolk. But the hundred testifies that Roger Bigot took (*recepit*) them before, as his fee. This is contradicted (*contradicit*) by Roger de Raismes by all law (*omni lege*).

2887 ii, 337b–338a (7-65) <u>Roger Bigot; Baylham</u>: TRE three freemen held twelve acres of land in Baylham. One, Wulfbald, was commended to Roger Bigot's antecessor Brun. Brun had nothing over the other two, but Ranulf Peverel's antecessor had their commendation. Now Werengar holds this from Roger Bigot.

2888 ii, 338a (7-66) <u>Roger Bigot; "Langhedena"</u>: TRE Ælfric, a freeman commended to Brun, Roger Bigot's antecessor, held ten acres of land in "Langhedena." Now Werengar holds this from Roger Bigot.

2889 ii, 338a (7-67) <u>Roger Bigot; Coddenham (near Needham Market)</u>: TRE Wigulf, a freeman commended to Toli the Sheriff, held seventy-six acres of land in Coddenham. There was half a mill there, but Hardwin, Earl Ralph's brother, took it away (*abstulit*) in the time of King William. In the same place twenty-seven freemen held seventy-five acres of land. Twelve of them were commended to Wigulf, Roger Bigot's antecessor, but Wigulf had nothing from the other fifteen. Now Werengar holds all of this from Roger Bigot.

2890 ii, 338a–b (7-68) <u>Roger Bigot; Hemingstone</u>: TRE Farman, a freeman commended to Wigulf, held five acres of land in Hemingstone. Now Werengar holds it from Roger Bigot. Roger de Raismes claims (*calumpniatur*) all the land of Wigulf and all of those freemen which Werengar holds from Roger Bigot. He says that it was delivered to him prior (*liberatum fuit priusquam*) to Roger Bigot. The hundred does not know how to tell the truth in this (*nescit ex hoc verum dicere*), because Werengar held from both Roger Bigot and Roger de Raismes. Nonetheless, Werengar vouches (*revocat*) it to the fee of Roger Bigot, and Roger de Raismes contradicts this by all laws (*hoc contradicit omnibus legibus*).

2891   ii, 338b (7-70) <u>Roger Bigot; Saxmundham</u>: TRE Northmann held 140 acres of land in Saxmundham. This manor is one of the three that King William returned (*reddidit*) to Northmann. Now Northmann holds this from Roger Bigot and has the soke.

2892   ii, 338b (7-71) <u>Roger Bigot; Saxmundham</u>: TRE Algar, a thegn of King Edward, held two carucates and forty acres of land in Saxmundham. In the same place seven freemen with forty-eight acres of land were added to this manor. They were commended to Algar. One of these men, Wulfnoth, was commended to Robert Malet's antecessor. Now Ranulf holds all of this from Roger Bigot.

2893   ii, 339a (7-75) <u>Roger Bigot; Brome, Oakley</u>: TRE Gode, a free woman commended to Archbishop Stigand, held a carucate of land in Brome and a carucate of land in Oakley. Now William Scudet holds this from Roger Bigot. There was also a freeman there with eight acres of land, who was commended to Ælfric. His wife was commended to Robert Malet's antecessor. Hugh de Corbon holds this from Roger Bigot.

2894   ii, 339b (7-78) <u>Roger Bigot; Hundred of Colneis</u>: [The following information appears in the chapter dealing with Roger Bigot's land, and may, therefore, suggest that Roger held illegally: "There is a pasture in the hundred of Colneis common to all men of the hundred (*communis omnibus hominibus de hundret*)."]

2895   ii, 339b–340a (7-79) <u>Roger Bigot; "Maistana"</u>: TRE Northmann held six freemen with one hundred acres of land in "Maistana." They were commended to him. Their names were Eadric, Burgric, Wulfbald, Ælfric, Almær, and Wulfric. Of these men, Wulfbald's father, Wulfheah, was half Robert Malet's antecessor, Eadric's, man.

2896   ii, 341a–b (7-98) <u>Roger Bigot; Falkenham</u>: TRE Eadric, a man commended to Northmann, held a carucate of land in Falkenham. There were seven and a half [*sic*] freemen with fifty-seven acres of land there commended to Northmann. Their names were Beorhtmær, Wulfmær, Godwine, Wulfweard, Godric, and Sweting. Roger Bigot was seised (*fuit . . . saisitus*) of Sweting, Leofric, and Leofstan. Now Ralph de Tourleville holds all this from Roger Bigot.

2897   ii, 342b (7-114) <u>Roger Bigot; Kirton</u>: Godric the Priest, a freeman with seven acres of land in Kirton, was commended to Eadric before he was outlawed (*utlagavit*) in the time of King Edward. After Eadric was outlawed (*utlagavit*), Godric was Northmann's man. Now Wihtmær holds this land from Roger Bigot.

2898   ii, 343a (7-121) <u>Roger Bigot; Kembroke</u>: TRE Northmann had the commendation of fourteen freemen in Kembroke with seventy-three acres of land. Now William de Bourneville holds this under Roger Bigot. The men of the hundred have this land worth (*pretiata*) 48s., but it used to and it now pays £6.

2899   ii, 343b (7-131) <u>Roger Bigot; Rendlesham</u>: TRE there was a freeman commended to Eadric in Rendlesham with eighteen acres of land. Now

Roger Bigot holds it. William Malet was seised (*fuit sesitus*) on the day he died.

2900   ii, 343b–344a (7-133) <u>Roger Bigot; Charsfield</u>: TRE Beorhtmær, a freeman commended to Ely Abbey, held thirty acres of land in Charsfield. There were five freemen there. All of them but one were commended to Beorhtmær. This one was commended to Earl Ralph, and he was seised (*fuit sesitus*) of sixteen acres of land. Another of these freemen was commended to Eadric, and William Malet was seised (*fuit sesitus*). Then this paid 30s., now its value is 20s. These men are in the same assessment, but they could not pay (*non potuerunt reddere*). Thurstan fitz Guy holds all of this from Roger Bigot.

2901   ii, 344a (7-136) <u>Roger Bigot; Blaxhall</u>: TRE eight freemen held sixty-six acres of land in Blaxhall. Five were commended to Northmann; two to the Abbot of Ely; and one, named Alwine, to Robert Malet's antecessor. Now Northmann holds this from Roger Bigot.

2902   ii, 344a (7-137) <u>Roger Bigot; Wantisden</u>: TRE Ælfric, Beorhtric, and Ealdhild, freemen under the commendation of Roger Bigot's antecessor, held eleven acres of land in Wantisden. Now Northmann holds this from Roger Bigot.

2903   ii, 344a–b (7-138) <u>Roger Bigot; Sternfield</u>: TRE Leofric, a man commended to Northmann, held fifty acres of land in Sternfield. William Malet held this manor on the day he died, as did Robert, his son. Now Northmann holds it from Roger Bigot.

2904   ii, 344b (7-139) <u>Roger Bigot; Farnham</u>: TRE Leofric held twenty acres of land in Farnham. William Malet and Robert Malet held it. Now Northmann holds it from Roger Bigot.

2905   ii, 344b (7-140) <u>Roger Bigot; Benhall</u>: TRE Wulfnoth, a freeman commended to Robert Malet's antecessor, held forty acres of land in Benhall. William Malet held it and was seised (*sesitus fuit*), as was Robert, his son. In the same place Beorhtmær, a freeman commended to the antecessor of Robert Malet, held sixteen acres of land. William Malet was seised (*saisitus fuit*) of this as well, and so too was Robert. Now Northmann holds all of this from Roger Bigot.

2906   ii, 344b–345a (7-143) <u>Roger Bigot; Sternfield</u>: TRE Eadric, a freeman commended to Northmann, held thirty-four acres of land in Sternfield. William Malet was seised (*saisitus fuit*) of this, and so too was Robert. In the same place Northmann had the commendation of seven and a half men, and Robert Malet's antecessor of three and a half – Eskil, Leofric, Osgeat, and half of Leofric Osgeat. William Malet was seised (*fuit sesitus*) of these, and so too was Robert. Now Roger Bigot holds all of this in demesne.

2907   ii, 345a (7-144) <u>Roger Bigot; Great Glemham</u>: TRE five freemen held fifty-four acres of land in Great Glemham. Four were commended to Robert Malet's antecessor. He was seised of this (*fuit inde sesitus*), and so was William, his father. Now Roger Bigot holds this in demesne.

2908   ii, 345a (7-145) <u>Roger Bigot; Bruisyard</u>: TRE Beorhtmær, a freeman commended to Eadric, Robert Malet's antecessor, held thirty acres of land in Bruisyard. Now Ralph holds it from Roger Bigot.

2909 ii, 345a (7-146) <u>Roger Bigot; Rendham</u>: TRE Blæcsunu, a freeman commended to Eadric antecessor of Robert Malet, held fifty-six acres of land in Rendham. William Malet was seised (*sesitus fuit*) of this. Now Ralph holds it from Roger Bigot.

2910 ii, 345a (7-147) <u>Roger Bigot; Swefling</u>: TRE Wulfric, a freeman of Harold, held sixty acres of land in Swefling. Three freemen under commendation were added with nine acres of land. Now Ralph holds this from Roger Bigot.

2911 ii, 345a (7-148) <u>Roger Bigot; Rendham</u>: TRE four and a half freemen held thirty-five acres of land in Rendham. Three of these men – Godric, Godric, and Tulf – were commended to Robert Malet's antecessor. William Malet was seised (*saisitus fuit*) of this. Now Ralph holds from Roger Bigot.

2912 ii, 346a (8-4) <u>Roger the Poitevin; Tuddenham (near Ipswich)</u>: TRE Leohtwine, a freeman of Healfdene antecessor of Geoffrey de Mandeville, held thirty acres of land in Tuddenham. Now Roger the Poitevin holds it.

2913 ii, 346b (8-8) <u>Roger the Poitevin; Hasketon</u>: TRE Alwine, a freeman of Ely Abbey, held forty acres of land in Hasketon. He could not grant or sell his land away from the abbey. There were also two and a half freemen there commended to Eadric, Robert Malet's antecessor. Now Roger fitz Arnulf holds all this from Roger the Poitevin.

2914 ii, 347b (8-22) <u>Roger the Poitevin; Monewdon</u>: TRE fourteen and a half freemen commended to Wulfmær held eighty-four acres of land in Monewdon. Humphrey the Chamberlain held half of one of these men, but Hertald took him away (*abstulit*). Now Roger the Poitevin holds.

2915 ii, 348a–b (8-32) <u>Roger the Poitevin; Ingham</u>: TRE Leofwine, a thegn of King Edward, held a carucate of land in Ingham. There were also ten freemen in Ingham commended to Roger's antecessor, who held forty acres of land. Now Roger the Poitevin holds this.

2916 ii, 348b-349a (8-35) <u>Roger the Poitevin; Thorpe Morieux</u>: TRE a freeman held four carucates of land in Thorpe Morieux. Norman fitz Tancred added seven freemen with twenty-five acres of land to this manor. Bury St. Edmund's had their soke and commendation. In the same place a freeman held one and a half carucates of land. Wihtgar, Richard fitz Gilbert's antecessor, had his commendation and soke. Bury St. Edmund's had the six forfeitures (*vi forisfactus*). Now Roger the Poitevin holds all of this.

2917 ii, 349a–b (8-42) <u>Roger the Poitevin; Mendham</u>: TRE three freemen held a carucate of land in Mendham, and William Malet was seised (*saisitus fuit*) of them. Two were commended to the antecessor of Robert Malet. The third, who held a fourth of this land, was Bishop Æthelmær's. In the same place there was a freeman commended to Ulf, Roger the Poitevin's antecessor, who had fifteen acres of land. Now Roger the Poitevin holds all of this.

2918 ii, 349b (8-45) <u>Roger the Poitevin; Brockley (near Whepstead)</u>: TRE three freemen held sixty acres of land in Brockley. Bury St. Edmund's had commendation over one of these men, and he could not sell. The King had commendation over the other two, but they could only sell in the soke of Bury St. Edmund's. Now Roger the Poitevin holds this.

2919   ii, 349b–350a (8-46) Roger the Poitevin; Boxted: TRE Wulfric, a thegn of King Edward, held two carucates of land in Boxted. There were three horses there when R. relinquished (*reliquit*) it. In the same place there were five freemen with two carucates of land, who were commended to and in the soke of Wihtgar. They could sell, but the King gave (*dedit*) them to Norman fitz Tancred. In the same place a freeman commended to Wulfric held forty-five acres of land. Thirty acres are in the soke of Ely Abbey; the other fifteen are in the soke of Northmann, antecessor of Ralph de Limesy, in Cavendish. In the same manor men held half a carucate of land under Bury St. Edmund's, which they could not sell without the abbot's consent; nonetheless, the King gave (*dedit*) it to Norman fitz Tancred. Now Roger the Poitevin holds all of this.

2920   ii, 350a (8-47) Roger the Poitevin; Preston (near Lavenham): TRE Wulf-weard, a freeman under Archbishop Stigand, held two carucates of land in Preston with the soke. In the same place there were three freemen commended to Wulfweard. Bury St. Edmund's had the soke and sake over two; and Wihtgar, Richard fitz Gilbert's antecessor, over the third. After-wards Norman fitz Tancred held this. Now Roger the Poitevin holds.

2921   ii, 350a–b (8-49) Roger the Poitevin; Buxhall: TRE Leofwine Croc held two carucates of land in Buxhall. He had soke and sake over the hall and the bordars. Norman fitz Tancred added three freemen commended to and in the soke of the King with twenty-four acres of land. Now Roger the Poitevin holds this.

2922   ii, 350b (8-51) Roger the Poitevin; Thorney: TRE a freeman of King Edward held sixty acres of land in Thorney, with soke and sake. He was there similarly after the coming of King William. Norman fitz Tancred took (*accepit*) him from this manor without livery (*sine liberator*). Later Gerald held him; and after Gerald, Roger the Poitevin.

2923   ii, 350b (8-53) Roger the Poitevin; Creeting St. Peter: There was a sokeman with three acres of forfeited (*foreface*) land in Creeting St. Peter. Roger the Poitevin holds it.

2924   ii, 350b–351a (8-55) Roger the Poitevin; Stonham (Earl or Little): TRE Wulfric, a thegn, held two carucates of land in Stonham. Now Roger the Poitevin holds it in demesne. There is a woodland there at sixty swine. A third of the woodland lay in Tunstall (in Nettlestead) TRE, a manor of William de Warenne. Raymond Gerald held it, and now Roger the Poitevin holds it. In the same place Wulfwine, a freeman commended to Wulfmær antecessor of Roger the Poitevin, held forty acres of land. Wulfræd, a freeman commended to Alflæd antecessor of Roger, also held twenty acres of land there. In the same place Ælfric, a freeman, held twelve acres of land. The

Abbot of Bury St. Edmund's had half his commendation. The other half was in the King's manor of Mendlesham. The abbot held half his commendation and half the land until Hertald was seised (*saisiuit*) of it. Now Roger the Poitevin holds all of this.

2925   ii, 351b–352a (8-59) Roger the Poitevin; Hemingstone: TRE twenty freemen held 142 acres of land in Hemingstone. One of these men, with thirteen acres of land, was commended to the Abbot of Ely, and he had the soke. Eight acres belonged there, which Hervey de Bourges took away (*tulit*). There was also half a church there. Fin, Richard's antecessor, took away (*tulit*) six acres which belonged to the church. Now Roger the Poitevin holds all of this in demesne.

2926   ii, 352a (8-63) Roger the Poitevin; Stonham (Earl or Little), Coddenham (near Needham Market): TRE Leofric, a freeman commended to the Abbot of Ely, held six acres of land in Stonham and three in Coddenham. In the same place Godwine, a freeman commended to Wihtgar antecessor of Richard fitz Gilbert, held ten acres of land. Raymond Gerald was seised (*fuit saisitus*) of this, and now Roger the Poitevin holds it. Roger de Raismes was seised with a prior livery (*de prima liberatione*), and the hundred testifies that it was first delivered (*liberatum fuit*) to him.

2927   ii, 353a (8-81) Roger the Poitevin; "Nordberia": TRE Edwin the Priest, a sokeman of the Abbot, held thirty acres of land in "Nordberia." Forty-nine freemen were added to this manor with 260 and a half acres of land. All of these men were in the soke and commendation of the abbot. Now Roger the Poitevin holds this.

2928   ii, 353a–b (9-1) William d'Ecouis; Blakenham (Great or Little): TRE the thegn Ælfric held a carucate of land in Blakenham. Hardwin added twenty-eight freemen with 171 acres of land to this manor. Now William d'Ecouis holds this. This manor was at farm for three years at £12 a year and once in three years an ounce of gold as a gift (*de gersumma*). But the men who took (*receperunt*) the farm as such were completely ruined (*fuerunt confusi*).

2929   ii, 353b (9-2) William d'Ecouis; Market Weston, Ixworth Thorpe: TRW Howard de Vernon holds a carucate of land in Market Weston and eight acres of land in Ixworth Thorpe from William d'Ecouis. TRE Ælfric, a freeman, held this land. Three freemen, moreover, held a carucate of land and twenty acres there in the time of King Edward. They could grant and sell their land, but the commendation, soke, and sake remained with Bury St. Edmund's. Hugh, William's man, has annexed (*invasit*) twenty-five acres of this land against the Abbot of Bury St. Edmund's. In the same place there were ten sokemen of Bury St. Edmund's TRE, with all customs and sixty acres of land. But Hardwin held them TRW.

2930   ii, 355a–b (12-6) Frodo brother of Baldwin abbot of Bury St. Edmund's; Lavenham: TRE Alwig held two carucates of land with soke in Lavenham under Bury St. Edmund's. He could not sell it without the Abbot's consent. Now Frodo, the Abbot of Bury's brother, holds from King William and claims (*reclamat*) it from his fee, saying that it was delivered (*liberata fuit*) to him.

2931 ii, 355b (12-7) Frodo brother of Baldwin abbot of Bury St. Edmund's; Buxhall: TRE twenty-five freemen in the King's soke held three and a half carucates of land in Buxhall. They were delivered (*fuerunt liberati*) to Frodo, the Abbot of Bury's brother, as a manor.

2932 ii, 359b (14-26) Bury St. Edmund's; Preston (near Lavenham): TRE Bury St. Edmund's held a freeman, who held three carucates of land in Preston in demesne. He could grant and sell his land. King William gave (*dedit*) this man and his land to Bury and to Abbot Baldwin with the soke and all customs. Arnulf now holds from Bury St. Edmund's.

2933 ii, 359b–360a (14-28) Bury St. Edmund's; Somerton: TRW Frodo holds a carucate of land in Somerton from Bury St. Edmund's. King William gave (*dedit*) this land to Bury with soke and commendation and all customs.

2934 ii, 360b (14-37) Bury St. Edmund's; Onehouse: TRE a freeman of Bury St. Edmund's held half a carucate of land in Onehouse. The soke and soke and commendation of all of this was Bury's, by gift (*ex dono*) of King Edward, so his writ and seal, which the abbot has, show (*sicut brevia et sigillum demonstrant, que abbas habet*). Afterwards King William granted (*concessit*) it, but the King's reeve has 4s. from one of the men for soke; be this just or unjust (*iuste vel iniuste*) neither the abbot nor his *ministri* knows. The hundred testifies that it did not know that Bury had been disseised (*fuisse dasaisitum*) of the soke after King Edward gave (*dedit*) it.

2935 ii, 360b (14-38) Bury St. Edmund's; Mickfield: TRE Bury St. Edmund's held sixty acres of land in Mickfield. The abbot now holds this land because Æthelric took (*accepit*) a wife TRE, who held this land freely in the soke of the King. But the abbot vouches the soke by gift of the King (*revocat socam de dono regis*). Berenger holds this from the abbot.

2936 ii, 360b (14-39) Bury St. Edmund's; Stonham (Earl or Little): TRE Wulfweard, a freeman in the soke of the King and the earl, held sixty acres of land in Stonham. Now Æthelbald the Priest holds this land. The Abbot of Bury has had it in mortgage (*in vadimonio*) for two marks of gold with the consent (*concessu*) of Engelric, since the English redeemed their land (*quando redimebant anglici terras suas*).

2937 ii, 361b (14-49) Bury St. Edmund's; Pakenham: TRE and TRW Bury St. Edmund's holds seven carucates of land in Pakenham. In the same place a freeman with a carucate of land petitioned (*impetavit*) the abbot to lease (*praestari*) him half a carucate by such an agreement (*tali conventione*) that all of his land, wherever it was, should remain (*remaneret*) in Bury after his death. Now the carucate lies in Pakenham in demesne.

2938 ii, 362a (14-52) Bury St. Edmund's; Bradfield (Combust, St. Clare or St. George): TRE and TRW Bury St. Edmund's holds three carucates of land in Bradfield. There were also nine freemen there with a carucate of land. They could grant and sell their land, but the soke and the service should remain with Bury, whoever might buy (*emeret*) the land.

2939 ii, 363b (14-68) <u>Bury St. Edmund's; Great Livermere</u>: TRE ten freemen held a carucate of land in Great Livermere. They could grant and sell their land, but the soke remained with Bury St. Edmund's. In the same place Frodo holds a freeman who had two carucates of land. He was a freeman of Eadric of Laxfield, and his wife was a free woman of Bury St. Edmund's. They could grant and sell their land, but the sake, soke, and commendation of the woman remained with the abbey. The King took (*accepit*) this man's land from the abbey and gave (*dedit*) it to Werno de Poix. Later, with the King's permission (*licentia*), Werno became a monk and returned (*reddidit*) the land to Bury.

2940 ii, 367b (14-101) <u>Bury St. Edmund's; Ixworth Thorpe</u>: TRW Robert Blunt holds nine freemen with a carucate of land in Ixworth Thorpe from the Abbot of Bury St. Edmund's. In the time of King Edward these freemen could grant and sell their land, but the sake and soke remained with Bury. In the same place Robert Blunt also holds a freeman with sixty acres of land. He could grant and sell his land, but the soke and sake remained with Bury. The abbot pledged (*invadiavit*) this land to the King's barons – that is, William bishop of Thetford, Engelric, and Ralph the Staller – for 100s.

2941 ii, 368a (14-104) <u>Bury St. Edmund's; Bedingfield</u>: TRE ten freemen held half a carucate of land in Bedingfield. One of these men, with thirty acres of land, could never grant or sell his land without the full permission of Abbot of Bury St. Edmund's: this is testified by the hundred. The other nine could grant and sell their land. Now Bury St. Edmund's holds.

2942 ii, 371a (14-146) <u>Bury St. Edmund's; Stoke Ash</u>: TRE Burgheard, a sokeman of the Abbot of Bury St. Edmund's, held fourteen acres of land in Stoke Ash. Roger Farthing, Godric Dapifer's man, claims (*calumpniatur*) this land is from the King's manor of Mendlesham. He says that Walter de Dol held it when he forfeited (*forisfecit*), and he wishes to prove this against (*vult probare contra*) the whole hundred by means of all laws (*omnibus legibus*).

2943 ii, 371a (14-152) <u>Bury St. Edmund's; Wickham Skeith</u>: TRE two freemen, Brunloc and Hereweard, men commended to Burgheard of Mendlesham, held five and a half acres of land in Wickham Skeith. Ordgar, the Abbot of Bury's reeve, holds them. Ælfric, who was reeve before him, annexed (*invasit*) them.

2944 ii, 372b (15-3) <u>Archbishop Lanfranc; Toppesfield</u>: TRE Leofgifu, a free woman, held two carucates of land in Toppesfield. She gave (*dedit*) half a carucate of this land to Christ Church after her death (*post mortem suam*) for another half carucate, which she was to hold from the archbishop during her life (*in vita sua*). This agreement was made (*conventio facta est*) in the time of King Edward. Leofgifu, moreover, was living in the time of King William and had been seised of this (*erat inde saisita*). John nephew of Waleran claims (*calumpniatur*) the land.

2945 ii, 372b (15-4) <u>Archbishop Lanfranc; Toppesfield</u>: TRE a freeman held twenty acres of land in Toppesfield. Wulfric, antecessor of the Abbot of Bury St. Edmund's, had this man's commendation and soke. Now Archbishop Lanfranc holds this.

2946 ii, 373a (16-1, 2, 3) <u>Odo of Bayeux; Haverhill, Seckford, Little Bealings</u>: TRE a freeman held twenty-four acres of land in Haverhill. The Bishop of Bayeux's antecessor had his commendation, and Bury St. Edmund's had the six forfeitures (*vi forisfacturas*). Now Tihel holds this from the bishop. TRE Ælfric son of Wulfgeat, a man commended to Harold, held two carucates of land in Seckford. Now Roger Bigot holds it from the Bishop of Bayeux. And in Little Bealings, Ælfric held fifty acres of land. Biorn, a freeman, held another fifty acres there. He bought (*emit*) it from the Abbot of Ely with the agreement (*conventione*) that after his death it should return (*rediret*) to Ely Abbey, by testimony (*testante*) of the hundred. Now Roger Bigot holds this from the Bishop of Bayeux, and W. de More holds from him. Earl Ralph held these three manors – Haverhill, Seckford, and Little Bealings – on the day he forfeited (*forisfecit*), and Hilary held from him.

2947 ii, 373b (16-6) <u>Odo of Bayeux; Charsfield</u>: TRE fourteen freemen held a carucate of land in Charsfield. Three and a half of these freemen were commended to Ely Abbey and Eadric of Laxfield. William Malet was seised (*fuit saisitus*) on the day he died. The others were commended only to the Abbot of Ely. Markulf, a freeman commended to Eadric of Laxfield, was also there. William Malet was seised (*fuit saisitus*) on the day he died. Now Roger Bigot holds all of this from the Bishop of Bayeux, and Ralph de Savenay holds from him.

2948 ii, 373b (16-8) <u>Odo of Bayeux; Kenton</u>: TRE five freemen held thirty acres of land in Kenton. Four were commended to Ely Abbey and one to Saxi, Ralph de Savenay's antecessor. Now Ralph de Savenay holds this from Roger Bigot, who holds from Odo of Bayeux.

2949 ii, 374a (16-11) <u>Odo of Bayeux; Creeting St. Peter</u>: TRE Ælfric son of Brun, a freeman commended only to Wihtgar, held a carucate of land in Creeting St. Peter in the King's soke. Now William de Bouville holds it from the Bishop of Bayeux. There were also five freemen there, commended only to the same Ælfric, with eighteen acres of land. They were delivered (*fuerunt liberati*) with the manor.

2950 ii, 374a–b (16-14) <u>Odo of Bayeux; Crowfield</u>: TRE Wudubrun, a freeman commended to Eadric, Robert Malet's antecessor, held twenty acres in Crowfield. Now Roger Bigot holds them from the Bishop of Bayeux.

2951 ii, 374b (16-15) <u>Odo of Bayeux; Stonham (Earl or Little)</u>: TRE Leofwine, a freeman commended to Eadric of Laxfield, held twenty acres of land in Stonham. Robert Malet was [seised] of this, as was his father on the day he died. In the same place Ælfric, a freeman commended to the antecessor of Richard fitz Gilbert, held twenty acres of land; and eleven freemen held fifty-two acres. Ten of these men were commended to this same Leofwine, who was commended to Robert Malet's antecessor. The eleventh, Sperun, was commended to Burgheard TRE, and he held eight acres of land. Roger Bigot now holds all of this from the Bishop of Bayeux.

2952 ii, 374b (16-16) <u>Odo of Bayeux; Olden</u>: TRE Ælfric, a freeman commended to Saxi, held sixteen acres of land in Olden. Roger de Raismes claims (*calumpniatur*) that he held this Ælfric from his fee when they were delivered (*postquam fuissent liberati*) to the bishop. In the same place there were six freemen with fifty-two acres of land. The Abbot of Bury had the commendation of one and a half of these men – Leofwine and Thormær – and Beorhtweald was commended to Eadric, Robert Malet's antecessor. Now Roger Bigot holds all of this from the Bishop of Bayeux, and Werengar holds from him.

2953 ii, 375a (16-20) <u>Odo of Bayeux; Coddenham (near Needham Market)</u>: TRE Almær, a freeman commended to the Abbot of Ely, held sixty acres of land in Coddenham. In the same place there were fifteen freemen with seventy-nine acres of land. Six of these men were commended to Saxi, Ranulf Peverel's antecessor. Odo of Bayeux now holds.

2954 ii, 375b (16-21) <u>Odo of Bayeux; Olden</u>: TRE there were eight freemen with forty acres of land in Olden. Four of these men, who held twenty-five acres of land, were commended to Saxi, Ranulf Peverel's antecessor. Now the Bishop of Bayeux holds this.

2955 ii, 375b (16-22) <u>Odo of Bayeux; Stonham (Earl or Little)</u>: TRE Wulfric, a freeman commended to the Abbot of Ely, held sixty acres of land in Stonham. In the same place Alweald the Priest and Godwig, both freemen commended to Saxi, Ranulf Peverel's antecessor, held forty acres of land. Now Odo of Bayeux holds this.

2956 ii, 375b (16-23) <u>Odo of Bayeux; Hemingstone</u>: TRE two freemen commended to Saxi, Ranulf Peverel's antecessor, held ten acres of land in Hemingstone. Ralph de Savenay now holds this from Roger Bigot, who holds from the Bishop of Bayeux.

2957 ii, 375b–376a (16-25) <u>Odo of Bayeux; Helmingham</u>: TRE Durand, a freeman commended to Eadric of Laxfield, Robert Malet's antecessor, held eighty acres of land in Helmingham. Now the Bishop of Bayeux holds it.

2958 ii, 376a (16-26) <u>Odo of Bayeux; Helmingham</u>: TRE Balki, commended to Æthelstan, held forty acres of land in Helmingham. In the same place Blachmann, a freeman half commended to a man commended to Eadric, Robert Malet's antecessor, and half commended to Saxi, held twenty-four acres of land; and Godric, a freeman half commended to a man commended to Eadric, Robert Malet's antecessor, and half commended to Saxi, held twenty acres of land. Also in Helmingham there were eleven freemen with seventy-one acres of land. Saxi, Ranulf Peverel's antecessor, had the commendation of two and a half of these men, and another half was commended to a man commended to Eadric, Robert Malet's antecessor. Now Odo of Bayeux holds all of this.

2959   ii, 376b (16-29) <u>Odo of Bayeux; Ulverston, Ashfield</u>: TRE Godwig held
fifteen acres of land in Ulverston and eight acres of land in Ashfield. In the
same place Gode, a freeman commended to a man commended to Eadric,
Robert Malet's antecessor, held fifteen acres of land. Now Odo of Bayeux
holds all of this.

2960   ii, 376b (16-30) <u>Odo of Bayeux; Ulverston</u>: TRE a freeman, Alwine the
Priest, a sixth of whom was commended to a man commended to Robert
Malet's antecessor, and five-sixths of whom was commended to Saxi, Ranulf
Peverel's antecessor, held forty acres of land in Ulverston. On the day he
died, William Malet had been seised (*erat saisitus*) of a fourth of this land and
of the priest who lived there. Now Roger Bigot holds this from the Bishop
of Bayeux, and Ralph de Savenay holds from him.

2961   ii, 377a (16-33) <u>Odo of Bayeux; Winston</u>: TRE twenty-one freemen held a
carucate of land in Winston. Two acres of this land were in Debenham, in
the demesne of Saxi, Ranulf Peverel's antecessor. One of these men, with
twelve acres of land, was commended to Bury St. Edmund's and was seised of
this (*fuit inde saisitus*) until Earl Ralph forfeited (*forisfecit*). Saxi had the
commendation of eight of these men; the Abbot of Ely had the commendation and soke over all the others except for two, that is, Alwine and Leofwine,
who were commended to a man commended to Eadric, Robert Malet's
antecessor. Now Odo of Bayeux holds this.

2962   ii, 377a (16-34) <u>Odo of Bayeux; Ashfield</u>: TRE Swærting the Priest, a
freeman in the soke and commendation of the abbot, held thirty acres of land
in Ashfield. Walter de Dol had been seised (*erat saisitus*) of this priest when
Walter forfeited (*forisfecit*) his land. Afterwards, Earl Hugh was seised, so the
hundred testifies. Northmann says that the King sent him a writ that he
should seise (*misit ei unum brevem ut saisiret*) Ralph de Savenay of all the
freemen over whom Hubert de Port had seised (*saisierat*) the bishop. Northmann thus seised (*saisiuit*) Ralph de Savenay of the priest. Northmann,
however, does not know if Hubert had first seised (*saisierat*) the bishop of the
priest. When they came into the county, the King's barons found the priest in
peace between (*invenerunt barones regis in pace inter*) Roger Bigot and Earl
Hugh, and so he shall be in peace until this be adjudged (*ita erit in pace donec sit
derationatus*).

2963   ii, 377b (16-38) <u>Odo of Bayeux; Ulverston</u>: TRE two freemen, Ælfric and
Leofwine, the first commended to Wihtgar and the second commended to a
man commended to Eadric, Robert Malet's antecessor, held thirty acres of
land in Ulverston. Now Roger Bigot holds this from the Bishop of Bayeux,
and Werengar holds from him.

2964   ii, 378a (16-41) <u>Odo of Bayeux; Raydon</u>: TRE Eadwig, a freeman, held a
carucate of land in Raydon. In the same place Smeri, a freeman commended
to Ælfric Kemp antecessor of Eudo Dapifer, held thirty acres of land. Now
the Bishop of Bayeux holds all of this.

2965   ii, 378b (17-1) <u>Ramsey Abbey; rubric</u>: [An "f," for "*fecit retornam,*" appears in the margin, opposite the rubric which marks the beginning of Ramsey Abbey's holdings, indicating that the abbey made a return.]

2966 ii, 379a (18-1) <u>Bishop of Thetford; Hoxne</u>: TRE Æthelmær bishop of Elmham held nine carucates of land in Hoxne. Now William bishop of Thetford holds it. There was a market in this manor both in the time of King Edward and after the coming of King William, and it was set up (*sedebat*) on Saturdays. William Malet made his castle at Eye, and he made another market in his castle on the same day that there was a market in the bishop's manor. Because of this, the bishop's market worsened (*peioratum est*), so that it has little value. Now it is set up on Fridays. The market at Eye, nonetheless, takes place on Saturday, and Robert Malet now holds it by the King's gift (*de dono regis*).

2967 ii, 379a (18-4) <u>Bishop of Thetford; Homersfield</u>: TRE Bishop Æthelmær held five carucates of land in Homersfield. Now William bishop of Thetford holds it. He has soke and sake over the ferding of South Elmham, except for the men of Archbishop Stigand. And Abbot Baldwin, through the testimony of the hundred (*per testimonium hundreti*), had a writ (*brevem*) of King Edward that he himself ought to have the soke and sake over the land and men of Bury St. Edmund's.

2968 ii, 379b (19-2) <u>Bishop of Thetford; Mendham</u>: TRE Ulf, a thegn, held a carucate of land in Mendham. Later Bishops Æthelmær and Herfast held it. Now William bishop of Thetford holds it. More land belongs to this manor, but it is in the returns of Norfolk (*in breviata in Norfolc*).

2969 ii, 379b (19-9) <u>Bishop of Thetford; Chickering</u>: TRE a commended freeman held twenty-eight acres of land in Chickering. In the same place a free woman held eight acres of land. Robert Malet's antecessor had her commendation. Bishop Æthelmær had soke and sake. Now the Bishop of Thetford holds.

2970 ii, 380a–b (19-16) <u>Bishop of Thetford; South Elmham</u>: TRE Alwine, a freeman commended to the thegn Ingvar, held two carucates and twenty acres of land in South Elmham. In the same place Alwig, a freeman commended to Eadric of Laxfield, held thirty acres of land. William Malet had been seised (*erat saisitus*) of this on the day he died. Now William holds all of this from the Bishop of Thetford.

2971 ii, 381a (20-1) <u>Bishop of Rochester; rubric</u>: [An "f," for "*fecit retornam*," appears in the margin, opposite the rubric which marks the beginning of the Bishop of Rochester's holdings, indicating that he made a return.]

2972 ii, 381a (20-1) <u>Bishop of Rochester; Freckenham</u>: TRE Gauti, a thegn of Earl Harold, held ten carucates of land in Freckenham. Afterwards, Lanfranc, by order of the King (*iussu regis*), adjudged it (*derationatus est*) to be in the bishopric of Rochester. Earl Ralph added four freemen to this manor, which he annexed (*invasit*), with eight acres of land. Now the Bishop of Rochester holds all of this.

2973 ii, 381b (21-2) <u>Ely Abbey; Rattlesden</u>: TRE a freeman, whose soke and sake was Ely Abbey's, held eight acres of land in Rattlesden. Falc, a man of Bury St. Edmund's, held these eight acres while Ely Abbey was in the King's hand, and he has held them until now. He denies, however, that he might have kept back service (*negat se detinuisse servitium*).

2974 ii, 382b (21-13) Ely Abbey; Buxhall: There is a sokeman in Buxhall with ten acres of forfeited land (*foreface terre*). Ely Abbey now holds.

2975 ii, 382b–383a (21-16) Ely Abbey; Barking: TRE Ely Abbey held seven carucates of land in Barking with soke and sake. Four freemen with six acres were added to this manor TRW. Hardwin had one and a half of these freemen when he forfeited (*forisfecit*). Now the Abbot of Ely holds all of this. The value of the manor was £16, and the Abbot gave (*dedit*) it at farm for £20.

2976 ii, 383a (21-17) Ely Abbey; Darmsden: TRE twenty-five freemen held a carucate of land in Darmsden, and Ely Abbey had the commendation and soke. Roger Bigot holds this land from the Abbot of Ely because the Abbot established his title against him in front of (*derationavit super eum coram*) the Bishop of St. Lô. Prior to this Roger held it from the King.

2977 ii, 383a (21-19) Ely Abbey; Horswold: TRE a freeman commended to and in the soke of Ely held twenty-two and a half acres of land in Horswold. Afterwards Roger d'Auberville held it from the King. The Abbot of Ely has established title (*derationavit*) against him, and now Roger holds from the abbot.

2978 ii, 383b (21-26) Ely Abbey; Barham: TRE Ely Abbey held four carucates of land in Barham. In the same place a freeman in the soke and commendation of the Abbot of Ely held thirty-five acres of land. Roger d'Auberville held this from the King. Now he holds it from the Abbot of Ely.

2979 ii, 383b (21-27) Ely Abbey; Sharpstone: TRE three freemen in the soke and commendation of the Abbot of Ely held eight acres of land in Sharpstone. Afterwards, William d'Ecouis held this from the King. Now he holds from the Abbot of Ely.

2980 ii, 383b (21-28) Ely Abbey; Winston: TRE and TRW Ely Abbey holds a carucate and forty acres of land in demesne in Winston. Alsige, a freeman in the soke and commendation of the Abbot, was added to this manor with thirty acres of land.

2981 ii, 383b–384a (21-29) Ely Abbey; Westerfield: TRE Asrøthr, a sokeman of the Abbot of Ely, held twenty-five acres of land in Westerfield. Now Hervey holds this from the abbot, by order of the King (*iussu regis*). In the same place Thorkil, a commended freeman, held eight acres of land. Afterwards Hervey held this from the King. Now, so he himself says, he holds it from the Abbot of Ely, by order of the King (*iussu regis*).

2982 ii, 384a (21-30) Ely Abbey; Pettaugh: TRE Thorkil, half commended to the Abbot of Ely and half to Gyrth, held twenty acres of land in Pettaugh. Afterwards, Hervey held this from the King, and now he holds from the abbot, by the King's order (*iussu regis*), so he himself says. The soke was half the abbot's and half Hugh's antecessor's.

2983 ii, 384a (21-31) <u>Ely Abbey; Debenham</u>: TRE a half freeman in soke and commendation held four acres of land in Debenham. Afterwards, Robert Malet held it from the King; now he holds from the Abbot of Ely.

2984 ii, 384b (21-39) <u>Ely Abbey; Wetheringsett</u>: TRE Ely Abbey held four carucates of land in Wetheringsett. Now Ralph de Savenay holds a quarter of this land from Ranulf Peverel. Ely Abbey holds the rest.

2985 ii, 384b (21-40) <u>Ely Abbey; Chedburgh</u>: TRE two freemen held two carucates of land in Chedburgh. The whole of this land lay in the demesne of Ely Abbey, with all customs except the six forfeitures (*sex forisfacturas*) of Bury St. Edmund's. Now Frodo holds it from the Abbot of Ely.

2986 ii, 384b (21-41) <u>Ely Abbey; Clopton (in Wickhambrook)</u>: TRE three freemen held twenty acres of land in Clopton. Ely had the soke, sake, and commendation. Now Ely Abbey holds this land. Bury St. Edmund's has the six forfeitures (*vi forisfacturas*).

2987 ii, 385a (21-45) <u>Ely Abbey; Wingfield</u>: TRE a freeman commended to Ely Abbey held two carucates of land in Wingfield. There were also thirteen freemen there with eighty acres of land. Robert Malet's antecessor had the commendation of one of these men. Roger Bigot claims (*reclamat*) this by gift of the King (*de dono regis*), but the Abbot of Ely has established his title (*derationavit*) against him. Now Roger holds through a postponement (*per respectum*).

2988 ii, 385a–b (21-46) <u>Ely Abbey; Monk Soham</u>: TRE a commended freeman held a carucate of land in Monk Soham. Robert Malet held this from the King. The abbot, however, has established title (*derationavit*), and Robert now holds from him.

2989 ii, 385b (21-49) <u>Ely Abbey; Trimley</u>: TRE Leofric, a freeman commended to the Abbot of Ely, held forty acres of land in Trimley. Afterwards, Roger Bigot held this from the King. The Abbot of Ely, however, has established title (*derationavit*), and Roger now holds it from him.

2990 ii, 385b (21-50) <u>Ely Abbey; Walton</u>: TRE Ælfgifu, a free woman commended to the Abbot of Ely, held sixteen acres of land in Walton. Now Hervey de Berry holds this from the Abbot of Ely. He used to hold it from the King, but the abbot has established title (*derationavit*).

2991 ii, 385b (21-52) <u>Ely Abbey; Kembroke</u>: TRE Godric, a freeman of Ely Abbey, held seven acres of land in Kembroke. Afterwards, Roger Bigot held this from the King, but the abbot has established title (*derationavit*). Now Roger holds from the abbot.

2992 ii, 386a–b (21-58) <u>Ely Abbey; Thistleton</u>: TRE Wulfmær, a freeman commended to Ely Abbey, held sixty acres of land in Thistleton. Five freemen were under him. Two of them were commended to Geoffrey de Mandeville's antecessor. Now the Abbot of Ely holds all of this.

2993 ii, 387b (21-83) <u>Ely Abbey; Bromeswell</u>: TRE two freemen commended to the Abbot of Ely held ten acres of land in Bromeswell. This is now in the Abbot of Ely's demesne. In the same vill, Hervey holds seventy freemen

whose commendation, soke, and sake the abbot had. Roger Bigot's antecessor had the commendation of one of these men with six acres of land.

2994 ii, 387b (21-85) Ely Abbey; Bredfield: TRE Robert Malet's antecessor held
six acres of land in Bredfield. Now Hervey de Berry holds it from the Abbot
of Ely.

2995 ii, 388a–b (21-95) Ely Abbey; Hoo (near Kettleburgh): TRE Ely Abbey held
three carucates of land in Hoo. William de Bouville took (*cepit*) one of these
carucates. Afterwards it was adjudged through the King's order, and the
Church was seised (*derationata est per praeceptum regis, et saisita aecclesiae*). But
William vouches his lord Geoffrey de Mandeville to warranty (*revocat ad
tutorem*), and he has given a pledge for it (*dedit inde vadem*). Now the land is in
the King's hand.

2996 ii, 388b (22-1) Gilbert bishop of Evreux; rubric: [An "f," for "*fecit retornam,*"
appears in the margin, opposite the rubric which marks the beginning of the
Bishop of Evreux's holdings, indicating that he made a return.]

2997 ii, 389a (23-1) Abbot of Bernay; rubric: [An "f," for "*fecit retornam,*" appears
in the margin, opposite the rubric which marks the beginning of the Abbot
of Bernay's holdings, indicating that he made a return.]

2998 ii, 389a (23-1) Abbot of Bernay; Creeting St. Peter: TRE a freeman held
twenty acres of land in Creeting St. Peter. Now the Abbot of Bernay holds it.
In the same place there was a freeman with five acres of land. The King gave
(*dedit*) this to the Abbot of Bernay from Hardwin's fee.

2999 ii, 389a (24-1) Chatteris Abbey; rubric: [An "f," for "*fecit retornam,*" appears
in the margin, opposite the rubric which marks the beginning of the Chatteris
Abbey's holdings, indicating that the abbey made a return.]

3000 ii, 389b (25-1) Richard fitz Gilbert; Clare: TRE Ælfric Wihtgarson held
twenty-four carucates of land in Clare. In the time of King Edward he gave
(*dedit*) this manor to the Church of St. John, Clare with the consent
(*concedente*) of his son. He put (*imposuit*) a priest there named Leodmær and
others with him. Having made a charter (*facta etiam carta*), he entrusted the
church and the entire place to the custody (*ad custodiendum commisit*) of Abbot
Leofstan and into the custody (*in custodia*) of Wihtgar, his son. The clerks
could neither grant nor forfeit (*nec dare vel forisfecere*) this land away from St.
John's. After King William came, however, the King seised it in his hand
(*saisiuit eam in manu sua*). Now Richard fitz Gilbert holds it.

3001 ii, 389b (25-3) Richard fitz Gilbert; Desning: TRE Wihtgar held twenty
carucates of land in Desning. It was valued at £30; later and now at £40.
Nonetheless, Richard fitz Gilbert gave (*dedit*) it to a reeve at farm for £65,
but the manor could not bear it (*non potuit pati*).

3002 ii, 390a-391a (25-4, 5, 6, 7, 8, 9, 10, 11, 12, 13, 14, 15, 16, 17) Richard fitz
Gilbert; Denston, Clopton (in Wickhambrook), Dalham, Denham (near
Bury St. Edmund's), Hawkedon, Hawkedon, Wratting, Stansfield, Hundon,
Farley, Brockley (in Kedington), Kedington, Boyton (in Stoke by Clare),
Stoke by Clare: TRE a sokeman held two carucates and ten acres of land in

Denston; two sokemen held a carucate and eighty-one and a half acres of land in Clopton; a sokeman held two carucates of land in Dalham; two sokemen held three carucates of land in Denham; a sokeman held a carucate of land in Hawkedon; a sokeman held another carucate of land in Hawkedon; a sokeman held a carucate of land in Wratting; a sokeman held a carucate of land in Stansfield; a sokeman held a carucate of land in Hundon; ten sokemen held another carucate in Hundon; a sokeman held seven acres of land in Farley; a sokeman held half a carucate in Brockley; a sokeman held thirty acres of land in Kedington; a sokeman held sixty acres of land in Boyton; and a sokeman held thirty-seven acres of land in Stoke by Clare. Now Richard fitz Gilbert holds this land, and various men hold from him. TRE Wihtgar held all these sokemen with all customs except the six forfeitures (*vi forisfacturas*) of Bury St. Edmund's.

3003 ii, 391a (25-18) Richard fitz Gilbert; "Wimundestuna": TRE three sokemen held sixty-five acres of land in "Wimundestuna." Now Richard fitz Gilbert holds it. His antecessor had all customs from these.

3004 ii, 391a (25-19) Richard fitz Gilbert; Wattisham: TRE a freeman held fifteen acres of land in Wattisham. Wihtgar had the soke, and Bury St. Edmund's had the six forfeitures (*vi forisfacturas*). Now Richard fitz Gilbert holds.

3005 ii, 391a (25-25) Richard fitz Gilbert; Timworth: TRE a freeman commended only to Wihtgar, Richard's antecessor, held sixty acres of land in Timworth. Now Richard fitz Gilbert holds it. The soke is Bury St. Edmund's.

3006 ii, 391a–b (25-27) Richard fitz Gilbert; Westley: TRE three freemen commended to Wihtgar held eighty acres of land in Westley. Wihtgar had the soke except for the six forfeitures (*vi forefacturas*) of Bury St. Edmund's. Now Richard fitz Gilbert holds.

3007 ii, 391b–392a (25-35) Richard fitz Gilbert; Cavenham: TRE Wihtgar, Richard fitz Gilbert's antecessor, held five carucates of land in Cavenham with the soke, as a berewick of Desning. Now Richard fitz Gilbert holds it.

3008 ii, 392a (25-37) Richard fitz Gilbert; Tuddenham (near Mildenhall): TRE Richard fitz Gilbert's antecessor held one and a half carucates of land in Tuddenham. Now Richard fitz Gilbert holds it.

3009 ii, 392a (25-40) Richard fitz Gilbert; Herringswell: TRE three of Wihtgar's sokemen held sixty acres of land in Herringswell. There was a sokemen in the same place with a carucate of land. Half his land and the soke were Wihtgar's, by testimony (*teste*) of the hundred, and half the land with the soke was Bury St. Edmund's. Now Richard fitz Gilbert holds all of this.

3010 ii, 392b (25-51) Richard fitz Gilbert; Shelland: TRE Fin, Richard fitz Gilbert's antecessor, held twenty-three acres of land in Shelland. Now Richard fitz Gilbert holds it.

3011 ii, 392b–393a (25-52) Richard fitz Gilbert; Ipswich: TRE Wihtgar held the Church of St. Peter, Ipswich with six carucates of land. Roger the Sheriff claims (*calumpniatur*) one hundred acres of this land, five villeins, and a mill for the King's manor of Bramford. Five villeins from the same manor testify for him, and they offer this by means of any law through which anyone might judge (*offerunt legem qualem quis iudicaverit*). But the half-hundred of Ipswich testifies that all of this lay in the church TRE, and that Wihtgar held it. They offer to establish title (*offerunt derationari*). Now Richard fitz Gilbert holds all of this. In the same borough Richard has thirteen burgesses whom Fin held TRE. Fin had soke, sake, and commendation over four of them, and one is a slave. He had the commendation only over twelve of these men, but they lived on their own land and paid all customs in the borough. This is from Fin's honor (*de honore Fint*).

3012   ii, 393a (25-53) <u>Richard fitz Gilbert; Badley</u>: TRE Eskil held two carucates and twenty acres of land in Badley. Now Richard fitz Gilbert holds it in demesne. The abbot claims (*calumpniatur*) half a carucate of this land, by testimony (*teste*) of the hundred. Twenty-six freemen with a carucate and forty-five acres of land were added to this manor in the time of King William. Richard fitz Gilbert holds all of these men in the manor which Fin held. Fin himself held them through a loan (*per acommodationem*) from the sheriff, so the sheriff himself says.

3013   ii, 393b (25-55) <u>Richard fitz Gilbert; Flowton</u>: TRE Godmann held two carucates of land in Flowton. Wihtgar had his commendation, and the King and the earl had the soke. Now Germund holds it from Richard fitz Gilbert. Germund added fifteen acres to this manor in the time of King William, which a priest held freely TRE in the soke of the King and the earl.

3014   ii, 393b (25-56) <u>Richard fitz Gilbert; Bricett (Great or Little)</u>: TRE Bondi, a freeman, held a carucate of land in Bricett. Queen Edith had the commendation only, but Richard fitz Gilbert claims (*clamat*) it from Wihtgar's fee. Roger d'Orbec holds this from Richard fitz Gilbert. Roger de Raismes claims (*reclamat*) this land by the King's gift (*de dono regis*), and he was seised (*saisitus fuit*) of it. In the same place Roger d'Orbec holds two freemen with fifteen acres of land. Roger de Raismes claims (*calumpniatur*) this as well, but Richard fitz Gilbert claims (*reclamat*) it from the fee of Wihtgar. In the same place Ranulf Peverel holds four acres of land which belonged to this manor TRE. Richard fitz Gilbert claims (*reclamat*) this from Fin's fee.

3015   ii, 393b–394a (25-57) <u>Richard fitz Gilbert; "Rigneseta"</u>: TRE Harthacnut, a freeman, held one hundred acres of land in "Rigneseta." Now Geoffrey holds it from Richard fitz Gilbert. In the time of King William, Fin added three freemen to this manor with twenty acres of land. Geoffrey holds this land and gave (*dedit*) it at farm for 70s., but he could only have 60s.

3016   ii, 394a (25-59) <u>Richard fitz Gilbert; Ashbocking</u>: TRE Wulfric, a freeman, held sixty acres of land in Ashbocking. TRW Fin added eight freemen with thirty-five acres of land to this manor, and a sokeman with twelve acres of land, who could not withdraw from Ely Abbey. Osbern of Wanchy holds all of this from Richard fitz Gilbert, who claims (*reclamat*) it from Fin's fee. Roger de Raismes claims (*calumpniatur*) two of these freemen from his own fee and was seised (*saisitus fuit*) of them. Fin had nothing from any of this in the time of King Edward.

3017 ii, 394a–b (25-60) Richard fitz Gilbert; Thurleston: TRE there were eighteen freemen in the demesne of Thurleston. Twelve and a half were commended to Ælfric the Priest, who was commended to Wihtgar. They held sixty-four acres of land. Richard fitz Gilbert's antecessor did not have the commendation of the others – Ælfric, Waldwin, Harold, Godwine, Wulfmær, and Ælfric. These men held twenty-four acres of land. Richard holds these men because Bishop Herfast held them when Richard established his title (*derationavit*) to the Church of St. Peter, Ipswich, against him. But now Richard did not know that they did not belong to his fee.

3018 ii, 394b–395b (25-64, 65, 66, 67, 68, 69, 70, 71, 72, 73, 74, 75) Richard fitz Gilbert; Shotley, "Torp," "Purtepyt," Kirkton, Erwarton, "Eduinestuna," unidentified land in Samford Hundred, Burstall, Boynton, "Toft," Raydon, Higham (near Brantham): TRE Ceolweald, commended to Ælfric, held sixty acres of land in Shotley; Osbern, a freeman of Ælfric, held one hundred acres of land in "Torp" and sixty acres of land in "Purtepyt"; Edmund, a freeman, held sixty acres of land in Kirkton; and Strangwulf, a freeman, held sixty acres there as well, as did Thorir, a freeman of Gyrth. And Huna and Godric, two freemen, held fifteen acres there. Ailbern, a freeman, held sixty acres of land in Erwarton; Godric, a freeman, held thirty acres of land in "Eduinestuna"; Godric, Edwin, and Leofric held thirty-three acres of land in Samford Hundred; Ælfric Stari, a man commended to Gyrth, held forty acres of land in Burstall; Leofstan, a freeman commended to Fin, held fifty acres in Boynton; Alwine, a freeman commended to Esger the Staller, held twenty acres in "Toft"; Leofric, a freeman, held thirty acres in Raydon; and Godric, a freeman, held a carucate of land in Higham. Fin, Richard fitz Gilbert's antecessor, had nothing from any of these freemen in the time of King Edward, except for the commendation only of one of them. The soke of the whole is in East Bergholt. Richard holds these men from Fin's honor (*ad honorem*).

3019 ii, 395b (25-77) Richard fitz Gilbert; Burstall: TRE Leofric, a man commended to Earl Ælfgar, held seventeen acres of land in Burstall. Richard fitz Gilbert vouches (*revocat*) this from Fin's land. Wulfmær now holds it from Richard.

3020 ii, 395b–397a (25-78, 79, 80, 81, 82, 83, 84, 85, 86, 87, 88, 89, 90, 91, 92, 93, 94, 95, 96, 97, 98, 99, 100, 101, 102) Richard fitz Gilbert; Stansfield, Depden, Clopton, Wratting, Haverhill, Hanchet, Withersfield, Wratting, Chilbourne, Poslingford, Boyton, Boyton (in Stoke by Clare), Hawkedon, Clopton (in Wickhambrook), Bradley (Great or Little), Thurlow (Great or Little), Kedington, Haverhill, Withersfield, Stoke by Clare, Poslingford, Wickhambrook, Stradishall, Hawkedon, Haverhill: TRE Eadric Spuda, a freeman, held two carucates of land in Stansfield; Wulfflæd, a freeman, held one; and Crawa, a freeman, held sixty acres. Beorhtric the Black, a freeman, held two carucates of land in Depden; and Blæcwine and Godwine held two carucates there as well. Leofgeat, a freeman, held one and a half carucates of land in Clopton; Gode, a freeman, held two carucates and thirty acres of land in Wratting; Frithebiorn, a freeman, held eighty acres in Haverhill; and Alwine, a freeman, held one hundred acres in Hanchet. In Withersfield Wulfmær, a freeman, held fifty-one acres of land; Leofwaru, a freeman, held one hundred acres there; and Alwine, a freeman, held three carucates there. Ailbern, a freeman, held three carucates of land in Wratting; Godwine, a freeman, held two carucates in Chilbourne; Eadric, a freeman, thirty-five acres in Poslingford; Wulfgar, a freeman, eight acres in Boyton; and Ainuar, a freeman, twenty-four acres there. Alwine, a freeman, held forty acres of land in Hawkedon; Roc thirteen acres in Clopton; two freemen sixty-nine acres in Bradley; ten freemen a carucate in Thurlow. Ten freemen held a carucate in Kedington; thirteen freemen held a carucate and sixty acres in Haverhill; nine freemen held one and a half carucates of land in Withersfield; twenty-one freemen held a carucate in Stoke by Clare; six freemen held eighty-five acres in Poslingford; a freeman held sixty acres in Wickhambrook; sixteen freemen held a carucate of land in Stradishall; eight freemen held thirty acres in Hawkedon; and two freemen held twenty-six acres in Haverhill. All of these freemen could sell and grant their land TRE, but Wihtgar, Richard fitz Gilbert's antecessor, had the soke and sake, except for the six forfeitures (*vi forisfacturas*) of Bury St. Edmund's, as we have said above (*ut superius diximus*). Now Richard fitz Gilbert holds all of this.

3021 ii, 397a (25-103) Richard fitz Gilbert; Bradley (Great or Little): TRE three freemen – Wulfwine, Leofric, and Leofwine – held fifteen acres of land in Bradley. A fourth freeman, Bondi, held a carucate of land there. Richard's antecessor did not have their commendation TRE; Bury St. Edmund's had all the soke. Now Richard fitz Gilbert holds.

3022 ii, 397a (25-104) Richard fitz Gilbert; Thurlow (Great or Little): TRE two of Eadgifu's sokemen, with all customs, held twenty-five acres of land in Thurlow. Earl Ralph held them when he forfeited (*forisfecit*). Now Widard holds this from Richard fitz Gilbert.

3023 ii, 397b (25-105) Richard fitz Gilbert; "Wimundestuna": TRE there were six freemen with two carucates and eleven acres of land in "Wimundestuna." The hundred does not know if one of these six men, Beorhtric, could sell his land or not in the time of King Edward. But it testifies that they saw him swear (*iurare*) that he could neither grant nor sell his land away from Richard's antecessor. Gerard now holds this from Richard fitz Gilbert.

3024 ii, 397b (25-108) Richard fitz Gilbert; Kersey: TRW Richard fitz Gilbert holds five acres of land in Kersey, which a freeman held TRE. His antecessor had the soke and commendation.

3025 ii, 397b (25-111) Richard fitz Gilbert; Whatfield: TRE three freemen held sixty acres of land in Whatfield. Now Richard fitz Gilbert holds it. His antecessor had their commendation TRE with soke and sake. Bury St. Edmund's had the six forfeitures (*vi forisfacturas*).

3026 ii, 397b (25-112) Richard fitz Gilbert; Stone Street (in Hadleigh): TRE a freeman held twenty-four acres of land in Stone Street. Now Richard fitz Gilbert holds it. His antecessor had half the commendation and the Abbot of Ely had the other half. Ranulf Peverel claims (*calumpniatur*) both half this land and that it was delivered to him (*fuit ei liberata*) in Loose.

3027 ii, 398a (26-1) William de Warenne; Rattlesden: TRE two freemen of Ely Abbey with soke and sake held land in Rattlesden. One of them, who held forty acres, could sell his land. The other, who held sixty acres, could not. Now Humphrey fitz Rodric holds this from William de Warenne. It is in exchange (*de escangio*) for Lewes [Sussex].

3028 ii, 398a (26-2) William de Warenne; Gedding: TRE two freemen commended to and in the soke of Bury St. Edmund's held sixty acres of land in Gedding. Now William de Warenne holds it. It is in exchange (*de escangio*) for Lewes [Sussex].

3029 ii, 398a (26-3) William de Warenne; Elvedon: TRE a freeman commended only to Ely Abbey and in the soke of Bury St. Edmund's, held two carucates of land in Elvedon. Now Nicholas holds it from William de Warenne. It is in exchange (*pro escangio*) for Lewes [Sussex].

3030 ii, 398a (26-4) William de Warenne; Herringswell: TRE a reeve, who was a freeman of Toki, held a carucate of land in Herringswell, but he could not sell it. It is from Frederick's fee, in the soke of Bury St. Edmund's. Now Roger holds it from William de Warenne. In the same place one of Frederick's antecessor's freemen held forty acres of land in the soke of Bury St. Edmund's. Now Nicholas holds this from William de Warenne.

3031 ii, 398a (26-5) William de Warenne; Buxhall: TRE Munulf the Priest, a man commended to Ely Abbey and in the soke of the King, held half a carucate and twenty acres of land in Buxhall. Now William de Warenne holds it in exchange (*pro escangio*) for Lewes [Sussex].

3032 ii, 398b (26-8) William de Warenne; Barnham: TRE Bosten held half a carucate of land in Barnham. Hugh fitz Gold now holds it from William de Warenne. There are also three freemen there with four acres of land. William's antecessor had their commendation.

3033 ii, 399a–400a (26-12a, 12b, 12c, 12d) William de Warenne; Wrentham; Henstead: TRE Eadric, a freeman, held two carucates of land in Wrentham. Thorkil of Wrentham also held two carucates there. He was a man of Eadric, antecessor of Robert Malet. Wulfric, a freeman, held another two carucates there; and twenty freemen held 360 acres of land. Now Robert de Pierrepont holds all of this from William de Warenne. In the same place Healfdene, a freeman, held three carucates of land; another freeman held half a carucate there; Ælfric of Sanford held fifty acres; and eight freemen held one and a half carucates and ten acres. Now William fitz Reginald holds all of this under William de Warenne. TRW Godfrey de Pierrepont holds a carucate of land in Henstead, which is a berewick of Wrentham. Two freemen with thirty acres of land have been added. From all of this, six acres of land were taken away (*sunt ablate*) from Count Alan: William's men took it away (*abstulerunt*) from him, by testimony (*teste*) of the hundred.

3034   ii, 400a (26-13) William de Warenne; Middleton: TRE Ælfric, a freeman, held two carucates of land in Middleton. Now Ranulf nephew of William de Warenne holds it from William. This Ælfric was a man of Eadric, antecessor of Robert, and William Malet and Robert were seised (*fuerunt saisiti*) of this land. Five freemen and half a priest with fifty-five acres of land were added to this manor.

3035   ii, 400a (26-14) William de Warenne; Thorington (near Dunwich): TRE Ælfric, a freeman, held two carucates of land in Thorington. Now Godfrey de Pierrepont holds it from William de Warenne. Robert Malet claims (*reclamat*) this land, as he does the other. This is testified by the hundred.

3036   ii, 400a–b (26-15) William de Warenne; Covehithe: TRE Eadric, a freeman, held two carucates of land in Covehithe. Fourteen freemen with 100 acres of land have been added to this manor. William's men have been seised (*habant sasitos*) of two halves of these freemen against Count Alan. Now William fitz Reginald holds all of this from William de Warenne.

3037   ii, 400b (26-16) William de Warenne; Burgh (near Woodbridge): TRE Æthelric, a freeman, held a carucate and twenty acres of land in Burgh. In the same place eleven freemen and three half freemen, commended to the same Æthelric, held fifty acres of land. William de Warenne took (*recepit*) the whole of this as a carucate of land, and Robert de Glanville holds from him.

3038   ii, 401b–402a (27-7) Swein of Essex; Aveley: TRE Brungar, a freeman commended only to Robert fitz Wimarc, Swein of Essex's father, held a carucate of land in Aveley. Bury St. Edmund's had the soke and sake. Now Swein of Essex holds. In the time of King Edward stolen horses were found (*fuerunt furati equi inventi*) in Brungar's house. The Abbot of Bury, therefore, who had his soke and sake, and Robert, who had commendation over him, came to a plea about this theft (*venerunt de hoc furto ad placitum*), so the hundred testifies. They left in friendship and without a judgment that the hundred has seen (*discesserunt amicabiliter sine iudicio quod vidisset hundret*).

3039   ii, 403a (28-2) Eudo Dapifer; Lakenheath, Brandon: TRE six sokemen held two carucates of land in Lakenheath and Brandon. Ely Abbey had the soke, and these men could not sell their land. They were delivered (*liberati fuerunt*) to Lisois, Eudo Dapifer's antecessor. Nonetheless, Lisois acknowledged (*recognovit*) afterwards that he held them from Ely Abbey. Eudo Dapifer held them with soke and sake.

3040   ii, 403a–b (28-6) Eudo Dapifer; Great Glemham: TRE Wulfric, half commended to the Abbot of Ely and half to Robert Malet's antecessor, held two carucates of land in Great Glemham, and William Malet was seised (*saisitus fuit*) of it. In the same place ten freemen commended to Wulfric with fifty-three acres of land have been added to this manor. Pirot holds this from Eudo Dapifer. William Malet was seised (*fuit saisitus*) of all of this.

3041   ii, 403b–404a (29-1) <u>Roger d'Auberville; Finborough (Great or Little)</u>: TRE Leofsunu, a freeman commended only to Guthmund, Hugh de Montfort's antecessor, held two carucates of land in Finborough. Now Roger d'Auberville holds it. In the same manor there were eighteen freemen, commended only to the same Leofsunu and in the soke of the King and the earl, with a carucate of land. Roger d'Auberville holds these in exchange (*pro escangio*). In the same place six sokemen belonging to Thorney, King Edward's manor, with commendation, sake, soke, and supply (*summagio*), had sixty-five and a half acres of land. Roger holds these in exchange (*pro escangio*). There were also two freemen there, commended only to Guthmund, Hugh's antecessor, and in the soke of the King and the earl, with eighty acres of land. Roger holds these in the same way. He also holds a freeman commended to Eustace's antecessor with four acres of land; a freeman commended to Leofstan of Looes with four acres; a freeman still commended to the King with twenty acres; a freeman with thirty acres, belonging to the commendation of Wihtgar, Richard's antecessor, but in the soke of the hundred; and four freemen with sixteen acres, in the soke of the hundred. Richard d'Auberville holds all of these freemen through exchange (*pro escangio*).

3042   ii, 404b (29-8) <u>Roger d'Auberville; Bricett (Great or Little)</u>: TRE Leofric, a freeman commended to Godric of Ringshall, William d'Auberville's antecessor, held ten acres of land in Bricett. Now Gilbert holds it from Roger d'Auberville.

3043   ii, 404b (29-9) <u>Roger d'Auberville; Horswold</u>: TRE Hearding and Tovi, freemen commended to King Edward, held twenty-two and a half acres of land in Horswold. Now William holds it from Roger d'Auberville. Roger d'Auberville holds this land from the Abbot of Ely, by order (*praecepto*) of the Bishop of St. Lô, so Roger himself says.

3044   ii, 404b (29-11) <u>Roger d'Auberville; Henley</u>: [The following information is enrolled under the rubric of Roger d'Auberville: TRE Tepekin, a freeman commended to Harold, held two carucates of land in Henley. Four freemen were added in the same place with eight acres of land. Now Eudo Dapifer holds this in his demesne.]

3045   ii, 405a (30-1) <u>William brother of Roger d'Auberville; rubric</u>: [An "f," for "*fecit retornam*," appears in the margin, opposite the rubric which marks the beginning of William brother of Roger d'Auberville's holdings, indicating that he made a return.]

3046   ii, 405b (30-2) <u>William brother of Roger d'Auberville; Ringshall</u>: TRE Eadric, a freeman commended to William d'Auberville's antecessor, held five acres of land in Ringshall. Now William d'Auberville holds it in demesne.

3047   ii, 405b (30-3) <u>William brother of Roger d'Auberville; Bricett (Great or Little)</u>: TRE Eskil, a freeman commended to Leofric Hobbeson, held sixty acres of land in Bricett. Now William d'Auberville has forty acres, but the whole was delivered (*liberatum fuit*) to him. Hugh d'Houdain took away (*tulit*) the twenty acres, so William and the hundred say. But Hugh himself is a prisoner of the King (*est in captione regis*), and was not, therefore, able to give a response (*non potuit dare responsum*).

3048 ii, 405b (31-2) <u>Hugh de Montfort; Wattisfield</u>: TRW Hugh de Montfort has nine freemen with sixteen acres of land in Wattisfield in demesne. Two of these men were commended to Bury St. Edmund's TRE and the other seven to the antecessor of Earl Hugh.

3049 ii, 406a–b (31-8, 13a) <u>Hugh de Montfort; Nacton</u>: TRW Hugh de Montfort holds two carucates of land in Nacton. On the day King Edward died, Guthmund held it from Ely Abbey in such a way that he could neither sell nor grant it away from the abbey, and through such an agreement that after his death it ought to return to the Church in demesne (*per istam conventionem quod post mortem suam debebat redire in ecclesia in dominio*). This is testified by the hundred.

3050 ii, 406b (31-15) <u>Hugh de Montfort; Burgh (near Woodbridge)</u>: TRE a freeman in Burgh, half commended to Ely Abbey and half commended to Robert Malet's antecessor, held twenty acres of land. Now there are three men there. This is held by Hugh de Montfort.

3051 ii, 406b (31-19) <u>Hugh de Montfort; Charsfield</u>: TRE two freemen commended to Ely Abbey and half of one commended to Hugh de Montfort's antecessor, held seven acres of land in Charsfield. Now Hugh de Montfort holds it.

3052 ii, 406b–407a (31-20) <u>Hugh de Montfort; Cretingham</u>: TRE Ælfric, a freeman of Harold, held two and a half carucates and fifteen acres of land in Cretingham. In the same place there were ten freemen commended to the same Ælfric with forty-six acres of land. William d'Arques claims (*calumpniatur*) two halves of these men and nine and a half acres of land. One of these freemen was commended to Eadric of Laxfield, and William Malet was seised (*fuit saisiatus*) on the day he died. Now Roger de Candos holds all of this from Hugh de Montfort.

3053 ii, 407b (31-34) <u>Hugh de Montfort; Rushmere (near Lowestoft)</u>: TRE a freeman commended to Gyrth held sixteen acres of land in Rushmere. Now Hugh de Montfort holds it in demesne. The hundred testifies that Walter de Dol was seised (*fuit saiatus*) of four [*sic*] of the abovementioned freemen on the day he forfeited (*se forisfecit*), and later Earl Hugh was. Now Hugh de Montfort holds, but he does not, by testimony (*teste*) of the hundred, hold through livery (*per liberationem*). Hugh de Montfort's men say that Walter himself held them from Hugh.

3054 ii, 408b (31-43) <u>Hugh de Montfort; Dagworth</u>: TRE seven freemen held two carucates of land in Dagworth. They were commended only to Guthmund, Hugh de Montfort's antecessor. They were in the soke of the King and the earl. Now Hugh de Montfort holds.

3055 ii, 408b–409a (31-44) <u>Hugh de Montfort; Dagworth</u>: TRW Hugh de

Montfort holds six sokemen with a carucate of land in Dagworth. They belong in the King's manor of Thorney and to the realm (*de regione*) with all customs. Hugh claims (*reclamat*) these six sokemen through livery (*ex liberatione*).

3056 ii, 409a (31-45) Hugh de Montfort; Wetherden: TRE seventeen freemen held two carucates of land in Wetherden. They were commended only to Guthmund, Hugh de Montfort's antecessor, and were in the soke of the King and the earl. Now Hugh de Montfort holds.

3057 ii, 409a (31-46) Hugh de Montfort; "Eruestuna": TRE ten freemen held half a carucate of land in "Eruestuna." They were commended only to Guthmund, Hugh de Montfort's antecessor. Now Hugh de Montfort holds.

3058 ii, 409a (31-47) Hugh de Montfort; "Torpe": TRE sixteen men commended only to Hugh de Montfort's antecessor and in the soke of the King and the earl, held a carucate of land in "Torpe." Now Hugh de Montfort holds it.

3059 ii, 409a (31-48) Hugh de Montfort; "Vltuna": TRE three freemen commended only to Guthmund, and in the soke of the King and the earl, held half a carucate and thirteen acres of land in "Vltuna." Now Hugh de Montfort holds it. There is a mill there, but the Count of Mortain claims (*calumpniatur*) half of it, and the hundred testifies.

3060 ii, 409a–b (31-49) Hugh de Montfort; Chilton (in Stowmarket), "Torstuna": TRW Hugh de Montfort holds sixteen sokemen in Chilton and "Torstuna' in demesne, through livery (*ex liberatione*), so Hugh says. All of these freemen and the soke were delivered (*fuerunt liberati*), so all Hugh's men say, for two manors of five carucates of land. But they belonged to King Edward's manor of Thorney with all customs, by testimony (*teste*) of the hundred.

3061 ii, 409b (31-50) Hugh de Montfort; Dagworth: TRE Breme, a freeman of King Edward, held one and a half carucates of land in Dagworth. Breme was killed at the Battle of Hastings (*fuit occisus in bello Hastingensi*), and his land was delivered (*liberata fuit*) to Hugh de Montfort in exchange (*de escangio*) as half a carucate. Now William fitz Gross holds this manor from Hugh de Montfort.

3062 ii, 409b (31-51) Hugh de Montfort; Old Newton: TRE Alwine of Mendlesham held a freeman with half a carucate of land in Old Newton. Now Hugh de Montfort holds this in exchange (*pro escangio*). In the same place Hugh holds two freemen in demesne through livery in exchange (*ex liberatione pro escangio*). They have twenty-seven acres of land, and their soke was in the hundred.

3063 ii, 409b–410a (31-53) Hugh de Montfort; Thorney: TRW Roger de Candos holds a carucate of land in Thorney from Hugh de Montfort, which was in the demesne manor and in the soke of King Edward. Ralph the Staller had it in mortgage (*in vadimonio*) from Toli the Sheriff, so the hundred heard say, but it saw neither writs nor livery (*non vidit breves neque liberatorem*). Ralph held it on the day King Edward died. Later, his son Ralph held it. This land, however, was delivered (*fuit liberata*) to Hugh. In the same place Roger holds two freemen with twenty acres of land from Hugh de Montfort. This is in exchange (*est de escangio*).

3064 ii, 410a (31-54) <u>Hugh de Montfort; Beyton</u>: TRE a freeman of Eadgifu the Fair held forty acres of land in Beyton. Now Hugh de Montfort holds it in exchange (*pro escangio*).

3065 ii, 410a (31-56) <u>Hugh de Montfort; Battisford</u>: TRE Ælfric, a freeman, held a carucate of land in Battisford. Hugh de Montfort added five freemen with a carucate and ten acres of land to this manor. This is in exchange (*pro escangio*) for the land of St. Augustine's Abbey. Now Roger de Candos holds all of this from Hugh de Montfort.

3066 ii, 410b (31-60) <u>Hugh de Montfort; Occold</u>: TRE Guthmund held a carucate and forty acres of land in Occold from his brother Wulfric abbot of Ely. Now Roger de Candos holds it from Hugh de Montfort. Eight freemen have been added to this manor with forty acres of land. Guthmund had the soke of all of this.

3067 ii, 411a (32-1) <u>Geoffrey de Mandeville; Creeting St. Peter</u>: TRE Wihtgar, a freeman commended only to the Abbot of Ely and in the soke of the King and the earl, held two carucates of land in Creeting St. Peter. Now Geoffrey de Mandeville has it as a manor by the King's gift (*ex dono regis*), and William de Bouville holds under him. It did not, however, belong to the fee of Esger, Geoffrey's antecessor. In the same manor there was a freeman commended only to Eadric, Robert Malet's antecessor, with sixteen acres of land. Now William de Bouville holds this under Geoffrey as well.

3068 ii, 412a–b (32-16) <u>Geoffrey de Mandeville; Shadingfield</u>: TRE Healfdene, a freeman commended to Harold, held a carucate of land in Shadingfield. Now Geoffrey de Mandeville holds it. In the same place there was a freeman commended to Archbishop Stigand with a carucate of land. This freeman was adjudged and seised for the King's use (*fuit derationatus et saiatus ad opus regis*), and afterwards Waleran was seised (*saisiuit*) of him, and has given a pledge (*dedit vadem*) for this.

3069 ii, 413a (32-28) <u>Geoffrey de Mandeville; Burgh (near Woodbridge)</u>: TRE three freemen commended to Healfdene held fifty acres of land in Burgh. In the same place Beorhtweald Mufla, half commended to Hervey de Berry's antecessor and half to Robert Malet's antecessor, held twenty-four acres of land. Now Geoffrey de Mandeville holds all of this.

3070 ii, 413b (33-1) <u>Ralph Baynard; Kedington</u>: TRE Æthelgyth held five carucates of land in Kedington. Now Ralph Baynard holds it. In the same place there were twenty-five freemen with two carucates of land. Ralph's antecessor had the commendation, soke, and sake of twenty-four of these men, except for the six forfeitures (*vi forisfacturas*) of Bury St. Edmund's. The twenty-fifth man was commended to the antecessor of Richard fitz Gilbert. But Ralph Baynard claims (*reclamat*) the whole of this through exchange (*pro escangio*).

3071 ii, 413b–414a (33-2) <u>Ralph Baynard; Poslingford</u>: TRE three freemen held a carucate and twenty acres of land in Poslingford. Ralph Baynard's antecessor had the commendation of two of these men and soke and sake, except for the six forfeitures (*vi forisfacturas*) of Bury St. Edmund's. Bury had the commendation of the third man. The King granted (*concessit*) Ralph Baynard this land, and we have seen a writ (*vidimus brevem*) concerning this. In the same place two freemen hold one and a half carucates of land each, and another two freemen hold 160 acres of land. Bury St. Edmund's has the six forfeitures (*vi forisfacturas*), and Ralph Baynard has the soke. This is in exchange (*pro escangio*).

3072 ii, 414a (33-3) <u>Ralph Baynard; Wixoe</u>: TRE Godwine, a thegn, held three carucates and fifteen acres of land in Wixoe. There were also two freemen there with twenty-five acres of land. Ralph Baynard's antecessor had their commendation and soke, and Bury St. Edmund's had the six forfeitures (*vi forisfacturas*). Now Ralph Baynard holds all of this.

3073 ii, 414a (33-4) <u>Ralph Baynard; Reydon</u>: TRE Thorth held five carucates of land in Reydon. Now Ralph Baynard holds it. In the same place there were thirty freemen with two carucates and five acres of land. In the time of King Edward, Ralph's antecessor had the commendation, soke, and sake. This is in exchange (*pro escangio*).

3074 ii, 414a–b (33-5) <u>Ralph Baynard; Brampton</u>: TRE eleven commended freemen, now ten, held two carucates and sixty acres of land in Brampton. Now Ralph Baynard holds it. It is in exchange (*pro escangio*).

3075 ii, 414b (33-6) <u>Ralph Baynard; Frostenden</u>: TRE Thorth held three carucates of land in Frostenden. The King and the earl have the six forfeitures (*vi forisfacturas*). In the same place eight freemen, now three, held 113 acres of land. Now Ranulf holds this from Ralph Baynard. This is in exchange (*pro escagio*).

3076 ii, 414b (33-7) <u>Ralph Baynard; Wangford (near Southwold)</u>: TRE Thorth held two carucates of land in Wangford. Now Ralph Baynard holds it. The King and the earl have the six forfeitures (*vi forisfacturas*).

3077 ii, 414b–415a (33-8) <u>Ralph Baynard; Henham</u>: TRE Alwine, a commended freeman, held a carucate of land in Henham. Now Robert of Blythburgh holds it from Ralph Baynard. This is in exchange (*pro escagio*).

3078 ii, 415b (33-12) <u>Ralph Baynard; Stanningfield</u>: TRE Alflæd, a free woman, held a carucates of land in Stanningfield under Bury St. Edmund's. Now Ralph Baynard holds this in exchange (*pro escangio*).

3079 ii, 415b (33-13) <u>Ralph Baynard; Shimpling</u>: TRE Æthelgyth, a free woman, held six and a half carucates of land in Shimpling under the glorious King Edward. Now Ralph Baynard holds this in exchange (*pro escangio*).

3080 ii, 416a (34-2) <u>Ranulf Peverel; Acton</u>: TRE Siward of Maldon, a thegn, held twelve carucates of land in Acton with soke and sake. Now Ranulf Peverel holds it. In Acton there are four freemen with fifty acres, which Ranulf took as a manor (*recepit pro terra*). There are five freemen with seventy-two acres of land in Great Waldingfield; in Little Waldingfield there are three freemen with fifty acres; in "Honilega" there is one freeman with fifty acres; and in Manton there is a freeman with fifty acres. Eleven of these men could sell their land and four could not, but Ranulf's antecessor had their commendation and soke, except for the one who was in the soke of Bury St. Edmund's. Ranulf Peverel took them all as a manor (*recepit pro terra*).

3081 ii, 416a–b (34-3) <u>Ranulf Peverel; Assington</u>: TRE Siward of Maldon, Ranulf Peverel's antecessor, held eight carucates of land with soke and sake in Assington. In the same place a freeman, delivered as a manor (*liberatus pro terra*), does not belong to the manor over which Ranulf's antecessor had commendation and soke. He held thirty acres of land. Now Ranulf holds all of this. The value was £10; afterwards £12; now £20, but it could not pay 100s. of this.

3082 ii, 416b–417a (34-6) <u>Ranulf Peverel; Onehouse</u>: TRE Ketil, a thegn of King Edward, held a carucate and twenty acres of land with soke in Onehouse. Now Ranulf Peverel holds it. Twenty-six acres of land in Onehouse belonged here TRE. Now Osbert Male holds it in the lands of the Church of Stowmarket. He held them before Ranulf had the manor of Onehouse.

3083 ii, 417a (34-8) <u>Ranulf Peverel; Bricett (Great or Little)</u>: TRW Ralph fitz Brian holds from Ranulf Peverel what Leofstan held TRE – that is, two carucates and four acres of land in Bricett. Fifty-four acres of this land lay in a certain church TRE, but now Ralph fitz Brian holds it in his demesne.

3084 ii, 417b (34-12) <u>Ranulf Peverel; Debenham</u>: TRE Saxi held a carucate and twenty-two acres of land in Debenham. Robert Malet's antecessor held eight of these acres TRE in the soke and commendation of the abbot. Now Ralph de Savenay holds all of this from Ranulf Peverel.

3085 ii, 417b (34-13) <u>Ranulf Peverel; Ulverston</u>: TRE Saxi held a carucate of land in Ulverston. Now Ranulf Peverel holds it. In the time of King Edward eight acres belonged in the demesne of this manor. Now Robert Malet's mother holds them.

3086 ii, 417b (34-15) <u>Ranulf Peverel; Clopton (near Woodbridge)</u>: TRE Eadric Grim held a carucate and forty-two acres of land in Clopton. He was half commended to Ely Abbey and half to Robert Malet's antecessor. Now Thurold holds from Ranulf Peverel.

3087 ii, 418a (34-17) <u>Ranulf Peverel; "Tusemera"</u>: TRE there was a carucate of land in "Tusemera" in the Abbot of Ely's demesne. Saxi held it for his shillings (*pro suis solidatis*). Now Ralph de Savenay holds it from Ranulf Peverel.

3088 ii, 418b (35-2) <u>Aubrey de Vere; Waldingfield (Great or Little)</u>: TRE Wulfwine, Aubrey de Vere's antecessor, held two carucates of land in Waldingfield under King Edward, with soke and sake. Now Aubrey de Vere holds it.

3089 ii, 418b (35-3) <u>Aubrey de Vere; Belstead</u>: TRE Toki, a freemen commended only, held eighty acres of land in Belstead. In the same place Thorgisl, a freeman commended only, held another eighty acres of land. These two manors were adjudged (*derationata sunt*) from Ralph Taillebois and Fin into the King's hand. Later Aubrey de Vere took (*accepit*) them without livery (*sine liberatione*), so the reeve and the hundred say.

3090 ii, 419a (35-7) Aubrey de Vere; Burgate (near Eye), Wortham, Thrandeston, Mellis, Thornham Magna, Gislingham, Wortham, Mellis: There is a free woman, Milde, in Burgate; and nine [*sic*] freemen in Wortham – Besi, Alwine, Godwine, Wulfgeat, Bote, Ordric, Stanheard, and Godric; two freemen – Fulcred and Alwine – in Thrandeston; four and a half freemen in Mellis – Leofric, Godric, Wulfwaru, Leofwine Benne, and half of Fulcred; a freeman, Wulfmær, in Thornham Magna; a freeman, Beorhtmær, in Rickinghall Superior; a freeman, Eadric, in Gislingham; a freeman, Coleman, in Wortham. There was also a free woman, Menleua, in Mellis. She held fourteen acres of free land, and she had granted (*concesserat*) it TRE to Bury St. Edmund's. Between them all, they held ninety acres of land, and Aubrey's antecessor had the soke and commendation of all of them. Æthelhelm now holds all of this from Aubrey de Vere.

3091 ii, 419b (36-4) Robert Gernon; "Manesfort": TRE Ramsey Abbey held a carucate of land in "Manesfort" in demesne. Ramsey Abbey also had the soke. Now William holds it from Robert Gernon.

3092 ii, 420a (36-5) Robert Gernon; "Alfildestuna": TRE Alwine, a freeman commended to Ælfric, antecessor of Robert Gernon, held thirty acres of land in "Alfildestuna." Harold had the soke. Now William d'Alno holds it from Robert Gernon.

3093 ii, 420a (36-6) Robert Gernon; "Turchetlestunam": TRE Grim, a freeman commended to Gyrth, held a carucate of land in "Turchetlestunam." Harold had the soke. Now William d'Alno holds it from Robert Gernon. Robert vouches (*revocat*) this in exchange (*pro escangio*) for Hugh de Montfort's land.

3094 ii, 420a (36-7) Robert Gernon; Brantham: TRE Grim held sixty acres of land in Brantham. Harold had the soke. Now William d'Alno holds it from Robert Gernon. Robert vouches (*revocat*) this in the same way [i.e. in exchange for the land of Hugh de Montfort].

3095 ii, 420b (37-1) Peter de Valognes; rubric: [An "f," for "*fecit retornam,*" appears in the margin, opposite the rubric which marks the beginning of the Peter de Valognes's holdings, indicating that he made a return.]

3096 ii, 420b–421a (37-1) Peter de Valognes; Great Fakenham: TRE Æthelstan, a thegn, held five carucates of land in Great Fakenham. In the same place Æthelstan had the commendation of twenty freemen with eighty acres. Peter de Valognes claims this by the King's gift (*reclamat de dono regis*).

3097 ii; 421a (37-2) Peter de Valognes; Ixworth Thorpe: TRE Spearhavoc, a freeman, held thirty acres of land in Ixworth Thorpe. He was a man of Queen Edith, and she gave (*dedit*) him to Peter de Valognes. After her death, the King granted (*concessit*) him to Peter. This Peter's men say.

3098 ii, 421a (37-3) Peter de Valognes; Sapiston: TRE three freemen held thirteen and a half acres of land in Sapiston. Now Peter de Valognes holds this by gift of the King (*de dono regis*).

3099   ii, 421a (37-5) Peter de Valognes; Wyken: TRE Æthelstan held a carucate of land in Wyken. Now Peter de Valognes holds it. In the same place there were eight commended freemen with a carucate of land. Peter has this through livery as a manor (*de liberatione et pro terra*).

3100   ii, 421b (38-3) Roger de Raismes; Ipswich: TRW Roger de Raismes has the Church of St. George in Ipswich, along with four burgesses and six waste messuages. One of these messuages was adjudged (*derationata fuit*) for the use of the Abbot of Ely, and he was seised (*saisitus fuit*) of it, by testimony (*teste*) of the hundred. But Roger says that he holds it from the King.

3101   ii, 421b (38-4) Roger de Raismes; Crowfield: TRE Eadric, a freeman, held twenty acres of land in Crowfield. Wigulf held thirty-five acres of land in the same place freely. The same Eadric held these thirty-five acres with his land when it was delivered (*liberata fuit*) to Roger de Raismes. Now Roger holds all this land.

3102   ii, 422a (38-5) Roger de Raismes; Coddenham (near Needham Market): TRE three freemen held thirty acres of land in Coddenham. Werengar held this land from Roger de Raismes, but Roger disseised him (*sed ipse desaisiuit*).

3103   ii, 422a (38-6) Roger de Raismes; Stonham Aspal: TRE Æthelmær, a freemen commended only to Eadric, Robert Malet's antecessor, held sixty acres of land in Stonham Aspal. In the same place there were eight freemen with thirty acres of land. Two of these men were commended to a man commended to Robert Malet's antecessor. William, Robert's father, was seised (*saisitus fuit*) of this. Now Miles holds all of this from Roger de Raismes.

3104   ii, 422b (38-11) Roger de Raismes; Akenham: TRE Godwine the Priest, a freeman, held a carucate and twenty acres of land in Akenham. In the same place Ælfric, a freeman commended to Saxi, Ranulf Peverel's antecessor, held forty acres of land. Now Roger de Raismes's daughter holds this from Roger.

3105   ii, 423b–424a (39-3) Ranulf brother of Ilger; Falkenham: TRE Beorhtmær held twenty-six acres of land in Falkenham. This Beorhtmær had several manors, and part were delivered on the King's behalf (*fuit liberata ex parte regis*) to Engelric, and the other parts to Ranulf brother of Ilger and Ralph Pinel. This particular manor was delivered (*fuit . . . deliberata*) to Ralph Pinel, so Ralph himself says. He also produces the testimony (*peribet . . . testimonium*) of the hundred that he was seised first (*fuit saisitus inprimis*). But they are ignorant as to whether or not he was seised on the King's behalf (*sed utrum ex parte regis nec non fuisset saisitus illud ignorant*). They say that Ranulf brother of Ilger claimed this land against (*calumpniatum super*) Ralph, and that Roger the Sheriff named a specific time to them that they should come together (*denominavit illis constitutum tempus modo ut ambo adfuissent*). Ranulf came, but Ralph did not. Therefore the men of the hundred judged Ranulf to be seised (*idcirco diividcaverunt homines hundreti Rannulfum esse saisitum*). He now holds it, but Ralph Pinel denies that he was summoned regarding this plea (*negat quod non fuit summonitus de eo placito*).

3106 ii, 424a (39-5) Ranulf brother of Ilger; Hemley: TRE Beorhtmær, a freeman half commended to Beorht and half to Ely Abbey, held twenty-two acres of land in Hemley. Now Ranulf brother of Ilger holds it from the King through livery (*per liberationem*) from his demesne. The Abbot of Ely, however, says that he ought to hold half from him. In the same place Wulfweard, a freeman commended to Godric, held twenty acres of land; Hardwin, a freeman half commended to N. and half to Eadric, held five acres of land; and Beorhtric, a freeman half commended to Beorhtmær and half to Stanmær, held nine acres of land. Ranulf brother of Ilger holds the whole of this through the King's livery (*per liberationem regis*), and William de Bosc-le-Hard holds from him. Ely Abbey has the soke.

3107 ii, 424b–425a (39-10) Ranulf brother of Ilger; Newbourn: TRE sixteen sokemen commended to Beorhtmær and his mother Cwengifu, and two half freemen commended to Ely Abbey, held a carucate and forty acres of land in Newbourn. There is a church there with twelve acres of land. It was Northmann's, by testimony (*teste*) of the hundred. Now Ranulf brother of Ilger holds all of this.

3108 ii, 425a (39-12) Ranulf brother of Ilger; "Aluredestuna": TRE Durand, a freeman of the antecessor of Robert Malet, held a carucate and eighty acres of land in "Aluredestuna." Now Ivo holds it from Ranulf brother of Ilger.

3109 ii, 425a (39-16) Ranulf brother of Ilger; Waldingfield (Great or Little): TRE Wulfric, a thegn of King Edward, held a carucate of land in Waldingfield. Now Ranulf brother of Ilger holds it as a manor by King William's gift (*ex dono regis*), with soke and sake.

3110 ii, 425b (40-1) Robert fitz Corbucion; rubric: [An "f," for "*fecit retornam*," appears in the margin, opposite the rubric which marks the beginning of Robert fitz Corbucion's holdings, indicating that he made a return.]

3111 ii, 425b (40-1) Robert fitz Corbucion; Brockley (near Whepstead): TRE Sægeard, a freeman under Bury St. Edmund's, held half a carucate of land in Brockley. He was in the soke of Bury, but he could not sell. Now Richard holds this from Robert fitz Corbucion.

3112 ii, 425b (40-3) Robert fitz Corbucion; Wenham: TRE Auti, a thegn, held three carucates of land in Wenham. He had soke over his demesne; but the soke of the villeins was in East Bergholt. Now Robert fitz Corbucion holds. Godwine, a freeman, also held ten acres of land in Wenham, which have been added to this manor.

3113 ii, 426a (40-5) Robert fitz Corbucion; Whatfield: The following information is enrolled under Robert fitz Corbucion's rubric: TRE a sokeman of Bury St. Edmund's held one hundred acres of land in Whatfield. Now Berard, a man of the abbot, holds this from Bury St. Edmund's.

3114 ii, 426a (41-1) Walter the Deacon; rubric: [A "*non*", for "*fecit non retornam*," appears in the margin, opposite the rubric which marks the beginning of Walter the Deacon's holdings, indicating that he had not made a return.]

3115 ii, 427a (41-11) Walter the Deacon; Dagworth: TRE a freeman who was only half commended to Teri, antecessor of [ ] of "Barthetona," and half commended to Guthmund, Hugh de Montfort's antecessor, held sixty acres of land in Dagworth. He could sell his land without their permission. Now William holds from Walter the Deacon. The same freeman held fifteen acres of land in "Weledana." Theodric, Walter the Deacon's antecessor, had this land without livery (*sine liberatore*), by testimony (*teste*) of the hundred.

3116   ii, 427b (41-18) Walter the Deacon; "Finesforda": TRE twenty-six freemen commended to Walter the Deacon's antecessor, held a carucate of land in "Finesforda," and Ely Abbey had the soke. Now Walter the Deacon holds it.

3117   ii, 427b (42-1) Tihel the Breton; rubric: [An "f," for "*fecit retornam*," appears in the margin, opposite the rubric which marks the beginning of Tihel the Breton's holdings, indicating that he made a return.]

3118   ii, 428a (43-1) Ralph de Limesy; rubric: [An "f r," for "*fecit retornam*," appears in the margin, opposite the rubric which marks the beginning of Ralph de Limesy's holdings, indicating that he made a return.]

3119   ii, 428a (43-1) Ralph de Limesy; Houghton: TRE Uhtræd held two carucates of land with soke in Houghton under Harold. He also held a carucate of land in Fenstead. Now Ralph de Limesy holds this as a berewick of Houghton. Uhtræd held it from Edgar, Ralph's antecessor.

3120   ii, 428b–429a (43-5) Ralph de Limesy; Bedingfield: TRE Ælfric, a freeman of Harold, held ninety-two acres of land in Bedingfield. In the same place there were six freemen with thirty-five acres of land. Ælfric had commendation over all of these men except half of one, who was commended only to Robert Malet's antecessor. Now Ralph de Limesy holds this.

3121   ii, 429a (44-1) Robert de Tosny; rubric: [An "f r," for "*fecit retornam*," appears in the margin, opposite the rubric which marks the beginning of Robert de Tosny's holdings, indicating that he made a return.]

3122   ii, 430a (45-1) Walter Giffard; rubric: [An "f," for "*fecit retornam*," appears in the margin, opposite the rubric which marks the beginning of Walter Giffard's holdings, indicating that he made a return.]

3123   ii, 430a (45-1) Walter Giffard; Blaxhall: TRE Godric, a freeman half under the commendation of Robert Malet's antecessor and half under the Abbot of Ely, held ten acres of land in Blaxhall. Now Ralph de Lanquetot holds this from Walter Giffard.

3124   ii, 430a (45-2) Walter Giffard; Great Glemham: TRE Starling held 180 acres of land in Great Glemham. He was half commended to the Abbot of Ely and half to William Malet, who was seised (*saisitus fuit*) of this. Twenty-four commended freemen were added to this manor with one hundred acres of land. Now Walter Giffard holds all of this.

3125   ii, 430b (46-1) Countess of Aumâle; rubric: [An "f r," for "*fecit retornam*," appears in the margin, opposite the rubric which marks the beginning of the Countess of Aumâle's holdings, indicating that she made a return.]

3126   ii, 431b (47-1) William d'Arques; rubric: [An "f r," for "*fecit retornam*," appears in the margin, opposite the rubric which marks the beginning of William d'Arques's holdings, indicating that he made a return.]

3127 ii, 431b (47-2, 3) William d'Arques; Clopton (near Woodbridge), Brandeston (near Framlingham): TRE Edmund the Priest, a freeman of Ely Abbey, held a carucate and twenty-two acres of land in Clopton. Now Bernard de St. Ouen holds it from William d'Arques. Edmund the Priest, who was commended to Ely Abbey, also held sixty acres of land in Brandeston. The land which he took (*cepit*) in Brandeston and Clopton with his wife, he put (*misit*) in Ely Abbey with the consent (*concedente*) of his wife, by such an agreement (*tali conventione*) that he could neither sell nor grant it away from the Church. Eighty acres, which were a manor TRE, were added to this manor. Now William d'Arques has all of this as a manor, but TRE there were two manors.

3128 ii, 432a (48-1) Drogo de la Beuvrière; rubric: [An "f," for "*fecit retornam*," appears in the margin, opposite the rubric which marks the beginning of Drogo de la Beuvrière's holdings, indicating that he made a return.]

3129 ii, 432a (48-1) Drogo de la Beuvrière; Sotherton: TRE Rada, a freeman, held two carucates of land in Sotherton from Harold. Now Frank holds it from Drogo de la Beuvrière. Drogo's antecessor Rada had soke and sake. Humphrey de St. Bertin has added a freeman with twelve acres to this manor, of whom his antecessor had commendation TRE.

3130 ii, 432a (49-1) Hugh de Grandmesnil; rubric: [An "f," for "*fecit retornam*," appears in the margin, opposite the rubric which marks the beginning of Hugh de Grandmesnil's holdings, indicating that he made a return.]

3131 ii, 432a (50-1) Ralph de Fougères; rubric: [An "f," for "*fecit retornam*," appears in the margin, opposite the rubric which marks the beginning of Ralph de Fougères's holdings, indicating that he made a return.]

3132 ii, 432b (51-1) Walter de St. Valéry; rubric: [An "f r," for "*fecit retornam*," appears in the margin, opposite the rubric which marks the beginning of Walter de St. Valéry's holdings, indicating that he made a return.]

3133 ii, 432b (51-1) Walter de St. Valéry; Creeting St. Peter: TRE Ælfric, a freeman of Eadric, Robert Malet's antecessor in commendation only, held one and a half carucates of land in Creeting St. Peter. Robert Malet held it, but afterwards he was disseised (*fuit desaitus*). Now Walter de St. Valéry holds it.

3134 ii, 432b (51-2) Walter de St. Valéry; Creeting St. Peter: TRE a freeman commended to Robert Malet's antecessor held sixty acres of land in Creeting St. Peter. Robert's father William was seised (*saisitus fuit*) of it. Now Walter de St. Valéry holds it.

3135 ii, 433a (52-1) Humphrey the Chamberlain; rubric: [A "*non*," for "*fecit non retornam*," appears in the margin, opposite the rubric which marks the beginning of Humphrey the Chamberlain's holdings, indicating that he did not make a return.]

3136 ii, 433a (52-1) Humphrey the Chamberlain; Otley: TRE Leofflæd, a free woman commended to Eadric, Robert Malet's antecessor, held one and a half carucates of land in Otley. William Malet was seised (*fuit saisitus*) on the day he died; afterwards Robert was, by testimony (*teste*) of the hundred. In the same place Lustwine, a man commended to Eadric, held half a carucate of land; and sixteen and a half freemen commended to Leofflæd held sixty-nine acres of land. William Malet had been seised (*erat . . . saisitus*) of all of this on the day he died, and afterwards Robert was. Now Humphrey the Chamberlain holds.

3137   ii, 433b (52-9) Humphrey the Chamberlain; Helmingham: TRE Grimulf, a freeman commended to Queen Edith, held 120 acres of land in Helmingham. It lies in the demesne of Otley. In the same place eleven freemen held sixty-eight acres of land. Nine were commended to Humphrey the Chamberlain's antecessor and two were commended to Beorhtweald. Now Anund holds all of this from Humphrey the Chamberlain.

3138   ii, 434a (53-1) Eudo son of Spearhavoc; rubric: [An "f r," for "*fecit retornam*," appears in the margin, opposite the rubric which marks the beginning of Eudo son of Spearhavoc's holdings, indicating that he made a return.]

3139   ii, 434a (53-1) Eudo son of Spearhavoc; Icklingham: TRE Anund, a freeman, held two carucates of land in Icklingham under Ely Abbey, but he could not sell. Now Morvan holds it from Eudo son of Spearhavoc, who holds it through (*ab*) Heinfrid, his antecessor.

3140   ii, 434a (53-2) Eudo son of Spearhavoc; Olden: TRE Sigeric, a freeman, held seventy acres of land in Olden. Now William holds it from Eudo son of Spearhavoc. In the same place thirteen freemen held forty acres of land. Roger's antecessor had the commendation of two of them TRE.

3141   ii, 434b (53-3) Eudo son of Spearhavoc; Battisford: TRE Cyneric, a freeman, held a carucate and twenty acres of land in Battisford. Now Iarnagot holds it from Eudo son of Spearhavoc. In the same place three freemen held twenty acres of land. Eudo son of Spearhavoc's antecessor had the commendation of two of these men.

3142   ii, 434b–435a (53-6) Eudo son of Spearhavoc; Westhorpe: TRE Wulfric Hagne held a carucate of land in Westhorpe. Now Geoffrey holds it from Eudo son of Spearhavoc. In the same place there were fifteen freemen commended to Wulfric with thirty-three acres of land. In the time of King Edward, Bury St. Edmund's had the soke and sake and commendation of this manor, and Wulfric Hagne could neither sell nor grant this land away from Bury St. Edmund's. Robert Malet's antecessor had the commendation over the fifteen freemen and over Wulfric, by testimony (*teste*) of the hundred, and Wulfric could neither sell nor grant his land from Bury.

3143   ii, 435a (53-7) Eudo son of Spearhavoc; Wattisham: TRE a freeman, who was commended to the Abbot of Ely, held a carucate of land in Wattisham. Now Iarnagot holds it from Eudo son of Spearhavoc. Bury St. Edmund's has the six forfeitures (*vi forisfacturas*).

3144   ii, 435a (54-1) William de Watteville; rubric: [An "f," for "*fecit retornam*," appears in the margin, opposite the rubric which marks the beginning of William de Watteville's holdings, indicating that he made a return.]

3145   ii, 435b (55-1) John fitz Waleran; rubric: [An "f," for "*fecit retornam,*" appears in the margin, opposite the rubric which marks the beginning of John fitz Waleran's holdings, indicating that he made a return.]

3146   ii, 435b (55-1) John fitz Waleran; Bures: TRE Wulfric son of Beorhtric held two carucates of land in Bures under King Edward. In the same place Tosti, a freeman under King Edward, held a carucate of land; and two of Harold's freemen held sixty acres there and could sell. These men were delivered to make (*fuerunt liberati ad perficiendum*) the manor. Now John fitz Waleran holds.

3147   ii, 436a (56-1) Humphrey fitz Aubrey; rubric: [An "f," for "*fecit retornam,*" appears in the margin, opposite the rubric which marks the beginning of Humphrey fitz Aubrey's holdings, indicating that he made a return.]

3148   ii, 436a (57-1) Hubert de Mont-Canisy; rubric: [An "f," for "*fecit retornam,*" appears in the margin, opposite the rubric which marks the beginning of Hubert de Mont-Canisy's holdings, indicating that he made a return.]

3149   ii, 436b (58-1) Gundwine the Chamberlain; rubric: [An "f," for "*fecit retornam,*" appears in the margin, opposite the rubric which marks the beginning of Gundwine the Chamberlain's holdings, indicating that he made a return.]

3150   ii, 436b (59-1) Sasselin; rubric: [An "f," for "*fecit retornam,*" appears in the margin, opposite the rubric which marks the beginning of Sasselin's holdings, indicating that he made a return.]

3151   ii, 437a (60-1) Robert de Verly; rubric: [An "f," for "*fecit retornam,*" appears in the margin, opposite the rubric which marks the beginning of Robert de Verly's holdings, indicating that he made a return.]

3152   ii, 437a (61-1) Ralph Pinel; rubric: [An "f," for "*fecit retornam,*" appears in the margin, opposite the rubric which marks the beginning of Ralph Pinel's holdings, indicating that he made a return.]

3153   ii, 437b (62-1) Isaac; rubric: [An "f," for "*fecit retornam,*" appears in the margin, opposite the rubric which marks the beginning of Isaac's holdings, indicating that he made a return.]

3154   ii, 438a (62-7) Isaac; "Redles": TRE a freeman of Archbishop Stigand's held half a carucate of land in "Redles." Now Isaac holds it. Fourteen acres of woodland lay in this manor, but William de Bourneville took them away (*abstulit*) and now holds them.

3155   ii, 438a (63-1) Northmann the Sheriff; Ipswich: TRW Northmann the Sheriff has two burgesses in Ipswich, one in mortgage to him (*in vadimonio contra eundem*) and the other for a debt (*pro debito*), but the King has the burgess's customs.

3156   ii, 438a (64-1) Iudhael the Priest; rubric: [An "f," for "*fecit retornam,*" appears in the margin, opposite the rubric which marks the beginning of Iudhael the Priest's holdings, indicating that he made a return.]

3157 ii, 438a (64-1) Iudhael the Priest; Stonham (Earl or Little): TRE Ælfric, a freeman of Eadric, Robert Malet's antecessor, held ninety acres of land in Stonham. Afterwards Robert was seised (*fuit saisitus*) of it, and now Iudhael the Priest holds it.

3158 ii, 438a (64-2) Iudhael the Priest; Stonham (Earl or Little): There is a church in Stonham with twenty acres there that was given (*dederunt*) by nine freemen for their souls.

3159 ii, 438b (65-1) Gerald the Marshal; rubric: [An "f," for "*fecit retornam*," appears in the margin, opposite the rubric which marks the beginning of Gerald the Marshal's holdings, indicating that he made a return.]

3160 ii, 439a (66-3) Robert Blunt; Great Ashfield: TRE Aki held three carucates of land in Great Ashfield. In the same place fourteen commended freemen held eighty acres of land; Ketil, a freeman, held a carucate; and three freemen under Ketil held twenty-two acres. Robert Blunt's antecessor had the commendation of these men. Now William holds from Robert Blunt.

3161 ii, 439b (66-5, 6, 7, 8, 9) Robert Blunt; Sapiston, Langham, Hepworth, Wyken, Ixworth: TRE two of King Edward's freemen held eighteen acres of land in Sapiston; Haret, a freeman commended to Bury St. Edmund's, held three carucates of land in Langham, and two other commended freemen held twenty acres there; half a freeman held forty acres of land in Hepworth; a commended freeman held sixty acres in Wyken; and a freeman held forty acres in Ixworth. Now Robert Blunt holds all of this. Concerning all these freemen, Robert Blunt vouches the King to warranty (*revocat regem ad warant*).

3162 ii, 440a (66-10) Robert Blunt; Ixworth: TRE Ketil, a freeman commended to Esger the Staller, held two hundred acres of land in Ixworth, and six freemen under him held twenty-nine acres of land. Ralph, Robert Blunt's brother, was seised (*erat saisitus*) when he died. Robert took (*recepit*) this from the King.

3163 ii, 440a (66-11) Robert Blunt; Whatfield: TRE five freemen held sixty acres of land in Whatfield. Bury St. Edmund's had the commendation of one of these men and the soke of all of them; and Robert Blunt's antecessor did not have commendation. In the same place there were four freemen with sixty-three acres of land. Now Robert Blunt holds all of this in exchange (*pro escangio*).

3164 ii, 440b (67-1) Hervey de Bourges; Thorney: TRE Beorhtric the Black held a carucate of land in Thorney under Wihtgar, Richard fitz Gilbert's antecessor. Beorhtric could not sell without Wihtgar's permission. Now Ewen holds this land from Hervey de Bourges.

3165 ii, 440b (67-2) Hervey de Bourges; Hemingstone: TRE Wulfmær, a freeman commended only to Eadric, Robert Malet's antecessor, held one hundred acres of land in Hemingstone. William Malet was seised (*fuit saisitus*) of this land on the day he died, and afterwards his son Robert Malet was. Now Reginald holds it from Hervey de Bourges.

3166 ii, 440b–441a (67-3, 4) <u>Hervey de Bourges; Pettaugh, Ashfield</u>: TRE Beorhtweald held a carucate and thirty acres of land in Pettaugh. Robert Malet's antecessor had his commendation. Now Hervey de Bourges holds it. The Abbot of Ely had half the soke and Earl Hugh's antecessor had the other half. The soke was the Abbot of Ely's and Earl Hugh's antecessor's. This manor was at farm for £3 15s., but the men were ruined (*fuerunt confusi*) by this, and now it is assessed at 45s. TRE Godmann, a freeman commended to Robert Malet, held thirty acres of land in Ashfield. Now Ranulf holds it from Hervey de Bourges. William Malet was seised (*fuit saisitus*) of the these two manors on the day he died.

3167 ii, 441a (67-5) <u>Hervey de Bourges; "Brutge"</u>: TRE Eadric, commended to Eadric, Robert Malet's antecessor, held 120 acres of land in "Brutge." Now Warner holds this from Hervey de Bourges. Eight freemen were added there with twenty acres of land. Concerning half this land, Hervey came to an agreement (*conciliatus*) with the Abbot of Ely. Afterwards he held it from the King.

3168 ii, 441a (67-6) <u>Hervey de Bourges; Beversham</u>: TRE Ælfric, a freeman in the soke and commended to the Abbot of Ely, held sixty acres of land in Beversham. Warner holds this from Hervey de Bourges, who came to an agreement (*est conciliatus*) with the Abbot of Ely concerning this manor.

3169 ii, 441a (67-10) <u>Hervey de Bourges; Grundisburgh</u>: TRE Godric, a freeman of Harold, held a carucate of land in Grundisburgh. In the same place Brun, commended to Eadric, Robert Malet's antecessor, held twenty acres from Eadric. Now Hervey de Bourges holds all of this.

3170 ii, 441a–b (67-11) <u>Hervey de Bourges; Great Bealings</u>: TRE ten freemen – Blachmann, Alwine, Stanheard, Ani, Wulfric, Thorbert, Eadric, Godwine, Alstan, and Anund the Priest – held eighty-four acres of land in Great Bealings. Healfdene had the commendation of Anund the Priest, and Ely Abbey had commendation over the other men. In the same place Wulfmær, a freeman of Healfdene, Geoffrey de Mandeville's antecessor, held 100 acres of land in demesne. And Wulfmær himself had three villeins under him. Now Hervey de Bourges holds all of this.

3171 ii, 442a–b (67-15) <u>Hervey de Bourges; Tuddenham (near Ipswich)</u>: TRE Eadric, Robert Malet's antecessor, was seised (*fuit . . . saisitus*) of a manor in Tuddenham, and when William Malet died, he was, and he could neither grant nor sell his land to anyone else. Now Bernard d'Alençon holds this from Hervey de Bourges.

3172 ii, 442b (67-16) <u>Hervey de Bourges; Thistleton</u>: TRE Frani, a freeman commended to Eadric, held thirty acres of land in Thistleton. Reginald holds this from Hervey de Bourges, but William Malet was seised (*fuit saisitus*) of this on the day he died.

3173 ii, 442b–443a (67-19) <u>Hervey de Bourges; Bredfield</u>: TRE Swærting, commended to Robert Malet's antecessor, held eighty acres of land in Bredfield. There were also twenty-one freemen there commended to

Swærting with a carucate and twenty-two acres of land; and a freeman commended to a man commended to Robert Malet's antecessor, with twelve acres of land. William Malet had been seised (*erat . . . saisitus*) on the day he died. Now Hervey de Bourges holds this.

3174 ii, 443a (67-20) Hervey de Bourges; Wickham Market: TRE Azur, a freeman commended to Eadric, held thirty-three acres of land in Wickham Market. Now Hervey de Bourges holds it, but William Malet was seised on the day he died.

3175 ii, 443a (67-21) Hervey de Bourges; Sutton: TRE Azur held sixty acres of land in Sutton. In the same place a freeman commended to Eadric held six acres of land. Now Erchenbald holds it from Hervey de Bourges, but William Malet was seised on the day he died.

3176 ii, 443a (67-27) Hervey de Bourges; Martley: TRE Beorhtmær, a man commended to Harold, held eighty acres of land in Martley. Now Hervey de Bourges holds it. There were ten freemen and two half freemen there commended to Beorhtmær with sixty acres of land. Robert Malet claims (*calumpniatur*) one of these.

3177 ii, 443b (67-28) Hervey de Bourges; Campsey Ash: TRE Swærting and Eadric, men commended to Eadric of Laxfield, held sixty acres of land in Campsey Ash. William Malet was seised (*fuit saiatus*) on the day he died. Now Hervey de Bourges holds.

3178 ii, 443b (67-29) Hervey de Bourges; Rendlesham: TRE Godgifu, a free woman half commended to Ely Abbey and half to Eadric of Laxfield, held sixty acres of land in Rendlesham. Now Bernard d'Alençon holds it from Hervey de Bourges. William Malet was seised (*fuit saisitus*) on the day he died.

3179 ii, 443b–444a (67-30) Hervey de Bourges; Potsford: TRE Wynning, half commended to Ely Abbey and half to Eadric, held eighty acres of land in Potsford. Now Odo holds it from Hervey de Bourges. In the same place there were eight freemen with thirty acres of land. Three of them forfeited (*forisfecerunt*) their land to the abbot, and after this, the hundred did not see that they redeemed (*redimeret*) it. The fourth man was the abbot's man, and the other four were commended to Wynning. William Malet was seised (*fuit saiatus*) on the day he died.

3180 ii, 444a (67-31) Hervey de Bourges; Glevering: TRE Beorhtmær, a man commended to Eadric, held forty acres of land in Glevering. Now Odo holds this from Hervey de Bourges. William Malet was seised (*fuit saiatus*) on the day he died.

3181 ii, 444a (68-1) Gilbert the Balistarius; rubric: [An "f," for "*fecit retornam,*" appears in the margin, opposite the rubric which marks the beginning of Gilbert the Balistarius's holdings, indicating that he made a return.]

3182 ii, 444b (68-5) Gilbert the Balistarius; Gislingham: TRE Alsige, a freeman, held two carucates of land in Gislingham. During the life of King Edward this manor was from the demesne of Leofstan abbot of Bury St. Edmund's. Abbot

Leofstan loaned (*accomodavit*) it to Alsige and his wife, with the agreement that after their death the Abbot should have his manor back (*tali conventione quod post obitum eorum rehaberet abbas suum manerium*) along with another of Alsige's manors called Euston. Now Gilbert the Balistarius holds it.

3183   ii, 445a (69-1) <u>Ralph the Balistarius; rubric</u>: [An "r," for "*fecit retornam*," appears in the margin, opposite the rubric which marks the beginning of Ralph the Balistarius's holdings, indicating that he made a return.]

3184   ii, 445a (70-1) <u>Reginald the Breton; rubric</u>: [An "f," for "*fecit retornam*," appears in the margin, opposite the rubric which marks the beginning of Reginald the Breton's holdings, indicating that he made a return.]

3185   ii, 445a (70-1) <u>Reginald the Breton; Lidgate</u>: TRE three freemen held four carucates of land in Lidgate. Now Reginald the Breton holds it, and he vouches (*revocat*) it as the King's alms. The men of William de Watteville, however, claim (*calumpniantur*) this land in William's fee.

3186   ii, 445b (73-1) <u>Wulfmær; "Lafham"</u>: TRW Wulfmær has twenty-four acres of land in "Lafham," and Bury St. Edmund's has the soke. In the same place Wulfmær holds another nine acres of land, which he mortgaged (*invadavit*) TRW from Ralph Pinel's antecessor for 21s. Roger the Sheriff had heriot (*herret*) from Wulfmær's father.

3187   ii, 446a (74-4) <u>Vavassors; Olden</u>: Four freemen in Olden – Radbodo, Leofric, Eadric, and Wulfric – with eight acres of land, were added to the farm of Olden in the time of King William. Roger is warrantor for this (*est warant inde*) for Wulfmær the Reeve, who added them. Roger did not know that they had been added, and that they did not belong to the farm. In the same place Wulfmær, a freeman, held a quarter acre of land. Beorhtmær the Beadle held this and has given a pledge (*dedit vadem*). Wulfmær the Reeve is surety (*fide iussor*).

3188   ii, 446a (74-7) <u>Vavassors; Hemingstone</u>: TRE Alwine, a freeman commended to Gyrth, held thirty acres of land in Hemingstone. Wulfmær the Reeve added him to the King's farm in Bramford. Roger the Sheriff is warrantor for him regarding this (*est ei inde warant*), and he pays 5s. each year.

3189   ii, 446a (74-8) <u>Vavassors; Thurleston</u>: TRE Rolf held twelve acres of land in Thurleston. Now his son Ælfric, a burgess of Ipswich, holds it. Earl Ralph was seised (*fuit saisitus*) when he forfeited (*forisfecit*).

3190   ii, 446a–b (74-9) <u>Vavassors; Ipswich</u>: TRW Ælfric, a burgess of Ipswich, holds the Church of St. Julian in Ipswich along with twenty acres of land. Earl Ralph was seised (*fuit saisitus*) of this church.

3191   ii, 446b (74-10) <u>Vavassors; Claydon</u>: TRE Ælfric, a freeman, held six and a half acres of land in Claydon. Ælfric held this land in mortgage, and he does not have a warrantor for it (*in vadimonio et non habet inde warant*). These acres are in the King's hand.

3192   ii, 446b (74-11) <u>Vavassors; Westerfield</u>: TRE six freemen – Alwine, Flint, Alwine, Eadric, Wulfric, and Æthelstan – held fifteen acres of land in Westerfield. One of them, Flint, has given a pledge (*dedit vadem*) for what they said they gave the farm in Ipswich. But the sheriff has established (*derationauit*) that he lied (*mentitus erat*). The sheriff is surety (*est fide iussor*) for this.

3193   ii, 447a (75-1) <u>Freemen in the King's hand; Ixworth Thorpe</u>: TRE a freeman held thirty acres of land in Ixworth Thorpe. Robert Blunt held him, thinking (*putans*) him to be from the fee of the abbot, and the same man confirmed (*confirmabat*) to Robert that he was in the abbot's fee. But the abbot is not his warrantor for this (*non est sibi warant*). Now, finally Robert has acknowledged (*recognouit*) that the man is not from the abbot's fee, and has handed him over (*dimisit*) into the King's hand, and has given a pledge (*dedit vadem*) for this.

3194   ii, 447a (75-2) <u>Freemen in the King's hand; Ixworth</u>: TRE there was a freeman with twelve acres of land in Ixworth. Bury St. Edmund's had half the commendation and soke and sake, and Peter de Valognes's antecessor had half the commendation. Richard, Robert Blunt's man, held this and has given a pledge (*dedit vadem*). Robert is not his warrantor (*non ei warant*).

3195   ii, 447a (75-3) <u>Freemen in the King's hand; Horham</u>: TRE a freeman held six acres of land in Horham. Herbert Blacun held this in the King's hand, by order (*iussu*) of Bishop Herfast, but Iudhael the Priest claims it by the King's gift (*reclamat de dono regis*) and was seised (*saisitus fuit*) of it. His antecessor had commendation TRE. The soke is in Hoxne.

3196   ii, 447a (75-4) <u>Freemen in the King's hand; Instead</u>: TRE a freeman commended to Bishop Æthelmær held ten and a half acres of land in Instead. William Malet held this, and afterwards so did his son, thinking (*putans*) that it was from his father's fee.

3197   ii, 447a–b (75-5) <u>Freemen in the King's hand; Bedingfield</u>: Two freemen with forty acres of land in Bedingfield remain (*remanent*) in the King's hand through the postponement of a plea (*per respectum placiti*) between the Bishop of Bayeux and the mother of Robert Malet. One of these men was commended to Archbishop Stigand and the other was half commended to Leofric, Robert Malet's antecessor, and half to Saxi. The soke is in Hoxne.

3198   ii, 447b (76-1) <u>Annexations (*invasiones*) against the King; Bradley (Great or Little)</u>: TRE three freemen – Wulfwine, Leofric, and Wulfwine – held fifteen acres of land in Bradley. A fourth freeman, Bondi, held a carucate of land there. Richard fitz Gilbert, the bad neighbor (*malus vicinus*), now holds it. His antecessor never had these men's commendation.

3199   ii, 447b (76-2) <u>Annexations (*invasiones*) against the King; Groton</u>: TRE a freeman commended only to Robert fitz Wimarc held sixty acres of land in Groton. Roger d'Orbec has annexed (*invasit*) this land and holds it under Richard fitz Gilbert. Richard's men vouch (*revocant*) it to the fee of Wihtgar, Richard's antecessor. But it never belonged there, so the hundred testifies, nor did the commendation or soke.

3200   i, 447b–448a (76-3) <u>Annexations (*invasiones*) against the King; Cavendish</u>: TRE Ælfric bother of Eadric, a man of Wihtgar, annexed (*invasit*) half his brother's land, that is sixty acres in Cavendish. Now Roger de St.-Germain holds it from Richard fitz Gilbert's fee, but it never belonged to this fee, nor did the commendation or soke.

3201 ii, 448a (76-4) <u>Annexations (*invasiones*) against the King; Cornard</u>: TRE there were two freemen commended only to Ælfric Kemp and in the soke of Bury St. Edmund's, with two carucates and forty acres of land in Cornard. After King William came, Wihtgar, Richard fitz Gilbert's antecessor, annexed (*invasit*) them before the agreement (*ante conventionem*) of Richard, who now holds them.

3202 ii, 448a (76-5) <u>Annexations (*invasiones*) against the King; "Saibamus"</u>: TRE a freeman, commended to Robert fitz Wimarc and in the soke and sake of Bury St. Edmund's, held a carucate of land in "Saibamus." But Wihtgar held this when he forfeited (*se forefecit*). Now Richard, his successor (*successor*), has it.

3203 ii, 448a (76-6) <u>Annexations (*invasiones*) against the King; Cavendish</u>: Alweald, a freeman commended to and in the soke and sake of Harold, held a carucate of land in Cavendish both TRE and after King William came. Now Richard has annexed (*invasit*) this.

3204 ii, 448a (76-7) <u>Annexations (*invasiones*) against the King; Cavendish</u>: TRW Richard fitz Gilbert has annexed (*invasit*) a freeman of King Edward, with a carucate of land in Cavendish, but his antecessor had nothing at all from him.

3205 ii, 448b (76-8, 9, 10, 11, 12) <u>Annexations (*invasiones*) against the King; Stanton, Knettishall, Bardwell</u>: TRE a free woman commended to Bury St. Edmund's held thirty acres of land in Stanton; Bury itself held thirty acres of land in Knettishall; and in Bardwell a freeman of Bury St. Edmund's held *mansiones*; a half freeman of Bury's held eight acres there, and a free woman of Bury's held ten acres. William de Parthenay has annexed (*invasit*) all of this against the Abbot of Bury St. Edmund's, and has the commendation of one of these freemen.

3206 ii, 448b (76-13) <u>Annexations (*invasiones*) against the King; Somersham</u>: TRE Wulfric, a freeman, held twelve acres of land in Somersham. Earl Ralph was seised (*fuit saisitus*) of this when he forfeited (*forisfecit*), and his antecessor had its commendation in Nettlestead. Wulfmær the King's reeve has annexed (*invasit*) it. He has given a pledge (*dedit vadem*). Roger Bigot is surety (*fide iussor*), and it is in the King's hand.

3207 ii, 448b (76-14) <u>Annexations (*invasiones*) against the King; Bricett (Great or Little)</u>: TRE Eskil held twenty acres of land in Bricett, which lies in the manor of William d'Auberville. Now Bothild holds it and vouches (*revocat*) Hugh d'Houdain to warranty (*ad warant*), but he is a prisoner of the King and cannot respond (*est in captione regis et non potest respondere*). Now it is in the King's hand, and Wulfmær the Reeve has custody of it.

3208 ii, 448b (76-15) <u>Annexations (*invasiones*) against the King; Baylham</u>: TRE and while she lived, Queen Edith held half a church in Baylham with twelve acres of land. Afterwards William de Bourneville held this. Now it is in the King's hand. William [or Wulfmær the Reeve?] has given a pledge (*dedit vadem*) for this, and Thurstan fitz Guy is surety (*fide iussor*).

3209 ii, 448b–449a (76-16) <u>Annexations (*invasiones*) against the King; Finborough (Great or Little)</u>: TRE a freeman, who was half commended to Roger d'Auberville's antecessor and half to Eustace's, held fifteen acres of land in Finborough. Afterwards Robert count of Mortain held this, but Roger d'Auberville held this man when he relinquished (*relinquid*) his land, and Robert the Balistarius held under him. Now Roger Bigot holds in the King's hand, until it be adjudged (*derationatus sit*).

3210 ii, 449a (76-17, 18) <u>Annexations (*invasiones*) against the King; Wissett</u>: TRE a freeman in Wissett with four acres of land lay in Count Alan's manor of Covehithe. Robert de Courson has annexed (*invasit*) this. Earl Ralph held it when he forfeited (*forisfecit*). Robert has given a pledge for this (*ex hoc dedit vadem*). TRE there was another freeman in Wissett with eight acres of land. William de Warenne's antecessor had his commendation only, and William had his land in exchange (*de sua terra pro escangio*). Robert de Courson has annexed (*invasit*) this land as well.

3211 ii, 449a (76-19) <u>Annexations (*invasiones*) against the King; Uggeshall</u>: TRE two freemen, Northmann and Ketil, held eighteen acres of land in Uggeshall. Berenger, a man of Bury St. Edmund's, has annexed (*invasit*) it, and he is in the King's mercy (*est in misericordia regis*). He had been ill, and could not come to the plea (*infirmus erat, non potuit venire ad placitum*). Now it is in the sheriff's custody (*in custodia*).

3212 ii, 449a (76-20) <u>Annexations (*invasiones*) against the King; Cavendish</u>: TRE Eadric the Deacon, a freeman of Earl Harold, who died with him in battle, held land in Cavendish. It was delivered (*fuit liberata*) to Baynard as a manor. Edgar added it to Cavendish after Baynard lost (*perdidit*) it. Now Ralph de Limesy holds it in demesne.

3213 ii, 449a (76-21) <u>Annexations (*invasiones*) against the King; Lavenham</u>: TRW Aubrey de Vere holds three freemen with fifty acres of land in Lavenham, who were commended only to Wulfwine, Aubrey de Vere's antecessor, and whose soke was in Bury St. Edmund's.

3214 ii, 449a–b (76-22) <u>Annexations (*invasiones*) against the King; Coddenham (in Boxford)</u>: TRE Walter de St. Valéry's antecessor had the commendation only of two freemen with twenty acres of land in Coddenham. Now Roger de Raismes holds this, but the hundred does not know how, nor is there anyone on his behalf who can say how (*nec fuit aliquis ex parte sua qui diceret quomodo*).

3215 ii, 449b (76-23) <u>Annexations (*invasiones*) against the King; Eye</u>: TRE Svartrikr, a freeman commended to Harold and in his soke, held 120 acres of land in Eye. Now Robert Malet holds this.

3216 ii, 450a (77-1, 2, 3, 4) <u>Concerning the claims (*de calumpniis*) between the Bishop of Bayeux and the mother of Robert Malet; Occold, Bedingfield, Aspall</u>: TRE Beorhthere, a freeman of Archbishop Stigand, held twenty acres of land in Occold. Stigand gave (*dedit*) this land to Robert Malet's mother. Afterwards she held it from the Queen. Now the Bishop of Bayeux holds it. In the same place Cyneric, a freeman half commended to Robert Malet's antecessor and half commended to Saxi, Ranulf Peverel's antecessor, held twenty acres of land. In Bedingfield the same Beorhthere and Cyneric held forty acres of land in the aforesaid manner. And in Aspall four freemen held eighty-six acres of land. One of these men, Deorwulf, was commended to the Abbot of Ely; Thurstan was commended to Saxi; Markulf was commended to Eadric, Robert Malet's antecessor; and Gunnulf was under the commendation of Robert Malet's antecessor. William Malet was seised (*fuit . . . saisitus*) of this land, so the hundred testifies, before the Bishop of Bayeux. Afterwards Hubert de Port came, and he adjudged (*derationavit*) it to be free land, and seised (*saisiuit*) the bishop of it because freemen had held it. On the day that Earl Ralph forfeited (*forisfecit*) and until the plea (*placitum*) at Odiham [Hants.], Robert Malet's mother had been seised (*saisita erat*) of it, by testimony (*teste*) of the hundred. Now it is in the King's peace (*in pace regis*), which the King has ordered (*praecepit*) between the bishop and Robert's mother.

3217 ii, 450a (unnumbered) Colophon: [The colophon of Little Domesday reads: This *descriptio* was made in the thousand and eighty-sixth year since the incarnation of the Lord, and in the twentieth year of William's reign, not only through these three counties, but throughout all the others.]

Part III
The indexes

Index of names

Index of places

Subject index

I Transactions

1 Agreed

acknowledged
  (*recognouit*)   900, 1355, 1951, 2360, 2379,
      2704, 3039, 3193
acknowledgment for a lease (*pro
      recognitione*)   1666, 1668
agreed
  (*concordavit*)   876, 880, 898, 1192
  (*convenit*)   1172
agreement
  (*conventio*)   478–9, 625, 630, 632, 834,
      1172, 1609, 1666, 2767, 2937, 2944,
      2946, 3049, 3127, 3182, 3201
  (*consilium*)   2137–8
  came to agreement (*conciliavit*)   3167–8
arranged (*constituit*)   1643, 2158, 2756
  arrangement (*constitutio*)   1643
    of ancient times   1643
leave plea in friendship   3038
pact (*pactio*)   630, 1022, 1179, 2763
settlement (*concordia*)   1037

2 Claimed

claimed
  (*calumniatus est*)   115, 127, 277, 279–82,
      298, 314–15, 321, 327, 330, 334–5,
      368, 481, 487, 508, 519, 534, 537–9,
      552, 554, 573, 597, 617, 620, 622–3,
      641–2, 648–9, 651, 653, 662, 742,
      748, 830–2, 837, 841, 890, 899, 902,
      939, 953–4, 956–7, 968, 990, 993,
      1006, 1058, 1066–7, 1071, 1092,
      1097, 1112, 1138, 1143, 1146, 1158,
      1164, 1169, 1190, 1215–16, 1218,
      1222–3, 1225, 1228, 1230, 1234–5,
      1237, 1239, 1252, 1305, 1328, 1332,
      1468, 1474–5, 1493, 1520, 1534,
      1550, 1582, 1597, 1604, 1611, 1625,
      1635, 1638, 1716–17, 1792, 1796,
      1804, 1819, 1822, 1830, 1864, 1891,
      1912, 1929, 1932–3, 1938, 1943,
      1958, 1962, 1997, 2001, 2030, 2047,
      2136, 2173, 2206, 2215, 2222, 2241,
      2251, 2254–5, 2258, 2285, 2297,
      2301, 2326, 2340–2, 2356, 2360,
      2376, 2378, 2399, 2403, 2435, 2441,
      2458, 2465, 2488, 2495, 2511, 2513,
      2540, 2552, 2556, 2558–9, 2561,
      2571, 2582, 2587, 2612, 2615, 2729,
      2808, 2845, 2848, 2886, 2890, 2942,
      2944, 2952, 3011–12, 3014, 3016,
      3026, 3052, 3059, 3105, 3176, 3185
  paid fine where claim was made   290
  (*clamavit*)   37, 42, 58, 273, 329, 486, 627,
      825–6, 829, 836–7, 838–9, 864, 867,
      971, 973, 991, 994–6, 1003, 1019,
      1021, 1025, 1030, 1034, 1038–9,
      1041–56, 1060, 1063, 1070, 1072,
      1077–9, 1081–2, 1096, 1098, 1102,
      1106–7, 1110–11, 1119, 1121,
      1123–4, 1130–1, 1138, 1140, 1142,
      1144, 1147, 1149–51, 1155–7,
      1159–60, 1162–3, 1175, 1177,
      1181–3, 1185–9, 1192–3, 1195,
      1227, 1620, 1732, 1734, 1736–8,
      1744, 1747–8, 1751, 1760, 1955,
      2272, 3014
  no one claimed   1732

2723, 2725–7, 2729, 2741–2, 2749,
2834, 2973, 2995, 3000, 3089, 3191,
3193, 3195, 3197, 3206–9

took/acquired

(*accepit*)   129, 313, 407, 468, 470–1,
496, 529–30, 575, 590, 611, 626,
874, 1253, 1262, 1478, 1485, 1502,
1527, 1586, 1650, 1655, 1680,
1807–8, 1812, 1844, 1848, 1861,
1882, 1927, 1940, 1988, 2165, 2184,
2410, 2453, 2630, 2922, 2935, 2939,
3089

(*adquisiuit*)   1134

(*assumpsit*)   508, 814

(*cepit*)   482, 532, 900, 916, 924, 1500,
2229, 2995, 3127

(*recepit*)   220, 225, 469, 503, 592, 623,
630, 647, 850, 906, 934, 1333, 1492,
1523, 1648, 1676–7, 1680, 1683,
1691, 1796, 1811, 1937, 1974,
2009–10, 2060, 2122, 2161, 2204,
2208, 2216, 2327, 2356, 2375, 2520,
2542, 2546, 2724, 2881, 2886, 2928,
3037, 3080, 3162

(*sumpsit*)   52, 147, 158, 167, 171, 173,
785–9, 801, 804, 806, 891

(*suscepit*)   2379

took away

(*abstulit*)

in the time of Cnut   1596

TRE   10, 140, 276, 283, 308, 462,
474, 477, 511, 584–6, 748, 763, 902,
905, 922, 1545, 1606, 1632, 1645,
1680, 2041, 2412

TRW   19, 28, 51, 162–3, 299–301,
305–7, 310–12, 315, 320, 340, 345,
351, 371, 375, 392, 401, 417, 423, 502,
515, 582, 608, 654, 660, 711, 747, 749,
760, 766, 790, 801, 817, 820, 836–7,
845, 864, 895, 901, 903, 920, 983–4,
1064, 1320, 1336–9, 1341–3,
1347–9, 1409, 1426, 1451, 1456,
1458, 1461, 1463, 1484, 1501, 1531,
1569, 1573, 1612, 1623–4, 1677,
1681, 1710, 1795, 1797, 1807,
1820–1, 1823, 1839, 1845, 1853,
1857–8, 1871, 1919, 1967, 2009,
2032–3, 2043, 2160, 2186, 2211,
2231, 2234, 2269, 2380, 2406, 2409,
2469, 2600, 2680, 2752, 2778, 2781,
2914, 3033, 3154

(*detulit*)

TRE   290

(*tulit*)

in the time of Cnut   1816

TRE   2404, 2925

TRW   465, 480, 767, 783, 1467,
1694, 1807, 1823, 1836, 1840, 1842,
1846, 1853, 1866, 1869, 1944, 1954,
2015, 2043–4, 2161, 2176, 2402,
2468, 2498–9, 2535, 2538, 2574,
2680, 2793, 2889, 2925, 3047

transferred

(*convertit*)   711, 1479, 1493

(*divertit*)   710

(*transportavit*)   132

(*transtulit*)   2749

withdrew (*retraxit*)   1258

II Agents

1 Beadle

could not withdraw without order from
King   1506

gave pledge   3187

2 Barons

sokemen commended to   2766

King's barons

came into county   2962

established claim before   360, 1674

gave judgment   900

gave pledge to   1190

mortgaged land to   2940

3 Earl

failed to seize a thief   256

gave

peace   252, 1702

third penny   1247

leased land in borough through   822

outlaws

expelled outlaws   1703

outlawed by   981, 1703

restored peace to outlaws   1703

put land elsewhere   504, 513

received forfeited land and goods   1246

received third of heriot   1115

III Antecessors and successors

1 Antecessors

English antecessor   18, 29, 37, 41–2, 44, 47,
    51–2, 94, 116, 126, 210, 243, 338,
    598–9, 608, 622–3, 635, 641, 658,
    708, 793, 795, 856, 893, 973, 1048,
    1055, 1061, 1063–5, 1067, 1069,
    1071–2, 1082, 1092, 1109, 1119,
    1138, 1140, 1159–60, 1162, 1168,
    1170, 1187, 1189, 1191–3, 1255,
    1494, 1508, 1518, 1644, 1734–5,
    1743, 1754, 1789, 1808, 1810, 1844,
    1847, 1879, 1891, 1914, 2000, 2037,
    2112, 2133–4, 2141, 2143–4, 2155,
    2202, 2218, 2225–6, 2285, 2322,
    2342, 2349–50, 2367, 2384, 2399,
    2404, 2422, 2433, 2544, 2588, 2614,
    2656, 2727, 2750, 2780, 2808, 2812,
    2815, 2820, 2919, 2924, 2959, 2961,
    2982, 3007–8, 3010, 3020, 3023–5,
    3081, 3084, 3088, 3115, 3119, 3129,
    3164, 3171, 3186, 3199, 3201
  antecessor's lease   244, 1189, 1508,
    1844, 1847, 1948, 2812, 3023, 3084
  antecessor's mortgage   973, 1065,
    1494, 2750, 2860, 3186
  not antecessor's   27, 132, 194, 211,
    332, 557, 570, 856, 1056, 1115,
    1129, 1155, 1160, 1251, 1446, 1526,
    1528, 1711, 1734, 2113, 2202, 2778,
    3067, 3081, 3199
English Kings' antecessors   792, 812
men of antecessor   21, 202, 214, 1914,
    1948, 1984, 1992–3, 1996, 1999,
    2004–6, 2115–16, 2172, 2200, 2203,
    2220, 2236, 2244, 2246–7, 2258,
    2264–5, 2272–4, 2278–9, 2292,
    2297–8, 2300, 2308, 2310, 2321–2,
    2342, 2344, 2349–50, 2365, 2370–1,
    2381–2, 2384–401, 2417–19, 2427,
    2437, 2439–40, 2442, 2444–5, 2447,
    2449, 2484, 2489, 2490–2, 2497,
    2501, 2505, 2521, 2527, 2531, 2537,
    2540, 2555, 2557, 2579–80, 2586,
    2588–9, 2591, 2605, 2616–18, 2620,
    2623, 2633, 2642, 2644–8, 2651–3,
    2655–73, 2688, 2691–3, 2702, 2710,
    2712, 2714–15, 2718–19, 2728,
    2730, 2733, 2749–50, 2755, 2766,
    2783–5, 2787, 2792, 2795–8,
    2800–7, 2809, 2811–12, 2816–20,
    2823–6, 2829–35, 2839, 2841,
    2843–4, 2846, 2848–9, 2852–61,
    2864, 2868–71, 2873–7, 2882–9,
    2892–3, 2895, 2901–2, 2905–9,
    2911–13, 2915–17, 2920, 2924–6,
    2945–6, 2948, 2950–8, 2960–1,
    2963–4, 2969, 2987, 2992–3, 3003,
    3005, 3018, 3023–6, 3030, 3032–4,
    3040–2, 3046, 3048, 3050–1, 3054,
    3056–8, 3067, 3069–73, 3080–1,
    3086, 3090, 3092, 3103–4, 3108,
    3115–16, 3120, 3123, 3129, 3133–4,
    3136–7, 3140–2, 3157, 3160,
    3164–7, 3169–70, 3173, 3194–5,
    3197, 3206, 3209–10, 3213–14,
    3216
  not men of antecessor   212, 793, 1452,
    2202, 2385, 2683, 2885, 2887, 2889,
    3017–18, 3021, 3163, 3198, 3204
Norman antecessor   20, 554, 558, 560,
    1326–7, 1836, 2172, 2285, 2342,
    2491–2, 2496, 2499, 2501, 2533,
    2737, 2743, 2777–8, 3039, 3139
William Malet, lands of   1718–19, 1733,
    1735, 1739–41, 1743, 1746,
    1749–50, 1755–6, 1761, 1777–85,
    1793, 2222, 2258, 2287, 2398, 2548,
    2589, 2704–6, 2788–9, 2790,
    2797–8, 2800–3, 2812, 2866,
    2869–71, 2876, 2878–9, 2899–900,
    2903–7, 2909, 2911, 2917, 2947,
    2951, 2960, 2970, 3034–5, 3040,
    3052, 3103, 3124, 3133–4, 3136–7,
    3165–6, 3171–5, 3177–8, 3179–80,
    3196, 3126
  probably William Malet's land   2225–6,
    2264, 2340, 2371, 2378, 2381–2,
    2591, 2605, 2750, 2755, 2766,
    2783–5, 2787, 2795–6, 2804, 2809,
    2868, 2877, 2883, 2892–3, 2895,
    2901, 2908, 2913, 2950, 2952,
    2957–9, 2961, 2963, 2969, 2983,
    2987–8, 2994, 3033, 3050, 3067,
    3069, 3084–6, 3108, 3120, 3123,
    3142, 3157, 3167, 3169, 3176

2 Successors

560, 766, 1683, 2234, 2240, 2354, 2509,
    2526, 2543, 3202

8 *People with third penny or third of rights, dues,*
   or customs

9 Proof (see also section IX, testimony)

10 Unfair payments

VII Means

VIII Offenses

1 Fines and forfeitures

2 Fines, dues, or pleas on special days

3 Individuals or places with fines and forfeitures

X Testimony and memory: times other than TRE and TRW

1 Dates given in years

2 Dates related to Domesday inquest or other legal meetings

3 Dates related to ecclesiastics

while Ely Abbey was in the King's
        hand   2973
while Peter bishop of Lichfield lived   1459

4 Dates related to English wars

after Battle of Hastings   116
after King Edward's death, but before King
        William came   614
as long as William Malet held land in
        Yorkshire   1741, 1743
as long as William Malet held the castle in
        York   1740
before Hereweard fled the country   1172
before the castle at York was captured   1718
in Harold's battle against the Norse   1683
in the first year after the destruction of the
        castle at York   1694
in the time of Harold   483, 1808, 2519
on the day Earnwine the Priest was captured
        and before   1001
on the day Hereweard fled   1128
on the day Rayner the Deacon left the
        country   1083, 1085, 1087, 1097
on the day Tonni was captured   1050
until Abbot of St. Augustine's was made an
        outlaw   131
until Danes captured William Malet   1793
until Skalpi went to York and died in
        outlawry   1951
until the castle at York was attacked   1735
until the castle at York was destroyed   1739
when Abbot of Ramsey was in
        Denmark   851
when Æthelric returned from a naval battle
        against King William   1832
when Earl Harold died   695
when Harold annexed the kingdom   584
when Harold reigned   585
when King William conquered
        England   2202
when Rayner the Deacon left this
        land   1087, 1097
when thegn went with Harold to battle in
        York   1835
when Whitgar forfeited   3202
while Ely Abbey was in the King's
        hand   2973

5 Dates related to forfeiture of Earl Ralph

after Earl Ralph forfeited   790, 2207, 2379,
        2439, 2535

before and after Earl Ralph forfeited   2612
before Earl Ralph forfeited   2194–5, 2231,
        2403, 2465, 2708
for one year before and one year after Earl
        Ralph forfeited   2326
for one year before and two years after Earl
        Ralph forfeited   2724
for one year before Earl Ralph
        forfeited   2360
for two years before and two years after Earl
        Ralph forfeited   2164
for three years before Earl Ralph
        forfeited   2227
in the time of Earl Ralph   1192, 2207,
        2256, 2259, 2262–3, 2283, 2314–15,
        2326, 2761
on the day Earl Ralph forfeited   805, 2163,
        2209, 2260, 2482, 2790, 2810, 2873,
        2946, 3216
on the day Earl Ralph wronged the
        King   194
one year before Earl Ralph forfeited   2538,
        2845
since Earl Ralph forfeited   2723
until Earl Ralph forfeited   2961
when division of lands was made between the
        King and Earl Ralph   2262
when Earl Ralph forfeited   2172, 2200–3,
        2213, 2215–17, 2219–20, 2222,
        2232, 2240, 2254, 2259, 2261, 2265,
        2280, 2326, 2326, 2376, 2379, 2393,
        2395–6, 2425, 2438, 2442, 2475,
        2487, 2531, 2538, 2582, 2595,
        2637, 2643, 2686, 2708, 2723,
        2726–8, 2741, 2745, 2759, 2789,
        2793–4, 2880, 3022, 3189, 3206,
        3210
when Earl Ralph forfeited and for three years
        before   2227
when Earl Ralph had power over his men
        and his lands   2455

*6 Dates related to forfeitures of Normans other
        than Earl Ralph*

after Walter de Dol forfeited   2809
    on the day Walter de Dol forfeited   2850,
        3053
        when Walter de Dol forfeited   2851,
        2942, 2962
when Hardwin forfeited   2975
when Humphrey forfeited   2285

XI Written word